Managing People in Changing Organizations

Managing People in Changing Organizations addresses the contemporary problems faced by managers in dealing with people, organizations, and change in a theoretically informed and practical way. It does so by drawing on classic studies in management, up-to-date research (including the author's own), case studies, and reflective exercises. This textbook approaches people management and organizational development from the perspective of practising and aspiring managers, making it a valuable alternative to existing texts on organizational behaviour, change management, and human resource management. This third edition incorporates new research and recent changes in technology, including artificial intelligence, work and job design, and additional insights into innovation, corporate governance, and sustainability.

Built around a chapter framework that connects different themes to managerial action and practices, this textbook covers a wide range of topics including: managing at the individual, group, and organizational levels; culture change; managing internationally; reputation management; managing creativity and innovation; and corporate governance, corporate social responsibility, and sustainability. There is an increased international flavour reflected in the range of contemporary case studies and literature used throughout, which explore business and management problems in the private and public sectors. The content also reflects the author's recent experience of consulting and managing at board level.

This text will be relevant to practising and aspiring managers studying leadership, people management, organizational behaviour and development, and change management on courses at later stage undergraduate, masters, doctoral, and executive education levels.

Graeme Martin is Professor of Management at the University of Dundee.

Managing People in Changing Organizations

THIRD EDITION

Graeme Martin

Routledge
Taylor & Francis Group

LONDON AND NEW YORK

Designed cover image: ©Getty Images

Third edition published 2025
by Routledge
4 Park Square, Milton Park, Abingdon, Oxon, OX14 4RN

and by Routledge
605 Third Avenue, New York, NY 10158

Routledge is an imprint of the Taylor & Francis Group, an informa business

First edition published by Elsevier Ltd 2006
Second edition published by Routledge 2016

British Library Cataloguing-in-Publication Data
A catalogue record for this book is available from the British Library

ISBN: 978-1-032-74536-7 (hbk)
ISBN: 978-1-032-74535-0 (pbk)
ISBN: 978-1-003-46971-1 (ebk)

DOI: 10.4324/9781003469711

Typeset in Berling and Futura
by Deanta Global Publishing Services, Chennai, India

Contents

List of Figures

List of Tables

CHAPTER 1

An introduction to managing people and organizations

LEARNING OBJECTIVES

By the end of this chapter, you should be able to:

- Describe and critically evaluate some of the key ideas underlying the management of people and organizations in changing contexts.
- Apply the notions of universalism and relativism to the key ideas and practice of modern management, especially to our understanding of 'best practice'.
- Understand the importance of frames of reference and mindsets in management, and how these influence practice.
- Understand how ideas about managing change, and how the institutional environment and the influence of management thinkers can cause changes in our understanding of good practice.
- Critically evaluate the role of management thinkers in producing useful knowledge for managers.

UNDERSTANDING MANAGEMENT

Introduction

According to Peter Drucker (1909–2005), who was one of the most prominent and most quoted business gurus of recent times, management is a timeless, human discipline. It has been used to build the Great Wall of China, to run empires and armies throughout history, and to guide the development of the joint stock company, which has been the key institution in the development of modern capitalism. During the later part of the twentieth century and the early part of the twenty-first century, management became one of the fastest-growing occupations because managers and their practices are

DOI: 10.4324/9781003469711-1

(but not always) seen to be essential to organizational and economic success (Bloom & Van Reenan, 2010; Glaister, 2014). Such developments, according to the Association to Advance Collegiate Schools of Business (AACSB, 2023, May 8), have been matched by the phenomenal growth in business schools over the past six decades and more (although recent evidence in the mid-2020s shows a slowing down). So, whether we work in the private, public, or voluntary sectors of the economy, managers and managerial work touch virtually every aspect of our economic, social, environmental, and political lives. Those of you who aren't yet a manager but aspire to become one most likely will have had direct experience of being led or managed by others. Sometimes this experience will have been positive, helping you achieve excellent results, and sometimes it will have been negative, perhaps causing you to underperform, experience undue levels of stress, lack of esteem, or lack of job satisfaction. Those of you who are experienced managers will also understand that the people you manage don't always respond in the ways in which you expect or want them to react to your ideas, actions, and/or evaluations of them. So, all of us need to be *critically reflexive* of our managerial potential, capabilities, and the roles we play in organizations, industries, and the grand societal challenges facing the world today, including climate change and recent technological developments such as artificial intelligence (AI). By critical reflexivity, we mean the constant need to query the relationships among ourselves as managers and those people we manage how we construct the world, and our assumptions and values, and our impact on inidividuals, organizations, and society (Cunliffe 2014; Robson, 2022). This is especially important in the current era of 'global polycrisis' – involving a tech cold war, retreat from hyperglobalisation, climate and demographic change – which is creating an imperfect storm (World Economic Forum, 2023). For many managers, however, who are naturally orientated to immediate action rather than reflection, this is an extremely difficult task, especially when faced with moral decisions that may go against the short-term interests of the firm (King & Learmonth, 2015).

With these points in mind, this revised and updated text is aimed at helping both aspiring and experienced managers explore and be critically reflexive of the *nature of management* and some of the key *processes of management*, specifically the key problems associated with *managing people and organizations*. To this end, this book has also been written from the perspective that the theory and practice of managing people and organizations are heavily influenced by the *context* in which ideas occur and how management is performed and that these contexts often *change* considerably over time.

Key questions on management knowledge

When we embark on any management education programme, it is important for us to understand the relationship between theory and practice, not least because we are usually taught theories that we rightly expect to be able to action. However, the gap between theory and practice seems extensive, with managers typically seeking simple guides to practice and academics often reluctant to provide them with such tools. With more than 40 years of experience teaching management students and executives in many different countries, I know this gap is sometimes questioned by readers or course participants. The kinds of questions practising managers raise are as follows:

1   Is there a one-best-way or set of best practices in management? Or, to put this question in slightly more formal terms: (a) is there a single set of truths about management that represents its core body of knowledge, and (b) if so, can this body of knowledge be applied in most, if not all, contexts?

2   Why is it that ideas about business and management seem to be a bit like the fashion industry, with new ideas and new jargon appearing almost every week?

3. Have managers, especially senior managers, become disconnected from organizations and societies they purport to serve. Have they literally becoming self-serving?

It is important that these questions are raised when studying management, or when contemplating ideas from consultants, conferences, or the increasing volume of business books found in airport bookshops and on the internet. Such questions are particularly relevant because managers generally seek knowledge that helps them simplify the world they must confront, especially given the increasingly complex nature of the environment in which they work. To be told there is the possibility of a 'magic bullet' or 'one-best-way' is an attractive proposition, because it means they don't have to think too much about what they are doing. And, as Henry Mintzberg (2011), one of the most insightful commentators on management, has pointed out, managers are very much focused on 'doing' rather than reflecting on academic theories concocted by people who have very little experience of practising management. However, the prospect of a magic bullet, contained in the nostrums of a single management book or PowerPoint presentation, is not something that usually accords with their experience of just how complex their world is. This disconnect is especially true when nearly all new books, courses, or consultants tell them there is a better way of doing things, which is usually *the* way advocated by the author, teacher, or adviser. Managers usually get little more from new 'guru-speak' than a recycling of even older ideas, often originating in the early 1900s, but given a makeover. Arguably, a good example is 'happiness studies', with its focus on subjective well-being at work and its own academic journal (Davies, 2015). Happiness is heavily promoted by governments and business but has its origins in early research in the 1930s on human relations (see Case study 1.1 on the development of human relations). Notwithstanding the respectability and merits of the various outputs of the *Journal of Happiness Studies*, many managers (and those on the receiving end of some of these practices) become sceptical or even cynical about any new business programme or form of management education (Martin et al., 2018). If such a process sounds familiar, then you are in tune with many of the critics of business education, business schools, and the management consulting industry (Ortenblad & Koris, 2022). For example, Khurana and Spender (2012) forcefully argued that American business schools and their 'products' (typically students who follow careers in management consulting) fashioned an intellectual inertia in management education that has promoted a disconnected managerialism that failed to serve practice and, more consequentially, was one of the principal causes of the Global Financial Crisis (GFC) of 2007–2008. Paradoxically, however, regardless of the extent to which the management education and consulting industries are challenged to explain their relevance by business leaders and politicians, their influence has become ever more widespread (Howieson & Robson, 2022). The demand for management education, outside of business school programmes, shows few signs of abating, fuelled by the growth of corporate universities and by executives willing to self-fund their development (AACSB, May 8, 2023).

So, in this chapter, and in the rest of the book, we shall address the three questions raised at the beginning of this section. We do so because it is in everyone's interests – teachers, students of management, and examiners alike – to avoid the reputation for lack of relevance that management knowledge enjoys with many practitioners (Pettigrew & Starkey, 2016) and for promoting a disconnected and self-serving managerialism (Ortenblad & Koris, 2022). With respect to lack of relevance, this has largely come about because dominant sections of the producer community of management knowledge – the producers of business guru books and the management consulting industry – have oversold the idea of the one-best-way in wave after wave of management fads (Collins, 2020; Pascale, 1999). Some years ago Francis Wheen (2004), rather amusingly, labelled much of this material, especially the self-help books by ex-business leaders, as 'old snake oil in new bottles,' pointing to the often-messianic salesmanship of banal aphorisms dressed up in jargon and pseudo-scientific phrases, such as 're-engineering, benchmarking, and downsizing.' Moreover, since we live in an increasingly changeable and arguably unknowable world, what we can usefully teach about management often has a short shelf life.

If the guru industry has not helped the relevance cause, neither have some management academics who claim to pursue a practical agenda and promote managerialism (a set of ideas and practices that are tied to promoting the interests of managers). Thus some critical management scholars argue that many, ostensibly practical, management academics and most consultants fail to engage in reflexive thinking over dominant business discourses (Cunliffe, 2014). Two examples of such a discourse are shareholder value, the belief that businesses exist to create value for shareholders only (Martin et al., 2016), and transformational leadership (Pettigrew & Starkey, 2016), which places managers at the centre of change programmes. Both are often expounded uncritically by those who benefit most from having such ideas accepted as truths – including, among others, highly paid leaders who benefit from share ownership, universities that benefit from running leadership courses, and the business press that promotes and feeds off celebrity leaders (Martin et al., 2018).

It is not only critical management scholars, however, that question the relevance agenda. Even 'mainstream' management academics and some practising managers acknowledge the limitations of their craft and the problems of becoming disconnected from the organizations they are employed to serve. The notion of sustainable governance (Martin et al., 2016), based on the Principles of Responsible Management Education (PRME) initiative, is a recent example of such questioning. PRME is a United Nations-backed movement to raise the profile of sustainability among management educators and businesses. It aims to work with academic institutions to draw attention to the United Nations Sustainable Development Goals when educating managers. There are 17 such goals, most of which have significant implications for all managers and management education. The goals are *No Poverty, Zero Hunger, Good Health and Well-Being, Gender Equality, Clean Water and Sanitation, Quality Education, Affordable and Clean Energy, Decent Work and Economic Growth, Industry and Infrastructure, Reduced Inequalities, Sustainable Cities, Responsible Consumption and Production, Climate Action, Life Below Water, Life on Land, Peace, Justice, and Strong Institutions, and Partnerships for the Goals.*

You may want to take some time to reflect on how management practice impacts on these goals. We will consider these in more detail in Chapter 11.

The ethics in business agenda, however, is not new. It was evident during a major soul-searching exercise run at Half-Moon Bay in California in May 2008 in the aftermath of the GFC, which brought together well-known academics and senior executives to redefine a more ethical notion of leadership. Take a few minutes to think about the outcomes of this exercise.

Time out: **Ethical leadership and management's grand challenges (based on Hamel, 2009)**

Well-known management scholar and consultant, Gary Hamel, brought together several prominent business school academics in 2008, including Henry Mintzberg and Jeff Pfeffer, and business leaders to develop a list of challenges that leaders would have to address following the growing criticism of businesses during the period leading up to and after the GFC. These challenges included:

1. Ensuring that managers serve a higher purpose to achieve socially significant goals.
2. Embedding notions of community and citizenship in their values and practices.
3. Modernising management's philosophical foundations and thinking to move beyond efficiency and focus on innovation.
4. Eliminating the focus on formal hierarchy as a solution to organization.
5. Reducing fear and building trust in management systems to create innovative cultures.
6. Recreating control systems to embed the notion of control from within rather than external control as being the most appropriate for innovation.
7. Redefining the current idea of leaders as heroic decision-makers to become architects and builders of systems.
8. Embracing diversity and pluralism as well as consensus.
9. Seeing strategy as emergent rather than planned and top-down.
10. Restructure or de-construct organizations into smaller, more flexible units.
11. Challenge the pull of the past and institutions that prevent change.
12. Distribute goal setting and leadership so that voice in the organization reflects insight, not power.

Questions

1. How do the PRME agenda and the UN Sustainable Development Goals challenge Hamel's thinking on ethical leadership?
2. Has your organization, or one with which you are familiar, adopted the UN Sustainable Development Goals or the issue of sustainability as part of its key strategic thinking?

The above time-out exercise may have helped provide an answer to the third of our three questions raised in the early part of the chapter concerning the disconnection between senior managers from their organizations and society. While there are a small number of high-profile organizations pursuing socially responsible and sustainable agendas, such ideas are not yet part of mainstream thinking among a majority (Mayer, 2013). Business schools, however, are leading the way in changing their own business models to help other organizations change theirs (AACSB, May 8, 2023).

To return to answering the first two questions raised in this chapter, we must go back in time to examine two concepts in management that go straight to the heart of the rigour-relevance debate. These concepts are *universalism* and *change*.

MANAGEMENT AS A SET OF UNIVERSAL TRUTHS

Universalism and relativism in management

There have been many books aimed at helping managers understand and improve their management skills, not just in people management but in other managerial functions such as managing information, budgets and finances, and operations. Many of these books take a *universalist* perspective on management.

> **Key concept: The universalist perspective on management**
>
> The proposition is that it is possible to discover a set of universal truths concerning principles, values, and morals that can be equally applied in all business and management contexts. These truths can be established either by reasoning from first principles or by empirical observation. The fundamental points of this perspective are its universal application and its relative permanence, though most universalists acknowledge that the gradual accumulation of new knowledge can improve our thinking. Such a perspective is associated with attempts to establish a science of management, and to establish universal codes of ethics for business behaviour that transcend national boundaries (Crane & Matten, 2019).

Such a view was evident before the end of the nineteenth century, best exemplified by the works of Frederick Taylor in the USA, the so-called father of scientific management, and by the French businessman-theorist, Henry Fayol. Both writers developed a set of principles of good management that formed the basis for much management education (Clegg et al., 2021), and their works are still discussed today in undergraduate and taught postgraduate classes in business and management all over the world. We shall return to their ideas later in this chapter.

Perhaps more controversially, the universalistic perspective contended that most of these management principles could apply regardless of cultural and institutional context. Jack Welsh, a former, well-known CEO of General Electric, best exemplified this view when he claimed what was good for his company was good for the rest of the world.

Welsh's view reflected the dominance of the American management model for most of the last century, which has influenced thinking and practice in many countries. There are at least three possible explanations for such dominance. These are: (a) the influence of US multinationals on global economic development (Foley et al., 2021); (b) the influence of management education programmes such as the MBA – an American invention in the late nineteenth century (Khurana & Spender, 2012); and (c) the influence of the global, but mainly US, management consulting and management guru industries (Armbruster, 2006; Collins, 2020).

There is undoubtedly something in the claims of universalists, given the history of post-Second World War reconstruction and the reliance on US finance and ideas to rebuild the economies of Europe and Japan. The UK, Germany, and Japan adopted many American ideas and accepted aid that, in turn, was dependent on their acceptance of American ways of managing (Locke & Spender, 2011). However, the adoption of American ideas did not, as some people claim, result in the 'Americanisation' of business and management in these countries. For example, in the 1970s and 1980s, Japanese companies came to dominate world markets in industries that the USA had traditionally owned (Pascale & Athos, 1981) by using techniques of quality management and production management that have since become popular in many Western organizations. Similarly, German companies developed their own way of managing and running businesses, based on their historical veneration of engineering specialists and the adoption of 'co-determination' before and after 1945, a practice that gave employees a much greater say in the running of companies (much to the distaste of some US occupying generals and CEOs). Consequently, there were severe limitations placed on the forces for convergence on and around the American model of management. This limitation of universalist principles is one of the key themes of this book.

Time out: Think about this: The history of co-determination in Germany

Historically, German business managers have had much less faith than the Americans or British in the powers of markets to regulate business and competition and have placed greater store in the power of national and state governments. Thus, co-determination in Germany has its origins in legislation passed in the early 1800s to give workers rights to social insurance and, later, in 1891, to rights to participate in management decision-making involving joint consultation on social matters at work. Following the First World War, in 1918, German employers, rather reluctantly, succumbed to pressure to give 'employees rights to co-determination with management in social policy and to be consulted in personnel and economic decisions' (Locke, 1996, p. 58). Subsequent legislation in 1920 allowed for the creation of works councils in firms employing more than 20 employees to act on social, personnel, and economic matters. Hitler and the Nazis dissolved works councils when they came to power in the 1930s, but following pressure from the Christian churches and trade unions after the Second World War, co-determination was re-established to give workers even greater rights to co-decisions in the running of firms on economic issues, including 'expansion, consolidations and shutdowns', and to joint consultation in the purchase and sale of equipment, changes in production methods, accounting procedures, and so on.

Such legislation was passed when Germany was in the hands of occupying forces, most notably the Americans. This was surprising in some respects because, without US approval, German discretion to pass legislation was severely limited. The American attitude to co-determination during the period varied from early acceptance – it wouldn't work in America but was perhaps good for Germany – to outright opposition. However, what became the official American line was that German business would lose control of its affairs, and thus the essential and inalienable rights of stockholders would be violated. Such opposition by the US to German attempts to reintroduce co-determination was exemplified by the role played by General Lucius Clay, leader of the occupying US administration, who obstructed and vetoed the rights of individual German states (the *Länder*) to pass such legislation for as long as he was able. Though, over time, American opposition to the rights of the German government to establish co-determination diminished, the business press and major figures in the US business community continued to see such legislation as an attempt to establish socialism in capitalist industry. To the extent that these people had influence over American aid through the Marshall Plan to German industry, German managers were perceived to be playing a dangerous game but nevertheless continued to do so. In this important sense, US attempts to impose on Germany a US-style 'best practice' and a way of managing failed: 'German entrepreneurs rejected American managerialism' (Locke, 1996, p. 64).

Source: based on Locke, 1996.

We can see from this example that the universalistic view on best practice in management has not always struck a chord with managers outside the USA, especially following events such as the GFC, which has had an acknowledged negative effect on the universal and enduring relevance of the American Business Model (Whitley, 2009). Moreover, the rise of the extended or BRIC+ economies and others in the Global South during the first few decades of the millennium have provided alternative models of growth. Similarly, many people working in the public or voluntary sectors of modern economies disagree that best practice developed in the private sector is superior or transferable to contexts that are not subject to the overarching goal of increasing the value of shareholders in the business. Consequently, we are witnessing a significant debate over the relevance of shareholder value as a dominant model of governing corporations in Western developed economies (see Chapter 11) and as a theory on which to base management principles (Martin et al., 2016; Mintzberg, 2015). These developments are leading to a serious examination of a *relativist* view among many management academics and practitioners, to which we now turn.

Key concept: Relativism in management

Relativism expresses the idea that it is not possible to establish a set of universal truths concerning principles, values, and morals about management that will not at some later time be abandoned and replaced by another set of truths. Relativism in management is often associated with the idea that management practices and values cannot be abstracted from the context in which they were produced and easily transferred to other contexts. Extreme versions of relativism in management hold that there is no such thing as reality, certainty, or 'social facts', and that all views about management are essentially value judgements. The principal aim of relativists in management is to give less powerful people and groups a greater voice in public discourse about how they should be managed.

A relativist perspective, for example, might point to the practice of management in France, which was thought to be different from the practice of management in the USA because of the relatively unique nature of the French business sector, its history, its national cultural characteristics, and institutional (legal, social, educational, and political) norms (Lawrence, 2002). Thus, it was argued, managers brought up in the French business system (or, indeed any non-US system) literally see through different eyes and listen with different ears compared with American managers. So, they are often not able to understand each other, even if they both use a version of American English. French business management is reputed to be hierarchical and individualist in nature and was unable to accommodate the bottom-up, group decision-making of quality circles, one of the fashionable techniques adopted by many global companies in the 1980s. Another example of an influential relativist perspective in management is the so-called *constructivist approach to learning* (Petit & Huault, 2008), which we shall discuss more fully in Chapter 7. The constructivist approach to learning is often contrasted with a cognitive or 'schooled' learning approach, in which abstract principles are taught to students in a classroom, as is often the case in many management courses. Constructivists argue that we learn most effectively through active participation rather than as a passive recipient of knowledge 'poured' into our heads through instruction in a classroom. However, when we engage in active learning, all such knowledge becomes personal to us. So, for example, my knowledge and understanding of what I am writing will be different from yours as an individual reader of this text, and it will also be different from that of others who read the same text. But, since all knowledge is personal and subjective, and not something that is literally 'out there' and ready to be grabbed like an apple on a tree, it is mainly tacit (in people's heads and hands) and highly specific to the context in which it is produced. Seen in this way, management is best viewed as a craft learnt in context rather than as an abstract science (Mintzberg, 2011). So, constructivists argue that learning to become a manager is most effectively undertaken by serving a long, on-the-job 'apprenticeship', often as part of a 'community of practice' in a particular industry, such as healthcare (Spilg et al., 2012) or a company (Wenger et al., 2002).

My position on this debate between extreme versions of universalism and relativism is somewhere in between the two, often depending on the context of application. Clearly, ideas about management developed in one situation can take root in other contexts. For example, the popularity of the MBA as a global form of management education would be unsustainable if this were not possible. Moreover, the success of multinational firms rests, in part, on their ability to transfer learning from one part of the world to another, often in the form of model practices and values. However, the perspective taken in this book is more relativist in the sense that context and individual interpretation of ideas are seen as very important in influencing action. Perhaps this is best explained by an organic, gardening metaphor. Highly regarded commentator on learning, John Seely Brown (2000), once likened transferring so-called best practices from one context to another to uprooting a tree from the fertile soil that gave it life and form, then replanting it into different soil, the properties of which are unknown or at least partially uncertain. It is unlikely that one can know with any certainty in advance the kind of tree, or anything resembling the original tree, that the soil and microclimate will produce. Thus, at best, the status of such best practices can be described as 'promising' (Leseure et al., 2004), but they are burdened by being deeply embedded into historically, culturally, and institutionally different contexts (Thornton et al., 2012), as I found out most vividly when carrying out research with a Chinese colleague into Sino-foreign joint ventures in China more than two decades ago (Zhang & Martin, 2003). This transfer problem also applies to industrial contexts, such as the transfer of private sector practices to the highly politicised public sectors of healthcare, education, and local government.

To return to the first of our three questions, concerning the possibility of a one-best-way of doing things or a set of best practices in management, our answer is a qualified yes and no. A 'yes' relates to the contention that there is a body of knowledge about management that we can legitimately teach and use in many different contexts, even though that body of knowledge has been developed for the most part in the USA and was founded on a private sector, market-driven, shareholder value model, which is different to many of the newly emerging economies (Davis, 2022). 'No' is an answer because there are no 'magic bullets' nor a 'one-best-way'. Our knowledge and practices should enjoy the status of no more than 'promising', and we must think deeply and sensitively when applying these in different contexts, whether these are national cultural, industrial, or company settings.

STABILITY AND CHANGE IN MODELS OF MANAGEMENT

Key features of models of management

If context is an important theme in recent management literature, a second key theme concerns the nature of *change and stability* in models and theories of management and their acceptance by managers. Like many relatively immature bodies of knowledge, the study and practice of management is no exception to the influence of fashionable or faddish ideas, with change being a recurrent theme in the literature, and the 'big' new idea being promoted every few years.

However, as some writers have pointed out, the debates over what constitutes the best way to manage show remarkable stability over time, especially regarding the choices among available models and theories. These models are often said to resemble paradigms, a scientific word referring to the existence of worldviews, which comprise a relatively coherent set of theories, metaphors, and practices. Paradigms are also notable for being relatively stable in a particular scientific community for many years until the next 'big idea' is developed, around which forms a competing paradigm.

In business and management, the term 'paradigm' tends to be used a little more loosely (Clegg et al., 2021), often describing a set of assumptions and values about how the organizational world works and how it should work. This is probably better described as a *frame of reference* (Fox, 1974), a notion that we have explored in some detail when examining trust in organizations (Siebert et al., 2015). Most managers operate and adhere to frames of reference that reflect their own career interests and identities, even though they are unable to articulate the assumptions and theories underlying them.

There are at least three important points about frames of reference. First, they are useful and limiting since a way of seeing is also a way of not seeing. Second, seeing the world through one frame of reference may lock us into our own 'psychic prison' (Morgan, 1997) and result in the self-perpetuation of tired and sometimes dysfunctional ideas. So, for example, Pierce and Aguinas (2013) have argued that managers are often guilty of implementing 'Too Much of a Good Thing,' which results in an apparent paradox in organizational life that ordinarily beneficial leadership and management interventions – such as empowering people, delegation, and communications – can actually cause harm to organizations when taken too far. Richard Pascale (1999) followed a similar line of reasoning when his research into business failure pointed out that 'nothing fails like success.' Success, he argued, was based on becoming highly attuned to, and skilled in, managing and organizing in one set of competitive circumstances. However, when these circumstances change, we are often unable to change our mindsets rapidly enough to produce the appropriate responses. In effect, what were previously held as core capabilities became core rigidities, leading Jeff Pfeffer and Robert Sutton (2006) to claim that being locked into a frame of reference explained why otherwise smart managers 'did dumb things.' This inability to see the world from different perspectives leads us to a third important point about frames of reference, which is that managers usually need to reflect critically on their assumptions, ethics, values, and short-term interests to produce the kind of change that may be needed in creating sustainable organizations. Much of the criticism of companies since the GFC, especially in the financial services sector, has been directed at managers' unswerving assumptions of shareholder value as the guiding principle for running companies since the early 1980s (Martin et al., 2016; Siebert et al., 2020), a critique we take up in Chapter 11.

These three points have given rise to what is probably one of *the* major debates in management theory over the last century between mechanistic forms of organization, characterised by 'top-down' modes of control, and organic forms of organization, characterised by 'bottom-up' modes of control, human relations principles, and the attempts to engineer strong organizational cultures (see Hoopes, 2003), issues to which we shall return in this book.

The mechanistic mindset

Many managers see their ideal organization as a well-oiled machine, in which everyone and everything is treated as a replaceable part. In such 'machines', predictability and control are the most important design features and are frequently accompanied by hierarchical organization structures. Not unnaturally, this view serves the interests of those managers who advocate such a perspective, since the people who are most important in machine-like organizations are the designers and planners (i.e., the managers). Thus, those managers who benefit from the machine view of organizations by running a 'smooth operation' tend to strive to keep things that way. They do so by imposing their mindsets on others and by the kind of actions they take, such as recruiting, developing, and promoting people with similar mindsets. Many years ago, Henry Mintzberg (1983) labelled these managers as the 'technostructure' – a term still used to capture their rational design and planning mindsets and characteristics.

This machine view of organizations is not in and of itself a problem, since classical machine-like organizations, such as public sector bureaucracies and armies, usually work well in stable and predictable circumstances – for example, in state-run, planned economies or when fighting conventional warfare. However, if the circumstances change – for example, if economies suddenly become open to market circumstances, as happened for a short time in the former Soviet bloc and in China, or if warfare becomes unconventional, as is the case with the 'war against terror' or the conflict in Ukraine being fought by drones and even robots – machine-like organizations often lack the intelligent capacity to take action themselves to adapt to these changing environments. This inability to adapt is a direct consequence of the frames of reference and actions of machine-like minds and of the vested interests of those who are in control. However, some organizations, such as those in the energy and extractive industries, often feel they have no other option than to be machine-like. This is because they operate in an 'unforgiving' social and political environment in which they are unable to learn because the financial and reputational costs of 'getting it wrong' – even once – are extraordinarily high. Thus, such organizations tend to centralise key management processes and exercise tight controls to ensure 'high reliability'. Good examples of organizations claiming to be high on reliability would be nuclear power plants, mining companies, and drilling companies working in oil and gas extraction (Weick & Sutcliffe, 2007). However, this mechanistic mindset may not be enough to manage risk effectively, as evidenced by disasters such as the Deepwater Horizon oil spill in 2010, which led to wholesale changes in how BP, the giant multinational, operates.

Beyond the mechanistic mindset

This machine view of organizations dominated much managerial thinking and action until the 1970s and continues to do so in industries where risk management has had to be prioritised over innovation and creativity. Healthcare might be considered a good example because the risks to patients are frequently prioritised over innovation by healthcare organizations for fear of litigation and reputational damage. However, with the changes that occurred during the last few decades of the previous century, it became increasingly obvious that the old ways of seeing had to give way to new paradigms based on the notion of open systems and the need for organizations to consider their external environments (see Chapter 4). Thus, we began to see a mindset developing among managers of organizations as adaptive systems, in which they had to consider what happened outside the organization, for example, changes in market structure and customer preferences, and be able to respond quickly and flexibly to these changes. Such a mindset or metaphor is often described as the *organic view*, reflecting the biological origins of open systems thinking and the relationship between living systems and their environments. This organic metaphor has become dominant in current managerial thinking and practice, especially in the economies of developed countries, in which uncertainty and, often fundamental, change are the key characteristics. These changes include the effects of disruptive technologies (Christensen, et al., 2015) that have essentially changed the rules of doing business in many industries, good examples being the expansion of the internet in retailing, social media in HRM (Martin et al., 2015), and 'cybernization' (Czarniawska, 2011) in the computerisation and automation of news production. More recently, we are now seeing the role of robotics and AI, based on large-scale machine learning, beginning to have a dramatic and highly disruptive effect on industry, education, and healthcare in ways we could have hardly envisaged, even a decade ago (Suleyman, 2023).

In the field of strategic management, the organic metaphor has become popular through the notion of dynamic capabilities (Teece, 2018). This theory is based on the idea that the sources of a firm's competitive advantage lie in its internal capabilities to:

(a) sense opportunities and threats in existing and developing markets and technologies;

(b) seize appropriate opportunities by making high-quality investment decisions in particular business models, products, and service architectures;

(c) constantly reconfigure its assets and structures, including its human resources, organizational structures, and culture, in response to market and technological changes.

Apple is one of the best examples of a company that has built its success on dynamic capabilities in developing the iPhone, iPad, the Apple Watch, Apple TV, and Apple Music.

In the energy and extractive industries, and others such as air traffic control and shipping, some researchers have argued that traditional views of high reliability may not be good enough to prevent problems occurring such as major oil spills and aeroplane crashes (Weick & Sutcliffe, 2007). Instead, they suggest that the lessons learnt from truly effective high-reliability organizations are that they are pre-occupied with failure, seek complex rather than simple analysis and solutions, are continuously sensitive to all operations in the field, are resilient enough to deal with emergencies, and open their normally closed hierarchical structures of control to inputs from those 'in the know' by sharing leadership and responsibility throughout the organization. These processes can reduce the 'blindspots' that cause catastrophic failures.

The key problem of managing human resources from both a dynamic capabilities and a high-reliability perspective lies in assisting managers to attend to the emotional and intuitive aspects of their work as well as the rational aspects. The solution in part involves creating supportive learning environments to avoid blind spots and help managers unlock their fixations by creating opportunities for safe reflection (Hodgkinson & Healey, 2011).

EXPLAINING CHANGING MINDSETS

The key questions

There are two key questions concerning the relationship between ideas and action that make it important for us to have some answers so that we can become more effective managers. The first question is: Why does a particular mindset, such as the mechanistic and organic one discussed previously, come to dominate managers' thinking at points in time? Though you may think that much of what you read in management texts is new, most of the so-called new ideas have their origins in much earlier theories, and those of us who have been around for a long time often get a sense of being sold 'old wine (or even old snake oil) in new bottles'. The second question arises from the first one and concerns the idea of progress in our thinking and practice. Much of what we read in management textbooks implies progress, involving a change from one mindset or model to another. This is particularly evident in the example of the mechanistic and organic mindsets, where we have come to believe that organizations (and their managers) that are 'fast, flexible, and friendly' are inevitably superior to those of more traditionally mechanistic styles. Understanding these questions is useful not merely to academics but also to practitioners because, as the famous British economist John Maynard Keynes once pointed out, everyone who claims to be practical is 'a slave of some usually defunct theory.' So, to provide answers to these questions on changing mindsets, we can briefly examine two sources of explanation. These explanations invoke changing models of national economic success and sources of institutional pressure to imitate new ideas and practice, such as the 'guru' theory and international management consulting organizations that diffuse so-called best practice (Collins, 2020).

National economic success and business

As has already been pointed out, for most of the last century and certainly since the end of the First World War, models of business and management have been drawn from the success of the American economy and from the teachings of US business gurus and business schools. American models of management, based on mass production, financial control, and the M-form or multidivisional organizational structure, came to dominate (Goold & Campbell, 2002; Clegg et al., 2021). As we have seen, their principles were exported overseas by the US government as a condition of aid for reconstruction, by US multinational companies, and by the growing number of business schools, academic research, and business gurus that began to influence European and Asian economies (Hoopes, 2003).

Interestingly, however, for a short period during the 1960s and 1970s, managers also began to look to Germany and Sweden for inspiration, following the economic success of these two countries during the same period. This was best exemplified by the interest shown in newer forms of work reorganization developed in companies such as Volvo and Saab, which adopted autonomous group working and job satisfaction as guiding principles to produce their automobiles. These ideas of autonomous groups and more democratic forms of decision-making were offered as a contrast to the more top-down models of low-skilled mass production associated with the US automobile industry.

The best example, however, of just how powerful a national economic success is in explaining the acceptance of ideas about management is the case of Japan in the 1980s and 1990s. During that period, Japanese organizations came to dominate in industries that the USA had once 'owned', including automobiles, consumer electronics, and business machines, such as electronic cash registers and photocopiers. They also became major players in other forms of manufacturing, including shipbuilding, heavy engineering, construction, and financial services. This was often explained by the quality 'revolution' initiated in Japan by Edward Deming, a US civil servant and academic who was neglected by senior US business leaders but idealised by Japanese senior managers after his lengthy visit following the Second World War. Japan was also notable for exporting ideas in labour relations, group working, and new forms of organization to the USA and Europe, most noticeably the 'lean production' system, during the 1980s and 1990s.

However, during the 1990s, America experienced eight years of unprecedented economic success under the Clinton administration, which when coupled with the relative decline of Japan and Germany during that same period, left the USA as the dominant world economic superpower. By the beginning of the current century, the wheel had turned full circle, with the American model of business being the only one to show sustained success, despite increasing challenges from economies such as China, India, and the Southeast Asian Tigers. Consequently, there have been many attempts to attribute such exceptional US economic and industrial success to the American way of managing and to American values and institutions (Collins & Porras, 1994; Collins, 2001), which, in turn, has pressured most other countries to accept US ideas, especially in respect of the virtues of flexible labour markets and freedom from government intervention. During this same period, the influence of US business gurus and the major US business schools has also been exceptional (Collins, 2020; Mintzberg, 2004), with the Master of Business Administration degree (MBA) becoming one of the world's major educational brands, especially when gained from prestigious universities in the developed world.

Just as in the 1960s, however, there have been limits to US dominance over ideas on effective business and management, especially following the problems of the collapse of major international companies such as Enron, WorldCom, and Tyco and the GFC of 2007 to 2008. The brand image of America and American companies began to be 'viewed as arrogant and indifferent to others' cultures; exploitative, in the sense that it extracted more than it provided; corrupting, in that it valued materialism above all else; and willing to sacrifice almost anything to generate profits' (*The Economist*, 28 February 2004, p. 76). Further studies showed little improvement in overseas perceptions of America's image, which took a major 'hit' following the election of Donald Trump as President (Pew Research, 2021). In the field of human resource management (HRM), this problem with the American model has been especially true for some considerable period. For example, many Europeans have questioned the appropriateness of much of

US employee relations practice, with its focus on individualism and 'short-termism', its morality in laying off employees without warning, and its appropriateness to social market economies that are based on employee participation in business decision-making (Pendleton & Gospel, 2013). As a result, there were various attempts to develop an alternative European way of managing people (Sparrow et al., 2004). Similarly, Australians sought to develop their own models of leadership and management, and the rapidly growing Chinese economy and indigenous industry attempted some years ago to embed mainly American ideas into their own culturally and institutionally specific ways of doing things (Zhang & Martin, 2003; World Economic Forum, 2023). Consequently, it was sometimes argued that there was a fragmentation of models, with no single set of ideas dominating the management agenda (Clegg et al., 2021). We also witnessed a major debate over the appeal of the US business and management model to the rest of the world. Some writers have described this debate as being between the forces of global convergence (largely those of American multinational corporations and consultants) and those of divergence, with its emphasis on the importance of national mindsets (local cultural and institutional ways of seeing and working) (Harzing & Pinnington, 2014). Recent evidence suggests there has been a retreat from globalisation and a return to nationalism, especially in the tech sector (World Economic Forum, 2023).

Dominant ideas and 'guru theory'

As we have noted, paradigms also appear to change because certain influential theorists or practitioners who make up the so-called management 'guru' industry develop new ways of working and thinking (Collins, 2020). Acceptance of these new ideas occurs not only because these ideas are in and of themselves somehow better than previous ones, but also because you need willing consumers as well as willing producers in the rapidly growing marketplace for knowledge. And, as many critics of management consultancy have noted, willing consumption is often associated with serving the career interests of particular groups of people in organizations or for non-rational institutional reasons such as the pressures to imitate other organizations because of what is expected by institutional shareholders or government officials, or adopt practices to conform to social network pressures – the fear of being 'left out' (Wheen, 2004).

James Hoopes (2003) described the role played by 'guru' academics, consultants, and practitioners who have had a major influence on new ideas and examples of so-called best practice in management during the last 100 years. Hoopes analysed two recurrent 'big ideas' in management and showed how interest in these two ideas has ebbed and flowed in popularity over time. These two ideas are *top-down control* and *bottom-up management*. Top-down control is best exemplified by Frederick Taylor and his school of scientific management in the late 1800s and early 1900s, which emphasised the importance and power of a new managerial 'cadre' in convincing or forcing workers to do what these managers wanted them to do. Usually, this involved heavy doses of close and direct supervision, and payment-by-results systems to motivate workers. Taylor and his followers, including Henry Gantt and Frank and Lilian Gilbreth, were important in spreading the gospel of scientific management. However, it took Henry Ford, the founder of the Ford Motor Company, to apply Taylor's ideas by linking them to technological control embodied in the moving assembly line, before they became practically important. As a result, Fordism became the dominant mode of organizing and managing during the twentieth century. It is usual in academic texts to trace some of the modern management techniques that we shall discuss during this course to Taylor and Ford's ideas of top-down control, including 'business process re-engineering' and 'lean production'.

In contrast, bottom-up management is associated with a more humanistic or, some would argue, realistic belief that such top-down control is ultimately self-defeating. At least two arguments have been used to explain the negative side of top-down management. The first of these, the *alienation thesis*, became fashionable in the 1930s and is still an important argument by many commentators on work and employment relations, especially in the low-skilled sectors of the economy. It concerns the nature and scale of opposition by employees during the twentieth century to having their work 'Taylor-made'. Indeed, this kind of thinking was used to explain the rise of trade unionism during that period and much of the industrial unrest that characterised industrial and labour relations in many advanced economies. The second argument, the *changing nature of work thesis*, has two variants, according to which sector of advanced industrialised economies is being put under the spotlight. The slightly *older variant* has focused on the nature of work in the growing service sector of most developed and developing economies. Jobs in this sector, it is argued, are characterised by employees having greater control over how they perform their jobs than in the traditional manufacturing sectors, largely because of the difficulties in measuring employee output. Services are more qualitative in nature because there is often no tangible output and, in the case of personal services, they are 'consumed' immediately. Think about the quality of service provided by checkout operators in a retail store and then think about the difficulties in measuring their output. High-performing retail organizations place great emphasis on the links between satisfied and engaged employees, high-quality service, and strong brand performance (see Chapter 3). This link between engaged employees and the service–profit chain became the major element in Kaplan and Norton's (2008) 'theory of the business,' to which we shall return.

The *newer variant* has developed because of the increased emphasis on knowledge work in modern economies, which became especially fashionable to emphasise following the 'dot-com' boom in the USA and Europe in the late 1990s. The argument here is that knowledge workers (and most skilled and professional employees can be labelled thus) enjoy genuine power *vis-à-vis* employers over the one scarce, non-substitutable resource that modern organizations use to compete, and that is knowledge and information (see Chapter 7). The adage that 'knowledge is power' has never been truer, it is argued, and in organizations that rest on knowledge as their distinctive competence, managing employees who have effective control over it has become a different proposition from managing large numbers of unskilled workers, whose prior knowledge has been effectively relocated into machines. So, for example, the models of top-down control employed in motor vehicle manufacture were not seen to be relevant in managing consulting firms, healthcare, or science-based industries such as biotechnology. Getting the best from employees in these kinds of industries, where expertise is often located in unwritten, tacit know-how built up over years of experience, usually requires organizations to provide them with high levels of involvement and voice in key decision-making rather than tell them what to do and how to do it, since managers often lack the expertise to do so. Think of the problems and conflicts that occur between hospital administrators and doctors, or between managers who do not have a technical background and technologists, and you begin to get a sense of the need to manage differently.

There are two final points worth highlighting in this section on dominant ideas and guru theory paradigms. The first is that our models of management change over time, often in a cyclical fashion. In connection with the two big ideas of top-down control and bottom-up management, it is clear they have ebbed in and out of fashion throughout the last 100 or so years. Often, this has been a reaction to the worst excesses of their application. This was the case with scientific management because it failed to deliver what was promised in the form of business process re-engineering. It has also been evident in some human relations prescriptions, more of which later. Change and changefulness are at the heart of business and management theory and practice because organizations are always in a process of 'becoming', especially given the, often turbulent, nature of their environments. Thus, any text and course on management must reflect such change and make it a central feature of the analysis.

The second point is to warn you about some of the worst excesses of guru theory and the kinds of material that you can often pick up in airport bookstalls. Willing consumers of management knowledge, looking for quick fixes, are sometimes motivated by the search for 'newness'. Consequently, we are witnessing the creation of a fads and fashion industry for management knowledge (Collins, 2020; Furnham, 2015). Rosenzweig (2007) identified many such fads that, in their day, laid claim to paradigm status, most of which have been discredited or else have been countermanded by other fads and fashions. Because of this faddist nature of management, the whole discipline of management has been characterised as little more than an immature body of knowledge lacking a proper scientific basis and bedevilled by inconsistencies and contradictions that would not be tolerated in any other area of scientific life. This faddish nature of much of management knowledge has been seen as the cause of the low status of business schools within the university community and has raised severe question marks over the role and content of courses such as the MBA.

So, by reading this book, I hope to help you avoid these pitfalls and help you learn useful, though often critical, ideas that have a longer shelf life than many of the guru books that dominate the market for management knowledge.

A FRAMEWORK FOR THE BOOK

Bearing in mind the issues previously raised in this chapter about the nature of management and change, our focus is on the problems of managing people and organizations in changing contexts. To help guide you through the rest of the book, let's look at Figure 1.1.

Any book on management must begin with an examination of the nature of what is being studied and practised, which is the subject of Chapter 2. In this chapter, we have adapted and reworked some ideas by well-known management theorists to produce a

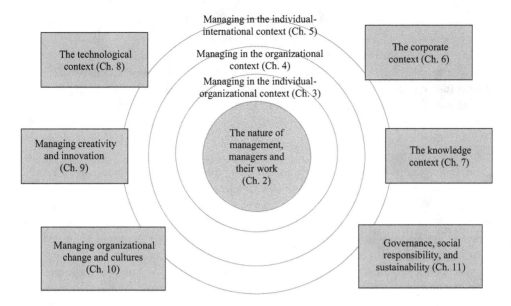

The technological context (Ch. 8)

The corporate context (Ch. 6)

Managing in the individual-international context (Ch. 5)

Managing in the organizational context (Ch. 4)

Managing in the individual-organizational context (Ch. 3)

The nature of management, managers and their work (Ch. 2)

Managing creativity and innovation (Ch. 9)

The knowledge context (Ch. 7)

Managing organizational change and cultures (Ch. 10)

Governance, social responsibility, and sustainability (Ch. 11)

FIGURE 1.1 A framework for the book

model of a rounded manager who can operate at different levels and in different contexts in modern economies. This model of management should help you to think more reflectively and, indeed, reflexively about your own job and others you may move into during your career.

The first premise of the model is that management is practised at different levels – managing on the inside, managing across the organization, and managing on the outside, which we discuss in Chapter 2. Managers who are unable to deal effectively with people at these different levels are increasingly unlikely to deliver strategic goals. This is equally true for human resource managers and many line managers, who have traditionally defined their roles as managing on the inside, as well as marketing managers, whose roles have naturally inclined them to manage on the outside.

The second premise of the model is that managers are being asked to manage in changing contexts., which, in some respects, are qualitatively different from the experience of managing even a few decades ago. Let's take an example from a real-life case of remote management I came across quite a few years ago. A senior sales manager, working for a leading international instrumentation company, was asked to take on the role of managing a global team of highly qualified, highly paid sales engineers, operating in ten countries. It made little sense to have these sales engineers relocate to head office, so the organizational structure had to be 'virtual' and the senior sales manager had to learn to manage at a distance and across time zones. This solution emerged because the company, Agilent Technologies, had grown rapidly through acquisition and had acquired these ten countries over a short period of time. His job was to instil a sense of corporate spirit into his engineers as well as support them in developing their own national markets. Thus, he faced the problems of managing a disparate group of people, from very different national and organizational cultures, to manage locally and integrate their efforts with each other.

This example throws up the problems of managing in multiple, changing contexts. Our senior sales engineer's initial problem required him to understand the different expectations, needs, and attachments that engage individuals with organizations – their psychological contracts – and how best to exercise leadership in circumstances where people are likely to differ markedly in their expectations, needs, and attachments. This is the subject of Chapter 3. Then he had to understand how organizational structures can influence individual and group behaviour, and how to design and operate in structures that were more complex and virtual than those he has previously experienced, which is the subject of Chapter 4. He also faced the problems of managing in an international context, which is sometimes defined in terms of overcoming the 'liability of foreignness': How should managers deal with the costs of doing business abroad, arising from unfamiliarity with the cultural and institutional environment and the needs for coordination across time and space? This is the subject of Chapter 5.

Moving on, the example raises problems of how to create a sense of 'corporateness' in a previously fragmented organization because the organization wishes to leverage its international brand for new markets. It also raises the problems of managing employees who are knowledge workers, many of whom are individualistic by nature and can exercise lots of power because of their understanding of local markets, and the issue of how technology might be used to achieve global integration of the sales team in a way that was close to impossible before the introduction of the internet. So, in Chapter 6, we shall look at the corporate context and examine the problems managers face in creating strong corporate reputations and corporate brands. In Chapter 7, we shall examine the changing nature of work, particularly the role of knowledge in creating value in organizations and the problems of managing so-called knowledge workers. In Chapter 8, we shall study the changing technological context, particularly the role of information and communications technologies, social media, and AI, in being positive and negative forces for change and jobs (OECD, 2023). In Chapter 9, we examine the problems of managing creativity, innovation, and teamworking. These issues have become an important context for firms in all countries as they strive to compete. Our senior sales engineer also faced the problems of managing the change process itself; how should he turn his plans for a globally integrated sales team into action? The old saying about the best-laid plans falling in the implementation phase is even more appropriate in an increasingly unknowable world, which is the subject of Chapter 10.

Finally, we end with Chapter 11, which deals with the increasingly important context of corporate governance and the related agendas of corporate social responsibility and sustainability. My recent research into corporate governance and managing people has convinced us of the importance of different governance models and how they influence every aspect of what goes on in organizations, sectors, and, indeed, national business systems(Martin et al., 2016). One only needs to consider the impact of the 2007/2008 GFC on economies such as the USA and the UK. Such events have given even further impetus to the corporate (social) responsibility and sustainability agendas, and a concern to inject ethics into business. We hope by covering such a wide range of ground that you gain a greater understanding of the need to 'complexify', rather than simplify, the problems facing managers in an increasingly unknowable world, but at the same time, find some ideas that you can put into practice. The adage that there is 'nothing so practical as good theory' is one I commend to you, and we hope you find enough in this book that is sufficiently well-founded theoretically and practical to justify the time you devote to reading the rest of the chapters.

LEARNING SUMMARY

In this chapter, we have learnt about some of the key ideas underlying the management of people in changing contexts, including the relevance of universalism and relativism to management practice and the importance of mindsets in shaping how we view management problems and solutions.

First, we argued that the idea of 'best practice' is flawed because management practices are always 'context bound' in the sense that practices are developed in unique mixtures of organizational, industrial, cultural, and historical 'soil'. Therefore, you cannot transfer practices easily from one situation to another without some adaptation and considerable time and effort to embed these practices in new fertile soil. Thus, practices can best be described as 'promising'; there is simply no 'one-best-way' to manage.

Second, we suggested that change is one of the few universals or constants of management. Therefore, understanding how contexts and ideas about management have changed and have often been recycled is important. However, such change is often cyclical, exemplified by *the* major debate in management theory and practice – top-down versus bottom-up management and organization. Management theory has been dominated at different points in history by the mechanistic mindset, which has resulted in bureaucratic organizations and control, and the organic mindset, which is revealed through a more bottom-up, humanistic, and people-orientated mode of management. These cycles of interest reflect models of national economic and business success – for example, the Japanese model and organic management – and the role of management gurus in shaping dominant ideas. All managers are searching for something new; often, however, the latest fad is little more than 'old wine in new bottles,' which usually turns into something quite disappointing. One good example is Case 1.1 on human relations; the basis of modern human resource management rests on many of its assumptions and studies, which have continued to disappoint business leaders, judging by the lack of credibility of the HR function in most organizations.

Finally, we have set out a framework for the book. This framework is based on the idea that management is practised at different levels and in changing contexts.. Above all else, however, management must produce change and innovation because, without these characteristics, organizations are destined for 'reversion to the long-term mean' for their 'asset class' or even terminal decline. Given the importance of organizations to our economic success and social well-being, making effective managers is one of the key goals of advanced industrial societies; the remainder of this book is aimed at helping you in this regard.

REVIEW QUESTIONS

1. What is the difference between a universalist and relativist perspective on management and organizations?

2. Is it possible for managers to engage in reflexive thinking about their careers and organizations? What might help them to do so and what might prevent them?

CASE 1.1 THE DEVELOPMENT OF HUMAN RELATIONS AND ORGANIZATIONAL BEHAVIOUR AND THE ROLE OF ACADEMIC GURUS

Zhong and House (2012) summarised the feelings of many management academics that few studies in management have had such a pervasive effect on organizational behaviour as the Hawthorne Studies. So, it is only natural to begin a book like this by introducing you to this landmark study and the problems it raised for the study and practice of management.

The conventional wisdom in many texts has been to attribute these studies to Elton Mayo, the founding father of what is now known as organizational behaviour but began as human relations. Mayo was of Scottish descent but grew up in Australia in the early 1900s. He attempted and failed at a medical education in Adelaide, Edinburgh, and London, but came to study economics and philosophy in Australia and was appointed to a lectureship in Queensland. How did this itinerant 'failure', with a rather conventional education, come to have such a huge influence on the study and practice of management for decades after his death in 1949?

Through a series of accidental meetings, Mayo became interested in the newly emerging discipline of psychology and psychotherapy and, following self-study, became Australia's first practising psychoanalyst. Because of previously formed interests in helping reduce conflict among workers and employers in Queensland, his adopted state, he wrote a book, published in 1919, entitled *Democracy and Freedom*, which warned against greedy employers and class-conscious workers and their unions pursuing their self-interests. Rather than see such a conflict of interests as a naturally occurring phenomenon during the early factory system, he described it in psychoanalytical terms as unconscious phobias. He proposed that the parties should act together to achieve a common social purpose through industrial cooperation and, in doing so, provide an alternative to political democracy. Intelligent managers, he argued, could, through therapeutic techniques and by allowing workers greater participation at work, promote social harmony, not only in industry but also in society at large. His message to the world became the importance of the human factor in an age that was dominated by the teachings of organizations as machines and the role of technology in transforming work and industrial enterprises.

Mayo decided to leave Australia in 1922 to return to London but, running out of money, ended up in California. Through personal charm, and an acute sense of opportunity, he managed to secure a research position with the influential Social Science Research Council, albeit aided by some rather dubious references he had created for himself. Through his heightened sense of networking as a way of getting career development, Mayo moved to the Wharton Business School and then to Harvard. By cultivating the attention of its Dean, Walter Donham, Mayo managed to establish himself at Harvard Business School. Once there, he introduced his ideas on psychotherapy into the curriculum and the notion that the manager's main mission was to produce social harmony in industry. While at Harvard, he secured some grant funds, which he used to cultivate a group of gifted young researchers, who collectively became known as the 'Harvard Human Relations Group'. He also made key connections with an anthropologist, W. Lloyd Warner, a statistician, T. N. Whitehead, and a biologist, Lawrence Henderson. This group would have an enormous influence on the progress of American industry and business education.

The most famous of their projects was the so-called Hawthorne experiments, begun in 1926–27 in the Western Electric subsidiary of AT&T, near Cicero, Illinois. This work began as a study of the effects of scientific management ideas on worker productivity and, in particular, the influence of natural or artificial lighting on worker output. However, manipulation of these variables seemed to have no effect. George Pennock, Hawthorne's technical superintendent who conducted these experiments, began to make other changes by introducing rest breaks, shorter hours, and mid-morning meals. Eventually, Pennock decided to set up an experiment by isolating five girls in the now-famous 'Relay Assembly Test Room' (RATR). Pennock asked them to work at a comfortable pace and examined the effects of changes in work conditions on their output. At the same time, however, he also introduced a strong, group-based economic incentive. The five girls were separated from the main hall, where 100 or so workers were employed and paid on a departmental-wide system; what individuals produced here didn't have much effect on individual earnings. Following a series of experimental changes to heating, lighting, length of the working day, rest breaks, and so on, productivity rose in the RATR by approximately 10 per cent.

The girls in the RATR had no supervisor, but Pennock introduced an observer called Homan Hilbarger, who initially became friendly with the girls, but gradually began to annoy them by making advances and unwanted remarks. Later on, Hilbarger created further problems when he overheard two of the girls discussing whether they would hold back their effort or go flat out. He told Pennock, who replaced them immediately. The result was record output levels. Pennock couldn't understand what the cause of the improvements was – the small group effect, lunches, rest periods, or whatever. He chose to reject the explanation of higher output for higher pay for reasons we can only speculate on.

Meanwhile, Mayo came across these experiments as the result of an invitation from the Personnel Director, following a talk Mayo had given in New York. He was asked to comment on what Pennock had found, and this he did with unbounded glee. Scarcely could he believe that he had come across a set of experiments that confirmed his thesis that men and women could use work as the basis for creating social harmony and quickly set about reinterpreting the 'data' to fit in with his prior ideas. Mayo originally analysed the conflict that emerged in the group through neurosis, but when he returned in 1928, Pennock had temporarily returned the improved working conditions of the RATR to their original state by removing all previous benefits. Productivity rose yet again, and Mayo, expecting the opposite to occur, was presented with the task of explaining this unwanted result.

Mayo turned to the now-famous theory that the more sympathetic supervision and counselling in the RATR, aided by the observer Hilbarger, had helped the workgroup establish a group spirit, a sense of belonging, and a sense of working for each other that could not be easily demolished by removing external conditions. He also castigated scientific management explanations for being unable to explain these rises in output. He went on to train supervisors in social therapy techniques so that they could interview workers and use these interviews as a valve for emotional release. However, he soon lost interest in the actual experimental side and gave control of the programme to some of his junior colleagues, who set up another experiment, the Bank Wiring Test Room. This experiment used more rigorous techniques of observation and found evidence that totally contradicted Mayo's thesis. However, Mayo chose not to report the Bank Wiring Test Room in the book he persuaded the Western Electric Company to sponsor, the 1933 edition of *Human Problems of an Industrial Civilisation*. In this book, Mayo devoted only 40 pages to Hawthorne but described it in eulogising terms – as a near-utopia in which the girls were never under pressure. Therapeutic supervision had managed to create harmony among a group that subordinated its own self-interests in favour of the right to participate in the greater good of the group. To create such communities of practice was the job of the new breed of managers trained in psychotherapy. The result would be a form of industrial democracy in which unreasonable democratic conflict would be removed from the industrial landscape.

A subsequent, and much larger, account of the Hawthorne experiments by his acolytes, Roethlisberger and Dickson (1939), was written in such a manner as to confirm much of what Mayo had suggested, preserving the idea that human relations should be concerned with the explanation of group dynamics and output changes, and not the more obvious scientific management explanations of pay and rewards (though they did recognise pay as a contributory factor). From what has been described as the 'dullest book ever written,' the 'scientific' study of human relations and organizational behaviour developed as a counter to Taylorism and the teachings of the day in American and European business schools.

Sources: Hoopes, 2003; Rose, 1975; Roethlisberger & Dickson, 1939; Zhong & House, 2012).

1 Why do you think Pennock chose not to report the possible explanation that output in the Relay Assembly Test Room rose because of the economic motivations of

the workers, and why did Mayo also reject the explanation that money was at the root of output increases?

2. Why did the ideas of human relations become so widely popular, despite the rather obvious flaws in the experiments and Mayo's reporting of them?

3. How have Mayo's ideas been adopted and transformed in modern management techniques?

4. How does the concept of universalism apply to this case, and how universal are the ideas of human relations?

REFERENCES

Association of Advanced Colleges of Business. (2023, May 8). *Changing the business model of business schools.* https://www.aacsb.edu/insights/articles/2023/05/changing-the-business-model-of-business-schools

Armbruster, T. (2006). The economics and sociology of management consulting, Cambrid, MA: Cambridge University Press.

Bloom, N., & Van Reene, J. (2010). Why do management practices differ across firms and countries. *Journal of Economic Perspectives, 24*(1), 203–224.

Brewster, C., & Harris, H. (Eds.). (1999). *International HRM: Contemporary issues in Europe.* Financial Times/Prentice-Hall.

Chartered Institute of Personnel and Development. (2002). *How do people learn? Research report.* CIPD.

Christensen, C.M., Raynor, M.E. & McDonald, R. (2015). What is disruptive innovation? *Harvard Business Review,*93, 44–53.

Clarke, T., & Clegg, S. R. (1998). *Changing paradigms: The transformation of management in the 21st century.* Collins.

Clegg, S. R., Kornberger, M., & Pitsis, T. (2021). *Managing and organizations: An introduction to theory and practice* (6th ed.). Sage.

Collins, D. (2020). *Management gurus: A research overview.* Routledge.

Collins, J. C. (2001). *Good to great: Why some companies make the leap ... and others don't.* HarperCollins.

Collins, J. C., & Porras, J. I. (1994). *Built to last: Successful habits of visionary companies.* HarperCollins.

Crane, A., & Matten, D. (2019). *Business ethics: Managing corporate citizenship and sustainability in the age of globalization* (5th ed.). Oxford University Press.

Cunliffe, A. L. (2014). Reflexive inquiry in organizational research: Questions and possibilities. Reprinted in H. Willmottand E. Bell (eds), *Qualitative Research in Business and Management.* London: Sage.

Czarniawska, B. (2011). *Cyberfactories: How news agencies produce news.* Edward Elgar

Davies, W. (2015). *The happiness industry: How the government and big business sold us well-being.* Verso Books.

Davis, J (2022). *Taming corporate power in the 21st century.* Cambridge: Cambridge University Press.

Dipoye, R. (2005). How I stopped worrying and learned to appreciate the gaps between academic HRM and practice. In R. J. Burke & C. L. Cooper (Eds.), *Reinventing HRM: Challenges and new directions* (pp. 91–112). Routledge.

Economist. (2015, May 15). *Keeping it on the company campus.* Economist Newspapers.

Evans, P., & Wurster, T. S. (2000). *Blown to bits: How the economics of information transformed strategy.* Harvard University Press.

Fox, A. (1974). *Beyond constract: work, trust and power relations.* London: Faber Faber.

Foley, C. F., Hines, J. R., & Wessel, D. (Eds.). (2021). *Global goliaths: Multinational corporations in the 21st century.* Brookings Institute Press.

Furnham, A. (2015, July 20). Fads and fashions in management. *The European Business Review.* https://www.europeanbusinessreview.com/fads-and-fashions-in-management/

Glaister, K. (2014). The contribution of management to economic growth: A review. *Prometheus, 32*(3), 227–244.

Goold, M., & Campbell, A. (2002). *Designing effective organizations: How to create structured networks.* Jossey-Bass.

Hamel, G. (2009, February). Moonshots for managers. *Harvard Business Review,* pp. 1–21.

Harzin, A–W., & Pinnington, A. (2014). *International human resource management* (4th ed.). Sage.

Hodgkinson, G. P., & Healey, M. P. (2011). Psychological foundations of dynamic capabilities: Reflexion and reflection in strategic management. *Strategic Management Journal, 32*(13), 1500–1515.

Hoopes, J. (2003). *False prophets: The gurus who created modern industry and why their ideas are bad for business.* Perseus Publishing.

Howieson, W. B., & Robson, I. (2022). The business school in ruins: Navigating the multi-stakeholder landscape of contemporary management scholarship. In A. Ortenblad & R. Koris (Eds.), *Debating business school legitimacy: Attacking, rocking, and defending the status quo* (pp. 25–145). Palgrave.

Kaplan, R. S., & Norton, D. P. (2008). *The execution premium: Linking strategy to operations for competitive advantage: How balanced scorecard companies thrive in the new business environment.* Harvard Business School Press.

Khurana, R., & Spender, J. C. (2012). Herbert A. Simon on what ails business schools: More than a problem in organizational design. *Journal of Management Studies, 49*(3), 619–639.

King, D., & Learmonth, M. (2015). Can critical management studies ever be `practical'? A case study in engaged scholarship. *Human Relations, 68*(3), 353–375

Lawrence, P. (2002). *The change game: How today's global trends are shaping tomorrow's companies.* Kogan Page.

Leseure, M. J., Bauer, J., Birdi, K., Neely, A., & Denyer, D. (2004). Adoption of promising practices: A systematic review of the evidence. *International Journal of Management Reviews, 5/6,* 169–190.

Locke, R. (1996). *The collapse of the American management mystique.* Oxford University Press.

Locke, R.R. & Spender, J-C. (2011). *Confronting managerialism.* London: Zed Books.

Martin, G., Parry, E., & Flowers, P. (2015). Do social media enhance employee voice just some of the time or all of the time, *Human Resource Management Journal, 25*(4), 541–562

Martin, G., Farndale, E., Paauwe, J. & Stiles, P.G. (2016). Corporate governance and strategic human resource management: four archetypes and proposals for a new approach to corporate sustainability, *European Management Journal, 34*(1), 22-35.

Martin, G., Siebert, S., & Robson, I. (2018). Conformist innovation: And institutional logics perspective on how HR executives construct business school reputations. *International Journal of Human Resource Management, 29*(13), 2027–2053.

Mayer, C. (2013). *Firm commitment: why the corporation is failingus and how to restore trust in it.* Oxford: Oxford University Press.

Micklethwait, J., & Woolridge, A. (1997). *The witch doctors: Making sense of management gurus.* Random House.

Mintzberg, H. (1983). *Structure in fives.* Prentice-Hall.

Mintzberg, H. (2004). *Managers not MBAs: A hard look at the soft practice of managing.* Financial Times/Prentice-Hall.

Mintzberg, H. (2011). *Managing.* New York: Berrett-Koehler.

Mintzberg, H. (2015). *Rebalancing society: radical renewal beyond left, right, and center.* New York: Berrett-Koehler.

Morgan, G. (1997). *Images of organization.* Sage.

OECD. (2023). *Artificial intelligence and jobs: An urgent need to act.* https://www.oecd.org/employment-outlook/2023/

Ortenblad, A., & Koris, R. (Eds.). (2022). *Debating business school legitimacy: Attacking, rocking, and defending the status quo.* Palgrave.

Pascale, R. (1999). Surfing the edge of chaos. *Sloan Management Review, 40*(3), 83–94.

Pascale, R., & Athos, A. (1981). *The art of Japanese management.* Warner.

Pendleton, A., & Gospel, H. (2013). Corporate governance and human resource management. In S. Bach & M. Edwards (Eds.), *Managing human resources* (5th ed., pp. 61–78). Wiley.

Petit, S. C., & Huault, I. (2008). From practice-based knowledge to the practice research: Revisiting constructivist research works on knowledge. *Management Learning, 39*(1), 73–91.

Pettigrew, A., & Starkey, K. (2016). The legitimacy and impact of business schools: Key issues and a research agenda. *Academy of Management Learning and Education, 15*(4), 649–664

Pew Research. (2021, June 10). *America's image abroad rebounds with transition from Trump to Biden.* https://www.pewresearch.org/global/2021/06/10/americas-image-abroad-rebounds-with-transition-from-trump-to-biden/.

Pfeffer, J. & Sutton, R.I. (2006). *Hard facts, dangerous half truths, and total nonsense.* Profiting from evidence-based management. Cambridge, MA: Harvard Business School Poress.

Pierce, J. R., & Aguinas, H. (2013). The "too-much-of-a-good-thing" effect in management. *Journal of Management, 39,* 313–338.

Robson, I. (2022). *The reflective leader: Reflexivity in practice.* Emerald Publishing.

Roethlisberger, F. J., & Dickson, W. J. (1939). *Management and the worker.* Harvard Business School Press.

Rose, M. (1975). *Industrial behaviour: Theoretical developments since Taylor. llen Lane.*

Rozenzweig, P. (2007). *The Halo effect…and the eight other business delusions that deceive managers.* Free Press.

Seely Brown, J. (2000). *The social life of information.* Harvard Business School Press.

Siebert, S., Martin, G., Bozic, B., & Docherty, I. (2015). *Looking 'beyond the factory gates': Towards more pluralist and radical approaches to intraorganizational trust research, organization studies, first published on May 7, 2015 as.* doi:10.1177/0170840615580010

Siebert, S., Martin, G. & Simpson, G. (2020) Rhetorical strategies of legitimation in the professional field of banking, *Journal of Professions and Organizations,* 7(2), 134–155.

Sparrow, P. R., Brewster, C., & Harris, H. (2004). *Globalizing human resource management.* Psychology Press.

Spilg, E., Siebert, S., & Martin, G. (2012). A social learning perspective on the development of doctors in the UK National Health Service, *Social Sciences and Medicine,* 75(9), 1617–1624.

Suleyman, M (2023). *The coming wave: Technology, power, and 21st century's greatest dilemma.* Bodley Head.

Teece, D.J. (2018) Business models and dynamic capabilities, *Long Range Planning, 31*(1), 40–49.

Thornton, P.H., Ocasio, W. & Lounsbury, M. (2012). *The institutional logics perspective: a new approach to culture, structure and process.* Oxford: Oxford University Press.

Weick, K.E. & Sutcliffe, K. M. (2007). *Managing the unexpected: resilient performance in the age of uncertainty* (2nd edition), Josey-Bass.

Wenger, E. (1998). *Communities of practice: Learning, meaning and identity.* Cambridge University Press.

Wenger, E., McDermott, R. & Snyder, W.C. (2002). *Cultivating communities of practice: a guide to managing knowledge.* Cambridge, MA: Harvard Business School Press.

Wheen, F. (2004). *How Mumbo-Jumbo conquered the world: A short history of modern delusions.* Perennial.

Whitley, R. (2009). US capitalism: a tarnished model? *Academy of Management Perspectives,* 23(2), 11–22.

Whittington, R. (2000). *What is strategy? And does strategy matter? Thomson International.*

World Economic Forum. (2023). *Welcome to the age of polycrisis: The global risks report, 2023.* https://www3.weforum.org/docs/WEF_Global_Risks_Report_2023.pdf

Zhang, H., & Martin, G. (2003). *Managing human resources in Sino-Foreign joint ventures.* Jiangxi Science and Technology Publishing.

Zhong, C.-B., & House, J. (2012). Hawthorne revisited: Organizational implications of the physical work environment. *Research in Organizational Behavior, 32,* 3–22.

CHAPTER 2

The nature of management, managers, and their work

LEARNING OBJECTIVES

By the end of this chapter, you should be able to:

- Understand the key roles and activities of a manager's job.
- Apply these roles and activities to your own job and those of your colleagues.
- Understand the importance of different contexts in shaping the jobs of managers.
- Understand how management competences relate to the different managerial roles and levels at which managers perform.
- Distinguish between management as a form of control and management as a form of leadership.
- Understand and recognise the components of wisdom and how they relate to sound judgement.
- Understand how the personal qualities of managers relate to effective managerial performance.
- Self-assess your personal qualities for management.

A FRAMEWORK FOR UNDERSTANDING MANAGERS AND THEIR WORK

Introduction

In Chapter 1, we examined some of the key ideas underlying the study of managing people in context, including universalism and relativism, the importance of changing contexts and their influence on managers' jobs, and the role of management thinkers in shaping our understanding of management. These ideas are further developed in this chapter, in which I drill down into some of the practicalities of management.

DOI: 10.4324/9781003469711-2

I have developed a framework for thinking about what it takes to be a 'rounded' manager by drawing on the work of some highly respected writers in this field. By rounded, I mean a manager who is competent across a broad range of activities rather than a specialist in a narrow field. This rounding-out framework integrates the personal qualities that managers bring to their jobs, the activities and contexts inherent in effective managerial work, and the different levels at which managers can act. It also introduces you to the notions of wisdom, a neglected area in the literature on management but very important for you to understand and be able to apply to your jobs and career.

Because this is quite a long and complicated chapter, I have interspersed the text with four activities that deal with specific aspects of the rounded manager framework. This should help break up the text and show how specific aspects of the framework can be applied to managers' jobs.

The background to the study of managerial work

To understand managers and the process of management, we can draw on a long tradition of research into the nature of managerial work – what managers do and what managers should be doing. Since the 1980s, much of this research has focused on defining, measuring, and developing managerial competences, especially in the USA and the UK. For example, the USA Office of Personnel developed a set of standards for supervisors and the UK government-sponsored research and development into producing new occupational standards for different levels and types of management, initially through the Chartered Institute of Management. These competence frameworks have become de rigueur even in fields such as medical leadership (Howieson et al., 2024). So, in this chapter, and in the rest of the book, I shall address the three questions raised at the beginning of this section. I do so because it is in everyone's interests – teachers, students of management, and examiners alike – to avoid the reputation for lack of relevance that management knowledge enjoys with many practitioners (Pettigrew & Starkey, 2016) and for promoting a disconnected and self-serving managerialism. With respect to the lack of relevance, this has largely come about because dominant sections of the producer community of management knowledge – the producers of business guru books and the management consulting industry – have oversold the idea of the one-best-way or best practice in wave after wave of management fads (Pascale et al., 2000). Some time ago, Francis Wheen (2004), rather amusingly, labelled much of this type of material, especially the self-help books by ex-business leaders, as 'old snake oil in new bottles,' pointing to the often-messianic salesmanship of banal aphorisms dressed up in jargon and pseudo-scientific phrases, such as 're-engineering, benchmarking and downsizing.' The same critique of what often passes for management knowledge is probably still relevant today, for example, in the leadership and engagement 'industries'. Moreover, since we live in an increasingly changeable and arguably unknowable world, what we can usefully teach about management often has a short 'shelf-life'.

If the guru industry has not helped the relevance cause, neither have some management academics who claim to pursue a practical agenda. Critical management scholars, a diverse group of academics who question the politics and values of managerialism (a set of ideas and practices that are tied to promoting the interests of managers), argue that many, ostensibly relevant, management academics and most consultants fail to engage in reflexive thinking over dominant business discourses (Cunliffe, 2014). Two examples of such a discourse are shareholder value, the belief that businesses exist to create value for shareholders only (Martin et al., 2016), and transformational leadership (Pettigrew & Starkey, 2016), which places managers at the centre of change programmes. Both are often expounded uncritically by those who benefit most from having such ideas accepted as truths – including, among others, highly paid leaders who benefit from share ownership, university business schools that benefit from running leadership courses, and the business press that promotes and feeds off celebrity leaders (Martin et al., 2018).

It is not only critical management scholars, however, that question the relevance agenda. Even 'mainstream' management academics and some practising managers are beginning to acknowledge the limitations of their craft and the problems of becoming disconnected from the organizations they are employed to serve. The notion of managerial sustainability by taking a longer-term time perspective (Martin et al., 2016) and the Principles of Responsible Management Education (PRME) are recent examples of such questioning. The ethics in business agenda is not new, however. It was evident in a major soul-searching exercise run at Half-Moon Bay in California in May 2008 in the aftermath of the Global Financial Crisis, which brought together well-known academics and senior executives to redefine a more ethically based notion of leadership.

Key concept: Management competence and standards

Management competences are the functions and activities that individuals with management and leadership responsibilities are expected to be able to undertake in their organization. Sometimes a distinction is made between competence and competency. Competence usually refers to the functions or activities undertaken by managers, such as developing people, whereas competency usually refers to the personal qualities an individual may bring to a job, such as networking skills or creativity. There have been various attempts to turn these competence frameworks into management standards – responsibilities that managers are expected to be able to undertake regardless of their industry sector or type/size of organization. The National Standards for Management and Leadership in the UK was an excellent example. These standards describe the level of performance expected for a range of management and leadership functions and activities, including managing and working with people, managing self and personal development, facilitating change, using resources, and providing direction and achieving results, all of which are examined in this book. More recently, the Management Chartered Institute in the UK has introduced level 3, 4 and 5 standards for different levels of managers. Level 5 includes building stakeholder relationships, delivering operational plans, managing projects, and managing finance, which they argue are needed for managers who typically report to a senior manager or business owner.

In this section, we trace the origins and trajectory of these developments and propose a new framework to help you think about the nature of management. This framework draws on different ideas from some of the leading thinkers on management and will provide the basis for much of the subsequent discussion in this course.

Reviewing the literature on the future of management some years ago, Harry Scarborough (1998) described two schools of theory on management. These are still relevant today, although we hear much less of the first of these – the *empiricist* perspective – probably because of the preoccupation with leaders and leadership. The empiricist perspective attempts to address the question: What do managers do? This stream of research was best exemplified by the various studies of effective managers' roles and behaviour, such as Henry Mintzberg (1973, 2011, 2013), John Kotter (1990), and the now-deceased Rosemary Stewart (1979). These writers developed rich descriptions of managerial behaviours and practices, classified them according to the functions they perform for organizations, and developed prescriptive theories of what managers should do. Probably the best known of these was Mintzberg's (1973) analysis of managerial work, which formed a point of departure for subsequent discussions of management and is still relevant today in describing what managers do (see Box 2.1 and Mintzberg, 2011, 2013).

Box 2.1 Mintzberg (1973/2011/2013): Managerial work – analysis from observation

Based on a one-week observation of the chief executives of five medium-to-large organizations in the early 1970s, Mintzberg suggested an answer to the question: 'What do managers do?'

He described the characteristics of the work of these managers in the following terms and found no reason to change this list more than 40 years later when he conducted a larger follow-up study:

- Managers performed a great quantity of work at an unrelenting pace.
- Managers' activity was characterised by variety, fragmentation, and brevity.
- Managers preferred issues that were current, specific, and ad hoc.
- Managers sat between the organization and a network of contacts.
- Managers demonstrated a strong preference for verbal media (telephone and meetings, as opposed to mail and tours).
- Managers appeared to be able to control their own affairs (despite the fact that they had so many obligations).

Mintzberg broke down the content of the work of a manager into the following roles:

- Interpersonal roles – arise directly from his formal authority and involve basic interpersonal relationships.
  - Figurehead: a symbol, attends ceremonial events, signs legal documents.
  - Leader: motivates subordinates, develops the work milieu.
  - Liaison: horizontal communication with other managers, informal relationships.

- Informational roles:
    - Nerve centre (monitor): the focal point for the movement of non-routine (internal and external) information, including contacts with people who are nerve centres in other organizations.
    - Disseminator: transmission of information and values to subordinates.
    - Spokesman: transmission of information to outsiders.

- Decisional roles:
    - Entrepreneur: looking for opportunities and potential problems that may cause him to initiate improvement projects.
    - Disturbance handler: handling situations that are not covered by the routine rules.
    - Resource allocator: scheduling their own and their subordinates' time, and authorising all significant decisions before they are implemented.
    - Negotiator: as part of being the organization's legal authority, its spokesman, and its resource allocator.

The second of the schools identified by Scarborough was the *essentialist* perspective, the various strands of which are characterised by the attempt to uncover the 'essence' of management and its relationship to the underlying functions management performs for organizations, such as planning, motivating, and controlling employees. This essentialism is closely related to the developments by the early writers on management, such as Taylor, Ford, and Fayol, to uncover a one-best-way or science of management (Clegg et al., 2021). Such a perspective has a long history and is underpinned by the universalistic principles discussed in Chapter 1.

Both perspectives have weaknesses, one of the most important of these being their neglect of the national institutional and cultural contexts in which management is practised, and how these change over time. As we have already seen from the illustration on Germany in Chapter 1, there has been resistance to management practices developed in the USA. Similarly, private sector practices, developed in contexts for which profit maximisation or shareholder value are the dominant concerns, may have less relevance in the public sector. The public sector tends to be characterised by multiple stakeholders, all of whom are deemed to have legitimate claims on organizational goals and resources (see Chapter 11 on corporate governance). Finally, neither perspective has much to say about the kinds of personal characteristics or competencies required of effective managers in different situations, a topic that has been the subject of work on leadership and emotional intelligence, and one to which we shall return in Chapter 3. In the remainder of this chapter, I have developed a framework for thinking about management that draws on the ideas of the eminent management thinkers who are widely acknowledged to have made a major contribution to the literature on management and organizational behaviour.

CASE 2.1 USING MINTZBERG'S DESCRIPTORS

1 Using the description of Mintzberg's work in Box 2.1, would you expect to find significant differences between managing in the public sector and managing in the private sector? If so, which roles would you expect to be more important in the public sector?

2 Again, using the description of Mintzberg's work in Box 2.1, think about someone who has had responsibility for your work. Which of the roles did he or she tend to perform most effectively and least effectively? How did his or her performance in these roles affect your work?

A FRAMEWORK FOR UNDERSTANDING THE ROUNDED MANAGER

Introduction to the rounded manager

Any selection of thinkers on management is bound to be restrictive because writing about the topic has become 'big business' and, as we noted in Chapter 1, there is a growing guru industry which has developed to meet the insatiable demand for new insights into management. High on anyone's list of experts would be Henry Mintzberg, a Canadian whose earlier work we have already discussed. Mintzberg has spent much of his academic career studying managers in context and developing models of management, with a view to setting out his ideas for a 'well-rounded manager' who would be able to function effectively in most business situations.

As we have already seen earlier in this chapter, Mintzberg's earliest work during the 1970s helped map out the territory by describing several roles that managers performed during his studies of managers. This work was notable because it was based on observation and what managers did in practice, not on what managers were supposed to do. However, in more recent formulations of the nature of management, Mintzberg (1994, 2011, 2013) attempted to 'round out the manager's job.' Prompted by criticisms of the 'atomistic' listing of managerial roles and competences taken by many organizations, Mintzberg offered a more holistic approach to management. He argued that the listings of well-documented roles and competences 'even if joined up in a circle' did not capture the integrated nature of a manager's job. Nor did they attempt to explain how different competences related to each other, except in a very general sense. For example, such a criticism could be made of the older version of the UK Management Standards, developed by the Management Charter Initiative in the early 1990s. In these standards, competences were categorised together under roles such as managing people or managing resources. Little or no attempt, however, was made to show how the competences related to each other, except as part of managing people, etc., or to show how the roles themselves related to the overall job of managing in different contexts. The newer version of the standards went some way to meeting these shortcomings but were still charged with being atomistic.

Mintzberg's rounding out of the manager's job is a holistic explanation that goes beyond a description of management. Building on his ideas, those of other key writers in this field, and some of our research in the healthcare sector (Martin et al., 2015), we have set out in Figure 2.1 a revised and extended model of his rounded-out manager. This new model also draws on Keith Grint's (2011) four approaches to studying leadership (*see* Figure 2.1) – management as a position, management as a person, management as results, and management as a process – and the work of other key writers and researchers in this field. While this framework is what we call an *entitative* framework, a logical abstraction that treats management as a homogenous group, we have tried to show how the context in which management is performed, and the vertical and hierarchical divisions among different levels and kinds of managers, shape managerial effectiveness.

The person in the job

The framework begins with Mintzberg's (2011) notion of the 'the person in the job.' People come to take on managerial jobs with an already formed self-concept or identity of who they are, a set of values about what is right and wrong, and ideas about acceptable behaviour for managers. They also bring with them a set of prior experiences that have helped them create a set of job and personal competences, and a body of job-related knowledge, such as professional standards, for example, those required by the Chartered Institute of Personnel and Development (CIPD) in the UK for entry into the HR profession. And, as we saw in Chapter 1, such knowledge and experience also help them develop frames of reference or mindsets through which to view their world and fashion solutions to the problems they face. These mindsets are a way of seeing and can lead to lots of creative insights, but they are also a way of not seeing (Morgan, 1997). For example, managers who lack knowledge and experience outside their own specific functions, organizations, or countries can run into trouble. If you can see from only one perspective, for example, as an accountant in XYZ organization in the UK, every problem will be framed in this way, summed up in the aphorism 'If you only have a hammer, every problem is likely to become a nail.' Mintzberg (2011, 2013), Finkelstein et al. (2009), and others suggest that specific combinations of individual differences, such as personality characteristics, values, experiences, competences, knowledge, and mental models, all go to make up a manager's personal style, which strongly influences how s/he tackles a job (Table 2.1).

In terms of individual differences, there are three key debates that I wish to raise because they are highly significant to practising managers. The first is the contribution of emotional intelligence, which has become a widely accepted idea among managers and the subject of much research (Goleman et al., 2002); the second is managerial judgement (Weick, 2001); and the third is the perceptions that managers bring to bear

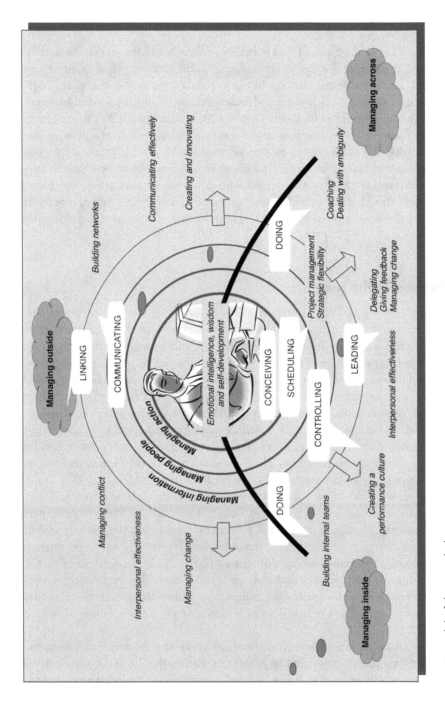

FIGURE 2.1 A model of the rounded manager

TABLE 2.1 The rounded manager

Person in the job	Frame	Context	Style	Level	Roles and associated competences (note that some competences are associated with two or more roles)	
Their values	Purpose of the job creation, maintenance, adaptation	Agenda of the work	Which role they favour: science, craft, or art	Managing information	Conceiving	Creating and innovating, exercising judgement
Their experience		Managing inside			Communicating	Effective oral and written communication, interpersonal effectiveness
Their knowledge		Managing within			Controlling	Creating a performance culture
Their models					Scheduling	Project management, strategic flexibility
Their degree of emotional intelligence	Purpose of the job creation maintenance, adaptation	Managing outside	How they perform the roles	Managing people	Linking	Building teams, managing conflict, networking, interpersonal effectiveness
Their self-development		The nature of the organization			Leading	Strategic flexibility, delegating, managing change, giving and receiving feedback, creating a performance culture Interpersonal effectiveness and intrapersonal effectiveness, making wise judgements and decisions
		The nature of the industry	The relationships among the roles	Managing action		
Their 'attitude of wisdom'	Position the product/ market strategy, structures, and systems of the business	The national institution and cultural context			Doing	Building teams, coaching, dealing with ambiguity, creating, and innovating

on what they see and how they see (Finkelstein et al., 2009). The basic argument in support of emotional intelligence is as follows. Managers usually need fairly high levels of what we call cognitive intelligence, which comprises several mental abilities associated with learning and performing, for example, numerical and verbal reasoning. This kind of intelligence has been shown to be a positive predictor of management success, as measured by achievements in levels of income and job status (Judge et al., 1999). However, cognitive intelligence is not regarded as sufficient to predict how well a manager will be able to perform in different organizational contexts. So, researchers then turned to examine the impact of personality factors such as the so-called 'big-five' (neuroticism, extraversion, openness to experience, agreeableness, and conscientiousness) on management outcomes (Barrick & Mount, 1991). Researchers found, for example, that factors such as conscientiousness were positively related to managers' career success while neuroticism (emotional instability and reactive to stress) was negatively related (Judge et al., 1999). They also found that situation strength (work was unstructured, employees had discretion to make decisions, etc.) exerted general and specific effects on the extent to which personality predicted job performance (Judge & Zapata, 2015).

Writers such as Goleman et al. (2002) have argued that emotional intelligence, which focuses on key personal qualities that managers bring to a job, is what will help managers perform effectively. Emotional intelligence was defined by Goleman as an individual's potential for mastering the skills of self-awareness, self-management, social awareness, and relationship management. These skills, in turn, become the basis for learnt abilities or competences. For example, self-awareness provides an accurate means for an individual to self-assess his or her strengths and weaknesses, a competence that is essential for someone seeking to manage a career. Emotional intelligence, however, is not something that one is necessarily born with, nor is it a fixed personality trait. One of its key features is that it can be developed in some people quite substantially. Quite how emotional intelligence differs from, and adds to, what the big-five personality factors can predict has been a subject of recent research. These works suggest that there is no strong evidence showing that emotional intelligence can predict key leadership and management outcomes beyond those already predicted by the big-five personality factors and cognitive intelligence (Harms & Credé, 2010). Indeed, some researchers have argued that emotional intelligence may be counter-productive because managers who are too sensitive to their own and others' emotions may be unable to make untroubled and dispassionate decisions (Antonakis, 2009). Nevertheless, the weight of research supports the positive effects of EI on those jobs that involve a high degree of emotional labour (Joseph & Newman, 2010), for example, the caring professions, retailing, and, indeed, some managerial functions such as HR

A second feature that forms an important input into what a person brings to a job is judgement, which has several dimensions to it, including wisdom (Weick, 2001), managerial hubris (exaggerated self-confidence), and overconfidence (Finkelstein, 2010). Again, we will discuss these in more detail later in this chapter. At this stage, however, it is worth pointing out that the ability to reflect critically on what one has learnt when acting and to be able to exercise sound judgement in making decisions are core skills that shape managerial performance in the long term. Reflexivity involves questioning our own attitudes and values when making decisions or acting these out, which has been a critical aim in recent 'learning from COVID-19' inquiries (Schippers & Rus, 2021). It may also be evident that there is a close relationship between wisdom, self-awareness, and the ability of managers to reflect critically on their actions – another point to which we shall return to in this chapter.

A third set of important person-related features that influence how managers do their jobs and the outcomes they achieve is what Finkelstein et al. (2009) call *key perceptual filters*. These draw on classic work by Herbert Simon (1916–2001) on managerial decision-making, and include:

- Bounded rationality, which refers to cognitive limits on managers' comprehension or cognitive biases over important elements that might influence decisions. For example, recent research has shown how physically attractive people do better at job interviews than unattractive people, even when attractiveness has no bearing on job performance.
- selective perceptions or cognitive biases, for example, what managers choose to 'notice' in memos, meetings, and interpersonal relations.
- Interpretation of stimuli or signals, which refers to the meanings they attach to these stimuli or signals, for example, the extent to which they see other managers or employees as helping or hindering their work, or the regard they hold them in.

An alternative to this rationalist perspective on how managers make decisions is managerial sensemaking (Weick, 1995; Weick et al., 2005), which we have used in our own research. Sensemaking refers to how we arrive at a plausible understanding of our situations, usually in relation to some triggering event like an organizational change. We create a mental map (or credible story) of the situation, usually in conjunction with others, and test it out through our experiences, conversations, and actions to produce a more refined and credible map. In this way, we often act our way into thinking rather than think our way into acting. It is important to understand that from a sensemaking perspective, there is no right or single story; instead, the story becomes more credible through our reflections, conversations, and actions, so that we can act with a degree of confidence rather than become trapped like rabbits in headlights. We take up this notion of sensemaking later in this chapter but note that educating managers in sensemaking is not only relevant for the present but also for making sense of the future. Managers constantly need to engage in looking into the future, especially for the purposes of creating novel and credible visions that provide a compelling and hopeful future for employees. In our research, we have found that merely making good on employees' undelivered expectations in the past and present is insufficient to ensure they engage with the organization in the future (Martin et al., 2023). Sensegiving of a hopeful future and evidencing such hope are key tasks of effective managers, especially when the 'going gets tough'.

The components of managers' jobs

Mintzberg's (2011) next key contribution lay in analysing managerial jobs into three components. The first is the *frame* of the job, the second is the *agenda* of the work to be undertaken, and the third is the *context* in which the work takes place.

The frame of the manager's job

The frame of the job is defined in terms of its purpose, perspective, and position. *Purpose* refers to what a manager is attempting to do with the unit he or she is managing. For example, the frame might be to run a business school to produce high-quality education, manage a hospital ward, or run a whole organization. Usually, the job is circumscribed by the collective *perspective* the organization has taken on the unit or department's role and how it fits into its 'theory of the business', or what has become known in everyday business language as the 'business model'. For example, the US-based Sears organization developed a customer–service–profit chain to describe how all units might work together to create profits through high levels of customer satisfaction (Heskett et al., 2008). This idea has underpinned the business models of many retailing and service companies over the last few decades. The final aspect of the frame of the job is its *position*, which broadly refers to how an organization or unit locates itself in its external product–market environment and how it proposes to do business. Michael Porter, a well-known writer on strategy, developed a positioning model of competitive strategy in the 1980s that is still used extensively. It poses three alternatives, all of which will have different implications for managers and how they manage people. These alternatives seek to compete by: (1) being cost-effective throughout the value chain; (2) being different from competitors in terms of quality or services; or (3) focusing on niche segments in the market either through costs or quality.

The frame of the job gives rise to the first of Mintzberg's key managerial roles in his original work, which is *conceiving*. This role is defined as 'thinking through the purpose, perspective and positioning of a particular unit to be managed over a particular period of time' (Mintzberg, 1994, p. 13). As he also suggests, managers interpret their jobs differently depending on their style and the circumstances of the organization. For example, some managers are forced to adopt a particular style because of external requirements or tight internal controls, whereas others can be more creative. Managers also vary according to how vague or sharp their frame is; some frames are characterised by a highly focused aim, such as achieving x per cent in sales revenue, whereas others are characterised by a more flexible desire to become the best company in a particular industry.

What does this conceiving role mean in practice? Gareth Morgan (1993) in a classic book described two general managerial competences that help managers 'imaginize' through new mindsets. These are:

* Creativity and innovation (which we explore in more detail in a later chapter).
* Strategic flexibility.

Creativity, to borrow from Marcel Proust, a nineteenth-century philosopher, is a voyage of discovery, and consists not in seeing new lands, but in seeing with new eyes. In his earlier well-known work, Morgan (1997) developed a range of different metaphors or 'eyes' for reframing problems based on the rationale that a way of seeing is also a way of not seeing. Thus, if organizations are to survive in an increasingly changeable world, managers need to use multiple lenses to analyse problems and be able to reframe them to produce novel and compelling solutions. He relabelled these metaphors as *mindsets*, the concept we shall use synonymously with different ways of seeing.

Being *strategically flexible* involves an attitude of mind as well as employing several practical competences. These include thinking about problems as opportunities for learning, anticipating major problems before they happen, learning through strategic planning by using techniques such as scenario planning, future sensemaking, and search conferencing, using multiple perspectives to analyse and solve problems, and challenging conventional organizational wisdom before it becomes a kind of 'psychic prison' that traps managers and their organizations into outmoded ways of working. For example, it has become commonplace in air travel to 'put customers first' by creating a business class for those who wish to pay extra money for superior service. This was not always the case; passengers in the 1980s were 'cargo to be transported rather than customers to be pleased,' with engineering and logistics dominating airlines' policies rather than marketing and customer considerations (Pascale et al., 2000). Consequently, airlines that failed to adopt a new 'customer-first' perspective went out of business during the early part of this century. As most of us know, however,this wisdom no longer holds with the advent of budget airlines, whose interests and business models have returned to providing low-cost travel for the masses. Similarly, those few retailers that have been slow to adapt to the internet are likely to have suffered badly in terms of market share because consumers' shopping habits have been changed by the online business models of firms like Amazon, especially following COVID-19.

The agenda of the work to be undertaken

Several management researchers, including Mintzberg (1994, 2011, 2013), Kotter (1990), and Grint (2010), pointed to the importance of agenda-setting as a key influence on managers' jobs. As Kotter cogently stated, agenda-setting refers to 'figuring out what to do, despite all the uncertainty of what is going on inside and outside the organization.' Managers must respond to issues that are framed by the job, in terms of position, purpose, perspective, and preferences, which are essentially dictated by their style. Such issues are usually 'chunked' into manageable tasks, where the key managerial role associated with setting and carrying out an agenda is *scheduling*. Scheduling is likely to involve prioritising activities and allocating time and resources to carrying out these activities on a day-by-day and week-by-week basis. In addition to strategic flexibility, project management skills are likely to be essential. The skills involved here include defining the scope and mandate for the project and developing a project mission, producing a project plan, creating and deploying a project team, keeping track of the project's progress, and being able to close the project once the goals have been achieved.

CASE 2.2 A CERTAIN KIND OF MANAGER

Mario Moretti Polegato is the owner of Geox footwear, an Italian company that makes sports shoes. His company has grown rapidly from a company that began life in 1997 as a 'hobby', employing five young people, and has grown into an established global retailer that employs 30,000 people in 1300 outlets worldwide.

According to an *Economist* article (March 2004), Polegato had several advantages. First, he is Italian, and Italy has led the world in footwear design and manufacture, especially in the region around Venice. Second, he brought some innovation to the business by attempting to solve the problem of foot odour and clamminess around the toes. This interest in solving the problems of sweat derives from his personal experience of running in the USA, during which time he developed an idea of a 'membrane that fitted between the sole and the foot and stopped water from getting in through the holes, but allowed the vapour from perspiration to get out.'

He patented this idea and others, which he took to the branded designers of sport shoes, including Nike and Adidas, but without success. So he turned to design and production himself, with his staff of five who still work with him. Polegato stressed the need for innovation in a BBC interview in 2014. He claimed that Italian schools and governments don't support innovation and that, although Italian entrepreneurs do well overseas, the political system discouraged innovators like him. Thus, he has had to battle against the tide and events such as the Eurozone crisis.

Like any business in the fashion industry, and sports shoes are a major part of it, tastes and circumstances can change. So, at the time of revisiting this case in late 2023, Polegato planned to close some of his outlets in Europe and open 400 new stores in Asia.

1. What are the kinds of values and experiences that Mario Polegato has brought to his job, and how have they shaped his business?
2. How does he display creativity and strategic flexibility?
3. Thinking about your thoughts on management, what values are likely to influence you as a manager - either now or in the future?

The context of the manager's job

So far, we have been describing the core of the manager's job., the person in the job, within a frame made operational through an agenda. We should note, however, that the core of a manager's job. is located *inside, within* and *outside* the organization (Mintzberg, 2011). The inside context is the department or unit in which the manager works, over which he or she may have direct control, and this context is often the focus for many middle managers. However, managers also must work within an organization and liaise with other departments to achieve their objectives. For example, sales managers must work with production departments, and HR managers rarely enjoy direct authority over other departments but must liaise with these managers and their units to achieve their HR objectives. Finally, managers achieve their objectives by working with people and resources outside the organization, often relying on these to get the job done, despite having no formal authority or leverage to draw upon to achieve their objectives. So, for example, the main activities of some chief executives often involve sitting on national committees or developing close relations with key customers or partners rather than managing their direct reports. This external context can provide the most difficult challenges to a manager and requires *networking, communications, and interpersonal* competences of a high order to achieve success. Nowadays, many recruiters in the UK who are responsible for taking on graduate management trainees emphasise communications and personal skills, rather than the class or type of degree, precisely because so much of modern work requires different forms of networking: operational networking with people you have to work with to get the job done; personal networking with people from outside of the organization to learn from them; and strategic networking with senior managers inside and outside the field to look for best practice and beyond the industry. Recent research by Marshall et al. (2024) have confirmed the importance of networking or 'relevant exchanges' (RE) as a core element of effective performance (P), alongside individuals' capabilities (C) and the opportunity to perform (O). This CORE model of effective performance is one thay is likely to become influential in the literature on managerial effectiveness.

Managing on three levels

To be effective, managers must translate their personal qualities (or, as they are sometimes known, personal competencies) into behavioural competences, inside, within, and outside their organizations. According to Mintzberg (1989, 2011), managers demonstrate these behavioural competences on three planes (or levels), moving outwards from the conceptual plane to the doing or action plane (see Figure 2.1). Thus, managers not only conceive and schedule, as we have just discussed, but also:

*   manage *action*, by doing things directly themselves;
*   manage *people* to get things done through others; and
*   manage *information* to influence people to act.

As Mintzberg pointed out, managers can choose to operate at any of these planes but have to understand that actions taken at one plane have 'knock-on' consequences for actions taken on other planes.

Managers are also stylised by the level at which they prefer to work: some administrators, accountants, or planners prefer to work at the informational level; 'people-orientated' managers prefer to work through others; whereas 'doers', often in front-line supervision, 'roll their sleeves up' and take direct action. In his 2004 book, Mintzberg reworked these issues of preferences in managerial styles and levels into a model of three

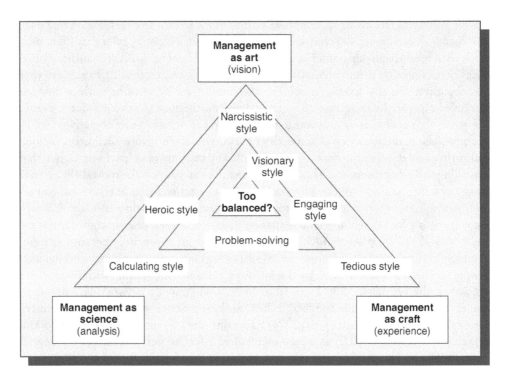

FIGURE 2.2 Managerial styles (*Source*: adapted from Mintzberg, 2004, p. 93)

poles of managing: management as a science, management as a vision, and management as a craft (see Figure 2.2).

Managers who prefer to work at the informational level are often influenced by the idea of *management as a science*, which involves applying rational techniques and thinking about leadership and strategy best achieved through systematic assessment and planning. Managers who prefer to work through people are more likely to be influenced by the idea of *management as an art*, which relies on creative insights and holding out a novel and compelling vision that others can buy into. Managers who prefer to work through action are influenced by the idea that *management is a craft*, learnt and practised through direct experience, experimentation, and action.

The critical point, according to Mintzberg, is that the rounded manager needs to function effectively at all three levels and achieve a degree of balance among the three poles in Figure 2.2. He contended there were three balanced styles:

- A *problem-solving style*, which combines the strengths of rational analysis with practical experience (and presumably just enough people-management intuition thrown in). Such a style, common among middle-level managers in production and engineering environments, is reminiscent of the Germanic model of management.
- An *engaging style*, which is people-orientated and experience-based, but with just enough science to take it out of the 'gifted amateur' category. Such a style is

associated with those managers who prefer to coach and facilitate and reflects an archetypical British style of manager.

- A *visionary style*, which is strong on art and vision, but is also rooted in experience, again with just enough science thrown in to give the ideas credibility. This style is one that is associated with successful entrepreneurs and is close to a stereotype of an American model of good management.

Note that his idea of balance among styles, however, lay in reconciling two out of the three, with just enough of a third style to keep things in check. His view was that if we try to achieve a balance among all three simultaneously, we run the risk of either having no style at all or of not making a choice over how to manage.

Mintzberg also highlighted the dangers of too little a balance in styles. *Calculating* managers who manage purely at the informational level run the risk of dehumanising the situation and lacking sufficient grounding in experience. This charge has often been made against the recruitment strategies of firms that target inexperienced MBA graduates and provide them with high degrees of responsibility early on in their careers. In Chapter 3, we shall look at the idea of talent management and some of its problems that exemplify this danger. *Tedious* managers, on the other hand, are often guilty of not being able to see the big picture because they rarely move out of their own comfort zone of experience. Often, this charge is made against engineers or other professionals who are promoted because they have been good at their professional 'craft', but who fail to provide people with a compelling vision or well-worked-out strategy. *Narcissistic* managers run the danger of being strong on vision, but with little else. Narcissism among managers has become a widely discussed topic among management researchers (Claxton et al., 2015; O'Reilly & Chatman, 2021), often associated with executives who become out of control and impulsive, lose contact with reality, have excessive confidence in their own judgement, and are disproportionately focused on image. Finally, *heroic* managers, according to Mintzberg (2013), are perhaps the most dangerous of all. Their style is influenced above all else by the need to promote shareholder value, which has involved a shift away from hard analysis but not from calculation. This time, however, the calculation is about how best to promote their careers (such as the account of Elton Mayo in the last chapter). The heroic style is largely about providing drama rather than true art and is focused on selling stories without substance to the investment community. Mintzberg's 'tongue-in-cheek' characterisation of heroic leaders involves: (1) looking out rather than in; (2) ignoring existing business, because anything established takes time to fix; then (3) doing anything you can to get the stock price up and cash in before you are found out.

We are now able to attach behavioural competences to each of these three levels of managing and their associated poles.

Managing by information and the problem-solving style

The first broad category of competences is *communication*, which is the collection and dissemination of information. John Kotter (1990), in his seminal work on general managers, pointed out that much of communication wasn't written and formal but oral and informal, sometimes operating at the non-verbal level – joking and kidding and talking about anything and everything remotely connected with the business with people inside and outside of the organization. Mintzberg (2011, 2013) reinforced this point when he suggested that nearly every serious study of managerial communications has stressed the informal and face-to-face nature of communications. However, given the availability of email, texts, other electronic means of communication such as mobile (aka cell) phones, video-conferencing, and social media, and the growth in 'virtual' organizations and globally distributed working that makes face-to-face communication more difficult, the emphasis on developing skills in electronic communication has become essential (see Chapter 8). Regardless of the medium, much of managerial work is concerned with building human networks to access information, sifting through this information, and sharing what is relevant with outsiders and insiders. Given this key role, communicating effectively through formal and informal means and acquiring interpersonal effectiveness skills are essential to effective managerial performance.

Morgan (1993) and Mintzberg (2011) provided some excellent insights into what managers need to be able to do to communicate effectively that have stood the test of time. They pointed to three clusters of competences associated with effective communication. These are:

- Developing self-awareness, self-regulation, motivation, empathy, and social skills such as influencing and listening.
- Monitoring all forms of useful information concerning internal and external events to become the 'Nerve Centre' of the organization.
- Communicating effectively by tailoring the message, ensuring clarity of communication, engaging in two-way listening, receiving feedback well, and understanding non-verbal communication.
- Giving feedback to your boss, colleagues, subordinates, and so on, and being able to deliver good news, bad news, and constructive criticism.

The second broad category associated with the informational role is using information in a *controlling* sense to get people to act. Such action is provoked by developing information systems, designing structures of control, and issuing directives for people to follow. For example, managers often spend lots of time creating and using planning and performance control systems, including budgets and appraisals. By defining responsibilities and creating hierarchies, they indirectly influence information flows. Managers can also issue instructions and directives, although as researchers have surprisingly pointed out, this directive style of management is not usually favoured in a Western context, which tends to regard authoritarian leadership as toxic (Cholkar et al., 2008; O'Reilly & Chatman, 2021), nor is it the traditional Japanese way of managing, which is focused on managing by consensus.

There is little doubt, however, that one of the key competences associated with controlling is the ability to create a performance culture in an organization. In addition to the three sets of competences above, we have pointed to the following sets of skills that leaders and managers need to be able to master (e.g., Beech & MacIntosh, 2012; Martin et al., 2015):

- Promote quality and continuous learning as core values in an organization.
- Create stretching benchmarks by measuring performance against practices from other organizations or industries and continuously raising the standards of these comparisons.
- Use problems as opportunities by using them as springboards for future success rather than treating them as barriers to change.
- Unlearn to create room for new developments because progress often requires managers to take a couple of steps back and unlearn previously held beliefs and attitudes to go forward.
- Challenge conventional wisdom by looking outside an individual or organization's conventional mindset for new solutions and ways of thinking, or by appointing 'deviants', 'heretics', or 'court jesters' to think and say the 'unthinkable'.
- Improve performance through action-based learning, which uses real, workplace-based problems facing the organization as the basis for learning and aims to produce solutions to these problems, rather than to use 'schooled' learning that is remote from practice.
- Understand and deal with resistance to change by 'knowing where people are coming from' and attempting to 'reframe' problems as opportunities for interested parties.
- Think 'win–win' by ensuring that all parties can achieve something of their aims without any one party being seen to dominate the agenda.
- Manage projects using the skills outlined in the previous section.

For example, one of my PhD students, Elena Pavlova, and I have been doing some work in the health service on the importance of perspective taking. Perspective taking refers to the benefits, challenges, and drawbacks of engaging with the viewpoints, thoughts, motivations, intentions, and emotions of others (Calvard et al., 2023). In a multi-professional context such as a hospital, perspective taking, which lies at the heart of some of Morgan's skills for managers, is central to understanding how professions relate to each other in more trusting and cooperative relationships at scale.

Managing through people and the engaging style

The second plane on which managers must act is through people, which is more direct than managing through information but not as direct as managing by action. As Mintzberg (2011) suggests, the focus here is on helping other people make this happen – in other words, *affect* not *effect*. Once again, most of the studies of management have stressed that much of a manager's time is taken up with managing people over whom they have no direct control, such as those individuals and groups within and outside the organization. However, you would not get that impression from reading some management texts, which lay great stress on the relationship between superiors and subordinates and are rooted in a model of pyramid-style organizations. Such a focus on hierarchical relationships, while not outmoded, is likely to form even less of a manager's time in the new forms of organization, such as the virtual, agile, and networked companies that dominate many industries (Billinger & Workiewicz, 2019) We shall look at these new organizational structures in Chapter 4.

We can identify at least three broad sets of competences associated with managing people within and without organizations. These are *leading*, *linking*, and *networking*, which have received lots of attention in the business literature. Of these three, leading is the one that has received the most attention in the literature and would require a book by itself to do this subject justice. For my purposes, however, I want to treat leadership as a subset of management rather than as a distinctive process. You cannot manage without leading just as you cannot lead without managing. Managers must exercise leadership at the individual, group, and unit levels in their organizations. *Individual leadership* refers to the ability of managers to inspire, motivate, coach, develop, drive, push, and mentor people. Morgan's (2003) model also highlights these competences, many of which are associated with managing change and developing people. *Group leadership*, which, according to some researchers, is the most important level at which leadership can be exercised, became a popular focus of attention following the 'rediscovery' of teamworking in the 1980s by Japanese organizations. Thus, building and managing relationally coordinated teams (Bolton et al., 2021) are key competences for group leadership. However, managers also must provide a different kind of leadership at the unit level, which is sometimes differentiated from the personal or group level by applying the label 'strategic leadership' (Schoemaker et al., 2013). Often, as we noted earlier, managers act as figureheads or in a symbolic role as strategic leaders, representing the organization to the outside world or at ceremonial events such as graduations. This level of leadership requires managers to be strategically flexible and resolute at the same time by creating a strong, performance-based culture (Morgan, 1993). In doing so, it also requires managers to be comfortable challenging their own and others' assumptions (an idea close to the notion of reflexivity we discussed in the first chapter) to learn from their mistakes and to deal with what Keith Grint has described as 'wicked problems' in an 'age of uncertainty' rather than purely 'tame' ones. As Grint (2022) has argued, wicked problems are:

- complex in that any action taken to solve a problem is likely to affect the environment which gave rise to the problem in the first place; and
- often intractable, since there is no obvious relationship between cause and effect, and thus can't be solved purely through rational analysis – what kind of problem you have depends on who and what you already know.

In essence, wicked problems are inherently contested and are often only resolved temporarily through political solutions. Such problems, almost by definition, are thought to be best tackled by teams rather than individual managers since no single person has the knowledge and abilities to address them by him or herself. Grint, however, argues that the collaborative efforts needed to address wicked problems are extremely difficult, if not impossible, to construct and maintain because of the requirements of trust among participants.

Following on from this need for managers to resolve wicked problems, Mintzberg (2011) suggested that nothing legitimises managers' positions and image more than their ability to connect and network with the world outside of their organizations or units. The exercise of leadership by advocacy of the managers' unit and by being the focal point of external pressures and information coming inwards is a core managing-people competence. Such a role is often underplayed in the texts on leadership but is increasingly important in complex organizational networks and newer forms of net-worked organization. For example, many managers spend much of their productive time promoting their units with managers of other units or with potential customers. At the same time, they act as a buffer or protector of their units from external pressures, such as the manager who spends his or her time taking criticism directly from irate customers when things go wrong because of actions taken by staff. Mintzberg used the metaphor of the manager as a valve to capture the essence of this role, which is probably more accurate than the use of the term 'gatekeeper'. Key competences associated with this linking and networking role are *interpersonal effectiveness, managing conflict*, and *communicating effectively*. It also requires elements of emotional intelligence. The dimensions of emotional intelligence most associated with the linking and networking roles include a high degree of self-awareness, empathy, and social competence. The networking aspect of the role also requires managers to create and develop a wide range of contacts to lobby effectively, provide information, and set agendas for action, as well as mediate between the pressures coming from the outside by disseminating information and delegating effectively. This is part of what has become known as a manager's social capital, which is defined as the ability to build 'bridges and bonds' with people inside and outside of the organization. Social capital has been found to be one of the most important drivers of organizational knowledge creation as well as creating positive external images of the organization (Martin et al., 2011), and is a key element in the CORE models of performance noted earlier in this chapter (Marshall et al., 2024).

Managing action and the visionary style

To manage effectively, managers usually need to take a direct involvement in actions. This is a controversial topic, with some writers preferring managers as thinkers rather than doers. However, in most Western industrialised settings, managers are required and respected for being able to act, which includes leading by example and avoiding being seen as disconnected from colleagues (Martin et al., 2015). As we have already discussed, the debate over managers as thinkers rather than doers is reflected at the national institutional level. For example, one researcher who studied how British employees in Japanese-owned factories felt about Japanese managers concluded that Japanese managers were more likely to obtain respect from their British employees because they were willing to become directly involved in sorting out problems on the shop floor, reflecting an engaging style. Similarly, senior German managers in the manufacturing industry tend to be highly qualified engineers who can solve technical problems, reflecting a problem-solving style. This ability to take direct action was contrasted with senior British managers in UK manufacturing firms, often with no technical background (Stewart et al., 1994). Mintzberg labelled this the *doing* role, which refers to getting closer to the action, sometimes managing the doing of action directly in a supervisory sense and sometimes doing the job themselves. Doing can be 'inside', carrying out projects and solving problems, substituting, and doing regular work such as a surgeon leading a medical team during a complex operation or a professor leading a research team by directly undertaking the work him or herself. In addition, doing can be 'outside', in the sense of doing deals and handling negotiations, essential components of many managers' jobs. Competences associated with this action level are being able to deal with ambiguity and helping others deal with ambiguity. On many occasions, especially during significant change, people will feel uncomfortable about the lack of clarity and certainty in their jobs. These feelings are related to personality and preferred learning and thinking styles. Understanding your own tolerance for ambiguity and being able to strike the right balance with others between imposing structure on the one hand and creating an atmosphere of openness and flexibility on the other are essential skills.

CASE 2.3 EXERCISE ON THE DISTINCTION BETWEEN MANAGEMENT AND LEADERSHIP

Background

In the preceding paragraphs on the nature of management, I have alluded to a distinction that is commonly made between management and leadership This following exercise is designed to help you examine this binary distinction and what underlies it. However, it also highlights the problems of binary thinking by pointing to possible overlaps between what might be labelled as management and leadership. It also helps to identify how you can implement leadership in your day-to-day jobs.

We know that organizational performance is increasingly a product of the engagement, motivation, and focus of the people an organization employs. I have also argued that a major influence on people's engagement, motivation, and focus is the quality of managerial performance, of which leadership is a key element in our model. Consequently, encouraging managers, supervisors, team leaders, and so on, to be better leaders is an important theme in management education and training.

Task 1

In Table 2.2 is a list of activities, some of which could be classified as managerial, some of which could be classified as leadership, and some of which could fall into both categories. Use Table 2.3 to position these activities.

Task 2

Reflect on why you have placed these activities in the various categories. What makes them management or leadership orientated? If you have placed some of the activities in the middle, why have you done so?

Source: adapted from Gillen, 2004.

TABLE 2.2 Lists of managerial and leadership activities

Delegate tasks	Act as an interface between team and outside
Motivate staff	Plan and prioritise steps to task achievement
Ensure predictability of performance	Explain goals, plan, and roles
Appeal to people's emotions	Inspire staff to achieve goals
Coordinate resources	Coordinate effort
Provide focus for staff	Share a vision
Guide their progress	Give orders and instructions
Create a 'culture'	Monitor feelings and morale
Check task completion	Monitor progress
Ensure people follow systems/ procedures	Create a positive team feeling
Monitor budgets and tasks	Ensure effective induction
Attempt to realise people's potential	Provide development opportunities
Monitor progress	Use analytical data to forecast trends
Take risks to innovate	Look 'over the horizon'
Role model desired behaviours	Appeal to rational thinking
Ensure the organization stays on track	Take advantage of situations to change direction

THE ROUNDED MANAGER

The process of rounding out the manager

It should now be evident that effective management requires the role holders to be 'rounded out'. Managers who emphasise one set of roles, style, or preferred level of managing at the expense of others are likely to become unbalanced and may fail to perform in the medium or long term. This is not to say that the context in which management is practised, and managers' preferred styles, are unimportant – indeed, I have already argued the opposite is more likely. However, rounding out a manager is likely to help him or her work effectively in changing contexts and to meet employees' valued expectations of meaningful work (Martin et al., 2023). This point was also made decades ago by Gareth Morgan (1997), whose seminal work on metaphors in management argued that managers need to be able to read situations through multiple lenses and act on these more complex readings to organize and manage effectively. He quoted F. Scott Fitzgerald, an eminent American writer during the 1930s, who suggested that 'The test

TABLE 2.3 Worksheet for Task 1

Very high on managerial work	Managerially orientated	Strong elements of both management and leadership	Leadership orientated	Very high on leadership

of a first-rate intelligence is the ability to hold two opposing ideas in mind at the same time and still retain the ability to function.' This is key competence for managers and is linked to the ability of managers to deal with paradox, ambiguity, and uncertainty (Lewis & Smith, 2014; Morgan, 1993; Nielsen et al., 2023).

As Mintzberg (2011) cautions, slavish adherence to some of the well-worn nostrums produced by the management gurus and leading practitioners – such as 'don't think, do', 'steady, fire, aim', or 'it's all about communications' – is inconsistent with rounded managers. Moreover, although it is conceptually possible to analyse managerial jobs into distinctive roles and knowledge-based competences, it is close to impossible to distinguish them behaviourally, because work is not practised as a set of independent or atomistic lists of competencies. Thus, managers who think 'their way into acting' at the expense of 'acting their way into thinking' or who manage well on the outside but fail to manage on the inside will, almost inevitably, fail to achieve significant positive results in the long run. Similarly, the core roles of leading, communicating, conceiving, linking, controlling, and doing cannot in practice be separated into outside and outside roles, nor can they be separated from each other, because they tend to infuse each other and blend into a mix of all.

If this is true of the key managerial roles, it is equally true of the competences that are associated with them. For example, interpersonal effectiveness is as important to linking and doing as it is to a leading role. Similarly, creating a performance culture and managing change are part of the roles most associated with managing on the outside as well as managing on the inside. Of course, how managers ultimately perform will be shaped by their preferred style as well as context. As Mintzberg argued, style will influence which roles a manager tends to stress, how he or she acts out these preferred roles, and how one role relates to another. For example, our research has shown that managers in the UK healthcare sector tend to prefer linking rather than leading because they are often dealing with autonomous and relatively powerful professionals who have been brought up in a fragmented culture in which doctors have considerable personal and positional power (Martin et al., 2021). On the other hand, the preferred management style in the US privatised healthcare sector, which has less of a history of employing autonomous, powerful, and highly rewarded professionals, is more likely to emphasise leading and controlling. In terms of the acting out of roles, managers in small organizations and entrepreneurial firms will probably favour doing (action) over conceiving (thinking). As Weick (2001) pointed out, however, these roles are related. Acting your way into think-ing about strategy, if done reflexively, has major benefits for managers over the think–lead–act style. The most obvious of these advantages is that it requires managers to learn through incremental actions and experience rather than implement abstract principles or theories without having knowledge beforehand of how they may influence outcomes.

Making wise decisions

I have already introduced this idea when discussing the person in the job in an earlier section. Surprisingly, making wise decisions through sound judgement is rarely discussed in the management literature. There were some early attempts to deal with this issue in the 1950s and 1960s when a group of researchers at American universities set out to find a more scientific method to make judgements. They created a discipline called 'decision science', which aimed to take the human element out of risk analysis, claim-ing it would provide a way of making soundly based decisions for a future fraught with uncertainties. This approach involved using computer models for forecasting, estimating the probabilities of possible outcomes, and determining the best course of action, thus avoiding the various biases that humans bring to decision-making. Such models, these researchers believed, would provide rational answers to questions such as whether and where to build a factory, how to deal with industrial relations negotiations, and how to manage investments.

Many business schools adopted management science as part of the core curriculum, in part because it gave them some legitimacy with their science colleagues, and even some senior policymakers were persuaded by the arguments. Decision science's high point was probably during the Vietnam War, in the 1960s and 1970s, when Robert McNamara, then America's Defense Secretary, used such techniques to forecast the out-come of the conflict (though, as it turned out, without much success). But, for the most part, the approach did not quite catch on, especially in the less rationally orientated countries such as the UK. Decision-makers, whether in business or politics, were loath to hand over their power to computers, preferring instead to go with their gut instincts (*The Economist*, 22 January 2004). If this lack of faith in the application of rational sci-ences to business was evident in the last few decades of the twentieth century, it is even more so now as we operate in an increasingly unknowable and unpredictable world, dis-rupted ever more frequently by technology such as AI and global trends such as climate change – issues that feature later in this book. Consequently, many managers have been grappling and will continue to grapple with the problem of how to exercise judgements that strike a balance between overconfidence and over-cautious doubt. This is the basis of much of the modern approach to risk management and corporate governance (Martin et al., 2016), which is encapsulated in the notion of an organization's risk appetite.

Reflection and judgement

Karl Weick (2001) began an engaging discussion on this issue when proposing that an attitude of wisdom would be one of the key management competences in the 'increasingly unknowable world.' Drawing on case research from studies of disaster management, when decisions can have immediate and life-threatening consequences, Weick examined 'wise' practices. So, for example, firefighters cited in his research operated by a maxim 'don't hand over a forest fire to an incoming crew during the heat of the day' because that was when winds were strongest, the temperature at its hottest, and humidity at its highest. Thus, a handover during the evening gave the incoming crew more time to learn and adjust to the conditions of uncertainty. Such maxims, he argued, revealed two initial properties of wisdom – *reflection* and *judgement*.

Reflection refers to a way of considering events in the light of their consequences in a wholly systemic fashion; in other words, it is about making considered decisions by articulating the 'big picture'. If reflection, as Weick argued, deals with the substance of decision-making, judgement is more about the process involved in coming to reflective decisions. Judgement has often been thought of as 'gumption' or 'common sense', which to most of us means bringing to bear common knowledge to the decision-making process. However, Weick believed bringing judgement to the reflective decision-making process is more than mere common sense and must involve using the 'non-obvious, significant, shrewd and clever' characteristics of decisions that deal simultaneously with *knowing* and *doubt*.

According to Weick, this process of judgement exercised during reflective decision-making focuses not so much on what is known but on how knowledge is held, shared, and used in practice – known as enactment. And, for him, having an attitude of wisdom was the key to exercising sound judgements, which is succinctly defined as knowing without excessive confidence or caution. Overconfidence, he argues, arises because managers and entrepreneurs find it difficult to doubt what they 'know' or admit to themselves that they can know only a small part of what is knowable about any situation. We have seen many examples of such overconfidence bias in events leading up to the Global Financial Crisis in 2007–2008 when banks such as the Royal Bank of Scotland, which sought to become a global player, continued to make acquisitions of other banks despite being warned by investment analysts that they were playing a dangerous game (Fraser, 2014; Martin & Gollan, 2012). Once people made confident decisions, they became excessively attached to them, defending their positions even in the light of contradictory evidence (Siebert et al., 2020). Such commitment to a course of action inevitably leads to blind spots and inattention to questions and alternatives; yet in business circles committed action is usually seen as preferable to doubt (Gu, 2023). This is because, as many writers have suggested, businesses and managers value action and anything that gets in the way of action – including reflection and wisdom – is likely to be discouraged. We know this from cases of politicians such as Boris Johnson, a UK Prime Minister who denied the role of expert reflection during the COVID-19 crisis and has been held to account for overconfident decisions.

If we accept the notion of excess confidence or overconfidence bias, though as we have pointed out this is less likely to be defined as a problem by practitioners, we can also be excessively cautious. On this last topic, there is a much larger literature because it is seen by managers and businesses as a greater threat to action. This is reflected in their criticisms of business schools, which have been characterised as institutions that produce analytical thinkers rather than 'doers' (Mintzberg et al., 1998). Excess caution, according to Weick, is a relative concept, depending very much on the position one starts from. So, if we admit we don't know (the answer) or if we notice we fail to notice (I've just discovered I was wrong and I should have accepted your alternative answer – you were right!), we begin to doubt ourselves. If those doubts begin from a position of over-confidence, then we move towards wisdom; if, on the other hand, we are too cautious to begin with, then we move further away from being wise. In short, wisdom is a fulcrum around which attitudes vary, and people make sense of their worlds differently depending on which side of the knowing–doubting scale they place themselves.

Improvisation and wisdom

The main problem for managers, according to Weick, is to act their way into confidence when confidence is already high because that is a position from which they will find it difficult to return. Instead, Weick, rather controversially, argues that the point of balance between knowing and doubting is best summed up as an intended oxymoron – the 'achievement of ignorance', based on Socrates' idea that it is best to begin with a sceptical attitude towards all knowledge. This he defined as the ability to act while remaining doubtful. And achieving ignorance, the sign of the wise manager, is based on his or her ability to *improvise* – the metaphor of the manager as a craftsman. Such improvisation is not the ability to make something from nothing, as is sometimes believed, but is the ability to rework existing knowledge and materials to deal with unanticipated ideas and problems during work. In doing so, we produce relatively unique solutions to 'local' problems set in context, rather than use preplanned recipes in an inflexible way (think again about the saying 'give someone a hammer and every problem becomes a nail'). To give an example, the wise manager is one who when presented with a novel problem – say, the need to get academics or doctors to become more business-orientated – can use his or her formal or informal knowledge of people to fashion a solution that will work in a specific context and timeframe. Thus, in the case of academics and doctors, financial gain may work with some people at certain career stages of their lives, whereas the opportunity for flexible work arrangements or to travel may work with others at different points in their careers (Martin et al., 2023). Such a wise course of action is qualitatively different from that taken by a manager who, following attendance on a business course where he read up on some theory or best practice on motivation through incentive schemes, then tries to apply these without regard to the local circumstances, history, or culture of the organization. Such an approach is to treat his or her knowledge as infallible. Instead, wise managers treat their knowledge as fallible, but at the same time have sufficient confidence to take what knowledge they have and combine it with other aspects of their repertoire to deal with new circumstances and problems. In short, this is a learning strategy whereby managers can act their way into thinking as well as thinking their way into acting.

In a special issue of a well-known journal devoted to wisdom in management, the editors (Nonaka et al., 2014) have summarised our discussion of wisdom by proposing a wise manager is able to cope with the unexpected and unknown by exercising two types of judgement. The first is an evaluation of what the experience means, not by relying on habit or previous experience but by sensitising oneself to what is going on, often from multiple perspectives and 'listening to a situation from within' (p. 373). Such evaluation should precede acting – a form of cool and considered reflection. The second is to act by 'making a stand' so that the situation is changed into an 'event with focus' (374), which allows those whom we manage to read into the situation a novel, credible, and, hopefully, compelling story. In Case 2.4, we ask you to apply some of these ideas to the case we researched of the Royal Bank of Scotland.

CASE 2.4 FRED GOODWIN AND THE ROYAL BANK OF SCOTLAND

The case of RBS has become a well-known landmark in management and organizational studies because it became the biggest failure in British corporate history in 2008 and almost led to the collapse of the UK economy. The excellent journalistic accounts of RBS, including two books by Ian Martin (2014) and Ian Fraser (2014), and our own research (Martin & Gollan, 2011; Siebert et al., 2020), all point to the role of erstwhile RBS CEO, Fred Goodwin, as a major factor in causing the demise of what was at the time the largest bank in the world with assets of 3 trillion pounds.

Goodwin is portrayed in most accounts as a kind of pantomime villain who enjoyed his nickname of Fred the Shred, bestowed on him by employees in his former bank for his ruthless cost-cutting approach to corporate turnaround. His background was modest and not untypical of middle-class children in the West of Scotland. Goodwins' academic career culminated in a law degree at the University of Glasgow, which he followed up by training as an accountant, working in the profession and then being appointed to a key role in the Clydesdale Bank based in Glasgow. He was subsequently headhunted by Sir George Mathewson in 1998 and promoted to CEO in 2001. This promotion coincided with the spectacular rise of RBS, for which he received much credit.

The Bank was deemed to be a small regional player from its inception in the early 1700s in Edinburgh right through until the late 1990s. Along with Mathewson, Goodwin set about the 'great aggrandisement' of the Royal Bank of Scotland (reduced to RBS for marketing purposes), through an ambitious, and some have argued nationalistic, programme of acquisitions of mainly financial institutions throughout the world. This began with a hostile takeover of NatWest, a bank three times its size, which propelled it into becoming a global player, i.e., Europe's second-largest bank and the fifth largest in the world by market capitalisation. Goodwin and his board proceeded to make further acquisitions, especially in the USA, culminating in the takeover of ABN Amro in 2007, just prior to the Global Financial Crisis.

Yet only a short time earlier, he hadn't even been a banker. In his early forties, he was feted by the British establishment and world financial press. In 2003, *Forbes* magazine awarded him the accolade of global businessman of the year, which was followed up by a report by Harvard Business School, which described him and his team as the 'masters of integration.' Perhaps understandably, Goodwin's ego entered the stratosphere, which was evidenced by the new headquarters built on the outskirts of Edinburgh, close to the airport which housed his private jet. Goodwin became notorious for his obsessive attention to detail in designing the new building, including choosing the colour of carpets and the design of fountains. He also took an intrusive interest in the commissioning and operation of the RBS Business School, which extended to making decisions on which cases his senior and middle managers should or should not study (one of our interviewees told us that Goodwin had written on a post-it note that a case of a top British retailer was unsuitable for learning in the Bank!).

Despite these obsessions and his notorious bullying behaviour towards his managers, which occurred weekly in the 'Monday Morning Beatings,' 'everyone wanted a slice of him.' This included the royal family, the Chancellor of the Exchequer, Gordon Brown, and other members of the British establishment that saw financial services as a way of restoring Britain's economy. So, in 2005, he was awarded a knighthood, which, according to his close colleagues, only fuelled his ego.

Goodwin's strategy appeared to be defined by a fixation on growth, despite warnings by financial analysts and his promises to his own board that he wasn't planning further acquisitions. Yet, he continued to plan for growth, often unknown to his board members. This culminated in the purchase of ABN Amro, a large Dutch-based bank, with interests in the USA and Asia. Although analysts warned against such a purpose and a major report on banking behaviour in 2000 recommended that banks should be restrained from becoming too big to fail, encouraged by politicians and his confidence, Goodwin was attributed with persuading his board in 'a moment of collective madness' (a description by one of our interviewees who was at the meeting when the decision was taken) to sanction the acquisition without performing the usual level of 'due diligence'.

A few months later, as the 'credit crunch' that led to the Global Financial Crisis began to take hold, the takeover of ABN Amro tipped RBS over the edge. It had extended itself financially to make the purchase during a period when it could not borrow the short-term money it needed to survive and discovered it had acquired a huge amount of toxic assets through its purchase and previous forays into investment banking, a field that Goodwin did not understand. The UK government, in one of the closest calls in history in which Britain came close to bankruptcy, was forced to bail out RBS.

Goodwin was eventually sacked and lost his knighthood but retired on an annual pension of £700,000. Yet, as Ian Martin (2014) pointed out, to focus only on Goodwin and let his board, the City, and government figures get away 'scot free' is wrong. At the time of writing, none of the bankers who caused the crisis have been jailed, which was a widespread public call. Moreover, huge incentives to engage in similar behaviour have not diminished despite attempts to curb bonuses, and regulation has amounted to tinkering rather than major institutional change (Siebert et al., 2020).

1. How does our discussion of wisdom help explain what happened at RBS?

A MODEL OF EFFECTIVE MANAGEMENT

Bringing these ideas together on the rounded manager, we can map out the relationship between the person in the job (i.e., what managers bring to a job) and their effectiveness as managers. The core relationship is set out in the horizontal sequence of boxes in Figure 2.3.

So, what I propose is that effective management performance is related to the person in the job, including:

- Their values, previous experience, age, career stage, and their models of management (assumptions).
- Their degree of emotional intelligence and their self-development.
- Their perceptual filters, which include their frames of reference and how these affect their interpretation of signals from external stimuli, bounded rationality and biases, and selective perceptions.
- Their sensemaking, shaped by their identities, perceptions, and collective interpretations of 'what's the story here'.

However, it is also clear from the previous discussions that the relationship between these personal qualities and management performance is directly influenced by two key *mediating* factors, which are:

- The roles they are required to play as part of their work, which include conceiving, communicating, controlling, linking, leading, and doing, and their identities – who do they want to be?
- The level of associated behavioural competences they demonstrate in performing their new roles, including creativity and innovation, communication, creating a performance culture, project management, strategic flexibility, managing conflict, building teams, networking, having an attitude of wisdom, and making wise decisions.

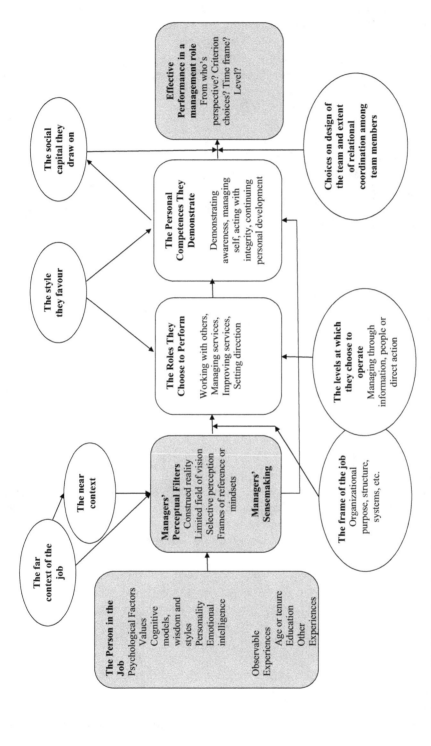

FIGURE 2.3 Modelling the relationship between the manager in the job and effective managerial performance

In addition to this direct 'line of sight' between what managers bring to the job and their effectiveness, the different contexts in which individual managers work will have an important *moderating* influence on this relationship. Moreover, within given constraints, managers have a choice in which roles they emphasise in their work and how they perform these roles (e.g., some managers are noted for emphasising close control over the work of their colleagues, whereas others prefer to delegate). These *contexts* and *choices* give rise to three related sets of moderating factors that we can place above and below the core horizontal axis or line of sight in Figure 2.3:

- *The frame of the job.* This refers to its purpose as set out by the organization, the theory of the business embedded in the organization (its assumptions regarding success and its business model), and its product/market position, structure of controls and systems, and so on.
- *The near and far contexts of the job.* The near contexts include the agenda set by the manager's bosses, the problems of managing inside the manager's department, the problems of managing within and across the organization, and the problems of managing outside the organization, including dealings with customers, suppliers, government departments, and employer associations. The far context refers to the nature of the organization, including its structure and so on, the nature of the industry (product/services/consulting, etc.), and the national and institutional framework in which the manager is undertaking his or her work.

The choices that managers can make can be set out in terms of the two interrelated factors that Mintzberg identifies as style and level. Most managers have a degree of discretion over:

- Their preferred *style*, including the roles they prefer to perform, how they perform their roles, and how they choose to configure and relate one role to another. The choice is between how they achieve balance between the three polarities of management – management as science, craft, or art.
- The *level* at which they choose to operate, which reflects their assumptions and preferred style of managing. They can choose to manage action directly, they can choose to manage other people acting, or they can influence other people by managing the information flows surrounding their jobs so that they take necessary actions.

Finally, our research over the past decades has pointed to two further moderating factors. The first is the *social capital* they draw on to make decisions, which refers to their ability to incorporate ideas from key people inside and outside the organization, and to the good relations and trust they may have built in the units they manage and with the people inside and outside with whom they network. The second is the degree of *relational coordination* they build in their teams, which refers to the intensity and nature of communications within the team and the levels of respect they have for each other. We discuss these concepts further in Chapter 3.

Of course, there is little point in studying and theorising about management if we are unable to specify the outcomes of good management, which has become an industry in its own right. However, this is not as easy as it seems, because there are many issues to 'bottom out' before we can do this. The first is specifying good performance, which raises the question: good performance from who's perspective? Often, what senior managers regard as good performance is at odds with what their employees might see as good performance. Some of our recent research has pointed to the need to understand in detail what employees regard as meaningful work – past, present, and future – which differs from managers' interpretations (Martin et al., 2023). Another is the choices and criteria that might be used, for example, whether to use 'hard' quantitative measures or 'soft' qualitative measures, and how to ensure these are content valid in covering all aspects of performance and are unbiased. There has been a tendency in recent times to focus on the quantitative, but we must be mindful of the adage, 'what is measurable isn't always meaningful, and what is meaningful isn't always measurable' (Small & Calarco, 2023). Yet a further problem of specifying outcomes is the time frame. Often, the results of managerial action or inaction can only be known fully after many years, yet organizations seek to performance manage and reward managers on a yearly or even more frequent basis. Finally, there is the issue of level: do we use the same criteria for senior, middle, and junior managers, or are performance outcomes attenuated by the level at which managers operate and the discretion they are allowed in their jobs? You may now be more aware of some of the problems of evaluating the performance of managers and leaders, which is one of the reasons why some consulting firms are moving away from attempting to regularly appraise their managers and reward them based on short-term outcomes. Perhaps when we come to write a fourth edition of this book, the performance appraisal of managers may look fundamentally different from where it is now.

Let's see if you can apply this model to understanding your job as a manager or a manager with whom you are familiar.

Time out: Self-reflection

Thinking either about yourself or a manager who is, or has been, close to you, use Figure 2.3 to analyse the relationship between what you (or they) bring to the job and your rating of yourself (or their) effectiveness as a manager. Use a sheet of paper to redraw and annotate the diagram because it will take up quite a lot of space if you do this correctly. Doing so should be a useful exercise in understanding yourself or your managerial colleagues and can lead you to think about your own self-development.

Questions

1. What personal qualities might you (or they) need to perform more effectively as a manager?
2. Which roles do you (or they) choose to emphasise more than others in your (or their) managerial work? Are these the right choices for managerial effectiveness, given the context of the job?

3. What are the most important contextual factors that influence how you (or they) perform their jobs? What can be done to influence these (if anything)?

4. How does the frame of the job influence the roles you (or they) perform? And can anything be done to shape the frame of the job to make you (or them) more effective as a manager?

5. What about your (or their) preferred style and the level at which you (or they) mainly operate at, i.e., through information, people, or directly through action? How can that be changed to make you (or them) more effective as a manager?

6. What are your (or their) key competences? Where are your (or their) shortcomings, and what can be done to improve them?

Doing this exercise should prove to be very useful in understanding yourself or your managerial colleagues and can lead you to think about your own self-development or the development of others.

LEARNING SUMMARY

The key learning points from this chapter are:

- The rounded manager brings values, attitudes, and experiences to the job, two of the most important of which are levels of emotional intelligence (in addition to cognitive intelligence) and the abilities and attitudes to engage in critical self-reflection and make sound judgements, which balance overconfidence and doubt.
- The frame of a manager's job., which includes its purpose, the mission of the organization or department, and the position of the organization in its chosen market milieu, will have an important influence on how the manager performs his or her key roles, and the roles the manager chooses to play.
- Managers spend much of their time figuring out what to do or setting agendas and priorities. Particularly at senior levels, they are rarely told what to do directly.
- How managers perform their key roles and the types and levels of competences they demonstrate will be influenced by the near and far contexts of their work. Effective management is strongly embedded in context, and being good in one situation doesn't always mean that someone will be good in another situation.
- Managers can operate at three related levels, indirectly through manipulating information flows, more directly through getting other people to act, or acting oneself. Effective managers operate at all three levels, depending on the context of the job and tasks at hand.
- Management is sometimes distinguished from leadership, in the sense that management focuses on stability and control, whereas leadership is necessary to produce change. The well-rounded manager has to have both of these characteristics in his or her repertoire.

- Having an attitude of wisdom, which means having enough self-confidence to act while remaining doubtful, is a key feature in effective management. Acting one's way into thinking can sometimes be a more effective strategy for managers than thinking one's way into action. The former is a learning approach whereas the latter is a planning approach. Usually, however, managers need to be good at both.

REVIEW QUESTION

During your appraisal, your boss tells you that he wants you to develop a 'performance-orientated culture' in your department. He then asks you for ideas on how to achieve this at the next meeting. How should you respond?

REFERENCES

Antonakis, J. (2009). "Emotional intelligence": What does it measure and does it matter for leadership?. In G. B. Graen (Ed.), *LMX leadership-- game-changing designs: Research-based tools* (Vol. VII., pp. 163–192). Information Age Publishing.

Barrick, M. R., & Mount, M. K. (1991). The big five personality dimensions and job performance. *Personnel Psychology, 44*(1), 1–16.

Beech, N., &MacIntosh, R. (2012). *Managing change: enquiry and action.* Cambridge: Cambridge University Press.

Billinger, S., & Workiewicz, M. (2019). Fading hierarchies and the emergence of new forms of organization. *Journal of Organizational Design, 8*(1), 1–6.

Bolton, R., Logan., C.& Hofffer Gittell, J. (2021). Revisiting relational coordination: A systematic review. *The Journal of Applied Behavioral Science, 57*(3), 290–322.

Calvard, T., Cherlin, E., Brewster, A., & Curry, L. (2023). Building perspective-taking as an organizational capability: A change intervention in a health care setting. *Journal of Management Inquiry, 32*(1), 35–49. https://doi.org/10.1177/10564926211039014

Chhokar, J. S., Brodbeck, F. C., & House, R. J. (Eds.). (2008). *Culture and leadership across the world: The GLOBE book of in-depth studies of 25 societies.* Taylor & Francis

Claxton, G., Owen, D., & Sadler-Smith, E. (2015). Hubris in leadership: A peril of unbridled intuition. *Leadership, 11*(1), 57–78.

Clegg, S. R., Pitsis, T. S., & Mount, M. (2021). *Managing and organizations: An introduction to theory and practice* (6th ed.). Sage.

Conzon, V. M. (2023).Mario Luis Small and Jessica McCrory Calarco. Qualitative literacy: A guide toevaluating ethnographic and interview research. *Administrative ScienceQuarterly, 68*(4), NP65–NP67.

Cunliffe, A.L. (2014).Reflexive inquiry in organizational research: questions and probabilities. In H.Willlmott & E.Bell (eds.) Qualitative research in business and management. London: Sage.

The Economist. (2004, January 22). Freud, finance and folly: human intuition is a bad guide to handling risk. *Economist Newspapers, print edition.*

The Economist. (2004, March 11). The Ferrari of footwear.

Finkelstein, S., Hambrick, D. C., & Cannella Jr., A. A. (2009). *Strategic leadership: Theory ad research on executives, top management teams, and boards.* Oxford University Press.

Finkelstein, S. (2010). *The 7 bad habits of unsuccessful people.* FT Press.

Fraser, I. (2014). *Shredded: Inside RBS, the bank that broke Britain.* Birlinn.

Gillen, T. (2004). *Leadership or Management: The differences.* CIPD.

Goldthorpe, J. (2003). The myth of education-based meritocracy. *New Economy, 10*(4), 234–239.

Goleman, D., Boyatzis, R., & McKee, A. (2002). *Primal leadership: Realizing the power of emotional intelligence.* Harvard Business School Press.

Grint, K. (2010) *Leadership: a very short introduction.* Oxford: Oxford University Press.

Grint, K. (2011). *Leadership: A very short introduction.* Oxford University Press.

Grint, K. (2022). Critical essay: Wicked problems in an age of uncertainty. *Human Relations, 75*(8), 1518–1532.

Gu, W. (2023). Impact of managers' overconfidence upon listed firms' entrepreneurial behavior in an emerging market. *Journal of Business Research, 155*(Part B), 113453

Harms, P. D., & Credé, M. (2010). Remaining issues in emotional intelligence research: Construct overlap, method artifacts, and lack of incremental validity". *Industrial and Organizational Psychology: Perspectives on Science and Practice, 3*(2), 154–158. doi:10.1111/j.1754-9434.2010.01217

Howieson, A.B.,Bushfield, S. Martin, G. (2024) Leadership identity construction in a hybrid medical context: 'Claimed' but not 'granted'. European Management Journal, https://doi.org/10.1016/j.emj.2023.04.012

Heskett, J. L., Jones, T. O., Loveman, G. W., Sasser Jr, W. E., & Schlesinger, L. A. (2008, July–August). Putting the service-profit chain to work. *Harvard Business Review.*

Joseph, D.L. & Newman, D.A. (2010) Emotional intelligence: an intrgrative meta-analysis and cascading model. Journal of Applied Psychology, 95(1), 54-78.

Judge, T., Higgins, C. A.,. Thoresen, C. J., & Barrick, M. R. (1999). The big five personality traits, general mental ability, and career success across the life span. *Personnel Psychology, 52*(3), 621–652.

Judge, T., & Zapata, C. (2015). The person-situation debate revisited: Effect of situation strength and trait activation on the validity of the big five personality traits in predicting job performance. *Academy of Management Journal, 58*(4). https://doi.org /10.5465/amj.2010.0837

Kotter, J. (1990). *A force for change: How leadership differs from management.* Free Press.

Nielsen, R.K., Bevort, F., Henriksen, T.D., Hijalager, A-M., & Lyndgaard, D.B. (2023) *Navigating leadership paradox: engaging paradoxical thinking in practice.* De Gruyter

Lewis, M., & Smith, W. K. (2014). Paradox as a metatheoretical perspective. *Journal of Applied Behavioural Science, 50*(2), 127–149.

Martin, G., Beech, N., MacIntosh, R., & Bushfield, S. (2015). Potential challenges facing distributed leaders in health care: Evidence from the UK National Health Service. *Sociology of Health and Illness, 37*(1), 14–29.

Martin, G., & Gollan, P. J. (2012). Corporate governance and strategic human resources management (SHRM) in the UK financial services sector: The case of the Royal Bank of Scotland. *International Journal of Human Resource Management, 23*(16), 3295–3314.

Martin, G., Gollan, P. S., & Grigg, K. (2011). Is there a bigger and better future for employer branding? Facing up to innovation, corporate reputations and wicked problems in SHRM. *The International Journal of Human Resource Management, 22*(17), 3618–3637.

Martin, G., Farndale, E.,Paauwe, J. & Stiles, P.G. (2016). Corporate governance and strategic human resource management: four archetypes and proposals for a new approach to corporate sustainability, *European Management Journal, 34*(1), 22–35.

Martin, G., Siebert, S.& Robson, I. (2018). Conformist innovation: an institutional logics perspective on how HR executives construct business school reputations. *International Journal of Human Resource Management, 29*(13), 2027–2053.

Martin, G., Schreven, S, Arshed, N., & Martin, A. (2023, July 6–8). *How healthcare staff make sense of their orientations to work(place) – past, present, and future.* Paper presented to the EGOS annual colloquium, University of Cagliari, Italy.

Martin, G., Siebert, S., Bushfield, S., & Howieson, W. B. (2021). Changing logics in healthcare and their effects on the identity motives and identity work of doctors. *Organization Studies, 42*(9), 1477–1499

Martin, I. (2014). *Making it happen: Fred goodwin, RBS and the men who blew up the British economy.* Simon & Schuster.

Marshall, J.D., Aguinas, H. & Beltran, J.R. (2024, forthcoming) Theories of performance: a review and integration. Academy of Management Annals,

Mintzberg, H. (1973). *The nature of managerial work.* Harper & Row.

Mintzberg, H. (1989). *Mintzberg on management: Inside our strange world of organizations.* Free Press.

Mintzberg, H. (1994, Fall). Rounding out the manager's job. *Sloan Management Review, 36*(1), 11–25.

Mintzberg, H. (2004). *Managers not MBAs: A hard look at the soft practice of managing and management development.* Pearson Education/Financial Times.

Mintzberg, H. (2011). *Managing. Financial Times/ Prentice Hall.*

Mintzberg, H. (2013). *Simply managing: What managers do - and can do better.* Financial Times Series

Mintzberg, H., Ahstrand, B., & Lampel, J. (1998). *Strategic safari: A guided tour through the wilds of strategic management.* Free Press.

Morgan, G. (1993). *Imaginization: New mindsets for seeing, organizing and managing.* Sage

Morgan, G. (1997). *Images of organization.* Sage.

Nonaka, I., Chia, R., Holt, R., & Peltokorpi, V. (2014). Wisdom, management and organization. *Management Learning, 45*(4), 365–376.

O'Reilly, C.A. &Chatman, J. A. (2021). When "me' trumps 'we': narcissistic leaders and the cultures they create. *Academy of Management Discoveries, 7*(3), https://doi.org /10.5465/amd.2019.0163

Pascale, R. T., Milleman, M., & Goija, L. (2000). *Surfing the edge of chaos: The law of nature and the new laws of business.* Three Rivers Press.

Pettigrew, A., & Whipp, R. (1991). *Managing change for competitive success*. Blackwell.

Pettigrew, A. M. & Starkey, K. (2016) From the guest editors: the legitimacy and impact of business schools – key issues and a research agenda. *Academy of Management Learning, 15(4)*, 649–664.

Scarborough, H. (1998). The unmaking of management? Change and continuity in British management in the 1990s. *Human Relations, 51(6)*, 691–716.

Schippers, M.C. &Rus, D. C. (2021). Optimizing decision-making processes in times of Covid-19: Using reflexivity to counteract information-processing failures. *Frontiers in Psychology*, 2021, 12:650525.

Schoemaker, P. J. H., Krupp, S., & Howland, S. (2013, January–February). Strategic leadership: The essential skills. *Harvard Business Review*.

Siebert, S., Martin, G., & Simpson, G. (2020). Rhetorical strategies of legitimation in the professional field of banking. *Journal of Professions and Organization, 7(2)*, 134–155.

Small, M. L., & Calarco, J. M. (2022). *Qualitative literacy: A guide to evaluating ethnographic and interview research*. University of California Press.

Stewart, R. (1979). *The reality of management*. Macmillan.

Stewart, R., Keiser, A., & Barsoux, J.-L. (1994). *Managing in Britain and Germany*. St Martin's Press.

Weick, K.E., (1995) *Sensemaking in organizations*. Thousand Oaks, CA: Sage.

Weick, K. E. (2001). *Making sense of the organization*. Blackwell.

Weick, K. E., Sutcliffe, K. M., & Obsfeld, D. (2005). Organizing and the process of sensemaking and organizing. *Organizational Science, 16(4)*, 409–421.

Wheen, F. (2004). *How Mumbo-Jumbo conquered the world: A short history of modern delusions*. Fourth Estate.

CHAPTER 3

Managing in the individual–organizational context

LEARNING OBJECTIVES

At the end of this chapter, you should be able to:

- Understand and apply the concept of psychological contracting to work situations.
- Recognise good practice in managing psychological contracts in organizations and take steps to influence these unwritten contracts.
- Understand the problems of managing talent, careers, employee engagement, and work–life balance.
- Use theories of employee engagement in your organizations to impact on key individual and organizational outcomes.

INTRODUCTION

In Chapter 2, I focused on managers' needs to understand themselves and reflect on how they can be more effective by managing at different levels and in different contexts. The model of the rounded manager has also highlighted a requirement for managers to develop their emotional intelligence, leadership competencies, and wisdom. In this chapter, I shall develop some of these ideas but, this time, focus on how managers can better understand the individual–organizational relationship and how they can provide more effective leadership that is sensitive to people's engagement with their jobs, with each other, and with their employers.

This topic is potentially vast, usually covered by texts and courses on organizational behaviour. These focus on understanding individual differences, motivation and job satisfaction, learning, group dynamics, leadership, and the like, so I shall not attempt to repeat what is already well-documented in such books. Instead, I will examine a key question, the answers to which have enormous importance for managers:

DOI: 10.4324/9781003469711-3

- What is the nature of the relationships between individuals and organizations, how has it changed and how is it likely to change in the future?

In addressing this question, I shall draw extensively on two concepts I've researched in the past that have become popular in the human resource management literature and are supported by the Chartered Institute of Personnel and Development (CIPD) in the UK as key ideas in understanding individual–organizational relationships. The first is the *psychological contract*, which we shall define and use to examine issues such as 'talent' management, careers, and employee commitment and identification, and the problems of over-identification, such as workaholism and burnout. The second is the related notion of employee engagement (Akingbola et al., 2023; Truss et al., 2013), a consultancy-generated term that has been promoted heavily by UK government agencies through the website, Engage for Success, as a way of aligning individual and organizational goals (Albrecht et al., 2015; see also http://www.engageforsuccess.org). While both provide significant insights, they also have their critics, which we shall also examine.

Let's begin by looking at some of the issues involved by examining the case in Box 3.1, which is based on some work I undertook on employee relations in the UK offshore oil industry. Although our research took place quite some time ago, it remains a good case for understanding the psychological contracts of employees in practice in an important sector of UK industry – the extraction of oil and gas – because our use of psychological contracting had an important impact on what subsequently happened in the management of employee relations in the sector – more of that later in the chapter.

Box 3.1 'Psychological contracts' among oil workers in the UK offshore drilling industry

The offshore drilling industry in the UK North Sea

In 1999, the industry comprised 14 companies employing some 6000 men and a limited number of women in onshore and offshore operations. The work of offshore drilling employees is usually depicted as hazardous, involving long hours in shifts and working away from home. Most employees on the drilling rigs were semi-skilled roustabouts, supervisors, and drilling technicians and technologists, most of whom had worked in the industry for several years. Despite the contracting nature of employment conditions, some employers and many employees tended to treat the industry as a source of a traditional career rather than as a pure wage-for-work relationship with limited job security and no career progression. Though mobility between companies was a feature of employment in the industry because of the contract nature of the work, many of the employers had an implicit policy of retaining good employees because of their personal knowledge of specific drilling rigs and their idiosyncrasies. Consequently, it was common practice in the industry to attempt to offer a degree of security during slack times by standing down men for a period on limited pay until new contracts became available. Such work protection practices, however, were not a feature of all companies, and this became a source of difference among employers, from the perspective of both employees and clients. By clients, I refer to the oil 'majors' operating in the North Sea, including companies such as BP, Shell, and Exxon. These client companies regarded a degree of employment continuity among the contractors' workforces as sufficiently important that they would sometimes 'foot the bill' to keep good workers on the books of drilling contractors, especially if a new contract was imminent. Traditionally, these workers had also been highly compensated in relation to comparable jobs onshore, though through time the differentials had been eroded to a point where recruitment had become difficult in 2000.

The UK offshore oil and gas industry as a body had been traditionally hostile to unions and union representatives. Consequently, unionisation was actively discouraged in the drilling industry and no company gave any form of recognition to the unions with members in the industry. In 1998, however, the UK government's White Paper on *Fairness at Work* was introduced with provisions to reintroduce the rights of unions to pursue recognition claims if they could be justified in terms of union membership.

The UK offshore drilling contractors, which operated drilling rigs on behalf of the oil and gas majors in the North Sea oil and gas fields, immediately saw themselves at risk to 'predatory' unions because they had been subject to attempts by a hostile union called OILC to organize members on the drilling rigs. So, when the employers became aware of the union recognition provisions of the White Paper, they interpreted the situation as a major threat because of OILC's potential for disruption to the 'mission critical', particularly if the union could recruit enough members to gain recognition under the legislation.

Thus, the drilling companies combined themselves into a consortium, now called the UK Drilling Contractors Association, to decide what their stance should be. This was achieved with the help of consultants who had the experience of working with trade unions that the individual companies lacked.

The first step the consultants recommended was that the companies should undertake a survey of all employees in the industry to assess their expectations of good employment, how they interpreted the key obligations of their employers, and whether these obligations were being met by their employers. The consultants also wanted the firms to understand the orientations of workers to trade unions so that they could advise the companies on how to proceed with union recognition. This survey involved all employees in the industry and achieved a relatively high response rate of more than 60 per cent. This response rate allowed the consultants to be relatively confident that the findings could be generalised to all employees in the sector.

The employee survey phase as a means of intervention

The survey data provided a wealth of information on employee perceptions, motivations, and orientations to trade unions. Tables 3.1 and 3.2 provide a selection of these data, which were presented to the drilling contractors' HR managers in a feedback session.

TABLE 3.1 Selected data from the employee survey on key elements of the psychological contract

Question	Mean average response of all employees on a five-point Likert scale
As far as could be expected the company has provided me with a reasonably secure job.	2.55
The company has provided me with fair pay for the work I do.	3.06
The company has provided me with good career opportunities.	2.94
The company has provided me with interesting work.	2.54
The company has ensured my fair treatment by managers and supervisors.	2.67
The company has helped me with the problems I have encountered outside work.	3.14
The company always provides me with a safe working environment.	2.33
The company provides me with good training for the job.	2.43

Scale: 1 = strongly agree; 3 = neutral; 5 = strongly disagree.

Given the sample size, for the purposes of interpreting these mean average responses, you should treat any result lying outside the range of 2.4 to 3.6 as statistically significant. Any figure lying within this range should be treated similarly to the mean average.

Based on these data and other findings and forms of analysis from the survey, the headline conclusions from the study, which were reported to the HR managers and their senior managers, were as follows:

- The standard predictors of why employees in non-union companies show little interest in joining unions are typically found to be: (1) high levels of job satisfaction; (2) positive beliefs about existing communications, consultation, and grievance-handling procedures; and (3) negative instrumental beliefs about the ability of unions to improve pay and conditions. From Tables 3.1 and 3.2, overall job satisfaction was found to be moderate and positive beliefs about existing communications were not high. However, unions were seen positively as a means of providing a voice on key issues and, of lesser significance, in improving terms and conditions of employment.

TABLE 3.2 Selected data from the employee survey on the need for union representation

Question	Mean average response of all employees on a five-point Likert scale
Employee relations in this company would be improved by having an employee representative who could speak to management on our behalf.	2.20
Management in this company usually consult employees on issues that affect them.	3.01
Management in this company usually give employees plenty of opportunity to comment on proposed changes at work.	3.16
Having an employee representative would generally be beneficial in securing fairer terms and conditions of employment.	2.31
There is definite need for better representation in this company to give voice to employee wishes and grievances.	2.18

Scale: 1 = strongly agree; 3 = neutral; 5 = strongly disagree.

- Employees did not perceive that they were well managed, particularly in relation to supervisors treating people poorly and to perceptions of a lack of trust in supervisors to work in employees' best interests.
- Employees were particularly interested in future employability, and the perception of a lack of career development by employees was strongly associated with positive attitudes towards unions as a means of representation and participation in decision-making.
- The lack of interactional justice (perceptions of fair treatment by the company and the lack of trust in managers) and the lack of affective commitment (attitudes towards the companies) were associated with positive attitudes towards unions as a means of representation and participation in decision-making.
- Expectations of job security were relatively low and, at the time of the survey, were worsening. *Source*: adapted from Martin et al. (2003).

THE PSYCHOLOGICAL CONTRACT

As I noted, the case on the UK offshore drilling industry discusses the levels of employees' attachment to their work, their orientations to trades unions, and to the companies employing them. It also introduces the notion of psychological contracts and shows how useful the concept can be to a real-life study of the relationships between employees and their organizations. First, however, we need to define what we mean by psychological contracts, look at how they are formed, and then transformed.

DEFINING AND FORMING PSYCHOLOGICAL CONTRACTS

Psychological contracts have been used to describe the expectations and beliefs that employees hold about the mutual obligations between themselves and their organizations, such as expectations about fair pay or career opportunities provided by their companies, or the amount of effort they might reasonably be expected to exercise in performing their work (Griep & Cooper, 2019; McDermott et al., 2013). So, the psychological contract mirrors the explicit legal contract by focusing on largely implicit and unwritten reciprocal obligations, though certain writers have included written 'promises' by employers, such as those evident in mission statements, for example, to treat people with dignity and fairness. Below is a basic but useful definition of psychological contracts:

> the employee's beliefs regarding the promises of the reciprocal exchange agreement between the employee and organization.
>
> *Suazo et al., 2009*

This definition needs some elaboration to tease out the key features of such contracts. To help us, we can draw on the insights into psychological contracts and the employment relationship provided by Conway and Pekcan (2019) and Sparrow and Cary Cooper (2003). These researchers have highlighted four key aspects of psychological contracts and how they come to be formed and changed:

- They are *subjective, unique, and idiosyncratic,* in that: (1) they reside in the subjective expectations and perceptions of employees (and employers); (2) every individual has his or her own interpretation of these expectations and perceptions; and (3) they vary from one person and organization to another. Therefore, you can gain an insight into psychological contracts by questioning only one party to the relationship because the contract 'is in the eyes of the beholder'.
- They are *reciprocal,* in that they emerge in the context of a *specific* mutual employment relationship. As there are two parties to this relationship, they each have their own expectations about the specific employment relationship (but not employment relationships in general).
- They are not objective 'facts' but are based on *beliefs and perceptions* held by individuals. However, because people act on their subjective perceptions, they are no less real in their consequences than if they *were* facts.
- They arise from beliefs and perceptions of *obligations* that, in the case of employees, are what they believe they are entitled to because of perceived *promises,* either explicit or implicit, made by the employer. In that sense, a psychological contract is more than just a set of expectations that can arise in the absence of a promise. Only

expectations relating to perceived promises are entitled to be considered as part of the psychological contract. Just what these promises look like in practice and how they arise are illustrated in Box 3.2.

Box 3.2 'Promises' in the employment relationship that create obligations

Promises arising from spoken and written communications:

- strategic documents, employer commitments to certain courses of action, mission and values statements, agreements, pledges, speeches;
- financial statements or employer reporting statements; and
- statements made on application forms, etc., by employees.

Promises arising out of behaviour and actions:

- observations of management or employee actions, e.g., how managers and employees act in relation to one another in treating each other with respect; and
- interactions with managers or employee representatives, such as how recruiters behave during the interview process.

BREACH AND VIOLATION OF PSYCHOLOGICAL CONTRACTS

Like legal contracts, psychological contracts can be breached or violated if employees feel that the significant terms have been broken, or that perceived obligations are unmet (Conway et al., 2011; Guest, 2017). The distinction between breach and violation is largely one of degree; breaches are treated as minor, more short term, and less significant, whereas violations are seen as more serious, more long term, and more significant in terms of outcomes. It is to the violation of psychological contracts that many researchers attribute major breakdowns in employee relations or failures in organizational change programmes. For example, the violation of psychological contracts has been used to explain strike action and rises in absenteeism and employee turnover; at the same time, violation has been used to explain rising levels of cynicism about never-ending 'programmes' of organizational change and lack of trust in managers to 'walk the talk' (see Chapter 10) (Martin et al., 1998).

One way of thinking about employee responses to contract violation is to distinguish between active and passive 'actions' on the one hand and positive and negative 'actions' on the other (see Figure 3.1). Note how apparent loyalty or silence by employees may occur as a response to management actions that breach, or even violate, expectations regarding promises. In one sense, this can be treated as a positive response to changes managers may make in the psychological contract because they have built up a store of trust and a reputation for integrity in the past. However, it may also be seen as negative because employees endure what they perceive as unfair treatment as they are unable to foresee alternatives

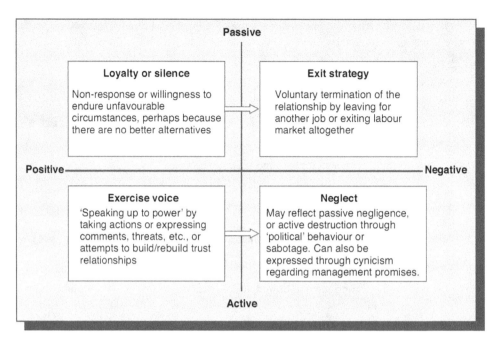

FIGURE 3.1 Range of employee responses to psychological contract violation (*Source*: based on Turnley & Feldman, 1998)

to their current employment. When the employment situation changes, however, they are very likely to adopt an exit strategy if the breaches continue. A further implication of this framework is that managers should do all they can to encourage employees to 'speak up to power', rather than suppress discontent. By encouraging such actions, managers can rebuild trust, an essential component of employment relations. Otherwise, they run the risk of employees adopting a negative, 'neglect' strategy.

Conway and Briner (2002) attempted to understand why and what happens when management actions, through design, accident, or miscalculation, result in breaches being treated as violations. They pointed to four characteristics of perceived promises that can have a major impact on employee responses to breach or violation, most of which were evident in a study we carried out on senior hospital doctors' intentions to retire from work in the NHS (Martin et al., 2023):

- The degree of explicitness of a perceived promise – the more explicit the promise, the greater the sense of injustice and the more active (positively or negatively) the employee response.
- Attributions of personal responsibility for contract breach or violation – the more personally responsible a manager or party is held to be for the perceived breach, the more intense the other party's reaction.
- The unexpectedness or infrequency of the breach – the more unexpected or infrequent the breach/violation (a break with past behaviour), the more intense or active the response will be from employees.

- The degree of importance the party attaches to the goal or relationship breached – the more important the interest/relationship breached, the more likely it will be treated as a significant violation and, hence, provoke a negative response.

The only one of the above we did not find in our research into doctors' premature retirement was the unexpectedness of the breach. Our respondents had significant experience of feelings of being let down over a period of a decade or more

---

Exercise 3.1

Drawing on the previous discussion on psychological contract breach and violation, do you think that the drilling companies should have recognised a union for bargaining purposes?

TYPES OF PSYCHOLOGICAL CONTRACTS

Though psychological contracts are individual in nature, resulting in as many contracts in an organization as there are people, psychologists have tried to classify some of their more general features. Three such classifications have emerged in the extensive research in this area. These are set out in Table 3.3 and reflect changes taking place in organizations and the wider economy.

During the 1990s in the USA, the traditional, relational contracts that many white-collar employees held with their employers – based on commitment in return for job security and career prospects – could no longer be sustained because of increased global competition (Cappelli, 1999) Consequently, this traditional, relational contract was replaced by a more transactional contract, but one with a slight twist on the model highlighted in Table 3.3. Organizations recognised that they could no longer offer stable employment to all, nor could they guarantee careers to all, even though they wished to retain the benefits of relational contracting from employees working 'beyond contract' and showing high levels of (temporary) commitment. Consequently, the notion of *employability* came into common usage: employers sought temporary commitment from employees if they remained in the job, in return offering the opportunity for employees for self-development and work on interesting and demanding projects. This employment proposition, which was a form of 'come and work for us and learn', was attractive to many mobile employees in fields such as computing and software development because it made them more employable for their next job. In effect, their career paths became boundaryless because they moved in and out of organizations and even occupations. This notion of employability, however, was much less widespread than much of the literature would have had you believe, especially outside of what became known as the 'new economy' based in the hi-tech regions of the USA and Europe (see Chapter 4). We shall examine this idea of changed psychological contracts later in this chapter and in

TABLE 3.3 Different types of psychological contracts

Dimension	Transactional	Relational	Ideological or Called
Organizational obligations	Degree of job security, safe work, and a 'fair day's pay'	To provide a career with training and education, promotion opportunities, meaningful work, and long-term employment prospects	Demonstrate credible commitment to a valued cause or moral and social purpose – the notion of a 'calling'
Individual obligations	'A fair day's work'	Go beyond contract by doing excellent work and demonstrating high commitment and identification with organization	Participate fully in the organizational mission/ cause by being a good organizational and societal citizen
Beneficiary	Self	Mutual interest between self and organization	The organization and employee share same passion/cause
Beliefs about human nature	Self-interested, instrumental worker who works for money	Socialised employee, who is collectively orientated and finds satisfaction in work itself	Principled involvement
Characteristics of violation	Black and white	Grey areas, which are negotiable	Grey (negotiable) but also non-negotiable, moral 'hot-buttons'
Typical response to violation	Leave organization	Withdraw commitment and revert to a transactional exchange	Principled organizational dissent/ disillusionment
Basis of attachment to work and organizations	Compliance and focus on the job	Identification with organization and career	Work as a calling

Source: based on Thompson & Bunderson, 2003, p. 575; Conway & Pekcan, 2019; Martin et al., 2023.

other chapters when we look at new forms of organization, technological change, and knowledge and innovation contexts.

Many organizations, however, are seeking through their mission and value statements to go beyond relational contracts and create ideological or 'called' relationships with individuals. This would include our healthcare system in the UK, which attempts to capitalise on employees' sense of calling to work for a higher social and moral purpose to attract, engage, and retain them (Martin et al., 2023). However, most mission-driven organizations aim to captivate employees by having them believe that they are working for a higher-level purpose, even in industries such as retailing. For example, Wal-Mart, the world's largest retailer, tries to engage employees by convincing them that they can 'give ordinary folks the chance to buy the same things as rich people.' In Chapter 6, we shall examine the effectiveness of such employer branding propositions in the development of ideological psychological contracts (Martin & Sinclair, 2018). However, it should be obvious to most readers that ideological contracts are more likely to be found among higher-level professionals in occupations with a sense of vocation, such as medicine, teaching, religion, and politics, or in voluntary organizations such as Save the Children or Cancer Research. Our recent research, however, shows that even those in 'dirty' or low-level work in healthcare often express feeling a sense of calling because of the moral and social purpose of the NHS (Martin et al., 2023)

Exercise 3.2

Drawing on the material in this last section, how would you describe the psychological contracts of most employees in the North Sea oil drilling industry, based on Table 3.3? How would you compare their psychological contracts with staff in healthcare?

MEASURING PSYCHOLOGICAL CONTRACTS

From a manager's perspective, it is clearly useful to be able to gain insights into employee perceptions of perceived promises because they have extremely important consequences for understanding the effectiveness of people management strategies and management actions (Guest, 2017). Figure 3.2 shows the relationship between what some researchers have found to be the important factors which shape psychological contracts, the key components or content of psychological contracts themselves, and positive and negative outcomes associated with the way in which psychological contracts are managed.

What most employees appear to expect from employers and what they regard as the most important employer obligations have been identified by several researchers. These items are often used in surveys to determine the health of psychological contracts in organizations:

- To provide an adequate procedure for induction into the job and training to make people more effective and safe.
- To ensure that the procedures for selection, appraisal, promotion, and lay-offs are fair.
- To provide justice, fairness, and consistency in the application of important rules and in discipline and dismissal.
- To provide equitable treatment on pay and rewards in relation to market circumstances and to be fair in the allocation of non-pay benefits to individuals and groups.

Key factors which shape psychological contracts	The content of psychological contracts	Key outcomes
Employee characteristics and expectations of perceived and important 'promises' by management ⇨	Perceptions of fair treatment by the organization ⇨	Employee behaviour and attitudes, including identification with work and the organization, employee commitment, employee citizenship behaviour ('going the extra mile')
Organizational characteristics	Trust in management to do the best for employees	⇕
The employment value proposition and HR policies and practices on recruitment, career development, training, rewards, employment security, etc.	The extent to what employees perceive to have been promised is actually delivered	Employee performance, including work effort, absenteeism, leaving, etc.

FIGURE 3.2 Inputs, content, and outputs of the psychological contract. (*Source:* based on CIPD, 2003; Conway & Briner, 2005; Martin et al., 1998.)

- To provide interesting work where possible.
- To provide fair pay for taking on responsibility in the job.
- To provide career development and support for employees to learn new skills.
- To allow people reasonable time off and flexibility to meet family and personal needs.
- To consult and communicate effectively on matters affecting employees.
- To allow employees reasonable autonomy in how they *do* their jobs.
- To act in a personally supportive way towards employees.
- To recognise loyalty and reward special contributions.
- To provide a safe and friendly work environment.
- To do what they can to provide employment security.
- To ensure that managers keep promises and commitments and do their best for employees.

Employers, on the other hand, expect employees to work extra hours when needed, take on work outside their responsibilities when circumstances dictate, look for better ways of undertaking the job and suggest improvements, be flexible, save costs, and adapt to changes in the work environment.

Exercise 3.3

Thinking back to the North Sea oil industry case in Box 3.1, design three written survey questions that might identify key elements of employees' psychological contracts.

MANAGING PSYCHOLOGICAL CONTRACTS

Managing the individual–organizational relationship by shaping the psychological contracts of employees in a positive manner comprises many elements. In this section, we want to discuss five such elements, especially in light of recent and forecasted changes in employment and trends in organizations:

- Managing talent
- Managing careers
- Managing organizational identification
- Managing work–life balance
- Managing employee engagement

These five management issues of the individual–organizational relationship are at the core of modern human resource management and have been the subject of intense research and speculation (Boxall & Purcell, 2022). As Brown and Edwards (2009) argued some years ago, the *individualisation of the employment relationship* has been one of the most important developments of recent times among organizations in most developed countries, evidenced by the decreasing influence of trade unions and the increased use of nonstandard forms of employment contracts. Such developments towards individualisation can be seen in two ways. On the one hand, some writers and critics have highlighted the negative side by pointing to how modern national states and large organizations have rejected their responsibilities for providing employment security and passed the onus on to individuals to make themselves employable through calls for self-development and displays of flexibility. On the other hand, researchers and proponents of these changes have argued that many employees are increasingly motivated by the need for autonomy and actively seek more career flexibility and the opportunities to follow different, boundaryless career and work patterns from those of their predecessors, a point discussed in the previous section. Many such individuals tend to work in knowledge-intensive occupations and organizations, such as business and financial consultants, professional engineers, entertainment, higher education, and healthcare. Because these people have such different orientations to work and because they tend to be in short supply, organizations increasingly find themselves competing for talent and having to devise new ways of managing them.

MANAGING TALENT

What is talent management? The term 'talent management' came into popular usage as a direct result of a major study by North American-based McKinsey consultants Ed Michaels, Helen Handfield-Jones, and Beth Axelrod, who undertook their original work in 1997 on the impact of how companies managed their leadership talent on corporate performance and followed it up with further research (Michaels et al., 2001). Prior to the deflation of the dot-com bubble in the USA in early 2000, the recruitment of talented people was seen to be the biggest single issue facing US business. Based on some in-depth research among business leaders, these writers concluded that the 'war for talent' was, and would continue to be, one of the most important problems facing industry and commerce in developed countries. The changed labour market circumstances following the downturn in economic prosperity in the USA associated with the dot-com collapse did nothing to diminish their beliefs, and subsequent research by them provided strong support for their thesis in certain industrial sectors and certain countries. Their work showed that only a small proportion of senior managers believed their organizations: (a) recruited talented people (their A-class high performers); (b) did all they could to identify and retain these talented performers, and to develop performers with potential (the B class); or (c) undertook to remove or replace low performers (whom they called C-class performers).

Talent management, they argued, required a new talent mindset among business leaders, because it was 'mission critical', and therefore could not be left to HR departments. Instead, it required the direct support of the organization's board and needed to be seen as a core element of the work of business leaders (see Table 3.4).

These authors proposed that organizations seeking to become top performers should implement three elements of a talent management strategy:

- Disciplined talent management, through rigorous and continuous assessment, development of managers, and matching them with jobs.
- Creative recruitment and retention through refined and meaningful *employee value propositions* (EVPs), which we shall discuss more fully in Chapter 6 on corporate reputation, branding and HR.
- Thoughtful executive development, using coaching, mentoring, and on-the-job experiences at key points in managers' development.

TABLE 3.4 The new talent mindset

Old HR mindset	New talent mindset
The vague leadership and HR rhetoric of 'people being our most important asset'	A deeply held conviction that talented people produce better organizational performance
The responsibility for people management lies with HR	The responsibility for managers to do all they can to strengthen the talent pool
Small-scale and infrequent programmes for succession planning and training managers in acquiring and nurturing people	Talent management as a central component of the business and part of the ongoing role of senior leaders
Managers must work with the people they inherit	Managers constantly take active and bold steps to attract and develop their talent pool and actively manage low performers

Source: adapted from Handfield-Jones et al., 2001, p. 4.

There is little doubt that this new talent mindset advocated in the last century is even more appropriate today, a claim to which we shall now turn.

NEW APPROACHES TO TALENT MANAGEMENT

A theory of talent management. Gradually, this Hollywood metaphor term has entered the lexicon of many organizations that once would have rejected such connotations to refer to the appointment and management of key people (McDonnell et al., 2017; Collings et al., 2018). While a somewhat cynical interpretation of the talent management bandwagon focused on the HR function's attempts to rebrand itself, we believe there is more to talent management than HR's constant claims for legitimacy. David Collings and Kamel Mellahi's (2009) original definition for strategic talent management set out the key claims when defining it as:

> the activities and processes which differentially contribute to the organisation's sustainable competitive advantage, the development of a talent pool of high potential and high performing incumbents to fill these roles, and the development of a differentiated human resource architecture to facilitate filling these positions with incumbents and to ensure their continued commitment to the organization.
>
> *(p.305)*

The first core element in their argument was the notion of an HR architecture, which differentiates the contribution and management of people according to the value they add to organizational performance and their scarcity in the labour market (Lepak & Snell, 2002). This approach segments the internal labour market of an organization into four quadrants (see Figure 3.3), all four of which require a focused approach to the recruitment, retention, development, and motivation of staff.

So, because knowledge-based workers in the top right-hand box (a) can add significant value to the strategic objectives of an organization and (b) are scarce or even unique, they require significant investment to develop and retain them. Good examples would be senior professionals such as engineers or scientists in high-tech or science-based industries, geologists and geophysicists in oil and gas companies, senior doctors or academics in hospitals and universities, top footballers, and, in some cases, high-performing managers. Workers in the bottom right box may add strategic value but are not as scarce; so, they are recruited, developed, and managed to perform predetermined jobs, such as craftsman, technicians, or middle/junior-level managers and administrators. Workers in the bottom left-hand box are neither high value-adding nor scarce, so they are likely to be employed on fixed-term contracts or be outsourced, with little or no investment in their training and development. Good examples include most workers in call centres, cab drivers, delivery drivers, some restaurant workers, care assistants, security staff, or semi-skilled workers on construction sites – the so-called precariat. Finally, workers in the top left-hand box may be scarce and talented but are not core to the strategic mission and operation of an organization. Examples of such workers can include employed professionals, such as accountants, HR staff, and computer programmers in certain types

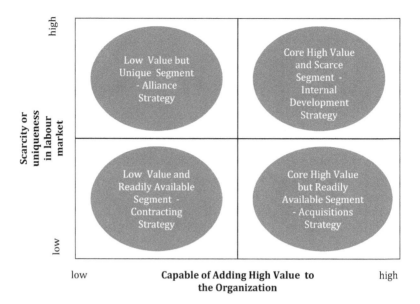

FIGURE 3.3 The segmented human resource architecture of the organization (*Source*: adapted from Lepak & Snell, 2002.)

of organizations. Most management consultants brought into an organization from time to time to help with special projects also fall into this category. These employees rarely enjoy significant career development or progression but may be rewarded highly for their (short-term) contribution.

The second core element is the notion of a talent pool, which is the internal reservoir of high-potential and high-performing employees that organizations usually rely on to undertake so-called 'pivotal' roles (Boudreau & Ramstad, 2007). Creating a talent pool by recruiting and developing talented individuals 'ahead of the curve' allows an organization to implement succession plans and develop new lines of business or ways of working. Sometimes, this means that organizations recruit high-quality staff for which no current job or vacancy exists; instead, they buy them in to develop their own role in the organization. This is a strategy frequently used by universities, the scientific sector, and the computing sector, all of which rely on constant innovation to compete in their respective marketplaces for ideas.

Bringing these ideas together, Collings and Mellahi (2009) proposed a useful theory of strategic talent management, which is depicted in Figure 3.4. They argue that the first step in talent management should be to identify the pivotal roles and pivotal performers in an organization – the so-called 'A' stars and 'A' positions, which correspond closely to the top right-hand box of the differentiated HR architecture in Figure 3.3. These positions are filled by a strategy of recruitment of high-performing individuals to the talent pool from an organization's internal and external labour market. In turn, they predict that this exclusive strategy should lead to high performance through improved work engagement, retention, and extra-role behaviour, sometimes labelled as organizational citizenship.

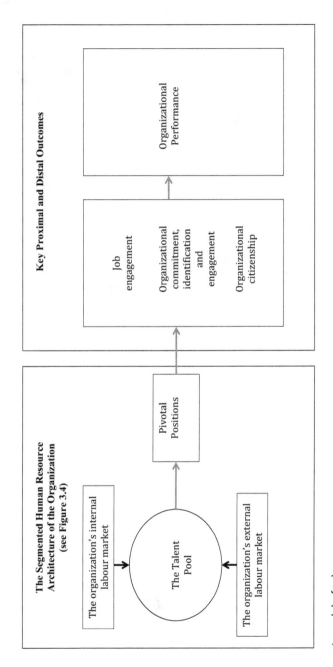

FIGURE 3.4 A model of talent management

(*Source:*   adapted from Collings and Mellahi, 2009)

Employer branding. One of the most important developments in talent management in recent years has been the incorporation of the language and theories of marketing into HR (Martin et al., 2011; Martin & Sinclair, 2018; Theurer et al., 2016) (see Chapter 6). This is most obvious in the recruitment process, which is seen by many companies as too important to be left to HR practitioners, especially those untutored in the language and methods of developing strong corporate reputations and brands. Marketing theories are increasingly evident in the proposals to segment internal labour markets, such as the architectural model described above, with firms attempting to different employer value propositions (EVPs) for each major segment or unit of labour. This idea of differentiating workforces internally to reflect the multiple, differentiated external strategies of companies has become one of the key HR messages in recent times. Mark Huselid and Brian Becker (2011) have argued that a differentiated HR architecture is necessary to support the implementation of firms' strategies. They focus on the need to identify strategic capabilities and strategic jobs as the most essential tasks in designing a 'workforce management system' design rather than use traditional hierarchies as the basis of segmenting the workforce. This has two implications. The first is that managers are not necessarily seen as core employees and may not be part of the talent pool; the second is that there is a need to develop employer brands and EVPs that appeal to an exclusive segment of core employees who have the necessary job-related, social, and networking skills to create high value. In effect, we are increasingly witnessing an exclusive approach to talent management and employer branding at odds with the more traditional inclusive approaches that organizations have usually followed (Thunnissen et al., 2013). Huselid and Becker's thesis is that 'best employer' schemes, which operate in many countries, are counterproductive because they attempt to appeal to, and include, all employees as 'talent' rather than a select group. As a result, they propose that organizations following undifferentiated talent management and employer branding approaches place 'golden handcuffs' on mediocre employees and fail to attract and retain high-value talent. This language of differentiation mirrors the ideas of psychological contracting in recognising the individual nature of psychological contracts and the different types of contracts. We return to this issue in the next section on managing careers.

Criticisms of talent management. Exclusive approaches to talent management and employer branding typically imply price segmentation in the form of highly differentiated rewards strategies in organizations. Given that talent, by definition, is in short supply or, in the language of economists, inelastic in the short to medium term, the price of talent has risen quite markedly over the last few decades in many countries. Thus, organizations are increasingly 'paying for the person' rather than having fixed rates and bands for staff, and the differentials between high performers and average performers are gradually increased to reflect market values and the kinds of economic rent that accrue to factors in short supply. There is certainly evidence of this having occurred since the 1980s, with ratios of salaries between the top-paid managers and the average salaries of employees having increased significantly in most countries. So, for example, the independent High Pay Centre (2023) in the UK reported that median CEO salaries among the top FTSE 100 firms in Britain were £3.41 million, approximately 103 times their median full-time workers pay of £33,000, with the gap increasing. These trends in rewarding talent in an increasingly global world, characterised by highly mobile executives, are associated with rapidly increasing inequality in many countries in the developed world. In Britain, for example, the share of income earned by the top 1 per cent more than doubled in the last decade although the public seems to be unaware of this trend in believing that social inequalities are diminishing (High Pay Centre, 2023).

These trends and the discourse of talent management have affected how all of us think about the increasingly individualised nature of the employment relationship, careers, and rewards in organizations, which may explain why societies seem to be more tolerant or even ignorant about growing inequalities. Such a discourse and set of associated HR practices, however, have not captured the imagination of all commentators and practitioners, especially critical theorists (Painter-Morland et al., 2019; Thunnissen et al., 2013), who question the ethical basis of an exclusive approach to talent management. Case 3.1 points to problems that can arise when individual talent management is overemphasised, especially at the expense of other members of the organization (Collings et al., 2019).

CASE 3.1 THE DARK SIDE OF TALENT MANAGEMENT

The 'talent mindset' is the new orthodoxy of American management. It is the intellectual justification for why such a high premium is placed on degrees from first-tier business schools, and why the compensation packages for top executives have become so lavish. In the modern corporation, the system is considered only as strong as its stars, and in the past few years, this message has been preached by consultants and management gurus all over the world. None, however, spread the word quite so ardently as McKinsey and, of all its clients, one firm took the talent mindset closest to heart. It was a company where McKinsey conducted 20 separate projects, where McKinsey's billings topped $10 million a year, where a McKinsey director regularly attended board meetings, and where the CEO himself was a former McKinsey partner. The company, of course, was Enron.

The Enron scandal became famous in 2001. The reputations of Jeffrey Skilling and Kenneth Lay, the company's two top executives, were destroyed. Arthur Andersen, Enron's auditor, was all but driven out of business, and attention turned to Enron's investment bankers. The one Enron partner that escaped largely unscathed, however, was McKinsey, which is odd, given that it essentially created the blueprint for the Enron culture. Enron was the ultimate 'talent' company. When Skilling started the corporate division known as Enron Capital and Trade in 1990, he 'decided to bring in a steady stream of the very best college and MBA graduates [he] could find to stock the company with talent.' During the 1990s, Enron was bringing in 250 newly minted MBAs a year. 'We had these things called Super Saturday,' one former Enron manager recalls. 'I'd interview some of these guys who were fresh out of Harvard, and these kids could blow me out of the water. They knew things I'd never heard of.' Once at Enron, the top performers were rewarded inordinately and promoted without regard for seniority or experience. Enron was a start system. 'The only thing that differentiates Enron from our competitors is our people, our talent,' Lay, Enron's former chairman and CEO, told the McKinsey consultants when they came to the company's headquarters in Houston. Or, as another senior Enron executive put it to Richard Foster, a McKinsey partner who celebrated Enron in his 2001 book (co-authored with Sarah Kaplan) *Creative Destruction*, 'We hire very smart people, and we pay them more than they think they are worth.'

The management of Enron, in other words, did exactly what the consultants at McKinsey said that companies ought to do to succeed in the modern economy. It hired and rewarded the very best and the very brightest – and it is now in bankruptcy. The reasons for its collapse are complex. But what if Enron failed despite its talent mindset but because of it?

1 Can organizations overrate talented people? What does the case highlight about the dark side of talent management?

Source: based on *The Talent Myth* by Malcolm Gladwell, available online at http://artsci.shu.edu/english/basicskills/02-exploratory/example-exploratory.htm.

Well-known American academics such as Boris Groysberg (2010) in the USA have pointed out the dangers of talent management and the trends towards individualisation of the employment relationship. The main thrust of their criticisms is that the competition created by talent management practices harms everyone, and not just the 'losers' or 'C' performers. This is because it undermines organizational loyalty, team-working, knowledge sharing, and the organization's overall ability to turn knowledge into action. To many people in the USA and UK, management practices that produce internal competition are so widespread nowadays that they seem unexceptional. Examples of such talent management practices include recognition awards given to individuals, such as 'employee of the month or year programmes'; forced distributions of individual merit raise budgets, so what one person receives another cannot; contests between departments or individuals for prizes; and published rankings of unit or individual performance. These practices often create a zero-sum contest in which the success or rewards of one person or department come at the expense of another, and thus there is a built-in disincentive to share knowledge. Other problems identified by Groysberg (2010) and his colleague (Ammerman & Groysberg, 2021) include the following:

- A focus on hiring outsiders plays down the abilities of insiders, who can rapidly become demotivated and often leave. Organizations that 'enjoy' such a reputation for favouring external 'new talent' can attract poor reputations among potential recruits as a 'hire-and-fire' company, as well as among dissatisfied insiders (a point to which we shall return in Chapter 6).
- A focus on hiring outsiders leads senior managers to expend considerable effort in finding the 'right people'. Such a commitment leads them to rationalise their

efforts by placing high value on talented outsiders and assuming they are better than insiders. Sometimes we refer to this as the 'neglect of prophets in their own land' syndrome. This syndrome is exemplified by the current fashion among many English Premier League football clubs for recruiting football managers and football stars from other countries, which is often played out in the popular press by a 'will they come, won't they come' storyline and frequently leads to a bidding war in which outsiders are paid much more than insiders. Such strategies are arguably self-defeating because they lead to internal dissatisfaction and a mercenary culture. Talented individuals who are attracted by money are equally likely to leave for money.

- A focus on individual talent often results in playing down the need to repair problems with the overall organization, such as the 'fit' among individuals, business processes, organizational cultures, and structures. Again, the football team example highlights the problems of relying on recruiting star players, a strategy that doesn't always lead to success.

- Arrogance and elitism often follow the recruitment of talented individuals – part of the problem at companies such as Enron and many of the investment banks. Such attitudes and behaviour run counter to cultivating an attitude of wisdom and reflection, a delicate balance between knowing and doubting, which is one of the hallmarks of good managers and leaders (see Chapter 2).

- The stars' 'shine' typically begins to decline because they are uprooted from their supportive, previous organization and workgroups, and replanted in often infertile soil. Stardom is over-attributed to personal qualities and under-attributed to the organizational context. Moreover, the performance of the group that must work with the new star usually suffers because of declining morale, communication problems, and interpersonal conflicts. These two consequences have related to declining valuations of companies following publicised appointments of stars in the financial services industry.

Last but importantly, the failure to break the barriers that still exist for women – the gender pay gap (Ammerman & Groysberg, 2021). This is a critical issue for many firms, industries, and, of course, women themselves. Recent evidence from the UK, however, is hopeful. A House of Commons report in 2023 pointed to the median hourly pay gap for full-time employed women being 7.7 per cent, a figure that has progressively declined since 1997 when it was nearer 17 per cent. Several factors were found to account for this gap, including age (with a substantial gap emerging for 40-year-olds plus), occupation, industry (especially high in financial services), sector (gap lower in the public sector), region (gap highest in the south), and pay (high earners have a larger gap) (Francis-Devine, 11 November 2023).

MANAGING CAREERS

We have already raised some of the issues concerned with managing newer patterns of careers in the previous sections. However, there are issues requiring elaboration so that managers are better able to understand and deal with the problems they are likely to face, both now and in the future. These issues can be subsumed under the general trend in career patterns towards fragmentation, segmentation, and/or idiosyncrasy.

The notion of boundaryless careers, employability, and the individualisation of employment have already been introduced in previous sections. Though there is still some argument over the objective evidence on the extent to which individual career expectations have changed, and whether there have been markedly different career behaviours exhibited by many employees, there is little doubt that the *rhetoric of careers* has changed since the 1990s (Arthurs, 2008). What seemed to be a widespread trend, among developed economies at least, was for employees to begin their disengagement from careers at an increasingly early age a few decades ago (Sparrow & Cooper, 2003). Until recently, however, demographic trends, changing attitudes towards older employees by employers, and projected labour shortages in certain countries over the next few decades led many people to remain at work well beyond traditional retirement age, with legislative changes making later retirement mandatory in countries with ageing populations (e.g., the UK and France). That trend has now reversed, especially since COVID, with the phenomenon known as the 'Great Resignation'. Our research into senior doctors exemplifies that trend with these specialist medical staff intending to retire or scale down their working commitments in ever-increasing numbers, causing major problems for the NHS (Martin et al.., 2023).

In the 1980s, Ed Schein (1990, Schein & Van Maanen, 2013) developed the idea of people having different *career anchors*, relatively stable orientations to one's organization and one's career(s). He identified eight such anchors (see Box 3.4), which have been widely used to analyse career development and to provide advice to managers, including, for example, assigning individuals to employment in other countries (Cerdin & Pangneux, 2012).

Box 3.4 Schein's career anchors

Edgar Schein identified eight career anchors and has shown that people will have prioritised preferences for these. For example, a person with a primary theme of security/stability will seek secure and stable employment over, say, employment that is challenging and riskier. Career anchors, he argues, are relatively stable, and people tend to stay anchored in one area, which will be reflected in their career and job choices.

- *Technical/functional competence.* This kind of person likes to become an expert at something and will work towards this end. They like to be challenged and then use their skill to meet the challenge, doing the job properly and better than almost anyone else.
- *General managerial competence.* Unlike technical/functional people, this individual wants to be a manager (and not just to get more money, although this may be used as a metric of success). They like problem-solving and dealing with other

people. They thrive on responsibility. To be successful, they also need emotional intelligence competences.

- *Autonomy/independence.* These people have a primary need to work under their own direction, rather than be controlled. They avoid standards and prefer to work alone.
- *Security/stability.* Security-focused people seek stability and continuity as primary factors in their lives. They avoid risks and are generally 'lifers' in their job.
- *Entrepreneurial creativity.* These people like to invent or innovate, be creative, and, most of all, run their own businesses. They differ from those who seek autonomy in that they will share the workload to accomplish things. They find ownership very important. They easily get bored. Wealth, for them, is a sign of success.
- *Service/dedication to a cause.* Service-orientated people are driven by how they can help other people, often more than using their natural talents (which may fall in other areas). They tend to work well in public services such as education and healthcare, or in management occupations such as HR.
- *Pure challenge.* People driven by challenge seek constant stimulation and difficult problems that they can tackle. Such people will change jobs when the current one gets boring, and their careers can be very varied.
- *Lifestyle.* Those who are focused first on lifestyle look at their whole pattern of living. They seek not so much balance between work and life but more to integrate work with their lifestyles. They may even take long periods off work in which to indulge in passions such as volunteering, sailing, climbing, or travelling, etc.

However, other researchers have shown the permanence implied by the notion of career anchors may be a little misplaced and that individuals who only have one dominant career anchor may also be mistaken (Wils et al., 2014). For example, Arthurs et al. (1999) found that 75 participants in their in-depth, longitudinal study over a period of ten years were less likely to involve upwards progression and were much less linear and idiosyncratic than most career theory had suggested, often involving movements outside the labour market and downwards and sideways moves. Thus, careers, they argued, sometimes lacked the objective rationality that was implied by these anchors, or else revolved around individuals' desire for personal fulfilment or maximization of their earnings or education, depending on their ambitions at a particular point in time.

- In relation to psychological contracting, it is likely that highly varied attitudes and expectations of such contracts can exist, even within the same industry and in the same country (the UK). So, once we move outside similar contexts, we are likely to find increased variations among typical psychological contracts (see Chapter 5). Thus, French respondents described their contracts as essentially exploitative, Canadians as instrumental, Chinese as custodial, and Norwegians as communitarian, which reflected their individualist versus collective national cultural values (Thomas et al., 2010)

- US researchers have found significant differences among career orientations and career-orientated behaviours of knowledge workers and managers in leading technology companies in America, Europe, Asia, and Israel (Finegold & Mohrman, 2001) (see Table 3.5). This work not only focused on what employees say in interviews about expectations and desires but also examined the relationship between key behaviours and levels of employee retention and commitment. The key point for managers from this research reinforces the idea introduced in the previous sections that organizations need to use their data on employees to refine their understanding of changing and varied employee expectations, psychological contracts, and career-driving behaviours, and to segment their workforces and develop appropriate EVPs and employer brands.

- Arthurs (2008) identified a broad category of contemporary careers, which are responsive to (1) changing boundaries in occupational, organizational, national, and global ways of working, (2) greater uncertainty arising from increased knowledge, and (3) increased choice among individuals consequent on changing occupational, organizational, national, and global boundaries and the greater range of job experiences available to people.

- One general trend, especially post COVID, is for people to seek more flexibility in the type of employment relationship (CIPD, 2022), especially in relation to where and how they work (Ashforth et al., 2023). We have referred to this as a place orientation in what they value and how they relate to meaningful work (Martin et al., 2023). Such flexibility, however, is more likely to be sought and granted to people whose skills are highly valued and who are in a relatively powerful position to negotiate flexible deals. They are usually high-status employees who are also highly mobile and marketable, including consultants, general practitioners, some academics and other professionals, or high added value contractors in short supply (Barley & Kunda, 2006). Denise Rousseau (2005), one of the most influential researchers of psychological contracting, has called this process *idiosyncratic dealing.* These I-Deals are different from psychological contracts because they are based on more than employee expectations and arise only when individuals negotiate different treatment from their employers than is normally the case with comparable others (Davis & Van der Heijden, 2018). Examples of such deals often involve working less than full-time contracts so they have time to work on their own behalf with other clients or can enjoy 'portfolio' careers, working significant time at home and negotiating special monetary and non-monetary arrangements, including special performance or commission arrangements, pension deals, vacation time, and so on (Collins et al., 2013). Idiosyncratic dealing, however, creates several problems for employers because it gives rise to a 'star' system that breaks normal conventions and can lead to some of the problems associated with talent management discussed earlier. Finally, Conway and Coyle-Shapiro (2016) proposed that I-Deals can damage employment relations and unit-level productivity.

TABLE 3.5 Potential variety in psychological contracts and career expectations

Sparrow's contractual deal (UK retail banking)	Herriot and Pemberton's career contracts (UK retail banking)	Finegold and Mohrman 'What employees really want' (technology industry/cross country)
Still ambitious – accept constraints of a new deal but believe they can still advance	*Career development core deal* – organization sought flexibility, commitment, involvement and performance, while employees accepted this and sought trust, security, employability, and career development	*Early career employees (30 and under)* seek career advancement, satisfaction with professional work environment, influence within organization, and to work for innovative company. Security less important
Frustrated mobile – disengaged mentally because managers did not understand need, and were on constant job search	*Autonomy* – organization looked for specific, short-term, project-type skills and capability to work unsupervised, while employees sought autonomy, freedom to do work and challenging projects	*Mid career employees (31–50)* seek degree of autonomy to manage own careers and professional satisfaction
Passively flexible – understood requirements for being flexible, but no enthusiasm for it	*Lifestyle or part-time deal* – organization wanted flexibility to match workload and part-time, and usually high-customer service skills while employees wanted flexible work patterns and workloads to match their lifestyle loads	*Late career employees (over 50)* These employees seek security above all else. Professional satisfaction and autonomy less important
Lifers – respected old relational contracts, and were not impressed with high pay and employability. Believed technical competence was a sufficient reason for advancement		
Buy me out – sought a deal to leave, but waiting for the right offer from employers		
Guidance seekers – sought and needed help to understand their career possibilities		
Don't push me too fast – understood the need for change but thought it was going too fast, too far		
Just pay me more – transactional outlook, and would accept most changes but at a price		

Source: adapted from Finegold & Mohrman, 2001; Sparrow & Cooper, 2003, p. 131.

Exercise 3.4

Think about your career. Which description, if any, fits your own career pattern or expectations? Would you say that your career expectations have changed over time? Do you agree that late career employees value security above all else or are some professionals concerned with other issues?

Our research into the career intentions of senior hospital doctors in the NHS does not fit into any of the above patterns (Martin et al., 2023). Instead, we found these doctors are increasingly likely to want to retire not only because of punitive pension taxation in the UK but because of progressive disillusionment with the NHS system's ability to provide resources and a diminishing lack of work centrality, comprising lowering work engagement and beliefs in the work they were doing had moral and social value. We argued this resulted from a violated psychological contract, especially after COVID, in which the promise of status, good pay, and autonomy in return for long and relatively paid training with unsocial hours had increasingly failed to be delivered. This point neatly leads us into the next section on the tools we need to understand the relations between employees and their work.

MANAGING ORGANIZATIONAL COMMITMENT AND IDENTIFICATION

We have repeatedly come across or used terms such as commitment, identification, citizenship, or engagement. These are different ways of describing the nature of the linkage between an employee and his or her organization and the factors that influence this relationship. For managers, it is important they understand the differences in these linkages, especially what they refer to and their implications for practice (see Table 3.6). For example, commitment, identification, and citizenship each have their own specific meaning, antecedents, and consequences, yet each is used to describe the nature of psychological contracts and the strength of employee brands or EVPs. Furthermore, many employee surveys conducted by 'blue-chip' organizations fail to distinguish between them or, even worse, confuse them. Therefore, HR managers often must rely on measures for A (e.g., identification) while hoping for B (e.g., commitment). In this section, we shall examine organizational commitment, organizational identification, and the notion of psychological ownership, three of the most important individual–organizational linkages.

ORGANIZATIONAL COMMITMENT

In the earlier case on the North Sea oil industry, our measures of employees' relationships with their organization focused mainly on commitment, a term that is used to refer to a few different types of attachment to work, including commitment to work itself, to specific jobs, to the union or workgroup, to a career or professional calling, or to the employing organization(s). It is the last of these that has received most attention because it has promised much in terms of desired organizational outcomes, such as loyalty, 'going the extra mile' (organizational citizenship behaviour), low absenteeism, and good performance.

Organizational commitment is an old concept usually defined in terms of the reasons underlying people's wish to join and remain with an organization and their feelings towards it (Cohen, 2014; Sparrow & Cooper, 2003). It is sometimes thought to have three components, which are set out in Box 3.5. An individual's commitment can be made up of one or more of these types of commitment, and usually a composite measure of all three is provided in general surveys.

Box 3.5 Three types of organizational commitment

1. *Affective (or attitudinal) commitment*, which is based on a willing acceptance of the organization's goals and an identification or emotional attachment with the organization and its values. Measures include items like 'I really feel as if this organization's problems are my problems'.

2. *Continuance commitment*, which refers to the extent to which employees are bound to the organization in terms of their intention to remain or leave. This may result from a weighing-up of the costs and benefits of staying or leaving, such as perceptions of alternative jobs, or the financial hardship associated with leaving. Measures include items like 'I would continue to work for this organization even though I received a better offer from another employer'.

3. *Normative commitment*, which refers to an individual's perceptions of obligation or loyalty to the organization. Measures include items like 'This organization deserves my loyalty'.

Sources: based on Meyer & Allen, 1991; Cohen, 2014.

There are several problems, however, with the notion of organizational commitment that renders it less useful in describing the strength of the relationship between individuals and their organization, especially in contemporary contexts. First, it is used as both an explanation and an outcome of individual–organizational linkages, which can cause confusion in trying to establish the causes of commitment. Second, the notion that individuals may be committed to only one organization may be becoming outmoded, especially in light of recent changes towards networking in organizations (see Chapter 4) and boundaryless careers discussed earlier. It is also the case that many professionals, including doctors and academics, often have little commitment to their employing organization but are more committed to their profession or the sector (Martin et al.,

2021). Third, the goals and values of a large organization are likely to vary from one part to another, such as in those organizations that have strong lines of business brands, and rejection of one specific value (or line of business brand) may coexist with the acceptance of other values (or other lines of business). This could be the case, for example, with organizations that have ethically dubious products such as cigarettes as part of their portfolio. Organizations with different sites or places of work also tend to have different cultures and thus attract varying levels of commitment, as we have found in the healthcare sector (Siebert et al., 2018).

Perhaps more than anything, however, the reason to be a little wary of the concept of commitment is its promised and expected relationship with desired organizational outcomes. Although high levels of continuance commitment are related to lower labour turnover and absence, and affective commitment is associated with job performance, the links between organizational commitment as a whole and job and organizational performance are quite weak. And given the changes in employment and careers, even this weak relationship may diminish over time.

ORGANIZATIONAL IDENTIFICATION

This concept has become more widely used over the last decade or so because of its more direct links with values-based management, EVPs, and employer branding (see Chapter 5). It differs from commitment, which is a more general term, and refers to only one component or type of commitment. However, psychologists who are experts in identity theory have claimed that organizational identification is a deeper and richer concept than the one measured by commitment scales. It also has a specific meaning. So, for example, He and Brown (2013) have defined it as 'the extent to which an organizational member defines himself/herself with reference to his/her organizational membership' (p.12).

Social identity theory, the basis of this idea, suggests that we define ourselves (our self-concept) through the links we have with important reference groups by forming a relationship in our minds between the identity of those groups and ourselves. We tend to highlight the similarities between our own self-identity and those of the group we aspire to relate or belong to and emphasise the distinctiveness between ourselves and those groups that do not fit in with our self-identity – in other words, we define ourselves by who we are not (Brown, 2017). For example, in recent studies we have conducted into the work of senior doctors in the National Health Service in Scotland, we found a significant division in attitudes to their jobs and organizations between hospital consultants who had worked in a medical management role and those without such experience (Martin et al., 2021). Many consultants in the latter group regarded consultants who had become medical managers as having undergone a significant identity change, one that was inconsistent with patient care as the primary goal of healthcare organizations. Medical managers were often described as having 'crossed a line in the sand' or having gone over to 'the dark side.' So, the less individuals believe the norms and values of an organization represent their own norms and values, the lower their level of organizational identification, which was certainly the case in our research.

From the perspective of managers, organizational identification theory holds out some promise because strong levels of identification have the potential capacity to be positively related to employee self-esteem, greater satisfaction, and motivation, perceived superior job performance by managers, high levels of loyalty, a more attractive place to work, organizational citizenship, and working beyond the contract. However, the links between it and financial performance are weaker and limited (He & Brown, 2013). Research also shows that measures of organizational support, especially employees' perceptions of the extent to which the employer values their contribution and cares for their well-being, have a positive effect on organizational identification (Edwards & Peccei, 2010), a finding we take up later in this chapter. Finally, a review of the antecedents of organizational identification points to four distinct factors that can lead employees to identify with their employers (Weisman et al., 2023). These are the organization's reputational characteristics and their fit with them; the social environment of the organization and interactions with leaders and peers; managerial policies and practices, and how these are experienced by employees; and the personal attributes of employees, including their orientations to work, identities, and needs. This framework has strong similarities with our own work on what healthcare employees seek from employment, past, present, and future (Martin et al., 2023), and with our work on organizational reputations, which I also discuss in Chapter 6.

PSYCHOLOGICAL OWNERSHIP

Strong claims are made for the incremental validity of psychological ownership over organizational commitment and organizational identification in predicting employee performance and organizational citizenship (Zhang et al., 2021). Two decades ago, Jon Pierce and his colleagues (2001) argued that although commitment and identification are important constructs for understanding the relationships and attachments between individuals and their organizations, neither is a complete or even a necessary explanation of psychological ownership, which they define as follows:

> As a state of the mind, psychological ownership … is that state in which individuals feel as though the target of ownership (material or immaterial in nature) or a piece of it is 'theirs' (i.e. 'It is MINE!'). The core of psychological ownership is the feeling of possessiveness and of being psychologically tied to an object.
>
> *(Pierce et al., 2001, p. 299)*

These authors contend that 'mine' is a small word, but with enormous consequences for organizations. Psychological ownership arises because people have an innate need to possess, or because it satisfies certain human motives, which are either socially derived or genetic (Avey et al., 2009; Van Dyne & Pierce, 2004; Zhang et al., 2021). These include:

- *Self-efficacy*, which refers to an individual's belief that they can achieve success in a specific task.
- The need to *control and be accountable*, in which ownership confers on us certain rights and abilities to shape our environment so that we can become more effective – for example, the degree to which we can determine our working times.
- *Self-identity*, which is formed partly through our interactions with what we possess and our reflections on what they mean – for example, company cars.
- The need to have a *place*, 'home' or 'territory' that we can call our own, which is not only a physical but also a psychological space – for example, employees not only seek office or workspaces they can call their own but also look for 'soul mates' they can metaphorically set up a home with while at work.

Ownership can be achieved by following one or more of three 'routes':

1. Having a strong degree of control over the object of our ownership, such as the job or the organization and its performance.
2. Coming to know the object of our ownership intimately by having a 'living' relationship with it – for example, the academic who comes to feel the university department belongs to him or her, having achieved tenure and worked in it for a long time.
3. Investing the self into the object of our ownership. Through time as we expend effort into shaping, creating, or making something, we feel that we come to own what we have shaped, created, or made, such as machines, ideas, and even people.

The consequences of psychological ownership are to create among individuals a set of perceived 'property' rights and responsibilities that help explain why individuals promote and resist change. Thus, self-initiated change by employees who have high levels of psychological ownership is more likely to be promoted and accepted because it enhances feelings of self-efficacy and control. Likewise, imposed change is likely to be resisted because it diminishes feelings of self-efficacy and self-control. This concept is extremely important in understanding the success or otherwise of stock or share ownership in organizations, often given as a form of reward to individuals and as a way of creating organizational identification. As several researchers have concluded, share ownership without psychological ownership will not produce the hoped-for benefits of greater organizational identification and motivated behaviour.

Finally, however, it is also worth noting that high levels of psychological ownership can also create pathological responses among those people who become separated from the objects of their ownership (Zhang et al., 2021). For example, many years ago I worked as a personnel manager in a construction company. Some senior managers in that company proposed laying off most of the young electrical apprentices who had spent many months installing electrical wiring in a new and high-profile building, on which many of these young electricians were naturally proud to have worked. On hearing of the proposed lay-off, in a deliberate act of sabotage, these young electricians systematically removed all the cabling and equipment they had installed, arguing they had property rights in this project. In effect, this was an act of sabotage from the employers view but psychological ownership from the young electricians perspective.

TABLE 3.6 The differences between commitment, identification, and psychological ownership

Criteria for distinctiveness	Organizational commitment	Organizational identification	Psychological ownership
Core proposition of concept	Desire to remain with organization	Use of organization's identity to define oneself	Possession of the 'organization', job or area of work
Questions answered for individuals	Should I remain?	Who am I?	What is mine?
Motivational bases	Security Belongingness Beliefs and values	Attraction Affiliation Self-enhancement	Control Self-identity Need for place
How it develops	Decision to remain with organization	Incorporating organizational values into self Emulating organizational characteristics	Active imposition/ investment of self on organization
Main consequences for practitioners from research findings	Organizational citizenship behaviour ('going the extra mile') Intention to leave or remain Attendance and absenteeism	Support for organizational values and participation in its activities Intention to remain Frustration/ stress Alienation Lack of integration into organizational values/ culture	Development of employee rights and responsibilities Promotion of/ resistance to change Frustration, alienation and sabotage Integration of employees with work Organizational citizenship behaviour

Source: adapted from Pierce et al., 2001, p. 306; Avey et al, 2009; Zhang et al., 2021.

Pierce and his colleagues have compared the three concepts of commitment, identification, and psychological ownership, the outcomes of which are highly relevant to managers who hope to manage psychological contracts and individuals' attachment to their organizations. We have adapted their table and subsequent work by Avey et al. (2009) and Zhang et al. (2021) to produce Table 3.6 to highlight the most important practical implications.

OVER-IDENTIFICATION AND WORKAHOLISM

In the previous section, we touched on negative or 'dark side' consequences of high levels of psychological ownership in terms of stress and sabotage. Among the most popular discussions among the organization and families of many employees, however, are the subjects of over-identification and workaholism, which tend to be treated as pathological responses to the pressures of organizations on individuals and as a form of addictive behaviour, like drug-taking. High organization identification among employees can lead them to overidentify with their employers. Over-identification manifests itself in strong feelings of psychological entitlement to preferential treatment as part of an in-group, unethical pro-organizational (mis)behaviour, and pro-social rule-breaking to benefit their employers (Irshad & Bashir, 2020). It is important for managers and employees to understand when faith in managerial decision-making becomes 'blind faith' or 'group-think' and to introduce structures, systems, and processes of decision-making that lead to reflexive questioning of organizational logics.

Workaholism is a related but different concept. A definition by Schaufeli et al. (2008) seems to capture the idea succinctly, when they describe it as 'a compulsion or uncontrollable need to work incessantly' (p. 175). The prevalence of workaholism, especially among professional workers and certain occupations, has been estimated in some studies to be around 20 per cent of employees in the groups studied. So, for example, one early study in the USA estimated that whereas 5 per cent of the population might be classified as workaholics, 23 per cent of a sample of doctors, lawyers, and psychiatrists were high on workaholism measures. Similarly, a study in 1996 of Japanese managers found that 21 per cent of the sample were workaholics (Burke, 2000). These figures have been confirmed by other surveys reported by Griffths (2015), who sees workaholism as a form of addictive behaviour, like gambling and playing video games. Interestingly, Avanti et al., (2012) found a curvilinear relationship between organizational identification and workaholism, with workaholism initially decreasing with increased identificatiion but when identification becomes too strong, workaholism increases. This relationship suggests managers need to strike a balance in pursuing identification strategies.

Thus, for managers, it is important to be able to identify workaholic behaviour (especially among themselves) to understand its negative consequences and how it can be managed for the good of both the organization and individual. These negative aspects include long work hours at work and home, waking times, refusal to delegate, not taking holidays, low levels of trust in others, perfectionist behaviour, and a range of attitudes associated with such behaviours.

Drawing on earlier work, Shimazu and Schaufeli (2009) suggested that a typical work addict is driven by strong internal factors that individuals are unable to resist, such as a desire for career advancement, rather than external factors, such as financial problems or organizational culture. They also distinguished workaholism from other types of engaged work behaviour in three ways. The first is the excessive amount of time workaholics spend on discretionary work – the behavioural dimension. The second is that workaholics are reluctant to disengage from work involvement, even thinking about work when not at work – the cognitive dimension. The third is that workaholics work beyond what could reasonably be expected of normal people to meet deadlines – the compulsive dimension. The outcomes of workaholism are often high levels of psychological distress and health problems. These factors are often associated with low levels of job satisfaction and life satisfaction (Shimazu & Schaufeli, 2009). We have also found a similar result in our study of consultant doctors, a significant proportion of whom could be categorised as workaholics (Martin et al., 2023). However, we know less about the impact of workaholism and job performance, leading some researchers to speculate that workaholics may well be poor performers, or at least not necessarily good (Schaufeli et al., 2008).

The lessons for practice from this research suggest that workaholism is associated with what Shimazu and Schaufeli (2009) call 'unwell-being' as distinct from well-being. These authors echo the epithet that the avoidance of workaholism and achieving work–life balance work calls for 'working smart' rather than 'working hard,' which leads us neatly into the next section.

WORK–LIFE BALANCE

Work–life balance (WLB) has become a major issue in many developed countries, with legislation being passed in many countries to limit the length of time spent at work by people in all kinds of employment (ILO, 2022). The basis for much of the debate is over the 'long hours culture' of some countries and of certain organizations within these countries, which is attributed to the adoption of new information and communications technologies, global competition, and job restructuring, and has resulted in greater pressure on employees to work harder and more flexibly. Table 3.7 shows the variations in average hours worked among selected countries and how working hours have varied over time. More recent evidence from the ILO (2022) shows that the average number of hours of work per week in paid work globally was approximately 43.9 hours prior to the COVID-19 pandemic (2019 or latest available year). However, there was substantial variation around this average, with workers in Asia and the Pacific working the longest (47.4), particularly in Southern Asia (49.0) and Eastern Asia (48.8). By comparison, workers in North America (37.9) and Northern, Southern, and Western Europe (37.2) worked the shortest hours.

The debate, however, has several angles to it, promoted even more vigorously because of COVID. The proponents of WLB suggest that work–life balance as a concept implies a balanced relationship between paid work and life outside work, with a presumption that the two are distinct and that people have and should seek a degree of control over their working lives. Often, the term is used in the context of an agenda that seeks to preserve the institutions of family life, caring for children and older people, and one that seeks to promote genuine equality of opportunity for women. Set against this balance are the forces of technology and more intensive competition, discussed in the previous section on workaholism, which have led some organizations to exercise pressures for long working hours, even though these extra hours may not be productive. For example, managers often talk about cultures of 'presenteeism', referring to situations where employees present themselves for work but don't actively engage in productive work ('there in body but not in mind'). Because of this tension, governments and some organizations have introduced policies to help mitigate 'colonisation' by long working hours and the increasing length of working lives over non-working hours and non-working lives. Central to this balancing act is the idea that the individual–organizational employment relationship

Country	2000	2004	2007	2010	2013
Japan	1821	1787	1785	1733	1735
Australia	1780	1741	1719	1695	1676
France	1535	1513	1500	1494	1489
Germany	1471	1436	1422	1405	1388
Korea	2512	2392	2306	2187	2163est
Poland	1988	1983	1976	1940	1918

TABLE 3.7 Annual total hours actually worked

Source: OECD.SatExtracts.

should be a negotiated psychological and legal contract that meets the expectations and obligations of both parties (Guest, 2017; Walsh and Bartikowski, 2013). The increasing degree of autonomy and control provided by this revised psychological contract is brought about by:

- Increasing the variety of ways individuals can integrate work and non-work activities by giving them choices over working hours or job sharing.
- Changing how employees balance work and non-work by constructing their own boundaries between work and non-work activities, such as working at home, telecommuting, sabbaticals, extended leave, unpaid leave, parental leave, and extended breaks for family responsibilities.

Policies that organizations develop to provide employees with these two forms of control have become more common. Box 3.6 illustrates how one UK company has attempted to put some of these ideas into practice.

Box 3.6 Work–life balance programmes in the UK

Constructing a better balance in Balfour Beatty. When Balfour Beatty Civil Engineering Major Projects surveyed their employees and found an overwhelming majority liked working for the company but that for 62 per cent, work–life balance was a problem. 'I love my job and feel proud when I drive past a bridge and know that I helped to build it' says engineer Chris Till, 'but I live in Preston and working on the M1/M25 means I live on site during the week and it can take me four hours to get home on a Friday.'

Balfour Beatty took these concerns seriously. 'We are always striving to improve both our service to our customers and the well-being of our employees,' said Commercial Director Nigel Roberts. 'A contented workforce leads to better productivity and fewer accidents on site.'

The Company employed flexible working specialists, Swiftwork, to help improve work–life balance. Working initially with the project team on the M1 construction site, the concept was tested. 'We had to be clear that the business case for this significant culture change was sound,' says Nigel Roberts. 'We wanted to ensure that performance was maintained and that our customers' and suppliers' needs were met. But we were also hoping that this would have a positive impact on recruitment and retention in an increasingly competitive market for highly skilled employees.'

Following a senior manager workshop, schemes were developed by local teams to target specific work and individual requirements. Each team devised new ways of working that suited its business needs. Most were variations on flexitime and, for some, compressed hours over the working week were introduced. One team developed cross-skilling to offer a broader depth of service to internal clients across the whole day. Cost savings were also made to night services supplied using a flexitime scheme that had previously been provided by an external consultant.

For Balfour Beatty, the business case is proven. 'We have realised operational improvements in efficiency,' says Nigel Roberts, 'for example, there is better interdependence and communication between teams, time recording is better, health and safety cover has increased – not decreased – with more flexibility. Now we're hoping to build on this and develop even smarter ways of working.'

Lynette Swift, of consultants Swiftwork, is confident that new ways of working have huge potential for achieving productivity gains and reducing costs. 'If it's not improving performance, you're not managing it right,' she says. 'To succeed, new initiatives should be people driven but also business focused, not just about acceding to individual requests for flexible work patterns.'

Despite the volume of research conducted on the relationship between working hours and key outcomes such as health and general well-being, few strong conclusions can be drawn (Walsh and Bartikowski, 2013). These may have changed over time, so providing some evidence for those who argue that generational differences matter. So, a meta-analysis conducted in 1997 found only a small, statistical correlation between working hours and health (Sparks et al., 1997) but a later one by Wong et al. (2019) concluded that long working hours were shown to adversely affect workers' health. Another meta-analysis by Faragher et al. (2005) found that job satisfaction was an important influence on the health of workers, which has been confirmed by later research. Finally, studies have concluded that perhaps the main justification for companies to introduce such programmes may have more to do with attracting and retaining non-traditional employees to organizations and contributing to meeting the expectations of individuals with respect to modern employment conditions. For example, Haar et al. (2014) found in a study of seven cultures that work–life balance was positively associated with job and life satisfaction and negatively related to anxiety and depression.

As we have already mentioned, however, there are some strong criticisms of the work–life balance agenda that suggest why the idea may have limited appeal to some organizations and to some employees. The first of these is the impact on productivity and output. Critics of work–life balance point to the example of the USA, which has relatively long working hours compared with other countries in the developed world, but also has among the highest levels of productivity growth. Indeed, this comparison has influenced the French government to change its legislation on working hours by increasing them only shortly after having reduced them. Another example of the importance of flexibility over working hours to productivity was an agreement negotiated by Volkswagen, the German motor vehicle company, with its German employees to trade flexible working (longer hours when required) for guarantees on job security.

Box 3.7 The importance of flexible working hours: VW's practice in Germany 2004–2015

A report in *The Economist* in late 2004 suggested that Volkswagen, Europe's largest vehicle manufacturer, was in trouble, especially with the Volkswagen brand. Losses had amounted to a €47m operating loss for the period January–September in 2004. The article pointed out that its production was less efficient than other German carmakers, including BMW and Chrysler Benz, with labour costs 11 per cent more than their competitors and wages 20 per cent higher than the union average. Nevertheless, this fact didn't stop unions putting in for an above-average 4 per cent pay increase. But, like all German industrial workers, the article went on to hypothesise 'what they really crave is job security,' which persuaded the workers to modify their demands and accept more flexible hours, sometimes translating into longer hours and a wage freeze until 2007, in return for job security until 2011.

VW's response was to pay its 100,000 plus workers €1000 each in cash as a flat-rate bonus, which it hoped would cut its labour costs by 10 per cent. However, this was only a small dent on its longer-term target, which was to reduce its wage bill by 30 per cent by 2011. The reaction of the investment markets to this news was to punish VW by devaluing its share price by 3 per cent for the 'compromise' deal that wouldn't go anywhere near to solving its long-standing productivity problem.

As *The Economist* noted in 2004, 'It sees that long hours are not enough to satisfy investors in Germany who also want to see traditional job security deals removed.'

Consequently, and after many years of negotiation with its unions and Works Council, Volkswagen developed a new working time model with its union representatives. According to the company website in 2015, this model:

offers its employees a high level of flexibility. Daily working hours are as variable as the number of shifts. Company weekly working hours – adjusted to market requirements and depending on the working time model – can be defined within a working time corridor of 25 to 34 hours per week. In addition, working time accounts ensure flexibility for the individual employees and the entire team over long periods...

Sources: adapted from *The Economist*, 'Darwin meets job creationism', 6 November 2004 and Working at Volkswagen (2015) (available online at http://www.volkswagen-karriere.de/en/what_we_stand_for/personnel_policy/flexibility.html, accessed 1/6/15).

The second criticism is the rather arbitrary distinction between work and life outside work, which the notion of work–life balance implies (ILO, 2022). Many employees see work and life as overlapping, since what they do for work is often the main source of meaning in their lives, whether or not they are being paid handsomely for it. This is often the case with professionals in the fields of medicine, academia, and in the creative professions, such as architecture and art, who are often seeking a form of calling or a higher moral and social purpose in their work (Martin et al., 2023). In essence, work–life balance is a subjective concept and will vary from one person to another. However, most commentators and governments would agree that organizations and their senior managers are obliged to ensure that they are not placing undue pressure on people to see the balance in such a way that it leads to ill-health and the detriment of family relationships.

MANAGING EMPLOYEE ENGAGEMENT

Since writing the first edition of this book, the topic of employee engagement has generated enormous interest among practitioners and, more recently, academics, as a way of integrating many of the ideas discussed in the chapter (Akingbola et al., 2023; Albrecht et al., 2015; Byrne, 2022; Peccei, 2013; Truss et al., 2013). While retaining a degree of scepticism over 'the desire to pour old wine into new bottles' by the management consultancy industry, I do believe the notion of employee engagement has something to offer as a way forward for understanding and managing individual–organizational relationships. This is especially relevant in economies, industries, and organizations that have relatively poor records of productivity growth and ensuring work–life balance, which has been recognised by the UK government in its funding of the 'Engage for Success' programme (see http://www.engageforsuccess.org).

In our research into hospital consultants (Martin et al., 2021), we drew on a set of ideas from contemporary research into employee engagement (Albrecht et al., 2015; Farndale et al., 2014; Sparrow, 2014; Truss et al., 2014) to develop a framework that might help us think about employee engagement more generally (see Figure 3.5). We proposed that employee engagement is best conceived in terms of four distinctive but related levels. The first is the well-researched and empirically verified concept of *work engagement* (Schaufeli, 2015). The second level is *engagement with each other*, especially in interdependent work groups, which draws on the notion of relational coordination, a construct that has been found to have a significant impact on performance outcomes in a range of industries (Hoffer-Gittell et al., 2010). The third level is *organizational engagement*, initially developed by consultants but which is now being treated in academic literature as an important driver of organizational performance (Farndale et al., 2014;

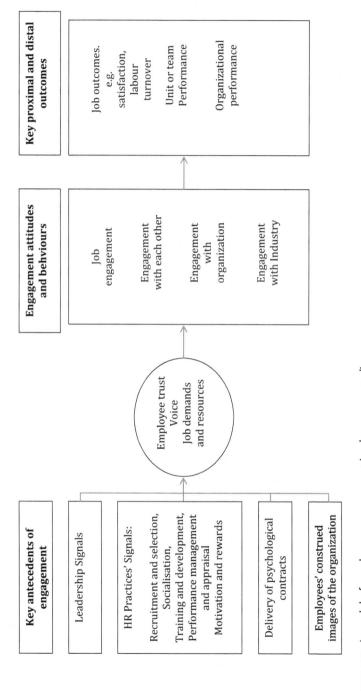

Key antecedents of engagement

Leadership Signals

HR Practices' Signals:

Recruitment and selection,
Socialisation,
Training and development,
Performance management
and appraisal
Motivation and rewards

Delivery of psychological
contracts

Employees' construed
images of the organization

Employee trust
Voice
Job demands
and resources

**Engagement attitudes
and behviours**

Job
engagement

Engagement
with each other

Engagement
with
organization

Engagement
with Industry

**Key proximal and distal
outcomes**

Job outcomes.
e.g.
satisfaction,
labour
turnover

Unit or team
Performance

Organizational
performance

FIGURE 3.5 A model of employee engagement (author generated)

Sparrow, 2014). The fourth level is industry engagement, which can be important in explaining employees' attachment to their work in certain sectors of economic life, such as the healthcare industry.

Work engagement. Work engagement studies are increasingly based on a *demand-resources model of work engagement* (Schaufeli, 2015). This model has identified three forms of connections that people have with their work: the *vigour* employees invest in doing the job, their levels of *absorption* or immersion and attachment to their work, and their *dedication* to their work. Work engagement has been shown to predict valuable outcomes such as positive evaluations of organizations, lower job turnover, and higher levels of individual and unit performance (Albrecht et al., 2015; Byrne, 2022). It is also positively associated with key job resources and challenging work. However, vigour, absorption, and dedication in work, if taken too far, can lead to over-engagement, or over-identification (as we have discussed in this chapter), or employee burnout. High levels of work engagement also tend to be associated with 'cosmopolitan' career orientations, which typically refer to the external career orientation of professionals such as the doctors in our own research (Martin et al., 2021) as distinct from the 'local' or internal career orientations of occupational groups such as health service managers.

Engagement with each other. Relationships among employees at a group or team level have also been found to lead to effective organizational performance. This has traditionally been theorised in terms of social capital and networking among employees to facilitate group and organizational learning. Over the last two decades, Jody Hofer Gittell and colleagues (e.g., Gittell et al., 2010; Bolton et al., 2021) have developed a theory of relational coordination to explain the impact of effective coordination among task-interdependent groups on achieving soft and hard desirable organizational outcomes. They defined relational coordination as 'a mutually reinforcing process of interaction between communication and relationships carried out for the purpose of task integration' (p. 3), which involves groups engaging in frequent and high-quality communications, sharing goals and knowledge, and showing mutual respect. While these authors restrict their analysis to the coordination of 'highly interdependent, uncertain, and time-constrained work,' we argue that the concept of relational coordination is relevant to most forms of work in modern organizations. It also provides an explanation of the link between the individualistic focus of employees' engagement with their work and employees' engagement with their organization and its senior management. This discussion of relational coordination is followed up in Chapter 9 on creativity and innovation, which are often associated with team engagement and effort.

Organizational engagement. Recent academic work has sought to define organizational engagement in terms of emotions and attitudes (state engagement) and behaviour engagement (the traditional interest of management consultants) (Farndale et al., 2014). Key components of these different types of engagement with the organization include organizational satisfaction and commitment, vigour, and absorption displayed towards an organization and positive organizational citizenship behaviours (Albrecht et al., 2015; Byrne, 2022). I add employee identification with an organization to these components, drawing on the well-established concept of organizational identification discussed earlier in this chapter. As noted, Martin Edwards and Ricardo Peccei (2010) proposed a three-factor explanation of employee identification with their organizations. The first factor refers to how employees self-categorise their personal identities. Employees differ in their career orientations and the extent to which their employing organization helps define their identities (Martin et al., 2023). The second refers to their sense of attachment and belonging to their organizations, often related to how long they have worked in it. The third refers to the extent to which employees share the goals and values of the organization and incorporate them into their own goals, values, and beliefs. In these studies, high levels of organizational identification were shown to predict all categories of workers' helping behaviours, turnover intentions, and feelings of being involved in the organization (Martin et al., 2023).

Industry engagement. Employees in particular industries often tend to identify with the sector in which they work rather than the firm, which reflects the notion of cosmopolitan versus local orientations to work discussed in the section on work engagement. This is closely related to the concept of a calling, which is usually taken to refer to a prosocial orientation to work on behalf of employees who seek a moral and social purpose from their work (Dobrow et al., 2023). We found in our study of the changing work experience of hospital consultants in the National Health Service in Scotland that many of these senior doctors were more attracted by working in the sector than any specific employer within it. Engagement with the values and purpose of the sector was high but engagement with their employers was only low to moderate (Martin et al., 2021). Moreover, we also found that consultant doctors identified more with the democratic values of the healthcare sector in Scotland than the more market-orientated healthcare system in England, even though the two sectors are part of a UK-wide National Health Service. Industry or sector engagement can also be explained by the notion of a *construed image.* What employees think about the industry and the organization in which they work is influenced by how significant others, including close friends and family, the media, and the general public, rate a sector or organization's reputation. So, for example, financial services rated only marginally better in reputation rankings than government and tobacco (Harris Poll Reputation Rankings, 2015), while the public in the UK has high levels of trust in doctors and nurses in the National Health Service.

State and behavioural engagement. A second element of engagement is the distinction made between state engagement, which refers to employees' attitudes and emotions (e.g., sharing the values of the organization), and behavioural engagement, which refers to the kinds of behaviours employees report when feeling engaged or disengaged. One of the most important of these is the employee net promoter score (e.g., I often recommend my employer as a place to work), which is sometimes referred to as the 'ultimate', engagement question. These distinctive *foci of engagement* (Byrne, 2022; Farndale et al., 2014) are very important in making engagement a worthwhile and useful subject of study and practice since most of the previous research into individual–organizational relationships has focused on attitudes and emotions rather than the arguably more important behaviours, such as advocating their organization as a place to build a career that risks putting personal reputations on the line.

The drivers of engagement and their impact on employee trust, voice, and job demands and resources. Our framework also identifies some of the most important antecedents of these different types of engagement discussed in this chapter. From my reading of recent research (e.g., Martin et al., 2021, 2023), the ones that have the most

impact are: (1) signals sent by the rhetoric and actions of senior leaders in the organization; (2) the signals sent out by the kinds of HR practices employed in the organization; (3) the extent to which the psychological contract is delivered; and (4) employees'
construed image of the organization or industry. The rhetoric-reality gap between
what leaders pronounce (usually a 'soft' version of people management as 'resourceful
humans') and how they behave both personally and in directing their organizations (a
'hard' version of people as 'human resources' or 'capital') has been a constant source of
tension in organizations (Legge, 2005).

We have covered the nature of signals sent out by senior managers and/or leaders in
Chapter 2, and the delivery of the psychological contract and the notion of a construed
image in this chapter, so little more needs to be said about these 'drivers' of engagement.
However, the nature of human resources practices requires further elaboration. Albrecht
et al. (2015) have usefully categorised these as recruitment and selection, socialisation,
training and development and performance management, including motivation and
rewards, and appraisal. To these we would add talent management and employer branding, job design, and employee relations practices, including the means and media used to
secure employees' involvement and cooperation (Martin & Sinclair, 2018). However, it
is not just the fact or existence of such practices, individually and collectively, regardless
of their sophistication, that is important, but the honesty of the signals they send out to
employees and how these signals are sensed or interpreted by them (Martin & Cerdin,
2014). This highly subjective process of interpretation by employees of the honesty or
authenticity of signals sent out by the organization shaped three key intermediate variables. These are: (1) employees' trust in the organization and its leaders; (2) the extent
to which they feel free to exercise voice and participate in decision-making; and (3)
their perceptions of demands placed on them and the quality of the resources available
to them to do their jobs.

Employee trust has become one of the most widely researched and sought-after phenomena in HR and organizational studies (Searle et al., 2018; Siebert et al., 2015). Trust
is manifested when employees place themselves in a vulnerable position and must rely
on their managers' competence, integrity (honesty), and benevolence (good intentions)
towards them. Following the Global Financial Crisis of 2007/2008, employee trust has
been lacking, especially in sectors badly affected such as financial services and the energy
industries. Instead of trust, we may be witnessing high and stable levels of distrust as the
norm in many sectors of the economy rather than lowering levels of trust. Our studies
of de-professionalisation among hospital consultants (Martin et al., 2021, 2023) could
be read that way. They showed a remarkable level of distrust of non-clinical managers
because of the 'dishonest' signals deliberately sent by recent government and managerial
strategies to reduce the once sacrosanct professional autonomy of doctors in healthcare
(Adler et al., 2008).

Employee voice is also a major influence on employee engagement at different levels.
This has been defined as 'the right to express opinions and have meaningful input into
work-related decision-making, which includes individual and collective voice, union and
non-union voice, and voice mechanisms that cover not only employment terms, but also
work autonomy and business issues' (Budd, 2014, p. 477). Voice researchers concern
themselves with whether employees feel free and able to speak up or remain silent,

whether voice is exercised in a socially constructive manner to improve decision-making, or as retributive justice exercised by employees over managers and the organization, and the extent to which employees enjoy democratic rights in their organizations and are able to exercise a degree of control or task autonomy in their work situations (Wilkinson & Fay, 2011). This literature has distinguished between direct, indirect, and hybrid voice channels, with the last of these represented by managers' attempts to secure employee voice through union or representative channels. In our study of doctors' deprofessionalisation (Martin et al., 2021), we found the lack of voice, individually and collectively, to be the most important factor in leading consultants to express low-to-moderate levels of engagement with their employers.

Of the theories that attempt to explain work engagement and its antithesis – burnout resulting from over-engagement – perhaps the most widely cited is the job-demands-resources model (Shaufeli, 2015). This model is based on the idea that resources can be of two types – functional job resources consistent with achieving work goals, personal growth, and/or reducing job demands – and personal resources, associated with personal resilience and self-belief in being able to control their immediate work environment. You might be able to think of the types of resources that your employer or university could provide you with to help you meet the demands of your job and career, such as appropriate technology, time to do the work, and low levels of bureaucracy; or, in the case of academics and students, a self-belief in their ability to produce good quality research papers in spite of what reviewers and tutors might write about you. However, if perceptions of demands are too great and your resources are insufficient, then this is likely to lead to health impairment, disengagement, and eventually to burnout. In our study of hospital consultants, greater demands for more intensive working and increased bureaucratic control over resources were also an important influence on their low levels of engagement with their employers. Nevertheless, this imbalance between demands and resources did not impact on work engagement or their engagement with colleagues in clinical teams.

The outcomes of engagement, improving engagement, and the influence of context. The research into engagement has predicted and shown positive effects on job, unit/team, and organizational performance (Byrne, 2022). At the level of the job itself, improved satisfaction, commitment, and lower levels of labour turnover have resulted from actions designed to raise engagement levels, such as providing the optimal mix of job demands and resources, enabling employees to improve their personal resources through training, and encouraging employees to engage in what are called 'job crafting' behaviours (Zhang & Parker, 2018). Reminiscent of the job redesign movement of the 1960s and 1970s, job crafting focuses on the ability of employees to shape their jobs by choosing tasks or specialisms that match their interests and abilities, negotiating different job content to enhance their skills, and assigning greater meaning to their jobs (for example, being seen as a mentor to less experienced people).

At the level of the team or work unit, improving relational coordination has been shown to have a highly significant impact on key outcomes. So, for example, improving the frequency, timing, accuracy, and quality of communications between doctors, nurses, social workers, physiotherapists, and managers, supported by shared goals, shared knowledge, and mutual respect in these clinical teams has a remarkable effect on surgical performance, as measured by patient satisfaction, post-operative freedom from pain and functioning, and days spent in hospital (Gittell et al., 2008).

Finally, Albrecht et al. (2015) report research findings that suggest higher levels of engagement can lead to greater organizational innovation, operational performance, financial returns, and competitive advantage. While these so-called 'distal' measures of performance are certainly desirable, for the most part, they remain part of the rhetoric of the 'engagement industry' rather than the reality on the ground, because organizational-level outcomes cannot easily be attributed to individual attitudes and behaviour such as leadership or employee engagement. Two examples might suffice to illustrate this point. First, from our research into organizational trust, we concluded that inaction can sometimes be a better strategy for repairing trust than direct action. Time can often be a great healer and taking direct action usually has unforeseen and, indeed, unknowable consequences (Siebert & Martin, 2014). This conclusion is supported by the so-called 'too-much-of-a-good-thing effect' in HR, which refers to the diminishing and indeed negative returns that often accompany programmes such as appraisal, rewarding people for performance and communications (Pierce & Aguinas, 2013). Second, organizational success is often down to external factors such as the vicissitudes of markets or, in the case of our doctors, factors outside of their control such as political priorities in spending. In other words, and to return to a central message of this book, context (and time) matters! Which is why I circumscribed the variables in Figure 3.4 by a box representing different levels of context – the societal, industry, and organizational levels.

In Chapter 4, we will discuss organizational contexts and show how organizational structures and processes shape people's attitudes, identities, and engagement. In Chapter 5, we examine the impact of societal-level institutions and national cultures on these same factors. And in Chapters 7 and 10, we look at the industry level when discussing knowledge workers and creative workers, whose attitudes, identities, and what they are engaged with are often very different from other types of employees.

LEARNING SUMMARY

In this chapter, we began by examining the idea of psychological contracts as a way of understanding the relationships between organizations and individuals at work. The concept of psychological contracts has become a popular one with both practitioners and academics and should help you understand your own relationships with your employer or potential employer. You should have learnt how to apply the idea of psychological contracts in analysing and designing work situations, including the importance of recognising the different types of contracts – transactional, relational, and ideological – the potential outcomes of breaching and violating contracts, and the questions used to measure psychological contracts.

We then examined the problems of managing psychological contracts at work, which include managing talent, managing careers, managing different kinds of individual–organizational linkages, and managing work–life balance.

Talent management has become one of the major issues for many employers in developed countries. It is generally defined as the ability to attract, inspire, and retain high-performing employees, and develop others so that they can perform more effectively. We examined the elements of a talent management strategy and new thinking in talent management, which focuses on the segmentation of internal labour markets and using different approaches to recruiting, developing, and retaining these groups. However, talent management has a dark side, especially if it focuses on external recruitment to the detriment of growing people inside the organization, and you should be aware of the shortcomings of many talent management programmes.

Managing careers has been characterised by general trends towards fragmentation and individualisation. The notions of employability and boundaryless careers have been used to illustrate these changes in psychological career contracts between employers and employees. There is little doubt that the evidence supports these changed expectations among employees who are seeking different things from careers at different stages of their working lives, and possibly greater variety, flexibility, and autonomy at work. Employers need to be aware of these changes, and design contracts to reflect the different groups within their workforces.

Psychological contracts can also be applied to the measurement of different kinds of individual–organizational relationships, including commitment, identification, and psychological ownership. The importance of these three concepts in managing relationships between people and their organizations cannot be overestimated; too many organizations engage in surveys of employees in which they are unclear as to what they are measuring and attempting to manage. Often, they measure and manage one aspect of individual–organization relationships while hoping for positive outcomes from some other, quite different, feature. Commitment is essentially focused on whether people will remain with the organization; identification focuses on a person's sense of who they are and the extent they can use the organization's values to define their identity; and psychological ownership indicates the extent to which an individual sees that organization as part of him or herself. These different constructs are associated with different outcomes, with identification arguably the most important when examining the extent to which individuals will provide behavioural support for the organization's values and branding strategies.

An area we also examined was the problems of over-identification and workaholism. Workaholism has been seen as a major problem by many employers and governments, which are attempting to reduce the negative consequences of people being too attached to their work. Workaholism has been attributed to three causes: family background and how young people learn addictive behaviour; personal beliefs and fears; and organizational values that encourage high levels of attachment. Many organizations have put programmes into place to deal with various dysfunctional consequences of workaholism, including flexible working, home-working, and culture changes focusing on working 'smarter' rather than 'harder'.

Finally, we examined the role of employee engagement, which has become a way of thinking about how employees connect with their work, each other, their organizations, and their chosen employment sector. We presented a model of engagement at these different levels, explained some of the antecedents of engagement, such as leadership, HR practices, delivery of the psychological contract, and construed image, and how they might work through employee trust and voice to impact on desired organizational outcomes. In summary, we have explored a wide range of ideas, research, and concepts that should be useful to you in practising management and in any writing you need to do for your courses.

REVIEW QUESTIONS

1. An exclusive approach to talent management is the way forward for organizations looking to gain a competitive advantage. Discuss.
2. Workaholism is not necessarily a bad thing. Discuss.
3. Can employees ever be over-engaged?

REFERENCES

Adler, P. S., Kwon, S.-W., & Hecksher, C. (2008). Professional work: The emergence of collaborative community, *Organization Science, 19*(2), 359–376.

Akingbola, K., Edmund Rogers, S., & Intindola, M. (2023). *Employee engagement in nonprofit organizations: Theory and practice.* Palgrave Macmillan.

Albrecht, S. L., Bakker, A. B., Gruman, J. A., Macey, W. H., & Saks, A. M. (2015). Employee engagement, human resource management practices and competitive advantage. *Journal of Organizational Effectiveness: People and Performance, 2*(1), 7–35.

Ammerman, C., & Groysberg, B. (2021). *Glass half broken: Shattering the barriers that still hold women back at work.* Harvard Business School Press.

Arthurs, M. B., Inkson, K. and Pringle, J. (1999). *The new careers.* London: Sage.

Arthurs, M. B. (2008). Examining contemporary careers: A call for interdisciplinary enquiry. *Human Relations, 61*(2), 163–186.

Ashforth, B.E., Caza, B.B., & Meister, A. (2023) My place: how workers become identified wih their workplaces and why it matters. *Academy of Management Review,* doi.org/10.5465/amr.2020.0442

Avanti, L., van Dick, R., Fraccaroli, F. & Sarchielli, G. (2012) The downside of organizational identification: relations between identification, workaholism and well-being. *Work & Stress, 26*(3), 289-307.

Avey, J. B., Avolio, B. J., Crossley, C. D., & Luthans, F. (2009). Psychological ownership: Theoretical extensions, measurement and relation to work outcomes. *Journal of Organizational Behavior, 30*(2), 173–191.

Bal, M. P., De Jong, S. B., Jansen, P. G. W., & Bakker, A. B. (2012). Motivating employees to work beyond retirement: A multi-level study of the role of I-deals and unit climate. *Journal of Management Studies, 49*(2), 306–331.

Barley, S. R., & Kunda, G. (2006). *Gurus, hired hands, and warm bodies: Itinerant experts in a knowledge economy.* Princeton University Press.

Bolton, R., Logan, C., & Gittell, J. H. (2021). Revisting relational coordination: A systematic review. *The Journal of Applied Behavioral Sciences, 57*(3), 1–33.

Boudreau, J. W. and Ramstad, P. M. (2007). *Beyond HR: The new science of human capital.* Cambridge, MA: Harvard Business School Press.

Boxall, P. & Purcell, J. (2022). *Strategy and human resource management* (5th edition), Bloomsbury.

Brown, A. D. (2017). Identity work and organizational identification. *International Journal of Management Reviews, 19*(3), 296–317.

Brown, W., & Edwards, P. (2009). Researching the changing workplace. In W. Brown, A. Bryson, J. Forth, & K. Whitfield (Eds.), *The evolution of the modern workplace.* Cambridge University Press.

Budd, J. (2014). The future of employee voice. In: A. Willkinson, J. Donaghey, T. Dudon and R. B. Freeman (eds), *Handbook of Research on Employee Voice.* Cheltenham: Edward Elgar, pp. 477–488.

Burke, R. J. (2000). Workaholism in organizations: Concepts, results and future research directions. *International Journal of Management Reviews, 2*(1), 1–16.

Byrne, Z. (2022). *Understanding employee engagement: Theory, research, and practice* (2nd ed.). Routledge.

Cappelli, P. (1999). *The new deal at work: Managing the market-driven workforce.* Harvard Business School Press.

Cerdin, J.-L., & Le Pangneux, M. (2012). Career anchors: A comparison between organization-assigned and self-initiated expatriates. *Thunderbird International Business Review, 52*(4), 287–299.

CIPD. (2001). *Married to the Job, CIPD survey.* CIPD.

CIPD. (2003). *Managing the psychological contract, factsheet.* CIPD.

CIPD. (2004). *Living to work, CIPD survey.* CIPD.

CIPD. (2022). *Trends in flexible working arrangements.* Chartered Institute of Personnel and Development. https://www.cipd.org/uk/knowledge/reports/flexible-working-trends/

Cohen, A. (2014). Organizational commitment theory. In E. H. Kessler (Ed.), *Encyclopedia of management theory* (Vol. 2, pp. 516–529). Sage.

Collings, D. G., & Mellahi, K. (2009). Strategic talent management: A review and research agenda. *Human Resource Management Review, 19*, 304–313.

Collings, D. G., Mellahi, K., & Cascio, W. F. (2019). Global talent management and performance in multinational enterprises: A multilevel perspective. *Journal of Management, 45*(2), 540–566.

Collings, D. G., Scullion, H., & Vaiman, H. (2015). Talent management: Progress and prospects. *Human Resource Management Review, 25*(3), 233–235.

Collins, A, M., Cartwright, S., & Hislop, D. (2013) Homeworking: Negotiating the psychological contract. *Human Resource Management Journal, 23*(2), 211–225.

Conway, N. (2015). The psychological contract. In C. Cooper (Ed.), *Wiley encyclopedia of management* (3rd ed.) . John Wiley

Conway, N., & Briner, R. B. (2002). A diary study of affective response to psychological contract breach and exceeded promises. *Journal of Organizational Behaviour, 23*, 287–302.

Conway, N., & Briner, R. B. (2005). *Understanding psychological contracts at work: A critical evaluation of theory and research.* Oxford University Press.

Conway, N., & Coyle-Shapiro, J. (2016). No so I-Deal: A critical review of idiosyncratic-deals theory and research. In M. Bal & D. M. Rousseau (Eds.), *Idiosyncratic deals between employees and organizations: Conceptual issues, applications, and the role of coworkers* (pp. 36–64). Routledge.

Conway, N., & Pecan, C. (2019). Psychological contract research: Older, but is it wiser? In Y. Griep & C. Cooper (Eds.), *Handbook of research on the psychological contract at work.* Edward Elgar

Conway, N., Guest, D. and Trenberth, L. (2011). Testing the differential effects of changes in psychological contractbreach and fulfillment. *Journal of Vocational Behavior, 79* (1), 267–276.

Davis, A. S., & Van der Heijden, B. I. J. M. (2018). Reciprocity matters: Idiosyncratic deals to shape the psychological contract and foster employee engagement in times of austerity. *Human Resource Development Quarterly, 29*(4), 329–355.

Dobrow, S., Weisman, H., & Tosti-Kharas, J. (2023). Calling and the good life: A meta-analysis and theoretical extension. *Administrative Science Quarterly, 68*(2), 508–550.

The Economist. (2004, April 19). Working hours.

The Economist. (2004, November 6). Darwin meets job creationism.

Edwards, M. R. (2013). Employer branding: Developments and challenges. In S. Bach & M. R. Edwards (Eds.), *Managing human resources* (5th ed., pp. 389–410). Wiley.

Edwards, M. R., & Peccei, R. (2010). Perceived organizational support, organizational identification, and employee outcomes. *Journal of Personnel Psychology, 9*, 17–26.

Faragher, E. B., Cass, M., & Cooper, C. L. (2005). The relationship between job satisfaction and health: A meta-analysis. *Occupational and Environmental Medicine, 62*, 105–112.

Farndale, E., Beijer, S., Van Veldhoven, M., Kelliher, C., & Hope-Hailey, V. (2014). Work and organization engagement: Aligning research and practice. *Journal of Organizational Effectiveness: People and Performance, 1*(2), 157–176.

Feldman, D. C. (2007). Career mobility and career stability among older workers, In K. S. Schultz & G. A. Adams (Eds.), *Aging and work in the 21st century* (pp. 179–197). Lawrence Erlbaum Associates.

Finegold, D., & Mohrman, S. (2001). *What do employees really want? The perception vs. the reality.* Report presented at the World Economic Forum 2001 Annual Meeting. Korn/Ferry International.

Francis-Devine. (2023, November 23). *The gender pay gap.* House of Commons Library.

Gittell, J. H., Seidner, R., & Wimbush, J. (2010). A relational model of how high-performance work systems work. *Organization Science, 21*(2), 490–506.

Gittell, J. H., Weinberg, D., Bennett, A., & Miller, J. A. (2008). Is the doctor in? A relational approach to job design and the coordination of work. *Human Resource Management, 47*(4), 729–755.

Greip, Y., & Cooper, C. (Eds.). (2019). *Handbook of research on the psychological contract at work*. Edward Elgar

Griffiths, M. (2015). Workaholism – a 21st century addiction. *The Psychologist.* https://thepsychologist.bps.org.uk/volume-24/edition-10/workaholism---21st-century-addiction

Groysberg, B. (2010) .*Chasing stars: The myth of talent and the portability of performance.* Harvard Business School Press.

Guest, D. (2017). Human resource management and well-being: Towards a new analytical framework. *Human Resource Management Journal, 27*(1), 22–38.

Guest, D., & Conway, N. (2002). Communicating the psychological contract: An employer perspective. *Human Resource Management Journal, 12*(2), 22–38.

Handfield-Jones, H., Michaels, E., & Axelrod, B. (2001, November/December). Talent management: A critical part of every leader's job. *Ivey Business Journal.* Retrieved May 14, 2005, from http://www.iveybusinessjournal. ca/view_article.asp?intArticle_ID=316

Haar, J.M., Russo, M., Sune, A., & Ollier-Malaterre, A. (2014). Outcomes of work-life balance on job satisfaction, life satisfaction and mental health: A study across seven cultures. *Journal of Vocational Behavior, 85*(3), 361–373.

Harris Poll (2015) Americans report declining trust in banks. Available online at www .theharrispoll.com/business/Americans_Report_Declining_Trust_in_Banks.html.

He, H. and Brown, A. D. (2013) Organizational identity and organizational identification:a review of the literature and suggestions for future research. *Group and Organization Management, 38* (1), 3–35.

Herriot, P. (2001). *The Employment Relationship: A psychological perspective.* Routledge.

Herriot, P., Manning, W. E. G., & Kidd, J. M. (1997). The content of the psychological contract. *British Journal of Management, 8*(2), 151–162.

High Pay Centre. (2015). *WPP CEO paid an astonishing £43 million in 2014.* Retrieved June 1, 2015, from http://highpaycentre.org/blog/wpp-ceo-paid-an-astonishing-43 -million-in-2014.

High Pay Centre. (2023, 18th December). Pay inequalities remain constant despite cost of living crisis.https://highpaycentre.org/high-pay-centre-analysis-of-ftse-350 -pay-ratios-2/.

Huselid, M. A., & Becker, B. E. (2011). Bridging micro and macro domains: Workforce differentiation and strategic human resource management. *Journal of Management, 37*(2), 421–428.

Huselid, M. A., Becker, B. E., & Beatty, R. W. (2005). *The workforce scorecard! Managing human capital to execute strategy.* Harvard Business School Press.

ILO. (2022). *Working time and work-life balance across the world.* International Labour Office. https://www.ilo.org/wcmsp5/groups/public/---ed_protect/---protrav/---travail/documents/publication/wcms_864222.pdf

Irshad, M., & Bashir, S. (2020). The dark side of organizational identification: A multi-study investigation of negative outcomes. *Frontiers of Psychology.* doi:10.3389/fpsyg.2020.572478. PMID: 33132980; PMCID: PMC7550469.

Legge, K (2005). *Human resource management: Rhetorics and realities* (Anniversary ed.). Palgrave Macmillan.

Lepak, D. P. and Snell, S. A. (2002) Examining the human resource architecture: the relationships among humancapital, employment and human resource configurations. *Journal of Management, 28* (4), 517–543.

Martin, G., Staines, H., & Pate, J. (1998). The new psychological contract: Exploring the relationship between job security and career development. *Human Resource Management Journal, 6*(3), 20–40.

McDermott, A.M., Conway,E., Rousseau, D. M., & Flood, P.C. (2013). Promoting effective psychological contracts through leadership: the missing link between HR strategy and performance. *Human Resource Management.52*(2), 289–310.

McDonnell, A., Collings, D. G., Mellahi, K., & Schuler, R. (2017). Talent management: Systematic review and future prospects. *European Journal of International Management, 11*(1).

Martin, G., & Cerdin, J. L. (2014). Employer branding and career theory: New directions for research. In P Sparrow, H. Scullion, & I. Tarique (Eds.), *Strategic talent management: Contemporary issues in international context* (pp. 151–176). Cambridge University Press.

Martin, G., Pate, J. M., Beaumont, P. B., & Murdoch, A. (2003). The uncertain road to partnership: An action research perspective on new industrial relations in the UK offshore oil industry. *Employee Relations, 25*(6), 594–612.

Martin, G., Gollan, P. J. and Grigg, K. (2011). Is there a bigger and better future for employer branding? Facing up to innovation, corporate reputations and wicked problems in SHRM. *International Journal of Human Resource Management, 22,* 3618–3637.

Martin, G., Schreven, S., Arshed, N., & Martin, A. (2023, July 6–8). *How healthcare staff make sense of their orientations to work(place) – past, present, and future.* Paper presented to the EGOS annual colloquim, University of Cagliari, Italy.

Martin, G., Siebert, S., Howieson, W. B., & Bushfield, S. (2021). Changing logics in healthcare and their effects on the identity motives and identity work of doctors. *Organization Studies, 42*(9), 1477–1499.

Martin, G., & Sinclair, K. (2018). Employer branding and corporate reputation management in global companies: theory and practice. In D. G. Collings, H. Scullion, & P. Caliguiri (Eds.), *Global talent management* (2nd ed.). Routledge

Martin, G., Staines, H. J., & Bushfield, S. (2023). *Senior hospital doctors' intentions to retire in NHS Scotland.* University of Dundee. https://discovery.dundee.ac.uk/en/ publications/senior-hospital-doctors-intentions-to-retire-in-nhs-scotlanmarti

Meyer, J. P., & Allen, N. J. (1991). *Commitment in the workplace.* Sage.

Michaels, E., Handfield-Jones, H., & Axelrod, B. (2001). *The war for talent.* Harvard Business School Press.

Painter-Moreland, M., Kirk, S., Deslandes, G., & Tansley, C. (2019). Talent management: The good, the bad, and the possible. *European Management Review, 16*(1), 135–146.

Peccei, R. (2013). Employee engagement: An evidence-based review. In S. Bach & M. R. Edwards (Eds.), *Managing human resources* (5th ed., pp. 336–364). Wiley.

Pfeffer, J. (2001). Fighting the war for talent is dangerous to your organization's health. *Organizational Dynamics, 29*(4), 248–259.

Pierce, J. L., Kostova, T., & Dirks, K. T. (2001). Towards a theory of psychological ownership in organizations. *Academy of Management Review, 26*(2), 298–310.

Pierce, J. R., & Aguinas, H. (2013). The "too-much-of-a-good-thing" effect in management. *Journal of Management, 39*, 313–338

Rousseau, D. M. (1995). *Psychological contracts in organizations: Understanding written and unwritten agreements.* Sage.

Rousseau, D. M. (2005). *What is an idiosyncratic deal?* Routledge.

Schaufeli, W. B., Taris, T. W., & Van Rhenen, W. (2008). Workaholism, burnout and engagement: Three of a kind or three different kinds of employee well-being. *Applied Psychology International Review, 57*, 173–203.

Schaufeli, W. B. (2015). Engaging leadership in the job demands-resources model. *Career Development International, 20*, 446–463.

Schein, E. (1990). *Career anchors.* University Associates

Schein, E. H, (1990). *Career anchors (discovering your real values).* Jossey-Bass Pfeiffer, San Francisco.

Schein, A.H. & Van Maanen, J. (2013) Career anchors: the changing nature of work and careers - particiapnat workbook. SanFrancisco, CA: Wiley

Scott, K. S., Moore, K. S., & Miceli, M. P. (1997). An exploration of the meaning and consequences of workaholism. *Human Relations, 50*, 287–314.

Searle, R. H., Nienaber, A.-M. I., & Sitkin, S. B. (Eds.). (2018). *The Routledge companion to trust.* Routledge.

Shimazu, A., & Schaufeli, W. B. (2009). Is workaholism good or bad for employee well-being? The distinctiveness of workaholism and work engagement among Japanese employees. *Industrial Health, 47*, 495–502.

Siebert, S., & Martin, G. (2014). People management rationales and organizational effectiveness: The case of organizational trust repair. *Journal of Organizational Effectiveness: People and Performance, 1*(2), 177–190.

Siebert, S., Bushfield,S., Martin, G., & Howieson, B. (2018). Eroding 'respectability': deprofessionalization through organizational spaces. *Work, Employment and Society, 32*(2), 330–347.

Siebert, S., Martin, G, Bozic, B., & Docherty, I. (2015). Looking 'beyond the factory gates': Towards more pluralist and radical approaches to intra-organizational trust research. *Organization Studies.*

Sparks, K., Cooper, C. L., Fried, Y., & Shirom, A. (1997). The effects of hours of work on health: A meta-analytical review. *Journal of Occupational Psychology, 70*, 391–408.

Sparrow, P. (2000). International reward management. In G. White & J. Druker (Eds.), *Reward management: A critical text* (pp. 196–214). Routledge.

Sparrow, P. (2014). Strategic HRM and employee engagement. In C. Truss, R. Delbridge, K. Alfes, A. Shanz, & E. Soane (Eds.), *Employee engagement in theory and practice* (pp. 99–115). Routledge.

Sparrow, P., & Cooper, C. (2003). *The employment relationship: Key challenges for HR.* Butterworth-Heinemann.

Suazo, M.M. (2009). The mediating role of psychological contract violation on the relations between psychological contract breach and work-related attitudes and behaviors. *Journal of Managerial Psychology, 24*(2), 136–160.

Swailes, S. (2002). Organizational commitment: A critique of the construct and its measures. *International Journal of Management Research, 4*(2), 155–178.

Taylor, R. (2004). *Skills and Innovation in Modern Britain*. ESRC Future of Work Programme Seminar Series.

Theurer, C. P., Tumasjan, A., Welpe, I. M., & Lievens, F. (2016). Employer branding: a brand equity-based literature review and research agenda. *International Journal of Management Reviews, 20*(1), 155–179.

Thomas, D. C., Fitzsimmons, S. R., Ravlin, E. C., Au, K. Y., Ekelund, B. Z., & Barzantny, C. (2010). Psychological contracts across cultures. *Organization Studies, 31*(11), 1437–1458.

Thompson, J. A., & Bunderson, J. S. (2003). Violations of principle: Ideological currency in the psychological contract. *Academy of Management Review, 28*(4), 571–586.

Thunnissen, M., Boselie, P., & Fruytier, B. (2013). A review of talent management: 'Infancy or adolescence?' *The International Journal of Human Resource Management, 24*(9), 1744–1761.

Truss, C. Shantz, A., Soane, E., Alfres, K., & Delbridge, R. (2013). Employee engagement, organizational performance and individual well-being: Exploring the evidence, developing the theory. *International Journal of Human Resource Management, 24*(14), 2657–2669.

Turnley, W. H., & Feldman, D. C. (1998). Psychological contract violations during corporate restructuring. *Human Resource Management, 37*(1), 71–83.

Van Dyne, L., & Pierce, J. L. (2004). Psychological ownership and feelings of possession: Three field studies predicting employee attitudes and organizational citizenship behavior. *Journal of Organizational Behavior, 25*, 439–459.

Walsh, G. and Bartikowski, B. (2013). Employee emotional labour and quitting intentions: moderating effects of genderand age. *European Journal of Marketing, 47*(8), 1213–1237.

Weisman, H., Wu, C.-H., Yoshikawa, K., & Lee, H.-J. (2023). Antecedents of organizational identification: A review and agenda for future research. *Journal of Management, 49*(6), 2030–2061.

Wilkinson, A. and Fay, C. (2011). New times for employer voice? *Human Resource Management, 50*(1), 65–74.

Wils, T., Wils, L., & Tremblay, M. (2014). Revisiting the career anchor model: A proposition and an empirical investigation of a new model of career value structure. *Industrial Relations, 69*(4), 813–838.

Wong, K., Chan, A. H. S., & Ngan, S. C. (2019). The effect of long working hours and overtime on occupational health: A meta-analysis of evidence from 1998 to 2018. *International Journal of Environmental Research into Public Health, 16*(12), 2102. doi:10.3390/ijerph16122102

Wolf, A. (2002). *Does education matter? Myths about education and economic growth*. Penguin.

Working at Volkswagen. (2015). Benefits and work life balance. https://www.volkswagen
-karriere.de/en/working-at-volkswagen/benefits-and-work-life-balance.html

Zhang, F., & Parker, S. K. (2018). Reorienting job crafting research: A hierarchical
structure of job crafting concepts and integrative review. *Journal of Organizational
Behavior, 40*(2), 126–146.

Zhang, Y., Liu, G., & Cheung, M. W.-L. (2021). Psychological ownership: A meta-
analysis and comparison of multiple forms of attachment in the workplace. *Journal
of Management, 47*(3), 745–770.

Managing in the organizational context

INTRODUCTION

According to John Child (2015), one of the best-known management researchers, the most fundamental task of senior managers is to set the strategy of the organization and design the organizational structures, systems, culture, and processes to deliver the strategy. While even the best firms in the world cannot make up for an unsound strategy, 'superior organization offers one of the best sustainable sources of competitive advantage' (Child, 2015, p 4). Designing organizations and managing in the organizational context refers to the tasks of understanding, analysing, and designing structures, systems, and processes to coordinate and motivate large numbers of people undertaking

DOI: 10.4324/9781003469711-4

interconnected activities, often in different locations (Roberts, 2004). At this level, managers must be capable of taking a macro and meso-level perspective, not only one that affects individuals and teams (Hatch, 2018; Rouleau, 2022). These decisions can have significant consequences for the strategic aims of the organization because it is through organizational structure that strategy becomes realised. Consequently, it is extremely important that you understand some of the basic design principles of organization and the potential advantages and drawbacks of adopting different organizational forms, including some of the newly emerging ones that have captured the imagination of the business press. So, in this chapter, we shall attempt to address the practical problems of organizational design, first by examining a case study and, second, by introducing you to some concepts and models that will help you understand the problems faced by senior managers in designing organizations and the solutions available to them.

You should read the case study of Innovative Petroleum Engineering, a pseudonym for an oil services company we shall use throughout this chapter to help you understand and apply key concepts. Your ability to understand some of the choices that managers face in designing organizations, analysing the problems faced by the case company, and your choice of design solutions should improve as you work your way through the chapter. We shall also look at cases of newer forms of organization that are becoming more popular in certain contexts and industries, especially those connected with knowledge-intensive, technologically based and creative organizations, which are discussed in Chapters 7, 8, and 9 of this book.

CASE 4.1 INNOVATIVE PETROLEUM ENGINEERING: AN INTEGRATIVE CASE STUDY

Innovative Petroleum Engineering is the pseudonym of a major subsidiary of a US multinational operating in Europe. It produces sophisticated drilling equipment, which is used by other major firms in the oil and gas industry. Its parent company is a well-known Fortune 500 company, with interests in many countries, and which is highly regarded in published lists of the 'Best Places to Work' in many of these countries. It has diversified into several related fields in recent years.

Innovative is an important part of the parent company's core business, but over the last five years, its performance has been patchy, owing largely to the downturn in the market for certain of its core products. The company built its reputation on technological breakthroughs in bits, tools, and other drilling products, based on extensive research and development. Each decade since the 1950s had seen success, with employees benefiting from the financial success. The company adopted an 'employer of choice' policy, in which highly talented people were recruited at all levels in the company and were paid well. These employees were treated well by Innovative, enjoying major benefits and privileges, internal career advancement, and time off to undertake education and training. It became known as one of the best places to work in the region, with a strong internally focused promotion and benefits system, which was associated with high levels of employee commitment and identification with the organization.

With the downturn in the oil and gas market because of the drive towards renewable energy, Innovative was forced to rationalise its activities and introduce a small number of compulsory layoffs for the first time in its 55-year history. Headcount management from the US parent company, which was also experiencing problems, made the situation worse a year or so later when more layoffs were implemented. However, the senior management at Innovative was confident matters would improve once the business cycle began to move into an investment phase for their principal customers, and employees were encouraged to 'weather the storm.' The company continued to pursue its 'employer of choice' policy, keeping benefits and career development at relatively high levels in anticipation of better times.

As the decade wore on, however, things didn't really improve. The technical developments by Innovative didn't really seem to be attractive to existing and new customers, and the company became ever more open to threats from new competitors. The mixture of less innovative developments and new competition resulted in losses being posted for the years 2010–2015 of more than 15 million euros per year, against a gross yearly revenue of between 450 million and 500 million euros. The true position, however, is unknown because of internal transfers between companies in the group of which Innovative was a part. Innovative was forced to use many of the services of sister companies and paid a premium price for some of these services, including some of the research and development on which technical breakthroughs were achieved. Innovative's management believed that real losses were probably much less than the 15 million euros per year, with the figure being 2 million euros according to senior managers.

The US parent company urged Innovative to maintain greater control of variable costs, mainly labour costs, and set targets for increased sales revenues. However, the US parent also insisted on using centralised research and development services and keeping local research to a minimum. This was troublesome for several reasons for Innovative's managers, most importantly because US products were not always suited to the mainly European markets served by Innovative. Consequently, they had always followed a local policy of encouraging new business ventures that showed promise to work around the parent company's strictures. However, cash constraints now prevented them from following this local product development strategy, and Innovative found itself having to make do with the core products that seemed to be unsuited to the local markets or required modification.

Innovative Petroleum's management team was mainly highly technically competent engineers. They regarded themselves as working for a leading-edge engineering company operating in the expanding upstream oil and gas industry, with first-class products, and despite current problems, always saw light at the end of the tunnel. The corporation was organized as a traditional bureaucracy, set within a global matrix structure. This meant that subsidiary companies such as Innovative were given responsibility for a specific geographical area but were expected to replicate the functional structure of the US parent company. Thus, people at the top levels of the organization and the functional heads dominated, with power concentrated in the hands of a powerful CEO at Innovative, who integrated the fragmented functions.

The CEO's power and control were exceptionally great, and he exercised his leadership through a careful reporting system of performance, costs, and other policies. He was also the single most important interface between the company and the US parent company and was also HQ's ambassador to Innovative. He had been in post for 15 years and followed the US parent company's policies to the letter without making local amendments. Though delivering excellent returns for the first ten years of his reign, like Innovative, his performance had suffered recently. His successor was John Fox, a 52-year-old British engineer, who had substantial experience in the US parent company in marketing. He had seen the problems of the ageing product range at Innovative and was committed to a turnaround but didn't really want to do anything that rocked the boat. He also believed the company had to be research and technology-driven, like his senior management in the parent organization. Fox suffered the problems faced by all senior managers in subsidiary companies caused by the tensions between demands for corporate control and local autonomy. However, in the final analysis, his decisions reflected the need to satisfy his career and senior management team in the USA.

Soon after his arrival, Fox had begun to make changes to the bureaucratic structure of Innovative by trying to foster closer collaboration between marketing, research and development, and the traditionally powerful production, sales, and engineering functions. He set up management teams incorporating these functional heads and new appointees to HR and Finance and gave them the mandate to work towards a more collaborative organization by 2020. Only the HR manager was female. This development was enabled by management 'away-days', based on a new vision and values framework, plans, and objective-setting. The head of HR experienced some problems with the male-dominated, 'rugby club' atmosphere, but gradually became used to the culture and worked her way into a powerful position, along with the new 45-year-old head of finance and accounting.

There were still lots of problems, however, partly associated with Fox's inability to 'walk the talk' through his actions. Although espousing teamwork values, he wasn't seen to be a good team player himself. When times were difficult, which were more and more frequent, he resorted to authoritarian behaviours and a 'bottom-line' performance mentality – 'it's the shareholders and parent company that pay your salary.' In addition, given the resource constraints of the US parent, there were problems associated with the allocation of resources among departments. Competition among departments led some members of the management team to pursue their own departmental interests and those of staff in their departments at the expense of overall company cohesion and team spirit. Thus, certain departments began to be run as personal 'fiefdoms' rather than contribute to the overall mission and goals of Innovative.

After functioning like this for some time, the management team made a decision to embark on a continuous improvement (CI) programme, which they labelled 'Project 2020,' signifying the desire to have this change programme last beyond the normal one to two years of many other initiatives introduced by the company. Continuous improvement through Project 2020 gave rise to several project teams that looked at issues such as quality improvement, Six Sigma, production improvement schemes, suggestion schemes, organizational development, and HR initiatives. The middle-level managers who staffed these teams were all sent on courses to develop their understanding of teamworking and help them develop new teamworking skills. Being selected for one of these project teams was seen as having 'arrived' because the management team selected only the fast-track, high-quality managers who were seen to be going places. Almost without exception, these people were highly committed to the company, technically very well qualified, and ready to go 'beyond contract' for the sake of the company and their careers.

The first year of this CI programme produced some excellent outcomes, with project team members being seen as highly engaged and highly productive in their tasks. However, not many of the team recommendations were taken up, except in a watered-down fashion. The management team was always full of praise, but usually found reasons not to implement recommendations, usually because of budgetary reasons, the time not being right, or that they didn't quite fit the strategic plans. This lack of implementation began to generate a great deal of cynicism and distrust, not only among the middle managers on the project groups but also among the members of the management team, who felt that the project teams weren't pursuing the interests of the company; nor were they coming up with the kinds of improvement that the management team would have suggested. Instead, they felt that nearly all improvements were 'bids for resources' rather than genuine, cost-effective improvements.

Project team members began to complain to each other that they didn't have the necessary information or policy guidelines to do their jobs effectively. The management team was rarely seen to issue 'straitjackets' (dictums that had to be followed) but let it be known through innuendo and hints what was and wasn't acceptable. Consequently, project teams often had to go through several iterations of improvement plans to learn what might really be acceptable. Most of the time, what they found out was rarely radical but only marginal improvements on the status quo. Complaints made along these lines to the management team caused the senior members of management to take a much more controlling approach to the workings of the project teams, often by dropping in on team meetings and overriding their discussions.

Gradually, the project teams began to become more sceptical of the management team's objectives, which, they determined, weren't really about improvements but about socialising them into the ways of Innovative Petroleum – what was acceptable and what wasn't. Naturally enough, those groups of middle managers who wished to get on began to play the game, which was concerned more with style than with substance, and 'second-guessing' what might be acceptable to their sponsoring managers in the management team. Over the next year or so, however, the project team members put in less effort and less commitment to the CI programme. As this project work wasn't rewarded in any specific way, and was over and above their departmental responsibilities, most project team members put their efforts into attaining good appraisals for their regular jobs.

After a further year of operation and wavering commitments by the management team and the project team members, it became clear that the CI programme wasn't going to deliver much in the way of transformational change, and even when the management team espoused the rhetoric of creativity and innovation, teams rarely believed that was what was required. Often, they ended up repackaging and producing 'old wine in new bottles' because, although innovation was called for, it was rarely implemented and never really rewarded tangibly or intangibly. This rather depressing vicious circle of cynicism was made worse by the management team's informal feedback sessions to the CI project teams, which, though designed as 'full and frank' discussions, often turned out to be blame sessions and calls for the teams to develop more teamworking skills and controls – this despite the company having a 'no-blame' culture as one of its aspirational values.

Following a further year of operation, the CI programme was still officially in existence but was essentially moribund. Few ideas that had been produced had been implemented, and although there were a few examples of success in quality controls, the senior management team had spent a lot of money on training and culture change for very little reward. If anything, they had produced a cynical and demoralised middle management group who played the game but weren't really committed. The management team settled down into a comfortable way of working with each other, in which formal relations were good but there was little in the way of team camaraderie. Fox's beneath-the-surface authoritarian streak and the latent rivalries within the management team continued to plague developments in Innovative and gradually their expectations of Project 2020 became much more modest.

At the time of writing, the company has shown little in the way of significant improvements, and most work is carried on through the formal, hierarchical structure of reporting relationships. The company management team continues to talk about innovation, entrepreneurship, and 'breakthroughs' from HQ, which will guarantee its future but know that the rhetoric bears little relationship to the reality of how they are doing.

Based on your current understanding of organizational design principles, and before you read the following text, answer the following questions:

1. How would you describe the organization of Innovative Petroleum Engineering?

2. What are the causes of the problems?

3. What changes would you make to the organizational structure to improve things?

ORGANIZATIONAL STRUCTURES

To help you provide an in-depth and more informed analysis of the problems faced by organizations such as Innovative Petroleum Engineering, we should begin by looking at some basic ideas from the organizational design literature (Clegg et al., 2021; Rouleau, 2022). A constant theme of the modernist (or traditional) theories of organization (Hatch, 2018) is that there is no one best way of managing and organizing; ultimately, firm performance and problems that arise in organizations such as Innovative depend on the degree of *fit* between the organizational design solutions, the strategies being pursued, and the context or environment in which they arise. This is a contingency theory of organizations that implies that there are no right answers, only those that fit the context (Child, 2015). Contingency theories arose as a challenge to the 'one best way or organizing' school associated with classical organizational theories such as bureaucracy and scientific management that we met in Chapter 1. So, to help us understand the case more fully, we should begin by defining different types of organizational structure, the problems to which they give rise, and the contexts that seem to influence their effectiveness.

Determinants of organizational structures

One very useful starting point in modernist approaches to organizational theory is to consider the well-known 'star model' of Amy Kates and the late Jay Galbraith (2010) as an approach to discovering universal principles of organizational design. They outlined the following six influences or 'shapers' of organizational forms relevant to the contemporary business environment:

- *Buyer power.* The new rules of competition, aided by access to information and communications technologies (ICT) and global sourcing, have shifted power to consumers and buyers, who are learning how to use that power effectively. Consequently, we are seeing a shift in organizations to reflect the desires of key customers and market segments.
- *Variety and solutions.* In response to customer demand and the segmentation of markets, organizations have developed increased numbers of products and services and have shown a willingness to customise their offerings. To do this, however, managers must be able to deal with ever more information, make more decisions, and set priorities – this means that more people should be involved in the decision-making process. Increasingly, business customers are seeking integrated solutions to their problems, not merely bundles of products and services. To provide such solutions, organizations must develop cross-product and cross-functional teams.
- *Information and communications technologies.* As we shall see in Chapter 8, the internet has been an incredibly powerful influence on organizations, especially in creating web-based portals and new business models such as those used by Amazon, Dell, and eBay, and new technology intermediators such as the 'e-lancing' firm, Uber (Aguinas & Lawal, 2013; Sostak & Kurz, 2020). The new economics of

information have altered the old-style trade-off between 'reach and richness' of information, allowing firms to do more of both simultaneously, which has had the result of deconstructing traditional industries (Christensen & Horn, 2008). Also, increasingly customers and staff require a single point of contact for their problems, so the functions of the organization, such as sales, delivery, call centre operations, and HR, must be coordinated.

- *Complexity.* Like many other writers in this modernist tradition, Kates and Galbraith (2010) identified environmental complexity, or what they label as 'multiple dimensions,' as a key factor in shaping organizations. Originally, companies were structured along functional lines, but as the environment became more complex, so organizations began to develop divisional (multi-product or multi-region) structures to reflect customer segments. Throughout the last century and the early part of the present one, the environments of organizations have become more complex in terms of the products, markets, and geographical regions they are serving; organizational structures have had to reflect this complexity.
- *Change.* One of the nostrums in the business of the last few decades has been 'the only constant is change', also a recurring theme of this book. As Hatch (2018) proposed, organizations are better examined from a process perspective, from which organizations are usually seen as in a state of 'becoming' rather than as static 'beings'. This process or symbolic philosophy has important implications for how we study organizations and organizing, which do not sit comfortably with some of the design principles we have outlined in this chapter but are very important in understanding organizational change and development. So, for example, we need to consider how the pace and direction of change in organizational environments have had a marked influence on how organizational structures and cultures have changed over time, particularly regarding information flows and decision-making structures. Changing environments and technologies have been at the heart of developments towards decentralised structures and cross-functional/departmental teamworking designs (Davis, 2022; Sostak & Kurz, 2020).
- *Speed.* The pace of change in customer demands and tastes has caused organizations to design along more flexible lines to meet these challenges. Demands for reduced operations and production cycle times and shorter lead times to market – for example, in the motor vehicle industry – have led to organizations changing their structures to cope with less inventory and increased response times. Thus, speed is associated with developments in outsourcing and decentralised structures, as well as increased take-up of ICT.

Kates and Galbraith (2010) argued that organizational designs able to meet the demands of these organizational 'shapers' were a source of real competitive advantage that could not be easily copied because they were a delicate and complex mix of different design features. They saw the choice of organization as a design issue in much the same way that buildings and machinery are designed to meet competing and often contradictory claims in which trade-offs must be made. For example, balances must be struck between time to market, with the focus on reduced design and production cycle time, and production organizations that achieve cost advantages through scale economies.

Consequently, effective organizational design is a constantly evolving balancing act between these environmental pressures and the policies that senior managers can use to influence appropriate design solutions. These policies are summarised in their 'star model' set out in Figure 4.1.

Corporate *strategy* refers to the mission, goals, and objectives of the organization, and sets out its basic direction. Business-level strategies refer to the products, services, and markets the organization seeks to serve. Different organizational designs are appropriate for centralised decision-making, whereas innovative strategies are likely to be better served by decentralised decision-making. Following a debate between outside-in and inside-out approaches to strategy in the 1990s (Child, 2015) and the growing importance attached by scholars to dynamic capabilities, Kates and Galbraith (2010) added strategic capabilities to the original model to refer to the internal, dynamic capabilities that firms use to differentiate themselves from their competitors. Dynamic capabilities refer to an organization's capacity to seek and create new opportunities by learning quickly and to reconfigure internal assets such as knowledge, technologies, people, and processes to ensure sustainable strategic advantage in rapidly changing environments (Teece, 2018).

Structure is concerned with the distribution of power and authority in organizations (Child, 2015, Clegg et al., 2021). The following are its main dimensions:

- *Hierarchy* – the hierarchical ordering of positions that gives rise to the chain of command.
- *Specialisation* – the number of jobs and job specialists found in an organization.
- *Span of control* – the number of people reporting to any specialist manager.

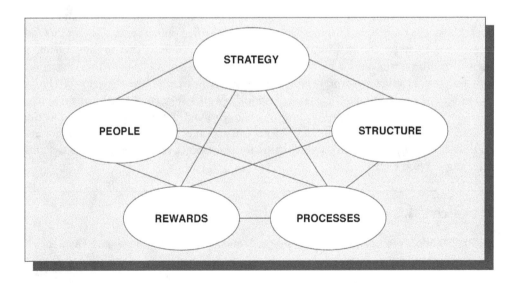

FIGURE 4.1 The star model

(*Source:* adapted from earlier work by Galbraith, 2002, p. 10)

- *Distribution of power* – this can be both *vertical*, referring to the levels of hierarchy in an organization, and *horizontal*, which refers to how close a particular department or manager is to the core, mission-critical decisions.
- *Departmentalisation* – the basis on which departments are developed, which can be functional, product-based, workflow-based, market-based, or geographically based.

Much of organizational life is influenced by the power in and around organizations, with organizational politics, conflicts, and contests for control being constant features of work in organizations (Hatch, 2018). Understanding the interests and perspectives of others is a fundamental skill of successful managers, alongside the ability to manage these different interests so that all parties gain – a so-called positive sum game.

Processes refer to the information and decision-making processes that are the lifeblood of any organization. Again, these can be vertical, reflecting hierarchical power, or lateral, with teamworking being a good example. *People* policies are one of the main subjects of this book, one that we have and will elaborate on in greater detail in later chapters. It is perhaps sufficient to point out at this stage that different structures require people with often contradictory abilities to make them work, with team-based organizations being a good example. Such organizations rest on the ability of people to *cooperate* rather than compete with one another, but at the same time, people in teams must show individual *initiative* (Fjeldstad et al., 2012). Selection and development policies for team selection should reflect these potentially opposing characteristics. Finally, the purpose of a *rewards* system is to align the needs and motives of employees with the goals and structure of the organization. To reuse the teamworking example, reward systems, which can be both monetary and non-monetary, need to be designed to facilitate interpersonal cooperation as well as be motivating to individuals.

Apart from warning us that the process of organizational design is a constant balancing act between the nature of the environment and the five policy areas of the framework in Figure 4.1, one of the main implications of the star model is that too much time is spent designing structures on paper and not enough time is given to thinking about how they might align with processes, people, and rewards. Given the pace of change facing many organizations, Kates and Galbraith (2010) suggested that processes, people, and rewards were more important in organizational design than formal reporting structures because they have the most direct impact on organizational performance and culture. However, they also recognised that the five points of the star must be dynamically aligned (see Figure 4.2).

Exercise 4.1

1. What are the key shapers of the organizational structure of Innovative Petroleum Engineering?

2. How does the star model in Figure 4.1 help us understand the problems of Innovative Petroleum Engineering?

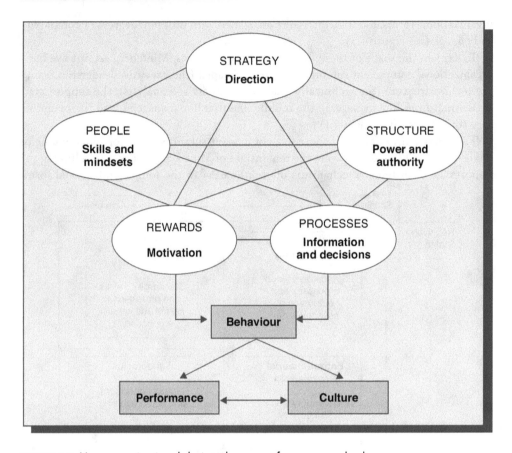

FIGURE 4.2 How organizational design shapes performance and culture

(*Source:*   adapted from Galbraith, 2002, p. 15)

MINTZBERG'S DIFFERENT TYPES OF ORGANIZATIONAL STRUCTURE

There have been several very useful attempts to classify structures according to how they relate to the environment in which they operate. Two such attempts have attained 'classic' status precisely because they are so useful in helping us understand the kinds of problems set out in our introductory case. The first is by Henry Mintzberg (1993), whose work on different forms of organization is one of the most often cited and is reflected in his thinking about management which we discussed in Chapter 2. The second is by Raymond Miles and Charles Snow (1984), whose constantly revised work has stood the test of time to provide excellent insights into the problems faced by modern organizations (Child, 2015).

Like Galbraith, Henry Mintzberg saw an organization's structure as shaped largely by the degree of environmental variety it faces. For Mintzberg, environmental variety was determined by *environmental complexity* and the *pace of change*. He identified five organizational forms, four of which were associated with different degrees of complexity and change (see Figure 4.3).

To explain the shape of these four organizational forms, Mintzberg set out five basic organizational component subunits: the strategic apex (the executive leadership team), the technostructure (the technically qualified planners and analysts), the support staff (as distinct from line managers), the middle line (the line managers), and the operating core (the 'doers') (see Table 4.1).

The relative importance of these five component subunits in any organization helps define its overall shape. However, the real insight of Mintzberg's work was in linking the importance of different mechanisms of coordination to the four organizational forms

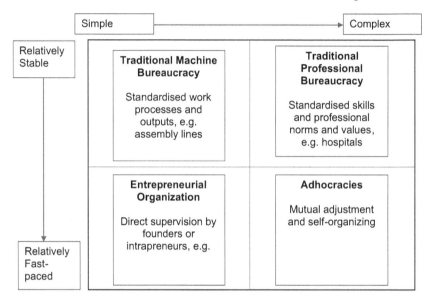

FIGURE 4.3 Four organizational forms related to environmental variety

TABLE 4.1 Basic component units of an organization	
Component subunit	**Possible positions from a firm such as Innovative Petroleum**
Strategic apex	Board of directors, chief executive officer
The technostructure	Corporate planning, HR, research and development, engineering managers
Support staff	Legal department, public relations, marketing
Middle line	Vice presidents of production, marketing, and sales
Operating core	Purchasing administrators, machine operators, assemblers, sales staff, dispatch staff

TABLE 4.2 Linking organizational form to coordinating mechanisms

Organizational form	Coordination mechanism
Machine bureaucracy	Standardised administrative procedures, work processes, and outputs, e.g., through quality assurance manuals, procedures, manuals, and strict templates for production or services (the nature of a telephone call in a call centre or the final product from an assembly line)
Professional bureaucracy	Standardised professional skills through education and training and operating norms through culture management techniques (e.g., a hospital or university that relies on the professional training and norms of medical or teaching staff)
Entrepreneurial organization	Direct and personal leadership, supervision, and control from the CEO (e.g., a newly formed business or a new department in an established organization)
Adhocracy	Mutual adjustment of ad hoc work teams (e.g., teams brought together to work on a one-off construction or engineering project, which have to develop their own ways of adjusting to each other, or a crew brought together to make a film, create a major conference, or sporting event)

depicted by his typology in Figure 4.3 and Table 4.2. His argument was that these four forms were dependent on very different mechanisms for coordination, which could vary from direct supervision through to the standardisation of operating norms or culture. Furthermore, in each form, different subunits tend to have greater influence.

The basic shapes of the four organizational forms, reflecting the relative importance of the component subunits and dominant mechanisms of coordination, are shown in Figure 4.4. Note how Mintzberg saw the importance of the operating core (e.g., the people who produce the services) in professional bureaucracies (e.g., hospitals and universities), and how unimportant they were in some versions of an adhocracy where many of the operations could be routinised or mechanised. Also note how he considered the strategic apex of an organization as less important in coordinating professional organizations and adhocracies, both of which form the basis of most of the knowledge-intensive and creative organizations discussed later in this book. However, traditional professional bureaucracies, such as healthcare organizations, accounting firms, and universities, are under increasing challenge from managers' attempts to control them to make them more accountable and to introduce into them an entrepreneurial spirit (Martin et al., 2021; Schachter, 2014).

Exercise 4.2

How would you describe the organization of Innovative Petroleum using Mintzberg's design framework? What are the principal methods of coordination used and are they appropriate to the teamworking structure?

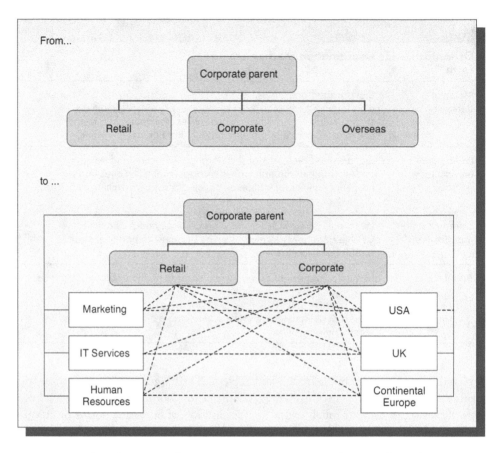

FIGURE 4.4 Evolving from a simple SBU structure to a more complex, interdependent structure

---

Box 4.1 Illustrating Mintzberg's organizational configurations: The organizational structure of a university

Universities used to be thought of as good examples of professional organizations or professional bureaucracy, dominated by academics and the core work of creating and disseminating knowledge. However, academic support units may be composed of other forms. For example, support units such as student accommodation or the maintenance department, which perform routine functions, may have a machine bureaucratic management structure, while technocratic subunits, such as HR or finance, may be administered as professional organizations themselves or as adhocracies.

As a university struggles to cope with the introduction of new information technologies in the areas of HR, student admissions, and online learning, and to the constant pressures to transform itself to improve reputational rankings, its overall organizational form may tend towards adhocracy in the form of new project teams. However, the stress of working in an adhocracy puts pressure on the organization to organize subunits according to one of the other forms. In other words, specialist departments are set up to take on board these new functions. One good example is international recruitment departments, recently established by many Western universities in the USA, UK, and Australia to capture a share of the lucrative overseas student market.

Finally, the logic of professionalism, which shapes the orientation of academics towards autonomy and the types of decisions they make, has come under increasing challenge from governments and managers, whose decision-making is governed by market, state, and bureaucratic logics. This political and managerial agenda has rendered often inexperienced students as knowledgeable 'customers', engendered competition through research and student experience rankings between universities, and sought to create disciplined compliance with quality and operating procedures. Consequently, universities are better characterised as hybrid organizations that attempt to align conflicting institutional logics of professionalism, bureaucracy, the state, and markets (Thornton et al., 2012).

Miles and Snow's strategy, structure, and process model

Alongside Mintzberg, Miles and Snow's 'strategy, structure and process' model of organizations is the best known and one of the most useful to managers who wish to improve their organization's competitive position through new organizational structures and processes. First developed in 1978 and refined in 1984, this model has stood the test of time and has been revised to show its application to contemporary circumstances (Miles et al., 2010).

Their original contribution began by setting out the idea of an adaptive cycle, which referred to how organizations adjust to changes in their environment (note, once again, the importance of matching organizations to their environments). The key proposition was that successful organizations needed to develop consistency in their strategy, their business model, which included the dominant form of technology, and their organizational capabilities, including human resource management practices. They viewed the adaptive process as addressing three problems – the entrepreneurial, engineering, and administrative problems – that an organization had to solve in a coherent way (see Table 4.3).

- The *entrepreneurial problem* focused on the choices of products/services and markets the organization would serve. In established organizations, these choices are constrained by history, and discussions typically focus on creating new ventures.
- The *engineering problem* focused on putting into operation the solutions to the entrepreneurial problem. Choices here revolved around which business model and types of technology to adopt and implement. The engineering problem is one that has been identified in many studies as one of the most critical in determining the success of organizations.

TABLE 4.3 The four organizational types

	Defender	Prospector	Analyser	Reactor
Entrepreneurial problem	Narrow market focus Limited external analysis Penetration of existing markets Limited development of existing products	Broad market focus Broad range of external analysis Growth through the development of new markets and new products Search for new technologies	Multiple markets, both stable and dynamic Steady growth through penetration of existing markets, with some product development Fast-follower strategy, rather than innovator	Poorly articulated or ambiguous strategy with no clear direction Often following strategic paths that are out of date
Engineering problem	Single core technology Relatively low on knowledge creation and work	Multiple technologies Low degree of routine operations High on knowledge creation and work	Dual technologies, stable core and innovative periphery Moderate degree of knowledge creation and work	No clear business model
Administrative problem	Functional organization Production and finance are predominant functions Relational psychological contracts and traditional careers Centralised control Coordination through standards and schedules Intensive planning	Product/geographical divisional structure Marketing and R&D heavily influential Transitory management structures and job tenure Many task forces and project teams Non-traditional careers and range of psychological contracts Decentralised control Extensive rather than intensive planning	Matrix structure Marketing and applied research are the main influences Moderately centralised control Complex coordination and planning	Organizational features not consistent with strategy Organizational features not consistent with each other Persistent strategy–structure imbalance of degree of fit
Risks and benefits	Good for defending existing markets and in conditions of little change. Unable to exploit new markets	Effective in dynamic environments but vulnerable because of low profitability and focus	Robust portfolio but needing constant review. Complex internal environment	Inability to respond to market changes. Poor performance

Source: adapted from Miles and Snow, 2003.

- The *administrative problem* related to the structure and processes of the organization, including its design and people management policies, is the topic of this chapter.

Miles and Snow's next contribution lay in developing a set of categories for organizations based on how they responded to the adaptive challenges. These categories were not intended to be static representations of reality but integrated organizational strategy/structure/process configurations that changed in a dynamic interaction with their environment. They identified four such archetypical configurations – the defender, the prospector, the analyser, and the reactor – the first three of which were coherent and sustainable in the long run. The reactor, by contrast, was incoherent and fragile (see Table 4.3).

Exercise 4.3

1 Based on Miles and Snow's typology, how would you classify Innovative Petroleum?

2 What would their typology suggest about the changes that need to be made in Innovative to make it more effective?

Developments from simple to more complex structures

These two approaches to understanding and designing organizational structures are relatively simple in the sense that they focus on single businesses or narrow product–market segments. Mintzberg's machine bureaucracy and Miles and Snow's innovator organizational configurations are good examples of such designs. Even as early as the 1930s, however, organizations such as Ford began to adopt an organizational design based on divisionalisation, which served a more complex, multi-product–market environment (Albert, 2023). This form of multidivisional structure (the M-form organization) became known as a *strategic business unit* (SBU) structure; it was, and still is, the dominant form of organizational design (Child, 2015). These SBUs had the following characteristics (Goold & Campbell, 2002):

- They were market- or customer-focused, serving specialist customer segments, e.g., small, family motor cars in Europe.
- They were largely autonomous, usually having a CEO, general manager, or president (or management team) who had the responsibility and authority to make key strategic and operating decisions that affected the results of the SBU.
- They generated revenues, incurred specific costs and were accountable for profits from serving their customer segments, and their managers were held to account for these revenues, costs, and profits (or losses).

Having such characteristics, SBUs developed a specific focus and were delegated sufficient control and authority to make key decisions without interference from the parent company. In effect, the role of the parent company (corporate headquarters) was to act as a central banker, allocating funds to the various SBUs on a strict 'return on investment' basis. Such SBU-based organizations were managed as portfolios of assets by the parent company, which treated the individual SBUs as independent businesses. As such, they provided an ideal training ground for general managers, who could step up to the problems of leadership at the corporate level.

However, SBUs also gave rise to the following important management challenges (Miles et al., 2010):

- Choosing the appropriate market focus for the SBUs and weighing up the trade-offs in such decisions. For example, some organizations have chosen to focus on geographically based customers, allowing them to develop local expertise in customs, cultures, and tastes. However, such a focus makes it more difficult to develop global products, develop global sourcing of materials, or reap the benefits of global branding or identities (Hatch, 2018).
- Silo management and achieving cooperation between SBUs. Organizing along SBU lines provides the advantages of local autonomy and the motivation for local managers to display initiative but inevitably creates 'silo' mentalities among SBU managers as they compete for resources from the parent company. This is another example of the cooperation–initiative dilemma referred to earlier. SBU managers are often accused of managing their own personal 'fiefdoms', like medieval barons, often striving to achieve their own units' objectives at the expense of others and the overall corporation. Achieving coordination between these units, especially when they act as internal suppliers or customers, or are required to share common services such as research and development or HR, is a frequent problem in many organizations. The motor vehicle industry is a good example of such supply chain issues.
- Parenting SBUs by adding value to them through, for example, setting stretching business objectives, providing shared critical services, such as research or marketing, or creating a powerful global brand reputation. Tensions often arise between the value-creating actions of the parent company and what SBUs may regard as local interference or value-destroying activity. For example, a global brand can be perceived as a strength and weakness, especially if they do not consider local tastes or identities (Hatch, 2018; Martin & Sinclair, 2018).
- Adapting to changing circumstances. Although SBUs are not inherently inflexible, they can become over-adaptive to local circumstances, or tied by design to specific customer segments that may decline in the long run. Such situations lead to 'skilled incompetence' (Argyris, 1985) in which SBUs become locked into their own 'psychic prison' and deny the existence of a changing world outside their purview. In effect, they become very skilled at what they have always done and incompetent at changing course.

To cope with the problems presented by SBU-based organizations, while retaining the benefits, large companies in the 1970s began to develop more complex structures., most of which revolved around the idea of a matrix structure (Miles et al., 2010) (see Figure 4.4). In Figure 4.4, we have simplified the original structure of a UK bank for the purposes of illustration into three autonomous customer segments – retail banking, corporate banking, and a small number of overseas clients who warranted special attention. Gradually, this bank has expanded into the US and continental Europe, creating multiple dimensions of focus but wished to retain the benefits of common marketing and product design, a shared IT platform and shared HR services, including the e-enablement of HR, training and development, and reward management. Figure 4.4 shows a simplified version of its structure in 2008.

These more complex structures. have the following characteristics:

- Multiple dimensions of focus are usually linked to serving differently defined market segments such as products, specific geographical areas, or industry groupings.
- Overlapping responsibilities, in which units will be much less self-contained and autonomous and more likely to work in collaboration with other units, or work in integrated project teams.
- Shared accountabilities, in which units are accountable for their own results and for how well they contribute to the work of other units and the company as a whole. This is a concept far removed from the profit and cost accountability of SBUs.

Like SBUs, however, these more complex structures pose significant management challenges (Hatch, 2018; Miles et al., 2010). First, decision-making can be slow and complicated because consensus is often required between the various units. Originally, the theory of matrix structures suggested a *balance* of authority between the different units so that, for example, country managers and customer managers would have an equal say in the marketing of a new product. Such balanced authority relationships have come to be seen as unworkable and time-consuming in resolving disputes, with the focus now on deciding which units will have the authority. These newer structures, however, are faced with the problems of either (a) deciding on the main sources of sustainable competitive advantage or (b) being able to change structures to reflect a competitive context in which there is no sustainable source of advantage, for example, where new technologies or sources of knowledge become readily available to all would-be competitors. Often, this means that organizations need to be designed on a *reconfigurable* basis, such as that described by the notion of dynamic capabilities discussed earlier (Teece, 2018). This reflects changes in the competitive environment, and enormous resources are now being put into organizational change or 'reinvention'.

Second, complex organizations need to deal with the challenge of coordination and collaboration across unit boundaries (Fjeldstad et al., 2012). Coordination and collaboration are rarely achieved through mutual self-interest and must be designed into organizational structures. Sometimes this is achieved through developing informal networks, but more often team-based or project-based methods of coordination are used to ensure that units collaborate to share knowledge. For example, customer teams can be set up if the main source of competitive advantage lies in serving a few large global customers well. An alternative solution might be to create a new role of a global account manager to ensure that country managers focus on globally important customers.

Third, more complex structures lead to less obvious accountabilities and are less exposed to market disciplines and self-correction when things go wrong. Complex structures mean that simple performance measures, such as unit profitability, are less relevant, and that there is a need for more rounded measures that consider the ability of a unit to collaborate and share its knowledge (Impink et al., 2020). As we shall see in Chapter 7 on managing knowledge, there are measures that can assist in this process based on ideas such as a balanced scorecard. These types of measures may reward unit managers and their teams for balancing the interests of key customers, geographical units, and product groupings, as well as implementing corporate HR and IT policies.

Exercise 4.4

Can some of the problems of Innovative Petroleum be attributed to the problems of the 'global matrix structure' of which the company is a part?

NEW APPROACHES TO ORGANIZATIONAL DESIGN

New organizational forms and networks

The approaches to analysing and designing organizations we have discussed have stood the test of time and provide excellent insights into most conventional forms of organizational structure. The principles underlying these structures, however, are based on hierarchy as a governance and control mechanism. During the 1980s and 1990s, the notion of flexibility became a much more important design principle, and organizations began to adopt more flexible structures, as presaged by both Mintzberg and Miles and Snow's earlier work on adhocracies and innovative organizations (Rouleau, 2022). Writing as far back as 1984 in the UK, John Atkinson proposed the model of the flexible firm based on the distinction between core and peripheral tasks. He noted that organizations were progressively segmenting their workforces between those employees who were 'mission critical' to the core tasks of producing and selling the key products and services of the company, and those employees who were peripheral. These peripheral employees were to be found at all levels of the organization. For example, they could be people such as accountants and HR staff, whose work could be outsourced, or whole departments, such as estate management or even manufacturing, if the organization saw its main capability as the marketing, design, or development of products and services, such as the sportswear firm, Nike. The periphery could also include work that could easily be undertaken by temporary employees who could be hired and fired when needed. The principle underlying this form of a flexible firm, which is similar in many ways to the architectural model of strategic human resource management we discussed in Chapter 3, was to translate as much of the fixed labour costs as possible in an organization into variable costs that could be adjusted to the fortunes and circumstances of the organization.

Around the same time, writers in the USA, such as Rosabeth Moss Kanter (1989) and Miles and Snow (1984), were proposing a model of the networked organization, based on the theory of loosely coupled systems of organization that operated throughout the value chain. Networked organizations began to develop in several forms (Kates et al., 2021; Rouleau, 2022). These included organizations that outsourced and offshored many of the functions, such as manufacturing in the case of consumer electronics and motor vehicles to Eastern Europe and China, and customer services, such as call centres to India. They also included so-called virtual organizations, which exist in space but are not bound by physical and legal structures – so-called imaginary structures. Jerry Davis (2022) argues that recent developments in technology have had the effect of helping reduce the size of most organizations in terms of the number of people employed while retaining their ability to earn revenues and profits through such structures. Davis, rather amusingly, pointed to an Amazon sensation of a Canadian entrepreneur using $350,000 of his own money to create a business based on a multi-functional electric cooking pot (the Instant Pot) that has sold in enormous quantities and generated substantial revenues but has almost no production, employment, marketing, financing, or distribution costs. We shall discuss these kinds of organizations later in this chapter. Finally, networked organizations also include strategic alliances, which cover situations where organizations engage in medium or long-term collaborations to realise the strategic objectives of all partners. Good examples of such alliances are to be found in oil and gas exploration, and in the staging of major international events such as the World Cup in Qatar or the Olympics in China.

Key definition: Tight and loose coupling

According to Aldrich (2008), a tightly coupled system is one where any changes in the organization's environment or design, or the fit between them, will result in compromised performance. In effect, organizations are designed to be aligned with one set of competitive circumstances, such as large-scale and hierarchical production plants, which used inflexible assembly line forms of manufacture to produce single models of motor vehicles for the mass-consumption markets in America during the 1970s and 1980s. Such tight coupling works well until the competitive conditions change – when the organizational design becomes a liability by preventing a change in strategy.

Loosely coupled systems are more flexible in design. They are less attuned to a particular set of competitive circumstances and offer the possibility of more rapid change when the environment changes. This is the thinking underlying the design of many modern motor vehicle plants, including the Toyota production system that we shall discuss in Chapter 8. We also raise it in Chapter 9 on creativity and innovation.

The ideas underlying many of these networked organizations emerged from places such as Silicon Valley in California, where rather unusual organization structures were being developed to take advantage of the rapid change associated with the high-technology environment. Agility and versatility became the bywords for organization design, rather than hierarchy and control (Kates et al., 2021). Many of these new organizations were more akin to loose federations or constellations of business units that relied on each other for expertise and know-how (Fjeldstad et al., 2012). Davis's (2022) earlier example of Instant Pot is an extreme illustration of such new organizations. He also uses the illustration of TikTok, a social media firm, partnering with Grubhub, a delivery service, and various ghost kitchens to create a virtual restaurant offering popular food items to order. A more 'traditional' example, though not based in Silicon Valley, is Microsoft with its Certified Partners programme. The illustration in Box 4.2, taken from Microsoft's website, gives you some insight into how organizations such as Microsoft have grown through networking with smaller organizations that can provide expertise in helping them develop their products and services and by providing channels to market for Microsoft products.

Box 4.2 An example of growth through networking

This is an extract taken from Microsoft's website for its partnership programme.

Microsoft Partner Program builds relevance and value into all the tools and resources we provide to help you thrive in the market. You'll find benefits and resources to support all stages of your business cycle, helping you to:

- *Plan your business.* The tools and resources to help you grow and develop your business.
- *Build and maintain expertise.* Assistance in building and maintaining expertise in your areas of specialisation through training resources and access to Microsoft software for development, support, sales or internal-use purposes.
- *Market and sell.* Marketing activities and resources to help you create demand and build sales around Microsoft software launches and new marketing initiatives.
- *Provide service and support.* The tools and services you need to aid in delivering and supporting Microsoft software and solutions.
- *Retain your customers.* Tools to help you connect with and strengthen your customer relationships.

Barber and Goold (2014), well-known authorities on organizational design and collaboration strategies, and, more recently, Davis (2022) have suggested that these kinds of organizations are one of the most compelling images of companies in the twenty-first century – the idea of such self-managed networks, free from bureaucracy, built on expertise and highly motivated, creative units interacting with each other in a mutually adjusting fashion (see also Case 4.2 on TCG). The image is particularly attractive because it contrasts markedly with the conventional, bureaucratic form many of us are used to working in, which is often characterised by a lack of innovation and internal political behaviour. Table 4.4 sets out the contrast between conventional and emerging network-based organizations in more formal terms. The table contrasts the two forms based on three dimensions: the process of strategic decision-making; how integration is achieved between units; and how the necessary differentiation is achieved within the organization. On this last point, note the implications for careers and attachments to organizations, and the changed basis of the psychological contracts discussed in previous chapters.

TABLE 4.4 Contrasting old and new organizations

Organizational activity	Conventional organization characteristics	Emerging organizational characteristics
Strategic management, goal-setting, and implementation	Top-down, centralised decision-making, tightly coupled	Decentralised goal-setting, loosely coupled
	Concentrated power and authority	Distributed power and authority and freedom from hierarchy
	Preference for large units and wide-scope SBUs, with a single-dimension focus to reflect relatively stable and simple environments	Preference for smaller units and multidimensional focus to reflect more complex and changing environments, the need for constant renewal and 'reconfigurability'
	Leader control, monitoring, and specific objective-setting through the use of formal authority	Leaders provide guidance and support, but also manage conflict and act as brokers
	Vision dictated by senior managers	Vision emergent often from middle
	Knowledge routine and knowledge secrecy	Knowledge intensive and knowledge sharing
	Focus on costs and 'playing within the rules of the game'	Focus on innovation and 'changing the rules of the game' by setting stretching targets
Maintaining necessary integration within organizational boundaries and defining organizational boundaries	Firms or SBU as a unit of analysis	The value chain or network as the unit of analysis
	Boundaries of organization are clearly specified and durable, with most support services undertaken in-house	Boundaries of organization permeable, fuzzy and flexible, with more outsourcing and markets for spin-offs and buy-outs
	Standards, reliability, and replicability as key bywords for managers	Flexibility as a key management principle
	Vertical communications	Horizontal communications

(Continued)

TABLE 4.4 (Continued)

Organizational activity	Conventional organization characteristics	Emerging organizational characteristics
	Rules and procedures dominant	Relationship-based and personal networking
	Assets, budgets, and investments linked to organizational units	Assets, budgets, and investments independent of organizational units and often focused on projects and initiatives
Maintaining necessary differentiation within the organization, including functions and roles, duties and rights, and governance	Specialised roles and detailed division of labour, with people hired for jobs	General roles and little heed paid to the division of labour, with people hired to fit organization
	Clear job and function definitions	Fuzzy job and function definitions
	Uncertainty absorption	Adaptation
	Relative permanence of jobs and careers based on relational psychological contracts	Relative impermanence of jobs and boundaryless careers, based on transactional psychological contracts and employability
	Efficiency orientation	Innovation orientated
Modes of integration		
Networking	Only with major stakeholders	Integral to the value chain
Outsourcing	Vertical integration into large units, little or no outsourcing	Horizontal integration between smaller units, non-core activities outsourced
Alliances	Avoided due to fears of loss of control	Extensively used
Organizing across borders	Either a loose financially coordinated conglomerate or coordinated via an international division	Complex multidimensional organization that attempts to gain the benefits of global integration and local responsiveness

Source: based on Aldrich, 2008; Barber & Goold, 2014; Child, 2015; Davis, 2022; Miles et al., 2010; Goold & Campbell, 2002; Malone, 2004; Roberts, 2004.

The virtual organization and networking

Thus, as the argument goes, networked organizations came together to create a 'virtual firm' (Rouleau, 2022). Such organizations are usually defined by what they are not (Aldrich, 2008). That is, they are not the conventional, vertically integrated and directed organizations described earlier in this chapter. Instead, they are 'virtual' in the sense that all or most of the activities in the value chain, from acquiring raw materials to customer relationships, are contracted out and loosely coupled. The result is a series of networked companies, focusing on doing what they can do most effectively and acting *as if* they were a single organization. In this sense, the network *simulates* a single company, which is why we use the term 'virtual'. Such organizational structures aren't new, as many industries have operated based on contracting out for many years. The construction industry is one such example, often with the architect acting as the network *'integrator'* on behalf of the client and managing the supply chain from design, through construction to handing over the building to the customer. The main advantages of this kind of organization lie in specialising in what they are good at and in being comparatively small when it is advantageous to be small while being able to scale up when size and scope are important. Such ideas are also applied in parts of the public sector to address the problems of the division of labour, task allocation, rewards allocation, and information provision, which are key issues facing many parts of the sector (Kennis & Raab, 2020). However, there is also strong resistance to such ideas in some countries for reasons that you may want to reflect on before we discuss the benefits and drawbacks of new organizational forms. A good example is the National Health Service in the UK, which has arguably decided to travel in the opposite direction by creating even larger integrated national (health)care systems.

Dell and Nike are well-known examples of virtual organizations, as are Benetton, the Italian fashion house. All these organizations contract out most, if not all, manufacturing, and act as network integrators in bringing together all aspects of their respective value chains to provide distinctive value propositions to their customers. It is not only organizations that are becoming virtual, but also major functions such as HR. Like all virtual organizations, the operations of the HR departments of Benetton, Dell, and BT have been made possible by new information and communications technologies in linking the various companies and outsourcing contractors together to provide a seamless service to their respective customers. One good example is the so-called e-Lancing firm, Uber (see Box 4.3).

Box 4.3 Uber: A technology mediator

Danial Pink wrote a book entitled Free Agent Nation in 2001 but could hardly have foreseen how technology would change the nature of freelancing to e-lancing. One company that has featured heavily in this new 'sharing' economy is Uber, a web-based taxi company that customers access through an app on their mobile phones. It originated in San Francisco in 2009 and became one of the fastest-growing technology start-ups by 2015, operating in 229 cities in 46 countries with a business model that has become a marker for many other firms.

Using an app on smartphones, Uber allows passengers to call drivers directly 'from the comfort of a sofa or bar stool,' which has caused a major shake-up in the taxi market. The interesting aspect of organizationally is that Uber does not own taxis but connects passengers with e-lancers, individuals who use their own vehicles in their own time to supply the rides. For this service, Uber charges a fixed 20 per cent of the fare. The strong networking effects of this type of business allow Uber to recruit more self-employed drivers, many of whom are part-time, which reduces pick-up times and thus attracts more passengers.

However, Uber is not without its critics, especially from the existing taxi companies and from some of its e-lancers. It is known for being a ruthless competitor in its market with its surge pricing model – raising rates during peak times to encourage more drivers on the roads – and also ruthless in its dealings with e-lancers. So, in June 2015, the Labor Commissioner in California ruled that a former driver was an employee and not a subcontractor, and thus entitled to be paid expenses for her mileage. This ruling has set off a class action by drivers who are seeking to be regarded as employees rather than e-lancers, receiving, for example, all tips. Such a decision, if repeated in other US states or other countries, could represent a major threat to Uber's business model and those companies that have adopted it.

Moreover, while e-lancing can be liberating for some, for others it can be a source of anxiety for two reasons. Schonfeld and Mazzola (2015) have shown how anxiety follows from the self-employed not knowing 'whether one is doing enough, or good enough work' because they lack a reference point with employee norms. In addition to performance anxiety (being good enough), Gianpiero Petriglieri from Insead described existential anxiety (who am I and why am I doing this – is it valuable?). One consequence is burnout, because, as Standing (2009) suggested, the 'profician' (e.g., lawyers, sports stars, IT professionals who are self-selling entrepreneurs) 'has to live a very frenzied and opportunistic life'.

As the above case highlights and as several writers have pointed out, virtual corporations have several disadvantages and face many challenges (Child, 2015; Pettigrew et al., 2000):

- The loss of proprietary knowledge, when providing information and learning to other members of the network. For example, when IBM contracted out its software and processor manufacture to Microsoft and Intel, they effectively gave away core competences. BT also suffered from losing control of proprietary knowledge in outsourcing much of its HR function to Accenture during the 1990s, a problem that took many years to overcome (Martin et al., 2008).
- The more an organization contracts out, the more potential profit through value-added services it loses. For example, in the IBM case in the previous bullet point, both Microsoft and Intel became larger than IBM. Perhaps as important, contracting out means that an organization has less control over the business process. If even one

of these processes is 'mission critical', any conflict that arises from disagreements can damage the reputation of the whole virtual network.

- The feasibility of networks, which depends on the attitudes of partners and the information available to them. In a virtual organization, success often depends on the personalities, emotional intelligence, motivations, and career trajectories of individual managers. It may be difficult for managers brought up in large SBU organizations, many of whom have been used to relatively rich resources, stable career paths, and competition, to work in smaller, often resource-poor, organizations with very different career structures, and expect them to collaborate and share their knowledge. Similar arguments apply to the public sector, with strong professions reluctant to lose power.

- A final problem with networks arises from the time and effort often required to create them. Because of the initial investment in management time, they are likely to become closed systems, resistant to new partners and future change.

Thus, designing effective virtual organizations is very much based on effective partnering, which writers such as Child (2015), Davis (2022), Galbraith (2014), and Miles et al. (2010) see as addressing the following issues:

1. Creating a partnership strategy in which companies play appropriate roles. These roles can range from being a specialist contributor, who performs only a few activities such as payroll services, to a network integrator such as Uber, Nike, Benetton, Dell, or even Boeing, the aircraft company. As discussed earlier, the network integrator must balance contracting out mission-critical and potentially profitable activities against the value of having expert outside suppliers contribute to the network.

2. Designing appropriate external relationships and coordination mechanisms, which can vary according to (a) the degree of control the integrator has or desires over other companies in the network, (b) the levels of day-to-day coordination necessary, and (c) the value the network integrator wishes to capture from the partnership: this refers to the proportion of total value added by the network supply chain that the network integrator seeks to appropriate for itself.

3. The design choices available range from developing pure *market or contracting relationships; sourcing and alliance partnerships*, often found in motor vehicle manufacture and large construction projects; *equity relationships*, in which an integrator may take out a financial stake in the other companies; and outright *ownership* of the other companies. As all these choices have their strengths and weaknesses, solutions are specific to the context of the partnership. For example, BT set up an equity relationship with Accenture in the 1990s to deliver HR services to other companies, which it subsequently relinquished in part because of problems of lack of trust between the partners (Martin et al., 2008). The BT group has now gone for an ownership strategy of four brands, BT, EE, Plusnet, and Openreach.

4. Partner selection is another and often critical design issue. In many respects, the issues here are like those involved in selecting individuals to fit organizations and revolve around having common aims and compatible cultures or characters. As Child (2015)

suggests, firms skilled at creating alliances, whether they be networks, sourcing alliances, joint ventures, or equity partnerships, spend a lot of time and effort evaluating potential partners for 'fit' during the selection process to ensure that all issues that may cause the partnership to go wrong are uncovered during the 'courtship' process.

5. Finally, supporting policies for people and reward policies, key components of the Star model in Figure 4.1, are critical design choices. As noted previously, the success of partnerships depends on the qualities and motivation of the managers who must make them work; these qualities are often different from those that are successful in competitive contexts. Key skills include the ability to influence without authority and negotiating and working with people from different corporate and international cultures. They also include the ability to cooperate and reveal information, as well as retain confidential information. Reward systems, like cooperating skills, must be based on the idea of a win–win scenario in which the deals and arrangements struck bring benefits to all parties (Barber & Goold, 2014).

CASE 4.2 TCG: AN EXAMPLE OF A VIRTUAL ORGANIZATION BASED ON CELLULAR PRINCIPLES

Technical and Computer Graphics (TCG), an Australian privately held information technology company based in Sydney and founded in 1971, is a classic example of a virtual organization based on cellular principles. As Miles et al. (2010) concluded since revisiting their original research in the firm in 1997, TCG has certainly evolved. In the 1990s, it focused on developing a wide variety of products and services, including portable and hand-held data terminals and loggers, computer graphics systems, barcoding systems, electronic data interchange systems, and other IT products and services. More recently, it moved into the development of business accelerators and technology parks, as well as business services. The network originally comprised 13 individual small firms as partners, the basis of the cellular approach. Drawing on the biological metaphor of a living organism, each firm or 'cell' had its own aims while living independently from the others, but all shared a common bond with other network members. For example, some TCG firms specialise in one or more product categories, whereas others specialise in hardware or software.

At TCG, the various partners had existing high levels of technical and business competence. However, the ambitions of the network were to ensure system-wide competence for the overall group. The process used to develop this overall partnership competence was called triangulation; it was how TCG developed new products and services.

Triangulation was based on a partnership model with three components: (a) a partnership among one or more TCG firms; (b) an external joint-venture partner, such as Hitachi, which may provide equity to the venture; and (c) a principal customer or client that can provide large orders and additional cash and resources to the partnership in return for contractual and intellectual property rights for the innovations or developments.

The process of venturing was critical to the partnership, with all TCG networked firms expected to search continually for new product and service opportunities. Once there was some interest shown by a potential client, the initiating TCG firm acted as project leader for the remainder of the venture. The first step in the triangulation process was to identify and collaborate with a joint-venture partner with specialist competence in the underlying technology or process involved. TCG sought funding for the project from the joint-venture partner and gained access to the key technology, etc. The second step was to locate and work with a potential customer for the new product, for whom they agreed to custom-design a product. By working with joint-venture partners and end users, TCG could produce high-technology solutions and products that met the demands of a client not taxed with having to set up a specialist in-house organization to innovate.

The credo of TCG ensures that the project leader firm in the network partnered with other firms in the group, not only for their specialist contribution but so that the collective competence and knowledge base of the network was enhanced. Triangulation thus served a dual purpose of building on collective expertise and enhancing it by diffusing the learning gained from business development, partnering, and project management. The principles of networking were interconnected at TCG and served to reinforce each other to bind the network together. First, acceptance of entrepreneurial responsibility is required for admission to the group and is increasingly enhanced by the triangulation process. Second, the principle of self-organization gave the individual firm both the ability and the freedom to adapt to changing partner and customer needs. Third, each firm's profit responsibility, as well as the guaranteed ability to take out equity in other TCG firms, provided the motivation and rewards for overall collective growth and use of each others' specific competences.

In revisiting this well-researched case, Miles et al. (2010) concluded that the process of multi-firm collaboration at TCG was mutually reinforcing, with knowledge sharing a key feature of this continuing collaboration (as stated on its website in 2015). Fjeldstad et al. (2012) proposed that such collaborations were built around organizational architectures that embodied three key features:

(1) organizational actors in the firms who had the capabilities and mindsets to self-organize,

(2) a common approach to accumulating and sharing resources, and

(3) enabling structures and processes that facilitated multi-actor collaborations.

Source: adapted from Fjeldstad et al. (2012); Miles et al. (1997, 2010).

1. To what extent does the TCG network embody effective partnering? Can you foresee any problems?

TESTS OF EFFECTIVE ORGANIZATIONAL DESIGN

So, what have we learnt about the kinds of problems faced by organizations such as Innovative Petroleum Engineering, and what can we do to help them restructure more effectively? During this chapter, you have been introduced to several ideas that might suggest useful ways forward from the perspective of Innovative and its parent company. You have also learnt about the virtues of new organizational forms that companies like Innovative may consider. However, I want to reiterate there is no single solution for organizations such as Innovative. Instead, there are only sensible general questions we can ask, the answers to which may help us design an organization appropriate for a particular context and time frame. To help us ask and answer such questions, I have integrated Goold and Campbell's (2002) nine design tests with those of Child (2015) and others (e.g., Fjeldstad et al., 2012; Barber & Goold, 2014; Kates et al., 2021), based on two fundamental concepts in organizational design:

- *Fit*, which is based on the idea that organizations should be fit for purpose.
- *Design principles*, which have been distilled from previous 'promising' practices in organizational design. Note we do not use the term 'best practice' because we do not believe there can be practices that are 'best' for all contexts other than at a very general level.

The four drivers of fit and the five design principles are best defined by the nine tests that Goold and Campbell associated with them (see Figure 4.5 and Table 4.5). Again,

FIGURE 4.5 Fit drivers and good design principles

(*Source:* Barber & Goold, 2014; Child, 2015; Goold & Campbell, 2002, p. 250; Fjeldstad et al., 2012; Kates et al., 2021)

TABLE 4.5 Linking fit drivers to fit tests

Fit drivers	Fit tests
Product–market strategy	Market advantage test: Does the design allocate sufficient management attention to the operating priorities and intended sources of advantage in each product market area? Structures should attend to the needs of customers in each product–market segment served by the organization, e.g., particular models of cars, and to the sources of advantage and major operating initiatives that will help them succeed in each product–market segment, e.g., supplier relationship management in motor vehicle manufacture and retailing.
Corporate strategy	Parenting test: Does the design allocate sufficient attention to the intended sources of added value and strategic initiatives of the corporate parent? The organizational design should reflect the chosen 'parenting' propositions, e.g., to provide research support for operating units, or to enhance the corporate brand, *and* to reflect key strategic initiatives or actions planned by the company, e.g., implement a corporate-wide customer relationship management system (CRM), outsource all ICT services or call handling.
People	People test: Does the design adequately reflect the motivations, strengths, and weaknesses of the available people? The structure should fit the available potential core talent needed to deliver the strategic aims, e.g., the kinds of recruits that will be needed for the future *and* the existing talent in the organization, e.g., the top management team or the core software team. This notion links closely to dynamic capabilities. If collaboration is a key feature of the design, are there actors with the values and capability to self-organize?
Constraints	Feasibility test: Does the design consider the constraints that might make the proposal unworkable? The requirements are to ensure that the external environment has been interpreted and sensed to identify all possible constraints, e.g., legal and government directives in setting up joint ventures in particular countries, and the robustness of the design against each constraint or possible source of failure, e.g., how will a major breakdown in one part of the organization affect the whole operation?

Good design principles	**Design tests**
Specialisation principle	Specialist subunit culture test: Do any units need to have specialist cultures that are different from sister units and layers above, and do these units have enough protection from the dominant culture, e.g., do innovative or research and development units have enough 'space'?
Coordination principle	Difficult links test: Does the organization call for any coordination benefits that will be difficult to achieve on a networking basis, and does it include 'solutions' that will ease the difficulty, e.g., does the organization require critical quality standards throughout the company that would be difficult to achieve on an informal basis? Are there protocols, processes and infrastructures that enable multi-actor collaborations?

(Continued)

TABLE 4.5 (Continued)

Fit drivers	Fit tests
Knowledge and competence principle	Redundant hierarchy test: Are all levels in the hierarchy and all responsibilities retained by managers at these levels based on knowledge and competence, e.g., do different levels of managers add value in terms of their specific knowledge and competence? Are there physical and virtual spaces where actors can accumulate and share resources?
Control and commitment	Accountability test: Does the design facilitate the creation of control processes for each unit that are appropriate to their roles and responsibilities, economical to implement, and motivating for the managers and employees in the unit, e.g., are customer-facing units given enough 'slack' or autonomy to meet their objectives and are they rewarded for doing so? To what extent is leadership effectively distributed in the organization to ensure that everyone with expertise can contribute? Is the design built on high trust dynamics?
Innovation and adaptation principle	Flexibility test: Will the design help the development of new strategies and be flexible enough to adapt to future changes, e.g., do innovative units have enough access to talent to meet demands for new products or services, and are they rewarded for learning, passing on their learning, and putting it into practice in the form of innovations? In a multinational context, is sufficient attention paid to the tensions involved in thinking global, acting local and transferring knowledge across borders simultaneously?

I believe these design tests have stood the test of time since writing the first edition of the book and remain extremely useful because they can be used to assess the strengths and weaknesses of existing organizations, those of major changes to an existing organization, or proposals for new organization forms such as the ones we have discussed in this chapter.

This practical set of principles would be a good place to begin to evaluate your own organization, focusing on its existing structure or on any proposed changes. Returning to the case of Innovative Petroleum, managers in the company would be well-advised to look at these design principles before continuing with their changes to the organizational structure. At the time of putting this book together, however, there is little sign of them doing so.

LEARNING SUMMARY

In this chapter, we looked at the kinds of problems faced by many large organizations that can cause them to underperform and, possibly, go out of existence. We looked at several classical frameworks that help us understand organizational analysis and design and applied these to the problems faced by Innovative Petroleum Engineering, a pseudonym for a real firm undergoing problems of change.

We have also examined developments in organizational forms, beginning with changes from simple to more complex structures, including the M-form and matrix structures. We also focused on the more recent introduction of virtual organizations and networking. These latter types are not yet widespread, but evidence suggests that they will become more common in all countries, creating new opportunities for businesses but also presenting new problems for managers, especially in managing situations with traditional levels of authority and power.

Finally, we looked at a highly practical test of good organizational design that I hope you will use in your future career to analyse the problems faced by the organization you work for or any changes proposed for its future.

REVIEW QUESTIONS

1. What are the key environmental factors that influence organizational design?
2. What are the strengths and weaknesses of new organizational forms?

REFERENCES

Aguinas, H., & Lawal, S. O. (2013). eLancing: A review and research agenda for bridging the science-practice gap. *Human Resource Management Review, 23*(1), 6–17.

Albert, D. (2023). What do you mean by organizational structure? Acknowledging and harmonizing differences and commonalities in three prominent perspectives. *Journal of Organizational Design*, 13, 1–11.

Aldrich, H. A. (2008). *Organizations and environments*. Stanford University Press.

Argyris, C. (1985). *Strategy, change, and defensive routines*. Pitman.

Atkinson, J. (1984). Manpower strategies for flexible organizations. *Personnel Management, 16*(8), 28–31.

Barber, F. & Goold, M. (2014) *Collaboration strategy: how to get what you want from employees, suppliers and business partners*. London: Bloomsbury.

Child, J. (2015). *Organization: Contemporary principles and practices* (2nd ed.). John Wiley

Child, J., & McGrath, R. G. (2001). Organizations unfettered: Organizational forms in an information-intensive economy. *Academy of Management Journal, 44*(6), 1135–1149.

Christensen, C. M., & Horn, M. (2008). *Disrupting class: How disruptive innovation will change the way the world learns*. McGraw-Hill.

Clegg, S.R., Pitsis, T.S.& Mount, M. (2021). *Managing and organizations: an introduction to theory and practice* (sixth edition). Sage.

Davis, G. F. (2022). *Taming corporate power in the 21st century.* Cambridge University Press.

Fjeldstad, O. D., Snow, C. C., Miles, R. E., & Lettl, C. (2012). The architecture of collaboration. *Strategic Management Journal, 33*(6), 734–750.

Galbraith, J. (2002). *Designing organizations: An executive guide to strategy, structure and process* (New and Revised ed.). Jossey-Bass.

Galbraith, J. (2014). *Designing organizations: Strategy, structure, and process at the business unit and enterprise level* (third edition). New York: Jossey-Bass.

Ghoshal, S. (2003). Miles and snow: Enduring insights for managers. *Academy of Management Executive, 17*(4), 109–115.

Goold, M., & Campbell, A. (2002). *Designing effective organizations: How to create structured networks.* John Wiley.

Gu, G., Wand, C. S., & Galinsky, A. D. (2015). The promise and perversity if perspective-taking in organizations. *Research in Organizational Behavior, 35,* 79–102.

Hatch, M. J. (2018). *Organization theory: Modern, symbolic and postmodern perspectives* (4th ed.). Oxford University Press.

Hunter, I., & Saunders, J. (2007). *Human resource outsourcing: Solutions, suppliers, key processes and the current market.* Gower.

Impink, S. M., Prat, A., & Sadun, R. (2020, May). Measuring collaboration in modern organizations. *American Economic Association Papers and Proceedings, 110,* 181–186.

Kanter, R. M. (1989). *When giants learn to dance: Mastering the challenges of strategy, management, and careers in the 1990s.* New York: Simon Schuster.

Kates, A., & Galbraith, J. R. (2010). *Designing your organization: Using the STAR modelto solve 5 critical design challenges.* John Wiley & Sons.

Kates, A., Kesler, G., & DiMartino, M (2021). *Networked, scaled and agile: A design strategy for complex organizations.* Kogan Page

Kennis, P., & Raab, J (2020). Back to the future: Using organizational design theory for effective organizational networks. *Perspectives on Public Management and Governance, 3*(2), 109–123

Ketchen, D. J. Jr (2003). Introduction: Raymond E. Miles and Charles C. Snow's organizational strategy, structure, and process. *Academy of Management Executive, 17*(4), 95–97.

Malone, T. W. (2004). *The future of work: How the new order of business will shape your organization, your management style, and your life.* Harvard Business School Press.

Martin, G., Reddington, M., & Alexander, H. (Eds.). (2008). *Technology, outsourcing and transforming HR.* Butterworth Heinemann.

Martin, G., & Sinclair, K. (2018). Employer branding and corporate reputation management in global companies: Theory and practice. In D. G. Collings, H. Scullion, & P. M. Caligiuri (Eds.), *Global Talent Management* (2nd ed. ed., pp. 144-164). Routledge.

Martin, G., Bushfield, S., Siebert, S., & Howieson, B. (2021). Changing logics in healthcare and their effects on the identity motives and identity work of doctors. *Organization Studies, 42*(9), 1477–1499.

Miles, R. E., & Snow, C. C. (1978). *Organizational strategy, structure and process.* McGraw-Hill.

Miles, R. E. and Snow, C. C. (1984). Fit, failure and the hall of fame. *California Management Review, 26* (3), 10–28.

Miles, R. E., & Snow, C. C. (2003). *Organizational strategy, structure and process: A Stanford business classic.* Stanford University Press.

Miles, R. E., Snow, C. C., Fjeldstad, O. D., Miles, G., & Lettl, C. (2010). Designing organizational to meet 21st-century opportunities and challenges. *Organizational Dynamics, 39*(2), 93–103.

Miles, R. E., Snow, C. C., Mathews, J. A., & Miles, G. (1997). Organizing in the knowledge age: Anticipating the cellular form. *Academy of Management Executive, 11*(4), 7–24.

Mintzberg, H. (1993). *Structure in fives: Designing effective organizations.* Prentice-Hall.

Pettigrew, A. M., Massini, S., & Numagami, T. (2000). Innovative forms of organising in Europe. *European Management Journal, 18*(3), 259–273.

Roberts, J. (2004). *The modern firm: Organizational design for performance and growth.* Oxford University Press.

Rouleau, L. (2022). *Organization theories in the making: Exploring the leading-edge perspectives.* Oxford University Press.

Schachter, H. L. (2014). New public management and principals' roles in organizational governance: What can a corporate issue tell us about public sector management. *Public Organization Review, 14,* 517–531.

Schonfeld, I. S., & Mazzola, J. J. (2015, February). A qualitative study of stress in individuals self-employed in solo businesses. *Journal of Occupational Health Psychology., 20*(4), 501–513.

Sostak, H., & Kurz, P. (2020). *Organizational design in the digital age: A systematic literature review.* https://papers.ssrn.com/sol3/papers.cfm?abstract_id=3658131

Standing, G. (2009). *Work after globalization: Building occupational citizenship.* Edward Elgar.

Teece, D. (2018). Business models and dynamic capabilities. *Long Range Planning, 51*(1), 40–49.

Thornton, P. H., Ocasio, W., & Lounsbury, M. (2012). *The institutional logics perspective: A new approach to culture, structure and process.* Oxford University Press.

Managing in an international context

INTRODUCTION

During the first four chapters of this book, we have discussed how important it is to understand business and management from an international perspective. As noted earlier, one of the dominant trends in the development of modern economies is the increased 'globalisation' of business, though as some writers have pointed out, this trend is the subject of several myths and misunderstandings (Reiche et al., 2017) and may also be in retreat according to the World Economic Forum in 2023 . Leaving aside this recent claim, globalisation has a significant influence on how we manage, not only in multinational enterprises (MNEs) but

DOI: 10.4324/9781003469711-5

also in our home-based companies because we often borrow ideas on promising practices from organizations in the advanced industrialised countries. Much of this borrowing, some might say copying, has come from US-based companies headlined in the international business press and much of the US-based academic literature as models of excellence, for example, Apple, Google, and Amazon, who are recognised as leaders to follow in their fields. Nevertheless, some researchers have argued US companies, partly because of the US government's generally isolationist approach to world affairs throughout much of its history (at least until the Second World War), were among the least well-equipped organizations to conduct effective global management in a multinational context. In essence, the argument is that US companies were 'reluctant globalisers', who did not want to sacrifice 'American jobs' to overseas subsidiaries. For example, only two US-based companies featured in the 'Global Top 100 Non-Financial Trans-National Corporations Ranked by Foreign Assets in 2014' list – General Electric and Exxon Mobil.

Yet, at the same time, several major US organizations have been at the forefront of the internationalising (if not globalising) process, initially in the UK and the rest of Europe after the Second World War, and more recently in their operations in the Asia-Pacific region (Preston, 2021). Such efforts at internationalisation, although generally successful in bringing economic success to the USA and to the host countries of US subsidiaries, have been plagued by problems. These problems are often the consequence of US 'exceptionalism' (a belief in the superiority of their own values), ethnocentrism, and attempts to export US-style 'best practice' in management to other countries, especially in the field of people management (Lawler & Boudreau, 2015). Consequently, major mistakes have been made by US companies in working overseas. By no stretch of the imagination, however, is such exceptionalism and ethnocentrism a feature only of American organizations. The political and economic history of the last four centuries is characterised by problems experienced by companies based in Europe, Japan, and the so-called 'newly emerging economies' such as China, Korea, and Thailand in internationalising (Jones, 2003; World Trade Report, 2023). Perhaps the most notable example of internationalisation was the British Empire, in which the UK attempted to create a world in its own image, reaching its high point in the early 1900s when it controlled 25 per cent of the world's land mass and 25 per cent of its population (Whittaker, 2023). This was internationalisation on a scale never seen before or since, and virtually every lesson in how to conduct global management – good and bad – can be drawn from Britain's imperialist era (Ferguson, 2003, 2004). Like the British East India Company, which once controlled most of India, European organizations have sometimes found that their internationalisation strategies have failed because of their excessive commitment to parent company values and practices, and a failure to understand the institutional and cultural characteristics of host countries and their subsidiaries. Amusing examples of such problems include the early attempts by Marks & Spencer, one of the most reputable British retailing organizations, to set up operations in France during the 1980s. So entrenched were their British values that they tried to operate a 'buy British' campaign in a country that has competed with England for hundreds of years (including a 100 years' war), and to sell Christmas puddings, a uniquely British dish, without any cooking instructions. French customers bought them and ate them cold, which only confirmed their already low opinion of British food products because they only taste good when heated.

Thus, we face the possibility of companies throughout the world destined to repeat many of the mistakes of history when operating in each other's territories. Therefore, it is critically important for globalising firms and SMEs with international growth ambitions to make sensible and contextually sensitive decisions in key areas of marketing, knowledge management, and human resource management. These decisions must consider institutional, cultural, and psychological differences between parent company institutions, values, and practices, those of host countries and those of third-country nationals employed to work in global organizations. Because there are so many lessons that can be drawn from the past, we shall also spend a little time taking a historical perspective on these matters.

So, in this chapter, we shall explore the international context of business and management and address three key questions often asked of practising managers and academics who research in this interesting area:

1. To what extent do countries differ in their business environments and how does this affect the practice of management in these countries?
2. What has been the impact of the internationalisation of business and the growth of so-called global firms on the practice of management?
3. What lessons can we learn from research and practice about managing people in an international environment?

The problems of internationalisation and its implications for management

In my academic and practitioner roles, I have spent some time living and working in several different countries. Consequently, when working for a brief period in the US, I was asked to provide advice to a US tech company in the online learning field that sought to establish operations in the UK and continental Europe. This company and its managers were not naïve; they appreciated the problems of 'going international', especially in countries of which they had little knowledge. The company was aware of what academics have referred to as the 'liability of foreignness' (Kim & Siegel, 2024), so, they took the sensible course of action to commission a European 'local' to provide a research-based insight into the European market for online learning in the business and education sectors. This liability of foreignness they faced is the cost of doing business abroad arising from the unfamiliarity of the environment, from cultural, political, and economic differences, and the need for coordination across geographic distances (see below).

Key concept: The liability of foreignness

This was originally defined by Zaheer (1995) as 'the costs of doing business abroad that result in a competitive disadvantage for a multinational enterprise (MNE)' and extended by Kim and Siegel (2024). These costs broadly refer to all the additional costs that a firm operating in a market overseas incurs that a local firm would not incur. Five such categories of costs are likely to arise:

1. Costs directly associated with distance, such as the costs of travel, transportation, and coordination over distance and across time zones.

2. Firm-specific costs based on a particular company's unfamiliarity with and lack of roots or embeddedness in a local culture and business system.

3. Costs resulting from the host country's environment, such as the lack of legitimacy of foreign firms and economic nationalism among governments and people.

4. Costs imposed by home country governments on doing business overseas, such as the restrictions on high-technology or weapons sales to certain countries.

5. Costs imposed by democratic countries on private sector firms from autocratic countries, especially the fees charged by professional corporate lobbyist firms to them (Kim & Siegel, 2024).

The relative importance of these costs, and the choices that firms can make to deal with them, will vary by industry, firm, host country, and home country. Regardless of its source, the liability of foreignness suggests, other things being equal, that foreign firms will have lower profitability than local firms and, perhaps, a lesser chance of survival.

The company, however, were also concerned with the liability of 'outsidership' (Johanson & Vahine, 2009), i.e., being locked outside of, or unable to access, networks of firms that can help them expand their business and innovate in new markets. Therefore, many companies, including this tech company, seek to exploit their assets by trading across international boundaries. In doing so, however, they are challenged by four basic questions. The first two relate to the now classical integration-responsiveness problem, which largely focuses on economic or profit advantages for international firms or multinational enterprises (MNEs) (Rosenzweig, 2006; Pucik et al., 2023). The second two focus on a need to develop intellectual and social capital in MNEs (e.g., Johanson & Vahine, 2009; Legnick-Hall & Legnick-Hall, 2012):

1. To what extent can or should they *standardise* their operations across national boundaries to exploit existing products and services, brands, intangible assets, and human resource management practices?

2. To what extent can or should they exploit the benefits of *localisation* by adapting these products and/or services, and policies to fit in with their overseas markets?

3. How can they best leverage their knowledge and learning in one part of the company to other units?

4. To what extent can they build trust and commitment to develop the necessary bonds and bridges between the firms in their network of relationships?

The balance between standardisation and localisation that a firm eventually settles on is based on the extent to which organizations assess their liability of foreignness or liability of outsidership in different market circumstances. Among other considerations, this calculation can turn on the extent to which these organizations assume that the countries they seek to enter are similar (convergent) to their own national cultures or are dissimilar (divergent) from their own national culture. The internationalisation strategies that organizations might choose can take a range of forms (see Table 5.1), dependent on the extent to which they seek to have equity (ownership) in their overseas ventures. However, all such strategies rest on the liability of foreignness perceived by a firm and

TABLE 5.1 Entry strategies into overseas markets

Non-equity modes	Forms	Characteristics
	Exporting	Selling overseas, which is usually low risk and requires little investment
	Licensing	Giving a local firm a legal right to produce or sell a product or service, which is usually low risk but may lead to problems of local quality control
	Franchising	Providing local firms with a complete package of trademarks, products and services, and operating principles
	Contract manufacturing and service provision	Contracting out non-core business activities to overseas operations, which requires no local ownership or investment. Problems associated with quality control and contracting out 'moral responsibilities' to local entrepreneurs who may have different standards and attitudes to labour management
Equity modes		
	International joint ventures	An agreement by two or more companies to produce a product or service together, usually involving an equity-sharing arrangement between a local partner and an MNE. Provides rapid entry into new markets and local knowledge, but is often associated with political problems between partners over the sharing of core technology and knowledge
	Fully owned subsidiaries	Can take the form of an overseas acquisition or merger, or a new business start-up. Acquisitions provide ready markets and local knowledge, but present major difficulties in merging cultures and creating new identities. New start-ups are most costly in terms of management time and highest risk, given levels of investment. However, they are often preferred as they minimise the cost of transferring knowledge to partners and sharing technologies.

their convergence–divergence assumptions. Should, for example, an internationalising firm invest in recruiting, developing, and rewarding managers in their own country so that they can be sent overseas to transfer their knowledge and practices to the local situation? Or should they rely on the 'insider' judgement of local managers and their knowledge and practices? If, as organizations are increasingly seeking to (or are required to) partner with local firms, should they enter a joint venture or a full-blown merger, and should they attempt to impose a homogeneous organizational culture by transferring home-based practices into the local firm?

Increasingly, however, international firms are being challenged by host countries to address a fifth question, which focuses on a need to act responsibly and ethically by adopting a stakeholder approach to their overseas operations (see Chapters 10 and 11). Often, this requires them to contribute to the development of local businesses and economies of the countries in which they locate through so-called 'local content' agreements. Moreover, they must comply with legislation on local labour, local cultural issues, and health and safety. Increasingly, international firms also seek to compete on the extent to which they implement socially responsible and socially sustainable policies and practices, which address the needs of local stakeholders by engaging in corporate citizenship activities and contributing to environmental improvements (Stahl et al., 2012).

NATIONAL DIFFERENCES IN THE BUSINESS ENVIRONMENT

Converging or diverging cultures?

To answer the questions posed in the previous sections, we need to understand not only how societies differ but also whether these differences are significant and growing, or are diminishing in importance. For instance, some people believe that societies are becoming alike, so understanding international differences and developing strategies to take these into account will be much less relevant soon. On this issue, informed opinion is divided over the extent and rate of convergence of national economies because of these changes. It splits between those who emphasise the forces for *convergence*, most notably the globalisation of business, and those who emphasise the forces for *divergence*, principally the existence of strong national institutions and institutional logics that constrain change (Cooke et al., 2017; Wilkinson et al., 2013). We shall examine this very important institutionalist perspective on why change is difficult later in this chapter.

Convergence and globalisation

The *convergence thesis* has become well-established in the international management literature (Kaufman, 2016; Pucik et al., 2023). It is based on evidence that organizations and their managers around the world embrace many of the same values, attitudes, and behaviours, and are increasingly likely to do so given the internationalisation of technology and markets. Convergence exists despite the influence of obvious historical differences in national culture and key institutions in these countries, such as the legal, political, and educational systems. A modified and more recent form of the convergence thesis is the *globalisation 'thesis'*, which has been used to herald the creation of worldwide markets and the growth of huge corporations with few roots in, or ties to, a specific country, some of them with revenues greater than many countries. According to some researchers (e.g., Kaufman, 2016), globalisation is an overworked concept because economic activity has always taken place across borders, and truly global companies, which are not tied to their home country in important ways, are limited in number. Others also point out the more negative connotations of globalisation as a form of neocolonialism and as a set of transformative social forces that lead to the exploitation of labour in the developing world (see Wilkinson et al., 2013) and major environmental problems such as global warming and depletion of natural resources. However, despite these arguments over the meaning of globalisation, most researchers broadly acknowledge the increased permeability of traditional boundaries of almost every kind, including those more tangible ones (time and space, nation-states and economies, industries, and organizations) and less tangible ones (cultural norms and assumptions of 'how we do things around here'). Thus, the proponents of this globalisation thesis propose that convergence among nations is occurring because of the globalisation of economies, techniques, and communications and that national mindsets and institutions are less important in understanding the nature and effects of international business and management. Perhaps more importantly, it is sometimes proposed by enthusiastic 'globalisers' – for example, the International Monetary Fund (IMF) – that in a global economy, national institutions and mindsets are an impediment to the modernisation and interests of business in a specific country (see Box 5.1). One good example was the insistence on the part of Greek creditors, especially the IMF, to reform the Greek economy from 2014 to 2015 by demanding pension reforms and the privatisation of businesses rather than increased taxes on the rich.

Box 5.1 Kultur clash

An *Economist* article in 2004 pointed out that Mannesmann, a leading German company, was taken to court in 2004 accused of breaches of German securities law, but not so serious to warrant any individual being convicted of a criminal breach of trust. This followed the Vodafone takeover in 2000 and the accusations against six senior managers of committing or abetting a breach of trust in awarding bonuses worth €57m to themselves.

The issue was portrayed in the German media as 'corporate greed' on trial and as a clash between two business cultures: the importation of Anglo-Saxon capitalism into the more socially oriented Rhineland variety. As an *Economist* article pointed out:

> Big German firms have traditionally been run by consensus: a German executive board has no real CEO, in the American sense. Each executive is directly answerable to the supervisory board, which contrasts with the autonomy enjoyed by the boards of American and British companies.

In German companies, however, it was unusual for a senior executive to be sacked, US style, by the supervisory board, though there have been some examples of this occurring. The article cited Ulrich Schumacher as one example, the American-influenced leader of Infineon, a semiconductor firm, when he was abruptly ousted by his supervisory board for his reputation for, among other things, lecturing his own executives 'like children.'

The norm in Germany was that some managers who may have been sacked under an Anglo-American regime would survive because they were adept at playing consensus politics with the supervisory boards, including Jurgen Schrempp, who was head of loss-making DaimlerChrysler. But, according to the article, if the Mannesmann trial led to more widespread adoption of Anglo-American management governance practices in Germany, it should also highlight the need to govern well, since 'the supervisory board of Mannesmann has been revealed as "Germanically" sloppy ... Adding American methods to traditional German business strengths may be a better strategy.'

There is evidence that just such a trend has begun to take root in German companies (Hilger, 2008). To fend off the US challenge, German companies began to adopt US-style management practices and, to an extent, corporate governance practices, as a way of catching up. So, is this a case of convergence around the American Business Model?

Sources: adapted from *The Economist*, 3 April 2004 and Hilger (2008).

One of the main engines for convergence and/or globalisation has been the role played by large, transnational corporations such as the Ford Motor Company, Toyota, and Volkswagen in the cross-border transfer of products, ideas, and processes to their subsidiaries, and indirectly to other organizations in those countries that copy them or are subject to their influence. For example, many multinational corporations seek to promote a corporate brand image and culture across all their subsidiaries. This practice sometimes extends to suppliers of those subsidiary companies and to local companies that imitate their 'winning formula' (see Chapter 6). This trend is being hastened by information and communications technologies (ICT), which allows new brands to become global at the touch of a keystroke (Steenkamp, 2020).

Few firms exemplify the globalisation thesis as much as McDonald's, the food retailing organization, which has had an enormous impact on eating habits and on business practices around the world. Until a change in strategy during the early 2000s, McDonald's, one of the world's most recognisable brands, was associated with promoting an American way of life around the globe and a one-best-way formula for fast-food retailing and for managing a franchise operation (see Case 5.2 for an example of changes at McDonald's).

In addition to MNEs, other important triggers, as we have pointed out, have been the growth in global management education and the growth of global consulting firms in the transfer of ideas and best practices (Khurana, 2007). Two decades ago, prominent UK HR researchers (Sparrow et al., 2004) suggested these triggering processes led to the development of a 'like-minded international cadre' of managers whose thinking has become 'de-nationalized' because of attendance at one of the 13,000 business schools in the world that broadly followed a similar syllabus and ethos of business in their MBA programmes or internal consultancy training. Since these authors reported on the effects of global management education in producing like-minded managers, convergence has probably become even more pronounced with the growing influence of 'triple' accreditation bodies for business schools, including the Association to Advance Collegiate Schools of Business (AACSB), the European Foundation for Management Development's EQUIS programme, and the Association of MBAs (Parker, 2018; Pettigrew et al., 2015; Zammuto, 2018).

Divergence, culture, and institutions

Although the convergence and globalisation theses have had many adherents, some writers believe that differences between national cultures and institutions have remained relatively marked and consistent over time (Pucik et al., 2023). These writers adhere to the *divergence thesis*, which is premised on two sets of observed and relatively enduring differences among societies. The first of these differences comprises the strength of locally held *cultural values* and their impact on management practices, despite obvious and growing economic and social similarities among nations (Hofstede et al., 2011). Such business-related cultural values typically include the extent to which national cultures endorse individualism and individual freedoms, the extent to which risk-taking behaviour by individuals is encouraged and rewarded, attitudes towards inequality and competitive behaviour, conceptions of time, and attitudes towards the open display of emotions (Trompenaars, 2012; Trompenaars & Hampden-Turner, 2004; Hofstede et al., 2011). We look at this cultural values approach in more detail in this chapter.

The second relates to the historically embedded *institutional differences* among countries (Morgan & Whitley, 2012; Whitley, 2007). These institutions refer to the social, political, economic, business, and labour market features of a country or region that have historically interacted to create a distinctive national business system. So, for example, we often talk about a distinctive American business system, Asian business systems, or the Chinese diaspora (Witt & Redding, 2014). This institutional difference argument is supported by recent events such as the Ukraine invasion by Russia, worries over food and energy security, trade wars, and the cooling of relations between the US with China which suggest globalisation may be in decline or a state of 'slobalisation', at least according to the World Economic Forum in 2023.

The *national business systems approach*, which has become more influential in the management literature since the 1990s, is a broader concept than culture and has emphasised the difficulties in borrowing and diffusing best practices from overseas countries created by enduring institutional differences (Morgan et al., 2010). Though competition among national business systems at the international level has led to borrowing and copying of practices, this process of diffusion does not necessarily result in convergence because the embedding of such practices must occur in pre-existing and nationally distinctive configurations of business practices. The consequences of this line of thinking for organizations seeking to export their values and practices are threefold: (1) they need to be aware of the historical and institutional configuration of the business system in which they seek to operate; (2) they are likely to meet with institutional resistance to such 'foreign' practices; (3) even if companies are initially successful in implanting their home-grown practices, they can never be sure how these transferred practices will interact with the existing systems to produce anything like the originally intended outcomes. Again, we shall examine these ideas in more detail later in this chapter.

To help you understand the role of institutional constraints, read the case of Walmart's entry into Germany in the late 1990s (see Case 5.1).

CASE 5.1 WALMART AND OVERSEAS EXPANSION

Traditionally, retailers are not very good at going abroad. Walmart is no exception. It has done well in America's border countries. It has been successful in Canada, for instance, and in Mexico, where Walmart is the biggest private employer. However, by 2020 it had put its UK subsidiary, ASDA – once a posterchild for overseas retail expansion – up for sale and had sold units in Japan. A *Forbes* article in 2020 headlined the question: 'Will Walmart Ever be Successful Overseas'?

In Germany, Walmart really ended up with egg on its face. Walmart entered Germany, the third biggest retail market after America and Japan, in 1997–98 by buying two local retail chains, Wertkauf and Interspar, for $1.6 billion. Whereas Wertkauf was well-known and profitable, Interspar was weak and operated mostly run-down stores. Walmart has lost money in Germany ever since. Problems have included price controls preventing below-cost selling, rigid labour laws, and tough zoning regulations that make it extremely difficult to build big stores.

Walmart also faced well-established rivals in Germany, such as Metro, and hard discounters such as Aldi and Lidl, already comfortable with razor-thin profit margins. Many retailers in Germany are owned by wealthy families, whose business priorities are not always consistent with maximising shareholder value.

But there was more to it than that. Walmart's entry was 'nothing short of a fiasco,' according to the authors of a 2003 study at the University of Bremen. At first, Walmart's expatriate managers suffered from a massive clash of cultures, which was not helped by their refusal to learn to speak German. The company has come to be seen as an unattractive one to work for, adds the study. In part, this is because of relatively low pay and an ultra-frugal policy on managers' business expenses.

Walmart eventually pulled out of Germany in 2006, with losses estimated by analysts at $200–300 billion per annum. The company has also had problems in Japan because of a failure to understand different consumer preferences and the preferred retail environment, and problems in gaining access to existing powerful supply chain networks. It has been claimed that Japanese consumers prefer to buy more frequently in smaller quantities and tend to equate high quality with high prices. Moreover, it persuaded Seiyu, its partner in Japan, to dismiss 25 per cent of headquarters staff and managers, which was a cataclysmic decision in a country known for lifetime employment practices. Similarly, Walmart had problems in South Korea because of a claimed failure to understand local consumer preferences for fresh food and for stores to be based in cities rather than the outskirts where Walmart sited most of its stores. Along with the French supermarket, Carrefours, it pulled out of South Korea in 2006.

This contrasts with Walmart's much smoother expansion into the UK, where it bought ASDA for $10.7 billion in 1999. ASDA already had a strong business competing on price, and it has since overtaken struggling J. Sainsbury to become the second biggest supermarket chain after Tesco. But that may say more about Sainsbury's difficulties in overcoming its problems than ASDA's successes. Unlike Tesco, Sainsbury was slow in responding to Walmart's expected arrival in the British market. It was late in expanding into non-food goods, the source of much of Tesco's growth.

1 What institutional features of the German system have prevented Walmart from making a successful entry into that country?

2 What could they have done to overcome these problems in Germany, and in Japan and South Korea?

3 Why do 'smart managers', such as those at Walmart, seem to do 'dumb things'?

More pragmatically minded writers have argued that the convergence–divergence debate isn't particularly helpful because it casts everything in terms of 'either/or' scenarios. Instead, they make a case for 'both/and' thinking in which nation-states, industries, and organizations deal with the tensions promoted by convergence and divergence in new, more appropriate ways. So, for example, nearly all MNEs seek to secure global economies of scale, promote consistent brand images, and have employees align with a single corporate identity and set of values. At the same time, they also seek to secure the benefits of differentiating their products and services in local markets and respecting local product and labour market circumstances by developing locally relevant practices. For these reasons, 'think global and act local' policies have been adopted by some MNEs, a process sometimes referred to as *'glocalisation'* (Martin & Hetrick, 2010) (see Case 5.2 on McDonald's in Europe).

Some researchers believe a glocalisation orientation is possible if organizations make a distinction between business *principles* and *practices* (Martin & Hetrick, 2010). Principles and values that many large MNEs espouse, such as respect for individuals and trustworthiness, tend to be more general and universal in application, but local context, contingencies, and firm-specific aspirations are likely to shape the practices that arise from such principles and value frameworks. In the remainder of this chapter, we shall elaborate on the problems of cultural differences, institutions, and business systems, and how managers should address these differences.

CASE 5.2 CHANGES AT MCDONALD'S: BACK TO THE FUTURE

McDonald's set out a new strategy in 2015 to reverse years of underwhelming results and customer loss. In an *Economist* article published in 2004, McDonald's appeared to be performing well in the USA; however, its European operations were not so good, except in the most unlikely country to adopt American ways – France. The article attributed the French performance to its French CEO, Denis Hennequin, who ran McDonald's in France and had been made head of McDonald's European operations.

Given the French love of *haute cuisine*, 'le fast food' was not expected to take off. Yet, the article claimed that 'France is the only place in Europe that has consistently loved McDonald's since the first outlet opened there in 1979.' Contrary to the popular image of the French distaste of everything American, particularly its pop culture, French families and children seemed to love McDonald's: so much so that it outperformed all its indigenous fast-food rivals and is the most profitable European subsidiary.

The answer, according to the article, lay in Hennequin's strategy for France as 'upgrading and transparency.' Put simply, restaurant décor was improved, the menu was widened and enhanced with better quality products, and relations with the difficult French unions over low pay – an often-made criticism of McDonald's – became relatively cordial.

The article also claimed that McDonald's was clever in adapting food and décor to local tastes and concentrating on children. The ham-and-cheese 'Croque McDo' was invented as McDonald's version of a *croque monsieur*, a French favourite. McDonald's teamed up with French companies to offer local fare – for instance, fruit yoghurts produced by Danone, coffee from Carte Noire, and the French soft drink Orangina. McDonald's in France also sourced most of its raw material from local farmers and has used this fact to enhance its reputation as a socially responsible company – at least in French eyes.

Hennequin's aimed to use the McDonald's France formula in the rest of Europe, where sales had dwindled. His innovations included a 'food studio' and a 'design studio' near Paris to research and innovate new products and interior designs for Europe's restaurants, under the supervision of a top French Michelin-star chef. One of the newest innovations was 'Salads Plus' to provide several healthier options to the often-criticised traditional McDonald's fare of burgers and fries. These were previously tried out in America to stave off litigation over its contribution to American levels of obesity. McDonald's calls the new salad menu 'a strategic change in the positioning of its menu in Europe.'

In 2015, a *Time* magazine article reported that McDonald's has experienced five years of underwhelming results and an exodus of customers due to increased competition and a 'menu that had grown bloated.' In 2023, the BBC in the UK reported that McDonald's managers in some of its UK franchises were guilty of harassment, racism, and bullying. The company has admitted that it had 'fallen short' in standards and has deeply apologised. Is this a case of the more things change, the more they remain the same?

> *Sources*: adapted from 'Burger and fries a la Francaise', *The Economist*, 17 April 2004, and How McDonalds plans to make a turnaround, Time Magazine, May 4th, 2015, BBC News (July 2023) McDonald's told to shut franchises over abuse claims, https://www.bbc.co.uk/news/business-66231131.

NATIONAL CULTURAL VALUES

Understanding national cultural values

We have already introduced the importance of national cultural values as a key factor in explaining the relatively enduring differences among countries and their approach to business and management. This 'cultural' school – which began with the work of Hofstede in the 1960s (Hofstede et al., 2011), continued with Trompenaars (2012), extended by the so-called 'Globe' studies of leadership and organizational effectiveness (House et al., 2014; Globe Project, 2020) – has resulted in many cross-cultural studies. These studies usually compare values and practices in a range of countries to shed light on the difficulties organizations may face in doing business outside their own territory, or to provide advice for managers on how to behave with 'foreigners'. The cultural values approach has been extremely influential in the management literature, but it is not without its critics, some of whom believe the 'national cultural card' was overplayed (Baskerville-Morley, 2005). In this section, we shall review the work of two of its most influential theorists and point out its limitations. First, however, we should describe what culture means in an international context.

Generally, in the management literature at least, national culture refers to systems of meanings, values, beliefs, expectations, and goals, shared by a particular group of people and distinguishing them from members of other groups. Ed Schein, one of the founding fathers of cultural studies in management, defined culture as:

> a set of basic assumptions – shared solutions to the universal problems of external adaptation (how to survive) and internal integration (how to stay together) – which have evolved over time and are handed down from one culture to another.
> *(Schein, 1985)*

This definition is appealing for two reasons. First, it links (a) the external but universal problem that all organizations face in searching for effective strategies and ways of addressing markets and customers with (b) the internal and often unique solutions for designing effective organizations and appropriate people management practices. Second, it points to the internalised ways in which people behave and in what they believe and value. Schein usefully distinguished between different levels of culture in an organizational setting (see Figure 5.1). These distinctions can also be applied to the international context, and indicate how we might discover these behaviours, values, and beliefs and the basic assumptions that underlie them.

Thus, translating Figure 5.1 into a national setting, the most visible levels of cultural artefacts might be exemplified by traditional modes of greeting each other, forms of address and title, dress codes, national symbols such as flags and buildings, and so on. For example, many emerging economies in the Global South seek to create buildings of national significance to reflect their aspirations to be a modern economy. The Petronas Towers in Malaysia in 1998, the Clock Building in Saudi Arabia in 2011, and Burj Khalifa in Dubai in 2012 are good illustrations. Older countries also use architecture to signify something distinctive about their national identity, such as the new Scottish Parliament Building in Edinburgh, Scotland, the Guggenheim Museum in Bilbao, Spain, and the Pompidou Centre in Paris, France. In greeting each other, Japanese businesspeople bow to show respect; the lower one bows the more respect one is thought to be showing, usually to seniors. Titles are used quite differently in different cultures, with Germans usually insisting on the use of titles such as professor and doctor in social as well as work situations, whereas in the USA the title 'doctor' may be dropped because it has elitist connotations. In the UK, doctor, used in a non-medical context, may even have negative connotations, reflecting the historically low value placed on higher education beyond first degree level (though these attitudes might be changing, especially in relation to business education). Office architecture is another good example of artefacts that reflect values, so, in Germany, one is likely to find enclosed offices with official titles on

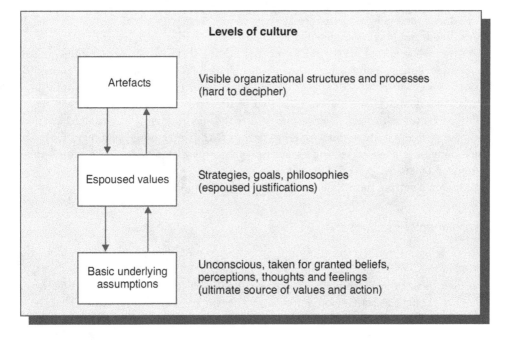

FIGURE 5.1 Different levels of culture

(*Source:* adapted from Schein, 1985)

the doors, whereas in the USA, open plan is quite normal (though people do attempt to personalise these spaces) (Hatch, 2018).

Espoused values and beliefs in a national setting refer to the goals, norms of behaviour, and everyday philosophies that guide actions in a particular country – for example, in relation to making money, displaying wealth, and promoting entrepreneurship in a society. As an illustration, it is widely accepted that national cultures vary in their beliefs and values about the criteria for success. Although somewhat stereotypical, the USA is well known for its business culture that promotes the 'divine rights' of shareholders, risk-taking behaviour, materialism, and open displays of wealth. In other countries such beliefs and values would be often considered an anathema, with the Japanese valuing customer service, market share, and obligations to colleagues, Swedes valuing the rights to be consulted, a rejection of the 'tall poppy' syndrome, job security, and social benefits, and the Germans (and Swedes) valuing product quality. German managers in the manufacturing industry will often place the high-quality design and reliability of their products over shareholder interests or customer satisfaction; engineering, producing, and selling are functions valued much more highly than marketing or finance. In France, the beliefs and values in technological leadership are paramount, with a high premium placed on engineering and science degrees, in sharp contrast to the UK, where the engineering professions have traditionally enjoyed lower status than doctors and lawyers. These international esteem indicators also extend to professions such as teaching, with enormous variation in teacher status indices between China and Malaysia that place high value on school teaching at one extreme compared with Brazil, Italy, and Israel, which appear not to value school teaching as a profession. Such differences in esteem seem to be related to the PISA scores by country of children's success in mathematics, science, and reading, with China ranking high while Brazil, Israel, and Italy ranking low in PISA outcomes (Varley Foundation, 2018).

At the deepest level, basic underlying assumptions refer to the unconscious, taken-for-granted beliefs, perceptions, thoughts, and feelings that shape values and guide actions. Schneider et al. (2014) have organized this idea of basic assumptions into three overlapping domains (see Figure 5.2). Two of these we have already discussed – how different cultures manage relationships with the environment (external adaptation) and how different cultures manage relationships with people (internal integration). The third domain is a set of linking assumptions on how different societies regard time, space, and language.

It is worth setting these assumptions out in a little more detail.

Environmental assumptions

Societies differ according to beliefs in their ability to *control nature*. So, for example, the notion of management implies control over nature, even though some economists argue that managers and management can exercise little such control (since, according to one school of thought at least – popular ecology – it is markets and competition that shape economic activity rather than managers). However, most Americans believe in the ability of managers to shape their destiny, so leadership has become a major preoccupation in US business teaching and practice over the last four or more decades. In contrast, fate or destiny is seen by Islamic cultures to be predetermined, so assumptions regarding

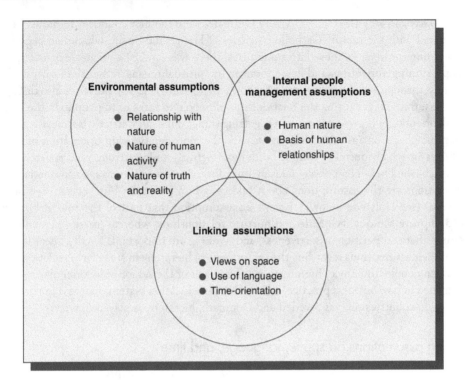

FIGURE 5.2 Underlying cultural assumptions
(*Source:* based on Schneider et al., 2014)

the power of leadership to shape the future, especially leadership of a secular kind, are limited. Linked to this belief in fate are beliefs in the power of *human activity*. So, for example, beliefs in control over the environment go hand in hand with acting and making decisions – to act one's way into thinking as Karl Weick (2001) insightfully put it.

It is also linked to the idea that achievement is a result of what a manager accomplishes. Contrast this 'American Dream' with societies that believe more in predetermined destiny. Arguably, this is the characteristic of French managers, who value reflection, analytical thinking, and planning – 'thinking their way into action' – and in 'being', which reflects the quality of their education and who they are rather than what they do. Finally, societies differ according to their assumptions about *truth and reality*. Anglo-Saxon cultures place emphasis on facts and science, whereas Asian, Latin European, and Latin American cultures are more likely to assume that truth(s) can be uncovered by intuition, feelings, and spiritual means – for example, by astrology, graphology, or fortune-telling in Brazil, France, and China, respectively (Schneider et al., 2014).

Internal people management assumptions

Societies differ according to their views of *human nature*, with some believing in the virtuous side of people (mainly those of a Protestant persuasion) and their ability to do 'God's work' on Earth by achieving material wealth through hard work. This argument has been used to explain why the UK, USA, and Germany were the first countries to industrialise compared with the mainly Catholic countries of France and Spain, which had been historical superpowers. In these latter countries, there was (and is) a greater expectation of people sinning, repenting, and being forgiven by spiritual means, rather than earning forgiveness through secular hard work (Anthony, 1977; Weber, 1930). Societies also differ in their assumptions regarding the relationships of people to tasks or to people. In the USA, a task orientation is pre-eminent, with 'getting things done' and 'strictly business' as guiding principles. Contrast this orientation with the more relationship orientation of Latin cultures in which business cannot be done effectively unless strong personal relations are established between people! Closely linked to these ideas about task and relationship orientations are the assumptions about taking care of people in business. In 'feminine' societies (see Hofstede below), there is an assumption that part of the role of business is to improve the quality of life and nurture relationships, whereas 'masculine' cultures assume that competition, assertiveness, and winning are important. Finally, societies differ in their assumptions regarding the importance of hierarchy in structuring relationships between people. In France, hierarchy and the power of the senior individual manager are enshrined in law, business practice, and the higher education system; whereas in northern European countries such as Sweden and Denmark, hierarchy is played down.

Linking assumptions on space, language, and time

Societies differ in their assumptions about *space*, which are expressed in the areas of architecture, personal space, and public–private space. For example, North Americans, probably because space is plentiful and available, place a great deal of emphasis on privacy and on geographic and professional mobility. In Japan and some other Asian countries where space is limited, assumptions regarding privacy and mobility are different, evidence, for example, by most people living in relatively small dwellings compared with North Americans.

Language is another, and critically important, linking assumption, because it helps us shape our thoughts as well as express them. So, for example, it is often claimed that Innuits who live in snowy climates have many different words to express snow, which help them 'see' different kinds of snow and convey their meanings to others. In 'high-context' cultures, communications between people are highly dependent on the person and the situation, so a great deal can be communicated by what is not said and how it is said, such as in Japan. In 'low-context' cultures, the assumption is that language and communication are means of expressing precisely what is meant, regardless of who is doing the saying and the nature of the situation. Such is the case in the USA, where short, to-the-point, written and oral communications are the norm. It is in such a society that PowerPoint slides have become the basis of classroom presentations, the bullet-point nature of which tends to exasperate and bore managers in the UK and continental Europe ('death by PowerPoint').

Finally, different cultures have quite different conceptions of time. The usual distinction is made between *monochronic and polychronic conceptions of time*. In Anglo-Saxon and northern European cultures, time is seen as a limited commodity and the clock as a crucial device in educating people about the value of time. Arguably, Anglo-Saxon capitalism could never have developed without the invention of the clock and synchronous time (Anthony, 1977). Time tends to be thought of as a linear sequence, with strict scheduling, clocking-in, and time management features of such societies, most notably Anglo-Saxon countries. Being 'on time' is an extremely important signifier of efficiency and in your respect of other people's limited time – the more important the person you are to meet, the more likely you are to be 'on time'. This contrasts with cultures in which time is seen as expandable to accommodate different activities concurrently. For example, in Latin and Middle Eastern cultures, engaging in several activities at the same time, without bothering too much about punctuality, would be the normal way of working, as I discovered when working in countries such as Cyprus, Greece, Malaysia, and Saudi Arabia. Assumptions also vary in relation to the importance of past, present, and future time, with older cultures such as the UK revering their past and traditions, whereas Americans are more inclined to look to the future (Schneider et al., 2014).

Box 5.2 Cultural assumptions and education

One good example of a basic national assumption over which societies differ is the belief in education as a way of advancement. In Chinese societies, learning and education are held in high regard, both as an end in themselves and as ways of advancement (see the Varley Foundation report on international attitudes to teachers and school education, 2018). Consequently, Chinese families are willing to sacrifice a lot for the education of their children, and educationalists, especially top-level university scholars, are held in great esteem. By contrast, education in England (as distinct from Scotland), at least historically, was not believed to be of such great value in defining who a person was and, consequently, as a way of advancing themselves in society (Weiner, 2004). This rather negative view of education as a way of getting on applied most notably to vocational education, such as engineering and, more recently, business studies (which began in earnest only in the 1960s in the UK compared with the late 1880s in the USA). Thus, vocationally based higher education in English universities and the academics who work in vocational subjects have not been held in high regard by the academic community or by the public in rankings of social esteem. It is these underlying assumptions that are the most pervasive aspects of national cultures. Nevertheless, they are the most difficult to surface and most resistant to change. Such is the legacy of the 'English disease' and its assumptions and attitudes to vocational education that nearly all governments since the 1960s have been forced to bring in never-ending programmes to generate interest in vocational subjects and vocational careers in areas such as engineering or, more recently, entrepreneurial activity.

Classifying national cultures according to fundamental dimensions such as values and beliefs has been of great importance to practitioners if only to explain the notion of cultural distance. This concept is self-explanatory and refers to the distance between one national culture and another in terms of values, beliefs, and deep-rooted assumptions. Thus, for example, the UK and the USA share elements of a common history, certain religious beliefs, language, and a legal system, so it should come as no surprise that the dimensions on which these countries are deemed to differ reveal very little cultural distance. The writers most associated with explaining national cultures according to key dimensions are the Dutchman Geert Hofstede (who died in 2020) and the Anglo-Dutch cooperation between Fons Trompenaars and Charles Hampden-Turner.

Hofstede and cultural values

Geert Hofstede began his work in 1967 on a large research project into national culture differences across subsidiaries of IBM, the computing MNE, in 64 countries. According to Hofstede, this original work and the follow-up studies by him and his colleagues identified and validated six independent dimensions of national culture differences (see Box 5.3).

Box 5.3 Hofstede's cultural values

Power distance

High- and low-power distance refers to the extent to which the less powerful members of organizations and institutions such as the family accept and expect that power is distributed unequally. This bottom-up view suggests that a society's level of inequality is endorsed by the followers as much as by the leaders. Power and inequality, according to Hofstede, are fundamental facts of any society, and the experience of living in different societies will lead anyone to the conclusion that all societies are unequal, but some are more unequal than others.

Individualism

This dimension is defined in contrast to *collectivism* and refers to the degree to which individuals are integrated into groups. In individualist societies, the ties between individuals are loose: individuals are expected to look after themselves and their immediate family. In collectivist societies, people from birth onwards are integrated into strong, cohesive groups, more often than not in extended families, which provide protection and a level of identity in exchange for unquestioning loyalty. Notions of the American and Sicilian Mafia come to mind here. It should be noted that Hofstede did not intend the notion of collectivism to have a political meaning, such as occurred in the old USSR. It refers to the group, not to an official state ideology.

Masculinity and femininity

Hofstede attracted much criticism for his use of terms here, especially from writers concerned with gender studies. However, he claims that he has been misunderstood or misinterpreted. His argument was that different societies distribute roles between the genders in different ways. His IBM studies revealed that: (a) women's values differ less among societies than men's values and (b) men's values from one country to another contain a dimension from very assertive and competitive (and very different from women's values in a country) to modest and caring (and like women's values in that country). The assertive pole he called 'masculine' and the modest, caring pole 'feminine'. The women in feminine countries he described as having the same modest, caring values as the men; in the masculine countries, they are somewhat assertive and competitive, but not as much as the men, so that these countries show a gap between men's values and women's values.

Uncertainty avoidance

This refers to a society's tolerance for uncertainty and ambiguity and how it deals with these issues. According to Hofstede, it refers ultimately to a society's search for and belief in a universal truth and indicates the extent to which a country's culture mentally programmes its members to feel comfortable in unstructured situations. Unstructured situations refer to new and perhaps surprising ones, different from those usually experienced. Uncertainty-avoiding cultures try to minimise the possibility of such situations by imposing laws and rules, safety and security measures, and at the philosophical and religious level by a belief in absolute truth. People in uncertainty-avoiding countries also tend to show more emotions in everyday interactions. By contrast, uncertainty-accepting cultures tend to be more tolerant of different opinions and new ideas, have fewer rules, and value rule-makers less, and on the philosophical and religious level, they are more relativist in their views (see Chapter 1). People within these cultures are more matter-of-fact and tend not to express emotions openly.

Long-term versus short-term orientation

This fifth dimension was brought to public notice by one of Hofstede's colleagues, Michael Bond, in a study among students in 23 countries around the world, using a questionnaire designed by Chinese scholars. Values associated with long-term orientation are thrift and perseverance; values associated with short-term orientation are respect for tradition, fulfilling social obligations, and protecting one's 'face'. Both the positively and the negatively rated values of this dimension are found in the teachings of Confucius, the influential Chinese philosopher who lived around 2500 years ago. However, the dimension also applies to countries without a Confucian heritage.

Indulgence versus self-restraint

Influenced by Michael Monkov's work, Hofstede introduced this sixth dimension, which refers to how some societies grant significant freedom to individuals to fulfil their desires and 'to have fun.' Examples often given are Latin America, some parts of Africa, the Anglo-Saxon, and Nordic countries. Other societies are more inclined to control instant gratification through strict norms of behaviour, typically East Asia and Eastern Europe.

According to his extensive research and further replication studies by other people, countries differ significantly along these dimensions, the ranking of which can be seen in Table 5.2.

TABLE 5.2 Country rankings according to Hofstede's values (N.B. the indulgence dimension is excluded because of a lack of comparable data)

Country	Power distance	Individualism	Uncertainty avoidance	Masculinity	Long-term orientation
Arab countries	80	38	68	53	
Argentina	49	46	86	56	
Australia	36	90	51	61	31
Austria	11	55	70	79	
Belgium	65	75	94	54	
Brazil	69	38	76	49	65
Canada	39	80	48	52	23
Chile	63	23	86	28	
China, mainland	No data available				118
Colombia	67	13	80	64	
Costa Rica	35	15	86	21	
Denmark	18	74	23	16	
East Africa	64	27	52	41	
Ecuador	78	8	67	63	
Finland	33	63	59	26	
France	68	71	86	43	
Germany FR	35	67	65	66	31
Great Britain	35	89	35	66	25
Greece	60	35	112	57	
Guatemala	95	6	101	37	
Hong Kong	68	25	29	57	96
India	77	48	40	56	61
Indonesia	78	14	48	46	
Iran	58	41	59	43	
Ireland	28	70	35	68	
Israel	13	54	81	47	
Italy	50	76	75	70	
Jamaica	45	39	13	68	
Japan	54	46	92	95	80
Malaysia	104	26	36	50	
Mexico	81	30	82	69	

(Continued)

TABLE 5.2 (Continued)

Country	Power distance	Individualism	Uncertainty avoidance	Masculinity	Long-term orientation
Netherlands	38	80	53	14	44
New Zealand	22	79	49	58	30
Norway	31	69	50	8	
Pakistan	55	14	70	50	
Panama	95	11	86	44	
Peru	64	16	87	42	
Philippines	94	32	44	64	19
Poland	No data available				32
Portugal	63	27	104	31	
Salvador	66	19	94	40	
Singapore	74	20	8	48	48
South Africa	49	65	49	63	
South Korea	60	18	85	39	75
Spain	57	51	86	42	
Sweden	31	71	29	5	33
Switzerland	34	68	58	70	
Taiwan	58	17	69	45	87
Thailand	64	20	64	34	56
Turkey	66	37	85	45	
Uruguay	61	36	100	38	
USA	40	91	46	62	29
Venezuela	81	12	76	73	
West Africa	77	20	54	46	16
Yugoslavia (former)	76	27	88	21	

Hofstede found that power distance scores tend to be high for Latin, Asian, and African countries and smaller for Germanic countries. Individualism prevails in developed and Western countries, whereas collectivism prevails in less developed and Eastern countries. Japan takes a middle position on this dimension. Masculinity is high in Japan and in some European countries such as Germany, Austria, and Switzerland, and moderately high in Anglo countries. It is low in Nordic countries and the Netherlands and moderately low in some Latin and Asian countries such as France, Spain, and Thailand. Uncertainty avoidance scores are higher in Latin countries, in Japan, and German-speaking countries, but lower in Anglo, Nordic, and countries with a dominant Chinese

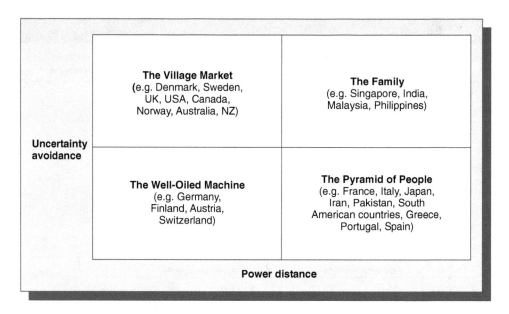

FIGURE 5.3 Hofstede's mapping of uncertainty avoidance and power distance

culture. A long-term orientation is found mostly in East Asian countries, especially in China, Hong Kong, Taiwan, Japan, and South Korea.

These rankings allowed Hofstede to map countries on two dimensions at a time to create typologies of cultural systems or maps. Perhaps the best known is his mapping of uncertainty avoidance and power distance, which was particularly relevant in explaining the relationship between national culture and organizational structures (see Figure 5.3). Countries high on both power distance and uncertainty avoidance, such as France and most South American countries, tended to favour bureaucratic or mechanistic organizational structures. This grouping was labelled the *pyramid of people*. Countries that were the opposite – low on both dimensions, such as Denmark and Sweden, and, to a lesser extent, the UK and the USA – tended to favour more flexible, decentralised, organic organizations that were less bound by rules and procedures. This grouping was called the *village market*. Countries high on uncertainty avoidance but low on power distance were called the *well-oiled machine*. These were located mainly in the Germanic region and were high on routines but low on the need for centralised leadership. Finally, those countries high on power distance and low on uncertainty avoidance tended to be in South-East Asia and exhibited the *family-like* tendencies of Chinese cultures. Organizations in these countries operate on centralised personal leadership rather than on routines and rules.

More recent research of a similar type has confirmed many of Hofstede's findings (Schneider et al., 2014). This research described variations in 'implicit' organizational models found in different cultures that closely resembled the pyramid of people in France and the well-oiled machine in Germany. The UK organizations researched in the study were found to reflect the more flexible village market, with British managers more willing to fit organizations to people, rather than the other way around. Similarly, studies in Asia have confirmed the family model in the Indian, Singaporean, and Hong Kong banking systems.

Trompenaars and Hampden-Turner and cultural values

Trompenaars and Hampden-Turner's (2004) work can be compared with Hofstede's approach in that both used bipolar dimensions to classify cultures. However, Trompenaars and Hampden-Turner began from a different position in drawing on ideas from sociology rather than empirical studies. Subsequently, they tested their ideas on cultural dimensions with 30,000 managers in companies across 28 countries. They have identified seven value orientations. Some of these value orientations described below are nearly identical to Hofstede's dimensions, whereas others offer different insights into culture.

- *Universalism versus particularism.* In universalist cultures, there is an emphasis on formal rules and contracts regardless of circumstances. Universalist countries take contracts very seriously and employ lawyers to make sure that the contract is kept. A good example is the USA, with probably the highest rates of lawyers per capita. Particularistic countries think that the relationship is more important than the contract and that a good agreement does not require a written contract; the relationship and trust between some people and the situation are more important than universal rules. Particularistic countries include Russia, China, and India.
- *Communitarianism versus individualism.* Very similar to Hofstede's individualist/collectivist dimension, in communitarian cultures, people stress allegiances to groups first and foremost, whereas, in individualist cultures, people stress individual freedoms, rights, and effort. Alongside Israel and Denmark, the USA is regarded as an individualist culture, with China and Germany seen as communitarian cultures.
- *Neutral versus emotional.* This value dimension refers to the extent to which emotional behaviour is used freely and openly in a business situation. In a neutral culture, emotions would not be seen as acceptable in interpersonal relations. Most South American and Latin European countries would be regarded as emotional, whereas China, Japan, and India would be regarded as neutral.
- *Diffuse versus specific.* A specific culture can be regarded as one in which a strong separation is made between work and private life so that the authority relationship that exists in a work situation is not carried over into wider social life. A manager is only a manager at work and not in the social community in which he or she lives. In diffuse cultures, authority relationships carry over into the wider social situation, where formal relationships are maintained. The USA would be regarded as a specific culture, whereas China, Russia, and Japan might be regarded as diffuse cultures.
- *Achievement versus ascription.* This value refers to the basis on which societies accord status to individuals. An achievement orientation is based on performance at work and through education, with the USA, UK, and Denmark scoring highly on achievement. An ascription orientation allocates status based on factors such as age (China), kinship (India), and gender (Japan). Other status factors also come into play, including the kind of school attended by children – private versus state (the UK).

Trompenaars and Hampden-Turner also refer to the two key dimensions of time and human nature, which we discussed in the earlier section on understanding cultures.

Of these seven value dimensions, two closely mirror the Hofstede dimensions of collectivism/individualism and, to a lesser extent, power distance. Trompenaars and Hampden-Turner's communitarianism/ individualism value orientation seems to be virtually identical to Hofstede's collectivism/individualism. Their achievement/ ascription value orientation, which describes how status is allocated in society, reflects Hofstede's power distance index, at least if one accepts that status is accorded by nature rather than achievement, and that this reflects a greater willingness to accept power distances. It is, however, not a complete match, as Hofstede's power index relates not only to how status is accorded but also to the acceptable power distance within a society. Trompenaars and Hampden-Turner's other dimensions seem to focus more on some resulting effects of underlying value dimensions. For example, their neutral/emotional dimension describes the extent to which feelings are openly expressed, i.e., a behavioural aspect rather than a value. Their universalism/particularism value orientation, describing a preference for rules rather than trusting relationships, could be interpreted as part of Hofstede's uncertainty avoidance dimension on the one side, and to some extent, the collectivist/individualist dimension. However, their diffuse/specific value orientation, describing the range of involvement, seems to have no direct link to any of Hofstede's dimensions.

The GLOBE studies

The GLOBE studies (2004), initiated by Robert House and subsequently extended into the international collaboration Globe2020, were an extension of Hofstede's work in showing how national cultures were both different and like each other. Built on an enormous body of research, this project identified nine dimensions of cultural similarity and differences in norms, values, and beliefs. These were:

1. Power distance – The degree to which members of a collective expect power to be distributed equally.
2. Uncertainty avoidance – The extent to which a society, organization, or group relies on social norms, rules, and procedures to alleviate the unpredictability of future events.
3. Humane orientation – The degree to which a collective encourages and rewards individuals for being fair, altruistic, generous, caring, and kind to others.
4. Institutional collectivism – The degree to which organizational and societal institutional practices encourage and reward collective distribution of resources and collective action.
5. In-group collectivism – The degree to which individuals express pride, loyalty, and cohesiveness in their organizations or families.
6. Assertiveness – The degree to which individuals are assertive, confrontational, and aggressive in their relationships with others.
7. Gender egalitarianism – The degree to which a collective minimises gender inequality.

8. Future orientation – The extent to which individuals engage in future-oriented behaviours such as delaying gratification, planning, and investing in the future.

9. Performance orientation – The degree to which a collective encourages and rewards group members for performance improvement and excellence.

Based on these dimensions, the many researchers associated with this project have been able to cluster cultures, most importantly to provide the basis for showing similarities and differences in outstanding leaders. These clusters were Germanic Europe, Anglo-American, Nordic Europe, Latin America, Confucian Asian, Middle East, Eastern Europe, Latin Europe, and Sub-Saharan Africa, which closely resemble a geographic description. The GLOBE researchers further identified how individuals in these clusters held implicit theories of leadership, showing how leadership is contextually embedded, eventually reducing the myriad of styles to six. A charismatic/value-based style and a team-oriented style appeared to be common to nearly all cultures, while participative, humane, self-protective (procedural, status-conscious) and autonomous (individualistic) styles varied in importance in the various cultural clusters identified above. So, for example, English-speaking Canadians viewed a participative style as very important in contributing to outstanding leadership, with a self-protective style inhibiting outstanding leadership, whereas Albanians and Egyptians tended to view self-protection as important in effective leaders. These studies have claimed to be the most rigorously researched and still attract a lot of attention in cross-cultural studies, but like all such studies, they have their critics.

PROBLEMS WITH THE CULTURAL VALUES APPROACH

Hofstede's work has been subject to several criticisms, which he acknowledged in his recent writings before he died. Five of the most important are discussed below (Baskerville-Morley, 2005; Jackson, 2020), some of which can also be levelled at Trompenaars and the GLOBE studies, though perhaps with less justification.

- Hofstede generalised the culture of national populations based on a small number of questionnaire responses from one organization, IBM, in particular countries. Small-sample research is prone to error. In addition, attempting to describe national variables while undertaking research at the level of the firm is a dangerous strategy. The corporate culture of the firm is always likely to influence respondents' answers.
- Nation-states are a relatively recent and often changing phenomenon, and sometimes don't have a national culture as such. A good example is the former state of Yugoslavia, which brought together six countries in 1918 but ended with a bitter inter-ethnic conflict and war in the late 1980s. Similarly, the break-up of the Soviet Union and arguably the conflict between Russia and Ukraine show that cultural differences within nation-states are often as great as differences between them!
- Hofstede didn't acknowledge the variation in cultures within countries that, as noted earlier, can often be greater than the variation between countries.

- Questionnaires are not a good means of identifying deep-rooted concepts such as culture. Many academics claim that survey methods only tap the surface of culture, which can only be fully understood by more in-depth qualitative research, or by ethnographic research using the methods of anthropologists.
- Hofstede claimed that culture was largely immutable, which goes against the evidence provided by convergence theorists.

These criticisms have sparked off a greater interest in qualitative and historical approaches to understanding national differences, including interest by Hofstede himself before his death. We can now turn to this focus on institutions, history, and business systems.

INSTITUTIONS, HISTORY, AND BUSINESS SYSTEMS

A definition of business systems

Sociologists and institutional theorists often refer to institutions in their analysis of societies, by which they typically mean the key 'pillars' of society such as the family, religion, education, the mass media, business and financial institutions, labour movements, and the state and its agencies. Recently, the concept of institutional logics has become a widely used framework for analysing how societal institutions guide human cognition, culture, identity, and actions (Thornton et al., 2012; Thornton, 2015). Such logics (or institutional orders) include the nature of state, corporations, religion, markets, the family, and the professions in different societies. These key institutional logics both shape and are shaped by national cultural beliefs, assumptions, and values. We have already seen this process at work when describing how the cultural values concerning education in different countries have been related to business success. In addition to the national institutional framework, we also must consider the role of supranational institutions, which include bodies such as the European Union (EU), the World Trade Organization (WTO), and the North American Free Trade Association (NAFTA). Thus, it is possible to make an analytical distinction, at least, between the more abstract notion of national culture, with its emphasis on values, assumptions, and beliefs, and the more concrete notion of institutions that refer to specific organizational forms and structures of behaviour that often define a society, such as its education systems or religious institutions.

In the business literature, institutional analysis has been used to describe the variety of national or regional models that provide alternative and often competing modes of operating in the global economy (Gooderham et al., 2019). We touched on this concept in Chapter 1 when examining the sources of ideas on management. As we have suggested, competition between national systems has led to much borrowing and diffusion of practices, but these cross-border developments have not resulted in the wholesale convergence predicted by the globalisation thesis. Institutionalists accept that national systems are increasingly interlinked and interdependent and that we are witnessing greater mutual influence among such systems, but they also point out that the picture is of a more complex pattern of simultaneous *convergence* and *divergence* in any system (Whitley, 2007). A little like the GLOBE researchers, these institutionalist writers have introduced the concept of national (or regional) *business systems* to describe these complex patterns, now an accepted way of comparing business and management issues in countries and regions of the world (Gooderham et al., 2019; Prince et al., 2022). We can get a better idea of what a business system might comprise by examining the following definition.

Key definition: A national business system

National business systems comprise the formal interlocking institutions, structures, patterns of behaviour, and norms and values that shape the markets, nature of competition, and general business activity of a country (or region) in capitalist economies. These institutions include the following: the industrial relations system; the systems of training and education of employees and managers; the typical structure of organizations; the typical relationships among firms in the same industry; typical firms' relationships with their suppliers and customers; the nature of financial markets of a society; the conceptions of fairness and justice held by employers and labour; the structure of the state and its policies for business; and a society's idiosyncratic customs and traditions, as well as norms, moral principles, rules, laws, and recipes for action.

Four elements are used to distinguish between national business systems: (1) the nature of property ownership (e.g., private, collective, or state); (2) access to capital (e.g., state, capital markets, banks); (3) the degree of integration of production and product markets into local, national, or international systems; and (4) relations between the state and the economy, for example, close relations in the case of France compared with distant relations, such as in the UK.

Sources: based on Hollingsworth & Boyer, 1997, p. 2; Gooderham et al., 2019; Martin, et al., 2011, p. 24; Whitley, 2007

As you can see, this definition refers to the cultural features of society, such as assumptions about fairness and justice, norms, moral principles, and recipes for action, but it also highlights the specific organizational forms, relationships, and systems that both reflect and give rise to these cultural features of a national or regional business system. Thus, for example, developing countries in the so-called 'Global South' such as Senegal and Cambodia have been studied to examine their readiness for the adoption of AI (Heng et al., 2022). While common challenges were found, such as persistent educational and digital illiteracy and a lack of a suitable data quality infrastructure, marked institutional differences suggested that Senegal was more likely to be ready for AI than Cambodia. These differences included the positive role of Pan-African organizations promoting a digital transformation agenda, while the role of regional organizations such as ASEAN in Cambodia constrained access to funding.

Like several authors, we believe that this wider conception of business systems and how they develop provides additional insights for practitioners, making the approach indispensable to gaining a deep understanding of how to manage in specific countries.

There are at least five characteristics of a business system approach that are worth highlighting:

1. The importance of a historical perspective.
2. The systemic and enduring nature of business systems.
3. The role of critical turning points in changing systems.
4. The basis for comparing business systems.
5. The interaction of national systems with regions and industry systems.

The importance of a historical perspective

The first of these insights is the emphasis on the *historical development of business systems*, an area that psychologists interested in international comparisons and cultures have either neglected or played down. To those of us who have lived and worked in different countries, this neglect of history may seem strange, as people in everyday situations are often proud of their history when describing their countries' distinguishing achievements and they make sense of their present by reference to the past. For example, ask the Scots, Israelis, or Greeks, all inhabitants of small countries with a previous tradition of educational excellence and a belief in the values of education as a way of getting on in life, what they have done for the modern world and they will point out a long list of mainly historical inventions, ideas, and people that they have 'gifted' to the 'New World'. Thus, 31 US presidents have claimed Scottish descent, as well as inventors of the telephone (Alexander Graham Bell), the steam engine (James Watt), the television (John Logie Baird), and the sciences of economics (Adam Smith) and sociology (Adam Ferguson) (Herman, 2001). So, to stick with these countries for the moment, it seems inconceivable that we could understand how international firms with origins in Scotland, Israel, or Greece operate abroad without some form of historical understanding of the relationships between education, innovation, and export of people to countries such as the USA, Canada, Australia, and New Zealand, for which these countries were, and (in some cases) still are, noted. Sadly, however, recent PISA scores have indicated a decline in educational excellence in Scotland in the school sector, which is a cause for national concern and reputation.

To widen the discussion, we might ask the question: Why is it that two countries as geographically (and, in some respects, as culturally) close as the UK and Germany have developed distinctively different forms of economic organization, industrial relations, and attitudes to management, particularly managing people? According to Peter Lawrence (2000) and others, the answer requires insight into the timing of industrialisation in these two countries, their relationship to the development (or absence) of political parties that supported the working classes, the development of trades unions, approaches to the development of managers, and the legacy of major events such as the two world wars during the twentieth century. As some researchers have pointed out, trade unionism in the UK developed prior to mass industrialisation in the eighteenth and nineteenth centuries to provide support for craft-based workers, and predated, by many decades, the political party (the Labour Party) that was created to support mass working-class interests. Consequently, the structure of trade unionism in the UK has been complex, with large numbers of unions pursuing different aims and often competing for members and for pay. Historically, many of these unions have had a strong political agenda because they were formed before the Labour Party, the consequences of which, according to some commentators, served only to increase the conflict between management and labour for most of the twentieth century in Britain. Strike activity, particularly unofficial strike action by small groups of workers, became a marked feature of industrial conflict after 1945, at least in the minds of the popular press, and gave birth to the phenomenon that became known, somewhat unfairly, as the 'British disease'.

Overlaid on these political and labour factors was a traditional approach to recruiting and developing business leaders and managers in the UK who were not experts in the task they were managing (witness the previously described attitudes to vocational education), but were noted more for social skills and graces, for which their education and social class backgrounds partially equipped them. It is not surprising that these 'gifted amateurs' defined their roles predominantly in terms of people management and external networking, rather than as managing through taking direct action or by managing sophisticated information flows, except in the field of accounting information (see Chapter 2). What might be more surprising, given the people-management bias of the traditional British manager, is that so much industrial conflict resulted. This can be partly explained by the historically marked differences in social class values that permeated UK management and labour. These differences exacerbated the 'arm's length' relationship created by the relative inability of managers to relate to their workers in terms of expertise or the task (Glover & Hughes, 1996; Stewart et al., 1994).

By contrast, much of German industry and its labour movement had to be reconstructed from scratch following the demise of Hitler and the Nazi Party and the devastation caused by the Second World War. The German trade unions were purposely reorganized, with British help, along industrial lines, so that the competition between unions for members and pay never developed to the same extent that it did in the UK. These factors, coupled with the return to a supportive system of labour legislation that had been developed by the social democratic political party prior to the 1940s and the new capital formation associated with much of German industry, resulted in a relatively peaceful industrial relations system for many decades. This state of relatively harmonious industrial relations has provided the stability necessary for rapid German economic development since 1945, and consensus between management and labour continued to be a feature of German industry even when economic development slowed down during the late 1990s.

Overlaid on these industrial relations factors and the effects of the Second World War was the traditional German attitude to education, particularly engineering education, and the beliefs of German managers in expertise and the importance of the task. German managers are noted for not distinguishing technical work from managerial work. Management is necessary to get things done, is not 'over and above' technical work, and is best done by acting (see Chapter 2 and the rounded manager model) rather than always delegating to others (Lawrence, 2000). Such an attitude, coupled with the higher technical education of many German managers, meant that they were able to define their jobs less as people managers and more as experts. So, given a more harmonious context, higher level of technical capability and greater respect from work-ers for this ability, it is not difficult to explain why the German business system might be different and why British managers may have difficulty in such a system.

Box 5.4 A business history approach

In an interview, Harvard Business School Professor Geoffrey Jones was asked what his research had told him about the success and impact of businesses around the world. He replied as follows:

> [It] shows how entrepreneurs and firms have occupied centre-stage in driving the wealth of nations. It also demonstrates that there has never been a single model for successful or unsuccessful capitalism.

To give only one example, business and economic historians have often taken a scepti-cal view of the merits of family-owned and managed firms. Harvard Business School's Alfred Chandler, the doyen of business historians, famously ascribed Britain's relative economic decline to the United States from the late nineteenth century to that country's proclivity towards family or 'personal capitalism.'

This was contrasted with the separation of ownership and control and the growth of professional management seen in the United States. That debate continues. But this book does report compelling research that shows that, historically, family ownership and management in many countries has been a dynamic force. Leading firms such as Michelin in France, Heineken in the Netherlands, or Cargill or Mars in the United States are the tip of a huge iceberg of successful and long-lived family firms world-wide. Even today around a third of *Fortune 500* companies are family controlled.

It may sound a simplistic conclusion that there has never been 'one best way' of achieving business success. However, this historical experience stands as a powerful corrective to over-simplistic management fads and fashions, and to slavish transfers of management systems and practices that might work well in one country but can be disastrous in another.

... I intended our chapter comparing British and Dutch business history to be pro-vocative. The business historians of these two countries have frequently made compari-sons with the United States, and sometimes Germany. Generations of British business historians explained their country's economic 'failure" by establishing what it did 'wrong' compared with US or German business. They then explained this by iden-tifying idiosyncratic factors in Britain's development, such as the class system, or an alleged industrial 'anti-industrial' bias of its social elite, or the post-1945 flirtation with socialism and extensive state intervention. We maintain that comparisons which use the United States as a benchmark can be misleading. The United States is an idiosyn-cratic country by virtue of its size and growth, high levels of entrepreneurial energy, legalistic culture, and several other unusual features.

In our work, we show that the business systems of Britain and the Netherlands shared many similarities. Both countries had an imperial and mercantile heritage.

Family business stayed important. The service sector was strong. Multinational activity was extensive and persistent. The two countries even shared the ownership of two of the world's largest multinationals, Shell, and Unilever. Many allegedly distinctive features of British and Dutch capitalism turn out to be part of a wider pattern for countries with shared geographical positions, cultural orientations, and historical patterns of development.

Source: adapted from an interview with Professor Geoffrey Jones talking about Jones and Sluyterman (2003).

The systemic and enduring nature of business systems

A second feature of business systems is the *interlocking and enduring nature of business-related institutions* in any country or region over time. We often find that new industries, developing in a particular country or region, call for new kinds of skills and work patterns. Good examples of such developments during the latter part of the twentieth century included moving call centres and software development to India, electronics manufacture to Malaysia, computing and mobile phone manufacture to China, and motor vehicle manufacturing to the southern states of the USA and Latin America. These new industries and the typical kinds of employment policies and practices associated with them were necessarily overlaid on the existing, dominant system of older industries and human resource management patterns. Although changes occurred in the business systems of the affected areas of India, China, Malaysia, the southern USA, and Latin American countries such as Mexico and Brazil, these changes were constrained by previous institutional frameworks, such as the dominant patterns of worker organizations, including trade unions, legislation, and patterns of business ownership (e.g., the importance of family-owned firms in Malaysia and the state ownership of traditional Chinese firms). For example, foreign companies wishing to set up in China were required to form a relationship with a local partner to form a joint venture, though this requirement was later relaxed because of legislative change. Such joint ventures were governed by a system of regulations on employment practices regarding contracts, union recognition, and safety that continue to reinforce the role of national and regional governments and the control of the Communist Party on economic development (Zhang & Martin, 2003). Thus, the rise of new industries and associated employment practices may herald some significant changes in certain aspects of the business system, but because these changes do not fit closely with the previously dominant business institutions, the interlocking and conservative nature of these previously dominant institutional arrangements means that the existing system remains largely intact, albeit in a modified form.

Some companies have understood this problem of institutional inertia only too well when setting up new facilities overseas. For example, most Japanese car manufacturers that entered the US market during the 1980s set up their production facilities in southern locations to avoid many of the institutional constraints associated with typical US vehicle manufacturing in the northern, 'rust-belt' states of the USA. Indeed, some researchers have pointed out that these Japanese firms tended to locate not in the major centres of population in these southern states but in formerly rural small towns to source employees without previously formed expectations of a manufacturing environment and without a previous history of trade union membership. This was reputedly the case with Toyota, which set up in 1986 one of its major US plants in Georgetown, Kentucky, a small town quite far removed in distance and 'mentality' from the major centres of vehicle manufacture in Michigan and neighbouring Ohio. This strategy has proven to be successful, with high-quality hybrids and premium cars being built for the US market and employment rising to 9,300 in 2022.

The role of critical turning points and changes in systems

A third feature of a business systems approach is the importance of aptly named *critical turning points* in bringing about radical change. These turning points include wars such as the Russian-Ukrainian conflict with its inevitable ramifications for East-West relations; economic crises such as the energy crisis resulting from the Russian-Ukrainian war and its implications for energy security; political upheavals such as Brexit in the UK; the COVID-19 pandemic; and, potentially, the agreement arising from the United Nations Climate Change Conference of 2023. Historically, Christian Caryl (2013) cited four events, all occurring in 1979, as the return of the market and religion with a vengeance – the election of Margaret Thatcher as Prime Minister in Britain, Deng Xiaoping liberalisation of the Chinese economy, Khomeini's establishment of an Islamic republic in Iran, and the rise of the Mujahideen in Afghanistan. Such events have often revealed severe problems in previously dominant systems and resulted in transformational institutional change. The new institutional frameworks that were imposed, for example, following the election of Margaret Thatcher in 1979 redefined the pre-existing relationship between employers and employees. Consequently, the changes in management–employee relationships became embedded in institutional arrangements (e.g., laws, bureaucratic systems, lobbying bodies) that persist to this day in the UK long after the upheavals giving rise to them. A further example can be taken from the USA and the New Deal era, following the critical turning point of the Great Depression in the 1930s that led to a new industrial relations framework, based on a highly codified system of collective contracts and trade union recognition, which exists to this day in the northern US states. As the inwardly investing Japanese car manufacturers attempted to point out in their location decisions, the New Deal institutional arrangement might have been appropriate during an era of mass production with an emphasis on a standard and limited product range and cost containment but was not suited to their novel 'lean production' strategy of providing high levels of quality, a wider product range, and even lower costs.

It is perhaps too early to say if COVID-19 can be considered a critical turning point in changing institutions or only amplifying trends already underway in many economies. However, there is evidence that COVID has influenced the institutions of work, especially in promoting remote and hybrid working. Evidence from the UK suggests that around one in ten people worked at least one day a week from home the previous week with around one in 20 reporting they worked mainly from home. These numbers increased markedly during the pandemic, but since restrictions were lifted, by September 2022, around one in five worked at least one day a week the previous week with around one in eight working from home exclusively (Muebi & Hobbs, 2022).

A more complex basis for comparing and contrasting international business systems

A fourth feature of the business systems approach is to allow comparisons of different national systems on a more complex range of key dimensions; simultaneously, it also reveals their unique nature. These key dimensions for comparison cover major institutional arrangements such as the nature of product, labour and capital markets, the organization of firms, the role of the state, systems of vocational education and training, and industrial relations. However, the unique character of any one system is guaranteed by the configuration of important dimensions and their interaction over time. In the example of the development of the US business system below, the timing or 'path dependence' of each of the key features of the system means that the US business system is unique (Jones, 2003), even though we can use most of these dimensions to compare it with other capitalist systems (see Box 5.5).

Box 5.5 Business systems analysis and the USA

Research by Almond and Ferner (2006), Davis (2009, 2022), Khurana (2007), Mayer (2013), and others show how different aspects on the American business system can be analysed using an institutionalist approach and how the features of this system affect managers of US multinationals managing overseas and developments in the global economy such as the Global Financial Crisis of 2007–2008, the war in Ukraine beginning in 2022, and the emergence of 'Trumpist' politics. Eight key components of the US business system can help us to compare it with other national systems:

- the development and nature of firms and product markets;
- the development and role of the state and interest associations;
- the development and nature of financial markets;
- the development and nature of labour markets;
- the developing relationship between capital and labour;
- the nature of work organization, the education and training system, and skills;
- the nature of management; and
- the development and organization of the HR function.

Firms and product markets

There are several key features of the ways in which US firms have developed, especially in their relationships with product markets:

---

1. The early emphasis on market competition and managerial capitalism as the main ethos in organizing economic competition and organizations, compared with the more cooperative form of market competition of Germany and the 'personal' form of capitalism that characterised the UK.

2. The early development of mass markets in the rapidly growing US, mass marketing techniques, such as the development of catalogue retailing and large stores, and the rise of multidivisional organizational structures associated with companies such as General Motors.

3. The mass production, standardisation, and large-scale organizations associated with the development of the application of scientific management and the moving assembly line in motor vehicle manufacture – for example, Ford's in the 1920s.

4. The early development and rise of a managerial class, functional management, including the growth of accountants and sales specialists, and the beginning of the separation of control by professional managers from the ownership of these large-scale organizations by financial institutions.

5. Early diversification overseas, including some of the earliest MNEs before and after the Second World War.

The role of the state and employers' associations

Historically, set out as an argument between 'big' and 'small' government in the USA, the state has been characterised by relatively weak central government as an economic actor, with a fragmented federal/state structure. Its role has been limited to creating a favourable climate for private sector investment and providing a limited safety net for its inhabitants in areas such as healthcare and social security. There was no explicit industrial policy, in contrast to countries such as Germany, Japan, France, and Singapore. The USA embarked on brief periods of direct global intervention, (e.g., Marshal Aid and GATT in the 1940s and 1970s, and more recently through the World Bank, IMF, etc.), but has traditionally been reluctant to provide economic aid to overseas countries or to become involved in major initiatives such as the limiting of global warming. However, there are signs that recent changes have occurred with the Biden administration taking a much more active role in international events. Its relatively weak business associations and industry groups reflect the historical weakness of organized labour. The USA, more than any other country apart from the UK (Mayer, 2013), has promoted the idea of economic coordination and performance through market forces and contractual relationships rather than trust-based, long-term relationships.

Financial markets

There has been a historical absence of close relationships between financial organizations and industry, with Wall Street having an arm's length relationship with corporate organizations. In comparison with other countries, the central bank and the banking system have been historically weak and have not intervened in industry. Like the UK, there has been a strong market for corporate control, involving many takeovers and mergers. Corporate control has been a key method of disciplining underperforming companies. This market for corporate control, coupled with the early development of equity markets, led to a rapid turnover of shares and charges of short-termism. The impact on long-term investment in areas such as strategy, R&D and training has been noticeable. Since the late 1970s, this system has been associated with a focus on creating shareholder value as a mode of corporate governance, cost control, and downsizing (Davis, 2009), which has become even more pronounced with the introduction of new players into the financing of businesses, such as hedge funds and private equity (Davis, 2022). However, the promise of extremely high rewards through 'playing' the financial markets has led to the large-scale development of new businesses and innovation.

Labour markets

Historically, the US labour markets have been highly flexible, with few restraints and with labour bearing the brunt of market difficulties. It was no surprise that the idea of human resource management was 'born in the USA' as costs to be cut rather than as people to be invested in. Consequently, among developed economies, the skills are standardised and there is a relatively high proportion of low-skilled workers in comparison with countries such as Germany, France, and Sweden. Traditionally, there have been highly rigid internal labour markets and career structures in organizations, with strong demarcation between groups, often based on education and qualifications. More recently, there has been a decline of organizational careers, with old-style psychological contracts offering job security becoming less important. Instead, there has been a growing importance in the idea of employability (a chance for individuals to learn new skills and make themselves more employable on the open labour market) in blue-collar and managerial labour markets. This is evident in the growth of self-employment and e-lancing discussed in Chapter 4. Historically, there have been few institutional constraints to flexible labour markets and insecurity apart from equal opportunities legislation. The consequence, according to some writers, has been a lack of incentives to invest in employees because of the short-term orientation of firms and the system of standardised mass production (see the section on work organization and skills).

The relationship between employers and labour

Traditionally, US employers have been anti-unionist, stemming from their beliefs in economic liberalism, which has also been the official ideology of the state. Both Democratic and Republican governments have provided state support for employers at the expense of labour, except during the New Deal era. Historically, labour relations have been marked by often violent and sustained anti-labour tactics, such as those employed by Ford during the 1930s. Apart from early flirtations with left-wing politics, the USA has lacked a radical labour movement that already had political rights. This contrasted with the labour movements of many European countries. Such a system resulted in company-based bargaining and 'business' unionism. This lack of a working-class movement was also brought about because the USA has historically been a middle-class, wealthy society (even during the eighteenth century), with the Frontier and the West a useful safety valve for minorities, and with high rates of social mobility that allowed such minorities to pursue the 'American Dream'. There has been a relatively recent and increasing division between classes in terms of income since the 1950s, which has been a feature of the end of the New Deal. America is now one of the most unequal advanced capitalist societies in the world, which shows no signs of declining.

The non-union model or sophisticated paternalism

The USA has been characterised by ever-declining levels of unionism since the middle of the last century or even earlier coupled with the resurgence of a sophisticated paternalism (human resources management) by naturally inclined, anti-union employers. This is a unitarist strategy, in marked contrast to the pluralist, New Deal strategy that governed much of labour relations before the 1970s. Such strategy has also been associated with the growth of US welfare capitalism, in contrast to European state capitalism (Davis, 2022; Martin et al., 2016). Employers have sought to employ 'high commitment strategies' designed to provide an alternative to unions, based on a heavy reliance on behavioural science techniques to secure compliance and commitment. Market-based pay became a guiding principle in the design of rewards systems, with a heavy emphasis on performance and shareholder value as criteria in determining pay differentials, which have widened markedly. This was accompanied by a decline of internal career progression and an increased reliance on recruitment from external labour markets and employability (employers offered high pay and the opportunity to learn but no guarantee of employment security in return for high commitment from employees).

The system of work organization and skills

The US work organization and skills profile is a legacy of mass production and the application of Taylorism to many aspects of US industry. Historically, it has been marked by the assertion of managerial control and the relocation of manual skills into technology and management. Managers have played a major role in innovation and leading teams, with the effect of broadening rather than deepening skills. The accompanying mass higher education system and the concern for vocational skills have been other marked features of the USA, with anti-intellectualism as a current in US society and the veneration of the 'practical' wo/man. This system has helped produce the focus on the external labour market and relatively low investment in training. Some economists have argued it has also produced a relatively inefficient use of cheap labour and a lack of investment in technological innovation.

Organization of the HR function

The HR function historically has been proactive and quite well developed in its pursuit of high commitment and welfare strategies, with a growing professionalism, assisted by bodies such as the Society for Human Resource Management (SHRM). Some researchers, however, have argued that HR has remained a minor administrative function compared with finance and marketing, and compared with HRM in countries such as the UK. Because of the absence of legal constraints, HR has had wider latitude in developing procedures for labour relations, especially when compared with the bureaucratisation and formalisation of other countries, for example, planning, testing, performance management, job evaluation, monitoring compliance, and affirmative action. There are, however, systematic differences between union and non-union firms and the priority assigned to labour relations.

Different types of business system

Like Hofstede, business systems writers have attempted to classify different types of systems according to key dimensions. Whitley's 2007 work is the most widely cited typology of business systems, in which he identified eight systems, four types of states, and six types of innovation systems. The eight systems, which were subsequently validated through large-scale analysis (Hotho, 2014), were:

1   *Fragmented systems*, which are dominated by small, highly competitive family businesses, with little overall coordination of economic activity, for example, Hong Kong. Short-term contracts are the basis for cooperation and employment.

2   *Project networks*, which were set up to be short term, narrow in scope but were highly integrated into ownership

3   *Coordinated industrial districts*, such as those existing in the northern Italian clothing industry. Here small firms are closely integrated across the value chain of an industrial sector and between sectors. High levels of employee commitment are the basis for innovation.

4   *Financial conglomerate*, in which holding companies operate businesses as financial investment vehicles. The UK has a high preponderance of such companies

5   *Integrated conglomerates*, which are characterised by high levels of ownership integration and high levels of scope (e.g., the Korean Chaebol),

6   *Compartmentalised systems*, associated with the traditional joint stock countries of the USA and UK. Large firms dominate, and activity between and across sectors is highly integrated. However, cooperation and commitment between firms, partners, and employees are based on contract rather than on trust.

7   *Collaborative systems*, such as those found in Germanic countries. Large alliances of inter-country collaborators, resting on interdependent relations between firms, managers, and employees. Comparatively high level of trust.

8 *Highly coordinated systems*, such as those found in Japan after the Second World War. Highly coordinated system of alliances and networks between and within sectors of industry, with government sponsorship.

Another approach is to compare the relative weight of different 'governance' mechanisms by which economic and business activity is coordinated in a country or region, and how these factors affect the management of people (Pendleton & Gospel, 2013; Martin et al., 2016). Traditional economic and organizational analysis has identified three such governance mechanisms:

1 *Market mechanisms*, which have emphasised the role of free markets, contracting and the price mechanism as the principal means of coordinating and controlling activities in organizations and economies during the nineteenth century and during the Thatcher–Reagan era of national economic policy, which was accompanied by large-scale deregulation of markets in the late twentieth century.

2 *Hierarchies*, which emphasised the increasing role of bureaucratic organizational structures, rules, rewards, and traditional career systems during the twentieth century to govern organizations and regulate economies.

3 *Corporatist structures*, which emphasised the interlocking roles of the state, informal networks, and associations. These corporatist arrangements have been especially important historically in the governance of European business systems and in Japan. The state refers to government and institutions, including government agencies. Informal networks refer to the loosely connected groups of key individuals and organizations in a business system that are influential in government–business relationships. These networks conduct their relations based on mutual trust and confidence rather than on a legally enforceable basis and are bound together by common values and/or dependence on resources (Almond & Ferner, 2006). Associations, of which employers' associations and unions are the most important examples in business systems, usually have a legal identity and are interest groups that enforce cooperative behaviour on their members and engage in collective contracts with other associations on behalf of their members.

In an interesting application of governance mechanisms to human resource management, Gooderham et al. (2006) identified four different contexts or business systems in Europe, which are still relevant today. They distinguished between such systems according to two dimensions, which reflect the ideas of Whitley and others. The first of these was the extent to which the state exercises a highly pervasive or limited role in labour relations. In turn, this influences the extent to which organizations can exercise choice in how they manage people. Thus, organizations in the UK, USA, Denmark, and Norway can exercise considerable freedom in human resource management, whereas firms in Germany, France, and Spain are highly regulated, albeit in slightly different ways. The second, which mapped onto the distinction between market and corporatist governance structures set out above, was the extent to which market individualist or communitarian infrastructures dominate in shaping business relations. Market

individualism refers to the belief in self-interest, market forces, and price as a coordinating mechanism, whereas communitarian infrastructures refer to a belief in high-
trust informal networks and mutually obligated associations as the most effective form
of shaping business relations. Gooderham et al. contrasted the UK and USA as having
a pervasive and strong market mentality that inherently leads to low-trust relations
and limited cooperation between managers and their employees with countries such
as Germany, Norway, and Denmark, in which firms are embedded in communitarian
obligations and relatively high trust relations. Figure 5.3 compares European countries
along these two dimensions.

MANAGING PEOPLE IN AN INTERNATIONAL CONTEXT

In the earlier chapters, we spent some time examining the nature of management and
produced frameworks for thinking about the rounded-out manager. In constructing
these frameworks, our desire was to make you aware that effective management had to
be related to the contexts in which it was practised. I referred to inner and outer contexts and to near and far contexts in these frameworks but only touched on the international context. This chapter has been written to provide you with a much greater insight
into this increasingly important international backdrop of how cultures and institutions
will affect the work of managers and their dealings with others. In this section, I provide
more detail on what internationalisation or globalisation might mean for managers in
their everyday working lives. We can do this by looking at the changing views of the
'international manager' and the kinds of characteristics, biographies, and competences
that seem to be necessary to work well in diverse cultural and institutional contexts.
We can also examine how organizations best approach the development of international
managers for such changing contexts.

Lessons from the field

Most companies first learnt about the international context through the stories told
by expatriate managers who may have been sent out on 'expeditionary' missions to
some new countries and returned to tell the 'horror' or 'wonderment' tales. These
tales were nearly always comparatively based, and for managers from developed
countries, the comparison was against their own national 'benchmark' cultures and
standards of behaviour. Such benchmarking is most apparent when managers are
confronted with situations that touch directly on their ethical or moral positions,
such as having to deal with requests for 'bribes', or where women are treated as
'second-class' citizens. These tales reflect the problems of expatriate adjustment on
international assignments (Chen, 2019). It has been estimated that around 30 per
cent of expatriates in US multinationals fail to complete their full term overseas,
with a large proportion of this rate put down to the failure of *cultural adjustment*
(Schneider et al., 2014).

This process of cultural adjustment to foreign countries is often thought to follow three phases:

1   The *honeymoon*, characterised by positive feelings and optimism.

2   The *morning after*, which is a period when the charm wears off and when interpersonal and/or work experiences become unsettling or annoying. This is the phase that creates the most difficulty for expatriates and can result in serious problems. Although these problems are more likely to occur because of several minor events or situations, the term 'culture shock' is used to describe feelings associated with this phase.

3   *Happily ever after*, when expatriates have become gradually adjusted to the new culture.

These phases are not universal, because expatriates have different family circumstances, prior experiences, and motivations, and are placed in different work situations. Moreover, the culture shock of moving between countries is usually related to the cultural and institutional distance between them. It should come as no great surprise that US MNEs invested more heavily in the UK than in any other European country following 1945, in part because of this lack of cultural and institutional distance.

Research has shown that adjustment evolves when expatriates acquire greater knowledge of the local culture and language and through positive work and social relations with local employees and people outside work. Stereotyping tends to diminish, and there is a greater likelihood of shared understandings and similarities. However, if work or social experiences are negative, then these tend to reinforce previously held views and make adjustment more difficult. Moreover, expatriate managers often need to resolve the dilemma of having formal responsibility over locals but not having the local 'knowledge' or resources to get things done. Consequently, they run the risk of managing at a distance, through information or different layers of hierarchy. As we have already seen, this is inconsistent with the model of the rounded manager, which requires people to manage directly through action on certain occasions.

International management competences

So, what is required to become a highly effective international manager, and how does this affect our model of the rounded manager? Again, we must consider the contexts of such work as set out in our model of the rounded manager in Chapter 2. These contexts include the agenda of the work, managing on the inside and managing on the outside. In this connection, international managers must interact with key stakeholders, including:

1.   *Owners*, who are mainly interested in short- and long-term returns for their investment and are often focused on financial and cost control.

2.   *Executive managers*, who are often interested in company growth and sometimes idiosyncratic issues that enhance their personal reputation and career prospects

3.   *Customers and suppliers*, whose interests lie in product/service quality, design, costs, availability, and so on.

4.   *Regulators and governments*, whose interests lie in compliance with legal, socio-cultural, and environmental norms.

5. *Employees*, whose interests lie in being treated with respect and in having interesting and rewarding jobs and long-term careers.

6. The public, who are interested in the long-term sustainability of the company and its impact on the environment

Such a focus on these stakeholders reminds us that managing in an international context often involves managing multiple and conflicting agendas, set by a wide variety of stakeholders, and that successful management is as much about managing on the outside as managing inside. It concerns managing one's own career, which is increasingly becoming defined as 'boundaryless', involving less hierarchical progression within a single organization and more national and lateral movement within and across organizational and national boundaries (and even outside organizations themselves, as people increasingly work for themselves or take career breaks) (see Chapter 3). Such career patterns are associated with changes in the willingness of organizations to guarantee secure employment, and with employees' changing career orientations, away from security to concerns with lifestyle, excitement, and psychological growth (Sullivan & Arthurs, 2006). According to Schein (1990), this concern for managing one's own career involves managing an

TABLE 5.3 Competences for managing abroad	
Interpersonal effectiveness	Usually seen as the key competence, this refers to the ability of managers to form relationships by building trust and getting along with others. The values of consensus and cooperation are important in developing such competences
Linguistic ability	Often, this means developing a feel for what language is important to others in a symbolic sense and being able to use this effectively in conversations, rather than complete mastery of a language in a technical sense
Cultural curiosity and the motivation to live abroad	Cultural curiosity of managers and families is based on a genuine interest in other cultures and experiences
Tolerance and dealing with ambiguity	Recognising that uncertainty and ambiguity is a normal state of affairs and that flexibility and multiple mindsets are necessary
Patience and respect	Again, these map onto the emotional intelligence of self-regulation (self-control) and empathy, but are even more important in an international context
Cultural empathy	Linked to the above, cultural empathy implies understanding the needs and cultural values of others without being judgemental
Strong sense of self-awareness	Another form of emotional intelligence refers to being in tune with your emotions and recognising that negative emotions, such as insecurity and a lack of self-identity, can hinder work performance
Sense of humour	A key social skill, which acts as a coping mechanism to help gain a sense of perspective and as a relationship-building skill

Source: adapted from Schneider et al., 2014; Pucik et al., 2023.

'external' career, which was concerned with objective notions of advancement upwards and between organizations, and managing the 'internal' career, which involves dealing with subjective, identity-related issues, such as 'where am I going in life?' and 'what kind of person do I want to be?'

Having an international career, however, doesn't always lead to objective notions of advancement because it will often take an individual away from the centres of key political decision-making. It comes as no surprise, then, that most lists of competences (e.g., Pucik et al., 2023) for such a career highlight the need for even greater emotional intelligence than may be conventionally inferred from our well-rounded manager model, and will include the *motivation to live overseas, cultural empathy*, and *linguistic abilities* (see Table 5.3).

In addition to expatriate managerial competences, which refer to what is required to work in another culture, international managers are increasingly required to work across many cultures and institutional contexts simultaneously. These situations also require managers to work across levels simultaneously. Often, this means managing a project in one situation but being a team member in another situation. This situation requires a further set of competences (see Table 5.4).

TABLE 5.4 Competences for managing internationally at home	
Understanding interdependencies	Usually seen as the ability to manage complex and interlocking systems that cut across hierarchy in organizational situations. This often means taking the lead in one situation and being a member in another
Responding to multiple cultures simultaneously	The ability to learn about multiple cultures and work with them simultaneously, which means dealing with people who are often different from each other as well as from yourself
Recognising cultural differences 'at home'	Cultural curiosity of managers and families is based on a genuine interest in other cultures and experiences
Being willing to share power and learn from others	Recognising that boss–subordinate relations are inappropriate in modern management situations, especially given increased educational levels and the importance of subsidiaries in MNE performance. This is associated with the acceptance of the reverse diffusion of ideas and practice
Thinking and acting with 'local worldwide' mindset	The ability to understand and work with the needs of companies to differentiate by thinking locally while integrating by thinking globally simultaneously
Adopt a 'culture-general' approach	This means understanding the dimensions along which cultures are likely to differ, rather than having a specific understanding of one culture
Rapidly learning and unlearning	The constant challenging of old assumptions and ways of doing things, and trying out new ideas and approaches – sometimes referred to as double-loop continuous learning

Source: adapted from Schneider et al. (2014) and Pucik et al. (2023).

Schneider et al. (2014) and Pucik et al. (2023) summarise these lists of competences for being able to manage internationally at home as having a *global mindset*. This meta-competence, or umbrella concept, refers to the ability of managers to think simultaneously about integration (global or corporate issues) and differentiation (local cultural or subsidiary issues) and to understand how such answers to specific problems of internationalisation may change over time. Returning to our discussion of multiple perspectives in earlier chapters, having a global mindset implies being able to work with competing ideas at the same time – in being open-minded rather than believing in a one-best-way. Above all, it implies a learning culture, which leads us nicely into a discussion of how we should develop managers for international roles.

DEVELOPING INTERNATIONAL MANAGERS

The problems of developing international managers

Let's begin with a short case in Box 5.6 that gets to the heart of some of the problems of developing managers for an international role, either at home or abroad.

Box 5.6 The problems of educating managers for international business

An old study by Reiss and Ones (1995) is still highly relevant in showing the unforeseen consequences of educating managers for international assignments. The study reported on attempts to internationalise US undergraduate and graduate courses by including substantial information about the global environment and cross-cultural differences in a business context may have backfired! The headline findings were that:

- Ethnocentric attitudes, as measured by standard questionnaire studies, increased during the period of the course.
- Most significant increase in ethnocentrism occurred when taught by US faculty members.
- 'International' faculty members, who had been recruited specifically to provide an international perspective, were associated with neither an increase nor a decrease of the subsequent ethnocentricism of these students.

This study showed that the conventional solution of education and training may not produce the intended outcomes: developing a global mindset or 'thinking global and acting local' is not an easy skill to develop, because of the paradoxical and ambiguous nature of the problem (Pucik et al., 2023). It requires us to link abstract issues such as global competition and outlook with concrete issues of 'place' and local identity. Moreover, as we noted in the criticisms of Hofstede earlier in this chapter, acting local usually assumes some kind of semi-fixed national cultural unity, itself a problematic concept. For example, can India, China, or Malaysia really be characterised as one culture, given the various historical ethnic, religious, and class divisions, despite political attempts to forge national identities? And can we reasonably talk of a British national culture, without offending the Scots, Irish, and Welsh? Clearly not in the case of Scotland, which in the last two decades is as far apart from the rest of the UK in terms of the identity of its people and its politics than at any time in the centuries-old history of the Union between Scotland and England.

Instead, in addressing this question, it is usually more useful to think in terms of the two options available to companies wishing to internationalise their managers that mirror the cooperation–initiative discussion raised in Chapter 4. The first is the *integration solution*, which focuses on creating cooperation through standardised structures, systems, processes, and, especially, development and training opportunities so that a strong corporate culture becomes the main point of reference for managers. Good examples of this integration approach include systems of managerial control. ABB, the well-documented Swiss-Swedish MNE, used a 'seven-ups' benchmarking system and international management development conferences to diffuse knowledge and best practice throughout the organization (Martin & Beaumont, 1998). Motorola and GE, like other MNEs, used their corporate universities to standardise the education of managers across their various subsidiaries in different countries. The second is the *differentiation solution*, which focuses on preserving variations in international cultures and institutions that are deemed necessary for local identity and initiatives and encouraging diversity among managers.

One way of thinking about this problem is to use the classic distinction made by Perlmutter (1969), whose work we adapted to discuss approaches to international staffing and deployment (Martin & Hetrick, 2010). Figure 5.4 draws on these integration–differentiation dimensions.

- *Ethnocentric* approaches are characterised by organizations with little interest either in developing a strong corporate culture across subsidiaries/markets or in establishing a strong local identity. Often, they have a strong belief in the virtues of their own culture and institutions and seek to export them overseas. The approach to staffing, deployment, and development is focused on head office interests and its predominant needs to maintain financial control. 'Exporting' home managers to run local subsidiaries with little or no thought given to the role and training of local managers is the usual approach to management 'development'. They may even see educating local managers as a dangerous strategy (too much knowledge!). This approach resonates with political or economic colonial/imperialist styles of management.
- *Polycentric* approaches are characterised by firms that have little knowledge of local product and/or labour markets, or which believe in the importance of differentiation above all else. Such an approach is evident in the hiring of local managers, developing them locally and in 'letting them get on with the job' with minimal interference.

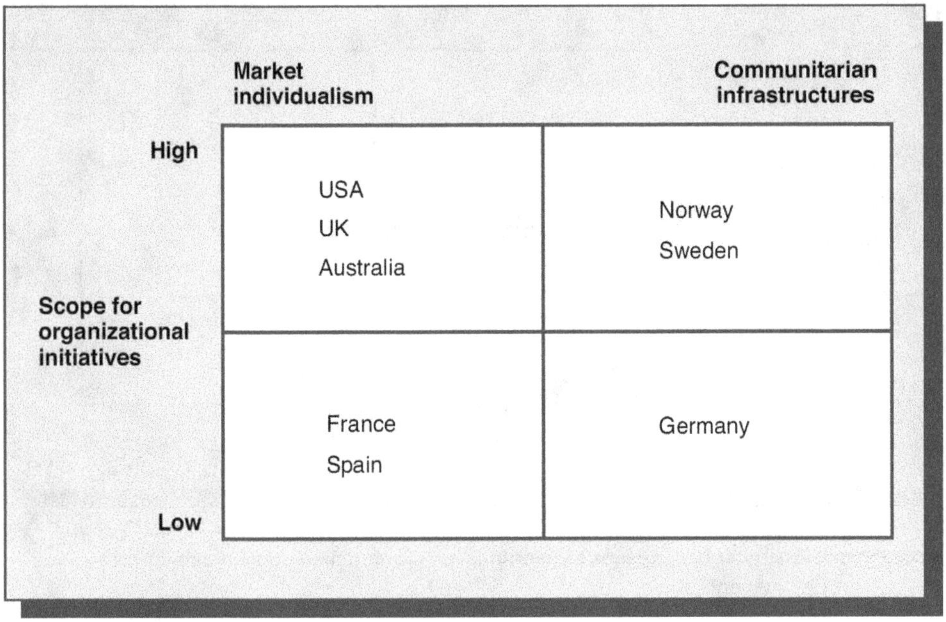

	Market individualism	Communitarian infrastructures
High	USA UK Australia	Norway Sweden
Scope for organizational initiatives	France Spain	Germany
Low		

FIGURE 5.4 Comparing key countries' governance structures. (*Source*: adapted from Gooderham and Nordhaug, 2003.)

- *Geocentric* approaches are characterised by a belief that nationality has no place in modern business and that home office 'imperialism' is bad for business because it promotes monocultures and inhibits change. High needs for integration and differentiation are thought to be reconcilable, but such organizations are relatively rare. They believe in recruiting managers from inside or outside the company, regardless of nationality, and in developing them to have a global mindset through education in international (academic and/or corporate) business schools and through frequent assignments in different countries.
- *Regiocentric* approaches are characterised by a strong emphasis on regional integration, such as having a strong regional brand, or regional corporate culture that reflects product and/or labour market features. Japanese firms setting up in Europe are good examples. Managers tend to be recruited from the home office, deployed in a particular region, and educated into a regional mindset.

It is important to note that no one solution is advocated as the best in all circumstances, although there is the implication in this kind of theorising that the geocentric approach is the most progressive. Even the ethnocentric approach has advantages and still dominates the HR strategies of many internationalising organizations. It also has some historical justification, as it was the basis of the British Empire's strategy for most of its 200-year dominance of world affairs (although there were periods and places when Britain pursued a more polycentric strategy). It has also been a strategy employed by many US MNEs as part of the USA's 'economic imperialism' at various points in recent history and in certain regional contexts.

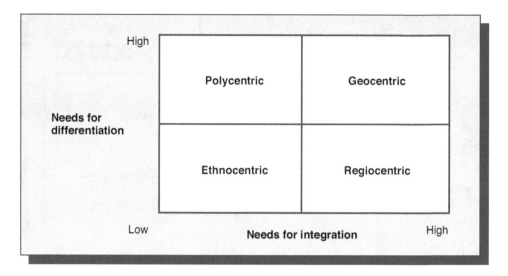

FIGURE 5.5 Classifying approaches to international management development and deployment.

Exercise 5.1

1 Think about the outcomes of the international management education programmes discussed earlier. Why should students have become more and not less ethnocentric during their international management courses?

2 What are the difficulties that organizations face in developing a geocentric strategy?

Management development for international managers

Developing global managers involves devising a set of policies and practices aligned with the needs of the organization for managerial talent and the needs of individual managers for continuous professional development (Harzing & Pinnington, 2014; Pucik et al., 2023). Such a process must be set in the external and internal contexts of an international organization. The critical factors which make management development in an international context different from developing managers for the domestic environment are as follows: (1) the competences needed to reduce the liability of foreignness, as discussed above; (2) the need for an international organization to create and transfer learning among its subunits for competitive reasons, often through the transfer or expatriation of managers to subsidiaries; and (3) the embeddedness of managers in the institutions and educational systems of their own countries.

Regarding the last of these three factors, it is quite clear that management development in international companies is strongly influenced by the institutions of their home countries. It is instructive to see how countries differ in their typical approaches, and these differences raise questions about the roles of managers and about management education. For example, when comparing systems of management development in the USA, France, Germany, Japan, and the UK, we get quite different views on the roles of managers and management education, as we have already seen in some of our illustrations. Although there is a growing convergence in that all these countries seem to require some form of self-development beyond their initial education, graduate education, based on the MBA model, is becoming more important in the UK, Germany, Japan, and France. On-the-job development in Germany, Japan, and, probably to a lesser degree, in the UK and France, is more planned than in the USA (Thomson et al., 2001; Wilson & Thomson, 2009). The UK was relatively unique in managers having low status compared with other occupational groups, traditionally a reflection of the low levels of qualifications of many managers. However, management education in Britain has improved markedly since the 1980s, in part because of systematic attempts to develop standards for management and leadership, and the growth of interest in executive development by organizations in all sectors because of the problems caused by talent shortages (Martin et al., 2018).

Attempts to draw comparisons in a few paragraphs are difficult, but Table 5.5 highlights some of the important traditional characteristics of national systems of management development, based on key features of national business systems. While there is evidence of greater convergence in these national systems, the research summarised in Table 5.5 remains relevant. We have strong reasons for believing institutional forces have an important influence on system divergence (Martin et al., 2018).

The main point of this comparison of approaches to developing managers is, once again, to reinforce the idea that there is no one-best way, though certain trends are observable. As we noted in Chapter 2, Henry Mintzberg (2004) is highly critical of management development that is not related to practice and context, and many of the more effective approaches to developing international managers require considerable periods of time spent in reflective practice while working in overseas countries. However, such reflection is aided by a critical understanding of where you stand, and one of the best exercises that can be undertaken off-the-job is to have managers understand how their views of others are influenced by the idiosyncratic nature of their institutional and cultural upbringing. To help you do this, we would like to end this chapter by asking you to engage in some personal reflection by attempting Exercise 5.2 for your own personal development.

Exercise 5.2 Personal reflection

1. Re-read Box 5.5 and then construct a brief analysis of your country's national business system, reflecting on:
   - the development and nature of firms and product markets;
   - the development and role of the state and interest associations;
   - the development and nature of financial markets;

TABLE 5.5 Differences among national systems of management development

	USA	France	Germany	Japan	UK
Status/role of managers in society	High recognition and increasing	High recognition, the 'cadre' mentality	Medium but increasing	High status and elitist	Medium status. gifted amateur model
Nature of labour market	Externally focused, decline of internal labour markets	Limited managerial mobility, except at top	Limited mobility, strong internal labour markets	Limited mobility but increasing. Strong internal labour markets	Changing from internal to external focus
Focus on 'off-the-job'/role of education	MBA as a screening device. Often criticised for lack of application	'Grandes Ecoles' (major universities) act as screening device. Seen as too intellectual	Middle status vocational schools providing Diplom Kaufmann. PhD for senior managers	Almost no graduate degrees in business. Undergraduate degrees as a screening device	Part-time MBA increasing. Professional qualifications also important
Focus 'on-the-job' development	Little emphasis. Rise of 'corporate universities' with strong emphasis on education	Considerable proportion of wage bill spent on management development for middle/lower managers	Strong apprenticeship system with job rotation	Integrated career structure, planned learning and mentoring, multifunctional approach	Relatively unplanned but improving. Development of corporate universities with a focus on experiential
Nature of education system/relationship to industry	Mass higher education. Rationalist focus of education. Unplanned 'system' of MD	Elitist and rationalist system of ESCs, linked to chambers of commerce. Planned system	Elitist universities supported by new polytechnic universities. Weak links with industry. Strong links with chambers of commerce and industry	Elitist universities, with a strong focus on technology and business. No strong links with industry	Moving to mass higher education, with some universities having strong links with industry

Source: based on Burgoyne et al, 2004; Lawrence, 2000, 2002; Thomson et al., 2001; Wilson & Thomson, 2009.

- the development and nature of labour markets;
- the developing relationship between capital and labour;
- the nature of work organization and the education and training system and skills;
- the nature of management; and
- the cultural values, norms, and standards of behaviour.

How does it differ from the example of the USA? And how do these differences influence how you see things at work?

(If you are from the USA, you can still benefit by choosing another country: reflect on how different its institutions and culture are from the USA and how that might affect how its people view American business practice.)

LEARNING SUMMARY

In this chapter, we have examined the problems of organizations 'going international' and the implications for managers. We began by examining the notion of the liability of foreignness and the practical problems to which that concept gives rise, such as whether firms should expatriate their own home country managers or use mainly local managers in overseas operations. Decisions such as these depend on the different entry strategies used by internationalising firms and on the experience and values of senior managers in the parent company.

They also depend on whether the parent company managers see the countries into which they are entering as convergent with or divergent from their own in terms of culture and institutional frameworks. In the middle section of the chapter, we examined the nature of national cultural differences and applied them to the analysis of different countries and their organizational and management practices. We also examined the idea of national business systems and applied these to the analysis of Walmart's entry into Germany to show how a lack of understanding of institutions, as well as culture, can seriously hamper ambitions to develop overseas markets. Indeed, one of the most practical exercises you can do as a manager charged with developing overseas markets or working overseas is to undertake an institutional and cultural analysis of the target country. It is also extremely beneficial for you to undertake a similar exercise on your own country to understand more fully your own idiosyncratic views and compare these with other countries. Such comparisons, however, are not without dangers, which are highlighted in Box 5.6.

The problems of educating international managers lead us into the final section on identifying key international management competences and developing managers for overseas assignments. The capability to think global and act local was a starting point for a more complex picture of competences required for managing abroad and managing internationally at home. These competences are quite distinct, requiring managers not only to understand one country but also to be able to work across many cultures and institutional contexts at the same time. Consequently, there is no one best way to develop international managers, with different countries taking different routes to prepare managers for their jobs. However, there is little substitute for reflective practice while working overseas to make you a more effective international manager. These kinds of reflections are assisted by having a deep understanding of how to analyse the institutions and cultures of your own country as well as those overseas.

REVIEW QUESTIONS

1. How easy is it to think global and act local? What are the best ways of developing a global mindset?
2. Compare and contrast a national cultures approach to international management such as Hofstede with a national business systems approach.

REFERENCES

Almond, P., & Ferner, A. (Eds.). (2006). *American multinationals in Europe: Managing employment relations across national borders.* Oxford University Press.
Anthony, P. (1977). *The ideology of work.* Tavistock.
Arthur, M. B., Inkson, K. I., & Pringle, J. K. (1999). *The new careers.* Sage.
Baskerville-Morley, R. F. (2005). A research note- the unfinished business of culture. *Accounting, Organizations and Society, 30*(4), 389–391.
BBC News. (2023, July 18th). McDonald's told to shut franchises over abuse claims. https://www.bbc.co.uk/news/business-66231131
Bjorkman, I., & Gooderham, P. (2012). International human resource management research and institutional theory. In G. K. Stahl, I. Bjorkman, I., & S. Morris, S. (Eds.), *Handbook of research in international human resource management* (2nd ed., pp. 472–489). Edward Elgar.
Burgoyne, J., Hirsh, W., & Williams, W. (2004). *The development of management and leadership capability and its contribution to performance: the evidence, the prospects and the research need* (Research Report RR560 Department for Education and Skills). HMSO.
Caryl, C. (2013). *Strange rebels: 1979 and the birth of the 21st century.* Basic Books.
Chen, M. (2019). The impact of expatriates' cross-cultural adjustment on work stress and job involvement in the high-tech industry. *Frontiers in Psychology.* https://doi.org/10.3389/fpsyg.2019.02228
Colvin, A., & Darbishire, O. (2012). International employment relations: The impact of varieties of capitalism. In G. K. Stahl, I. Bjorkman, I., & S. Morris, S. (Eds.), *Handbook of research in international human resource management* (2nd ed., pp. 52–75)). Edward Elgar.

Cooke, F.L., Veen, A., & Wood, G. (2017). What do we know about cross-country comparative studies in HRM? A critical review of the literature in the period 2000-2014. *International Journal of Human Resource Management, 28*(1), 196–233.

Davis, G. F. (2009). *Managed by markets: How finance re-shaped America*. Oxford University Press.

Davis, G. F. (2022). *Taming corporate power in the 21st century*. Cambridge University Press.

Economist. (2004, April 3). Kultur clash.

Economist. (2004, April 17). Burgers and fries a la Francaise.

Ferguson, N. (2003). *Empire: How Britain made the modern world*. Allen Lane.

Ferguson, N. (2004). *Colossus: The rise and fall of the American Empire*. Allen Lane.

Ferner, A. (2001). *The embeddedness of US multinational companies in the US business system: Implications for HR/IR. Paper available at the School of Business*, De Montfort University, Leicester, UK.

Ghoshal, S., & Nohria, N. (1993). Horses for courses: Organizational forms for multinational corporations. *Sloan Management Review, 34*, 23–35.

GLOBE 2020. (2020). *A unique large-scale study of cultural practices, leadership ideals, and generalized interpersonal trust in 150 countries in collaboration with nearly 150 researchers*. https://www.globeproject.com.

Glover, I., & Hughes, M. (Eds.). (1996). *The professional managerial class; Contemporary British management in pursuer mode*. Avebury.

Gooderham, P., & Nordhaug, O. (Eds.). (2003). *International Management: Cross-boundary challenges*. Blackwell.

Gooderham, P. Nordhaug, O., & Ringdal, K. (2006). National embeddedness and calculative human resource management in US subsidiaries in Europe and Australia. *Human Relations, 59*(11), 1491–1513.

Gooderham, P., Mayerhofer, W., & Brewster, C. (2019). A framework for comparative institutional research on HRM. *International Journal of Human Resource Management, 30*(1), 5–30.

Harzing, A.-W., & Pinnington, A. H. (Eds.). (2014). *International human resource management* (3rd ed.). Sage.

Hatch, M. J. (2018). *Organization theory: modern, symbolic, and postmodern perspectives* (fourth edition), Oxford: Oxford University Press.

Heng, S., Tsilionis, K., Scharff, C., & Woutlet, Y. (2022). Understanding AI ecosystems in the Global South: The cases of Senegal and Cambodia. *International Journal of Information Management, 64*, 102454

Herman, A. (2001). *How the scots invented the modern world*. Three Rivers Press.

Hilger, S. (2008). 'Globalisation by Americanisation': American companies and the internationalization of German industry after the second world war. *European Review of History, 15*(4), 375–401.

Hofstede, G. Hofstede, G. J., & Minkov, M. (2011). *Cultures and organizations, software of the mind: intercultural cooperation and its importance for survival*. McGraw-Hill.

Hotho, J. J. (2014). From typology to taxonomy: A configurational analysis of national business systems and their explanatory power. *Organization Studies, 35*(5), 671–702.

House, R. J., et al. (2004). *Culture, leadership and organizations: the GLOBE study of 62 societies*. Thousand Oaks, CA: Sage.

House, R. J., Dorfman, P., Javidan, M., Hanges, P. J., & de Luque, M.S. (Eds.). (2014). *Strategic leadership across cultures: The GLOBE study of effective CEO leadership behavior and effectiveness in 24 countries*. Sage.

Hollingsworth, J. R., & Boyer, R. (Eds.). (1997). *Contemporary capitalism*. Harvard University Press.

Jackson, T. (2020). The legacy of geert hofstede. *International Journal of Cross Cultural Management, 20*(1).

Johanson, J., & Vahine, J.-E. (2009). The Uppsala internationalization process model revisited: from liability of foreignness to liability of outsidership. *Journal of International Business, 40*, 1411–1431.

Jones, G., & Sluyterman, K. (2003). Multinationals. In F. Amatori & G. Jones (Eds.), *Business history around the world* (pp. 353–371). Cambridge University Press.

Joynt, P., & Warner, M. (Eds.). (2002). *Managing across cultures: Issues and perspectives* (2nd ed.). Thomson Learning.

Kaufman, B. E. (2016). Globalization and convergence-divergence of HRM across nations: New measures, explanatory theory, and non-standard predictions from bringing in economics. *Human Resource Management Review, 26*(4), 338–351.

Kaufman, H. (2009). *The road to financial reformations: warnings, consequences, reforms*. Wiley

Khurana, R. (2007). *From higher aims to hired hands: The social transformation of American business schools and the unfulfilled promise of management as a profession*. Princeton University Press.

Kim, J. H., & Siegel, J. (2024). *Paying for legitimacy: Autocracy, nonmarket strategy, and the liability of foreignness*. Administrative Science Quarterly. https://doi.org/10.1177/00018392231217676

Lawler, 111, E. E., & Boudreau, J. W. (2015). *Global trends in human resource management: A twenty-five year analysis*. Stanford University Press.

Lawrence, P. (2000). Management development in Europe: A study in cultural contrast. In M. Meddenhall & G. Oddou (Eds.), *Readings and cases in international human resource management* (3rd ed., pp. 169–183). South West College Publishing.

Lawrence, P. (2002). *The change game: How today's global trends are shaping tomorrow's companies*. Kogan Page.

Legnick-Hall, M. L., & Legnick-Hall, C.A. (2012). IHRM and social network/social capital theory. In G. K. Stahl, I. Bjorkman, & S. Morris, S. (Eds.), *Handbook of research in international human resource management* (2nd ed., pp. 490–508). Edward Elgar .

Lorbiecki, A. (1997). International management learning: Towards a radical perspective. In J. G. Burgoyne & M. Reynolds (Eds.), *Management learning: Integrating perspectives in theory and practice* (pp. 265–281). Sage.

Martin, G., & Beaumont, P. B. (1998). Diffusing 'best practice' in multinational firms: prospects, practice and contestation. *International Journal of Human Resource Management, 9*(4), 671–695.

Martin, G., Farndale, E., Paauwe, J., & Stiles, P. G. (2016). Corporate governance and strategic human resource management: Four archetypes and proposals for a new approach to corporate sustainability. *European Management Journal, 34*(1), 22–35.

Martin, G., & Hetrick, S. (2010). Employer branding and corporate reputations in an international context. In P. S. Sparrow (ed.), *Handbook on international human resource management* (pp. 293–321). John Wiley.

Martin, G., Gollan, P. S. and Grigg, K. (2011). Is there a bigger and better future for employer branding: facing upto innovation, corporate reputations and wicked problems in SHRM. *International Journal of Human Resource Management*, 22 (17), 3618–3637.

Martin, G., Siebert, S., & Robson, I. (2018). Conformist innovation: And institutional logics perspective on how HR executives construct business school reputations. *International Journal of Human Resource Management*, 29(13), 2027–2053.

Mayer, C. (2013). *Firm commitment: Why the corporation is failing us and how to restore trust in it.*Oxford University Press.

Mintzberg, H. (2004). *Managers not MBAs: A hard look at the soft practice of managing and management development.* Pearson Education/Financial Times.

Morgan, G, Campbell, J., Crouch, C., Pedersen, O., & Whitley, R. (Eds.). (2010). *The Oxford handbook of comparative institutional analysis.* Oxford University Press.

Morgan, G., & Whitley, R. (Eds.). (2012). *Capitalisms and capital in the twenty-first century.* Oxford University Press.

Muebi, N., & Hobbs, A. (2022, October). *The impact of remote and hybrid working on workers and organisations.* Parliament Postbrief 49. https://researchbriefings.files .parliament.uk/documents/POST-PB-0049/POST-PB-0049.pdf

Parker, M. (2018 April 27). Why we should bulldoze the business school. *The Guardian.* Retrieved November 5, 2023. https://www.theguardian.com/news/2018/apr/27/ bulldoze-the-business-school

Pendleton, A., & Gospel, H. (2013). Corporate governance and labour. In M. Wright, D. Siegel, K. Keasey, & I. Filatochev (Eds.), *The Oxford handbook of corporate governance* (pp. 634–657). Oxford University Press.

Perlmutter, M. V. (1969). The tortuous evolution of the multinational corporation. *Columbia Journal of World Business*, 4(1), 9–18.

Pettigrew, A. M., Cornuel, E., & Hommel, U. (Eds.). (2015). *The institutional development of business schools.* Oxford University Press.

Preston, A. (2021). America's global imperium. In P. F. Bang, C. A. Bayly, & W. Scheidel (Eds.), *The Oxford world history of empire: Volume two: The history of empire* (pp. 1217–1248). Oxford University Press.

Prince, N., Krebs, B. Prince, J. & Kabst, R. (2022). Revisiting Gooderham et al. (1999) "Institutional and Rational Determinants of Organizational Practices: Human Resource Management in European Firms". *Journal of World Business*, 57 (6).

Pucik, V., Bjorkman, I., Evans, P., & Stahl, G. (2023). *The global challenge: Managing people across borders* (4th ed.). Edward Elgar.

Reiche, S. B., Stahl, G. K., Mendenhall, M. E., & Oddou, G. (Eds.). (2017). *Readings and cases in international human resource management* (6th ed.). Routledge.

Reiss, A. D., & Ones, D. S. (1995). *Does international management education work? Reduction in ethnocentrism and negative stereotyping.* Paper presented to Academy of Management Conference, Vancouver, Canada.

Rosenzweig, P. M. (2006). The dual logics behind international human resource management: pressures for global integration and local responsiveness. In G. K.

Stahl & I. Bjorkman (Eds.), *Handbook of research in international human resource management* (pp. 16–34). Edward Elgar.

Schein, E. (1985). *Organizational culture and leadership.* Jossey-Bass.

Schein, E. (1990). *Career anchors.* University Associates.

Schneider, S. C., Barsoux, J.-L., & Stahl, G. K. (2014). *Managing across cultures* (3rd ed.). Financial Times/Prentice Hall.

Sparrow, P. R., Brewster, C., & Harris, H. (2004). *Globalizing human resource management.* Routledge.

Stahl, G. K., Bjorkman, I., & Morris, S. (Eds.). (2012). *Handbook of research in international human resource management* (2nd ed.). Edward Elgar.

Steenkamp, J.-B. E. M. (2020). Global brandbuilding and management in the digital age. *Journal of International Marketing, 28*(1), https://doi.org/10.1177/1069031X19894946

Stewart, R., Keiser, A., & Barsoux, J.-L. (1994). *Managing in Britain and Germany.* St Martin's Press.

Sullivan, S. E., & Arthurs, M. B. (2006). The evolution of the boundaryless career concept. Examining physical and psychological mobility. *Journal of Vocational Behaviour, 69*(1), 19–29.

Thornton, P. H. (2015). Culture and institutional logics. *International Encyclopedia of the Social and Behavioral Sciences* (2nd ed., pp. 550–556), Elsevier.

Thornton, P. H., Ocasio, W., & Lounsbury, M. (2012). *The institutional logics perspective: A new approach to culture, structure and process,* Oxford University Press.

Thomson, A., Mabey, C., Storey, J., Gray, C., & Iles, P. (2001). *Changing patterns of management development.* Blackwell.

Trompenaars, F. (2012). Cultural dimensions relating to people. In J. Dumetz et al (Eds.), *Cross-cultural management textbook: Lessons from the world-leading experts in cross cultural management* (pp. 117–146). Create Space Independent Publishing.

Trompenaars, F., & Hampden-Turner, C. (2004). *Managing people across cultures.* Capstone.

Varley Foundation. (2018). *Global teacher status index, 2018.* https://www.varkeyfoundation.org/media/4790/gts-index-9-11-2018.pdf

Weber, M. (1930). *The protestant ethic and the spirit of capitalism.* Unwin University Books.

Weick, K. E. (2001). *Making sense of the organization.* Blackwell.

Weiner, M. J. (2004). *English culture and the decline of the industrial spirit, 1850–1980.* Cambridge University Press.

Whitley, R. (2007). *Business systems and organizational capabilities. The institutional structuring of competitive competences.* Oxford University Press.

Whittaker, N. (2023). *Geopolitics and identity in British foreign policy discourse: The global race.* Routledge.

Wilkinson, A., Wood. G.T., & Deeg, R. (2013). (Eds.). *The Oxford handbook of employment relations: Comparative employment systems.* Oxford University Press

Wilson, D., & McKiernan, P. (2011). Global mimicry: Putting strategic choice back on the business school agenda. *British Journal of Management, 22*(3), 457–469.

Wilson, J. F., & Thomson, A. (2009). *The making of modern management: British Management in an historical perspective.* Oxford University Press.

Witt, M. A., & Redding, G. (2014). *The Oxford handbook of Asian business systems.* Oxford University Press.

Wolf, A. (2002). *Does education matter? Myths about education and economic growth.* Penguin.

World Trade Organization. (2014). *World trade report 2014.* WTO. Retrieved June 3, 2015, from https://www.wto.org/english/res_e/publications_e/wtr14_e.htm

World Trade Organization (2023) World trade report 2023 – re-globalization for a secure, inclusive and sustainable future, https://www.wto.org/english/res_e/publications_e/wtr23_e.htm.

Zaheer, S. (1995). Overcoming the liability of foreignness (Special research forum: International and intercultural management research). *Academy of Management Journal, 38*(2), 341–364.

Zammuto, R. E. (2018), Accreditation and the globalization of business. *Academy of Management Learning & Education, 7*(2). https://doi.org/10.5465/amle.2008.32712623

Zhang, H., & Martin, G. (2003). *Human resource management practices in sino foreign joint ventures.* Jiangxi Science and Technology Press.

CHAPTER 6

The corporate context, organizations, and managing people

LEARNING OBJECTIVES

At the end of this chapter, you should be able to:

- Understand the importance of the corporate context and the role of managing people in creating corporateness.
- Identify the different concepts that contribute to the corporate image of an organization.
- Apply theoretical frameworks to the analysis of organizational identity.
- Understand the importance of employer branding in organizations.
- Understand the complex relationships between people management, organizational identity, corporate branding, and corporate reputation.
- Apply the model of the relationship between people management, organizational identity, corporate branding, and corporate reputation to an organization seeking to develop a strong corporate brand and reputation.

INTRODUCTION TO CORPORATE REPUTATION, IDENTITY, BRANDS, AND PEOPLE MANAGEMENT

There can be few better justifications for a chapter in a book on management than the importance of its intended topic to the fate of a nation and its major corporations – in this case, the USA. Take a few minutes to read this case, which I have updated with new data on America's image abroad since it was originally written.

DOI: 10.4324/9781003469711-6

CASE 6.1 AMERICA'S CHANGING IMAGE ABROAD: REPUTATION MANAGEMENT, BRANDING, AND AMERICAN FOREIGN POLICIES

In the first edition of this book, I used a case study based on an *Economist* article written in 2004 referring to Keith Reinhard, the chairman of DDB Worldwide, whose challenge was to sell American business and American brands to the world following the Iraq war. He exclaimed: 'I love American brands, but they are losing friends around the world, and it is vital to the interests of America to change this' was the message of a talk to an audience at Yale University Business School in February 2004. He argued that the reputation of America abroad was at an all-time low and that this perception, however misguided, was damaging the economy.

To tackle the problem, Reinhard, with senior executives in America's advertising industry and some academics, set up Business for Diplomatic Action (BDA) to improve the reputation of the USA overseas. The idea wasn't new – President George W Bush had speculated on the reasons as to why 'everyone hates America' after 11 September 2001. But Reinhard felt the need to use consumer research to tell American business what most people outside the USA seemed to know about America's declining image.

His worries were reinforced by a DBB study covering 17 countries, which provided the feedback that 'America, and American business, was viewed as arrogant and indifferent toward others' cultures; exploitative, in that it extracted more than it provided; corrupting, in how it valued materialism above all else; and willing to sacrifice almost anything to generate profits'. Further evidence came in the shape of a survey of global brands by Roper ASW, which showed a marked decline in support for and trust in American brands.

Since writing this case illustration almost two decades ago, there have been several investigations into America's image abroad, including a House of Representatives hearing and conference on the topic in 2007. So, for example, Condoleezza Rice, US Secretary of State in the Bush Administration, announced the creation of a new annual award for a company, university, or other non-governmental institution that excelled in promoting America's image abroad. A public relations coalition, which was an offshoot of this initiative, argued that despite US companies and individuals donating much more money overseas than in the overall US aid budget, the image was still in decline. This decline was to be further exacerbated by the role played by American financial services companies during the Global Financial Services Crisis in 2007–2008.

Since then, however, matters seem to have improved a little, at least according to Pew Research (2014, 2021), a prestigious 'think tank'. Although there were major critics of the USA and American companies, especially in the Middle East (Egypt, Jordan, Palestine, Lebanon), Turkey, Greece, and Germany, all of which had predominantly unfavourable images, there were blocks of the world where America's image and those of its companies, were generally positive, including most of Europe, Asia, sub-Saharan Africa, and the traditional 'suspects' such as Israel and Italy. There were also some very surprising results on favourability, with France entering the top ten nations of 'Fans' of America for the first time. The image held by UK citizens declined markedly from 2002 until 2008 but recovered a little by 2015 with approximately two-thirds of those surveyed holding a favourable image of the USA and its companies in 2015.

The election of Donald Trump had a negative impact, especially on US allies and partners, but according to Pew Research (2021), Joe Biden's victory restored some of the previous levels of trust in American foreign policies.

> In each of the 16 publics surveyed, more than six-in-ten say they have confidence in Biden to do the right thing in world affairs... In France, for example, just 31% expressed a positive opinion of the U.S. last year, matching the poor ratings from March 2003, at the height of U.S.-France tensions over the Iraq War. (In 2021) 65% saw the U.S. positively, approaching the high ratings that characterized the Obama era.

And in 2023, Pew Research reported that people in 23 countries tended to see President Biden in a more positive light than President Xi Jinping regarding world affairs – and by a big margin. However, the support provided by the US for Israel's actions in Gaza may well have undone these high ratings.

Sources: adapted from 'Selling the flag', *The Economist*, 26 February 2004 and 'Which Countries Don't Like America and Which Do?' Pew Research Center (2014); 'America' image abroad rebounds with transition from Trump to Biden' Pew Research Center (2021).

1 In your view, what are the causes of the USA's changing reputation abroad?

2 What can or should the American government and businesses do to improve it in the medium and long term?

3 What role can more effective leadership and people management play in improving the brand image and reputation of American companies and the USA generally?

The above illustration sums up the growing realisation that organizations and even nation-states (see Dinnie, 2022) need to create and maintain strong ideas of 'corporateness' for competitive advantage and foreign policy. The case also raises issues of the USA's image abroad and that of its major corporations, invoking notions such as identity, branding, and reputation. These corporate-level concepts have become key areas of strategic interest among the boardrooms of companies in sectors as diverse as financial services, information, and communication technology (ICT), retailing, food and beverages, hospitality and tourism, healthcare, local and national government, and charities. They also provide one of the key future contexts for shaping the nature of people management (Harvey & Morris, 2012; Veh et al., 2019) and consumer behaviour (Huber, 2018).

As we have already discussed, there are strong negative reasons driving organizations throughout the world to focus on their corporate identities, brands, and reputations, including:

- *The decline in general levels of trust and consumer confidence* following the highly publicised cases of *questionable corporate governance* and *questionable ethics*. Good examples of these are the Enron, Andersen Consulting, and WorldCom financial scandals during the early 2000s, British financial services companies such as RBS, the Bank of Scotland, and Barclays in the lead up to and following the Global Financial Crisis, and global companies such as Starbucks and Amazon, which continue to incur public wrath over their attempts to minimise the taxes paid in particular countries (e.g., the UK) by legitimate but questionable tax approaches and methods.
- *Problems associated with inferior and dangerous lines of business products and services.* Examples here include BP and the Deepwater Horizon oil spill disaster in 2010, Toyota and its frequent recalls of cars from 2010 onwards, Ryanair, the low-cost airline, which was named the worst company for customer service in 2015, the data breach at Facebook-Cambridge Analytica in 2018, and Tesco, whose reputation suffered markedly because of the UK horsemeat scandal in 2013 (Bozic et al., 2019).

More positively, however, organizations also see strong corporate brands, identities, and reputations as significant intangible assets, sometimes worth up to twice the book value of their tangible assets. For instance, one of the world's best-known brands, Apple, has been estimated to be worth $277.51 billion in 2023, and the brand images of companies such as UK-based Virgin, the budget airline EasyJet, and Apple itself have allowed them to extend their product–service offerings into completely new areas of business, for example, Apply Pay and Apple Music. So, a firm's corporate brand and reputation can lead to significant strategic advantage through the power to differentiate itself in the marketplace (Barnett & Pollock, 2012; Huber, 2018). Moreover, this differentiation is often difficult to copy, precisely because the sources of differences are intangible and take many years to create (see Table 6.1 on the most reputable companies in 2023). Note the absence of many of the tech companies, which have dropped out of the rankings, and the dominance of longstanding brands.

The illustration in Case 6.1 of the reputation of American organizations abroad also serves to highlight another important feature of corporate brands, identity, and reputation, which is the role of *people* in creating and maintaining these valuable assets (Martin & Hetrick, 2006; Martin & Sinclair, 2018). Corporate image usually refers to how diverse groups of receivers react to communications of the corporate identity projected by an organization (Melewar et al., 2012). It is largely created through the *unscripted and discretionary* actions, attitudes, talk, and behaviours of employees, which lead customers, investors, and the public at large to infer favourable or unfavourable impressions of the company (Sjovall & Talk, 2004; Huber, 2018). The key point is that it is not only

TABLE 6.1 The world's most reputable companies

Position	Company
1	Lego
2	Bosch
3	Rolls Royce
4	Harley-Davidson
5	Canon
6	Rolex
7	Miele
8	Sony
9	Nintendo
10	Mercedes Benz

Source: Reputation Institute (2023) Global Reptrak Study.

the formal communication of corporate identity an organization wishes to portray that is important, but also the informal impressions created by employees in the normal day-to-day conduct of their work that, in turn, lead key stakeholders to attribute to the company fundamental attributes, such as its culture, character, or reputation. This is one of the central messages of the example of 'America abroad', particularly its conduct of recent wars, its support for Israel in Gaza, and the actions of its managers in some multinational companies such as the Walmart example in Chapter 5. So, many organizations have come to recognise that one of their few unique and inimitable assets is their *human resources* in creating *reputational capital*, because their products and services, and many of their internal management processes, including financial engineering, supply chain management, and purchasing strategies, are all tangible sources of capital, so are open to copying and therefore provide little sustainable differentiation.

The business literature is replete with anecdotal evidence of how customer service, linked to good human resource management, makes a significant difference in consumer purchasing decisions, including a number of those firms listed in Table 6.1. However, a note of caution – since writing the first edition of this book in 2006, companies previously cited as excellent no longer enjoy such a reputation, including firms such as Nokia, British Airways, Tesco, and RBS, all of which have suffered reputational decline or reversion to the mean in reputational terms. We should not be surprised at this finding, however, since it mirrors the pattern of studies of so-called excellent companies in the 1980s which failed to remain excellent or failed completely (Rosenzweig, 2007). Thus, we must look for more solid justifications for this proposition in widely cited sources we examine later in this chapter. These are:

- Mary Jo Hatch and Majden Schultz's (2008/12) and Schultz (2022) work on more than 100 leading companies in the USA and Europe, which found that organizations wishing to create a strong corporate brand had to align three essential, interdependent, and largely intangible elements – the organization's vision, its culture, and its image. These included the top management's aspirations for the company, the organization's values, and the way employees felt about their organization and the image (or reputation) held of the organization by its major stakeholders – customers, shareholders, the business media, and potential employees.
- Charles Fombrun and colleagues' work on corporate reputation management since the early 1990s has demonstrated a close link between the financial fortunes of companies worldwide and their reputations (Fombrun & Van Riel, 2004; Fombrun, 2012; Fombrun et al., 2015). They found that bottom-line returns, operating performance cash flows and growth in market values were closely tied to their reputation quotient (RQ) measure and to their new reputation toolkit – RepTrak® – both of which include important people and culture management variables.

In this chapter, we shall look at the relationship between corporate-level concepts such as brands, identity, and reputations, and their relationships with human resource management, as this is one of the most important areas in which the effective management of people has been proven to impact directly on performance. First, we shall address the rather vague notion of 'corporateness' and corporate reputation (Veh et al., 2019) to clear up some of the confusion of ideas in this area. Second, we shall look at some of the human resource-based literature to see what it can add to our understanding. Then we shall examine a framework we have created that brings these two sections together to show the links between people management, branding, identity, and corporate reputation. Finally, we shall use this model to analyse one of the cases we have researched so that you can learn to use it in real-life situations.

DEFINING AND EXPLAINING 'CORPORATENESS'

There is little doubt that the concept of corporateness, a term coined by marketing specialists Balmer and Greyser (2003, 2006) to refer to a raft of corporate-level concepts, has featured more prominently in the management literature in recent years (Veh et al., 2019). This is because the promise of benefits derived from strong corporate brands, images, and reputations for social responsibility and sustainability is now being taken seriously by businesses on a global scale. At the same time, the notion of corporateness provides a new and powerful lens through which to reveal how corporations can improve performance. It also creates confusion because of the myriad of concepts competing for prominence (Fombrun, 2012). This confusion has arisen because of the different disciplines and interests contributing to the growing body of ideas, evidence, and practice that has served only to mystify practitioners and academics.

To help clear up this situation, Balmer and Greyser (2003) set out six questions that remain important to anyone working in this area (see Table 6.2). These questions

TABLE 6.2 What 'corporateness' means: six questions and related concepts

Key question	Key concept
What are the corporation's distinctive attributes?	Corporate identity
To whom and what do/should we communicate?	Corporate communications
What is our corporate promise or pledge?	Corporate branding
What are organizational members' affinities, or 'who are we'? (see Chapter 3)	Organizational identity
How are we perceived as time goes on?	Corporate reputation
How are we perceived right now?	Corporate image

Source: adapted from Balmer & Greyser, 2003, p. 4.

related to six corporate-level concepts that are often used synonymously, thus producing much of the confusion of terminology in this field. When brought together, however, and defined in more exacting terms, they seem to capture the notion of corporateness.

Balmer and Greyser pointed out that each of these concepts has been popular during different time frames since the 1970s, reflecting the problems that organizations faced at the time and the various disciplinary interests and ambitions of those contributing to the debate. For example, corporate branding was the concept favoured in the last decade, perhaps because marketing specialists made an all-out attempt to colonise this field of study and practice for their own ends. Interestingly, Balmer and Geyser, both of whom are marketeers, identified a potential for bringing together these concepts and interests under the umbrella of 'identity studies', which comprise the various definitions of identity, branding, and reputation discussed in this chapter. We shall return to this proposition later in this chapter because the notion of identity has become very popular in recent years. More recently, Veh et al. (2019) have identified clusters of research interest in corporate reputations, including auditing, initial public offerings, trust, entrepreneurial networks, and industries in which corporate reputations are critical, such as tourism and electronic commerce. However, from our perspective, and to repeat the core message, what is common to these concepts is the critical importance of people in helping 'make or break' them.

Let's look at some of these definitions and distinctions in a little more detail before building our model.

Corporate branding

Branding of products and services has played a significant part in the marketing strategy of firms for many years, with several products and services having worldwide recognition and helping create market values exceeding book values. We have already highlighted the example of Coca-Cola. Another good example from the service sector is the MBA

– the single most recognisable global brand in educational services. The classic case of branding lines of products, however, is often associated with Procter & Gamble, the American multinational, which is attributed with 'inventing' the branded strategy for its household cleaning, personal hygiene, baby, and pet care goods. Although some of its brands are global, such as Oral-B toothpaste, Ariel washing powder, and Old Spice aftershave, others are specific to countries.

Nevertheless, it is the *branding of companies* that has become increasingly valuable, especially in industries such as financial services, and consumer goods and services (Schultz et al., 2012; Miller & Merrilees, 2013; Veh et al., 2019). Marketing jargon for company or corporate branding is *monolithic branding* because it reduces the need for firms to promote individual lines of business or products/services. Such developments are not new: some strong corporate brands have retained their place in the top 100 global brands for 50 years or more, including Coca-Cola, Hewlett-Packard, Gillette, Heinz, Volkswagen, and Kellogg's. In the case of the MBA, it is Harvard that is mostly associated with this brand. So, to some extent at least, the fact of the continued existence of these organizations reflects the power of corporate brands to bestow the following advantages on their companies by:

- building long-term trust by increasing customer loyalty and convincing consumers of the benefits of their products and services;
- reducing customers' search costs for perceived quality products and services and also conferring on them certain psychological rewards; and
- ensuring repeat purchases, assisting in the development of new product launches, facilitating market segmentation by communicating directly to the intended customers of the product or service, and facilitating premium pricing.

As we noted, branding specialists began to stake out a claim for the whole area of corporate-level studies and practice because it was a concept used more and more by organizations, especially multinationals, to express their distinctiveness (Huber, 2018). A website for a major branding consulting company put the inclusive case for corporate branding as the key unifying concept, which was, the author suggested:

> no less and no more than the face of business strategy, portraying what the corporation wants to be known for in the marketplace. The corporate brand is the overall umbrella for the corporation's activities and encapsulates its vision, values, personality, positioning, and image among many other dimensions. (Hatch & Schultz, 2008)

Given its popularity and inclusiveness, Balmer and Greyser (2003, 2006) believed that the concept of the corporate branding philosophy offered the 'superior organizational lens.' It was the *explicit covenant* between an *organization and its key stakeholder groups.* The corporate brand had to articulate its agreement with these stakeholder groups – consistently and over time – to indicate that it kept its word or pledge. In this sense, it resembled the concept of corporate identity, which we discussed in the introduction. But it was also quite distinctive in several important ways:

- Corporate branding usually applied only to organizations, whereas identity could apply to individuals, groups, organizations, regions, and countries.
- Corporate brands usually took longer to develop than identities.
- Corporate brands focused mainly on the external world.
- Corporate brands usually attempted to achieve high visibility.
- Corporate brands typically required support through organizational communications and designers, e.g., through logos and symbols.
- Corporate brands could be portable – extended to cover new products and services – in a way that identities could not.
- Corporate brands could be valued financially in terms of goodwill.

Corporate branding, however, is also important for a further reason, which is the ability to *engage* the 'hearts and minds' of employees. The reverse is also true, however, since corporate branding *depends* on the hearts and minds of employees, because, as we have already seen, much of the value of corporate brands is delivered through people, having employees identify with the brand and align their efforts behind the brand (Martin et al., 2011; Martin & Sinclair, 2018). Marketing professionals have become more willing to recognise the role of employees in delivering the brand: as a result, corporations have begun to use the language and tactics of branding internally to create employers' brands, which, as we suggested in Chapter 3, is quite widespread in the USA, Europe, and Asia. One good example is HSBC, which is a bank that grew rapidly through acquisitions on a global scale during the early part of this century to be number one in the world as measured by Tier 1 capital. It has since retained a place in the top ten banks in 2022. Part of its secret of success was its ability to transfer the brand equity of these acquired firms into the corporate brand equity, so that customers and employees identify with the corporation rather than the local banks they used to be served or employed by. We shall return to this idea of employer branding later in this chapter.

However, not every organization wishes to, or needs to, have a corporate brand. Indeed, many large organizations have chosen to continue with a devolved branded strategy or have gone for a halfway-house – a so-called *endorsed brand strategy* – in which business units enjoy brand status but derive benefits from carrying the overall corporate brand. For example, before its rapid decline from 2008, RBS allowed its acquired brands such as NatWest, Ulster Bank, and Citizens in America to retain their identities, albeit referring to the RBS Group in the strapline. Interestingly, the tables have recently been turned in this company following the RBS failure after the GFC in 2007/2008. In 2016, NatWest became the corporate brand and RBS, rebranded as the Royal Bank of Scotland, the devolved brand. This rebranding was seen as an attempt to distance the company from its recent past associations with failure and to reconnect RBS to its Scottish heritage.

Corporate reputation and image

Organizations have always had a concern for their image and in the 1950s academics began to examine the idea of image in terms of personality theory in the retailing sector (see, for example, Martineau, 1958). This concern led several commercial research organizations to conduct image studies, such as Marketing and Opinion Research International (MORI) in the UK and the Opinion Research Center (ORC) in the USA. The concept of image and image research, however, has been bedevilled by problems because it has been used to refer to different aspects of an organization. These include the transmitted image (the visual image or desired image, transmitted by the corporate designers), the received image (how stakeholders perceive the brand, corporate reputation, or organizational symbols), and the construed image (how, for example, employees believe that customers see the organization). Consequently, image is a concept that is difficult to pin down and, consequently, has ceded ground to the idea of corporate reputation as a more useful concept. So, from the 1990s onwards, the study of corporate reputation has grown rapidly, bringing together scholars and practitioners from marketing and branding, economics, organizational studies, communications, and strategic management (Barnett & Pollock, 2012; Chun et al., 2019; Dowling, 2016; Fombrun, 2012, Ravasi et al., 2018; Veh et al., 2019), and from HRM (including our own work, e.g., Martin & Hetrick, 2006; Martin et al., 2010, 2011; Martin & Sinclair, 2018).

Though branding and corporate reputation have a common origin in being concerned with the external image of an organization, corporate reputation claims to be a distinctive and, arguably, a higher-order concept than either branding or image because it includes past as well as present and future impressions of a company's image, a wider range of measures of corporateness, and a wider range of stakeholders. In this sense, corporate reputation currently competes with branding and identity to be the superior organizational lens. Corporate reputations have become the subject of several influential press ratings, including *Fortune* magazine, *Asia Business*, and the *Financial Times*, which have lent it credibility with the public and other stakeholders. As I indicated earlier, such a positive reputation can lead to significant financial advantages. However, it has also become notable because of its ability to help defend an organization when it encounters adverse publicity (Elsbach, 2012). For example, Apple has been able to draw on its reputation for control, innovation, and privacy following the problems it experienced with the slowing down of old iPhones in 2017 and problems in fixing bugs in 2022. Similarly, Johnson & Johnson was able to survive the catastrophic, malicious tampering with Tylenol, one of its core products, by recovering well from a small decline in its market value because of the company's past reputation for good business principles – its reputational capital. Other companies, when facing similar disasters, have suffered more severe and sustained declines in market value because they did not have the depth of reputational capital to sustain them through their crises (Rhee & Kim, 2012). Recent examples include Pret a Manger and Boeing. Corporate reputations have also become more important in the wake of recent corporate governance and financial irregularities following the GFC of 2007–2008, because they act as a form of moral control by creating a culture of ethical values and standards of behaviour that help guide employees in their dealings with customers, clients, and governments (Barnett & Pollock, 2012). In effect, they answer the question: Would my actions be in line with the organization's reputation? An interesting example of this notion is a UK proposal developed by senior bankers to have their pay determined by how they advance the 'standards' (read reputation) of their companies.

So, what do we understand by corporate reputation? One of the most insightful and practical answers to that question was provided by Mary Jo Hatch and Majken Schultz (2008/2012), who saw it as the interaction between the objective and subjective evaluations of existing and potential stakeholders, comprising three interrelated dimensions:

- *Informal* interactions among stakeholders – for example, through sales meetings, employee storytelling, or accounts from satisfied or dissatisfied customers. These incidents strongly influence an organization's reputation or external image but are largely uncontrollable.
- *The business press,* such as the rankings of the best places to work and industry press ratings of organizations, as outlined above.
- *Potential stakeholders,* such as possible recruits, shareholders and other funders, government organizations, and the community at large.

Perhaps the best-known practitioner-orientated work on corporate reputations, however, is by Charles Fombrun and his colleagues at the New York-based Reptrak Company (formerly the Reputation Institute) (Fombrun, 1996, 2012; Fombrun et al., 2015). The definition of corporate reputation used by Fombrun and his collaborators has seven characteristics:

- They are socially constructed through interactions between companies, stakeholders, and environments.
- They are rooted in past actions and achievements as well as the present, and stakeholder assessments of them.
- Corporate reputations can attract and repulse people, so they have a powerful effect on how people perceive and enact reputations.
- Because they are diversely perceived by different stakeholders, they are only partly shaped by company communications and corporate identity management.
- They are affected by the degree of alignment that develops between parts of the system and the system as a whole.
- They signal the relative attractiveness of a company to potential stakeholders and result from long-term investments in creating distinctiveness.
- They are an important intangible source of economic value for organizations and can be used to position the organization against competitors and benchmark against the best ones.

Fombrun and Van Riel (2004) developed a widely used measure of corporate reputation – the *reputation quotient* – which was developed into a more sophisticated consulting tool in 2010 – the RepTrak® measure of global companies used in Table 6.1 (Fombrun et al., 2015). This aggregate measure is based on seven dimensions of reputation (see Table 6.3) that influence the extent to which stakeholders hold the organization in high esteem, have positive feelings/emotions about it, admire it, and trust in its competence, integrity, and benevolence. The RepTrak® model has been validated across five stakeholder groups in six countries, which confirmed the existence and stability of the seven dimensions

TABLE 6.3 The RepTrak® reputation dimensions

Products and services	The organization stands behind products and services. It offers high-quality products and services at good value. Meets customer needs
Innovation	Innovative products and services, and processes of producing them; first to market and quick to adapt to change
Leadership	Well-organized, appealing leaders, excellent management team, and a clear vision for the future
Workplace environment	Offers equal opportunities, rewards people fairly, and is known for looking after employee well-being
Governance	Fair in business, behaves ethically and is open and transparent in its decision-making
Citizenship	Environmentally responsible, positive influence on society, and supports good causes
Financial performance	Record of profitability, strong prospect for future growth, and typically produces results that are better than expected

Source: Reputation Institute (available at http://www.reputationinstitute.com/about/RepTrak).

The interest in corporate reputation management had its origins in earlier work on organizational identity, discussed in Chapter 3. In a classical interpretation of the concept, there were three central principles that could be used in any assessment of organizational identity (Albert & Whetten, 1985; Pratt et al., 2018):

of the model and so makes it a good academic and practitioner tool for measuring and managing stakeholder images of different companies.

We can now define corporate reputation as 'a collective representation of a firm's past actions and results which describe its ability to deliver valued outcomes to multiple stakeholders. It gauges a firm's relative standing with employees and externally with stakeholders, in both its competitive and institutional environments' (Fombrun et al., 2015).

Corporate and organizational identity

- it should capture the essence or 'claimed central character' of the organization.
- it should set out its claimed distinctiveness.
- it should show continuity over time.

This last principle has been subject to challenge, especially in the modern environment of continuous change, with other writers claiming that fluidity and flexibility are requirements for organization identities to cope with environmental turbulence (Gioia et al., 2013; Pratt et al., 2018). Note, for example, how a firm such as IBM has managed to make the transition from a computer hardware manufacturer to business, software, and consulting services as pressures on manufacturing costs increased because of global competition from countries such as China.

A second feature of identity noted by several authors is the idea that organizations have multiple identities (Pratt et al., 2018). This concept runs counter to the notion of a monolithic corporateness but is probably a more realistic image of most organizations. For example, hospitals can be seen as a business, a caring organization, and a professional organization in which to build a career at one and the same time (Reay & Hinings, 2009; Martin et al., 2021). So, how you see an organization at any point in time thus depends on your perspective –the perspective of a politician or financier looking for value for money, as a patient looking for high levels of care, or as a doctor looking for a place to practise his or her craft and develop a reputation (Martin et al., 2021). This feature leads us to a third characteristic, that the issue of an organization's identity surfaces and resurfaces at different points in its career or life cycle. For example, during the start-up phase, the concern will be to establish an identity, whereas during a period of retrenchment, the concern will be with embracing the need for change but retaining previously held identities for acting in good faith so that they are able to retain valued employees (Pratt et al., 2018). Again, IBM is a good example of this characteristic.

However, as we have already pointed out, in addition to the notion of organizational identity, we can also talk about corporate identity. Stretching (some might say, straining) the concept even further, Balmer and Greyser (2003) contend that identity has five meanings, which incorporate the notions of corporate and organizational identities but also include others that broadly coincide with our ideas of corporate image, strategic vision, and corporate strategy (see Figure 6.1). They also contend that the field of corporate-level studies can cohere around the management of these *multiple identities* of

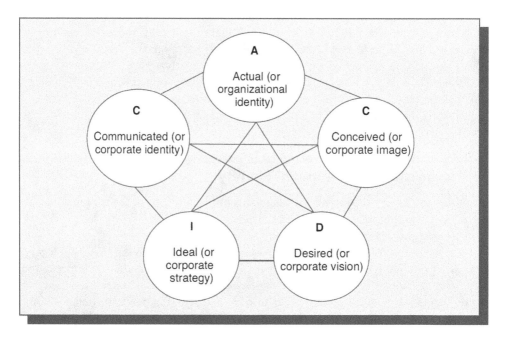

FIGURE 6.1 The AC²ID framework

(*Source*: adapted from Balmer & Greyser, 2003, p. 17)

a corporation, and they proposed an interesting though somewhat simplistic multidisciplinary approach – the AC^{2}ID *framework* – to the management of image and identity.

- The *actual identity* is defined as the current attributes of the corporation, including the values shared by management and employees. It is close to, but not synonymous with, the notion of organizational identity discussed in Chapter 3, and broadly addresses the question: Who are we? The actual identity is shaped by leadership styles, organizational structure, ownership characteristics, and the businesses and markets in which the organization operates, as well as the psychological contracts and motivations of organizational members.
- The *conceived identity* refers to the perceptions or interpretations of image, branding, and reputation held by stakeholders. Managers must make judgements about which of these to focus on.
- The *ideal identity*, the optimum positioning of the corporation in its given markets at a point in time, is based on an analysis of external environmental–internal resources fit. This identity is associated with the work of strategic planners, which is close to the notion of corporate strategy and strategic positioning.
- The *desired identity* is synonymous with the vision of the organization held by its leadership. It is not the same thing as ideal identity, which is mostly the result of serious analysis. The desired identity is very often a personal and egotistical statement made by senior leaders.
- The *communicated identity* is the 'official' identity put into the public domain through the corporate communications function – the official rhetoric of the organization that communicates what the organization wishes to be. It is also, however, communicated by less controllable media, such as 'word of mouth' and the financial press, which require a great deal of management time spent on internal communications and public relations.

Although the idea of an actual identity runs counter to identity being seen as a socially constructed phenomenon (Pratt et al., 2018), the main practical value of this framework is the proposition that all five identities need to be broadly aligned over time. If any two of these are out of alignment at a particular time, this is manifested as a 'moment of truth' from which a corporation's reputation is in danger of suffering serious damage. So, for example, the dangers of communicated identity (or corporate identity) running ahead of the actual identity (or organizational identity) can, as we pointed out in Chapter 3, lead to persistent cynicism among employees, leading to a breach of trust among customers if this cynicism is communicated by disaffected employees. Our recent work with doctors evidences this problem, with politicians and some managers in the NHS consistently overpromising what patients can expect in the form of waiting time targets without providing the means and human resources for such promises to be realised. As a result, doctors have become increasingly disillusioned and seek to withdraw from work prematurely (Martin et al., 2023). Another situation could be where redundancies lead to mass disaffection among employees (organizational identity) who are simultaneously being exhorted to 'live the brand' image that claims to 'put people first' (the conceived identity).

CONNECTING CORPORATE BRANDING, REPUTATION, AND IDENTITY TO PEOPLE MANAGEMENT

Let's turn to the human resource management literature and practice to see what else we can learn about the concept of corporateness. The key message – that good employee relations is a necessary (but not sufficient) condition for creating and maintaining corporate brands, reputations, and identities – is lent considerable support by five streams of writing and practice in the HR-related fields. These are the culture–excellence movement, the strategic HRM literature, the employer of choice thesis, employer branding, and the corporate reputation management literature itself.

The culture–excellence movement

One reading of the corporate branding and marketing literature is that it demonstrates close parallels with the 'culture–excellence' movement, which dominated much of management thinking and practice during the 1980s and 1990s (Godard, 2014). This movement, which began with Peters and Waterman's (1982) well-known book *In Search of Excellence*, fuelled the idea that the search for business success began with a serious examination of the internal culture of the organization. They promoted the message that, as the environment of most organizations was increasingly unknowable and uncontrollable, the 1970s focus on 'outside-in', rational management techniques was misplaced. Instead, it was to feelings and people – the organizational culture – that they turned for an explanation of excellence. Excellence was achieved through a strong emphasis on customer focus, which, they argued, 'all began from people.' This focus on culture as a source and driver of success has re-emerged over the past two decades from its earlier human relations incarnation, which we discussed in Chapter 1. It has influenced many of the 'business guru' writers and the development of the new resource-based view of strategic management, which focuses on internal resources as the key driver of competitive success.

Peters and Waterman took some of their ideas from Ed Schein (1992), who defined the major problem of organizations as one of simultaneously managing external adaptation to the changing environment of organizations with internal integration. This process of alignment, which we encountered earlier in this chapter, involved managing cultures and people to fit with the external image of the organization. However, the process is not a simple one and requires managing dualities, paradoxes, and tensions. Such notions have become key features of the organizational change and culture literature to be examined in Chapter 10.

The culture–excellence literature, however, was roundly criticised by economists and strategic management scholars for its overemphasis on the internal workings of organizations at the expense of market analysis and socioeconomic explanations, for the belief that managers can control organizational cultures, and from an ethical standpoint by critical management writers who see culture management as little more than indoctrination (Hatch, 2018; Pratt et al., 2018) (see Chapter 10). We return to these criticisms in the final two chapters, but there is little doubt that the managerially orientated, 'optimistic' literature on culture management has had an unquestionable influence on the practice of many organizations. Culture management and its associated 'toolkit' approach have provided a strong rationale for both strategic human resource management and the corporate reputation and branding literatures with their emphasis on vision and values (Giorgi et al., 2015; Pratt et al., 2018).

The strategic management literature

A second important stream of literature is the new strategic management or *resource-based view* (RBV) of the firm (Barney, 2002; Boselie, 2013; Ravasi et al., 2018) and its derivative, *strategic human resource management* (Boxall & Purcell, 2022). This approach has developed as a counter to the traditional 'outside-in' approaches, in which the starting point for thinking about strategic management and competitive advantage is the external environment. The work of Michael Porter is most associated with this outside-in perspective. The resource-based view on strategy and, by extension, on people management sees the fundamental, and indeed only, sustainable route to competitive advantage as arising from how you put together unique and enviable combinations of internal resources – the most important of these being people and their relationship to other key systems in the organization, such as knowledge and information. Such a perspective has led some writers to argue that how organizational cultures are managed and how employees are selected, developed, rewarded, and organized are the source of competitive advantage among firms, especially in knowledge-based industries or the growing service sectors in Europe and the USA (Boxall & Purcell, 2022; Pfeffer, 2010). Thus, the resource-based view has strong links with humanist ideas on learning organizations and organizational learning (Easterby-Smith & Lyles, 2011) (see Chapter 7).

Like the earlier outside-in approaches, however, these 'inside-out' theories have in common a tendency to offer a one-best-way solution, regardless of context, and to proselytise employees at the expense of other aspects of the business. As Porter (1996, 2008) argued, resources in and of themselves are of no competitive value; it is how and in what context such internal resources are used that leads to value creation. The two camps are beginning to recognise, however, that the answer to this fundamental question of competitive strategy probably lies somewhere in the middle, with both perspectives having something to offer (Boxall & Purcell, 2022). Nevertheless, the RBV has managed to rebalance the debate, based on the rationale that you don't move a seesaw by sitting in the middle (Boselie, 2014). This view has also provided a major intellectual and empirical justification for HR and its links to key strategic decisions on issues such as branding (Boxall & Purcell, 2022).

Consistent with the RBV, another stream of strategic management literature has been influential in explaining effective and sustainable strategic advantage, which is based on the notion of *core internal competences* (Hamel, 2007) and the complementary idea of the *balanced scorecard* (Kaplan & Norton, 2001; Kaplan, 2008). The balanced scorecard is particularly relevant to the links between HR and branding because it makes explicit and very practical links to balancing the needs and measurement of satisfying customers and financial objectives with the effective management and measurement of internal business processes, including people, and individual and organizational learning and growth. Kaplan and Norton also developed a strategy map or *theory of the business* that was, in summary, a cause-and-effect model to help managers understand the relationships between critical performance drivers and their associated outcomes. Especially in the context of service industries, such as retailing and financial services, there have been several important contributions linking the marketing of services and customer satisfaction to internal market and human resource management. The best known of these is the old but still relevant employee–customer service–profit chain identified by the Sears corporation in the USA (Kirn et al., 1999; Boxall & Purcell, 2022) (see Figure 6.2).

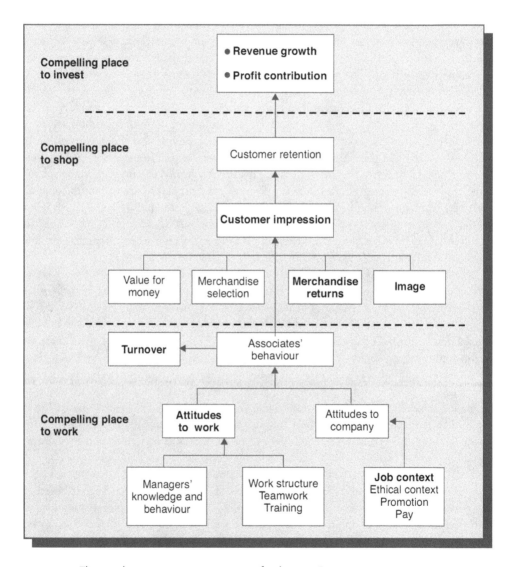

FIGURE 6.2 The employee–customer service–profit chain at Sears
(*Source:* adapted from Kaplan and Norton, 2001)

Employers of choice

As we discussed in Chapter 3, during the 1990s, an important stream of literature emerged on *new psychological contracts* based on the need to become an employer of choice (Leary-Joyce, 2004). This argument served as an antidote to the business process re-engineering, delayering, and downsizing exercises undertaken by many organizations during the early part of the 1990s and led employers to think more closely about the connections between employee satisfaction and retention, hiring, customer satisfaction, branding performance, financial performance, and corporate reputation.

According to some consultants, becoming an employer of choice is a deliberate business strategy that has driven some large US and UK employers to benchmark themselves against others in rankings of the 'best place to work', published by *Fortune* magazine in the USA and *The Times* in the UK. Although such ideas and strategies have their roots in a decade of unprecedented economic growth in the USA during the 1990s, when recruitment and retention became among the most important business issues for American employers, they appear not to have diminished in importance, despite recurrent economic crises as we saw in Chapter 3.

For many organizations, following an employer-of-choice strategy means little more than more sophisticated and sensitive recruitment practices, such as improving recruitment design, online recruitment, sensitive induction, retention analysis, cafeteria compensation and benefits, and 'growing your own' talent. For others, it meant a new, more contextually sensitive, version of the old-style, relational psychological contract (Cappelli, 1998) in which long-term commitment from employers, demonstrated through the organization's goals, values, and trust initiatives, was matched by high commitment and low turnover responses from employees. Such a psychological contract is characterised by highly competitive remuneration and benefits, often including elements of contingent pay, interesting, challenging, and varied projects, a commitment to training and development tailored to individual needs, flexible working arrangements, family-friendly policies, and a motivating work environment.

This consulting recipe for an employer-of-choice strategy is reminiscent of the classical and still influential work by Pfeffer (1998), in which he identified seven practices of highly successful companies from his review of the US and European literature (Boxall & Purcell, 2022). The list encompassed prescriptions on employment security, selective hiring, self-managed teams and decentralisation, high compensation contingent on organizational performance, extensive training and development, reduced status distinctions, and extensive information sharing on performance and financial issues. Contrary to some fashionable ideas during the 1990s, which advocated changes in the terms of the traditional psychological contracts to a new, transactional employment contract based on employability and no long-term commitment to individual careers inside an organization (e.g., Cappelli, 1998), Pfeffer (2010) made it a central part of his argument that employment security provided the necessary 'table stakes' for sustainable organizations. He reviewed several studies that showed the negative consequences of downsizing, including important connections between downsizing and the adverse impact on organizational performance with its strong, negative correlations between employee turnover and positive assessments of customer service, a vital factor in establishing and maintaining strong brand identities. If downsizing had to be undertaken, Pfeffer argued that it could be accomplished sensitively and sensibly, in a way that retained the morale of those surviving and minimised the impact on the company's image in concurrent and future hiring campaigns. It should be noted, however, that certain academics have criticised the notion of employer of choice as a recipe for breeding mediocrity in organizations by sending untargeted signals to people that everyone is welcome and encouraging underperforming staff to remain. Thus, Becker et al. (2009) argued for an 'employee-of-choice' approach, which signals that only highly qualified, motivated, and performing people should apply and expect to be retained in the organization.

For newer sectors of employment, however, these traditional psychological contracts have been difficult to sustain. This is especially evident in online sharing platform organizations such as Uber, DiDi, and LYFT, in which the psychological contract of drivers is with customers directly as well as with the platform enterprise (She et al., 2020). This link with customers makes such contracts difficult to identify and concepts such as employer of choice a much less relevant notion to sustain. Clearly, more research into these new forms of organization is needed.

Employer branding

A final stream of work deals most directly with issues of branding and attempts to use branding and marketing concepts to align employees behind strong corporate brands (Martin & Sinclair, 2018). Our research into employer branding and organizational reputations (e.g., Martin & Hetrick, 2006/2009; Martin et al., 2011; Martin & Cerdin, 2014; Martin & Sinclair, 2018; Sinclair & Martin, 2019) has led us to define an employer brand as:

> a generalised recognition for being known among key stakeholders for providing a high-quality employment experience, and a distinctive organizational identity which employees value, engage with and feel confident and happy to promote to others.
>
> (Martin et al., 2011)

The process by which branding, marketing, communications, and HR concepts and techniques are applied externally and internally to attract, engage, and retain potential and existing employees is known as employer branding. Prior to the GFC of 2007/2008, most practitioner and consulting work focused on talent attraction because of longstanding labour market conditions in developed and developing countries. Thus, employer branding became associated with the external application of marketing and communications tools. Since then, however, as we noted in Chapter 3, much of the focus of employer branding has been internal and aimed at establishing a sense of 'who are we'.

Employer branding is now big business, with several consulting firms specialising in helping firms create distinctive identities. One good example is Universum, a British company that specialises in developing distinctive employer brands through the development of a unique employer value proposition (EVP). They claim that an EVP must be an attractive, accurate (true), credible, distinctive, and sustainable representation of an organization, which has its roots in the notion of compelling strategic narratives. The key questions to be addressed by organizations are:

1. What is the compelling, novel, and credible story that employees can tell about working here?

2. How can we convey that story to potential and existing employees and significant others (parents, suppliers, customers, universities, etc.) in compelling, credible, and novel ways?

Universum's employer branding process involves establishing EVPs through internal and external research into four areas: (1) the current employer branding strategy, since all organizations have one – deliberate or accidental; (2) senior managers goals and visions for the organization – the story they want to tell to employees; (2) their corporate branding strategy, which is largely orientated to external stakeholders; and (4) how competitors position themselves in the labour market. Based on research into these four areas, they recommend developing EVPs for different employee segments/audiences, in much the same way that we discussed in the section on talent management in Chapter 3. For example, it has been estimated that by 2025, in the UK, Gen Z will comprise 23 per cent of the workforce, alongside millennials (born between 1980 and the early 2000s) who will make up 39 per cent. And by the late 2020s, Generation Alpha (born between 2010 and 2024) will also enter the workforce . The proposition here is that EVPs need to consider not only the current workforce but also future generations, who may have different interests and ambitions. Thus, for example, Universum claims that millennials are interested in an EVP that stresses a sense of purpose and innovation. They seek to be inspired by an organization's values and wish to be given opportunities to develop and grow, which is why firms like Google, J.P. Morgan, Apple, and the large management consulting firms such as PwC and KPMG were the most attractive organizations to work for in 2023. They also claim that men and women differ in their motivations to join an employer. While both are looking for work–life balance, women place greater value than men on career security, international experience, and ethical employment. Our recent research into consultant doctors' intentions to retire from the workforce provides some tentative support for generational differences in values, especially in relation to work–life balance, and the need for the NHS to reflect such differences in the 'offer' to potential doctors (Martin et al., 2023).

To return to EVPs, once they are established, they must be communicated to relevant audiences through appropriate channels. These channels are usually categorised as internal (e.g., leadership modelling, training, employer brand ambassadors), external offline (e.g., school lectures, job fairs), and external digital (campaigns, career websites, etc.). Social media are increasingly signalled as key channels for younger age groups, with firms making extensive use of social networking sites such as Facebook in sophisticated ways (Parry et al., 2019; Martin et al., 2015).

The final stage of a typical consulting process is to evaluate the messaging, both prior to launch to test out the message and post-launch to evaluate if the employer branding signals are being interpreted as intended (Martin & Cerdin, 2014). This stage is critical because it completes the loop by telling an organization whether the signals align with the EVPs as intended, whether the signals are attractive to the target group and consistent with the corporate brand, and whether they help differentiate and legitimise the organization.

The corporate reputation approach

The corporate reputation literature itself has contributed directly to our understanding of how people, culture, and organizational identity are linked to those corporate-level concepts discussed earlier (Harvey & Morris, 2012; Dowling, 2016; Ravasi et al., 2018). Three practical contributions are of particular interest and are reflected in our model.

The first of these is the work by Davies et al. (2003) and Davies (2010), which sought to develop a unified and objective way of measuring the gaps between external image and internal identity. The core argument is that reputation is 'the collective term referring to all stakeholders' views of corporate reputation' (Davies et al., 2003, p. 62), including internal (organizational) identity and external image, which they define as the views of the company held by external stakeholders, especially customers. Their framework is set out in Figure 6.3 and highlights the potential for gaps between desired image, actual image, and internal identity.

It is how these gaps are measured, however, that is of most interest, because they use a single concept and set of measures to gauge differences, which is very unusual in this type of research. To get a clear line of sight between internal and external perceptions of the organizations, they make use of the concept of stakeholder perceptions of the *organization's personality*, a construct borrowed from the psychology literature to describe generic organizational personality types. Organizational personality is defined in terms of agreeableness, trustworthiness, enterprise, chicness, competence, masculinity, ruthlessness, and informality. Questions have been derived to assess these personality dimensions, and internal and external stakeholders are provided with the same questions. By doing so, the extent of the gaps can be measured and used to realign the

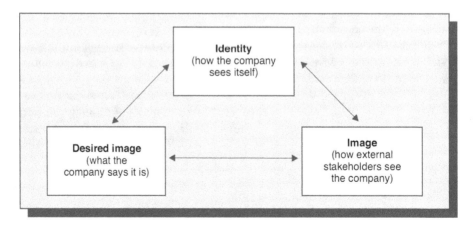

FIGURE 6.3 Gaps in reputation

(*Source*: based on Davies et al., 2003, p. 62)

three components of reputation. This work has been extensively used in research and consulting, so it is useful in helping us understand the various views of the organization held by different stakeholders using the same set of measures.

The second is the work of Hatch and Schultz (2008) and Schultz et al. (2012), which we have already discussed. These researchers developed a tripartite framework, based this time on corporate image, corporate vision, and organizational culture. By image, they mean key stakeholders' impression of the company, including customers, shareholders, the media, and public. Vision refers to what senior managers aspire to for the company, and culture refers to the organization's key values, behaviours, and attitudes (p. 130). Hatch and Schultz argued that to build an effective corporate brand or corporate reputation, organizations must ensure these three elements of an organization – the *three strategic stars* – are aligned. They also pointed out how misalignments occur when there are significant gaps in the following areas:

- The *vision–culture* gap results from senior managers moving the company in a direction that employees either do not understand or do not support. Sometimes this is a consequence of the pace of change, in which the vision is too stretching, whereas at other times, it results from visions that sit uneasily with ethical or traditional values, such as the attempted rebranding of the UK Royal Mail as Consignia more than a decade ago, which had to be undone within two years. The public and media deemed the attempt to undo 500 years of history as misplaced, despite the name being more representative of the new vision of the company.
- The *image–culture* gap usually results from organizations not putting into practice their brand values, leading to confusion among customers about the company's outside image. This gap is usually most apparent when employees' views of the company are quite different from those held by customers. Our recent research into the NHS shows how this problem can arise (Martin et al., 2023).
- The *image–vision* gap occurs when there is a mismatch between the external image of the organization and senior management's aspirations for it. The example used by Hatch and Schultz was an attempt by British Airways to globalise its image by removing the Union Jack from its tailfins. These actions led to a major public and press reaction, a cabin crew strike, and key customers threatening to switch to different carriers. Similarly, it was argued the Royal Bank of Scotland changed its logo to RBS to avoid the negative connotations of 'royal' in their expansion into America.

Hatch and Schultz have developed a framework (or 'toolkit') that comprises a series of diagnostic questions to assess the extent of misalignment between these three strategic stars (see Figure 6.4). These questions do not break new ground in assessing culture, but do point to the complex relationships between the external and internal aspects of managing effective corporate branding, placing equal weight on these dimensions.

Finally, Van Riel and Fombrun (2007) tackled the direct people management contribution to corporate reputation building by developing an *employee-expressiveness quotient* (EQ), which, in turn, is linked to strong identification with companies and to supportive employee behaviours (see Figure 6.5). They contended that companies must express themselves to employees to build emotional appeal, comprising good feelings about the

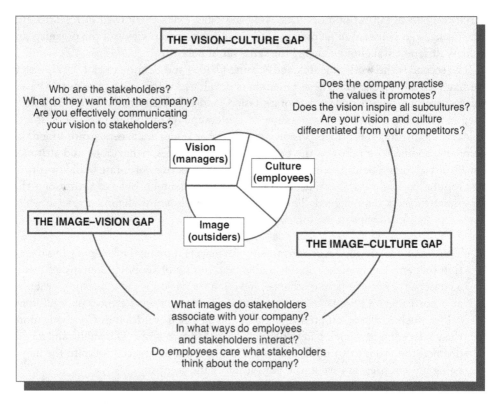

FIGURE 6.4 The corporate branding toolkit
(*Source:* adapted from Hatch & Schultz, 2008)

company, admiration, respect, and trust in the company. Expression, in this context, refers to the corporate communications process in which companies are willing to 'put themselves out there, to convey who they are and what they stand for' (Fombrun & Van Riel, 2004, p. 95). Figure 6.5 shows the drivers of expression for employees and their relationship to the EQ. You can probably infer the implied proposition, which is, that the greater the EQ, the greater the emotional appeal of the company to its workforce.

The EQ is close in tone and language to the notion of employer branding, both of which share an interest in telling credible, novel, and compelling stories to employees as to why they should identify with the company. Van Riel and Fombrun (2007) also posited a two-way relationship between identification with the company and expressiveness: the greater the level of identification, the greater the expressiveness and resulting reputation. High levels of identification were likely to lead to employees engaging in supportive behaviours, such as managers 'walking the talk', senior executives constantly communicating results, and front-line, customer-facing staff communicating honestly with customers, behaviour that, in turn, will enhance the corporate reputation over time. Conversely, the better the reputation of the company, the more likely that employees would identify with the company and its mission, acting as 'ambassadors' for the

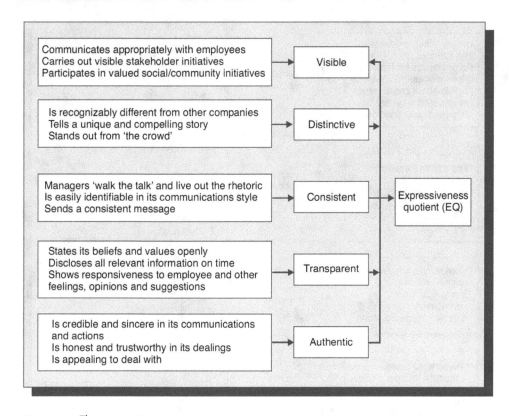

FIGURE 6.5 The expressiveness quotient

(*Source:* adapted from Fombrun & Van Riel, 2003, p. 96)

company to potential recruits, to other less-committed employees and, of course, to customers.

This cause-and-effect model is set out more formally in Figure 6.6, which shows how reputation building, personalised communications, the quality of communications, and the EQ (or emotional appeal) are linked through increased levels of organizational identification with behaviours that are supportive of corporate reputation. The model also highlights the questions used to assess the levels of organizational identification. Interestingly, these mirror much of our discussion on psychological contracts and identification outlined in Chapter 3.

MODELLING THE RELATIONSHIP BETWEEN PEOPLE MANAGEMENT, IDENTITY, BRANDS, AND REPUTATION

I have integrated some of these ideas above and some of our own work into a new framework of the relationship between people management and corporate reputations. First, however, we must decide on which of the corporate-level concepts discussed in this

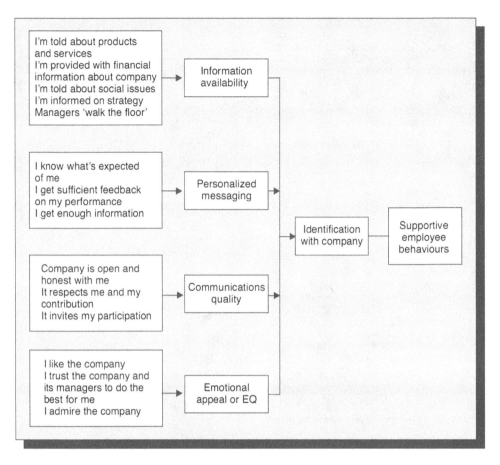

FIGURE 6.6 Measuring identification with the company and the links with employee behaviours

(*Source:* adapted from Fombrun & Van Riel, 2003, p. 100)

chapter are to be the *explained* variables and which are the most important *explainers*. As noted, a number of these compete for preeminence in corporate-level studies, and we need to be clear about our position on this issue.

Based on the evidence and arguments as they stand, I believe that corporate reputation and corporate brand are the two most important variables impacting directly on the market value of a firm and its capacity to compete in the future. However, marketing academics and trust researchers have argued these concepts are linked: brands follow from the trust key stakeholders have in an organization's reputation for competence, benevolence, and integrity, and the continued support for its products and services. These concepts, then, need to be explained by a combination of other, important corporate-level concepts and people management variables. The case made by Balmer and Greyser (2006), Pratt et al. (2018), and Hatch (2018) for identity as the superior lens is a strong one, but it is still too closely aligned with the notion of corporate identity, logos, symbols, and the output of the communications and graphic design industries. Corporate branding is also a powerful and practical concept in describing corporateness, but cannot stand alone, because as pointed out earlier, it is not a state to which all organizations aspire. Corporate reputation also has detractors: strong reputations are no guarantee of organizational success or longevity, and it is still redolent of public relations 'spin'. However, the arguments of Fombrun, his colleagues in the emerging corporate reputation field, and researchers on organizational reputations (e.g., Barnett & Pollock, 2012; Deephouse et al., 2016) make a compelling case for reputation being closely linked to business success and failure and its broader application to public sector and voluntary sector organizations, which make up large parts of the national economies.

So, this framework is based on explaining the interrelated concepts of corporate branding and corporate reputation and their links with people management explainers. In turn, these work through organizational identity and the process of identification (see Figure 6.7).

The core lessons of the model

The core lessons of the model for managers are threefold:

- Corporate reputation and evaluations of corporate brand strength (trust, confidence, and support) are strongly influenced by a series of people management strategies, including the nature of HR strategies, formal and informal organizational communications, policies designed to influence psychological contracts, and the main processes connecting individuals to their organizations (the individual–organizational linkages). These processes focus on building identification, commitment, and psychological ownership, as discussed in Chapter 3.
- These people management strategies and actions are, in turn, shaped by important corporate-level antecedents, including the corporate vision of leadership in the organization, the more analytical elements of corporate strategy, and the expressed corporate identity.
- Finally, the people management strategies work through the reciprocal relationships between organizational identity and supportive employee behaviours to influence the corporate reputation and the corporate brand.

I believe that organizations can take several important steps in people management to improve their corporate reputations and, if they so choose, their corporate brands. These are as follows.

Accurately measure what you are trying to achieve

- Organizations should design appropriate measures of corporate reputation and corporate brands, including quantitative measures and qualitative assessments of stakeholder perceptions of reputation and brands at regular intervals.
- Regular assessments should also be made of the organizational identity/identities and the kinds of behaviours associated with organizational identity. This process

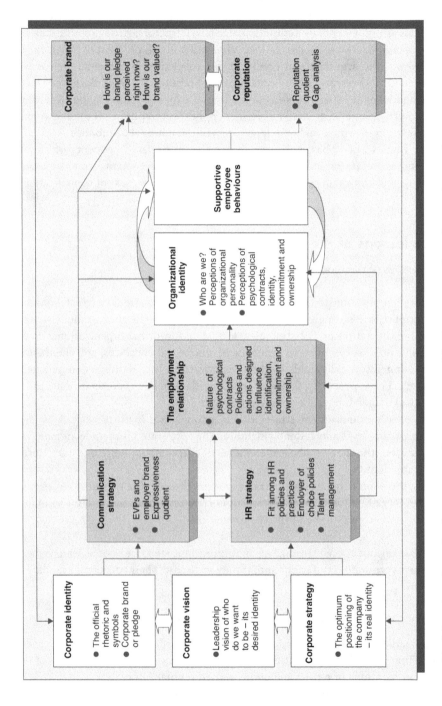

FIGURE 6.7 Modelling the relationship between people management, identity, corporate branding, and reputation

might include measures of the organization's personality or character, such as the one by Davies (2010) or the RepTrak® approach. It should also include assessments of psychological contracts and whether expectations are being met, and measures of identification with the organization, commitment to it, and feelings of psychological ownership in the organization (see Chapter 3). Finally, the performance management literature suggests that regular assessments should be made of the behaviours displayed by employees, using individual and group-level appraisals, although recent claims by consulting companies have suggested this process may be too burdensome in terms of time in relation to the benefits gained.

Understand the nature of the employment relationship and its potential to influence organizational identity

* Managers should understand the various types of psychological contracts that exist in their organizations, including the balance between transactional, relational, and ideological contracts (see Chapter 3). They might consider segmenting their employees by psychological contract type and designing appropriate mixes of policies and communications to influence and meet employee expectations (see also Chapter 3), though remaining cognizant of the problems of doing so which we take up in the next section.

Use appropriate communication strategies to influence psychological contracts, identity, and supportive employee behaviours

* This should begin with the development of a relevant EVP for the company as a whole and specific or tailored EVPs for each of the different segments of employees identified by psychological contract type. We should also consider possible generational differences and the future workforce. Above all, EVPs should contain a novel, compelling, and credible story of why people should work for the organization.
* It might also include a tailored employer-branding 'toolkit', which sets out the EVPs, the appropriate behaviours, values, and the ethical standards required by the organization.
* Personalised, face-to-face messaging that involves senior managers engaging at all levels with employees throughout the process of establishing an identity is usually required, supported by online communications and appropriate written materials. Daniel Diermeier (2023) has gone further in arguing that reputation management is so important to organizations that they should consider establishing a reputation council to act as stewards of the organization's reputation involving managers, employees, and other key stakeholders. Their job would be to monitor all business decisions and their potential influence on reputation, using game theory, psychology, and text analytics. It's interesting to note that the organizations that have been the most enthusiastic about nascent reputation councils are universities, which have gone to great lengths to build and sustain their own.
* The key messages should be expressed in such a way as to engage the emotions of employees by having managers become visible and 'walking the talk', making distinctive promises, stating beliefs and problems openly, being willing to listen,

being timely in communications, and being credible and honest. Managers should consistently measure their 'expressiveness quotient', as outlined earlier in the chapter.

Develop an appropriate mix of HR strategies that will facilitate segmentation of psychological contracts and influence organizational identification, commitment, and psychological ownership

- Employ appropriate talent management strategies, as discussed in Chapter 3, but avoid the dark side of the 'star system'. This should include clear identification of different performance levels, written action plans for each group, making leaders responsible for developing their talent pool and thoughtful executive development. However, the focus on external recruitment should be viewed with caution because there is strong evidence that the business of hiring 'stars' is very risky, often leads to companies underperforming, and is detrimental to identification by existing employees (Groysberg, 2010).
- Consider developing an 'employer-of-choice' strategy but remember that there is no 'one-size-fits-all' approach that will work in every situation. This is especially the case when employees are segmented by psychological contracts and when expectations and what is important are likely to vary by group and over time.

An integrative case study: Volvo Cars Employer Branding

To bring some of these ideas together, and to help you understand the value of the model in Figure 6.7, let's look at the case of Volvo Cars Katie Sinclair and I put together from 2017 to 2018 (Martin & Sinclair, 2018).

Volvo Cars: History, strategy, and organization

Volvo Cars was established in 1927 and remained part of the Volvo Group (Sweden) until 1999 when it was bought by Ford Motor Company (US). In 2010, Zhejiang Geely Holding Group, one of the largest independent private car manufacturers in China, acquired Volvo Cars from Ford. They addressed the global integration/ local responsiveness problem by keeping its main headquarters in Gothenburg, Sweden. This Swedish heritage and the location of the headquarters influence all aspects of its corporate culture, ethos, values, and practices. However, with aspirations to become a truly global brand, Volvo Cars currently manufactures in Sweden, Belgium, and China with plans to enter the USA and India. They have also established design hub centres in Barcelona, Shanghai, and Los Angeles. The published growth figures in 2015 showed the measured progress towards achieving its global aspirations, which saw Volvo Cars selling over half a million cars for the first time since its creation. This figure represented an increase of 8 per cent over the previous year. Moreover, during the same period, 2014 to 2015, sales increased in Europe by 10.6 per cent, the USA by 24.3 per cent, and China by 11.4 per cent. In 2017, Volvo Cars employed 30,000 people worldwide (with 62% in Sweden, 15% in Belgium, 14% in China, and other countries accounting for 9%) and sells in 100 countries across 2300 dealerships.

The company attempted to answer the 'who are we' question by describing itself as 'a company with a purpose' – *people*. This corporate identity is consistent with Geely, which proclaims employees as their 'first resource' using a '人本' (RenBen) management method. This translates into 'people are the base of every activity and every activity should be conducted in consideration of people' . However, Volvo Cars' focus on people is not new: since its founding in 1927, it has consistently presented *the safety of people* at the heart of its corporate message. The original owners' philosophy, Assar Gabrielsson and Gustav Larson, is reflected in corporate messaging that 'cars are driven by people. The guiding principle behind everything we do, is – and must remain – safety' (*Volvo Cars*, 2015).

Volvo Cars has continually dedicated its innovation and technological advancement to develop this corporate identity. Thus, for example, Nils Bohlins, a Volvo engineer, created the first three-point seatbelt in 1959 (which he subsequently gave away its patent for so all cars would benefit from this safety – essentially the creation of a global safety mechanism), and in 1976, the company's engineers created the first catalytic converter that reduced harmful exhaust emissions by 90 per cent.

In 2017, Volvo Cars developed an even greater focus on sustainability and human life, with the landmark move as the first multinational car manufacturer to say that from 2019 all new cars launched by the company will be partially or completely batter powered (battery only or plug-in hybrid) to meet EU carbon targets. The corporate communications of Volvo Cars embodies the safety of people, captured in its 'Vision 2020' 'that by 2020, no one should be killed or seriously injured in a new Volvo car' (Hakan Samuelsson, President and CEO, Volvo Car Group Annual Report, 2017).

This focus on people and safety has also been expressed in its employer brand, which is a core part of its corporate vision. As the company's 2017 annual sustainability report highlighted, its vision is: '*to be the most desired and successful transport provider in the world by...*

1. *Have leading customer satisfaction for all brands in their segments – the only true measure of customer satisfaction.*

2. *Be the most admired employer in our industry – by being the most admired employer we attract and retain the best people – create a culture of highly-engaged employees.*

3. *Have industry leading profitability – through strong performance we are able to invest in products, services and people – and our own destiny.*

being the most admired employer in our industry. Leading and embracing change. Attracting people with a strong business instinct and developing a skilled and agile workforce with the optimal knowledge and competencies at all levels. Trusting and empowering colleagues to use their intuition and make the right decisions.'

The Background

The context for the case is one in which the motor vehicle industry was, and is, facing multiple challenges, an unpredictable global economy, accelerated impact/change of digital technologies such as autonomous driving, social change in how cars are used (diverse or shared), mobility issues such as a demand for 'city' cars, and sustainability policies (on issues such as carbon emission targets, tightening regulations on cars being cars allowed in cities, and a demand for electric and hybrid vehicles). These changes are forecast to create opportunities, not only for existing car producers but also for different players from new industries and collaborations outside the 'traditional' automobile networks. For example, the advancing technology for autonomous driving has seen new entrants such as Tesla, Apple, and Google enter the industry. As the industry diversifies into new technology, companies have identified recruiting talented employees with different types of skills as a fundamental competitive requirement, thus the need for credible, novel, and effective employer brands/branding strategies has become a core HR problem.

As noted earlier, Geely acquired Volvo Cars in 2010, but largely left control of the company's operations and decision-making to its headquarters and management team in Gothenburg, Sweden. This decision was aided by the degree of compatibility of Geely's RenBen management philosophy and methods. During a discussion with the authors when visiting Volvo Cars in Gothenburg, senior HR staff stated that Geely management had left the Swedish-based team very much in charge of its Swedish heritage and culture, which shapes its corporate identity, communications style, and signalling. These moves and their interpretation by senior Swedish HR staff point to Volvo Cars remaining a company with a strong Swedish identity but needing to find a solution to how an inherently Swedish-infused message would resonate across different national and cultural contexts. Thus, much of its global messaging, advertising, and corporate communications are linked to its Swedish heritage, culture, and landscapes. Nevertheless, they also created sophisticated social media advertising and merging of branding and employer branding campaigns to target specific national regions in which they operate, particularly in the UK. To do so, Volvo Cars (UK) has entered a unique collaboration with premium telecommunications company, Sky UK Limited. This collaboration shows how a company's corporate objectives can be signalled differently across international contexts with the assistance of unique collaborations outside the car industry. In addition, Volvo Cars has made the strategic decision to promote and 'tell their story' of how they build/intend to build their brand by becoming involved with a firm of international employer brand strategists. According to senior HR staff, this cooperation was intended to send a powerful message to employees, potential recruits, and competitors in the industry of the extent to which they are dedicated to becoming an 'employer of choice.'

Designing the brand

Volvo Cars make extensive use of social media content, especially advertising and YouTube clips, to promote their corporate and employer brands. In 2014, VC HR staff elaborated how they felt the need to update communication channels with a new global career site structure, a global umbrella strategy for employer branding in social media, along with a new 'tone of voice,' and new visual guidelines for recruitment ads . Thus, the company introduced what they labelled as a people-centric message in their flagship advert Volvo – Made by People' (2016), a portrayal of a day in the life of an average employee. This short film shows a range of employees of diverse age groups, backgrounds, nationalities, and religions. The clip was intended to capture what it was like to work in the company: people waking up at home, going to work, and employees interacting and enjoying their work in an environment, attempting to send a message of an ethos of design, craftsmanship, engineering, teamworking, and innovation. The clip finished with the message:

> MADE BY CROATIA, GREECE, BELGIUM, FINLAND, GERMANY, CHINA, FRANCE, NORWAY, THE NETHERLANDS, POLAND, REPUBLIC OF KOREA, SPAIN, TURKEY, UK, MADE BY SWEDEN, MADE BY PEOPLE.

The company's corporate and employer branding focused on this simple message of 'Made by People' and lists of diverse countries contributing to the creation of Volvo Cars in all its communications literature, video clips on TV, and YouTube in an attempt to send honest brand signals to a range of audiences worldwide, which were important in creating an employer brand image, including those that refract the image such as powerful media.

In one of its most sophisticated campaigns, Volvo Cars (UK) became the official sponsor of Sky Atlantic in 2014. Building upon the initial globally reaching story for 'Volvo – Made by People', this unique collaboration saw the later creation in 2016/2017 of a campaign called Human Made Stories:

> a depiction of the Volvo philosophy centred around people ... Human Made Stories is a series of short films portraying defiant pioneers. People who do things differently and go their own way. Whose relentless pursuit of craft and innovation will change our world. These are the types of people that inspire each and every one of us at Volvo every day. We hope their stories will inspire you too.
> ("http://www.volvocars.com/uk/about/humanmade/discover-volvo/defiant
> -pioneers" }).

These short films were made in a highly refined and stylish manner. With behavioural nudges towards the company's Swedish heritage, they sought to engage with a broad audience as they covered a range of identifiable issues, including art, engineering, music, sustainability, and technology. They can be seen as representing a highly differentiated collaboration between a car manufacturer and a premium TV network to create a sophisticated approach to building an internal and external employer brand. These messages in the films were aimed:

1. Internally, by projecting an organizational culture intended to resonate with current employees and help create, or further embed, a strong personal and organizational identification.

2. Externally, to potential recruits, with the intention that they interpret these clips in line with their self-identity – their work ethic, values, and attitudes – and begin laying foundations for psychological contracts.

Employees' voices were communicated to audiences through the theme underlying the challenges depicted in the clips. However, these messages were communicated subtly: the clips did not explicitly tell the viewer what it is like to work day-to-day at VC, since the 'Made by People' clip creates this narrative but sought to create an impression of culture and work ethic that characterise Volvo Cars.

The release of a second set of chapters in August 2017 of the Human Made Stories reaffirmed the relationship the company wished to portray between their core values and innovation ethos. These chapters introduce a father and son, with no farming experience, finding a solution to ensure a successful harvest – literally, under the sea. However, it is in the final chapters that the underlying Volvo Cars corporate identity is fully revealed. One of these stories concerns a young aspiring violinist 'robbed of her speech and movement in a tragic car accident. Twenty-eight years later, she learns to create music again, using only the power of her mind' through current technology and innovation.

Building on these chapters, the company released the advert for their flagship Volvo XC60, which portrays a young child telling her mother the story of what she wished for the rest of her life; friends, university, career, marriage, and children of her own. The end of the advertisement shows the latest vehicle release using modern 'stop technology' to brake as the young child crosses the road – depicting that a car accident could have happened. Volvo Cars describes this advertisement, and thus the new technology, as 'sometimes the moments that never happen, matter the most' thus allowing her 'future' to continue.

Evaluating the Brand

One of the main future trends in employer branding lies in employers becoming better acquainted with identifiable, relevant, and unique ways of measuring the effectiveness of their employer brands as well as perfecting the employer brand processes. To that end 'big data' has become a topic of interest for HR managers interested in aligning their activities with key business objectives. Big data has been defined as unstructured datasets that are too large for the average database programs to effectively obtain, manage and use. These vast datasets tend to originate in collections of data generated and shared by a wide range of public bodies, businesses, and non-profit organizations. Big data can offer insights into the everyday life of habits and actions of millions of people by capturing, integrating, and transforming data into forms usable for analysis by businesses – a process sometimes referred to as 'datafication'.

Volvo Cars have used 'big data' very effectively to measure the responsiveness of its employer branding activities when it became the official sponsor of Sky Atlantic. This sponsorship deal allowed the company to access Sky's data management platform (DMP), which is described on the Sky website as:

Delivering a digital campaign to viewers of a particular show, group of shows or genre (for example, those who watch food programmes, movie fans, Game of Thrones viewers). Its core to the proposition is the viewing data Sky collects from households on our viewing panels, this data is aggregated at either a programme, ad spot or sponsorship level and fed into the DMP. Within the DMP the viewing data is matched to online data to link household viewing with online cookies which allows cross platform targeting ... At the heart of Sky AdVance is data – Sky Media has expanded its TV audience measurement capabilities to now gather data from 3 million households, providing second by second viewing data. This massive scale allows insights from the Sky platform covering over 500 TV channels, providing programme, spot and sponsorship viewing as well as regency and frequency data. This combined TV, online and mobile knowledge opens the door to advanced understanding and delivery. (https://www.skymedia.co.uk/skyadvance/)

Using the Sky platform has allowed Volvo Cars to use Sky Atlantic's capabilities to target specific audience segments by (a) collecting and analysing data on who is watching and engaging with their clips, then (b) repeating these clips online and across other Sky Digital platforms (such as phones and tablets), with accompanying advertising banners, which are targeted at specific users based on their historical web 'cookies'. In short, Volvo Cars can deliver advertisements to specific audiences based on their TV viewing habits and all other data held by Sky. Using this approach, the company in the UK has also gained the ability to use data to direct Human Made Stories to potential employees, which is, as Sky proffers, 'the next level of connected campaigns.'

External engagement. At the time of writing this case, Sky Atlantic reported high levels of audience engagement with 'Human Made Stories', citing 'strong identity for the series and the quality of the brand' (*Sky Media*, 2016). These audiences not only included potential vehicle purchasers, but also potential and existing employees, and significant others who refracted the brand image. Results showed the initial chapters for the 'Human Made Stories' gaining similar amounts of views since their release in 2016. The newer releases of chapters (August, 2017) achieved substantially higher levels of online engagement – almost double that of the first set of chapters – less than two weeks after their release. As Sara Axling, Volvo Cars previous employer brand manager proposed, 'collaborations with the best employer brand strategists, market research companies and creative agencies worldwide, you can bring an outstanding team to drive your employer brand strategy.'

Internal engagement. While it is difficult to gain independent evidence of the internal impact of 'Human Made Stories', VC reported increased engagement and performance since the promotional campaign began. Their 2016 Volvo Group Attitude Survey (VGAS), based on a 93 per cent response rate, showed an increase in engaged employees over the previous two years. In addition, their Global People Survey which specifically measures employee engagement asked employees for their opinions on their work and teams. A 90 per cent response rate was recorded as showing employees as 'engaged and customer-orientated and have a good knowledge of corporate culture and ethical issues' (*Volvo Annual and Sustainability Report*, 2017).

Questions

1. How do you assess Volvo Cars' approach to employer branding at the time of writing the case? What were its strengths and weaknesses?
2. Undertake a follow-up web-based investigation into employer branding in Volvo Cars. What have you learnt?

LEARNING SUMMARY

In this chapter, we have discussed the importance of corporateness as a new lens through which to view organizations. Many organizations in all sectors of the economy view corporate reputation and a strong corporate brand as an essential component of their corporate strategy, so have invested heavily in image and brand building. This is especially true of international companies seeking to operate in global markets and *leverage the benefits of trust and confidence in their products and services* worldwide. However, it is not only large organizations that need to secure trust and confidence, small companies, public sector organizations, and not-for-profit organizations are especially vulnerable to problems connected with trust and confidence. Investment in strong trust relations has been associated with superior organization performance in the long term because trust and confidence in an organization and its corporate brand result in customers, employees, and other stakeholders continuing *to support the company* by purchasing existing products and services, buying new ones (brand extension), and recommending other people to do the same. Perhaps of equal importance, especially in modern knowledge- and service-based economies, trust and confidence in the organization result in existing and potential employees providing essential support through increased motivation, commitment, identification, and psychological ownership. Indeed, as some writers have argued, and which is a central theme of this chapter, creating employee trust and confidence in an organization is the most *important, necessary prior condition* for building, maintaining, and defending *reputations and brands.*

One of the key problems bedevilling the development of this field is the proliferation and confusion of terms: to follow the old management adage, if you can't define something accurately, you can't measure and manage it. As a result, we have spent some time defining the concepts associated with corporateness, including corporate identity, organizational identity, corporate image, corporate strategy, corporate vision, corporate communications, and the key outcomes of strong corporate reputations and brands. The AC²ID framework was used to illustrate these ideas and show you how it might be applied to the analysis of organizational problems.

Returning to the importance of people management in creating, sustaining, and defending corporate reputations and brands, I have created a framework to show how the complex relationships between HR strategies, communications strategy and the nature of employment relationships can impact organizational identity and employee behaviours that, in turn, shape corporate brands and corporate reputations. This framework has been built from extensive research in the field and has been used by HR and marketing practitioners to analyse the process of building reputations and brands and to design appropriate people management policies. From the model, I also drew some practical lessons concerning the measurement of reputations and brands, understanding the nature of the employment relationship, the use of appropriate communications strategies to influence employment relationships, and the use of different HR strategies to facilitate more refined segmentation of psychological contracts. I concluded the chapter by asking you to apply the model to a case study of Volvo Cars to illustrate its practical relevance.

REVIEW QUESTIONS

1. What strategies are most likely to create long-term *reputational* capital?
2. The HR department in a company has been given the task of developing a compelling employer brand to help develop employee attraction and engagement. How might they go about doing this?

REFERENCES

Albert, S., & Whetten, D. (1985). Organizational identity. In L. L. Cummings & B. M. Staw (Eds.), *Research in organizational behaviour* (Vol. 7, pp. 263–295). JAI Press.

Alessandri, S. W., & Alessandri, T. (2004). Promoting and protecting corporate identity: The importance of organizational and industrial context. *Corporate Reputation Review, 7*(3), 252–268.

Aperia, T., Simic Bronn, P., & Schultz, M. (2004). A reputation analysis of the most visible companies in Europe. *Corporate Reputation Review, 7*(3), 218–231.

Balmer, J. M. T., & Greyser, S. A. (2006). Corporate marketing: Integrating corporate identity, corporate branding, corporate communications, corporate image, and corporate reputation. *European Journal of Marketing, 40*(7/8), 730–741

Balmer, J. T., & Greyser, S. A. (2003). *Revealing the corporation: Perspectives on identity, image, reputation, corporate branding and corporate-level marketing.* Routledge.

Barnett, M. L., & Pollock, T. G. (Eds.). (2012). *The Oxford handbook of corporate reputation.* Oxford University Press.

Barney, J. (2002). Strategic management: From informed conversation to academic discipline. *Academy of Management Executive, 16*(2), 53–58.

Barry, D., & Elmes, M. (1997). Strategy retold: Toward a narrative view of strategic discourse. *Academy of Management Review, 22*(2), 429–452.

Becker, B. E., Huselid, M. A., & Beatty, R. W. (2009). *The differentiated workforce: Transforming talent into strategic impact*. Harvard Business School Press.

Boselie, P. (2013). Human resource management and performance. In S. Bach & M. R. Edwards (Eds.), *Human resource management in transition* (5th ed., pp. 18–36). Wiley.

Boselie, P. (2014). *Strategic human resource management: A balanced approach*, 2nd edn. London: McGraw-Hill.

Boxall, P., & Purcell, J. (2022). *Strategy and human resource management* (5th ed.). Bloomsbury.

Bozic, B., Siebert, S., & Martin, G. (2019). A strategic action perspective on organizational trust repair. *European Management Journal, 37*(1), 58–66

Cappelli, P. (1998). *The new deal at work: Managing the market-driven workforce*. Harvard University School Press.

Chun, R., Argandoña, A., Choirat, C., & Siegel, D. S. (2019). Corporate reputation: Being good and looking good. *Business & Society, 58*(6), 1132–1142

Davies, G. (2010). The meaning and measurement of corporate reputation. In R.J. Burke, G. Martin, & C. L. Cooper (Eds.), *Corporate reputation: managing opportunities and threats* (pp. 45–60). Gower.

Davies, G., Chun, R., Da Silva, R. V., & Roper, S. (2003). *Corporate reputation and competitiveness*. Routledge.

De Chernatony, L. (2001). *From brand vision to brand evaluation*. Butterworth-Heinemann.

Deephouse, D. L., Newbury, W., & Soleimani, A. (2016). The effects of institutional differences and national culture on cross-national differences in corporate reputation. *Journal of World Business, 51*(3), 463–473.

Diermeier, D. (2023). *Reputation analytics: Public opinion for companies*. University of Chicago Press.

Dell, D., & Ainspan, N. (2001, April). *Engaging employees through your brand* (Conference Board Report, No. R-1288-01-RR). Conference Board.

Dinnie, K. (2022). *Nation branding; Concepts, issues, practice* (3rd ed.). Routledge.

Dowling, G. R. (2001). *Creating corporate reputations: Identity, image and performance*. Oxford University Press.

Dowling, G. R. (2016). Defining and measuring corporate reputations. *European Management Review, 13*(3), 207–223.

Easterby-Smith, M., & Lyles, M. A. (2011). The evolving field of organizational learning and knowledge management. In M. Easterby-Smith & M. A. Lyles (Eds.), *Handbook of organizational learning and knowledge management* (pp. 1–21). Wiley.

Elsbach, K. D. (2012). A framework for reputation management over the course of evolving controversies. In M. L. Barnett & T. G. Pollock (Eds.), *The Oxford handbook of corporate reputation* (pp. 466–486). Oxford University Press.

The Economist. (2004, February 26). Selling the flag.

Fombrun, C. J. (1996). *Reputation*. Harvard Business School Press.

Fombrun, C. J. (2012). The building blocks of corporate reputation: Definitions, antecedents, consequences. In M. L. Barnett & T. G. Pollock (Eds.), *The Oxford handbook of corporate reputation* (pp. 94–113). Oxford University Press.

Fombrun, C. J., Ponzi, L. J., & Newbury, W. (2015). Stakeholder tracking and analysis: The RepTrak® system for measuring corporate reputation. *Corporate Reputation Review, 18*, 3–24.

Fombrun, C. J., & Rindova, V. (2000). Reputation management in global 100 firms: A benchmarking study. *Corporate Reputation Review, 1*(3), 205–214.

Fombrun, C. J. and Van Riel, C. B. M. (2003). *How successful companies build winning reputations.* Upper Saddle River, NJ: Pearson Education.

Fombrun, C. J., & Van Riel, C. B. M. (2004). *Fame and fortune: How successful companies build winning reputations.* Financial Times/Prentice-Hall.

Gioia, D. A., Patvardhan, S. D., Hamilton, A. L., & Corley, K. (2013). Organizational identity formation and change. *The Academy of Management Annals, 7*(1), 123–193.

Giorgi, S., Lockwood, C., & Glynn, M. A. (2015). The many faces of culture: Making sense of 30 years of research on culture. *The Academy of Management Annals, 9*(1), 1–54.

Godard, J. (2014) The psychologisation of employment relations? *Human Resource Management Journal*, 24(1),1–18.

Groysberg, B., Nanda, A., & Nohria, N. (2004, May 5). The risky business of hiring stars. *Harvard Business Review, 82*, 92–100.

Guest, D. E. (1998). Is the psychological contract worth taking seriously? *Journal of Organizational Behaviour, 19*, 649–664.

Groysberg, B. (2010). *Chasing stars: The myth of talent and the portability of performance.* Princeton, NJ: Princeton University Press.

Haig, M. (2004). *Brand royalty.* Kogan Page.

Hamel, G. (2000). *Leading the revolution.* Harvard Business School Press.

Hamel, G. (2007). *The future of management.* Cambridge, MA: Harvard Business School Press

Handfield-Jones, H., Michaels, E., & Axelrod, B. (2001, November/December). Talent management: a critical part of every leader's job. *Ivey Business Journal.* Retrieved May 14, 2005, from http://www.iveybusinessjournal.ca/ view_article.asp?intArticle _ID=316.

Harvey, W. S., & Morris, T. (2012). A labor of love? Understanding the influence of corporate reputation in the labor market. In M. L. Barnett & T. G. Pollock (Eds.), *The Oxford handbook of corporate reputation* (pp. 341–360). Oxford University Press.

Hatch, M. J. (2018). *Organization theory—modern, symbolic, and postmodern perspectives* (4th ed.). Oxford University Press.

Hatch, M. J., & Schultz, M. (2002). The dynamics of organizational identity. *Human Relations, 55*, 989–1018.

Hatch, M. J., & Schultz, M. (2008). *Taking brand initiative: How the company can align strategy, culture and identity through corporate branding.* Wiley.

Huber, C. (2018). *The corporate reputation of multinational corporations: An analysis of consumers' perceptions of corporate reputation and its effect across nations.* Springer Link

Joyce, W., Nohria, N., & Robertson, B. (2003). *What really works: The 4+2 formula for sustained business success.* Harper Collins.

Kaplan, R. S. (2008). Conceptual foundations of the balanced scorecard. In C. Chapman, A. Hopwood, & M. Shields (Eds.), *Handbook of management accounting research* (Vol. 3). Elsevier.

Kaplan, R. S., & Norton, D. (2001). *The strategy-focused organization*. Harvard Business School Press.

Kirn, S. P., Rucci, A. J., Huselid, M., & Becker, B. (1999). Strategic human resource management at Sears. *Human Resource Management, 38*(4), 329–335.

Leary-Joyce, J. (2004). *Becoming an employer of choice: making your own organization a place where people want to do great work.* CIPD

Martin, G., & Beaumont, P. B. (2003). *Branding and people management: What's in a name? Chartered Institute of Personnel and Development.*

Martin, G. and Cerdin, J.-L. (2014) Employer branding and career theory: new directions for research. In: P. R.Sparrow, H. Scullion and I. Tarique (eds), *Strategic Talent Management: Contemporary issues in international Context.* Cambridge: Cambridge University Press, pp. 151–176.

Martin, G., Gollan, P. J., & Grigg, K. (2011). Is there a bigger and better future for employer branding? Facing up to innovation, corporate reputations, and wicked problems in SHRM. *International Journal of Human Resource Management, 22*(17), 3618–3637.

Martin, G., & Hetrick, S. (2006). *Corporate reputations, branding and HRM.* Butterworth-Heinemann.

Martin, G. and Hetrick, S. (2010). Employer branding and corporate reputations in an international context.In: P. S. Sparrow (ed.), *Handbook on International Human Resource Management.* Sussex: John Wiley Sons,pp. 293–321.

Martin, G., Gollan, P. J., & Grigg, K. (2011). Is there a bigger and better future for employer branding? Facing up to innovation, corporate reputations and wicked problems in SHRM. *The International Journal of Human Resource Management,* 22(17), 3618–3637.

Martin, G., Parry, E., & Flowers, P. (2015). Do social media enhance constructive employee voice all the time or just some of the time? *Human Resource Management Journal, 25*(4), 541–562.

Martin, G., Siebert, S., Bushfield, S., & Howieson, W.B. (2021). Changing logics in healthcare and their effects on the identity work and identity motives of doctors. *Organization Studies, 42*(9), 1477–1499.

Martin, G., & Sinclair, K. (2018). Employer branding and corporate reputation management in global companies: theory and practice. In D.G. Collings, H. Scullion, & P. Caligiuri (Eds.), *Global talent management* (2nd ed., pp. 144–164). Routledge.

Martin, G., Staines, H. J., & Bushfield, S. (2023). *Senior hospital doctors' intentions to retire in NHS Scotland.* University of Dundee. https://discovery.dundee.ac.uk/en/publications/senior-hospital-doctors-intentions-to-retire-in-nhs-scotland

Martin, J. (1992). *Cultures in organizations: Three perspectives.* Oxford University Press.

Martineau, P. (1958, January/February). The personality of the retail store. *Harvard Business Review*, p. 47.

McEwen, B., & Buckingham, G. (2001, May). Making a marque. *People Management, 7,* 40–44.

McKenzie, A., & Glynn, S. (2001). Effective employment branding. *Strategic Communications Management, 5*(4), 22–26.

Melewar, T. C., Sarstedt, M., & Hallier, C. (2012). Corporate identity, image and reputation management: A further analysis. *Corporate Communications: An International Journal, 17*(1), 1–5.

Michaels, E., Handfield-Jones, H., & Alexrod, B. (2001). *The war for talent.* Harvard Business School Press.

Miller, D. and Merrilees, B. (2013) Rebuilding community corporate brands: a total stakeholder approach. *Journal of Business Research, 66* (2),172–179.

Miller, J., & Muir, D. (2004). *The business of brands.* John Wiley.

Mitchell, C. (2002, January). Selling the brand inside. *Harvard Business Review,* pp. 34–41.

Ogbonna, E., & Harris, L. C. (1998). Managing organizational culture: Compliance of genuine change? *British Journal of Management, 9*(2), 273–288.

Parry, E., Martin, G., & Dromey, J. (2019). Scenarios and strategies for social media in engaging and giving voice to employees. In P.Holland, J. Teicher, & J. Donaghey (Eds.), *Employee voice at work* (pp. 2001–2015). Springer.

Peters, T. J., & Waterman, R. H. Jr (1982). *In search of excellence.* Harper & Row.

Pew Research Center (2014). Which countries don't like America and which do? Available online at www.pewresearch.org/fact-tank/2014/07/15/which-countries -dont-like-america-and-which-do/.

Pew Research Center. (2021). America's image abroad rebounds with transition from Trump to Biden. https://www.pewresearch.org/global/2021/06/10/americas-image -abroad-rebounds-with-transition-from-trump-to-biden/.

Pfeffer, J. (1998). *The human equation: Building profits by putting people first.* Cambridge, MA: Harvard Business School Press.

Pfeffer, J. (2010). Building sustainable organizations: The human factor. *Academy of Management Perspectives, 24*(1), 34–45.

Porter, M. P. (1996, November/ December). What is strategy? *Harvard Business Review,* pp. 61–71.

Porter, M. P. (2008, January). The five competitive forces that shape strategy, *Harvard Business Review,* pp. 79–93.

Pratt, M. G., Schultz, M., Ashforth, B. E., & Ravisi, D. (Eds.). (2018). *The Oxford handbook of organizational identity.* Oxford University Press.

Reay, T. and Hinings, C. R. (2009). Managing the rivalry of competing institutional logics. *Organization Studies, 30* (6), 629–652.

Rhee M and Kim T (2012). After the collapse: A behavioral theory of reputation repair. In: Barnett ML and Pollock TG (eds), *The Oxford Handbook of Corporate Reputation.* Oxford: Oxford University Press, 446-465.

Rosenzweig, P. (2007). *The halo effect* . . . and the eight other business delusions that deceive managers. New York: Free Press.

Ravasi, D., Rindova, V., Etter, M., & Cornelissen, J. (2018). The formation of organizational reputation. *Academy of Management Annals, 12*(2), 574–599

Roll, M. (2004). *Understanding the purpose of a corporate branding strategy.* Retrieved December 5, 2004, from http://www.brandchannel.com/brand-speak.asp?bs_id=81.

Ruch, W. (2002). *Employer brand evolution: A guide to building loyalty in your organization.* http://www.versantsolutions.com.

Schein, E. (1992). *Organizational culture and leadership.* Jossey Bass.

Schultz, M. (2022). Balancing the past and future in corporate branding. In O. Inglsias, N. Ind, & M. Schultz (Eds.), *Routledge companion to corporate branding* (pp. 408–416). Routledge.

Schultz, M., Hatch, M. J., & Adams, N. (2012). Managing corporate reputation through corporate branding. In M. L. Barnett & T. G. Pollock (Eds.), *The Oxford handbook of corporate reputation* (pp. 420–445). Oxford University Press.

Sjovall, A. M., & Talk, A. (2004). From actions to impressions: Cognitive attribution theory and the formation of corporate reputation. *Corporate Reputation Review, 7,* 269–281.

She, S., Xu, H., Wu, Z., Tian, Y., & Tong, Z. (2020). Dimension, content, and role of platform psychological contract: Based on online ride-hailing users. *Frontiers in Psychology, 11.* https://doi.org/10.3389%2Ffpsyg.2020.02097

Sinclair, K., & Martin, G. (2019). *Internal perceptions of employer branding: A review and conceptual framework.* Paper presented to the British Academy of Management Annual Conference, Aston University, Birmingham.

Sparrow, P. R., Brewster, C., & Harris, H. (2004). *Globalizing human resource management.* Routledge.

Van Riel, C. B. M. and Fombrun, C. J. (2007). Essentials of corporate communication: Implementing effective reputation management. Oxford: Routledge.

Veh, A., Göbel, M., & Vogel, R. (2019). Corporate reputation in management research: A review of the literature and assessment of the concept. *Business Research, 12,* 315–353.

Volvo Cars (2015). Safety. Available at: https://www.volvocars.com/uk/v/safety/culture-vision.

CHAPTER 7

The knowledge context, organizational learning, and managing people

LEARNING OBJECTIVES

By the end of this chapter, you should be able to:

- Understand the nature of knowledge in society, its role in creating strategic advantage in knowledge-based enterprises, and the role of people management
- Understand what knowledge is and its relationship to learning.
- Describe the processes of knowledge management in organizations and use them to analyse an organization.
- Understand how organizations create and share knowledge and learning.
- Understand the relationship between knowledge and learning, especially the importance of tacit knowledge.
- Apply a knowledge management perspective to an organization.
- Understand the notion of intellectual capital and advise on how it might be measured in different types of organizations.
- Use measures of intellectual capital to evaluate an organization.
- Understand how different forms of knowledge relate to organizations and processes and the issue of managing people.
- Advise managers on the nature of 'knowledge workers' and the issues connected with managing knowledge workers.
- Advise on an appropriate performance management system for knowledge workers.

DOI: 10.4324/9781003469711-7

UNDERSTANDING THE NATURE OF KNOWLEDGE MANAGEMENT AND ORGANIZATIONAL LEARNING AND THE IMPACT ON ORGANIZATIONS AND PEOPLE

Introduction

Received wisdom in the strategic management literature is that organizations that integrate disparate sources of *knowledge* across their boundaries will be those that survive and prosper. These disparate sources include not only formal, written, or coded forms of knowledge but also the possession of some advantageous, intangible, knowledge-based assets (Hislop et al., 2018). Indeed, as we have seen in Chapter 4, some writers on innovation go further to claim that the primary reason for an organization's existence is its ability to transfer knowledge and learning more effectively and efficiently than through external market mechanisms (Gupta & Govindarajan, 2004). This is especially true of international organizations, many of which have previously relied on establishing subcontracting relationships, based purely on market relations and the price mechanism, to extend their operations beyond their domestic boundaries. Nowadays, they are more likely to engage in networks or strategic alliances, as we discussed in Chapter 4. However, these arguments may also be applied to smaller and medium-sized organizations that operate in mainly domestic markets in the developed world, as they increasingly find themselves in a knowledge-based economy, with intellectual rather than physical or financial capital being the source of their competitive advantage (Durst & Edvardsson, 2012). Consider the following illustration of a Scottish financial services company, which I researched years ago (and which now exists under a different name and form as part of Standard Life Aberdeen).

CASE 7.1 STANDARD LIFE INVESTMENTS: KNOWLEDGE TRANSFER AND BUSINESS DEVELOPMENT OVERSEAS

Standard Life Investments (SLI) was a global investment company, which focused on managing institutional investments for clients in a range of countries. It was formed as a separate division of the parent company, the Standard Life Assurance Company, founded in 1825, floated on the London Stock Exchange in 2006 and was a FTSE 100 company. When I worked with the company, most recently in 2006, SLI had offices in Boston, Hong Kong, Paris, Beijing, Sydney, London, Dublin, and Seoul, and joint ventures in India and Japan. The company was headquartered in Edinburgh, Scotland, employed 1100 people, and managed assets worth £246 billion on behalf of clients throughout the world. This represented a three-fold increase in the number of employees and a five-fold growth in managed assets since 1998. The company had consistently won awards for its fund performance and levels of service to clients.

The company provided skilled investment experts to manage the assets that many organizations, including its own parent company, entrusted to SLI. These investment experts were of two kinds. First, client fund managers, who were responsible for the full range of their clients' performance and servicing needs: in effect, they were customer relationship managers who provided a tailored portfolio-management service to key customers. Second, asset class managers focused on identifying investment opportunities and generating performance. Both categories of staff were scarce, highly talented, and experienced individuals, much of whose work was both esoteric and skilled. And both were attracted, motivated, and rewarded by exceptional remuneration packages. The fund and asset managers were supported by a large 'back-office' team of marketing, information systems, and HR professionals.

The company employed an investment philosophy and process that involved asset allocation, stock selection, portfolio development, risk management, and dealing. It was research-intensive and built on a 'Focus on Change' philosophy, which provided early and detailed information on key drivers that affected markets and the dynamics that influenced the investment environment, particularly the pricing of stock. The webpage of the SLI explicitly stated its knowledge credentials at the time:

We believe in a collaborative approach to business where knowledge and expertise are shared openly. When we work together, we work more effectively as a team. Our team-based approach encourages us to share ideas across asset classes, business areas and worldwide locations. We do this daily through cross-team communication and webcasts with our global offices.

Investment decisions were based on five guiding questions:

- What are the key market drivers?
- What's changing?
- What expectations are priced in?
- Why will the market change its mind about these expectations?
- What will trigger these changes?

These questions represented a common language used to guide all decision-making in all regional offices and on all asset classes. The Focus on Change philosophy also recognised that different factors drove markets at different times, and that prices were not inherently responsive to internal growth or momentum. Consequently, fund managers had an opportunity to outperform others during a cycle, but only if they were able to understand markets better than fund managers in other companies. So, for example, through having deep knowledge of a macroeconomic analysis of China or of key competitors in the USA, they were better able to predict the price of stock in the UK. As one of their internal company documents stated: 'The more pieces of corroborating evidence we can amass, the greater the conviction we can take behind these investment positions.'

Investment knowledge was gained from top-down and bottom-up information and was expressed in a house view by the chief investment officer and his team of analysts, who provided strategic direction for SLI. As stated earlier, the success of the company also depended on its ability to learn from its offices in other parts of the world; in turn, they required high-quality sources of knowledge on which to make their decisions. The company prided itself on global teamworking and on its people management philosophies and practices, for which they had won awards. SLI had established a culture based on team autonomy and trust, and a strong employer brand that was used to attract and retain top talent (see Chapters 3 and 6).

SLI grew rapidly through acquisitions, including a major one in 2014 with the UK company, Ignis, and joint ventures. However, it only acquired companies that could exhibit similar business cultures and sound business processes, or at least ones that were complementary. When first researching this case, senior managers explained that India was a natural and desirable target for expansion because of a common language, laws, and business practices. Conversely, however, their efforts to expand into the fast-growing Chinese market left managers challenged by the slow pace and rather 'exotic nature of the negotiation process,' learning the language, ambiguities in the regulatory environment, and simply finding a partner willing to accept SLIs' business model.

SLI's origins and culture lay in the mutualised heritage of its parent company, which changed in 2006. Prior to demutualisation, the parent company was a type of partnership of members (policyholders) in which the company reinvested all profits for the benefit of the members. Standard Life Assurance, the parent company, fought a long battle to resist demutualisation but, given the pressures placed on it by some members and trends among most large insurance businesses in Europe, demutualisation become inevitable. In addition to internal pressures and industry trends, the arguments for demutualisation include increasing efficiency, gaining access to capital for expansion, increasing commercial flexibility, and unlocking the value of ownership rights and benefits for staff, customers, and future shareholders. Demutualisation involved floating the company on the stock market and, second, changing the mindsets of managers to act in the interests of its new shareholders as well as its other stakeholders. It also brought with it the potential for takeover or merger, especially if it underperformed. Such a changed environment from 2006 onwards led the company to think very seriously about its knowledge management and human resource policies.

1   In what ways did SLI rely on knowledge to operate its business?

One very useful way of thinking about this case and, indeed, the whole subject area of the knowledge context is to draw on a framework I have adapted from a classical model of strategic knowledge management by Choo and Bontis (2002) (see Figure 7.1). I continue to use this framework because it raises six sets of questions that organizations such as SLI need to address. Like many other companies, SLI competed with others on their ability to manage the *knowledge assets* they hold and the *processes they use to learn* from each other (Hislop et al., 2018; Webb, 2017).

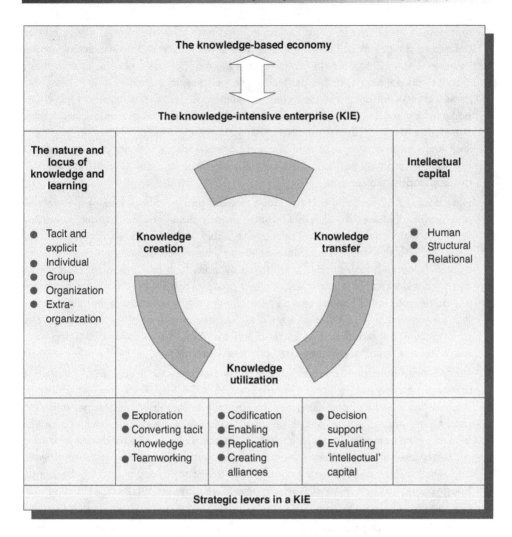

FIGURE 7.1 A framework for understanding knowledge in organizations
(*Source*: based on Choo & Bontis, 2002; Hislop et al., 2018)

1. Why is knowledge seen as a strategic asset in modern societies, and why should organizations become more interested in managing knowledge and their intellectual assets?

2. What does a knowledge-based enterprise (KBE) or in Choo and Bontis's language, a knowledge-intensive enterprise (KIE), look like? What are the essential features of such organizations? What makes them different to traditional organizations? And can we learn about them from studying traditional knowledge-based organizations, such as universities and consulting firms?

3. What are the processes by which KBEs *create, transfer,* and *utilise knowledge* within and beyond their boundaries, and how effective are they? Organizations, such as those

represented in the above case, generate value from what they know, which can be defined as their stock of *intellectual capital* at a point in time. This intellectual capital, however, depends on an organization's ability to manage the processes of knowledge creation, dissemination, and exploitation. The key questions connected with these processes are: What are the best means for such organizations to convert *tacit knowledge* (which resides in employees' heads and organizational processes) into *explicit knowledge* (which is formal, usually written, codified knowledge)? How can they share such knowledge among their subunits and partners across national and international boundaries and time periods? How can they integrate and coordinate knowledge to develop goods and services?

4. How does a KBE facilitate and help *feed-forward* and *feed-back* knowledge creation and learning *between the different levels* in organization—individual, group, organization, and extra-organizational networks? Arguably, only individuals can learn about work, but how they learn, and from whom and where they learn, are matters of some debate. Is learning for work best undertaken by individuals in a 'schooled' environment away from work, or is learning essentially a group process that is most effective when it is carried out in the context of work? Equally important is to ensure that the learning that takes place in individuals and small groups becomes part of the wider processes of organizational learning, and in certain cases, extra-organizational learning (e.g., suppliers, customers, government, and other key stakeholders).

5. What is the *nature of the intellectual capital* generated by the processes of knowledge creation, transfer, and utilisation, and how can it be exploited? Intellectual capital is often described as comprising *human capital* (the learning, knowledge, and skills residing in people, groups, and in an organization's unique culture, which cannot be owned by the company in any strict sense), *structural capital* (the hardware, software, organizational structure, databases, trademarks, and brands that support employees, and which are owned by the company), and *relational or social capital*, the bonds, bridges, and trust developed with customers, employees, suppliers, and other key stakeholders.

6. What *strategic levers* can be 'pulled' to improve the processes described above? These levers include the following: methods of promoting knowledge creation through groups, etc.; forming cross-functional work teams; establishing enabling conditions for knowledge creation through appropriate human resource management practices; replicating organizational routines across different parts of an organization, for example, building in automatic environmental scanning; methods of codifying knowledge to make it explicit and capable of being stored; designing decision support systems; and measuring and evaluating an organization's intellectual assets.

We shall use this framework to organize our discussion of knowledge management and organizational learning by examining in turn the nature of the 'knowledge-based economy', KBEs, the nature of knowledge and learning, the processes of knowledge creation, transfer and utilisation, the strategic levers that can be pulled to enhance knowledge management, and the outcomes of KIEs and the creation of intellectual capital.

THE KNOWLEDGE-BASED ECONOMY

The idea of a knowledge-based economy (KBE), which advances the notion that knowledge industries, knowledge workers and knowledge assets are the most important sources of economic growth, has been around since the 1980s (Brinkley, 2008; Bolisani & Bratianu, 2018). Nevertheless, it remains a contested concept (James et al., 2011). Following the problems associated with the de-industrialisation of many Western economies, in which the traditional mass-production industries of America and Europe declined in importance, there was the search for a new, more optimistic theory of economic development. As Western economies moved from being powerhouses of manufacturing to becoming largely service-driven economies, a major, and seemingly intractable, problem presented itself: how to increase productivity in an economy based largely on services so that living standards could continue to rise. Because living standards are highly sensitive to productivity increases, economists were quick to point out that productivity in services industries was notoriously difficult to increase, as there are natural limits to the levels (both quantity and quality) of service that customers desire – for example, in eating out at restaurants, attending concert halls, undergoing education, having new tyres fitted on their cars, having their investments managed, and in taking holidays. Increasing inputs in customer care, it was argued, would yield rapidly diminishing returns (and eventually negative ones, as people came to resent the intrusive service in some restaurants, car showrooms, holiday locations, etc.). Thus, economies such as those in the West, which were rapidly changing to include high proportions of such workers in their employment structure, would eventually move towards a position of zero productivity growth, and thus no rises in standards of living. Such a view is consistent with the evidence of consistently low productivity in developed economies such as the UK, which has relied heavily on services for economic growth and continues to do so – as pointed out by the International Monetary Fund in 2023.

Following the emergence of the new computer-based and digital technologies in the USA in the 1980s, the entrepreneurial spirit to which these gave rise, and the resurgence of the American economy in the 1990s, a set of new theories of economic growth began to emerge (Evans & Wurster, 2000; see also Chapter 8 on the technological context for more details). For example, an influential OECD report published in 2001, entitled *The New Economy: Beyond the Hype*, identified information and communication techniques (ICT), education levels, and the proportion of knowledge-intensive employment as key factors in explaining differential growth rates among advanced industrialised countries. These ideas have continued until the present day, witness the example of the influential UK-based Centre for Cities (2022) calling for a £14 billion growth package to build innovation districts built on the knowledge economy in three key UK cities – Birmingham, Glasgow, and Manchester. The core proposition of all of these theories was that sustained economic wealth was most effectively created by focusing on knowledge and knowledge-based products and services – in effect, moving from a *hardware world* of bricks and mortar and manufactured goods to a *software-dominated world* of computer code, DNA-based biotechnology, educational and consulting services, and e-trading, all of which were reliant on new ICT, social media, and newer technologies for their 'transport infrastructure' (Alavi & Denford, 2011). This knowledge-based version of economic growth was inherently optimistic because it was not associated with a future based on diminishing returns or deteriorating productivity growth. Knowledge could be applied an infinite number of times with no decline in value, was relatively durable through time and space, and could be stored at very little cost using digital media. The uses to which knowledge could be put were also thought to be infinite, as innovation promised new ranges of products and services to new markets. Thus, for example, although people in the West might have natural limits to the levels of services they required, the emerging markets in Eastern Europe and the Global South were thought to be infinitely susceptible to McDonald's franchises, digitised music, online degrees, and low-cost air travel, all of which are forms of knowledge-based products and services.

Thus, the new economics of knowledge, especially with developments in artificial intelligence (AI) (Suleyman, 2023), focuses on knowledge as a key factor in economic and technological growth (see the annual Word Economic Forum's Global Competitiveness Reports and the Centre for Cities Report, 2022). And, rather obviously, since knowledge is essentially a human construction (or, arguably, was), the new economics of knowledge and the new knowledge economies were seen to be largely dependent on the *quality and management of people* (Hislop et al., 2018). There are at least five strands to this argument:

1. Knowledge is seen as an important economic factor input, in the same way as the traditional economic factors of production – land, labour, and capital. Like capital, knowledge can accumulate over time and is seen to be an important engine of economic growth. For example, as we have seen, the growth rates of economies are often linked to spending by organizations and governments on research and development (R&D), and world competitiveness is linked to technological growth, so the proportion of knowledge workers in an economy and their levels of knowledge are thought to be critical (World Economic Forum Global Competitiveness Report, 2020).

2. Knowledge, however, is a rather different type of concept from the term 'information', which is widely used in ICT. Information is defined in terms of the codifiable 'know why' and 'know what'. As we have seen, however, much knowledge is tacit and is embedded in people and contexts – so-called 'know-how' – so the economic returns to knowledge workers tend to be high because of their relative scarcity value. This is most obviously reflected in the net worth of senior business figures and of certain engineers and scientists. Twenty-two per cent of the world's wealthiest people in 2015 had an engineering degree, while a further 20 per cent held degrees in mathematics or science, showing the value of the so-called STEM (science, technology, engineering, and mathematics) subjects. Rishi Sunak, a UK prime minister, led such an initiative in 2023 to bolster STEM subjects, especially mathematics. Such people are said to earn *economic rent* – payment for relatively scarce knowledge and skills that are inelastic in supply. The same argument is also used to explain the high earnings of sport stars, investment managers, pop musicians, and even some academics.

3. Most knowledge is not of the pure, 'research and development' type, associated with scientific breakthroughs, but is embodied in products such as software, digital

media, databases, financial bonds, video games, and online courses. Organizations in knowledge-based industries, such as those offering these products, have been traditionally characterised by high fixed development costs but low marginal production costs, and have had major problems in recovering these costs in price-sensitive markets. Consequently, there was great pressure on these organizations to protect their intellectual property rights and reduce their fixed costs by 'off-shoring' some of the knowledge work to emerging economies such as India in the fields of software writing and call centres, which has now built significant capabilities of its own in these fields.

4. Knowledge is thought to *spill over* and be *localised*. Thus, breakthrough ideas created by one firm are thought to spill over to other firms and industries in a local region more quickly than between regions. Consequently, we often witness the clustering of firms in knowledge-intensive sectors such as financial services, software and games, mobile telephones, learning, biotechnology, and artificial intelligence, where face-to-face interaction and the rapid transfer of employees between firms in a region are thought to be important in knowledge transfer. These locally clustered labour market factors are extremely important in developing career opportunities and establishing attitudes to work. Silicon Valley in California and Bangalore in India are among the best-known examples.

5. Enormous emphases have been placed on the emergence of *knowledge networks* that facilitate the kinds of interactions between people and ideas central to the previous point concerning clustering. The diffusion of tacit knowledge is facilitated by such networks, so access to these networks is becoming critical for knowledge workers and knowledge transfer. However, these networks are heavily dependent on integrating increasing numbers of members for their added value, within and between organizations, as they seek to learn from each other and share out the costs of innovation. To succeed, these networks have had to develop a new form of integration, based more on trust and less on market/price coordination or hierarchical/authority coordination (Hislop et al., 2018). This renewed emphasis on trust has enormous implications for the management of employment relations, and in recruiting, developing, motivating, and retaining talented, trustworthy people (Siebert et al., 2015). At the same time, such networks are thought to create lock-in effects, which mean that past decisions shape collective choices about new technologies and other forms of knowledge. Thus, being part of a network provides access to new ideas, but it can also create a form of 'psychic prison' that limits innovation and creativity (see Chapter 9).

In the early part of this century, Taiwan was often cited as an excellent example of an economy that linked its desire to develop a national economic development strategy based on the growth of KBEs to a corporate branding strategy. An *Economist* article in 2005 pointed out that three-quarters of the world's laptop computers, two-thirds of LCD panels, and 80 per cent of personal digital assistants were made in Taiwan in 2000, but few people had heard of a Taiwanese brand. By 2005, Taiwanese manufacturers had transferred nearly all production to China. Companies such as BenQ and Acer design and manufacture many ICT products for other companies. These companies began as original equipment manufacturers (OEMs), producing the designs of other companies, but gradually took over substantial parts of the design processes themselves to become original design manufacturers (ODMs). However, BenQ was the first company to try to build a world-class brand when it was spun off from Acer; it had 40 per cent of its business as its 'own brand' by 2005. Since then, Acer has established a brand name and is one of the largest personal computer brands in the world, ranking sixth in 2022 just behind Apple and Asus in units shipped. Taiwan has also established itself as the dominant player in the world's advanced microchip industry through the Taiwan Semiconductor Manufacturing Company, which by 2023 had become the number one most valuable semiconductor company in the world and one of the most indispensable.

KNOWLEDGE-INTENSIVE ENTERPRISES

A definition and example

At the core of the arguments for the new, knowledge-based economy were so-called *knowledge-intensive enterprises*. This notion of knowledge intensity indicated the relative nature of the reliance on knowledge in organizations. KIEs have been differentiated from other forms of organization because of their ability to bring together the knowledge of specialists more effectively than through contractual relations, the spot market, and price mechanisms (Foss & Mahnke, 2011). In other words, they were 'knowledge-integrating institutions', seen as a bridging concept that explains how firms based on knowledge assets and knowledge workers are different from traditional organizations (Del Giudice et al., 2017). To explore the nature of KIEs and what makes them different, it is worth examining one of the oldest forms of knowledge-intensive institutions with which readers are familiar. Here, we are referring to universities, and we need to look no further than university business schools, which are among the newest (and often most resented) departments in higher education, to reveal some of the problems and tensions that KIEs face (Pettigrew et al., 2014).

Box 7.1 Universities as the archetypical KIE: The case of the business schools

Contrary to the normal professional bureaucracy (see Chapter 4 on the organizational context) found in most universities, it would certainly be possible to operate a 'virtual' business school with a very small core staff of administrators and rely on creating market-based, pay-for-performance, contract relations with academics from around the world to write and teach students. This approach became apparent to universities during COVID-19. Such virtual schools can be more effective and efficient in operating a 'delivery model of education' and more flexible in responding to signals from the educational markets they serve. However, most university business schools have not followed that route, preferring to retain the 'brick' schools that reflect the traditional university model, staffed by traditionally employed experts on full-time contracts. This traditional brick or campus-based form of organization has remained the dominant one, despite the fashion for retrenching to core competences.

Arguably, this conservatism is because most university business schools see their core competences not only as transmitting knowledge through teaching, which, in its most basic form, can be seen as an individual relationship between teacher and student but also as producing knowledge through research and transferring it through academic papers and books, consulting, executive education, and so on. There are major threats to the traditional business schools, however, from the new corporate universities and consulting companies on the one hand and, on the other hand, from the university–corporate collaborations, which are moving rapidly into developing sophisticated business models for delivering high-quality online learning through so-called MOOCs (Massive Online Open Courses) on a global basis.

This example also illustrates the following three key features of KIEs:

- Their need to access core, advanced, and innovative knowledge.
- Their need to build communities of knowledge workers, in this case, academics.
- Their need and capacity to absorb new knowledge and transform it into useful products and services.

Core, advanced, and innovative knowledge

It is often argued that all organizations need core knowledge merely to compete in an industry (based on the existing 'rules of the game'). So, for example, all university business schools need to have access to certain core knowledge to teach MBA courses. However, certain schools invest heavily in advanced knowledge, often through unique, research-based content over which they have established some intellectual property rights, or through different methods of learning, such as online or hybrid learning. They do so to differentiate themselves from other schools by attempting to change the existing rules of the game and their business models. However, business schools seeking to dominate the industry on a regional or global basis will need to draw on truly innovative knowledge to change the basis of competition (continuing with the metaphor of the game, to change the game itself). It is this innovative aspect of KIEs that makes them important to modern economies and provides them with a potentially powerful source of long-term strategic advantage. Much of the recent focus on innovation has been on the evolving power of ICT, social media, and AI in KIEs. In the context of university business schools, especially post-COVID, ICT, social media, and AI are seen as critical to extending their outreach into other countries, not only through, for example, online learning and MOOCs but also through social networking in such a way that those on the periphery of a business school's main campus feel socially connected to each other and to the centre. They must also develop strategies for using AI to enhance staff and student learning potential as well dealing with the potential misuse of AI by students to maintain the integrity of traditional assessment methods.

The communal nature of KIEs

The business school example illustrates a second feature of KIEs, which is the need for community and a sense of shared identity (see Chapter 3). KIEs, including financial services, business schools, and healthcare organizations, tend to rely on a strong sense of shared identity to reduce communication costs and minimise the degree of bureaucracy required for regulation purposes, an argument that reflects the importance of trust as a coordinating mechanism in the previous section on knowledge-based economies. However, the shared identity of KIEs also contributes to the propensity for organizations to learn by creating *communities of practice* that support individual learning and knowledge sharing (Wenger, 2011). We shall define and discuss such communities of practice later in this chapter, but the essential point is that communities are forms of social networks that create the social capital of an organization, doing so more effectively than through a purely market relationship. Such social capital, in the form of a set of unique relations between people (sometimes called *cultural capital*), is leveraged to produce an organization's intellectual capital. And it is this aspect of organizations that provides them with a distinct and non-reproducible source of differentiated, competitive advantage. Thus, university business schools have traditionally seen themselves in the roles of facilitating and building knowledge production in research communities, encouraging learners to participate in learning communities, and developing long-standing social networks that, by definition, require academics, students, practitioners, and alumni to work together and share their ideas (Pettigrew et al., 2014).

The absorptive capacity of KIEs

A KIE uses both knowledge as a key input to its core business and produces knowledge as a key output for customers. Returning to our example of the business school, competitive advantage is more likely to accrue to those schools that have a well-developed capacity for absorbing leading-edge knowledge from industry and from other academic networks, such as alumni. Such a capacity is known as *absorptive capacity*. This refers to an organization's ability to *acquire, assimilate, transform*, and *exploit* new knowledge (Martin & Reddington, 2009; Muller et al., 2021) (see Figure 7.2). Thus, any KIE, including our business school example, seeking to create new knowledge and create innovative products, services, or processes, needs a high *potential* for:

- identifying and acquiring new knowledge with greater speed, intensity, and focus than others; and
- assimilating this new knowledge into the KIEs current routines and processes more effectively than others.

They must also realise their potential by:

- transforming this knowledge by developing it and fusing it with existing knowledge to provide some novel ideas, products, or processes; and

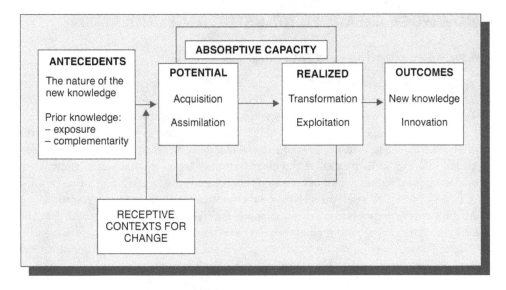

FIGURE 7.2 A KIE's absorptive capacity for new knowledge
(*Source:* based on Zahra & George, 2002; Martin & Reddington, 2009; Muller et al., 2021)

• exploiting this newly transformed knowledge by leveraging existing learning competencies or developing completely new competencies.

The extent to which a KIE has the potential absorptive capacity for new knowledge is, however, dependent on key *antecedents*, including: (1) the nature of the knowledge it possesses; (2) whether it has had any previous exposure or experience with related knowledge; and (3) whether this new knowledge complements its existing body of knowledge. It is also likely to be influenced by the existence of receptive contexts for change, such as a crisis in the organization, new legislation that supports the need for new knowledge, or new leadership and/or a new strategic direction.

Exercise 7.1 **The future of university business schools and Standard Life Investments**

1. Continuing with our example of university business schools, what practical measures could an established school implement to increase its absorptive capacity? What constraints can you envisage in increasing absorptive capacity in this context?

2. In the case of Standard Life Investments at the beginning of the chapter, to what extent was absorptive capacity one of its key factors for success? What problems do you think it should have foreseen in the company exploiting its absorptive capacity in its overseas ventures?

3. What receptive contexts for change might have influenced the absorptive capacities of the university business school and Standard Life Investments?

KNOWLEDGE CREATION, TRANSFER, AND UTILISATION

Knowledge creation and learning

To deepen our understanding of the knowledge context, we need to address the nature of knowledge and learning, namely what knowledge is (and is not), the different forms of knowledge, how knowledge relates to learning, and the relationships between different forms of knowledge and organizational structures (Hislop et al., 2018). Usually, the first distinction made in texts on the subject is between information and knowledge, in which information is treated as the organization of basic 'factual' data. Information becomes knowledge only when people apply their minds to change information in some way, for example, how academics change data 'findings' from their research into theory. In effect, knowledge is a human creation and is inherently subjective, whereas data and information are seen in a more objective and basic sense. It is this human and subjective quality of knowledge that makes it different from other factor inputs into organizations and, as we have seen, makes it a unique source of competitive advantage. There are at least three perspectives we can take on the nature of knowledge creation and learning (Hislop et al., 2018):

1. To see knowledge as the *outcome of learning*. As individuals (and groups), we learn to acquire knowledge and use knowledge to learn about something important to us. For example, in learning about the nature of knowledge in this book, hopefully you gain new knowledge to use in your workplaces.

2. To view knowledge as something *conscious and actionable* – people need to know what they know, know why they need to know, and enact their knowledge. For, as some commentators believe, it is only through conscious reflection and action that we truly understand (Weick, et al 2005). This perspective on knowledge and learning has become important in the field of training and development and is embodied in the principles of action learning, which are based on the idea that you only really know about something – for example, the organization in which you work – when you need to change it (Coghlan, 2019). So, some learning theorists argue that understanding theory and concepts to analyse a situation only takes us so far in learning; the real problems and deep learning come at the implementation stage, and then only if we consciously reflect on what worked (or didn't work) and why.

3. To see knowledge as a *dynamic, social construction* – that is, knowledge is continuously created, sustained, and changed by people, usually working in conjunction with others. This dynamic characteristic of knowledge places more importance on knowing than on knowledge itself. For example, it is often argued that knowing and teaching facts is less important than learning how to learn. The argument underpinning this claim is that the useful lifespan of knowledge in modern societies is often short; therefore, we need to learn the skills of knowing to be able to operate in an increasingly unknowable world and in learning 'how to be(come)' (Brandi & Elkjaer, 2011). This is often the case related to knowledge in HRM and people management (Ogbonnaya et al., 2022).

Explicit and tacit knowledge and learning

Another major issue that taxes most people in the field of knowledge management and learning is how you convert tacit knowledge into explicit knowledge. For example, in the case of Standard Life Investments, one of its biggest problems was converting the largely tacit knowledge of its 'star' fund managers into explicit knowledge. It needed to do so to transfer its expertise to its overseas offices and joint ventures and retain these fund managers so that their expertise didn't 'walk out of the door'. Let's look at a 'classic' take on tacit knowledge by John Seely Brown, one of the key thinkers in knowledge management and organizational learning over the last few decades. This work is worth quoting at length because it continues to be relevant in a world of hybrid working and especially a world changed by AI from which organizations must learn to capture value from knowledge applications like chatbots (Berg et al., 2023).

CASE 7.3 JOHN SEELY BROWN ON LEARNING AND BRICOLAGE

This material is quoted verbatim from a presentation made by John Seely Brown in 2004, who was talking about his work as Chief Scientist at Xerox before he became an academic and consultant.

'There was also a second defining moment, a kind of event for me. I was initially trained in theoretical mathematics and hard-core computer science. The event that actually transformed me…showed me that there was a lot that a theoretical mathematician understood about how the world really works.

This had happened before, before I was working in Xerox. It's actually ironic that we are in this particular building. I had been doing a lot of work on troubleshooting for the Navy, and also how to build really hard-core computer science systems, these job-performance aids, for actually figuring how to really get people to be much more effective at troubleshooting. So, I joined Xerox some time ago, and after a while, Xerox discovered my background in having worked for the Department of Defense (DoD), and the Navy in particular, and really rethinking troubleshooting.

So, they said, "John, you really have to, kind of, help us." Most days, those machines broke down. No comment. (Laughter.)

So, I said, "You know, it would be really helpful if I could actually meet some expert troubleshooters."

They said, "Fine, we've got a great expert troubleshooter, actually in Leesburg, Virginia, about 20 miles from here. Why don't you go meet him?"

So, I said, "Well, great, I'll go and meet him." And they called in advance and said that this guy is coming.

Well, the first mistake that happened, I walked into the office, wearing a suit. This was not good.

He was a real kind of guy who fixes real machines. So, he was not happy. He was saying to himself, "Now here's a suit, and it's going to be a total loss. And he's an academic, even more of a loss. Clearly, he has his head up in the sky somewhere. How can I get rid of him?"

And he kind of looks at me, and he says, "John, this letter says that you are an expert troubleshooter. I'm going to give you a little problem. Here is the problem. This is a relatively high-speed copier. And this copier has an intermittent copy quality fault. Now those of you who have done any troubleshooting know that an intermittent fault is nasty. You know, if it's always broken, it doesn't take too much to figure it out. But if it's intermittent, it's tough."

So, he says, "This is The Official Xerox Procedure for fixing an intermittent quality problem. It has five steps. So, you take this brilliantly conceived computer-generated test pattern. And you put it on the platen. That's where you put the normal paper. We have a fancy term for everything. You dial in, '5000 copies.' And you push the START button." And then he said, "What do you do next?"

I said, "You get some coffee." So, I scored one point. I can compute 50 pages into 5000. You know, a total loss.

He said, "Yes, that's what you do. You go get some coffee. A few minutes. Maybe half an hour. Then you come back and the next step is that you take this pile of 5000 copies, ten reams of paper by the way, and you kind of plough through this pile until you find an example of something bad, and then you save that. And you plough through the pile some more until you get something and then you save that. And that's how you do this."

And then he said, "You, John, would surely have a better idea than that, how to fix this machine, right? So why don't you tell me how you would go about doing this. Because clearly you are cleverer than this rote procedure."

And I hummed and hawed and I tried to put off answering, and was trying to get him to say something, an old trick in the Navy. (Laughter.) So, for about ten minutes, I danced around, and then he got really impatient, and he said, "Blah, blah, dammit, tell me how you do it?"

And I said, "I can't. I mean, I would use something similar."

And he said, "I thought so!"

So, I said, "Paul, how would you do it?"

And he looks at me and he says, "It is obvious what you do!" Probably some of you have already figured it out. He said as he walked across the room and he found the waste basket next to the copier. He takes the waste basket, picks it up and walks over to a table like this, dumps it on the table, quickly files through the paper, and about 30 seconds later, comes up with brilliant sets of copy quality problems.

And he said, "You know, John, what do you do if you discover a copy quality problem? You know, you don't classify it as a copy quality problem. You classify it as a damn bad copy and you throw it away. So why don't you let the world do a little bit of the work for you. Why don't you work with the world and see that there's a natural way to have the world collect this information for you. Just step back and read the world a little bit."

Now maybe you can see where I'm heading with you. "Read the world a little bit" is almost a kind of judo, or a better term from the French, *bricolage*. And so, he said, "This waste basket was ready at hand. It was already there. It was already full of this stuff. Learn to work with the world, and you're going to find your life a lot simpler."

And I walked out and I thought to myself, "This guy is a genius." I also realized that it was very hard to build computer systems that could do this.'

1. Would it be possible to take the knowledge of the expert troubleshooter in this illustration and turn it into explicit knowledge?

2. What does this case suggest about the limits of hybrid working and the use of artificial intelligence?

Explicit knowledge is what most of us in education have long since regarded as the most important form of knowledge and, in Western societies at least, it has been credited with material and scientific progress. Explicit knowledge can be formally stated and is relatively easy to codify, document, transfer, share, and communicate. Typically, the learning of explicit knowledge is undertaken through books, manuals, and computer-coded content and through educational or training institutions – so-called 'schooled' or 'delivery-based' learning. Precisely because explicit knowledge is accessible, especially with the development of web-based knowledge and artificial intelligence, KIEs have focused on this form of knowledge to develop their core competences. For example, until relatively recently, university business schools in most countries focused on developing content in the form of teaching 'packages' rather than on research (Pettigrew et al., 2014) and putting the changing purpose of business at the heart of what it does (British Academy, 2022). Accessibility has also underlain the growth of the knowledge-management industry, which has sought to develop a wide range of technology-based knowledge-management tools to make use of the explicit properties of knowledge and to sell these onto KIEs. These software tools include coordinated databases, groupware systems, intranets, and internets, and, more recently, AI chatbots (Berg et al., 2023). However, codified explicit knowledge is synonymous with information and must rely on people to understand and apply it subjectively. Thus, according to Polanyi (1966), who is credited with inventing the distinction between the two forms of knowledge, a wholly explicit knowledge was unthinkable.

So, in an important sense, all knowledge is either tacit or rooted in tacit knowledge. By tacit, we mean the often subconsciously understood or applied ideas and skills that we have but that are difficult to articulate in any formal sense. Tacit knowledge is learnt from direct action and experience and shared through informal means such as conversations and storytelling. Polanyi argued that tacit knowledge was personal, context specific, and therefore difficult to put into words. It could also be compared with acquiring skills such as riding a bike or playing football (soccer). Though we can read manuals or generate ideas from chatbots to perform such activities, these do not explain the reality of performing such skills in context. For example, riding a bike on the roads is very different from riding a bike off-road. Similarly, playing five-a-side football in a gym with friends is a very different game from playing professionally in front of thousands of people. Thus, tacit knowledge is not generally revealed to us through texts or images but is based on intangible thoughts and therefore comprises assets embedded in personal beliefs, experiences, and values.

The idea that all knowledge is tacit implies that we can distinguish between different types of tacit knowledge, perhaps in the form of a spectrum (see Figure 7.3). At one end, we can have semiconscious and unconscious knowledge held in people's heads and bodies, which is unlikely to be codified; at the other end, we can have a pure form of explicit knowledge that can be codified and made available to anyone. For example, experienced selection interviewers often talk about 'gut instincts' when making decisions, rather than relying on objective information about candidates. However, ask an interviewer who relies on instinct or intuition to articulate why they know that this candidate is right for the job, and it is unlikely they will be able to explain their reasoning fully. Indeed, as some studies have shown, forcing people (such as interviewers) to explain what they thought they knew about the process of learning (in this case, learning about a candidate) may lead to a deterioration in performance (in this case, making wise decisions about candidates) (Leonard, 2011). Often, however, it is necessary to force interviewers to explain their decisions to combat the problems of unconscious bias and discrimination, which are inherent in selection interviewing and why we are increasingly turning to AI and expert systems to mitigate such problems. This kind of reasoning is also applicable to the world of making judgements in legal cases, which is why judging is one of the occupations most likely to be affected by AI in the future (Berg et al., 2023)

Tacit knowledge is also a property of groups as well as individuals. For example, some writers analyse organizational structure and stability through the notion of organizational routines, collective ways of working, or embedded forms of tacit knowledge that no one person could articulate. However, these routines 'automatically' nudge people into behaving in certain ways. This idea is very similar to the concept of culture, which we shall study in Chapter 9.

In discussing the process of innovation, one of our key outcomes of KBEs, Leonard and Sensiper's (2002) highly cited framework described three types of group-level, tacit

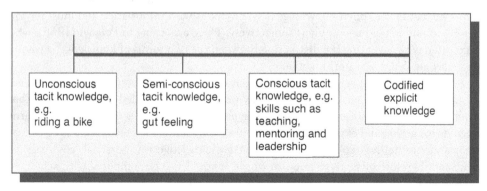

FIGURE 7.3 A spectrum of tacit knowledge

knowledge that need to be managed. These types formed a hierarchy of abstraction, as represented in Figure 7.4.

- *Overlapping specific tacit knowledge* refers to the build-up of shared knowledge at the interfaces between specific domains. For example, in a case I researched on NCR, the world's largest producer of automatic teller machines for the financial services industry, a multifunctional design teamworking on a new form of automatic teller machine for a major UK bank spent considerable time with its clients and customers trying to understand from first-hand observation what their problems were. On returning to work, the different functions represented in the design team had different tacit understandings of the bank and its customers' problems and issues, but the visits provided enough overlapping, common knowledge to create a shared understanding of the issues involved.

Quite often 'apprenticeships' are used, especially in industries where the technologies are new to build shared specific tacit knowledge because the sciences involved are immature and rarely completely codified. In such a context, apprenticeship means working directly with people who are highly experienced so that the apprentices can learn their craft from them.

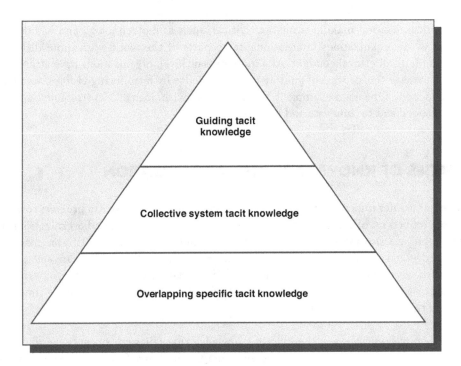

FIGURE 7.4 A hierarchy of group-level, tacit knowledge
(*Source*: based on Leonard & Sensiper, 2002)

- *Collective system tacit knowledge* is community-based, tacit knowledge developed through the interactions between members of groups as they attempt to address common problems. Such knowledge resides largely in people's heads and is transmitted through stories and tales. We shall discuss this very powerful source of tacit knowledge when examining communities of practice. A good example, however, might be the shared understandings and ways of working of a top-class sports team. Even though their on-field and even training performances may be made public to anyone who wants to take the time to watch, it is almost impossible to imitate because the knowledge and skills are largely tacit and diffused throughout the team. A similar argument is often used in the context of top business teams that are often only too ready to invite others to watch and learn from them, knowing full well that deep learning is available only to those people willing to engage in a significant period of apprenticeship in the organization and actively participate in the team.

- *Guiding tacit knowledge* is the tacit knowledge about the overall direction of the organization that goes beyond the explicit value statements frequently adopted by organizations. As innovations of products, processes, or organizations break new ground, there is often little guidance for exercising judgement available to groups in the form of explicitly stated rules, or even mission and values frameworks. Thus, innovative groups need to develop tacit visions of the organization's unstated mission, often in a highly abstract way, so that they can function effectively. Good examples of guiding tacit knowledge are likely to be found in industries in which ethical decision-making is mission critical, such as biotechnology and healthcare, or when organizations internationalise to parts of the world with quite different standards of ethical conduct. At a more prosaic level, organizations have attempted to manage this process of guiding tacit knowledge by introducing vision statements and logos. One good example is Nike, with its 'swish' logo and its strapline referring to speed and to 'innovate and inspire'.

IMAGES OF KNOWLEDGE AND ORGANIZATION

With our greater understanding of tacit and explicit knowledge, we can progress towards a more refined set of perspectives on knowledge, knowledge work, and organizations. In this regard, classic discussions by Blackler (2002) and Blackler et al. (2016) on images of knowledge and learning help increase our understanding of KIEs. These are *embrained, embodied, encultured, embedded,* and *encoded* images, all of which connote properties of people or a system; the sixth image is 'knowing'. It is worth spending a little time discussing this highly cited work.

- *Embrained knowledge* is the kind of knowledge that relies on conceptual and cognitive skills, often referred to as knowing about something. This kind of knowledge is usually abstract and involves higher levels of reasoning and understanding to make connections and explain what is going on around us. It is often the kind of knowledge associated with the world of theory and of 'schooled learning'. For example, chatbots will provide a teacher not only with knowledge about theoretical concepts but also how to design a plan to teach students about the concept and the types of exercises that might help students learn.

- *Embodied knowledge* is knowledge usually acquired in action, for example, by undertaking a project or apprenticeship, and is partly explicit and partly tacit. Sometimes it is described as 'know-how' and is contrasted with embrained knowledge. Embodied knowledge is not just gained through working on something, but depends on face-to-face interaction and discussion, emotional and sensory information, physical cues, and so on. It is also knowledge rooted in specific contexts, such as when a mechanic learns how to repair a specific make of automobile but using only particular kinds of tools or a footballer learning how to play against a particular type of team, such as a defensive one. As such, it is often not readily transferable to other situations, for example, other types of cars or other games against different types of teams. As a result, embodied knowledge is much more difficult to transfer through new forms of online learning that rely on platforms such as Teams and Zoom, or ChatGPT.

- *Encultured knowledge* refers to the process by which we arrive at shared understandings of our group, organization, or even national, cultures. Learning about cultures is usually linked to the socialisation (or indoctrination) processes and to acculturation, i.e., how we come to adapt and take on cultural or professional norms, or the 'way we do things around here'. Learning about cultures (and professions) is heavily dependent on sharing a common language and on negotiated meanings – for example, people coming to accept common metaphors about what an organization means to them. Thus, some people find it easy to work with the idea that their organization is like a soccer team, characterised by team players of different abilities playing on the same side to score into the opponent's goal. Other groups may use another kind of sporting metaphor to describe their version of teamworking, such as the relay race, or even American football, which differs from soccer in its approach to organization and winning through its heavy reliance on off-the-field, some say tyrannical, coaching (Harvard Business Review et al., 2018).

- *Embedded knowledge* is knowledge located in organizational routines or capabilities or, at the societal level, in the social and institutional arrangements or institutional logic configuration of a particular country or region. It has strong connections with our previous discussions in Chapters 1 and 2 on managerial work and the international context of people management in Chapter 5. Embedded knowledge can be found in systems of relations between, for example, technologies, the roles people perform, the formal procedures of the organization, and the emergent routines. Thus, an organization's distinctive capabilities (or competences) are deeply embedded in how these factors come together or are consciously and unconsciously coordinated to produce skilled performance. Think about the example of what makes a great orchestra or soccer team. The distinction is often made between the expert knowledge or skills of the players and coaches or conductors and the 'architectural' or relational knowledge they require (or the coaches and conductors require) to work together to produce first-class performances. This refers not only to the way they work together (e.g., teamworking), but also to the tools they use (selection techniques, quality of equipment, arenas, etc.), the explicit codes of conduct (e.g., whether certain behaviours are demanded or prohibited), and the habits and ways of working (practising their skills and dietary regimes, who works best with whom, etc.). Thus, embedded knowledge is systemic and requires an understanding of how all these factors interact to produce skilled performance. This notion may help explain why the talent transfer system doesn't always lead to immediate results for football teams or organizations that seek to buy in the best players. It also helps explain why you cannot uproot the best players or the 'best' practices from one context and transplant them into another context with the immediate expectation that they will take root and flourish in the expected or predicted fashion. Our example of the problems of talent management in financial services in Chapter 3 illustrates this point well.

- *Encoded knowledge* is close to what we have previously defined as information, which is more easily transmitted by signs and symbols. Written texts, drawing on abstract forms of language or pictorial language, have been the usual repositories of encoded knowledge, but it is increasingly to computer code, digital signals, and artificial intelligence that we look to transmit such knowledge, hence the coining of the term 'information and communications technologies. However, we should not assume that such knowledge is neutral, because it must be abstracted from the context in which it was produced; this process can be highly selective in the impression it conveys. So-called 'factual reporting' on newscasts during wars, in which the horrors of wars are told from the perspective of one side or against a particular backdrop, illustrates this feature of the context-boundedness of information. The 'special military operation' conducted by Putin and his regime in Ukraine illustrated this point dramatically, as did reporting in the Israeli-Hamas conflict. Nor can we assume that encoded knowledge will be equally acceptable to people in different cultures. We found this during our earlier research into online learning when it first emerged in Europe during the early 2000s. Our data in those days showed that people in France and Germany found the method of delivery to be culturally alien to them when compared with people in the USA and UK. Thus, the acceptability of online learning was quite different in influencing the absorptive capacity for online learning in German educational and corporate organizations (Martin et al., 2003). We also found that similar problems occurred during the roll-out of e-HR programmes in major multinational companies in later research (Martin et al., 2008).

- *Knowing.* Blackler (2002) argued that it may be more important to concentrate on the verb 'knowing' than on the subject/object of knowledge because organizations are always in the process of becoming something other than they are. Another way of saying the same thing is that the process of change in organizations is normal, whereas equilibrium is temporary. We shall consider this view of organizations in more detail later in the book when we look at change and learning organizations. At this point, however, it is necessary to explore the image of knowing in greater depth because it has been an extremely influential perspective in the knowledge management literature and in practice.

Knowing as an image of organization

There are at least two sets of ideas built on theories of knowing and learning which help us shed light on how organizations innovate and change, discussed further in Chapter 10. The first focuses on the relationship between tacit and explicit knowledge discussed earlier, which is based on a set of ideas concerning knowledge conversion in innovative Japanese organizations. The second has its roots in encultured knowledge and refers to the notion of communities of practice.

Knowledge conversion and learning

One of the most frequently cited studies in knowledge management came about because of the participation of Ikujiro Nonaka, with his colleagues Hirotaka Takeuchi and Kenichi Imai, at a Harvard Business School colloquium (Nonaka & Takeuchi, 1995). Following this colloquium, they agreed to do a joint project to study the innovation processes at several Japanese companies. Drawing especially on Polanyi's work, they conceptualised knowledge in terms of tacit and explicit knowledge and argued that the dynamic interaction between the two led to organizational knowledge creation and innovation. This interaction between the two types of knowledge leads to four modes of *knowledge conversion*, which they labelled (1) socialisation, (2) externalisation, (3) combination, and (4) internalisation (see Table 7.1).

Socialisation, involving tacit-to-tacit conversion, is conducted by individuals, sometimes without language. For example, apprentices often learn from their masters in this way. The key is learning from experience and experienced people by sharing such knowledge. Combination, which involves learning through combining different bodies of explicit knowledge, can be found in meetings, telephone conversations, and computer program exchanges. These media create new knowledge by sorting, re-categorising, or re-analysing these different bodies of knowledge. Internalisation, which involves learning from explicit knowledge to create tacit knowledge in individuals, is like traditional notions of learning. Externalisation, which involves learning from tacit knowledge to create explicit knowledge, is much less well understood and, as we have pointed out, is much more difficult to achieve.

Nonaka (2002) described the process of knowledge creation as a double spiral movement between (a) tacit and explicit knowledge and (b) individual, group, divisional, and corporate levels in organizations (see Figure 7.5). Thus, although each of

TABLE 7.1 Four modes of knowledge conversion

	To tacit knowledge	To explicit knowledge
From tacit knowledge	Socialisation	Externalisation
From explicit knowledge	Internalisation	Combination

Source: based on Nonaka and Takeuchi, 1995.

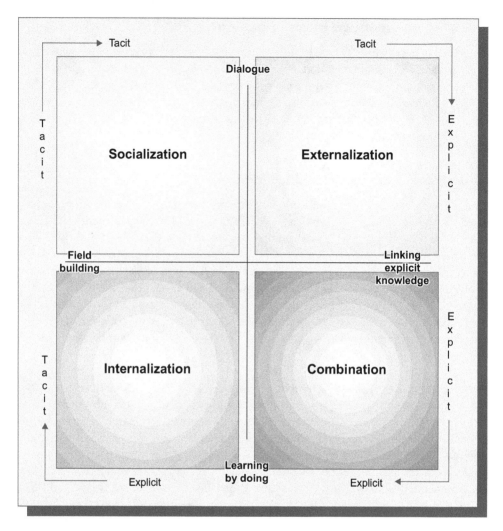

FIGURE 7.5 The spiral of organizational knowledge creation
(*Source*: based on Nonaka & Takeuchi, 1995)

these four modes of knowledge conversion can create new knowledge, it requires the dynamic interaction of all four to produce real innovation over sustained periods of time. It also required organizations to manage the process in the form of a continuous cycle. These management activities included (1) team building to facilitate the sharing of tacit experiences, (2) meaningful dialogue to allow members to externalise their tacit knowledge in the form of metaphors and concepts, (3) coordination and integration of teams into the wider organization, and (4) the documentation of the knowledge that is produced.

According to Nonaka, the basis for all organizational knowledge was an individual's tacit knowledge, built up through experience. Experience, however, can be a poor teacher unless it is of a particular quality. Two factors influence the overall quality of a person's experience. The first of these is the *variety of experiences* an individual has, especially of the non-routine type. We have all heard the criticism that many older people may have many years of experience, but it is often the same, routine experience repeated year after year. The second factor is the *knowledge of experience*. Because he came from an Asian culture, Nonaka drew on the Asian notion of the 'oneness of body and mind', in which people learn not only with the brain but through bodily recognition or realisation. Though difficult to translate into Western terms, this seems to mean that deep learning can take place only through lived experience rather than concepts. He illustrated this idea by explaining how Japanese managers learn on the job through interactions with customers, shopfloor employees, and reflective action rather than through courses such as MBAs. Such learning, however, was counterbalanced with combination methods of knowledge conversion in which people share their different bodies of explicit knowledge in meetings and seminars.

To create organizational knowledge, however, the process must move beyond individual learning, which remains personal unless it is amplified through interacting with the group and the organization levels. Nonaka used the concept of a *field* (of play) where people can come together as a self-organizing team to work out their conflicts and collaborate in the knowledge-creation process. He further argued that to be effective, a team needed to be self-organizing, which connotes ideas of mutual self-interest, voluntarism, and lack of hierarchy. Such teams also needed to be diverse in backgrounds to bring to the 'party' the basic ideas from the different functions and specialists who have something to add, sufficient variety to ensure that no function dominates, and just enough redundancy of information so that more than the basic ideas are brought to bear on the problems at hand. More recently, Nonaka and Takeuchi (2021) have argued that to cope with increasingly volatile and complex work, managers must engage in practice-based wisdom for strategy and learning in organizations to become more future-orientated and morally acceptable if companies are to survive in the long run. Much of this future orientation can be realised through strategic narratives that emphasise the idea of a calling we encountered in Chapter 3.

Communities of practice

The term – *communities of practice* – is associated with the work of Lave and Wenger (1991), Wenger (1998, 2000, 2011), Seely Brown and Duguid (2000), and Seely Brown et al. (2017). Like Nonaka, these writers saw learning as an act of membership of a group but used the term 'community' rather than 'team'. Most of the writing on communities of practice seeks to understand the structure of naturally occurring, work-based communities, how learning occurs in them, and how to put that learning into practice. In our own research, we have also applied the idea of communities of practice to three different eras of the training and development of doctors, during which inexperienced medical practitioners acquired the necessary tacit knowledge and skills to become accepted as full-fledged practitioners by working alongside more experienced doctors in clinical communal settings (Spilg et al., 2012). Our findings supported the situated or social learning approach and the apprenticeship model rather than the educational competence approach in enabling the acquisition of tacit knowledge so important in developing medical expertise.

Etienne Wenger, one of the main proponents of communities of practice (1998) originally put the case for community-based learning as follows:

> Communities of practice are everywhere. We all belong to several of them – at work, at school, at home, in our hobbies. Some have a name, some don't. We are core members of some and we belong to others more peripherally. You may be a member of a band, or you may just come to rehearsals to hang around with the group. You may lead a group of consultants who specialize in telecommunication strategies, or you may just stay in touch to keep informed about developments in the field. Or you may have just joined a community and are still trying to find your place in it. Whatever form our participation takes, most of us are familiar with the experience of belonging to a community of practice.
>
> *(http://www.co-i-l.com/coil/knowledge-garden/cop/lss.shtml)*

Members of a community are informally bound by what they *do* together, whether this is engaging in discussions around the metaphorical water cooler, brown-bag lunches, or solving important problems through informal professional networks. In other words, action and experience are central to such communities. They are also bound by what they have *learnt* together through their shared engagement in these activities. In these two senses, a community of practice is different from an interest group or a geographical community, as neither implies shared learning by doing.

A community of practice can be defined in terms of three dimensions (Wenger, 1998):

- What it is about – the continuously evolving and negotiated understanding of the joint aims of the community.
- Its mode of operation – how members mutually engage with each other to form a distinctive social entity.
- What it produces – the *shared repertoire* of resources, which include routines, group attitudes, artefacts, language, and styles of operating, about which, as members develop over time, they learn.

To expand on these ideas, communities of practice are based on the following assumptions:

1. *Learning is a social, rather than individual, process.* The argument is that people organize their learning around the communities to which they belong. Thus, for example, business schools are at their most powerful as learning environments for students whose outside social communities connect with the school in some important ways, for example, local SME communities, professional communities, and alumni networks.

2. *Knowledge and learning are integrated into the life of communities that share values, beliefs, languages, and community routines.* Thus, real knowledge is integrated into doing or action in the social relations and networks and in the expertise of these communities. This is most obvious in professional communities, such as medicine and the law (Siebert et al., 2017).

3. *The processes of learning and membership in a community of practice are intertwined.* Since learning is bound up with membership in the community, as we learn more, our identity and our relationship to the community change through continued participation. Thus, we go from being a peripheral 'apprentice' knowing very little to becoming a fully engaged and committed master or mistress of practice, able to teach and mentor others. This process is very much evident in the older style training of hospital doctors in the UK, who learnt their craft through an apprenticeship process rather than the more modern education and training approach (Spilg et al., 2012).

4. *Knowledge is inseparable from practice.* Some argue it is not possible to truly know without doing. Through action, we learn new skills and we change our ideas by reflecting on our practice (Nonaka & Takeuchi, 2021). This is the basis of reflective and reflexive learning we discussed in the first two chapters of this book.

5. *Empowering people to contribute to a community creates the greatest potential for learning.* By creating a set of circumstances that allows people to engage in meaningful action with real consequences for both participants and the community, one can create the most powerful learning environment. Again, this is an argument for action learning in which participants work on 'live' problems with real consequences and are allowed to make and learn from mistakes. Such an idea is associated with the notion of a 'no-blame' culture where organizations are encouraged to let employees learn from mistakes and 'false starts'.

Drawing on the concept of communities of practice, Seely Brown and Duguid (1991, 2017), who worked at the Institute for Research on Learning at the Xerox Corporation, saw learning as the bridge between working and innovating. They led a cross-disciplinary approach to learning research, involving cognitive scientists, organizational anthropologists, and traditional educators, and have become leading figures in organizational learning. They have argued that communities of practice, through their constant adaptation to changes in membership and changing environmental circumstances, are significant sources of innovation and learning in organizations. They proposed that, to foster working, learning, and innovating, organizations needed to re-conceive themselves as *communities of communities.* By building on and legitimising the naturally occurring communities at work, which often cut across the officially sanctioned work teams and formal practices in the organization, organizations could derive lasting benefits. They continued with the construction metaphor in suggesting ways in which such independent communities could be linked together to form an organizational architecture that preserved the autonomy of these communities but built interconnections and bridges between them. Developing his ideas, Seely Brown (2012) saw technology, the internet, and social media as a way of creating such an architecture because many organizations operate without the physical proximity and stable relationship needed for more traditional communities of practice. Presumably, he would endorse a similar message regarding the need to capture value from AI by Berg et al. (2023).

Let's look at another classic example of learning at work by John Seely Brown and Paul Duguid that illustrates different kinds of knowledge and learning, including the idea of communities of practice.

CASE 7.4 MENDING PHOTOCOPIERS

In what is regarded as a classic piece of research, Orr, an early anthropological collaborator of Seely Brown, provided various examples of how photocopier technicians diverged from established practice. For example, on one service call a 'rep' (technician) confronted a machine that produced copious raw information in the form of error codes and obligingly crashed when tested. However, the error codes and the nature of the crashes did not tally. Such a case immediately fell outside the official instructional training and documentation provided by the organization, which ties errors to error codes. Unfortunately, the problem also fell outside the rep's experience. He called his technical specialist, whose job combined 'troubleshooting consultant, supervisor and occasional instructor.' The specialist was equally baffled. Yet, though the canonical approach (the officially sanctioned procedures of the organization) to repair was exhausted, with their combined range of unofficial practices, the rep and technical specialist still had options to pursue.

One option – indeed, the only option left by official practice now that its strategies for repair had been quickly exhausted – was to abandon the repair and replace the machine. This was deemed to be a loss of face and not good for the reputation of the company or for themselves. Such loss of face or faith was not just about embarrassment. The rep's ability to engage the future support of customers and colleagues would be jeopardised because there was strong social pressure from a variety of sources to solve problems without exchanging machines. In addition to maintaining machines, the job of the rep was to enhance the social standing of the company. As Orr suggested, 'A large part of service work might better be described as repair and maintenance of the social setting.'

Solving the problem without removing the machine required constructing a coherent account of the malfunction out of the incoherence of the data and documentation. To do this, the rep and the specialist embarked on a long storytelling procedure. The machine, with its erratic behaviour, mixed with information from the user and memories from the technicians, provided essential ingredients that the two aimed to account for in a composite story. The process of forming a story was, centrally, one of diagnosis. This process, it should be noted, began as well as ended in a common understanding of the machine, one that was unavailable from the official sources.

While they explored the machine or waited for it to crash, the rep and specialist (with contributions from Orr himself) recalled and discussed other occasions on which they had encountered some of the present symptoms. Each story presented an exchangeable account, which could be examined and reflected upon to provoke old memories and new insights. Yet more tests and more stories were thus generated.

Orr continued his account. The rep and his boss were faced with a failing machine displaying diagnostic information that had previously proved worthless and in which no one had any particular confidence. They did not know where they were going to find the information they needed to understand and solve this problem. In their search for inspiration, they told stories. The storytelling process continued throughout the morning, over lunch and, back in front of the machine, throughout the afternoon, forming a long but purposeful progression towards a finally coherent account. The process lasted five hours, during which a dozen anecdotes were told during the troubleshooting, taking a variety of forms and serving a variety of purposes.

Ultimately, these stories generated sufficient interplay among memories, tests, the machine's responses, and the ensuing insights to lead to diagnosis and repair. The final diagnosis developed from what Orr described as two different versions of the same story, in which the two characters talked about personal encounters with the same problem, but their two versions were significantly different. Through storytelling, these separate experiences converged, leading to a shared diagnosis of certain previously encountered but unresolved symptoms. The two characters had constructed a common interpretation of until now uninterpretable data and individual experiences. The rep and specialist were now able to modify previous stories and build a more insightful one. They both increased their own understanding and added to their community's collective knowledge. Such stories were passed around and became part of the repertoire available to all reps. Orr reported hearing a concise, assimilated version of this particular false error code passed among reps over a game of cribbage in the lunchroom three months later. Thus, the story, once in the possession of the community, was used – and further modified – in similar diagnostic sessions.

Source: adapted from Seely Brown & Duguid (1991).

1 What kind of knowledge does the rep and his boss draw upon to mend the photocopier and how much does it depend on a community of practice?

2 What are the implications for capturing value from technologies such as chatbots?

THE RELATIONSHIP BETWEEN DIFFERENT IMAGES OF KNOWLEDGE, ORGANIZATIONAL STRUCTURES, AND MANAGING PEOPLE

Knowledge and organizations

How do these different versions of knowledge and learning relate to organizational structures and people-management problems? Blackler's (2002) work drew on two dimensions central to the production of knowledge to produce a typology of organizations based on knowledge and learning. As Crane (2013) argues, his work is among the most insightful in the field because he emphasised the role of social learning and language, and takes a constructivist approach to understanding learning in organizations (see Figure 7.6). The first dimension Blacker used was whether knowledge is seen as

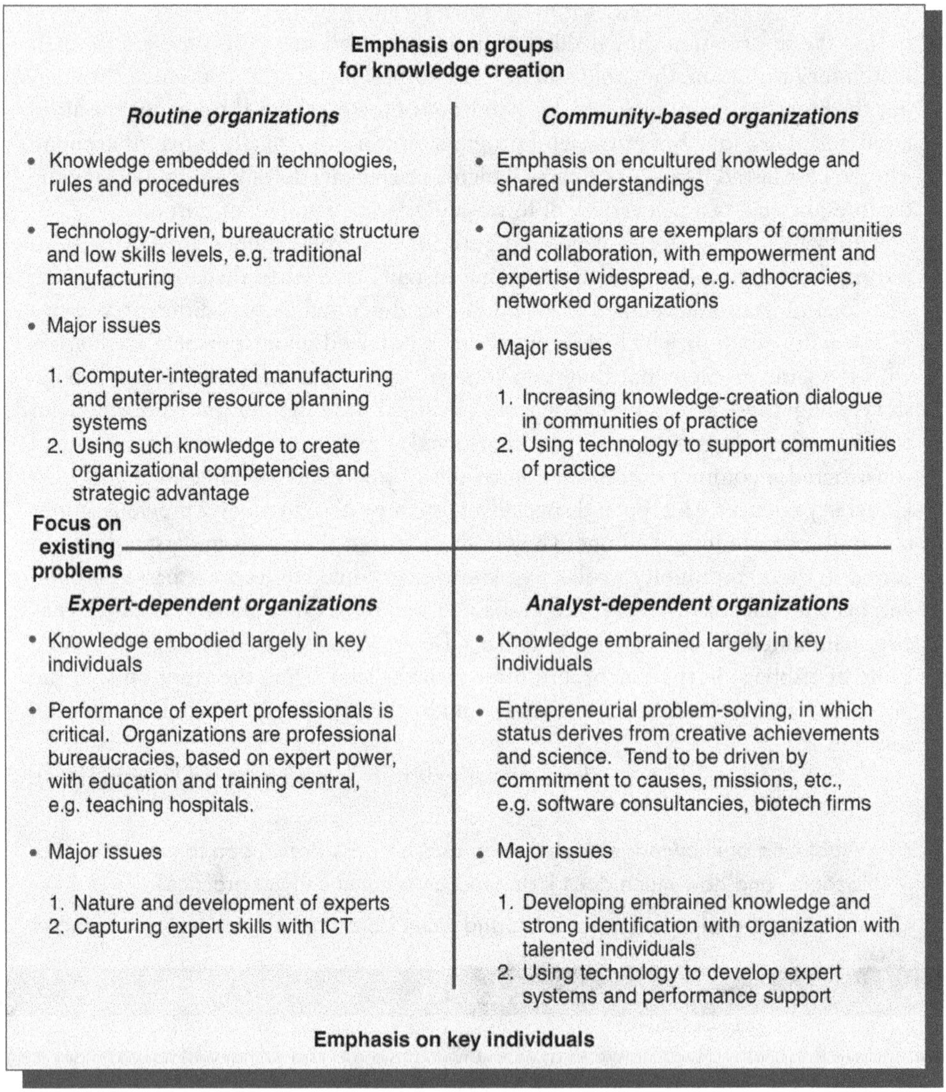

**Emphasis on groups
for knowledge creation**

Routine organizations	*Community-based organizations*
• Knowledge embedded in technologies, rules and procedures	• Emphasis on encultured knowledge and shared understandings
• Technology-driven, bureaucratic structure and low skills levels, e.g. traditional manufacturing	• Organizations are exemplars of communities and collaboration, with empowerment and expertise widespread, e.g. adhocracies, networked organizations
• Major issues	• Major issues
1. Computer-integrated manufacturing and enterprise resource planning systems 2. Using such knowledge to create organizational competencies and strategic advantage	1. Increasing knowledge-creation dialogue in communities of practice 2. Using technology to support communities of practice

**Focus on
existing
problems**

Expert-dependent organizations	*Analyst-dependent organizations*
• Knowledge embodied largely in key individuals	• Knowledge embrained largely in key individuals
• Performance of expert professionals is critical. Organizations are professional bureaucracies, based on expert power, with education and training central, e.g. teaching hospitals.	• Entrepreneurial problem-solving, in which status derives from creative achievements and science. Tend to be driven by commitment to causes, missions, etc., e.g. software consultancies, biotech firms
• Major issues	• Major issues
1. Nature and development of experts 2. Capturing expert skills with ICT	1. Developing embrained knowledge and strong identification with organization with talented individuals 2. Using technology to develop expert systems and performance support

Emphasis on key individuals

FIGURE 7.6 A typology of organizations based on knowledge
(*Source*: based on Blackler, 2002)

the product of individuals or of groups, which reflects the debate over communities of practice. The second is whether the organization deals with essentially familiar or routine problems (manufacturing repeatable solutions to known problems) or is tasked with providing innovative solutions to new problems. This dimension reflects the often-used distinction between *wicked* and *tame* problems (Rittel & Weber, 1984). A wicked problem is difficult to solve because of incomplete, contradictory, and changing requirements that reflect complex interdependencies in organizations. Much of clinical leadership in healthcare falls into this category (Grint, 2022; Martin et al., 2021), which is contrasted with tame problems that may be complex but have known or routine solutions, such as many routine surgical procedures.

Many organizations in industrialised countries are moving away (or being exhorted to move away) from organizing and strategising based on routine knowledge, given the opportunities provided by access to information and communications technologies and social media to enhance communications and performance support. However, Blackler also pointed out that these four boxes are bi-polar typologies, thus it would be a mistake to think of these different types of knowledge as independent of one another. Many organizations reveal aspects of all four images in their implementation of strategy, sometimes simultaneously. For example, different departments or divisions in the same company may see their knowledge management and HR problems through one of these images and use this dominant image to frame solutions to their perceived problems. Alternatively, organizations may strive to move between these images over time, using them as a form of blueprint and as a set of organizational development techniques.

Exercise 7.2 Standard Life Investments

Re-read the case of Standard Life Investments and its progress to demutualisation. Which of these four images of organization does Standard Life Investments most resemble and what problems does this imply for the future of the company?

Managing knowledge workers

These different types of organizations raise several issues concerning the management of knowledge workers, including the management of expertise, developing expertise, and encouraging and facilitating knowledge workers to share their expertise with others (Child & Rodrigues, 2011; CIPD, 2022; Newell, 2015). As we have already suggested, knowledge work and knowledge workers are nothing new, a notion reflected in the image of the *routine organization* in Figure 7.6. Thus, the focus of much attention in HR is on the role of knowledge workers who are seen to play a key part in value creation, which we have already discussed in relation to talent management in Chapter 3 and shall touch on in the next section on intellectual capital.

Traditional economic approaches to management in these organizations are based on the so-called *agency model*, consisting of a 'principal' employer, an 'agentic' employee, and the relationship between them (see Chapter 11). The motivations of these actors can be stated quite simply in economic terms: an agent (e.g., a senior manager) is not motivated to expend effort but is motivated by getting paid; the principal (investors and owners) dislikes paying the agent but likes the valuable work that the agent does. In this scenario, the objectives of the principal and agent are set in opposition to one another. The agent wants as much pay as possible for as little work or effort as possible, whereas the principal wants to get as much work as possible from the agent while paying as little as possible. Devising an appropriate contract for wages in return for work – the employment contract – is complicated by the fact that the principal is rarely around to see how much effort the agent is expending but can only observe the result or output of the agent's work. These wage–effort bargains and output control are also subject to a set of random factors over which the principal has little or no control, including the agent's tacit knowledge and skills, and factors connected with clients and customers, which also depend on random factors. However, the primary conclusion of agency theory is to link pay to performance to provide employees with appropriate incentives.

As we have already discussed, this model runs into problems with knowledge workers, especially expert professionals such as doctors, lawyers, consultants, and academics, for several reasons:

1. There are the problems of observing knowledge work and even understanding what is going on. For example, hospital managers, unless they have clinical training, have major problems in making reasoned judgements on what goes on in an operating theatre or on the results of the operation (Martin et al., 2021). At times, this can result in unfortunate consequences, such as 'rogue' doctors and nurses being allowed to continue harming, even when warning signs have been raised by other clinicians. The cases of Ian Patterson, a surgeon who operated inappropriately for financial gain, and Manish Shah, a GP, who received three life sentences for serious sex offences are recent UK examples. Lucy Letby, a nurse, who was found guilty of murdering seven babies and trying to kill six others, was perhaps the most infamous recent case.

2. Agency models that focus on output incentives may be inappropriate for knowledge workers, who are likely to be driven by their calling, including the socially desirable nature of the work itself and a need to be known as an expert. Some workers in public services, for example, would fall into this category, including academics, doctors and nurses, and social workers, whose orientations to work are more about moral and social purpose than financial gain (Newell, 2015). Agency models are not particularly helpful in leveraging such desires and may even be counter-productive, although this does not mean that professionals in the public sector are uninterested in pay (Martin et al., 2023).

3. Agency models are frequently unidimensional in their measures of productivity. Usually, this is seen as a simple relationship between inputs, such as how hard someone works, and, often crude, measures of outputs such as sales or customer satisfaction ratings. However, knowledge work is much less capable of being measured by single, short-term criteria; it is often related less to how hard someone works and more to how smart someone works. Therefore, agency-based incentive schemes can sometimes distort effort allocations of knowledge workers by forcing them to apply effort in measurable, but not necessarily meaningful, directions. Again, this is evident in recent research we have undertaken on doctors who are measured against targets set to reduce waiting lists, regardless of the severity of the clinical need to see patients in line with how long they have been waiting (Martin et al., 2021).

4. Work in routine organizations, which is often characterised by production environments, usually requires major initial investments in technologies and processes, such as when designing and building a new automobile. Consequently, planning and linear

thinking tend to dominate because getting something right the first time will avoid the problems of retooling and scrapping. However, in organizations that focus on tackling novel problems, linear planning and making 'big decisions' can be counter-productive by locking organizations into a fixed strategic direction. This approach to strategy through planning is often inconsistent with innovation and change, which require knowledge workers to 'act their way into thinking' and to evolve emergent strategies for changing contexts. Thus, forcing knowledge workers into a planning and measurement straitjacket can be extremely counter-productive in innovative environments.

The images of organizations depicted in Figure 7.6 pose a range of different problems for KIEs, especially in the management of knowledge workers. The growing literature in this area, however, suggests two main principles for the future of management in a knowledge context (Newell, 2015; Wang & Noe, 2010):

- The first suggests a move away from traditional incentives and an emphasis on developing collaboration, trust, and professionalism, based on employer-of-choice policies, developing strong internal employer brands, and changed psychological contracts (see Chapter 6 on the corporate context). As we saw in Chapters 3 and 6, the management of employee engagement and the management of external and internal corporate reputations or brands to attract, retain, and motivate knowledge workers is likely to become an even more important issue than it currently is.
- The second emphasises emergent strategising and planning and iterative work structures, rather than linear planning and structured forms of organization. Knowledge creation and diffusion often iterate daily and are based on alternative periods of unstructured work in communities of practice or small groups.

Finally, we should be aware of the impact of new technologies such as AI on the future of knowledge work occupations. Forecasts suggest that AI will be most useful in creative jobs and industries, such as publishing, advertising, music, television, app development, haute cuisine, architecture, and live entertainment (Berg et al., 2023). But this is only likely to be so if the professionals in these industries hone their creative human and social capital. We should also be aware that some professions and industries may be negatively affected, such as certain kinds of teachers, judges, and healthcare workers.

THE NATURE OF INTELLECTUAL CAPITAL

In the introduction to this chapter and in Figure 7.1, I referred to the nature of intellectual capital as an outcome of the knowledge management process in organizations. The term is increasingly being used to refer to the knowledge assets of organizations (Serenko & Bontis, 2013). In this section, we explore what is meant by intellectual capital in more detail, the components of intellectual capital, some of the problems involved in measuring intangible assets, and the methods currently used to value intellectual capital. This is an important discussion because there is pressure on organizations in many countries to value human capital and to include it on the balance sheet.

Approaches to intellectual capital management

The term 'intellectual capital' began to enter the field of management in the late 1960s and has become part of the standard terminology of knowledge management, with endorsement by highly respected scholars, consulting organizations, and companies. And, like many academic disciplines, it now has a journal devoted to research in the field (Belluci et al., 2021). There have been several generic attempts to show how knowledge assets and intellectual capital relate to each other and business performance (Bamel et al., 2022). Perhaps the best-known of these is the well-known *balanced scorecard*, which we examined in Chapter 6. The approach sets out cause-and-effect relationships between strategic success and four areas of measurement that relate directly to knowledge management: financial measures; customer measures; internal process measures (e.g., cycle times, levels of waste); and learning and growth measures. A second generic approach is the *knowledge assets map*, which was designed to help companies identify and measure their knowledge-based assets and their contribution to the firm (CIMA/ Cranfield, 2004; Carlucci & Schluma, 2011). This approach identifies a hierarchy of knowledge assets (see Figure 7.7).

The nature and examples of these assets to which this hierarchy refers are illustrated in Table 7.2. It should be noted that these measures are illustrative and must be related to the context of the organization.

Defining and measuring intellectual capital

Edvinsson, the architect of the well-known Skandia framework, has suggested that intellectual capital comprises the hidden factors of human and structural capital (Edvinsson & Malone, 1997). *Human capital* is the combined current stock of knowledge, skills, innovativeness, and abilities of an organization's individual employees. The distinguishing feature of human capital is that it cannot be owned by the company, and 'walks out

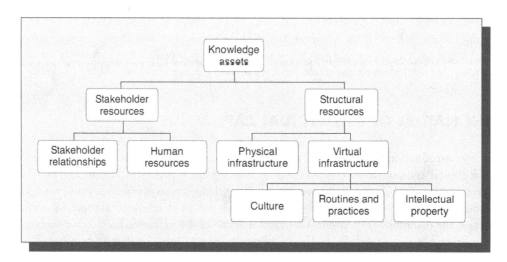

FIGURE 7.7 The hierarchy of knowledge assets

TABLE 7.2 Knowledge asset indicators

Stakeholder relationships	All forms of relationship established by the company, including numbers of partnering agreements; number/quality of licensing agreements; market share; public opinion surveys, partnership satisfaction index, customer retention, brand loyalty, customer complaints
Human resources	All knowledge provided by employees in the form of competencies, commitment, motivation, and tacit knowledge. Measures include: • Demographic indicators: number of employees, ages, etc.; length of service, per cent full-time employees; diversity measures, including the number of woman managers, ethnic minorities, foreign nationals • Competence indicators: employees with degree qualifications and above; average years' service with company; competence levels • Attitude indicators: employee satisfaction; commitment or engagement levels, stress levels, new ideas generated by staff, employee net promoter scores, etc. • HR practice indicators: training expenses per employee; time in training, recruitment indicators; rankings in best places to work for league tables Physical infrastructure All infrastructural assets, including structure, ICT, and AI assets, including scalability/capacity measures; number of computers per employee; server response times; use of knowledge-sharing facilities, use of AI tools
Culture	Corporate culture/reputation/internal branding, e.g., number of internal disputes, engagement surveys, organizational personality surveys and strength of psychological commitment, external measures of best places to work
Routines and practices	Covers internal practices and virtual networks, including process quality, number of codified processes, intranet use; widespread usage of generative AI aligned with human capital
Intellectual property	Sum of patents, copyrights, brands, and processes owned by the company, e.g., revenues from patents, number of patents, value of copyrights, brand recognition surveys

Source: adapted from CIMA/Cranfield, 2004; Marr, 2008; Rus et al., 2019.

of the door' most evenings. *Social capital*, which refers to bonds (in the form of shared culture and values), bridges (the strength of networks), and trust within and between organizations, is another key form of capital (Kwon & Adler, 2014). *Structural capital*, which includes the hardware, software, organizational structure, patents, databases of customers, logos, and so on, is what supports employees. These more tangible assets, which are left behind when employees leave or go home at night, are capable of being owned by the company and are tradable. Structural capital also generates a third form of capital, which Edvinsson originally described as *customer capital*. This class of asset has been widened to incorporate not only customers but all stakeholders and is increasingly known as *relational capital*. Subramaniam and Youndt (2005) found that social capital is often the most important in developing the intellectual capital of organizations. Without social capital, human capital does not come into play and investing only in human capital through the recruitment of stars can lead to a deterioration in intellectual capital, as we saw in Chapter 3.

> all the resources linked to the external relationships of the firm – with customers, suppliers or partners in research and development. It comprises that part of human and structural capital involved with the company's relations with stakeholders (investors, creditors, customers, and suppliers), plus the perceptions that they hold about the company. Examples of this are image, customer loyalty, customer satisfaction, links with suppliers, commercial power, negotiating capacity … and environmental activities.
>
> *(CIMA/Cranfield, 2004)*

Often, when an organization is being sold to a new owner, it is the relational capital that is being purchased, along with the human and structural capital. The key point about this framework is that intellectual capital is set alongside financial capital (see Figure 7.8) and can account for the difference between a company's traditional balance sheet assets and investors' valuations of companies.

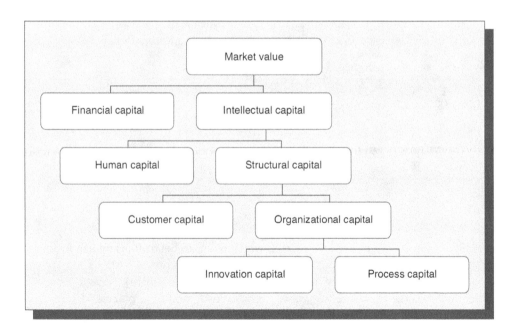

FIGURE 7.8 Skandia's value scheme

(*Source*: adapted from Bontis, 2001)

LEARNING SUMMARY

In this chapter, I have described and evaluated one of the major contexts of modern organizations and its implications for managing people. Knowledge and learning are important in all organizations. They are a major source of strategic advantage for many organizations in most developed countries. I began by raising six questions that all organizations need to address based on the framework of knowledge management in Figure 7.1. The key 'takeaways' from these questions and framework are as follows:

- The knowledge-based economy and the new economics of knowledge are heavily dependent on the quality of so-called knowledge workers and on finding more appropriate ways of managing knowledge workers.
- Knowledge is seen as the key factor input into the generation of wealth and organizational success, is the source of high economic returns for people whose knowledge is scarce, is localised in certain regions, leading to an important local labour market for knowledge, and depends for its successful transfer on knowledge networks.
- Knowledge-intensive enterprises (KIEs) are knowledge-integrating organizations that rely on access to and the creation of advanced and innovative knowledge for sustained strategic success. They also tend to be based more on communal relations and trust than on markets and price mechanisms for their effective operation. Finally, they need to have high levels of absorptive capacity to create new knowledge.
- Knowledge is different from information because it is essentially a human creation, which makes it much more difficult to manage.
- Knowledge is usually depicted in terms of the split between its tacit and explicit forms; it is the tacit nature of knowledge that makes it difficult to manage. However, it is more useful to think of knowledge as a spectrum, ranging from unconscious tacit knowledge, through to semiconscious tacit knowledge to explicit knowledge, because all knowledge has tacit roots.
- Tacit knowledge is also to be found in groups as well as individuals, and learning is often undertaken in groups. Indeed, group-based learning is often seen as superior to individual learning in the field of innovation.
- We can think of different images of organizations based on the type of knowledge they most use. Tacit and explicit knowledge can be related to individual and group-based knowledge to produce four different images of organizations, raising different problems for managing people.
- Agency models of management, which rely heavily on traditional structures and financial incentives, are mainly relevant to organizations that use knowledge in a routine way. Other images of organizations require different solutions to managing knowledge workers. These solutions are to be found in new forms of trust, commitment, and development models, and in more flexible and less directive forms of organization.

- Developing and converting tacit knowledge to explicit knowledge is *the* key managerial problem in KIEs. Developing tacit knowledge by increasing the variety and quality of experience among knowledge workers is critical in increasing the knowledge stock of a KIE.
- Creating and harnessing naturally occurring communities of practice are the principal means by which tacit knowledge can be increased and transferred in organizations. Communities of practice are based on community theories of learning and assume that learning and practice are intertwined. Empowering people to create such communities unleashes organizational potential for learning and knowledge creation.
- Intellectual capital must be placed on the same level as financial capital in organizations and must be measured and managed. New methods of valuing intellectual capital may change the focus of many organizations and their reporting systems towards knowledge management.

REVIEW QUESTIONS

1. What distinguishes a KIE from other forms of organizations?
2. How do communities of practice facilitate organizational learning and the creation of intellectual capital?
3. How does AI change the nature of knowledge work?

REFERENCES

Alavi, M., & Denford, J. S. (2011). Knowledge management: Process, practice and Web 2.0. In M. Easterby-Smith & M. Lyles (Eds.), *Handbook of organizational learning and knowledge management* (2nd ed., pp. 105–124). Wiley.

Bamel, U., Pereira, V., Del Guidice, M., & Temouri, Y. (2022). The extent and impact of intellectual capital research: A two-decade analysis. *Journal of Intellectual Capital, 23*(2), 375–400.

Bellucci, M., Marzi, G., Orkando, B., & Ciampi, F. (2021). Journal of intellectual capital: A review of emerging themes and future trends. *Journal of Intellectual Capital, 22*(4), 744–767.

Berg, J. M., Raj, M., & Seamans, R. (2023). Capturing value from artificial intelligence. *Academy of Management Discoveries, 9*(4), Guidepost.

Blackler, F. (2002). Knowledge, knowledge work and organizations: An overview and interpretation. In Y. Choo & N. Bontis (Eds.), *The strategic management of intellectual capital and organizational knowledge* (pp. 47–64). Oxford University Press.

Blackler, F., Crump, N., & McDonald, S. (2016). Organizing processes in complex activity networks. In D. Nicolini (Ed.), *Knowing in organizations: A practice-based approach* (2nd ed.). Routledge.

Bolisani, E., & Bratianu, C. (2018). The emergence of knowledge management. In E. Bolisani & C. Bratianu (Eds.), *Emergent knowledge strategies: Strategic thinking in knowledge management* (pp. 27–47). Springer Link.

Bontis, N. (2001). Assessing knowledge assets: A review of the models used to measure intellectual capital. *International Journal of Management Reviews, 3*(1), 41–60.

Brandi, U., & Elkjaer, B. (2011). Organizational learning viewed from a social learning perspective. In M. Easterby-Smith & M. Lyles (Eds.), *Handbook of organizational learning and knowledge management* (2nd ed., pp. 23–42). Wiley.

Brinkley, I. (2008). *The knowledge economy: How knowledge is reshaping the economic life of nations.* The Work Foundation

British Academy. (2022). *Teaching purposeful business in UK business schools.* https://www.thebritishacademy.ac.uk/publications/future-of-the-corporation-teaching-purposeful-business-in-uk-business-schools/

Carlucci, D., & Schluma, G. (2011). A knowledge assets mapping methodology to view knowledge-based value creation dynamics. In G. Schluma (Ed.), *Managing knowledge assets and business value creation in organizations: Measures and dynamics* (pp. 67–86). IGI Global.

Cappelli, P. (1998). *The new deal at work.* Harvard Business School Press.

Centre for Cities. (2022). *At the frontier: The geography of the UK's new economy.* https://www.centreforcities.org/publication/at-the-frontier-the-geography-of-the-uks-new-economy/

Child, J., & Rodrigues, S. (2011). Social identity and organizational learning. In M. Easterby-Smith & M. Lyles (Eds.), *Handbook of organizational learning and knowledge management* (2nd ed., pp. 305–330). Wiley.

Choo, C. W., & Bontis, N. (Eds.). (2002). *The strategic management of intellectual capital and organizational knowledge.* Oxford University Press.

CIMA/Cranfield. (2004). *Understanding corporate value: Managing and reporting intellectual capital.* www.cimaglobal.com/downloads/ intellectualcapital.pdf

CIPD. (2004, June). Outsourcing: Is the appeal of offshoring diminishing? *People Management, 3*, 34–39.

CIPD. (2022). *Knowledge work performance: An evidence review.* https://www.cipd.org/uk/knowledge/evidence-reviews/evidence-knowledge-work/

Coghlan, D. (2019). *Doing action research in your own organization* (5th ed.). Sage.

Crane, L (2013). A new taxonomy of knowledge management theory: The turn to knowledge as constituted in social action. *Journal of Knowledge Management Practice, 14.*

Del Giudice, M., Carayannis, E. G., & Maggioni, V. (2017). Global knowledge intensive enterprises and international technology transfer: Emerging perspectives from a quadruple helix environment. *The Journal of Technology Transfer, 42,* 229–235.

Durst, S., & Edvardsson, I. R. (2012). Knowledge management in SMEs: A literature review. *Journal of Knowledge Management, 16*(6), 879–903.

Easterby-Smith, M., & Lyles, M. (2011). *Handbook of organizational learning and knowledge management* (2nd ed.). Wiley.

Edvinsson, L., & Malone, M. S. (1997). *Intellectual capital: Realizing your company's true value by finding its hidden brainpower.* HarperCollins.

Evans, P. and Wurster, T. (2000). *Blown to Bits: How the new economics of information transforms strategy.* Cambridge, MA: Harvard University Press.

Foss, N., & Mahkne, V. (2011). Knowledge creation in firms: An organizational economics perspective. In M. Easterby-Smith & M. Lyles (Eds.), *Handbook of organizational learning and knowledge management* (2nd ed., pp. 125–153). Wiley.

Fuller, S. (2002). *Knowledge management foundations.* ButterworthHeinemann.

Grant, R. M. (2004). *Contemporary strategic analysis.* Blackwell.

Grint, K. (2022). Critical essay: Wicked problems in the age of uncertainty. *Human Relations, 75*(8), 1518–1532.

Gupta, A. K., & Govindarajan, V. (2004). *Global strategy and the organization.* John Wiley.

Harris, R. G. (2001). The knowledge-based economy: Intellectual origins and new economic perspectives. *International Journal of Management Reviews, 3,* 21–40.

Harvard Business Review, Ferguson, A., Parcells, B., Abdul-Jabbar, K., & Giradi, J. (2018). *HBR's 10 must read leadership lessons from sport.* Harvard Business School Press.

Hislop, D., Bosua, R., & Helms, R. (2018). *Knowledge management in organizations* (4th ed.). Oxford University Press.

Hsu, I. C., & Sabherwal, R. (2012). Relationship between intellectual capital and knowledge management: An empirical investigation. *Decision Sciences, 43*(3), 489–524.

James, L., Guile, D., & Unwin, L. (2011). *From learning for the knowledge-based economy to learning for growth: Re-examining clusters, innovation, and qualifications.* Published by the Centre for Learning and Life Chances in Knowledge Economies and Societies. http://www.llakes.org.

Klinger-Vidra, R. (2023, June 9). The microchip industry would implode if China invaded Taiwan, and it would affect everyone. *Conversation.* https://theconversation.com/the-microchip-industry-would-implode-if-china-invaded-taiwan-and-it-would-affect-everyone-206335

Kwon, S.-W., & Adler, P. S. (2014). Social capital: Maturation of a field of research. *Academy of Management Review, 39*(4), 412–422.

Lave, J., & Wenger, E. (1991). *Situated Learning: Limited peripheral participation.* Cambridge University Press.

Leonard, D. (2011). *Managing knowledge assets, creativity and innovation.* World Science Publishing.

Leonard, D., & Sensiper, S. (2002). The role of tacit knowledge in group innovation. In C. W. Choo & N. Bontis (Eds.), *The strategic management of intellectual capital and organizational knowledge* (pp. 485–500). Oxford University Press.

Makini, J., & Marche, S. (2010). Towards a typology of knowledge-intensive organizations: Determinant factors. *Knowledge Management Research Practice, 8,* 265–277.

Marr, B. (2008). *Impacting future value: How to manage your intellectual capital.* Society of Managements Accountants of Canada/ Institute of Certified Public Accountants/

the Chartered Institute if Management Accountants. http://www.cimaglobal.com /Documents/ImportedDocuments/tech_mag_impacting_future_value_may08.pdf .pdf

Martin, G., Massy, J. and Clarke, T. (2003). When absorptive capacity meets institutions and (e)learners. *International Journal of Training and Development, 7*(4), 222–244.

Martin, G., Beaumont, P. B., Doig, R. M., & Pate, J. M. (2005). Branding: A new performance discourse for HR. *European Management Journal, 23*(1), 76–88.

Martin, G., & Reddington, M. (2009). Reconceptualising absorptive capacity to explain the e-enablement of the HR function (e-HR) in organizations. *Employee Relations, 31*, 515–537.

Martin, G., Reddington, M., & Alexander, H. (2008). *Technology, outsourcing and transforming HR*. Butterworth Heinemann.

Martin, G., Siebert, S., Bushfield, S., & Howieson, W. B. (2021). Changing logics in healthcare and their effects on the identity motives and identity work of doctors. *Organization Studies, 42*(9), 1477–1499.

Martin, G., Staines, H. J. & Bushfield S. (2023). Seniro hospital doctors' intentions to retire in NHS Scotland. https://discovery.dundee.ac.uk/en/publications/senior -hospital-doctors-intentions-to-retire-in-nhs-scotland

Morgan, G. (1997). *Image of organization*. Sage.

Muller, J. M., Buliga, O., & Voigt, K.-I. (2021). The role of absorptive capacity and innovation strategy in the design of industry 4.0 business models – a comparison between SMEs and large enterprises. *European Management Journal, 39*(3), 333–343.

Newell, S. (2015). Managing knowledge and managing knowledge work: What we know and what the Future holds. *Journal of Information Technology, 30*(1). https://doi.org /10.1057/jit.2014.12

Nonaka, I. (2002). A dynamic theory of organizational knowledge creation. In C. W. Choo & N. Bontis (Eds.), *The strategic management of intellectual capital and knowledge creation*. Oxford University Press.

Nonaka, I., & Takeuchi, H. (1995). *The knowledge-creating company*. Oxford University Press.

Nonaka, I., & Takeuchi, H. (2021). Humanizing strategy. *Long Range Planning, 54*(4). https://doi.org/10.1016/j.lrp.2021.102070

Ogbonnaya, C., Daniels, K., Messersmith, J., & Rofcanin, Y. (2022). A theory based analysis of null causality between HRM practices and outcomes: Evidence from four-wave longitudinal data. *Journal of Management Studies, 60*(6), 1448–1484. doi:10.1111/joms.12881

Pettigrew, A. M., Cornuel, E., & Hommel, U. (Eds.). (2014). *The institutional development of business schools*. Oxford University Press.

Polanyi, M. (1966). *The tacit dimension*. Doubleday.

Rittel, H., & Webber. M. (1984). *Dilemmas in a general theory of planning, policy sciences* (Vol. 4, pp. 155–169). Elsevier Scientific Publishing Company, Inc., 1973. [Reprinted in N. Cross (Ed.), *Developments in design methodology* (pp. 135–144). Wiley Sons.

Rus, A. I. D., Achim, M. V., & Borlea, S. N. (2019). Theoretical and methodological approaches on the intellectual capital. *Sciendo, 29*(2), 1–16.

Seely Brown, J. (2012). *Cultivating the entrepreneurial learner in the 21st century.* http://www.johnseelybrown.com/el.

Seely Brown, J., & Duguid, P. (1991). Organizational learning and communities-of-practice: Toward a unified view of working, learning, and innovation. *Organization Science, 2*, 40–57.

Seely Brown, J., & Duguid, P. (1996, July/August). Universities in the digital age. *Change: The Magazine of Higher Learning, 28*(4), 11–19.

Seely Brown, J. and Duguid, P. (2000). *The social life of information.* Cambridge, MA: Harvard University Press.

Seely Brown, J., Duguid, P., & Weinberger, D. (2017). *The social life of information (updated).* Harvard Business School Press.

Serenko, A., & Bontis, N. (2013). Investigating the current state and impact of the intellectual capital academic discipline. *Journal of Intellectual Capital, 14*(4), 476–500.

Siebert, S., Martin, G., Bozic, B. and Docherty, I. (2015). Looking beyond the factory gates: A critique and agenda for organizational trust research. *Organization Studies, 36*, 1033–1062.

Siebert, S., Wilson, F., & Hamilton, J.R.A. (2017). 'Devils may sit here': The role of enchantment in institutional maintenance. *Academy of Management Journal, 60*(4), 1607–1632.

Staples, D. S., Greenaway, K., & McKeen, J. D. (2001). Opportunities for research about managing the knowledge-based enterprise. *International Journal of Management Reviews, 3*(1), 1–20.

Spilg, E., Siebert, S., & Martin, G. (2012). A social learning perspective on the development of doctors in the UK national health service. *Social* Science and Medicine, *75*, 1617–1624.

Subramaniam, M., & Youndt, M. A. (2005). The influence of intellectual capital on the types of innovative capabilities. *Academy of Management Journal, 48*(3), 450–463.

Suleyman, M. (2023). *The coming wave: A.I., power and the 21st century's greatest dilemma.* Bodley Head.

Teece, D. J., & Al-Aali, A. (2011). Knowledge assets, capabilities and the theory of the firm. In M. Easterby-Smith & M. Lyles (Eds.), *Handbook of organizational learning and knowledge management* (2nd ed., pp. 505–534). Wiley.

Van Wijk, R., van den Bosch, F. A. J., & Volberda, H. W. (2011a). Organizing knowledge in social, alliance and organizational networks. In M. Easterby-Smith & M. Lyles (Eds.), *Handbook of organizational learning and knowledge management* (2nd ed., pp. 477–504). Wiley.

Wang, S., & Noe, R. A. (2010). Knowledge sharing: A review and directions for future research. *Human Resource Management Review, 20*(2): 115–131

Webb, S. P. (2017). *Knowledge management: Linchpin of change.* Routledge.

Weick, K. E., Sutcliffe, K. M. & Obsfeld, D. (2005). Organizing and the process of sensemaking. *Organization Science, 16*(4), 409–421.

Wenger, E. (1998). *Communities of Practice: Learning meaning and identity.* Cambridge, UK: Cambridge University Press.

Wenger, E. (2000). Communities of practice and learning systems. *Organization*, 7(2), 225–246.

Wenger, E. (2011). *A brief introduction to communities of practice: National Science Foundation*. http://hdl.handle.net/1794/11736

World Economic Forum. (2020). Global competitiveness report special edition: how countries are performing on the road to recovery.

Zahra, S. A., & George, G. (2002). Absorptive capacity: A review, reconceptualization, and extension. *Academy of Management Review*, 27, 185–203.

CHAPTER 8

The technological context, organizations, and managing people

LEARNING OBJECTIVES

By the end of this chapter, you should be able to:

- Understand the nature of technological change and its relationship to people management and organizational change
- Understand the trends in technological developments and use these trends to analyse your strategic environment.
- Apply the notion of a technological system to your workplace (or one with which you are familiar) to analyse its essential components.
- Distinguish between how technologies are used to empower and disempower people at work.
- Apply the concepts from the chapter to designing systems of work and work roles that enhance employees' sense of meaningful work and minimise the negative influences of new (and old) technologies on people.

UNDERSTANDING THE NATURE OF TECHNOLOGICAL CHANGE AND ITS RELATIONSHIP WITH MANAGING PEOPLE

Introduction

This chapter synthesises a wide range of literature and research from different disciplines, including some of my own research over the previous two decades, to help you *understand* the importance of technological change to the management of people and be able to *use* these ideas to improve your thinking and performance as a manager. The relationship between changing technologies, organizations, and people is an extremely

DOI: 10.4324/9781003469711-8

important one, which has been at the heart of nearly all management thinking and a good deal of economic policy in various countries for many years. It is also clear that this relationship is an ever-moving target because there is nothing new about new technologies; they are always with us and always presenting managers and workers with new problems as well as new opportunities. These ever-present dynamics have never been more obvious than during recent times, following the widespread use of digital information and communications technologies (ICT) in the 1980s and, now, artificial intelligence (AI), which is the simulation of human intelligence by computer systems (Barrat, 2023; Stone et al., 2022; Budhwar et al., 2023).

The rate of recent technological progress, the ubiquity of ICT at most workplaces, and the cluster of related technologies to which ICT has helped develop – for example, biotechnology, nanotechnology, synthetic biology, new material science, robotics, mobile technologies, cloud computing, social media, and AI – has radically changed many businesses and economies. However, we need to be careful in getting carried away with some of the hype. If we focus on these new technologies, much of the recent work by academics and practitioners is on ICT and AI as *general-purpose technologies* and their relationship with economic growth, productivity, and the future problems and opportunities at work created by new business models (e.g., Barrat, 2023; Suleyman, 2023). In the past two decades since writing the first edition of this book, much of this work has focused on the impact of mobile technologies and social media on people management, a research direction to which we have contributed over the years (e.g., Martin et al., 2015; Parry et al., 2019). This interest was initially generated by comparisons in the early 2000s between the so-called 'new economy' and the old economy, as many countries sought to play 'catch-up' with the long-standing perceived American advantage in technologically led productivity (Obijiofor, 2015).

There has been a considerable debate, however, over the extent to which a new economy truly existed and whether it was fundamentally different from the old economy, even in the USA where the concept first saw daylight. This debate began following the bursting of the dot-com bubble in 2000 when the American securities market for technology stocks collapsed. It continued after the Global Financial Crisis (GFC) in 2007/2008, when the increasing 'financialization' of economies such as the USA and the UK became a source of significant problems for most taxpayers, many of whom were forced to bail out financial services companies that used technology *in extremus* to develop new products and services that turned out to be worthless (Thompson, 2011). But, if we accept the idea that there is something quite different about economies such as the USA and its continuously impressive productivity record, can other countries hope to match it by creating an economic and industrial structure based on new types of business models to which new technologies have given rise? The evidence on this question is mixed. Certain countries in northern Europe, such as Finland and Sweden, smaller states such as Singapore, and some Asian countries, such as Taiwan and South Korea, have been successful in creating technologically advanced economies and organizations. For example, I have already referred in Chapter 7 to Taiwan's dominance of the semiconductor industry that has put it centre stage in international relations between China and the USA, both worried about the extent to which Taiwan could be controlled by the other and the effects that would have on many other industries. Companies in these countries have tended to follow a *'high-road'* competitive strategy (see Box 8.1) (Osterman, 2018).

Box 8.1 High and low 'roads' to economic growth

A *high-road strategy* to economic growth is based on having a high proportion of either significant ICT-producing industries, such as chip manufacturers, software developers, and games companies, or significant ICT-using industries, such as financial services, fintech, pharmaceuticals, motor vehicles, and education, to create high added-value products and services based on high levels of education, skills and meaningful work as measured by work quality, work intensity, working time quality, and a good physical environment. Such a relationship between technology, products and services, and skills is thought to create a self-reinforcing equilibrium. Silicon Valley, Boston, and North Carolina in the USA and Cambridge in the UK are the traditional examples of such clusters of companies linked with world-class universities, although these examples are gradually extending to certain European and Asian city regions.

A *low-road strategy* is associated with minimal effective use of ICT in organizations, coupled with a self-reinforcing concentration on products with low skill requirements, often meaningless jobs, and competition based on low costs and prices. Such a strategy is thought to produce a negative dynamic because it generates a workforce unable to operate effectively in a high skills/advanced technology environment. Nor does the strategy provide any incentive for employees to acquire and be paid for advanced technology-based skills.

Source: based on CIPD, 2014; Finegold & Soskice, 1988; Taylor, 2004; Osterman, 2018

However, one of the key messages from research has shown that most companies still follow or have no choice but to follow a *'low-road'* strategy (Osterman, 2018), even in countries as technologically advanced as the UK (which might be better characterised as following a hybrid strategy) (Hanley & Douglass, 2014). The dominance of a low-road strategy among companies in a national economy is often used to explain why these economies lag the USA, with the UK being the example *par excellence* of technology-lag productivity. For example, the UK recorded approximately 9 million people, which is a quarter of its adults of working age, with low basic skills (Kuczera et al., 2016). The UK also recorded the largest proportion of young people compared to the generation approaching retirement in any OECD country with low basic skills. Only the USA and Italy had a greater proportion of its working-age population in the 16–24 age group with lower basic skills than the UK. If this is the case among developed OECD countries, what price the success of the developing world, particularly if they lose their current comparative advantages in low labour costs due to high growth rates? Thus, nearly every country in the world has a policy on how to take advantage of the new technologies to create successful firms and generate economic progress. India is a good example of such a country in the developing world, with its significant cluster of ICT-based companies in Bangalore. Taiwan and South Korea are other good examples, with their strategy of building branded goods on the back of high levels of research and development into new computing technologies. Finally, China is investing hugely in its universities and science to generate economic development by following a high road to growth strategy, which has become evident through the inclusion of a growing number of Chinese universities entering the elite, top-50 reputation rankings since 2012, and the development of electric cars by Chinese companies.

It follows that taking advantage of technological change is usually seen as the *necessary* condition for economic and business success for all countries in the long run, but, as we shall see, technological investment in firms by itself is not a *sufficient* condition. Most researchers agree that it is the *interrelationships* among technology, institutions, organizations, and people that seem to matter in delivering the promises made for new technologies (Berg et al., 2023). In this chapter, we shall explore these interrelationships and the implications for managers by addressing three sets of related questions:

1. To what extent are organizations in the new economic environment different in their requirements for people and the experience of people working within them? To what extent are they different in making use of technology, particularly investment in ICT and AI, to produce innovations and productivity growth? And how can we best manage the relationship between investment in new technologies and the exploitation of knowledge as discussed in Chapter 7?

2. To what extent do we have a choice in shaping such technological change to become a progressive and empowering force for the people working in the new economy? Can we design jobs and organizations so that adopting new technologies will lead to liberating employees from routine and boring jobs and enhance their ability to use knowledge for their own good and for the good of the firm? Or will the choices we make result in dominating employees, perhaps leading to widespread deskilling for most people?

3. What can managers do to prepare themselves to make appropriate choices in the technology–people management relationship?

DEFINING TECHNOLOGIES AND NEW TECHNOLOGIES: A COMBINATION OF 'HARDWARE AND SOFTWARE'

A technological system

Often, one of the most puzzling aspects for managers and management students, especially those coming from a non-technical background, is to understand what is meant by technology. Defining technology in a general sense helps us understand not only what we mean by new and old technologies, but also their distinctive nature. However, a problem arises when different writers and traditions in the literature have different conceptions of where technology begins and ends, so to speak. This is especially so in relation to the 'hardware' of material objects, such as networked computers and computer code, and the software of organizations, including structures, systems, and processes. In the field of business and management studies, technology is traditionally seen as how a desirable outcome or goal is achieved, such as the development of a new product (e.g., electric vehicles or cobots in warehouses), new services (health benefits resulting from wearable technologies, ChatGPT-4 to improve search engines, write screenplays, create lessons plans in education, etc.), or the development of new processes (e.g., online and hybrid learning, AI-generated medical diagnosis). From this perspective, technology can be defined by the three elements in Box 8.2.

Box 8.2 Defining technology

- The physical objects or artefacts – products, tools, and equipment – that are used to create these outcomes (e.g., moving assembly lines and robots to produce automobiles, applications of AI to produce healthcare expert systems, or virtual learning environments to facilitate online learning).
- The activities or processes that constitute the method of production (e.g., the design of flowline production methods to produce automobiles, software programming to network computers for a talent management system, or online discussions and online assessments).
- The knowledge needed to develop and apply the physical objects and processes to produce a particular output (e.g., the know-how to design and assemble an automobile or a generative AI application such as ChatGPT-4, the knowledge of specific healthcare interventions, or the knowledge of a field of study to be learnt and knowledge of how people learn online).

Source: based on Hatch (2018).

1. Think about your own work organization or one with which you are familiar. Use the above definition and the three elements of artefacts, processes, and know-how to describe the technology of the organization or department.

This view of technology is grounded in an open-systems perspective, which sees the organization as a technological process converting inputs from the environment into outputs. It allows us to relate organizational technologies to resource requirements and to the objects of technology such as automobiles, improved communications through social media, or elaborated knowledge structures in the heads of employees.

We usually distinguish between an organization's core technology, which is the technology it uses to produce its key products or services (e.g., flowline technologies in manufacturing or knowledge transfer in higher education), and technologies that maintain the production process (such as autonomous work groups or online learning), or technologies used to adapt organizations to their environment (such as planning and market research in both vehicle manufacture and higher education). We shall use this broader definition of technology throughout this chapter because it steers us away from a purely 'technicist' perspective, which has restricted discussions in this important field of study to discussions of ICT hardware and digital systems. It also helps explore the interfaces between the various components of a given technical system and its relationship with the management of people.

Exercise 8.1

Use Figure 8.1 to map out a basic systems view of your organization or department, or one with which you are familiar.

1. What are the key inputs and outputs?
2. What are the key features of the technical system? Here you may wish to refer to the review question in Box 8.2.

Stages in technological development and new technologies

One of the key questions raised earlier in this chapter was the distinction between old and new generations of technologies and their different impact on organizations and people management. A conventional way of thinking about this is to refer to the stages of technological development described in Box 8.3. Stages 3 and 4 broadly correspond to what we mean by the new technologies, all of which, to a greater or lesser degree, are based on computers and computing power for their emergence and impact. Stage 3, which is based on computing and information systems, became important in the 1980s with the development of the microchip. However, it was not until the late 1990s and the widespread adoption of the internet and ICT that we saw new business models emerging, in the form of e-commerce in retailing and m-businesses based on mobile apps. Well-known international examples are Amazon, Apple, and eBay, which have transformed the retailing, computing, and auction industries, respectively.

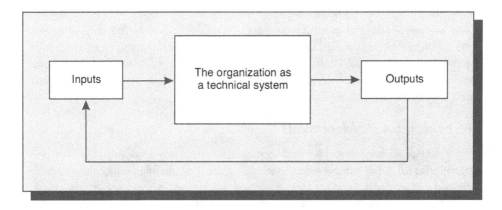

FIGURE 8.1 A basic open-systems model of organizations

Box 8.3 Stages in technological development

- Stage 1. Use of machines driven by steam power to replace labour in the transformation of raw materials into products.
- Stage 2. Use of electrically powered machines to move materials between machines and to power moving assembly lines and flow production.
- Stage 3. Use of electronics-based ICT to coordinate and control the transfer of information and tasks.
- Stage 4. Use of several related technologies, all of which reinforce each other and are based on increasingly cheap computing power and the internet. These include biotechnology to analyse and synthesise the genetic basis of plants, animals, and humans, nanotechnology, robotics, and advanced forms of materials to transform the production of goods and services, big data analytics to use large data sets to uncover hidden trends, unknown correlations, market, customer and employee attitudes, and so on, cloud computing, social media, and AI to store digital information, enhance communications, learning, and knowledge sharing, and mimic human intelligence and even human forms.

Such has been the progress in technological development over the last decade that much of what was new even a few years ago is rather old hat now or is at an advanced stage. This is especially true for AI (see Box 8.4).

Box 8.4 The future of artificial intelligence: Transformative potentials and ethical considerations

Here is a short essay I asked ChatGPT to write on the future of AI in November 2023. The question at the end asks you to critically evaluate its predictions.

Introduction

Artificial intelligence (AI) has emerged as a transformative force that is reshaping the way we live, work, and interact with the world. As we stand on the cusp of a new era, the future of AI promises unprecedented advancements, raising both excitement and concerns. This essay explores the potential trajectories of AI development, the profound impact it may have on various aspects of society, and the ethical considerations that must accompany its evolution.

Technological advancements

The future of AI is marked by continuous technological advancements that push the boundaries of what machines can achieve. Machine learning algorithms, neural networks, and deep learning techniques are becoming increasingly sophisticated, enabling AI systems to process and interpret vast amounts of data with remarkable accuracy. The convergence of AI with other emerging technologies such as quantum computing, robotics, and the Internet of Things (IoT) is amplifying its potential, paving the way for intelligent systems capable of autonomous decision-making and problem-solving.

Transformative impact on industries

AI is poised to revolutionise various industries, unlocking new possibilities and efficiencies. In healthcare, AI-powered diagnostics and personalised treatment plans have the potential to enhance medical outcomes and reduce costs. In finance, predictive analytics and algorithmic trading are reshaping investment strategies. The manufacturing sector is witnessing the rise of smart factories where AI-driven automation optimises production processes. The fusion of AI with augmented reality is transforming education, offering personalised learning experiences tailored to individual needs.

Societal implications

As AI permeates different facets of society, its impact on the job market and employment landscape is a subject of intense debate. While AI has the potential to create new job opportunities and boost productivity, there are concerns about the displacement of certain jobs through automation. Striking a balance between technological advancement and workforce adaptation will be crucial to mitigate potential social and economic disruptions.

Ethical considerations

The rapid evolution of AI raises ethical questions that demand careful consideration. Issues related to bias in AI algorithms, data privacy, and the potential misuse of advanced AI systems underscore the need for robust ethical frameworks. Ensuring transparency, accountability, and fairness in AI development and deployment is essential to prevent unintended consequences and protect fundamental human rights.

Human-AI collaboration

The future of AI is not necessarily a tale of machines replacing humans but rather one of collaboration. Human-AI partnerships hold the promise of addressing complex challenges that require a combination of human intuition, creativity, and emotional intelligence with AI's computational power and analytical capabilities. Ethical guidelines must be established to govern these collaborations and define the boundaries of AI involvement in decision-making processes.

Conclusion

The future of AI is an unfolding narrative with profound implications for humanity. As we embrace the potential benefits of AI, we must also navigate the ethical challenges it poses. Striking a balance between technological innovation and ethical considerations will be pivotal in ensuring that AI serves as a force for positive change, enhancing the quality of human life while upholding principles of fairness, transparency, and accountability. The collaborative synergy between humans and AI holds the key to unlocking a future where intelligent systems contribute to the betterment of society.

Question

To what extent have its predictions been realised, and what ethical concerns are emerging?

Robotics is one good illustration of the revolutionary potential of AI in lowering costs of the technology and its applications in industries such as vehicle manufacture. For example, cobots (collaborative robots that work alongside people) have begun to change the way in which products are manufactured. Industries as diverse as acting, education, criminal justice, and healthcare are being transformed by the introduction of generative AI in the form of expert systems, natural language processing, speech recognition, and machine vision. As the ChatGPT-generated content argues, some of these changes, are controversial and, indeed, create huge risks for society as well as benefits (Berg, 2023; Budhwar et al., 2023; Suleyman, 2023), which we shall discuss later in this chapter.

Clearly, as we highlighted in the introduction, different forms of technology and technological change have been at the heart of people management problems and the work of human resource professionals for many years. There is also a long and distinguished history of research and writing linking technology and technological change in the broadest sense of these terms to economics, organizational studies, psychology, and HRM. For example, the work of notable figures in economics and management, such as Adam Smith, Karl Marx, and Frederick Taylor, was concerned with the role of technology. In more recent times, however, the role of ICT, especially AI, in transforming societies, transforming economic progress, and in how we work in such societies has resulted in a renewed interest in the relationship between these new technologies and the management of people (Budhwar et al., 2023; Suleyman, 2023)

As we also flagged in the introduction, some academics are sceptical about the competitive advantages of investment in ICT for organizations, a point to which we shall return (Osterman, 2018). Most informed opinion, however, points to at least the potential for ICT, AI, and other new technologies to have a major impact in transforming economies, organizations, and how people work (Berg, 2023; Deranty & Corbin, 2024). Researchers typically point to at least five reasons for such transformative potential:

1. ICT has driven down the costs of information flows and speeded up the transmission of information, which, in an increasingly knowledge-based economy, is a critical success factor. In addition, low costs increase the adoption and diffusion of information. As technology gathers pace, advanced economies are combining technology with knowledge to create a new basis for competition and competitive advantage, drawing on knowledge management, social media, and AI. The Fitbit device is a good example of how

wearable technologies using AI can transform healthcare by detecting and monitoring early heart and respiratory problems.

2. The lowering of costs and ubiquity of information has assisted companies in developing new international markets and in internal coordination and learning in multinational companies. Good examples are AI-generated automated hiring system platforms that have been developed by companies such as PeopleStrong and HireVue to assist companies in their recruitment and selection processes.

3. ICT has led to new applications and business models. It is not just a technology but is also a marketplace, a method of manufacturing and a means of communication. We are also witnessing a new agenda made possible by these technologies in promising new ways of organizing work, including virtual and hybrid working, and e-lancing.

4. ICT has the potential to make all kinds of work more productive, because it increases access to information and makes markets more efficient. Good examples are the way in which Amazon has changed retailing and firms such as Uber have changed personal transport services in many countries. The education sector will likely be transformed by the application of generative AI, with many aspects of teaching and different types of teachers radically affected by chatbots (Berg, 2023)

5. ICT speeds up the adoption of new techniques and innovation by connecting people and organizations, often across time zones and distances. However, there is a developing concern about the idea of community and how internet technologies such as Teams and Zoom, used to link up people across time and space, can impact negatively on communities of practice. It is partly this factor that has led to firms such as Apple, Google, and Meta to request staff show up to their offices at least three days a week following a long period of remote working during COVID

Other strategic management writers have pointed to how the new economics of information have transformed business strategy by changing the traditional trade-off in information between reach and richness (Hitt et al., 2008). Reach is easily understood, being the number of people exchanging information; richness is more complicated, referring to bandwidth, the customisation of information, connectivity, and the reliability, security, and value of near-instant information. Their claim is that this traditional trade-off, a basic law of economics, has been disrupted, leading to simultaneous greater reach and richness, and thus the deconstruction of traditional industries such as retail banking and automobile retailing, and the creation of new ones in virtual entertainment (e.g., Netflix), gaming (e.g., Rockstar), and music provision (e.g., Spotify and Apple Music).

In addition to these more general reasons, our own research (Martin et al., 2009) singled out technology as the most important transformative force foreseen by senior HR managers in international companies, especially social media, due to its impact on the creation and transfer of knowledge among firms. Few of these managers, however, could have foreseen just how much their jobs would be threatened by technologies such as AI (Barrat, 2023; Budhwar et al., 2023), even allowing for the hype generated by figures such as Elon Musk. Some of the jobs most under threat, as we discussed in Chapter 7, are in the knowledge-based professions such as medicine, higher education professionals, lawyers, teachers, writers, and even politicians (Berg et al., 2023). As we have also discussed in previous chapters, access to instant knowledge and learning from others is one of the key strategic drivers of global companies in industries as diverse as news media, investment banking, and manufacturing. One good example from our research was IBM, which developed social media platforms for internal use before turning it into a source of revenue by selling its solutions to other organizations and supporting the solutions-based business of IBM more generally (Martin et al., 2009). However, managing the volume of information or 'overflow' generated by these technologies is becoming as much a problem for firms as not having enough information (Czarniawska & Lofgren, 2012). This is also a significant problem for academics and students alike!

This brief discussion of the new technologies leads us to ask the following important set of questions: Are there common issues confronting old and new technologies and their relationship with work and people management? If so, what can we learn from the introduction of older technologies? Or are new technologies, based on the internet and perhaps even newer ones such as biological sciences, nanotechnology, robotics, materials sciences, social media, and AI, raising new questions (Suleyman, 2023)? In the next part of this chapter, I shall attempt to shed some light on these questions with a brief examination of two lines of enquiry concerning the relationship between technology and people management:

- The new economics of knowledge and technology, and the rise of knowledge-intensive enterprises, which we have already discussed in previous chapters.
- The organizationally based, micro-level research into technology, knowledge work, and knowledge workers.

Following this examination, I have developed a simple framework to help us understand the key issues concerning technology and the 'human condition', which can help us think about new technologies and people management. I also suggest some pointers for organizations that wish to improve their performance in technology investment.

DEVELOPING A FRAMEWORK FOR EXPLORING THE RELATIONSHIP BETWEEN TECHNOLOGY AND HUMAN RESOURCE MANAGEMENT

The new economic environment: Combining technology, knowledge, and organizational change

We addressed the new economy literature in the last chapter on knowledge work discussing the relationship between the knowledge-based economy and knowledge-intensive enterprises (KIEs). That discussion, however, did not really examine the fundamental role of technology in shaping that relationship, to which I will now turn in a little more detail.

The story of the new economy began with the emergence of the new computer-based and digital technologies in the USA during the 1980s, the entrepreneurial spirit to which these gave rise, and the resurgence of the American economy in the 1990s.

Following these developments, a set of new theories of economic growth, which econo-mists labelled the *new economy*, emerged in the USA during the late 1990s. However, just what the new economy looked like, and whether this model has been replaced by newer variants, is a matter of some debate.

On the one hand, some writers equated it with ICT and its sectoral consequences. For example, various OECD reports have examined the impact of ICT on the *ICT-producing industry* itself, including manufacturers of semiconductors, computer equipment and peripherals, telephony, and software companies. They also examined the *ICT-using industries* – intensive ICT users such as retailing, pharmaceuticals, financial services, news media, academia, healthcare, and consulting. The general conclusions of these reports were that the ICT-producing sector was characterised by very high rates of pro-ductivity growth and economic performance in the countries where significant clusters of such companies were found, such as South Korea, Finland, Ireland, Sweden, Japan, and the USA. Regarding the ICT-using sector, the picture was still positive because it was associated with productivity growth, particularly labour productivity, but it had a different international distribution. For example, the contribution of ICT-using indus-tries in Sweden and Finland to economic growth was modest; by contrast, it was large for countries such as the UK, Australia, Canada, and the USA. In part, this was explained by the importance of intensive ICT-using industries to an economy, such as retailing and wholesaling, and financial services (e.g., securities). On the other hand, Sweden and Finland were not traditionally noted for having a high preponderance of these intensive ICT-using industries.

Other commentators took a broader perspective on the new economy, more akin to the knowledge-based economy discussed in the last chapter. Indeed, some equated the new economy with a form of post-industrial society, in which not only knowledge work but also services have replaced manufacturing as the dominant sectors in the economy. Two decades ago, Diana Coyle (2004) introduced the metaphor of *weightlessness* to char-acterise an economy in which creating value relies less on physical mass and more on intangibles, such as building intellectual capital through knowledge and creativity, and performing 'emotional labour' (continuously being required to be pleasant to unpleasant customers and patients, smiling, etc.,) in delivering high-quality services. This metaphor of weightlessness remains a revealing one and has recently been extended to include what has been termed the *sharing economy* (Sundararajan, 2013), which provides access to products, services, and unique skills beyond single ownership, for example, ride and car sharing, garden sharing, or short-term property sharing, such as Airbnb. This new form of economic and organizational structure is based on the application of web-based technologies to work, resulting in people shifting from being employees working under a contract *of* services to becoming independent workers, freelancers and e-lancers, work-ing under a contract *for* services. Good examples are the hundreds of thousands of part-time 'driver-partners' who are contracted to Uber, a firm that claims to provide taxi services cheaper and more convenient in major cities in many countries, and the many thousands of property owners who have let out their apartments on a short-term basis.

Support for these trends in advanced economies is evidenced by the changing occu-pational structure in countries such as the UK with employment manufacturing fall-ing from around 25 per cent to 10 per cent over the 50-year period to 2018, while employment in services reached 80 per cent (Source: Office for National Statistics, 2021). These figures confirm a significant increase in these knowledge-intensive occupations, which require high levels of education and skills acquisition. However, it also confirms a significant increase in service occupations such as care assistants in homes for the elderly and hospitals, which are relatively low-skilled occupations and low users of ICT. Indeed, ICT may well replace many of the functions carried out by such occupations, with the advent of 'ubiquitous computing' and the 'Internet of Things' (see Box 8.5). At the time of writing, the impact of AI on replacing functions and jobs is unknown but is subject to a great deal of speculation (Budhwar et al., 2023; Suleyman, 2023) and discussions on the ethics and regulation of its impact, as our ChatGPT-generated essay in Box 8.4 alluded to.

So, whether an economy can be described as new, weightless, sharing, or the latest variation, circular (Stahel, 2019), which focuses on recycling or re-using our resources, all these metaphors allow for a prominent role for ICT, especially to its contribution at the level of the firm. Studies on the economic impact of ICT over the last two decades (e.g., OECD, 2004; Fernández-Portillo et al., 2020) have shown the following:

- Enterprise-level studies showed that ICT use typically had a positive but variable effect on company performance, demonstrating the fact that investment in ICT was not enough by itself to guarantee success. This variable effect has been demonstrated in the gradual reversal of working from home (Economist, 2023, June 28)

Box 8.5 Ubiquitous computing and the Internet of Things

An alternative vision of ICT promises to transform work, which is where computing is 'made to appear everywhere and anywhere', forcing computers to live out there in the world of people. The notion of ubiquitous or pervasive computing is based on cheap and low-powered computers with convenient displays embedded into our everyday environments, including homes, work, hospitals, offices, and public places. These devices are wired or wireless networked and supported by applications software. The ubiquitous nature of computing will pervade common places and be embedded in clothing or the fabric of buildings. The computers can deal with many inputs, including voice data, acoustics, images, motion and gestures, light, heat, moisture, and pressure.

Examples of the applications of ubiquitous computing have been demonstrated at the Xerox PARC laboratory. As soon as people enter the work environment, they are immediately authenticated, thereby triggering a range of resources available to them, including visual displays, computing devices, and knowledge resources. These resources can be easily manipulated to create rapid analysis and synthesis of new knowledge in a range of visual and textual forms much faster than using conventional means.

This notion of ubiquitous computing is also being used in environments such as care homes for the elderly, in which diagnostic computers are embedded into the clothing of old people to provide constant monitoring of the location and, in a limited sense, state of health. Residents carry dual-channel radio frequency locator tags, which serve as their apartment keys and emit periodic infrared pulses to the sensors in each room. Beds have embedded weight sensors. Each apartment has motion and health vital sensors plus a networked computer with a touch interface screen, enabling communication through email, video conferencing, and voice communication. These systems and sensors feed personalised databases to monitor personal health, activity levels, interactions with medical attention, and the status of medication. Managers use the information to monitor staff performance, and residents use the information to monitor themselves. Residents in such environments claim greater control and autonomy, feeling that if they become disorientated or wander, and require help or medicine, assistance will be at hand immediately.

- Some ICT technologies had a bigger impact than others on productivity and performance, with *communications networking* being especially important in industries such as financial services, and mobile phones in small businesses. This point begs the question: how does remote work affect productivity and how productive are workers who choose remote jobs? The answer to this question was partly provided by Emanuel and Harrington (2023) in a longitudinal study of a Fortune 500 call centre company that employed remote and on-site workers in the same job. The results were complicated. During COVID-19, when the call centres closed, the productivity of formerly on-site workers declined by 4 per cent compared with existing remote workers. However, an 8 per cent productivity gap remained, indicating that much of the productivity gap was due to negative worker selection into remote work. They also found that remote work resulted in poorer call quality, especially for inexperienced workers. These findings show just how important the person-job fit is in decisions on remote working.
- Researchers have also shown that there were important sectoral differences in the impact of ICT on performance at the level of the enterprise, with firms in the service sectors of retailing and financial services making large gains from ICT investment, and larger firms benefitted from e-commerce and other e-business applications.
- Significantly, ICT effectiveness has been found to be complementary to *human capital investment*. For example, studies in different countries showed that the use of ICT was linked to higher levels of skills and that they became even more productive as they became more experienced in using these technologies. The same is claimed for AI (Berg et al., 2023). Yet others found that firms that adopted advanced technologies also increased their expenditure on education and training while reducing their demand for less skilled people.
- Finally, ICT effectiveness was complemented by investment in successful *organizational change*, also helping to explain the first set of findings. For example, studies (e.g., Martin et al., 2015) found close relationships between ICT investment and performance, but only when combined with complementary changes in new strategies, business processes, and/or new ways of organizing and working. These organizational

changes included teamworking, flattening out of hierarchies, employee involvement schemes, and improved communications.

Thus, this new economics, based on the knowledge-based economy and on new KIEs (see Table 8.1), has two important implications for the relationship between technology, organizations, and the management of people. The first of these implications focuses on knowledge, education, and skills as one of the key factors in productivity and performance, and a general-purpose *enabling technology* such as ICT as both the key *input* and key *output* of knowledge creation (Brynjolfsson & McAfee, 2011, 2014). For example, if we map out a basic, open-systems model, the development and diffusion of genetic profiling, a new form of knowledge, is dependent on ICT, but also advanced biotechnological know-how and complementary organizational inputs are synonymous with a KIE. In turn, it is hoped that these inputs, transformed by the KIE, will lead to improvements in the quality and reductions in the costs of key healthcare technologies such as cancer treatment and heart disease. These improvements arise not only from the development of new treatments, but also in improving the intangible aspects of existing treatments such as convenience, timeliness, quality, and choice available to patients. In addition, increased productivity through improved quality and reduced costs also arises through the development of new forms of organization and know-how to be able to take advantage of these discoveries (see Figure 8.2).

The second implication, and perhaps more important from the perspective of human resource management practitioners, is that the new economics of knowledge and technology, both of which are essentially human constructs, depend largely on the management of intangible assets. Most notably, these include the *quality and management of people and their tacit knowledge, and how they are organized*. This has been the explicit message of well-known researchers in the field such as Brynjolfsson and McAfee (2011), who argued that a significant component of the value of ICT investment is its ability to enable complementary organizational investments, such as new business processes and new forms of working, to become effective (see the classic case of MacroMed below). These MIT-based researchers, who described themselves as 'digital optimists' argued that while the GFC, off-shoring of jobs, taxes, and regulations all had an impact on jobs in the United States, technology was also a significant factor in shaping employment practices. Claiming that advanced economies such as the USA were facing a 'Great Restructuring,' they argued that ICT-based technologies were racing ahead but many skills and organizations were lagging. Thus, it was necessary to understand these technologies and phenomena, discuss their implications, and derive strategies that allowed people to 'race with machines instead of raging against them.' In their later book, they argued the second machine age was characterised by the automation of many cognitive tasks, heralding the development of AI in all its forms (Brynjolfsson & McAfee, 2014). While recognising the benefits of these technologies, they also foresaw increasing inequalities resulting from uneven access to them. To what extent have they been proven prescient? A tentative answer has been provided by a panel of leading HR academics from different parts of the work to discuss 'human resource management in the age of generative AI' (Budhwar et al., 2023). They concluded that there is a great deal of uncertainty over whether AI will result in job creation, job displacement, or just shift people

TABLE 8.1 The old and new economies compared		
Issues	Old economy	New economy
Economy-wide characteristics		
	Industrial	Weightless, post-industrial
Markets	Stable	Dynamic
Scope of competition	National	Global
Organizational form	Hierarchical, bureaucratic	Networked
Structure	Manufacturing core	Services core
Source of value	Raw materials, manufactured goods, financial capital	Knowledge and skills, human and social capital, emotional labour
Business		
	Fordist	KBEs
Organization of production Key drivers of growth	Mass production/Fordism	Flexible Innovation/knowledge and skills
Key technological driver	Mechanisation and electrical power	Digitisation and related technologies
Source of competitive advantage	Lowering costs through economies of scale	Innovation, quality, and speed through whole supply chain
Importance of research/ innovation	Low–moderate	High
Relations with other firms	Go it alone, competitive	Alliances and collaboration, outsourcing
Workplace relations	Adversarial	Collaboration and partnership
Nature of employment	Stable	Marked by insecurity, risk and opportunity
Consumers		
Tastes	Stable	Rapidly changing
Skills	Job specific	Broad, transferable skills and adaptability
Educational needs	Craft skill or degree: one-off requirement	Lifelong learning
Government		
Business–government relations	Impose regulations	Encourage growth opportunities
Regulation	Command and control	Market tools, flexibility, and devolved government
Government services	Nanny state	Enabling state

Source: adapted from Coyle & Quah, 2004.

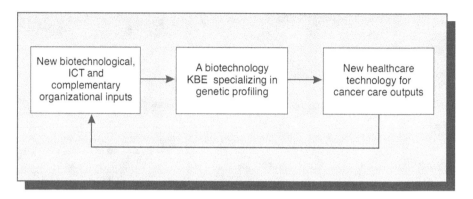

FIGURE 8.2 A basic open-systems model of knowledge-based enterprise in the biotech industry

into trivial applications of AI without any significant practical implications. But they do believe generative AI such as ChatGPT-4 has 'ramped up the AI arms race.' This has created uncertainty for workers, and increased risks of problems such as misinformation, bias, privacy, and ethical dilemmas. Such a conclusion also aligns with industry experts such as Mustafa Suleyman (2023), who wrote of the 'coming wave' of advances in AI and synthetic biology in making science fiction possible but also raised the many risks associated with such transformative developments. These risks, he argued, should generate a wide discussion over how they can be constrained because of their implications for work, the distribution of wealth in societies, bad actors who can use these technologies for highly damaging purposes, and, indeed, the ability of nation-states to constrain their use.

CASE 8.2 MACROMED

MacroMed Inc. was a US-based medical products manufacturer founded in 1995. In 2006, it was acquired by a UK-based biopharmaceutical company and now trades as MacroMed Ltd. Before being bought out, it embarked on a major investment in computer-integrated manufacturing to provide greater customisation and variety. This investment coincided with several other changes in people management, including eliminating payment by results, giving workers authority for scheduling machines, decentralising decision-making, more frequent and richer interactions with customers and suppliers, increased communications and teamworking, and changes in skill levels and organizational culture.

However, the new system fell way below expectations for greater flexibility and responsiveness to customer demands. Investigations into the causes of the problem showed that employees still retained many old ways of doing things, not to be deliberately obstructive, but because that was the way they had always done their jobs.

Ironically, the new machines were so flexible that workers could operate them and work in the same old ways, but without securing the improvements promised by the new computer-controlled technology.

Management decided after some time to set up operations on a new, greenfield site, with a set of handpicked, younger employees who had not been part of the old culture of work practices. The improvements in productivity were sufficiently dramatic to make the management team paint the windows of the new factory black so that competitors could not look in.

1 Can you explain the causes of the dramatic productivity improvements?

2 Given its current position as a world leader in its field, were management justified in worrying about competitors 'seeing into the new factory'? Or would they have done just as well had they allowed competitors to see in?

Despite the findings of these digital optimists and the hype generated by notions such as the new economy and sharing economy, events such as the 'dot-bomb' crisis in 2000 and the GFC in 2007/2008 provoked a major backlash and widespread criticism among economists and business academics. These critics argued that the new economy was 'stillborn,' especially in countries such as the UK and much of Europe where, according to some economists and politicians, these countries still followed a low road to growth. So, for example, a UK Commission on Employment and Skills (2015) pointed out that despite having a highly skilled workforce, UK productivity had 'tanked.' According to the UK National Institute of Economic and Social Research (2022), the UK continued to have a problem because of chronic underinvestment in the business and public sectors.

Thus, a key question arises: Is there really anything new or special about the new economy knowledge work and knowledge workers? To answer this, we need to examine some of the older research on the relationship between technological change, organizations, and people management.

The old orthodoxy: Technology, knowledge work, and knowledge workers in the old economy

Some commentators suggests that there is little that is new in new technologies. 'New' technologies and various forms of knowledge work have always combined to create a form of 'new economy', represented by stages 1 and 2 in Box 8.3. Indeed, the history of management studies can be portrayed in terms of the evolving relationship between technological change, knowledge work, and the management of knowledge workers (see Chapter 7). This concern is associated with Taylor and his disciples, whose work was characterised by an attempt to relocate the knowledge of craft workers – skilled machine-tool men who fashioned the major parts of early motor cars by brain and by hand – into procedure manuals and machines, a subject discussed in Chapter 1. These developments culminated in the era of Fordism, often stylised as the application of technology to Taylorism, to create the dominant mode of production in the last century. Another answer is to draw on the data we used earlier in this chapter to show how the occupational structure of the UK is changing. Thus, although the use of ICT in some occupations has advanced rapidly over the last two decades (e.g., in medicine, accounting, and academia), it has not done so among large sections of the population of manual, unskilled, and personal service workers – at least until now.

Before embarking on a review of more contemporary work, it is necessary to revisit some of the earlier, 'classical' studies to see what we can learn and use in our understanding of new technologies and the kinds of problem managers are likely to confront. Four competing perspectives on the effects of technology on work help us here, each of which portrays technology in a different light:

* Technological determinism.
* Labour process theory.
* Strategic choice perspectives.
* New theories linking technology and the experience of work.

Technological determinism

In any history of management and organizational studies, the 1950s marked something of a watershed. From that time, technology became the favoured variable for explaining how people behaved at work (Child, 2015; Clegg et al., 2021), rather than the nature of the human relations climate, which had characterised most of the writing between the 1920s and 1940s (Rose, 1975). This relationship between technology and people was sometimes treated as a direct one, in that the nature of the technology itself was thought to have an immediate effect on work behaviour. For example, producing motor vehicles using craft-based technology had a different impact on skills and levels of job satisfaction from production methods associated with assembly line, mass production technology. Often, however, this impact was assumed to refer to a complementary relationship between the technological 'hardware' – plant and machines – and a form of organizational 'software'. Such changes were thought to shape work behaviour in the following ways:

* The first was the system of rules that governed management and employee relations in the industry or workplace where unions were recognised. For example, technology shaped the kinds of people who were employed, and collective bargaining agreements between managers and unions would often dictate which trades or occupations were allowed to use or supervise machines or tools in industries such as engineering, construction, motor vehicle manufacture, and printing.
* The second was the form of production systems and work processes, i.e., the methods of production and knowledge required to develop and use the technology determined the work behaviour.

Four such works serve as good illustrations of these links between technological hardware, organizational forms, and human behaviour, which are still relevant today. The first was Woodward's (1965) studies of the effects of organizational structure on the performance of 100 manufacturing firms operating in the south-east of the UK. Initially, she could make little sense of her findings, which seemed to show that the form of organization (as measured by factors such as spans of control, levels of management, or centralisation) had little relationship with performance. Only when these structural characteristics were related to the different types of technology she identified (unit and small batch production, mass production, the types of continuous production found in chemicals, etc.) did they make any sense. That is, the highest levels of performance found in her sample of firms were correlated with either mass production technologies being combined with mechanistic organizations, or unit/small batch technologies and continuous process technologies being combined with organic organizations.

The second work was Leonard Sayles' (1958) research, which found different types of workplaces were marked by high rates of grievance activity that were wholly unrelated to variations in managerial policies or style. At that time, this was a counterintuitive finding because the dominant explanation of industrial conflict focused on human relations and management style as key variables in explaining the quality of employee relations in organizations. His research showed that different types of groups, which he labelled apathetic, erratic, strategic, and conservative, were products of different types of technological systems found in the 30 companies in his study. In short, it was different types of technology, and not managers, that he believed caused high and low levels of grievance.

The third was the well-known study by Robert Blauner (1964), who claimed that the most important single factor that determined an industry's character was its technology. Blauner attempted to show a direct relationship between worker *alienation*, which was made up of objective conditions and feeling states, and different forms of technology. He classified alienation in terms of powerlessness (the lack of control over conditions of work), meaningless (the work and its products have no meaning for employees), isolation (referring to the lack of community in certain types of plants), and self-estrangement (roughly comparable to current notions of employee identification with the work and organization). Blauner related scores on these different forms of alienation to four types of technological systems, comprising craft production, machine tending, mass production and process production. We return to this issue of alienation in a later section of this chapter.

The fourth work was by Charles Perrow (1986), a well-known American organizational theorist. Perrow's major contributions were in recognising that the same organization may have several different core technologies and producing a typology of the relationship between technology and organization that is still highly influential. He proposed that different units and subunits of an organization can be compared along two dimensions relating to its core tasks:

- *Task variability* was defined in terms of the number of exceptions from standardised procedures evident in the application of a given technology. For example, moving assembly lines are portrayed as dictating how workers perform their tasks, whereas design engineers have considerable latitude in how they arrive at solutions.

- *Task analysability* was defined in terms of the extent to which there were well-known analytical methods for dealing with any exceptions to standard procedures. For example, lower-level administrators are always able to refer problems to higher-level managers, a well-documented procedure for dealing with problems, whereas scientists in leading-edge computing or biotechnological research often lack the procedures or training to deal with exceptions to the rule. In effect, they must invent them.

Combining Perrow's two dimensions resulted in four different forms of organizational technology:

1 *Routine technologies* were characterised by low task variability and high task analysability, exemplified by assembly-line work and lower-level clerical work. Many modern call or service centres and some types of care work fall into this category.

2 *Craft technology* was described by low scores on both dimensions. For example, workers on a building site face few exceptions to standard operating procedures laid out by architects' plans and building regulations, but when they do, they often have to invent new ways of dealing with a lack of materials or mistakes made by the architect. In effect, they must craft a solution based on their tacit knowledge and experience of such work.

3 *Engineering technologies* were characterised by high scores on both dimensions. For example, though software engineers are likely to face many exceptions to standard practices in creating new programs, the increasing body of knowledge in this field and their specialised education and training provide them with known and codified methods of solving such problems. The work of many human resource management departments falls into this category.

4 *Non-routine technologies* were high on task variability and low on task analysability. Such technologies of organization are to be found in advanced research work, high-level consultancy, some branches of medicine, managerial work, and entrepreneurship.

The significant lesson about Perrow's work, which has much modern-day application to new technologies and knowledge workers, is the distinction between *routine* technologies, which allow for few exceptions to known procedures and provide well-documented ways for dealing with any exceptions that arise, and *non-routine* technologies, which permit many exceptions and rely on high levels of worker discretion and levels of tacit knowledge to deal with these exceptions. This is a point that informed our discussion of knowledge management in Chapter 7, and to which we shall return later in this chapter.

Labour process theory

Much of the above work was prescriptive and treated technology as a progressive and optimistic force in the economy, or at least neutral when applied to work and workers, i.e., neither good nor bad. Accompanying these studies throughout the last century, however, were those of a more critical and pessimistic bent. From the perspective of the authors of these critical management studies, technology was seen to have a 'dark side': it was rarely seen as neutral in its political impact on work and workers, nor was it viewed as a necessarily progressive force in society. In these senses, many of these studies were influenced by Marx's dialectical method of social theory, which turned on the idea that every theory of technological progress created its own antithesis. This dialectical theory of technological change was illustrated by the widespread opposition in some countries to the introduction of biotechnology and genetics, particularly in relation to GM food technology and genetic engineering. More recent illustrations include the opposition to the development of new oil fields in the North Sea in an era of climate change and the development of AI applications, such as the use of expert systems in influencing legal decisions on who to parole in the UK criminal justice system, or who to hire for important jobs.

They were also influenced by Marx's class conflict theory of societies and organizations. Nowhere was this more apparent than in the writings of the labour process school, whose inspiration was Harry Braverman's (1974) criticism of Taylorism and the organization of manual and knowledge work during the twentieth century. Braverman's deskilling thesis claimed that the development of capitalism as an economic system had given rise to a mode of production and work organization that was being systematically fragmented and deskilled in the pursuit of rational efficiency. The logic of deskilling was to replace expensive and powerful craft (and knowledge) workers with more easily trained and less expensive unskilled labour and, eventually, machines (read computers and AI in modern parlance). Such deskilling led to a reduction in employee bargaining power and, thus, to maximising profits. It also had the effect, following Blauner and others, of alienating employees from their work and from the products of their labour. For example, studies showed that workers on an assembly line rarely felt committed to their work or organization, nor did they feel that they had contributed to the overall product or feel any sense of ownership for mistakes or successes. More modern expressions of this aspect of alienation are to be found in call centres, textile factories in the Global South, and in some types of public sector work (e.g., Conway et al., 2020).

The earlier literature portrayed Taylor as the arch-enemy of workers and was heavily critical of Fordist systems of production. During the early 1980s, when the labour process school was probably most prominent in academic terms, it influenced the more practical concerns of trade unions in some countries. Many of these adopted a defensive posture in opposing the introductions of microprocessor-based technologies during the early 1980s, especially if it were to be used to deskill the labour process and lead to even greater unemployment than existed at the time. This resistance to technological change is an underlying cause of many industrial disputes and can often help explain why some countries and some organizations are able to adapt to technological change more effectively, and why others are less able or willing to adapt.

In the 1990s the focus of this work turned to the effects of computing technology on work and work behaviour, with a series of articles and books produced by critical theorists writing from a labour process perspective and, increasingly, producing 'gloomy analyses of emerging factory regimes in which workers lose even the awareness of their own exploitation' (McKinlay & Taylor, 1997, p. 3). This kind of thinking has infused more recent HRM literature on the 'dark' use of AI in exacerbating already biased selection decisions and the deprofessionalisation of doctors in the NHS (Martin et al., 2021). Thus, various reports on the 'information society' and the role of ICT have found that many employees are unwilling to give up knowledge or have resented the introduction. One good example was the strike by actors in Hollywood in July 2023, with one of the principal causes being the uses to which AI was put. As the *Conversation* (2023, July 24) notes:

> When they perform on film sets, their image and voice are digitally recorded at extremely high resolution, providing producers with huge amounts of data. Actors are concerned the data can be reused with AI. New processes such as machine learning – AI systems that improve with time – could turn an actor's performance in one movie into a new character for another production, or for a video game.

The central message of this literature, in contrast to the digital optimists, is not the limitations of technological forms of control, but that the logic of capitalism as an economic system ineluctably leads to a degraded form of knowledge work, regardless of how individual firms might behave. In that sense, managers have very little control over how they use technology because it is the logic of profits or cost reduction that dictates how technology and work are related (see Chapter 11).

Strategic choice perspectives

If gloom was the character of much of the writing on technology during the twentieth century and beyond, the strategic choice perspective has represented something of a balance between the optimism and political neutrality of the technological determinist school and the 'dismal science' predictions of the labour process school. Strategic choice implied that introducing new technologies did not need to result in deskilling or in any form of predetermined work organization. Instead, different groups of employees and managers had different objectives for any form of technology, based on their values and perceptions of their power, and the eventual outcomes of any technological innovation depended on negotiations between these groups (Child, 2015; Clegg et al., 2021). Perhaps the original inspiration for such work was the sociotechnical systems approach of the Tavistock Institute of Human Relations in the UK (Trist et al., 1963), which set out the choices of social organization available for any given form of technological system. This work focused on the importance of meshing technology with the needs, characteristics, and attitudes of workers to optimise outcomes. People were organized into groups or autonomous work teams, completed whole tasks with minimal external supervision, and experienced variety, support, and recognition in achieving the goals that were set. The work of the Tavistock group had a major influence on subsequent attempts to operationalise sociotechnical systems during the 1980s in Sweden and Germany, most notably at Volvo and Saab. For example, during the 1980s, both organizations undertook major experiments that eliminated assembly-line technology and introduced autonomous, multi-skilled workgroups, which built the major parts of a motor vehicle. These experiments were seen as a partial return to the traditions of craft-based manufacture, enhanced by modern manufacturing technologies.

More modern expressions of what might be called a sociotechnical approach to organizational studies and HRM were to be found in the 'lean production' literature that had such a major impact on vehicle manufacture during the 1990s and on services in the decades following. This work was provoked by a major series of studies, culminating in the book *The Machine That Changed the World* (Womack et al., 1990). The book set out the findings on world motor vehicle manufacture and the choices facing vehicle manufacturers in developing organizations and work teams. One of the key messages of the book and associated studies was that managers had a technological and organizational choice over how to produce motor vehicles and that Japanese organizations seemed to have reached an optimal compromise between the tightly coupled design based on standardisation and economies of scale of Fordism on the one hand, and the more loosely coupled design based on innovativeness and quality on the other, by using teams and employee involvement strategies (see also Chapter 4). These studies have had an enormous influence on current ways of organizing work in many different industries, especially in the USA and Europe, and provide the stereotypical model of modern manufacturing. Nowadays, lean production ideas are also being applied to the public sector in an administrative setting because productivity improvements in services are required. However, bringing lean ideas into service industries has not been as easy as first thought (Staats & Upton, 2011). Not all ideas and principles of the Toyota system translated from the factory floor to the office.

CASE 8.3 LEAN PRODUCTION, THE TOYOTA SYSTEM, AND ITS MODERN APPLICATION

Assembly-line technology and social organization have dominated manufacturing methods for nearly all of the last century, especially in the motor vehicle industry and among component suppliers for motor vehicles. Such systems of manufacture have allowed companies to reap enormous benefits from economies of scale by producing vehicles and components for inventory. However, they have been associated with unwanted stocks, poor quality, and high levels of employee dissatisfaction due to the mechanical pacing of jobs and lack of autonomy on behalf of workers. In the 1980s, companies such as Volvo and Saab attempted to do away with assembly lines and introduced state-of-the-art factories built around the concept of autonomous workgroups of multi-skilled people who would build a major part of a car by themselves. These experiments generated a lot of interest, which has recently been rekindled in Sweden by Volvo.

Lean production as a method of manufacturing is an alternative to traditional mass production and the more craft-based, autonomous workgroups. It is an assembly-line manufacturing methodology developed originally for Toyota and the manufacture of automobiles. It is also known as the Toyota Production System. The goal of lean production is described as 'to get the right things to the right place at the right time, the first time, while minimising waste and being open to change.' Engineer Ohno, who is credited with developing the principles of lean production, discovered that, in addition to eliminating waste, his methodology led to improved product flow and better quality.

Instead of devoting resources to the planning required for future manufacturing under mass production, Toyota focused on reducing system response times so that the production system was capable of immediately changing and adapting to market demands. In effect, their automobiles became made-to-order. The principles of lean production enabled the company to deliver on demand, minimise inventory, maximise the use of multi-skilled employees, flatten the management structure, and focus resources where they were needed.

During the 1980s, the practices summarised in the ten rules of lean production were adopted by many manufacturing plants in the USA and Europe, and, more recently, they have been adopted in services. The management style was tried out with varying degrees of success by service organizations, logistics organizations, and supply chains, and more recently in knowledge work (Staats & Upton, 2011). Since the mid-2000s, there has also been a renewed interest in the principles of lean production in manufacturing, particularly as the philosophy encourages the reduction of inventory and waste. Dell Computers and Boeing Aircraft have embraced the philosophy of lean production with great success. However, researchers have found that the implementation of lean production in manufacturing has been variable, especially over how it impacts employee learning and job quality. For example, Sterling and Boxall (2013) found that only where line managers had given up some control and employees had the necessary levels of literacy did mutually beneficial learning tend to result. Even then, these positive outcomes were dependent on the level of production pressures and investments by firms in developing supervisor and worker literacy.

The 17 rules of lean production can be summarised as follows:

1. Set up cross-functional design and development teams.
2. Develop a *kaizen* philosophy of continuous improvement.
3. Flexible machines, low set-up costs.
4. Broad product lines.
5. Targeted markets.
6. Eliminate waste.
7. Minimise inventory.
8. Maximise flow.
9. Pull production from customer demand – make to order rather than for stock.
10. Meet customer requirements.
11. Do it right the first time.
12. Empower workers through quality circles and improvement groups.

13. Develop highly skilled and cross-trained workers.

14. Design for rapid changeover.

15. Partner with suppliers.

16. Create a culture of continuous improvement, involving workers on the shop floor.

17. Build long-term, trusting relationships with key suppliers.

Note that these features are complementary to one another, and adopting only some of them will not produce the gains that Toyota experienced. This has been one of the reasons why many firms in the West have not been able to achieve Toyota's quality and productivity levels.

1. How do you think that workers in manufacturing outside of Japan would respond to lean production techniques?

2. Why might these rules be difficult to apply to the service sector, especially public services?

3. What lessons does the Toyota model have for firms seeking to take advantage of AI?

The influence of socio-technic systems thinking is also evident in the debate over meaningful work that has been resurrected by worries over trends such as the 'great resignation' and 'quiet quitting' in the early years of the 2020s. Some of the literature in this field has invoked the socio-technic prescriptions of achieving a balance between technology and the employee's sense of, and desire for, meaningful work (Bailey et al., 2019). Such a desire is also evident in the UN Sustainable Development Goal of decent work and economic growth and in the debate over generative AI (Budhwar et al., 2023).

New theories linking technology and the experience of work

The above theories tended to separate out technology from work and to see technology in a deterministic way, as if it was something out there, independent of our own interpretations of what technology meant and how it influenced our work behaviour. So, by the 1990s, researchers began to view technology as socially constructed by people in their everyday work experience and to investigate how the same technological hardware and software might generate quite different outcomes, for example, as something which dominated us or something which liberated us, or both simultaneously. Theoretical perspectives have been influential in this respect. The first is *sociomateriality* (Jarzbkowski & Pinch, 2013), a deliberately fused term, signifying an approach to understanding how technologies are used by people in their day-to-day actions in a process that Orlikowski and Scott (2008) have described as 'constitutive entanglement.' In other words, they focused on how the social and the material entwine and mutually constitute each other.

One good example of research in this tradition has been the examination, *in situ*, of how email or social media platforms are used differently by different people, resulting in a change in the material nature and meaning to users. For example, in December 2023, National Records of Scotland revealed that the Scottish Government in 2008 considered email led to a lack of professionalism among civil servants because of the way in which email was being used to provide poorly written advice to ministers that could lead them to misinterpret information. The solution posed was to provide formal templates to introduce a more 'professional' way of communicating important information. You might want to reflect on how you use email and whether you see it as unprofessional or as an invasive technology to be avoided outside of working hours, or as a liberating technology, allowing you to keep in touch and exercise influence over your work situation 24/7.

A second variation of this theme is Stephen Barley's (2015) *role theory*. This approach focuses on how the introduction of specific technologies changed the tasks that people did. Because of these changes, people may begin to interact differently with co-workers in their 'role-set' and even begin to interact with new people outside of the traditional role-set. Barley argued that if these role relations change, then relations within the social network may also change, and thus the material nature of technology can be said to change a work system. In turn, however, the changed work system can also lead to changes in the technology and how it is used. For example, his early research examined how the introduction of ultrasound and CT scanners altered professional power between technologists who produced traditionally produced X-rays and radiologists who interpreted them. With the introduction of these new technologies, technologists who understood how computerised images were produced acquired greater power and autonomy, which in turn changed the nature of hierarchical relations in the hospital department. He also cited a study on the introduction of minimally invasive cardiac surgery in 16 hospitals in the USA. The introduction of this technology worked best when there was greater relational coordination and collaboration, and less hierarchy among surgeons, nurses, technicians, and anaesthesiologists in departments.

Is there something different about new technologies and their effect on the world of work?

As we have already noted, social scientists, Erik Brynjolfsson and Andrew McAfee, are two of the most respected researchers in this field. In three books (Brynjolfsson & McAfee, 2011, 2014) and McAfee & Brynjolsson, 2017, they attempted to answer this question. First, they saw the new digital technologies, the linked systems of computer hardware, software, and networks referred to in this chapter, as driving forces in improving productivity and growth. Second, they saw these changes as largely beneficial because they could increase the variety and volume of consumption, including information, entertainment, and expertise from teachers and doctors. Such volume and variety, they claim, have altered the basis of traditional economic theory from resource scarcity to abundance. Third, as we noted earlier in this chapter, digitalisation brings with it the problems they discussed in the 'Race Against the Machine' thesis: that these technologies are racing ahead of the capabilities of workers and managers to keep up with them, a perspective in line with some of the commentators on AI (Budhwar et al., 2023; Suleyman, 2023). Like other researchers in the field, they see the divergence between highly skilled and lower skilled workers, between the highly scare superstars and everyone else, and between capital and labour becoming much greater, trends borne out by economic data in the developed world. Their predictions also extend to greater dislocation between economies in the Global North and Global South. Their pessimism is tempered only to the extent that workers and managers learn to use new technologies as assets and allies rather than adversaries by destroying jobs and opportunities. They also argue for national and supranational constraints on the uses to which such technologies can be put.

A framework for explaining the relationship between new technology and managing people

This review of some of the classic and newer studies in which technology, organization, and people management are linked raises two sets of important questions that have helped us develop a framework (see Figure 8.3) for thinking about newer technologies, including ICT, digital technologies, and managing people:

1. To what extent are the new *non-routine, knowledge-intensive organizations* different from old-style *knowledge-routinised organizations*? To what extent are the new non-routine, knowledge-intensive organizations different in making use of technology, particularly investment in ICT and AI, to produce innovations and productivity growth? And is there, as much of the literature suggests, a direct relationship between investment in these new technologies and the exploitation of knowledge in organizations?

2. To what extent is there a choice for managers between using ICT and technologies such as AI as *dominating and centralising forces*, perhaps leading to a deskilling of employees, or as a potentially *liberating and empowering force*, enhancing the role of employees and HR managers and in re-skilling work? This dualism between control and freedom has been an important feature in the organizational writing on technology (e.g., Brynjolfsson & McAfee, 2011, 2014; Stone et al., 2022), and posits a role for managers as strategic enablers of business directions and visions rather than as passive recipients or 'handmaidens' of technological investment and general economic trends.

The answers to these sets of questions, we argue, lie along two continua, which, when related orthogonally, create four scenarios or images of organization. These images can then be used as prisms to view the relationship between newer technologies, organizations, and people management. Each of these images reflects a dominant view of organization within a firm or characterises certain departments or divisions within a firm. The critical point is that, although one image may be a way of seeing technology and people management, it is also a way of not seeing.

One of the best uses to which these images can be put is to generate four sets of questions managers might ask about the relationship between new technologies and the management of people, the answers to which are of enormous practical value:

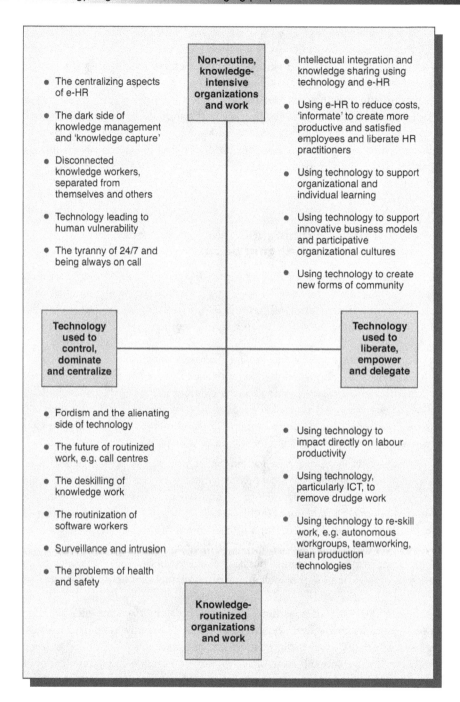

FIGURE 8.3 Mapping out the relationships between new technology and managing people

1. To what extent might these new technologies facilitate advances in intelligent relationships between organizations, groups, and individuals that are based on increased employee voice dialogue and participation (Martin et al., 2015) rather than through existing patterns of control and domination?

2. How might these new technologies allow organizations, groups, and individuals to make things happen (i.e., create new business models to make and sell innovative products and services) rather than have things happen to them in the context of organizational and societal goals (Barrat, 2023; Brynjolfsson & McAfee, 2011, 2014; Stone et al., 2022; Suleyman, 2023)? How might these technologies facilitate employee productivity? How might organizations use technology to follow a high-road route to international competitiveness?

3. In what ways can these new technologies create new forms of community and new forms of organization, bringing together organizations, groups, and individuals that up until now have been separated by time, space, and culture? Or will they lead to new forms of social disintegration by alienating people who once worked together?

4. In what ways can new technology create new ways of limiting the damage caused by economic pressures on organizations, groups, and individuals (i.e., deskilling and work intensification), or will these new technologies lead to even greater damage (e.g., stress and intrusion problems, health and safety problems, data breaches and ethical problems, increased human vulnerability and the '24/7 – always on' problems) (Budhwar et al., 2023)?

Inevitably, this framework and these questions imply an ideal to be achieved of progress through technology, with a movement in the general direction of greater freedom for most employees in knowledge-based organizations. We need to suspend judgement, however, because much of the evidence is running behind the rhetoric.

NEW TECHNOLOGIES AND MANAGING PEOPLE: THE ROLE OF SOCIAL MEDIA IN COLLABORATION, SHARING KNOWLEDGE, COMMUNICATING, AND EXPRESSING VOICE

One of the most notable developments over the last decade or so has been the introduction of social media into organizations and the world of work. By social media, we refer to the ICT tools that have enabled people to create, share, and exchange digital information, ideas, pictures, and videos in virtual communities and networks, including blogs, wikis, media-sharing sites, and social networking, which have been with us for decades. We also refer to the more recent developments in video conferencing, team chat, virtual assistants, and virtual reality worlds, some of which are enabled by AI. In this final section of the chapter, we shall discuss the role of these social media and their relationship with work organization and people management since they have had a highly significant impact on employees' experience of work and the capacity of businesses to innovate because of accessibility and immediacy in cyberspace. As a McKinsey report stated some time ago, if Facebook were a country, it would be the world's sixth most populous one, with more than 175,000,000 people. One method of answering this question is to explore the potential for social media by undertaking some scenario analysis (Parry et al., 2019).

Social media, AI, and engagement

As we noted earlier, a technological system comprises not only hardware and software but also embraces the knowledge needed to use the technologies and the work organization to implement it. As an example, mass production is a technology based on the hardware of a moving assembly line to produce, for example, motor vehicles, software in robots, work organization based on a detailed division of labour, and relatively low levels of employee knowledge and skills to work on an assembly line.

Thus, how we make choices on technological systems and the choices we make have a significant impact on work organization and people management. One of the most important influences on these choices has been the extent to which employees and managers are *engaged* by and with them. By engagement in this context, I draw on my definition in Chapter 3 to mean whether employees:

* *identify* with a particular technology (does it help employees express their personal and organizational identity – who am I?);
* *internalise* the technology's built-in values (does the technology embody the values employees hold?); and
* feel a degree of *psychological ownership* over it (to what extent is the technology their own and no one else's?).

So, with respect to social media and AI, a key question we need to answer is: how easy is it for employees to engage with these technologies to collaborate, share knowledge, communicate, and express an authentic voice in their organizations? By easy, we mean not just ease of use and access, but also identification, internalisation, and psychological ownership. Indeed, identification with technological change by employees has been shown to be one of the key factors in technology acceptance (Tripas, 2008). Evidence suggests new generations of employees are much more likely to identify and engage with these social media technologies than previous generations (Calvo-Porral & Pesqueira-Sanchez, 2020) despite the 'silver surfer' characterisation of some 'baby boomers'. And there is little doubt that many generations of employees will find chatbots easy to deal with as portable personal assistants, given the extremely rapid uptake of these technologies (Suleyman, 2023).

Thus, we can think of technological engagement in terms of an answer to the question: how easy is it for employees to identify and engage with a particular technology to collaborate, share knowledge, and express their voice in their organizations? At one end of the scale, technologies can be highly engaging for certain groups of employees and facilitate their voice and collaboration; on the other end of the scale, some technologies can disengage employees and inhibit voice and collaboration (Parry et al., 2019).

Social media, AI, and organizational control

Control is another widely discussed and contested idea in management and employee relations, especially in relation to the distribution of power between employers and employees in organizations. In the context of social media and AI, control seems to be expressed in the answer to another important question: how easy or difficult is it for organizations to cope with the power employees enjoy from easy access to decentralised and open forms of communication and collaboration? Some of the earlier discussions on the introduction of social media into organizations seemed to suggest that many HR managers at least saw the answer to this question as a 'zero-sum' game – the more control and power employees had, typically to misuse these social media at work for personal reasons, the less control organizations and HR were able to exercise (Martin et al., 2009, 2015). Our research showed social networking and blogging were typically banned from organizations, resulting in a time-consuming battle of blocking and unblocking sites from view. This control focus was also evident in legal cases and advice by lawyers on the use by employees of social media technologies during the latter part of the last decade. Consequently, lawyers began to advise employees not to post any comments online that could remotely relate to their employer's business.

However, we also found that the introduction of social media into organizations was not always seen as a win–lose scenario: employees and employers were able to gain if they agreed to a 'win–win' solution (Martin et al., 2009, 2015; Parry et al., 2019). Participants in several cases we researched spoke of a 'positive sum' game, in which organizations and employees both gained from better morale, not being seen to ban freedom of speech, and encouraging experimentation with these media technologies which resulted in significant innovation.

Thus, organizational control can be conceived as the extent to which technologies are put into the hands of employees to express authentic voice, learning, and collaborating over the means and ends of their working lives in organizations. At one end of this continuum, employees enjoy maximum autonomy and high trust from managers; at the other end, employees enjoy minimum autonomy and experience low trust from managers in how they use technologies (Parry et al., 2019). This latter perspective characterises much of the discussion over the use of AI by students and the furore it has generated among academics who are having to deal with the consequences for assessment and learning. A more positive view is how AI can be used as a personal tutor and enabler to both staff and students in helping them achieve their educational aims much more effectively.

Four scenarios for the future of social media and AI in organizations

Combining engagement and control, we propose four scenarios that describe modes of communication, knowledge sharing, collaboration, and voice in organizations (see Figure 8.4).

These scenarios help us think about the challenges faced by HRM and the possible choices organizations can make when using social media and AI.

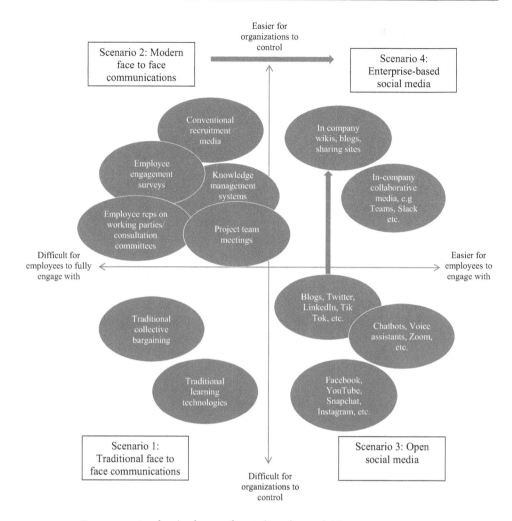

FIGURE 8.4 Four scenarios for the future of social media and AI in organizations

Scenario 1: Traditional face-to-face communication and collaboration

This scenario represents the typical, existing face-to-face system of collaboration and communication, the latter of which is typically conducted through the formal collective bargaining system. Union representation provides the main medium for employee voice, and knowledge management and collaboration continue to be viewed as a 'contested terrain'. Knowledge and skills are seen as issues to be bargained over since knowledge is power and not something to be readily given up by employees, who seek to capitalise on their tacit knowledge and skills.

In this scenario, the challenges to both managers and union representatives are that:

- new generations of employees begin to use social media as a means of expressing their own, often negative, voice, as unions are seen by an increasing number of workers to be less relevant in expressing their interests (Martin et al., 2015); and

- employees don't engage in much formal or informal collaboration and knowledge sharing with one another since their tacit knowledge and skills are their main source of power to enhance their careers at work. Social media and AI are rarely used to enhance voice and collaboration.

Managers view employees' use of these technologies in a largely negative light, often attempting to proscribe their use at work, or else ignore them as a means of finding out what employees think and want to discuss. Such a scenario may be typical of many organizations in traditional manufacturing and service industries and certain parts of public services with high levels of routine manual and administrative grades. The earlier illustration of the Scottish Government's 2008 desire to formalise email exemplifies this control approach.

Scenario 2: Modern face-to-face communication and collaboration

This represents a modern, consultative system in which communication takes place through working parties, joint consultation, and regular attempts to tap into employee voice through attitude surveys, exit interviews, appraisals, and focus groups. Collaboration and knowledge management are typically based on face-to-face teamworking, project teams, and traditional employer-centred knowledge management systems, which attempt to capture knowledge and store and disseminate it in a top-down fashion.

Again, in this scenario, the challenge to managers and representatives is that new generations of employees begin to adopt social media and generative AI as a means of expressing their own voice, learning, and collaborating in naturally occurring communities of practice. These employee initiatives remain largely untapped and unmanaged as in Scenario 1. HR continues to rely (a) on top-down means of assessing what really matters to employees, such as attitude surveys, and (b) on representative forms of workplace democracy/participation to allow employees to express concerns and take part in decision-making. Knowledge management continues to be formal, drawing on traditional non-participative software systems that are relatively inaccessible to employees.

Such a scenario is probably typical of most organizations in many of the knowledge-intensive and creative sectors of the economy, including 'professional bureaucracies' such as healthcare, education, professional services, defence, and prison and police services, and in industries such as financial services and others. Data protection in these organizations is a sensitive issue, as are concerns over protecting brand identities and the desire to exercise a duty of care to employees. HR's role in this scenario remains focused on policing, rather than encouraging the innovative and experimental use of social media and AI.

Scenario 3: Open social media and AI

This scenario, drawing on open social media such as Facebook, blogs, Twitter, Zoom, Alexa, and other voice assistants, represents a relatively anarchic situation in which some organizations may find themselves in the not-too-distant future. Organizations may begin in Scenarios 1 and 2 but come to resemble a more decentralised system of informal bottom-up communications and knowledge sharing as more and more people, especially members of the net generation, become employees. Much communication becomes virtual, in which knowledge sharing and employees voicing their concerns take place *outside of formal employer-controlled media*, especially in locations geographically and functionally distant from head office among remote workers and higher educated and paid networked workers. It is this scenario that seems to worry HR professionals and, indeed, many educational institutions confronted by generative AI being in the hands of students. As we have noted, it is the lack of organizational control over social media and the ease with which employees can engage with various applications that causes many organizations and HR professionals to worry about these media, with some organizations placing outright bans on their use at work or substantially restricting the ability of employees to access them at work. Time-wasting at work and the potential for organizational misbehaviour by disenchanted employees has dominated the HR agenda with firms ready to discipline employees for using social networking sites during working time and banning the use of such sites at work. Thus, for example, reviews of social media by UK government departments have posed several barriers to its more widespread adoption, despite the official line that encouraged the use of these media to communicate and engage users in dialogue. These barriers were:

- A lack of understanding and expertise among civil servants, especially higher-level ones.
- Following on from this lack of understanding, a lack of high-level support for wider use.
- A lack of data and uncertainties about the costs and benefits of various media.
- The risk of public exposure, damage to customer and employer brands, and general loss of control.
- The limitations placed on social media by IT departments that didn't want to damage the integrity of their systems.
- Problems in monitoring what employees were sharing.

Underlying such concerns were the very features that make social media attractive to organizations and employees. These were its openness, the ease of use for employees and users to engage with these media (spontaneity, conversational, and democratic), its new rules of engagement and the different behaviours required by civil servants, and its newness and experimental nature.

Scenario 4: Enterprise-based social media and AI

This scenario is the one that represented the best solution for many of the case study companies in our research (Martin et al., 2009, 2015; Parry et al., 2019) and seems to be the route larger organizations seek to follow (Bondarouk & Olivas-Lujan, 2013). Advocates of enterprise-based social media recognised that social media are fast becoming a fact of life among the more educated and more highly paid networked workers and new generations of employees. This scenario is based on one in which organizations are driven by younger generations or by the need to secure collaboration and the voice of increasingly geographically dispersed workers, often in other countries, working from home, or who rarely visit head office locations. Organizations attempt to regain control by developing social media and generative AI applications inside of firewalls and by encouraging or facilitating employees to make use of these technologies (see Box 8.4 and the case of KPMG).

According to Andrew McAfee, who is usually credited with coining the term 'Enterprise 2.0', this route is probably the most promising way forward for organizations seeking the benefits of social media but also seeking to minimise the downside. He defined Enterprise 2.0 (his term) 'as the use of emergent social software platforms *within* companies and their partners or customers.' He used the term 'social software' to describe how people meet, connect, and collaborate through computer-mediated communication and form online communities. Platforms are defined as 'digital environments in which contributions and interactions are widely visible and persistent over time.' Emergent means the software is freeform, in the sense that people can choose to use it or not, is egalitarian, and can accept different forms of data. He ruled out (a) open web-based platforms, such as Wikipedia, YouTube, Flickr, and Facebook, because they were widely available to individuals, (b) corporate internets because they are not emergent, and (c) traditional email and messaging services such as WhatsApp because they weren't persistent.

Figure 8.4 shows a potential trend away from the very open social media towards Enterprise 2.0. A good example of enterprise-based media is Microsoft Teams, which can be used in conjunction with a collection of apps as a multipurpose platform for collaboration, communications, and teaching and learning. The diagram also hints at the potential trend away from traditional media used to give employees a say in decisions, such as face-to-face representation in consultative committees, focus groups, and online surveys towards Enterprise 2.0 read-write media. Just as the web has allowed the so-called power law to operate in firms such as Amazon by allowing them to cater for the long tail of profitable customers comprising only 20 per cent of its total sales, so organizations can now reach out to the 'long tail' of employees. These comprise previously marginalised or disengaged groups who weren't economically possible to reach or who rejected the normal consultation process through union representation and organizationally determined (and often meaningless to them) questionnaires.

Box 8.5 Lloyds Register and the 'Future of Work Lab'

Lloyds Register is a global engineering, technical, and business services organization employing over 9000 people in 78 countries. In 2015, the energy team, comprising 2500 employees globally, embarked on a business transformation programme to change from a regional matrix structure to a global service line structure. The company wanted to both make the change quickly and involve employees in the new organization design so that it reflected local needs and fostered collaboration and employee engagement. Despite existing voice channels, they decided to adopt the social research tool 'Future of Work Lab' (FOWlab) to engage a large and geographically dispersed workforce in a focused discussion.

330 Technology, organizations, and managing people

FOWlab allows 'firms and employees guidance and methodologies to identify problems and build practical solutions that will pre-empt risks and enhance 'good work' when designing and developing AI systems' (Company website). It allows large groups of employees to have their say, shape the change process, and identify concerns, challenges, and solutions. The tool is accessible online, and users have named accounts because the company saw it as a means to ensure professional and constructive contributions. Lloyds Register posted several questions or provocations so that managers could frame the debate but also allowed employees to raise their own issues and questions. Each 'jam' was online for 72 hours constantly to promote intensive involvement and discussion on a particular issue and allow a narrow focus. The company undertook extensive marketing work via emails, messaging from senior management and line managers, and a video to facilitate take-up. The role of senior managers in both promoting the tool and in taking part themselves was seen as essential.

Out of 3066 employees who were invited to take part, over 1275 did so, posting 1400 comments. Staff were seen to be co-creating ideas and projects together and supporting innovation. The company also perceived an impact on employee engagement and perceptions of voice as employees felt 'genuinely consulted' and that they had a greater buy-in to decisions as 'when the solution comes out of the Jam, they're not surprised ... [at the] solution they've identified.' Interviewees in Lloyds Register emphasized the importance of acting on the information coming out of the Jam because 'if you're expecting people to give up their time, you need to do something with it' (Source, Parry et al., 2019).

Question: Why might some individuals or groups who did not participate be sceptical about using such a tool for collaboration and knowledge sharing?

LEARNING SUMMARY

In this chapter, we have attempted to show how new technologies and the changing technological context can impact on organizations, groups, and individuals. New technologies, especially ICT, and, more recently, AI, have had an enormous impact on the work of many individuals in a variety of industries. From the perspective of managers, investment in new technologies often delivers less than it promised because it is poorly implemented or misaligned with the necessary organizational and human factor changes. From the perspective of ordinary employees, sometimes the introduction of new technologies has been perceived as positive by empowering or liberating these people; sometimes it has been perceived as negative by increasing perceptions of lack of control and removing decisions and tasks that once were essential and desired parts of jobs. Managers need to understand the complexities associated with the introduction of new technologies, especially the impact on productivity and people, before embarking on major programmes of technical change. Understanding the concepts, examples, and cases in this chapter should help them do so.

REVIEW QUESTIONS

1. What do you understand by a *high road to growth strategy*?
2. You have been asked to evaluate the strengths and weaknesses of using social media and AI to encourage collaboration, learning, and knowledge sharing in your organization. What would you advise and why?
3. Discuss the merits of the optimistic and pessimistic scenarios for AI. How can we develop a way forward for dealing with the pessimistic future?

REFERENCES

Aker, J. C., & Mbiti, I. M. (2010). Mobile phones and economic development in Africa. *Journal of Economic Perspectives, 24*(3), 207–232.

Bailey, C., Yeoman, R., Madden, A., Thompson, M., & Kerridge, G. (2019). A review of the empirical literature on meaningful work: Progress and research agenda. *Human Resource Development Review, 18*(1), 83–113.

Barley, S (2015). Why the internet makes buying a car less loathsome: How technologies change role relations. *Academy of Management Discoveries, 1*(1), 5–35.

Barrat, J. (2023). *Our final invention: Artificial intelligence and the end of the human era.* Quercus.

Berg, J. M., Raj, M., & Seamans, R. (2023). Capturing value from artificial intelligence. *Academy of Management Discoveries, 9*(4), Guidepost/

Beirne, M., Ramsay, H., & Panteli, A. (1998). Developments in computing work: control and contradiction. In P. Thompson & C. Warhurst (Eds.), *Workplaces of the future* (pp. 195–209). Macmillan.

Birkinshaw, J., & Pass, S. (2008). *Innovation in the workplace: How are organisations responding to generation Y employees and Web 2.0 technologies? [online].* Chartered Institute of Personnel and Development. http://www.cipd.co.uk/subjects/maneco/general/_inwrkplgny.htm.

Blauner, R. (1964). *Alienation and freedom: The factory worker and his industry.* Chicago University Press.

Bondarouk, T., & Olivas-Lujan, M. R. (2013). *Social media in human resources management. Advances series in management* (Vol. 12). Emerald

Braverman, H. (1974). *Labor and monopoly capital: The degradation of work in the twentieth century.* Monthly Review Press.

Brynjolfsson, E., & Hitt, L. (2000). Beyond computation: Information technology, organizational transformation, and business performance. *Journal of Economic Perspectives, 14*(4), 23–48.

Brynjolfsson, E., & McAfee, A. (2011). *Rage against the machine: How the digital revolution is accelerating innovation, driving productivity, and irreversibly transforming employment and the economy.* Digital Frontier Press.

Brynjolfsson, E., & McAfee, A. (2014). *The second machine age: Work, progress and prosperity in a time of brilliant technologies.* Norton.

Budhwar, P., Chowdhury, S., Wood, G., Aguinis, H., Bamber, G. J., Beltran, J. R., Boselie, P., Lee Cooke, F., Decker, S., DeNisi, A., Dey, P. K., Guest, D., Knoblich, A. J., Malik, A., Paauwe, J., Papagiannidis, S., Patel, C., Pereira, V., Ren, S., . . . Varma, A. (2023). Human resource management in the age of generative artificial intelligence: Perspectives and research directions on ChatGPT. *Human Resource Management Journal*, 33(3), 606–659. https://doi.org/10.1111/1748-8583.12524

Calvo-Porral, C., & Pesqueira-Sanchez, R. (2020). Generational differences in technology behaviour: Comparing millennials and Generation X. *Kybernetics*, 49(11), 2755–2772.

Child, J. (2015). *Organization: Contemporary principles and practice* (2nd ed.).Wiley.

Choo, C., & Bontis, N. (Eds.). (2002). *The strategic management of intellectual capital and organizational knowledge*. Oxford University Press.

CIPD. (2014, February). *Industrial strategy and future skills policy, research insight*. Chartered Institute of Personnel and Development. http://www.cipd.co.uk/binaries /industrial-strategy-and-the-future-of-skills-policy_2014.pdf

Clegg, S. R., Pitsis, T. S., & Mount, M. (2021). *Management and organizations: An introduction to theory and practice* (6th ed.). Sage

Conversation. (2023, July 24). *Actors are really worried about the use of AI by movie studios – they may have a point*. https://theconversation.com/actors-are-really -worried-about-the-use-of-ai-by-movie-studios-they-may-have-a-point-210034

Conversation. (2023, July 26). A black box AI system has been influencing criminal justice decisions for over two decades – it's time to open it up.

Conway, E., Monks, K., Fu, N., Alfes, K., & Bailey, K. (2020). Reimagining alienation within a relational framework: Evidence from the public sector in Ireland and the UK. *International Journal of Human Resource Management*, 31(21), 2673–2694.

Coyle, D., & Quah, D. (2004). *Getting the measure of the new economy*. The Work Foundation. http://www.theworkfoundation. com/research/isociety/new_economy .jsp

Czarniawska, B., & Lofgren, O. (Eds.). (2012). *Managing overflow in affluent societies*. Routledge.

Deranty, JP., Corbin, T. (2024). Artificial intelligence and work: a critical review of recent research from the social sciences. *AI & Society*, 39, 675–691.

Divoli, R., Edelman, D., & Sarazin, H. (2012, April). *McKinsey quarterly*. Retrieved July 20, 2015, from http://www.mckinsey.com/insights/marketing_sales/demystifying _social_media

Emanuel, N., & Harrington, E. (2023, May). *Working remotely? Selection, treatment, and the market for remote work* (Rederal Reserve Bank of New York. No. 1061). https:// www.newyorkfed.org/medialibrary/media/research/staff_reports/sr1061.pdf?sc _lang=en

Evans, P., & Wurster, T. S. (2000). *Blown to bits: How the new economics of information transformed strategy*. Harvard Business School Press.

Fernández-Portillo, A., Almodóvar-González, M., & Hernández-Mogollón, R. (2020). Impact of ICT development on economic growth. A study of OECD European union countries. *Technology in Society*, 63. https://doi.org/10.1016/j.techsoc.2020 .101420

Finegold, D., & Soskice, D. (1988). The failure of training in Britain: Analysis and prescription. *Oxford Review of Economic Policy, 4*, 21–53.

Hanley, C., & Douglass, M. T. (2014). High road, low road, or off road? Economic development strategies in the American states. *Economic Development Quarterly, 28*(3), 220–229.

Hatch, M. J., & Cunliffe, A. (2012). *Organization theory: Modern, symbolic, and postmodern perspectives* (3rd ed.). Oxford University Press.

Hatch, M. J. (2018). *Organization theory: modern, symbolic and postmodern perspectives*. Oxford: Oxford University Press.

Hitt, M., & Duane Ireland, R. (2008). *Strategic management concepts: Competitiveness and globalization* (10th ed.). South-Western

Jarzabkowski, P., & Pinch, T. (2013). Sociomateriality is 'the New Black': Accomplishing repurposing, reinscripting and repairing in context. *M@n@gement, 16*, 579–592. https://doi.org/10.3917/mana.165.0579

Kuczera, M., Field, S. & Windisch, H.C. (2016) Building skills for all: a review of England. OECD. https://www.oecd.org/education/skills-beyond-school/building -skills-for-all-review-of-england.pdf

Obijiofor, L (2015). *New technologies in developing societies: From theories to practice.* Palgrave MacMillan.

Orlikowski, W. J., & Scott, S. V. (2008). Sociomateriality: Challenging the separation of technology, work and organization. *Annals of the Academy of Management, 2*(1), 433–474

Li. C., & Bernoff, J. (2008). *Groundswell: winning in a world transformed by social technologies.* Harvard Business School Press

Malone, T. W. (2004). *The future of work: How the new order of business will shape your organization, your management style, and your life.* Harvard Business School Press.

Martin, G., Beaumont, P. B., Doig, R. M., & Pate, J. M. (2005). A new discourse for HR: Corporate reputation management. *European Management Journal, 23*(1), 76–88.

Martin, G., Reddington, M., & Alexander, H. (2007). *Technology, outsourcing and transforming HR.* Butterworth

Martin, G., Reddington, M., & Kneafsey, M. B. (2009). *Web 2.0 and human resource management: 'Groundswell' or hype?* Chartered Institute of Personnel and Development.

Martin, G., Parry, E., & Flowers, P. (2015). Do social media enhance constructive employee voice all of the time or just some of the time? *Human Resource Management Journal, 25*(4).541–562.

Martin, G., Siebert, S., Bushfield, S., & Howieson, W. S. (2021). Changing logics in healthcare and their effects on the identity motives and identity work of doctors. *Organization Studies, 42*(9), 1477–1499.

McAfee, A.& Brynjolfsson, E. (2017) *Machine, platform, crowd: Harnessing our digital future.* Norton

McKinlay, A., & Taylor, P. (1997). Foucault and the politics of production. In A. McKinlay & K. Starkey (Eds.), *Foucault, management and organization* (pp. 98–114). Sage.

OECD. (2004). *The economic impact of ICT: Measurement, evidence and implications.* Organization for Economic Development.

(OECD). (2014). *OECD skills outlook 2013 – first results from the survey of adult skills.* OECD. http://dx.doi. org/10.1787/9789264204256-en

National Institute of Economic and Social Research. (2022). *Why is UK productivity low and how can it improve?* https://www.niesr.ac.uk/blog/why-uk-productivity-low -and-how-can-it-improve

Osterman, P. (2018). In search of the high road: Meaning and evidence. *Industrial and Labor Relations Review, 71*(1), 3–34.

Parry, E., Martin, G., & Dromey, J. (2019). Scenarios and strategies for social media in engaging and giving voice to employees. In P. Holland, J. Teicher, & J. Donaghey (Eds.), *Employee voice at work* (pp. 201–2016). Springer Link.

Perrow, C. (1986). *Complex organizations: A critical essay* (3rd ed.). Random House.

Rose, M. (1975). *Industrial behaviour: Theoretical developments since Taylor.* Allen Lane.

Rosenberg, M. (2001). *E-Learning: Strategies for delivering knowledge in the digital age.* McGraw-Hill.

Sayles, L. R. (1958). *The behavior of industrial workgroups: Prediction and control.* John Wiley.

Staats, B., & Upton, D. M. (2011, October). Lean knowledge work. *Harvard Business Review.*

Sterling, A., & Boxall, P. (2013). Lean production, employee learning and workplace outcomes: A case analysis through the ability-motivation-opportunity framework. *Human Resource Management Journal, 23*(3), 227–240.

Stahel, W. R. (2019). *The circular economy: A user's guide.* Routledge.

Stone, P., Brooks, R., Brynjolsson, E., et al. (2022). *Artificial intelligence and life in 2030: the one hundred year study on artificial intelligence.* Computers and Society. https:// doi.org/10.48550/arXiv.2211.06318

Suleyman, M. (2023). *The coming wave: AI, power and the twenty-first century's greatest dilemma.* Bodley Head

Sundararajan, A. (2013, January 3). From zipcar to the sharing economy. *Harvard Business Review.*

Taylor, R. (2004). *Skills and innovation in modern britain.* ESRC Future of Work Programme Seminar Series. http://www.leeds.ac.uk/ esrcfutureofwork/download s/fow_publication_6.pdf.

Thompson, P. (2011). The trouble with HRM. *Human Resource Management Journal, 21*(4), 355–367.

Thompson, P., & Smith, C. (Eds.). (2010). *Working life: Renewing labour process analysis. Critical perspectives on work and employment.* Palgrave Macmillan

Trist, E. L., et al. (1963). *Organizational Choice.* London: Tavistock Institute of Human Relations.

Tripas, M. (2008). *Technology, identity, and inertia through the lens of 'the digital photography company'* (Harvard Business School Working Paper, 09-042). Retrieved May 20, 2015, from http://www.hbs.edu/faculty/Publication%20Files/09-042.pdf

United Kingdom Commission for Employment and Skills. (2015). *Working futures, 2012-2022.* Retrieved May 20, 2015, from https://www.gov.uk/government/publications /working-futures-2012-to-2022

United Nations Conference on Trade and Development. (2011). *Measuring the impacts of information and communications technology for development.* Retrieved May 20, 2015, from http://unctad.org/en/docs/dtlstict2011d1_en.pdf

Weick, K. E. (1990). Technology as equivoque: Sensemaking in new technologies. In P. S. Goodman, L. S. Sproull, & Associates (Eds.), *Technology and organizations*, pp. 1–44. Jossey-Bass.

Womack, J. P., Jones, D. T., & Roos, D. (1990). *The machine that changed the world.* Ranson.

Woodward, J. (1965). *Industrial organizations: Theory and practice.* Oxford University Press.

Work Foundation. (2004). *You don't know me but ... Social capital and social software.* Work Foundation. http://www. theworkfoundation.com/research/isociety/index .jsp

CHAPTER 9

Managing creativity, innovation, and teams

LEARNING OUTCOMES

By the end of this chapter, you should be able to:

- Understand the difference between creativity and innovation.
- Understand the shift from the individualistic approaches to creativity towards a systems perspective.
- Evaluate the ways in which creativity and innovation can be managed through effective teamworking.
- Analyse the relationship between networks and creativity.

INTRODUCTION

In this chapter, I want to explore three organizational processes that are closely related to change – creativity, innovation, and teamworking in organizations. These three processes have become more important because in times of fierce business competition, with shorter product and service life cycles, and more demanding customers and service users, success depends on creating new products and services and a need to constantly adapt to the changing environment by developing new organizational systems and processes. It is not only business that requires creativity and innovation, however. The public sector is also pressed to find new ways of delivering services to boost productivity and keep up with the ever-increasing demand for health and social care, cultural life, housing, transport, waste disposal, and so on. So, we begin this chapter with some basic definitions and an examination of the concepts of creativity and innovation.

One of the most frequently cited definitions of workplace creativity and innovation is provided in Anderson, De Dreu et al.'s (2014, p.1298) review:

> Creativity and innovation at work are the process, outcomes, and products of attempts to develop and introduce new and improved ways of doing things. The

DOI: 10.4324/9781003469711-9

creativity stage of this process refers to idea generation, and innovation to the subsequent stage of implementing ideas toward better procedures, practices, or products. Creativity and innovation [...] will invariably result in identifiable benefits.

This definition is useful because it suggests that not all creative ideas lead to innovation; some ideas are never commercialised or implemented. Organizational creativity refers to the generation of novel and useful ideas, organizational innovation is used to describe the realisation of those ideas, for example, new product development, a new process, or a new service. In other words, creativity is the starting point of innovation, a necessary but not sufficient condition for the process of innovation to be realised (Hughes et al., 2018).

Reflection

Most innovative ideas never get a chance to be implemented. When employees hear dismissive comments from their managers, they become increasingly frustrated and either give up trying to be innovative or move to a different organization. Why are some managers reluctant to support innovation? What are other possible reasons why some ideas are dropped, whereas others are picked up and lead to the development of innovative products, processes, or services?

Although creativity and innovation are crucial to the survival of organizations, some organizations and managers seem to want to stifle new ideas. Kanter (2013) claims that many leaders operate hidden principles aimed at preventing innovation. Her list of anti-rules includes being suspicious of new ideas, invoking past experiences, over-burdening people with work, confining strategic plans to a small group of people, and punishing failure. Innovative ideas are usually risky and uncertain, so many leaders will see them as threats to stability and profitability and react accordingly by shelving them. Why is this the case? The answer to this question probably lies in the politics of organizations, which we examined in Chapter 4. McCalman et al. (2015) define organizational politics as 'the use of power through influencing techniques and tactics (sanctioned or unsanctioned) aimed at accomplishing personal and/or organizational goals.' The presence of politics in organizations cannot be denied, and it often affects all aspects of management. Managers engage in 'turf game tactics' to further their own agendas, even if it sometimes means destroying the enterprise of others, and these include people's creativity and innovative initiatives (Afzalur Rahim, 2023). So how can we help organizations become more innovative? One answer is by applying theories of creativity to the problem.

CHANGING APPROACHES TO CREATIVITY

There have been numerous attempts to develop theories of creativity. One of the most influential theories was proposed by Teresa Amabile (2012). She developed the five-stage componential model of creativity, which identified three key components: task motivation (intrinsic and extrinsic motivation which trigger the creative process); domain-relevant skills (skills that determine the approach); and creativity-relevant skills (variables of personality and individual differences). Amabile's stages of the creative process were:

1. Task representation – the creative process is triggered by extrinsic and/or intrinsic motivation.

2. Preparation – this is when individuals gather information before generating responses.

3. Response generation happens when individuals search through different solutions to come up with a response.

4. Response validation – individuals draw on their domain-relevant skills to validate the value of the product/response.

5. Outcome evaluation – outcomes are evaluated based on evaluation in stage 4.

If the outcomes are successful or unsuccessful in the final stage of this process, the process ends. If the outcomes are partially achieved, the process then returns to stage 1.

CASE 9.1 'ROBOT SURGEONS SLASH HOSPITAL STAYS AND WAITING LISTS FOR PROSTATE CANCER IN TAYSIDE' – HELEN MCARDLE, HEALTH CORRESPONDENT ON THE *GLASGOW HERALD*, APRIL 28, 2023.

'More [than] 400 patients in Tayside have undergone robotic-assisted surgery since the technology was first introduced at the end of 2021. The health board [NHS Tayside] has recorded the highest number of robotic procedures using a single robot of any region in Scotland, with the machines now being deployed in the majority of prostate cancer operations. It has also been credited with a significant impact on waiting times – with no waiting list at all currently for prostate cancer surgery' wrote *Glasgow Herald* Reporter, Helen McArdle.

She continued her report, 'NHS Tayside's robotic assisted surgical service first began operating on patients at Ninewells Hospital in Dundee [at] the end of 2021 and has since expanded significantly. As well as being used in prostate cancer surgery, it has been used to perform complex procedures in colorectal, upper gastrointestinal, urology, gynaecology and ear nose and throat specialities. The approach sees surgeons manoeuvre the arms of the robot surgeon using a control panel, with a screen and headset enabling them to view and guide the procedure with extremely precise movements.'

The outcomes are very impressive in reducing the risk of infections and reducing the time it takes patients to recover from surgical trauma because it is minimally invasive. Consequently, it reduces so-called 'bed-blocking', one of the main issues facing health and social care, because it leads to patients being able to leave hospital significantly earlier. The initiative has been led in Dundee by consultant urology surgeon, Professor Ghulam Nabi, who carries out robotic-assisted radical prostatectomies. He spent several years researching the benefits of robotic technology and eventually persuaded the Board of NHS Tayside to invest in an advanced surgical system robot. This robot features a three-dimensional endoscope and image-processing equipment that provides a magnified view of nerves and blood vessels surrounding the prostate gland, so mitigating the risk of surgical damage. Persuading the Board to invest in the robot, however, was no easy task because it faced considerable pressures on its finances and alternative claims for investment. Professor Nabi and his surgical colleagues had to overcome sceptics from within the medical directorate of NHS Tayside of the merits of such investment and convince the Board of the payback through the presentation of a rigorous business case.

Helen McArdle's interview with Professor Nabi continued with him stating: 'It really is an innovative step up from laparoscopic [keyhole] surgery. The benefits of using precision instruments and keyhole surgical techniques for patients are evidenced in reduced blood loss and time spent recovering in hospital. Patients who have had robotic surgery for prostatectomies are generally able to be discharged the next day...Robotics surgery has increased capacity and thereby decreased the 31 days waiting target for surgery.'

He continued: 'We have no waiting list for prostate cancer surgery currently... Robotic surgery is the least invasive surgical treatment option available today and this surgical option is now very much embedded in the treatment of urology patients.'

Coincidentally, Dundee has a history of significant medical innovation. Sir James Whyte Black developed the first beta-blocker drugs in Dundee, which earned him the Noel Prize for Medicine in 1988, while laparoscopic [keyhole] surgery was developed at Ninewells Hospital in Dundee by Sir Alfred Cushieri, who performed the first keyhole operation in 1986. Professor Cusheri carried out many experiments over a period of ten years to prove to colleagues and patients that this kind of surgery was safe. It also took him over a year to find a patient who would agree to undergo such new surgery.

Sources: McArdle, H. (2023) https://www.heraldscotland.com/news/23488551 .robotic-surgery-boost-tayside-prostate-cancer-patients/. Tocher, K. (2019) https:// www.meetdundeecityregion.co.uk/blog/major-surgical-innovation-in-dundee-and -angus.

Questions

1. Which elements of Amabile's theory does the case illustrate?
2. What other aspects of creativity and innovation does the case illustrate?

Our understanding of creativity has been changing over the years. In the past, creativity was often associated with an ability granted only to a few very talented people, usually working in isolation. It also relied on a set of cognitive factors such as mental flexibility, the ability to 'think out of the box', originality of thinking, and the ability to link remote associations (Andripoulos & Dawson 2010). Creativity was also associated with personality traits such as risk-taking, self-confidence, tolerance of ambiguity, non-conformity, and a motivation to achieve. However, examinations of biographies of great artists and inventors from the past proved largely inconclusive in finding the magic ingredient of a genius. Little evidence of creative competences was found, as many brilliant inventors did not appear to share similar personality traits. This growing scepticism of individual, trait-based approaches in recent years resulted in a noticeable shift towards the approaches based on groups of individuals working together as the robotic surgery case illustrates (Amabile, 2012). Researchers have also begun to question the cause-and-effect relationship – whether certain traits result in creativity, or whether the pressures of creative work result in certain psychological consequences (Bilton & Cummings, 2010).

THE CONTEXT FOR CREATIVITY AND INNOVATION

There is a wider, although not universal (see Straub et al., 2023), recognition that creativity exists in communities and that the creativity or collective intelligence of a group or a team is greater than the sum of creative traits and abilities of individuals within them (Hughes et al., 2018). There is also a marked recognition of the context for creativity, i.e., external conditions that either hinder creative thinking or facilitate it. Mihaly Csikszentmihalyi (2014) argued that creativity is as much a cultural and social as it is a psychological event that takes place within a certain environment. For him, there are two aspects of the creative environment: the domain (for example, Florence in the fifteenth century, or Silicon Valley since the 1970s), and the field i.e., the social context within which creativity takes place. Creativity understood in this way is a process that can be observed at the intersection of individuals, domains, and fields (Anderson, Potocnik et al., 2014). To an extent, Case 9.1 illustrates this intersectionality. Csikszentmihalyi's argument led him to develop the system's theory of creativity whereby the creative individuals are embedded in informal networks of collaboration, which extend horizontally – through peer-to-peer relationships, and vertically – through supply chain relationships in the process of cultural production. This means that creativity requires the act of creation, but also a system of relationships underpinning this act of creation (Anderson, De Dreu et al., 2014). What it means in practice is that to be successful it is not enough for an individual to have a good idea, but also to have a network of contacts that will facilitate the development of the idea. Bilton (2010) summed it up: 'the bright sparks of illumination only catch fire when the right combination of elements is assembled.'

Exercise

Csikszentmihalyi (1999) suggested that some conditions in the external environment are more conducive to creativity than others. Think about different contexts and consider these questions:

- Are big cities more conducive to creativity than small villages?
- Are some cities more creative than others?
- Are rich people more creative than people who are less well-off?
- Does external threat mobilise creativity?
- Are egalitarian societies more likely to support the creative process than societies with aristocracies and oligarchies?
- Do young people tend to be more creative than older people?
- Is necessity the mother of invention?

To understand better how the environment may influence creativity, let's look again at the case study of the city of Dundee, where I am based.

CASE 9.2 DUNDEE AS THE CREATIVE AND INNOVATIVE INDUSTRIES HUB

Csikszentmihalyi (2014) argued that the domain is very important for creativity, you will recall the example of Florence in the fifteenth century as a place particularly conducive to creativity. A question arises of whether the domain itself can be created? *The Guardian* in an article entitled 'Dundee: From black sheep of Scottish cities to "living cultural experiment"' throws some light on this question.

Dundee used to be perceived as one of the most deprived places in Scotland. Heavy industry began to disappear from the 1970s onwards, leaving behind a scarred industrial landscape. Although Dundee has a population of only 150,000 (down from 180,000 a century earlier), its post-industrial problems often overshadowed those encountered by larger Scottish cities such as Glasgow.

But despite pockets of severe deprivation still visible to visitors, Dundee's image is changing, and the city is reinventing itself as a creative hub. Now over 3000 people work in Dundee's creative industries, which generate a turnover of £200m. DC Thomson, the famous publishing house, is one of the major employers in producing comics and newspapers in the UK. In 2014, Dundee received the UK's first UNESCO City of Design award for its contributions to the world.

Dundee is particularly known for its video games. Chris Van Der Kuyl set up his first video game company in Dundee in the mid-1990s, which then helped develop Minecraft. Dundee is the heart of Scotland's gaming industry with around 40 gaming firms based there. There are also long-established links between Dundee's universities and the creative industries in gaming. For example, in 1997, Abertay University designed and delivered the world's first degree in computer games technology and in ethical hacking.

But Dundee is known not only for games development but also for its cultural offerings. The Dundee Contemporary Arts Centre (DCA) was opened in 1999, and it now contains a print studio, cinema, a gallery, and a cafe. Thousands of children every year attend screenings at the two-week Children's Film Festival there. As the *Guardian* article proclaimed 'there are also some exciting developments on the banks of the River Tay.'

- The Victoria and Albert Museum, the only branch of the V&A museum outside London, was opened in 2018.
- A new digital headquarters on the city's docks.
- Plans to implement a £120m project to bring a film studio to Dundee.
- A hotel, retail units, and apartments, as part of an ambitious regeneration project to connect Dundee city centre to the water.

In 2015, the *Guardian* observed: 'Dundee was known as the city of "jute, jam and journalism". Now, with the mills gone and the printing presses quieter, [Dundee] has a rather different claim to global fame: not just Minecraft but Grand Theft Auto and other classic video game titles were born or raised on the banks of the River Tay.' This video games industry has also given rise to a vibrant software sector, with games entrepreneurs founding other software firms in conjunction with experienced entrepreneurs. One examples is Waracle, one of the UK's leading mobile app, internet of things, and virtual reality companies, which grew rapidly from 2017 to 2023 (Martin & Arshed, 2020).

The change in Dundee's image does not only involve investment; it also required a change in the attitudes of the citizens of Dundee. Dundee still has its economic and social problems. Even when the cultural offering in Dundee is better, there are still going to be barriers for some people to access it. A lot needs to be done to avoid polarisation where the new creative sector is separated from the citizens of Dundee. The change in attitude is being achieved by collaboration between schools, universities, and businesses to mentor young people to show them how culture and entrepreneurship can change their lives. A lot is done to attract people to come and live in Dundee and encourage those who left to return.

Some argue that Dundee has shaped its own future and has become an example of culture-led regeneration 'partly by accident, partly by design, building on what was already' (The Guardian, 2015) At the time of rewriting this chapter in 2024, Dundee continues to be known as a creative hub for games development and other software development and digital product firms such as Waracle, which specialises in working with fintech, medtech, and energy businesses. It also relies on Dundee's two universities, along with nearby St Andrews University, working in close partnership with the region, the NHS, and local companies to support them. And, as we have already seen in the case of robotic surgery earlier, the region, despite its location and relative poverty, has a history of creativity and innovation in medicine and life sciences. Life sciences has been particularly impressive. So, for example, the University of Dundee was named in 2023 as the best university in the UK for supporting spin-out companies that commercialise university research. Most of these occurred in life sciences, including the £2.2 billion IPO of Exscientia on the US NASDAQ, one of the largest ever UK university spinouts, and biotech firms Tay Therapeutics and Vyne Therapeutics. Related to these developments in life sciences, the University of Dundee and NHS Tayside have initiated a collaboration called TIME. TIME is an acronym for the Tayside Innovation Medtech Ecosystem, whose mission is to 'Advance MedTech innovation through effective partnerships among academia, the NHS, industry, and Tayside Region for the betterment of health and wellbeing and the promotion of economic growth in the region.' TIME connects directly to the Tay Cities Innovation Hub, providing resources to stimulate and support the commercialisation of MedTech innovation.

Source:
http://www.theguardian.com/cities/2015/jun/22/dundee-scotland-design-v-and-a
-culture-regeneration-minecraft-grand-theft-auto.

Questions

1. Does the case of Dundee provide convincing evidence for having a supportive environment for creativity and innovation?

2. How important has the role of the universities been in promoting creativity and innovation? What further action could they take?

3. As the case study demonstrates, financial investment was crucial in the city reinventing itself. But is such investment enough? What can be done to promote a culture of creativity, innovation, and entrepreneurship among people who traditionally worked in older industries?

So, while creativity may be a solitary act of a talented individual, it is also a social experience, and today's theories of creativity overlap with management theories of teamwork, the study of networks, knowledge management, and organizational learning. In the following sections of this chapter, we will consider creativity and innovation through the lenses of teamworking and networks.

TEAMWORKING, CREATIVITY, AND INNOVATION

We start our discussion of teams with a short discussion exercise about your own experiences of working in teams.

Reflection

Drawing on your experience of working in teams in the past – at work, at school, or university, and in other contexts, what are the advantages and disadvantages of working in teams? Why do teams sometimes fail?

A classic but still useful definition of a team is 'a small number of people with complementary skills who are committed to a common purpose, set of performance goals, and approach for which they hold themselves mutually accountable' (Katzenbach & Smith, 1993, p. 113). Teamworking became established as an alternative to repetitive work routines many decades ago because it allowed for the rotation of tasks within a team, which was believed to enhance employee engagement. There is also evidence to suggest that teamworking can improve organizational performance (Mortensen & Hass, 2018), mainly because it constitutes a move away from control towards more participative forms of management. Teamworking was an integral part of the Japanese and Nordic models of management, socio-technical systems theory, the quality of working life movement in the 1980s, Japanese Total Quality Management, and Business Process Re-Engineering. It was also strongly advocated by management 'gurus' such as Peter Drucker (1988) and Tom Peters (1989). In their seminal book, Katzenbach and Smith (1993) argued that teams would become the primary unit of performance because they are based on mutual accountability and allow team members to take responsibility for their own contribution to the achievement of the common goals. Such predictions have turned out to be generally true but with an important caveat. Arguably, teamworking under current conditions is different from teamworking in the past; teams nowadays are far more dynamic, dispersed, and diverse and often must work together digitally. The enabling conditions for such teamworking, according to Haas and Mortensen (2016), are having a compelling sense of direction with challenging goals, a supportive context, a shared mindset, and a solid structure, the last of which refers to the mix, diversity, and number of members.

On this diversity issue, management scholars have studied teams extensively and produced various classifications of team roles. Perhaps the best known to practitioners is Belbin's study of effective teams, which focused on the roles people assume when they work in teams. For him, team role is 'a pattern of behaviour that characterises one person's behaviour in relation to another in relation to the progress of the team' (Belbin, 2000). Team roles are different from functional roles (such as an engineer, a marketing expert, or an accountant); they are the ways in which team members contribute to the working of the team. Thus, Belbin argued that people can contribute to team effort in the following nine ways: coordinating the teams' efforts, imparting drive, creating ideas, exploring resources, evaluating options, organizing the work, following up on details, supporting others, and providing expertise.

Based on these ways of contributing, he proposed a classification of team roles (Belbin, 2024:

- **Plant** – creative and generates new ideas but does not always communicate effectively.
- **Resource investigator** – outgoing and communicative but tends to lose interest when enthusiasm has passed.
- **Co-ordinator** – mature and confident, identifies talent but can be seen as manipulative.
- **Shaper** – thrives on pressure, has the determination to overcome obstacles but is prone to provocation and sometimes offends people.
- **Monitor-evaluator** – sober and strategic, sees all options and judges them accurately but lacks drive and the ability to inspire others.

- **Teamworker** – cooperative, perceptive, and listens to others but indecisive and avoids confrontation.
- **Implementer** – practical reliable and efficient, turns ideas into action but sometimes inflexible.
- **Completer finisher** – conscientious, polishes, and perfects but reluctant to delegate and inclined to worry
- **Specialist** – single-minded and dedicated, provides knowledge and skills but tends to dwell on practicalities.

The diagnostic tool for identifying the primary and secondary team roles is Belbin's self-perception inventory (SPI), which sometimes is accompanied by an observer checklist. According to Belbin, an individual can function well both in primary and secondary team roles and can contribute to more than one team at the same time. The key idea behind Belbin's classification is the notion of a 'balanced team', i.e., it is crucial who works together in a team. Belbin found that complementary combinations of people tend to be far more effective, and making up a team of people who tend to contribute in very similar ways might be counterproductive.

Belbin's classification of team roles is not without criticism. For example, Senior (1997) argued that the meaning of team performance was usually far more complex, and Belbin's perspective fails to capture this complexity. In her view, teamwork was not always about winning or losing; different people may define team success differently and team members' contributions may be different depending on their subjective sense-making. From the methodological point of view, Belbin's inventory was criticised for two further reasons. First, it relied too heavily on self-perceptions; second, not enough research has been done on the psychometric properties of the inventory and its validity (Wilson, 2014). However, it should be noted that Van Dierendonck and Groen (2011) found the Belbin inventory broadly constructed and was valid in a large-scale study, which provided some support for the approach and its key messages.

Reflecting on Haas and Mortensen's (2016) concern that teams have a compelling sense of direction with challenging goals and a supportive context, a further and highly impactful perspective on understanding effective teamworking is the notion of relational coordination. Developed in the 1990s by Jody Hofer Gittell, relational coordination is based on the proposition that coordination among team members is a key element in effective teamworking. Such relational coordination is enhanced by shared goals, shared knowledge, and mutual respect, supported by frequent, timely, accurate, and problem-solving communications, and vice versa (Bolton et al., 2021; Gittell et al., 2010). The theory is especially important when the kind of work people undertake is highly inter-dependent, uncertain, and time-sensitive, which is often the case in creative teams, and where work is characterised by siloed thinking, such as in professional bureaucracies like healthcare.

Bolton et al. (2021) produced a systematic review proposing a more dynamic theory of relational coordination almost 30 years after Gittell developed her original ideas. This is conceptualised in Figure 9.1, which I have adapted to include the dimension of organizational antecedents as a key aspect of relational coordination and people and culture as a key outcome. The adapted figure has three components. The first is relational

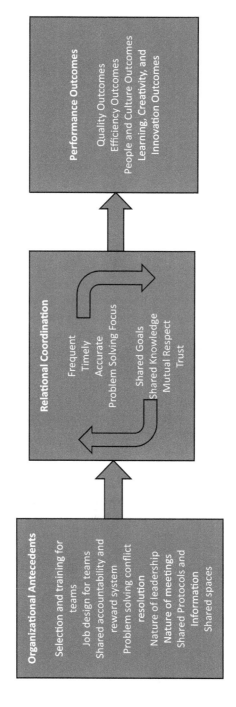

FIGURE 9.1 A revised framework for understanding relational coordination's antecedents and outcomes (adapted from Bolton et al., 2021)

coordination as a recursive process for bringing teams together, which refers to the nature of communications within a team and the nature of shared goals, knowledge, mutual respect, and levels of trust in colleagues, competence, benevolence, and integrity. The second is the cross-cutting organizational structures and processes needed to strengthen relational coordination (the antecedents), which include, among other factors, the selection and training for teamworking, formal and informal structures for teambuilding such as 'agile' teams, huddles (in healthcare), 'scrums' (in software development), and shared (identity) spaces, accountability, and reward systems geared to teams rather than individuals, shared information, and protocols. The third is the outcomes thought to result from high levels of relational coordination. These include people and culture outcomes, and learning and innovation as well as the more traditional outcomes of quality improvements, productivity, and meaningful work.

PROBLEMS WITH TEAMS AND TEAMWORKING

Like most solutions to management problems, however, the overall notion of teamworking is not without its critics and controversies. One of the problems raised by critics such as Wilson (2014) relates to the potential for inequality in teams. Although teams are meant to be largely more democratic, the team members often bring in their status from outside the team, and consciously or subconsciously try to reconstruct it in the team. Team members who are normally in lower rank positions very often assume a background role in the team. Wilson referred to this phenomenon as the 'seduction of hierarchy.' Different positions of individuals in a team can also be determined by the unequal distribution of resources, different educational backgrounds, and simply different levels of self-confidence. This phenomenon is especially likely to occur in professional bureaucracies such as healthcare, higher education, and the legal profession, in which professional power is often strong.

A second problem related to teams often raised in the literature is the phenomenon of conformity and groupthink. Conformity occurs when people change behaviour/attitudes to match those of the group, because of real or imagined group pressure. In his seminal study, Asch (1956) tried to answer the question of what happens when established norms are wrong. In his experiment, he found that when faced with peer pressure, his experimental subjects made significantly more errors than his control group subjects. Asch found that conformity to the group pressure resulted in distortion of perception, distortion of judgement, and distortion of action. In other words, when subject to group pressure, individuals were more likely to give wrong answers to the questions asked. Such results have been supported by Koriat (2015), who found that group interaction not only impaired accuracy but also enhanced confidence in erroneous decisions during experiments aimed at assessing people's judgements.

Conformity to group pressure is also referred to as groupthink, which was popularised in the 1950s by William H Whyte. He used it to discuss the problems of American management and the tyranny of groups that destroyed employee individuality or challenged the collective view. The usual prescriptions focus on how managers and leaders sense and enact strategies to prevent groupthink from occurring, including encouraging internal and external critical evaluation, leaders avoiding excessive influence by absenting themselves from certain discussions and avoiding taking the lead in offering opinions, and ensuring all alternatives are discussed by formally assigning roles to group members to play 'devil's advocate' in advancing alternatives. The bottom line is that ensuring the 'psychological safety' of group members is a necessary condition to avoid conformity and groupthink (Edmondson & Verdin, 2018).

The context of the creative industries also leads to teams having problems (Hesmondhalgh, 2019). Bilton (2010) warned, somewhat counterintuitively, that team-based organizations can sometimes appear as constraining as traditional bureaucracies, which are based on a detailed division of labour. This is because the horizontal lines of communication within project-based teams cross with vertical lines of functionally based hierarchies. Also, the focus on the task at hand and the planned outcomes of the project sometimes hindered a team's ability to see the big picture. Furthermore, where teamworking was associated with projects, a lack of continuation of such project work could negatively affect further learning (Grugulis & Stoyanova, 2011). Again, the focus on the task may reduce opportunities for the self-fulfilment of individuals. These last findings have been supported by research into contexts when groups perform better than individuals. Thus, Straub et al. (2023) found during experimental conditions that dyads gradually improved in performance on a specific set of tasks but did not experience a collective benefit compared with individuals during most tasks. They also found having an individual expert in the team improved accuracy. They concluded that the costs of collaboration can, in certain contexts, exceed the benefits of collaboration in performing complex tasks. Their data showed the extent of training received by individuals, the complexity of the task, and the desired performance indicators were critical factors that needed to be considered when discussing the benefits of teamworking.

Creativity and teams

One of the earlier but still highly practical attempts to understand creativity in teams is Michael Kirton's (1984) theory of complementary opposites, i.e., adaptation-innovation theory (A-I Theory). Kirton argued that creativity requires a connection between opposite thinking styles. So, he developed the Kirton Adaptation-Innovation Inventory (known as KAI, http://www.kaicentre.com/) to explore individuals' thinking styles to indicate what roles they might play in creative teams. He researched teams of engineers and found that everyone could be located on a continuum ranging from highly adaptive to highly innovative.

Adaptors are individuals who produce ideas based closely on, but stretching, existing definitions of the problem and likely solutions. They usually proceed within the established theories, policies, and practices of organizations, and their effort is directed at improving things. Innovators on the other hand are more likely to reconstruct the problem, separate it from the accepted paradigms, and produce much less expected solutions. In other words, innovators were interested in doing things differently. Kirton did not argue that one type is in any way superior to the other, and successful teams and organizations need a mixture of both. Innovators usually come up with new concepts but they need adaptors to develop these concepts into practical solutions. He contended that balanced teams are most effective, while teams consisting of one type were less successful. For example, teams consisting of innovators were unable to move their ideas forward, whereas teams with the most adaptors lacked the initial impetus to initiate new ventures. We found similar processes among senior HR leaders when making key decisions over partnering with business schools to develop their executives (Martin et al., 2018). Most were what we labelled as 'conformist innovators' after Karen Legge's well-known description of the HR function. These HR directors effectively outsourced their decisions to reputation rankings rather than engage in 'deviant innovation'. Deviant innovators, of which there were few in our sample of large international companies, were more likely to engage in rational choice decisions by considering schools that might be less prestigious but more inclined to offer tailored and more innovative solutions to executive development.

This phenomenon reflected the finding that organizations differ in what thinking styles they favoured, with the mean KAI score reflecting the organization's ethos. For example, some banks, certain types of hospitals, and government organizations tended to employ adaptors to reflect their low-risk appetite because of external regulation and institutional pressures. Similarly, bureaucratic organizations want to minimise risk and they tend to encourage adaptation, i.e., precision, reliability, and efficiency that come with it. On the other hand, adapters were usually in short supply in the creative industries. Kirton noted that adaptors were found in departments where solutions to problems come from within the unit, whereas innovators are found in departments that act as interfaces (i.e., cross-disciplinary boundaries).

Kirton's idea was extremely influential on theories of innovation because it drew managers' attention to the fact that creativity and innovation in organizations can be *managed* through recruitment and selection, as we have already noted. Selecting candidates for jobs cannot involve only choosing the most qualified or experienced candidate, but should also involve candidates' creativity, the roles they assume in teams, and how they collaborate with others. Taking into consideration these other characteristics, and designating candidates as psychological types, led to a more widespread use of psychometric tests for talent management (see Chapter 3). This approach was justified by research by Von Wittisch and Antonakis (2011), which showed that KAI scores were mostly predicted by the 'big five' personality dimensions and gender. Thus, it is debatable whether style constructs like KAI added much to what we already knew about innovation.

MANAGING CREATIVITY

An interesting starting point for managing creativity is to reflect on whether change can be managed, or is best 'left alone' to those involved in the creative process. Organizational scholars have differing opinions on this question. Some believe that organizations need to manage change in line with the organizational strategy, business environment, and available resources. Others advocate 'letting things happen'. Thus, Robert Chia (2014) was highly sceptical of the leader-centric theories of heroic action which see change as highly visible, dramatic, and rapid interventions, often associated with top-down, system-wide management initiatives. Chia called such interventions 'owned' processes as they privilege management agency and play down the role of serendipitous chance. On the opposite end of the spectrum, there are 'unowned' change processes that consider the complexity of context within which organizations operate. Change, seen from this perspective is a naturally occurring phenomenon, and managing change simply means relaxing organizational orders and letting change happen.

The team-based approaches to creativity and innovation sit somewhere in the middle on this question. They result from the systems' theories of creativity as well as from the observable shift away from an economy based on material production to a creative economy based on ideas and knowledge. In manufacturing product development, teams draw on expertise from across the organization and utilise the insights of engineers, programmers, designers, and artists.

Creative teams in the creative industries also rely on social networks. Creative individuals rarely operate on their own and are often embedded in systems and networks (Florida, 2002; Torr, 2008). And although individual talent still needs to be valued and celebrated, this embeddedness must not be ignored as creative processes in the creative industries are essentially collective. Bilton (2008) also noted that individualisation and specialisation of creative work results in high levels of mutual dependency. This mutual dependency is largely determined by the structural characteristics of the sector, for example, the predominance of project work in IT, which requires access to networks of self-employed specialists. Such work is often conducted on a temporary contract basis.

Mutual dependency is also a feature of creative organizations. Such organizations are often small, and individuals working in them must be able to step into different roles when needed. This tendency towards multi-tasking facilitates creativity because swapping roles allows for changes in perspective and promotes a holistic understanding of the business. On the other hand, Bilton observed that people in small organizations face the danger of over-familiarisation. When they become too familiar with each other, they no longer question each other, resulting in like-mindedness and groupthink, which in turn negatively affects creativity. As the organization grows, multi-tasking gives way to specialisation, and individuals begin to assume more clearly defined roles. They specialise in selected areas of the business – design, marketing, operations, finances, and so on. The danger of this tendency is over-specialisation where individuals are not able to step into the roles of other team members. This may result in alienation where individuals retreat into predefined roles.

So, can a creative team be managed?

Before we attempt to answer the question of whether creative teams can be managed, it is important to look at the role of a manager (see also Chapter 2). Mayle (2006) and Chia (2014) argued that close control and supervision on the part of the manager are often seen as detrimental to creativity. Creative teams, however, required managerial involvement, not through command and control but through monitoring and modifying the relationships that underpin this process. The advice often given to managers and leaders of creative teams is 'don't try to be a boss, act like a coach instead'. Micro-managing the creative process may be detrimental, and too much intervention might lead to unnecessary confrontation. Excessive focus on one talented individual might be damaging to the team spirit and other members' motivation.

There are some areas, however, where a manager has an important role to play. As we have noted, one of the key areas is recruitment and managing the allocation of roles in creative teams. Bilton (2008) suggests a powerful theatrical metaphor of managing teams being like casting actors in a play. Recruiting team members is not about who is the best for this job, but what kind of character a certain team or an organization needs. This is where understanding team roles discussed above is important. By bringing new people into the team, managers can disrupt consensus, avoid the development of groupthink, and create an opportunity to realign existing roles. Each new individual provides an opportunity to recast the others, and this is when the manager can have a role in managing creativity by brokering relationships within a team and connecting people with different talents. By being outside of the teams, managers often see 'the big picture' which team members miss. They should also build an internal culture of communication and collective ownership of the task. Related to culture is trust, and to achieve creative collaboration between individuals, team members need to develop mutual trust and respect.

As we have already noted, a team manager's role in encouraging team diversity is critical. The link between the diversity of a team and a team's creativity has been explored extensively by researchers in recent years. What most studies suggest is that diversity positively impacts creativity. Diverse teams may include people from different genders, cultural and national backgrounds, ages, and specialities. Such diversity allows for the interplay of different perspectives and experiences, which in turn disrupts consensus, so disrupting the drift towards like-mindedness. However, it is not only a business case for diversity that requires to be addressed. Arguably, more compelling is a strong moral and social case that is made by advocates of equality, diversion, and inclusion (EDI). This case emphasises the rights of individuals not to feel threatened or intimidated by differences between people but to value and promote them. In relation to work, it also promotes the belief that everyone should have an equal right to access to employment and career development, based purely on merit. These beliefs and rights are enshrined in the UN SDG goals, which form the basis of much of the work of business schools.

CASE 9.3 LINKLATERS

(used with kind permission of the Arts Council England)
Linklaters is one of the five largest global law firms in London, with its origins as far back as 1838. In 2023, it had 31 offices in 21 countries, and nearly 5600 staff, including 2550 lawyers and 560 partners. It works only on the most complex deals and cases, with 70 per cent of its work being on multi-country or multi-practice issues.

It has very strategically and consciously embraced diversity, which features in its core values statement. Some years ago, the global diversity manager put the case for diversity very simply, and in words which certainly find an echo in arts rhetoric: 'As a talent-driven organisation, Linklaters needs to attract the most talented people it can, to attract the kind of customers it wants to serve to meet its business goals.'

An even stronger business case for diversity has been developed and accepted within the organization. This responds to three external pressures as well as the case for talent. First, there is increased regulation of diversity and equality issues. Second, the media increasingly scrutinises the age, ethnicity, and gender of lawyers, especially in high-profile cases, and looks for diversity. Third, and perhaps most crucially, clients increasingly ask for diversity information – driven by their own shareholders or by regulatory contexts. Clients increasingly expect to see diverse teams working on projects, rather than all-male, all-white teams, for instance – an obvious parallel with the arts sector.

Linklaters describes itself as essentially a people business, based on relationships as well as legal expertise. Its corporate responsibility strategy is built around three pillars: colleagues, clients, and community, with diversity sitting across all three strands.

One rationale for this derives from key demographics for Linklaters. More than 40 per cent of law graduates in London are non-white, and there is now a 50-50 gender split. The workforce, especially at partner level, understandably lags behind this, but it is crucial to recruitment for the firm to demonstrate that it is taking positive steps. There are parallels with the steps taken in the cultural sector to change the face of organizations to attract those who might not have previously recognised themselves in the image of certain institutions.

Culture change is a process that takes time. Elements of working practice continue to challenge culture change, especially for the fee-earning lawyers who may find it very difficult to work flexible hours to allow for caring and child-care responsibilities. It is a highly competitive culture, with a 24/7 service to clients leading to elements of unpredictable and long-hours working, with a heavy emphasis on intellectual prowess and influence rather than a clear, structured hierarchy. Consequently, Linklaters introduced its agile working policy in 2020 empowering its staff to work 20 to 50 per cent of their working hours remotely as long as notice is given, and operational role requirements are fulfilled.

Linklaters has developed several affinity groups, including groups based on faith and gender and a lesbian, gay, bisexual, and transgender network. The latter has moved over time from being invitation-only, and run off-site, to being open, internal, and running client-focused events, sharing the development of a more diverse culture with clients and stakeholders. The faith groups began working together some years ago to run 'Faith in the City' events and collaborate with clients. Work is client- or colleague-facing rather than 'issue awareness' building: there is always a strong business rationale for activity.

Linklaters is cautious regarding the effectiveness of specific diversity training and coaching, preferring to build understanding and skills into its general approach to professional development. They network with other firms including competitors and clients to draw on others' expertise.

Sources:
based on
http://www.creativecase.org.uk/creativecase-linklaters and Linklaters website.

Question

1. What are the benefits of workforce diversity for Linklaters? How can they improve on their current approach?

THE IMPORTANCE OF NETWORKS

Networks are critical to developing and maintaining creativity and innovation (Perry-Smith & Mannucci, 2015; Townley & Beech, 2010). This is because creativity lies in organizing a system of relationships, and the act of creation depends on the system of relationships. According to systems theory, creativity is dependent on the relationships between individuals in organizations and between organizations. Networks of individuals and organizations also underpin creative, project-based work (Flew, 2012; Zhou & Rouse, 2021). Creative industries are often fragmented and consist of small creative organizations that cannot sustain the permanent employment of specialists. When faced with such fragmentation, the industry often counteracts fragmented organizational structures by fostering cooperation between organizations and individuals. Seen in this way, networks are not only used as an informal recruitment method (Burt, 2021, Van Hoye et al., 2010) but also as a way of sourcing expertise and creative input from others.

Networks in the creative industries

Creativity and innovation are crucial to all organizations. However, the sector where they are particularly important is the creative and cultural industries (Burt, 2021). The UK Government Department for Culture, Media and Sport defined creative industries as those industries that 'have their origin in individual creativity, skill and talent and which have a potential for wealth and job creation through the generation and exploitation of intellectual property' (DMCS, 2016). The creative sectors include arts, design, film, advertising, music, publishing, computer games, interactive media, TV, and radio, but they overlap with cultural industries, which also include cultural tourism, heritage, museums, libraries, and cultural events. Although classified as separate by the DMCS, creative and cultural industries sectors are similar in the type of work and the patterns of work that individuals undertake.

The nature of work in the creative and cultural industries is primarily based on a post-industrial, employment relationship (Hesmondhalgh, 2019; Zhou & Rouse, 2021), which includes portfolio careers with workers being in multiple jobs including self-employment, working freelance, or running a business. This non-linear career progression pattern does not appear to change over time and remains the same, often decades into individuals' careers. Because of the pattern, work in this sector has become increasingly precarious, i.e., uncertain, volatile, and competitive (Godart et al., 2014). To engage in creative work, individuals rely on networks as a source of economic and social benefits. Networks are said to foster collaboration, trust, and cooperation; they also lead to personal a economic advantage in the labour market. Forming and maintaining social and professional contacts has been found to be crucial in securing employment in the creative and cultural industries, but it is also important in fostering creativity and sharing knowledge.

Various studies into creativity in the creative and cultural industries draw on seminal research by Mark Granovetter (1973), who introduced the ideas of weak and strong ties. Granovetter highlighted the importance of interconnectedness among members of a social network and emphasised the role of weak ties in gaining personal advantage. 'Weak ties' are loose links that are indispensable to individuals' opportunities and their integration into communities. In contrast to weak ties, strong ties are links with close family and friends. They breed social cohesion but can lead to overall fragmentation (1973, p. 1378). Consequently, weak ties offer individuals several advantages over strong ties, for example, in finding employment opportunities. Granovetter's study also suggested that informal 'weak' ties might lead to greater innovation than strong ties. This is because strong ties are developed between people who are similar so they produce 'more of the same'; whereas weak ties may lead to the development of wider networks and promote creative thinking. This point is highly relevant to the EDI agenda and to the next approach to innovation.

The Triple Helix Model

Perhaps the best known formal model of the power of networks in creativity and innovation is the Triple Helix Model (Etzkowitz & Zhou, 2018). This model proposes a shift from single-source or dual-source innovation to one that brings the main actors of industry, government policymakers, and academia together, at local, regional, sectoral, national, and supranational levels. Of the institutional actors, universities have benefitted most from this shift in being seen as more of an equal partner than previously was the case. Indeed, at times, universities have taken the lead in commercialising their research, as Case 9.2 has shown, with its Life Sciences and Medical School/NHS TIME initiatives.

The Triple Helix Model can be found all over the world, with some well-known examples, such as the Swedish Governmental Agency for Innovative Systems and various European Union initiatives, leading the way in attempting to meet the so-called Grand Challenges of global warming, energy supply and security, poverty, water scarcity and quality, food supply and quality, ageing society, public health, international terrorism, and changes in the global economy. Yet, like all networks, they face their own grand challenges. Some of these relate to the different institutional logics (Thornton et al., 2012) governing decision-making and ways of thinking, feeling, and acting among these three actors in the Triple Helix. For example, university academics are often deeply embedded in a strong professional logic, policymakers in bureaucratic and state logics, and industry actors in market logics, so how possible is it to reach shared visions and durable ways of working together? Similarly, the notion of strong and weak ties also applies to the innovative potential of Triple Helix arrangements. Strong ties that develop among actors over a period may provide socio-emotional support for innovation, but they are also likely to lead to groupthink and a lack of diversity. Thus the 'strength of weak ties' allows for greater innovation because people with whom you have weaker ties are more likely to have useful knowledge or connections.

Recent empirical data on the strong versus weak ties debate in relation to labour market mobility has shown it is not a case of the 'weaker the better' or the 'stronger the worse' (Rajkumar et al., 2022). Innovation seemed to be associated with moderately weak ties, especially in creating job mobility between sectors in high-tech, which is seen as beneficial for transferring new knowledge.

Finally, perspective-taking theory can be applied to making networks such as the Triple Helix Model more effective but also explain potential challenges. As Ku et al. (2015, p. 79) argued, perspective taking involves 'the active cognitive process of imagining the world from another's vantage point or imagining oneself in another's shoes to understand their visual viewpoint, thoughts, motivations, intentions, and/or emotions.' Such a process can be of significant help in bringing people and organizations together to form effective collaborations with increasing collective understanding and decision-making, knowledge complexity, creativity, liking, cognitive closeness and cooperation, and decreasing prejudice and stereotyping. However, it also can result in perverse effects, such as groupthink and the weaknesses of strong ties, and preferential treatment for one group over another. Thus, for example, taken too far, it can also lead to greater stereotyping of others because one party is often asked to use stereotyping as the basis for their perspective taking of others. Finally, in contexts where collaboration is forced and better characterised by competition, perspective takers can behave more egotistically or self-serving than before.

MANAGING INNOVATION

'Innovate...or die' is a mantra of many of the executives of contemporary organizations. To avoid bankruptcy or oblivion, organizations need to develop new ideas for products, services, and processes (Tidd & Bessant, 2020). By pursuing innovation, companies stay ahead of the competition for markets and for staff. Kanter (2009) refers to the need to stay ahead as the 15-minute competitive advantage, i.e., 'changing in short fast bursts rather than waiting for the breakthrough that transforms everything.' To illustrate her point, Kanter evoked a Woody Allen comedy routine about humans' first contact with UFOs on Earth. Instead of worrying about alien civilisations that are light years away in technological advancement, humans should worry about civilisations that are just

15 minutes ahead of us – 'That way they'd always be first in line for the movies, they'd never miss a meeting with the boss…and they'd always be first in every race.'

The case study of Deutsche Bank demonstrates how the need to fend off threats from competitors leads to companies engaging in new ways of doing business.

CASE 9.3 DIGITAL INNOVATION IN DEUTSCHE BANK

Banks are under constant pressure from other businesses that take over the functions traditionally performed by banks. The main driver for innovative change has been the rapid advances in technology, especially digital and mobile solutions. These advances forced the banks to rethink the traditional model of working with clients, which mainly relied on branch banking. The launch of Apple Pay allowed iPhone users to pay with their mobile phones was one of the initiatives seen as a potential threat to the traditional banking model. Because of the competition from innovative solutions such as Apple Pay, and to improve the use of digital technology, banks around the world began to make links with so-called fintech firms (financial technology), often by investing in them (FT, 2015).

One such example was Deutsche Bank, Germany's largest bank, which decided in 2015 that it was going to open innovation hubs in London, Berlin, and Silicon Valley. The Bank's collaborators in this initiative were IBM in Silicon Valley, Microsoft in Berlin, and HCL in London. In these hubs, Deutsche Bank planned to work with start-up fintech companies and researchers from universities to develop ideas to improve internal processes and develop new products, initially planning to evaluate more than 500 start-up ideas every year. They saw this change as a way of signifying a shift away from the reliance on 'bricks-and-mortar branches' towards capitalising on novel IT systems and utilising digital capabilities. As part of this change, the Bank proposed to close about 200 of its 700 retail branches in Germany and to focus on investing up to €1bn into digital initiatives.

Henry Ritchotte, Deutsche's chief operating officer, was given responsibility for the Bank's digital transformation. This change was part of a wider programme of changes involving a management reshuffle, a recent deal with Hewlett-Packard, and other attempts to reduce the bank's cost base. Since 2015, Deutsche Bank has continued to invest in fintechs, seeing them as partners rather than competitors in the innovation process – with one big advantage over banks. They have created the role of Head of Strategy and Innovation Networks, whose present incumbent, Gil Perez, made the case for their approach to innovation:

Fintechs have one major advantage that sometimes goes under the radar – they don't need to deal with a legacy environment. They begin with an infrastructure that is modern and easy to update. They can focus on looking at financial services from a different perspective, testing new technologies and bringing their new ideas to life – in a segment where they can win.

Banks have been around a lot longer and have complexity in their technology and areas where transformation must take place. It's too risky and costly to throw it all out and start again. But as a bank, our strengths are our understanding of our industry, our ability to comply with different regulations and our global network, which has been established over a number of decades...

I strongly believe that banks and start-ups can bring their comparative advantages together.

Sources:

The Financial Times (2015) Deutsche Bank to create innovation hubs to boost technology, http://www.ft.com/cms/s/0/402ced62-09d0-11e5-a6a8-00144feabdc0.html #axzz3dyhLXrnl accessed on 24/6/2015

Deutsche Bank (2023) Banks and fintechs: potential partners, rather than competitors. https://www.db.com/what-next/digital-disruption/dossier-future-financial -industry/banks-and-fintechs-potential-partners?language_id=1

Question

1. Is Gil Perez wise in his assessment that banks such as Deutsche and fintech start-ups can work together as partners? Are there any disadvantages to this approach? Can you think of the arguments for banks to sustain the traditional branch-based ways of providing banking services?

I have already referred to the conventional way of distinguishing between three types of innovation: product, service, and process innovation (Smith, 2015). Product innovation is concerned with the development of a new product. This is usually achieved by using new technology, re-configuring old technology, or meeting new consumer needs. Service innovation focuses on the offer of a new/different service to consumers or service users, for example, new ways of online retailing, wearable technology to diagnose health and well-being levels, or online delivery of education. Process innovation is about developing new ways of making things or delivering services, such as Toyota's just-in-time production or using robotics to undertake surgical inventions.

Exercise

Think of one well-known innovation and try to answer these questions:

- What was so innovative about this product or service?
- Did it solve an existing problem?
- Who came up with the idea and when?
- What were the potential difficulties in the process of innovation?

The challenges of innovation

As mentioned earlier in the chapter, innovation is sometimes a contested terrain. Organizational change often triggers resistance on the part of employees, and so does innovation, which is sometimes seen as a threat to the established order. Resistance often comes from those who have done well under the old system and are fearful of the future, so innovative solutions to running a business may bring about risks of losing position, control, and reputation (Hatch, 2018).

It is also worth remembering that innovation is not always for the better. The Global Financial Crisis of 2007–2008 is a good example of how 'innovative banking practices' in investment banking beyond the understanding of senior management led to the collapse of many banks. The RBS case in Chapter 2 is a good example. We also found a close relationship between how senior bankers justified their practices during the Global Financial Crisis to a UK Parliamentary committee, which shared similar characteristics to the ways in which criminals legitimised their own behaviour (Siebert et al., 2020).

Finally, Case 9.4 illustrates that the perceptions of organizational initiatives aimed at innovation may be evaluated differently by different stakeholders. As the classic pluralist perspective on organizations tells us (Fox, 1966), an organization is often characterised by different rather than shared interests, and managers are wise to recognise that conflict is not always unavoidable, or even desirable.

CASE 9.4 INNOVATION IN GOOGLE

Google is a company that cultivates a culture of innovation to stay at the forefront of innovation. One of the initiatives aimed at promoting innovation in Google was the 80/20 Innovation Time Off (ITO) model.

The 80/20 ITO model, which dates to 2007, allowed Google employees to spend 80 per cent of their time on their substantive projects, and 20 per cent (which usually amounts to around one day per week) on innovation activities that are of interest to them. These activities were believed to keep employees engaged in their work, empowered, and constantly challenged to come up with new ideas. When freed from the pressures of deadlines and targets, employees were said to be more creative. As part of the programme, employees formed 'Google grouplets' comprised of engineers who shared an interest in a novel idea and aimed to work on it to bring the idea to fruition. These grouplets did not have budgets, or any decision-making powers, but were aimed at attracting individuals who were keen on pursuing innovation together.

The 80/20 ITO model was said to have built the foundations for many successful business ideas. Google claimed that many of its new products including Gmail, Google News, and AdSense came into existence because of employees' involvement in the ITO program.

Perceived as a good idea, the ITO programme was emulated in other companies, for example, HootSuite. However, the 80/20 model had its problems and was discontinued.

One of the issues was employee scepticism of Google acting in good faith. The 80/20 rule is said to violate the 'normal expectations of corporate life' (Wired), and was seen as ineffective when the organizational culture in general does not support innovation. An article in *Wired* states: 'Innovation never happens in a vacuum. Which is why the focus on the 80/20 rule is a red herring. It's merely the iceberg-tip of a much larger, and more fundamental, set of issues plaguing modern corporations.' Over time, the programme narrowed in scope, and employees who wanted to take advantage of the 20 per cent time off for innovation had to seek approval from their managers, who for the sake of efficiency and productivity were not always willing to support it.

The scepticism of the 80/20 ITO model comes from the idea that innovation cannot be achieved by giving employees time to engage in innovation activities, innovation also needs proper investment (staff and funding) and management endorsement.

Sources:

http://www.cloverleafinnovation.com/blog/secrets-innovative-companies
-innovation/

http://www.wired.com/2013/08/innovate-or-die-why-googles-8020-rule-is-a-red
-herring/

http://www.fastcompany.com/3015877/fast-feed/why-google-axed-its-20-policy

Questions

1. What are the benefits and challenges of introducing a formal innovation system such as Google's 80/20 Innovation Time Off model?

2. The 80/20 ITO model resonates with the idea of employee empowerment – employees are given more discretion in deciding how to spend 20 per cent of their time if the activities are company-related. Does empowerment necessarily enhance innovation?

KEY LEARNING POINTS

This chapter was focused on three concepts that are important for understanding the management of organizations – creativity, innovation, and teamworking. We defined the concepts, explained the differences between them, and discussed a shift away from the creativity of an individual towards more distributed conceptions of creativity as a feature of a system. While creativity is a solitary act of a talented individual, it is also a social experience, and today's theories of creativity overlap with management theories of teamwork, the study of networks, knowledge management, and organizational learning. We considered creativity and innovation through the lens of these theories. The central question raised in this chapter is whether creativity and innovation can be managed, and if so, what are the possible ways of doing it.

REVIEW QUESTIONS

1. Based on the reading of this chapter and your own observations, do you agree that creativity in organizations can be managed? If so, what are the ways in which manager can manage creativity?

2. Not all ideas are implemented and lead to innovation. What are the factors that enable or hinder innovation in organizations?

REFERENCES

Afzulur Rahim, M. (2023). *Managing conflict in organizations* (5th ed.). Routledge.

Amabile, T. (2012). *Componential theory of creativity* (Harvard Business School Working Paper, 12-096). Harvard University. https://edisciplinas.usp.br/pluginfile.php/4927777/mod_resource/content/0/TeresaAMabile.pdf

Anderson, N., Potocnik, K., & Zhou, J. (2014). Innovation and creativity in organizations: A state-of-science review, prospective commentary and guiding framework. *Journal of Management, 40*(5), 1297–1333.

Anderson, N., De Dreu, C., & Nijstad, B. (2014). The routinization of innovation research: A constructively critical review of the state-of-science. *Journal of Organizational Behavior, 25*(2), 147–173.

Andripoulos, C., & Dawson, P. (2010). *Managing change, innovation and creativity.* Sage

Antcliff, V., Saundry, R., & Stuart, M. (2007). Networks and social capital in the UK television industry: The weakness of weak ties. *Human Relations, 60*(2), 371–393.

Asch, S. E. (1956). Studies of independence and conformity: I. A minority of one against a unanimous majority. *Psychological monographs: General and Applied, 70*(9), 1–70.

Banks, M. (2007). *The politics of cultural work.* Palgrave Macmillan.

Belbin, R. M. (2000). *Beyond the team.* Butterworth-Heinemann.

Belbin, R.M. (2024). Belbin team roles. https://www.belbin.com/about/belbin-team-roles

Bilton, C. (2008). *Management and creativity: From creative industries to creative management.* Blackwell Publishing

Bilton, C., & Cummings, S. (2010). *Creative strategy: Reconnecting business and innovation.* Wiley

Bolton, R., Logan, C., & Gittell, J. H. (2021). Revisiting relational coordination: A systematic review. *Journal of Applied Behavioral Sciences, 57*(3), 290–322.

Burt, R. S. (2021). Social networking and creativity. In L. Zhou & E. D Rouse (Eds.), *Handbook of research on creativity and innovation* (pp. 82–104). Edward Elgar.

Catmull, E. (2014). *Creativity, Inc.: Overcoming the unseen forces that stand in the way of true inspiration.* Bantam Press.

Chia, R. (2014). Reflections in praise of silent transformation – allowing change through 'letting it happen'. *Journal of Change Management, 14*(1), 8–27.

Csikszentmihalyi, M. (1999). A systems perspective on creativity. In: R. J. Sternberg (ed), *Handbook of creativity.* Cambridge: Cambridge University Press, pp. 313–335.

Csikszentmihalyi, M. (2014). *The systems model of creativity: The collected works of mihaly csikszentmihalyi.* Springer. ISBN 978-94-017-9084-0

Delarue, A. Van Hootegem, G. V., Proctor, S., & Burridge, M. (2008). Teamworking and organizational performance: A review of survey-based research, *International Journal of Management Reviews, 10*(2), 127–148.

DCMS. (2016), DCMS Sectors Economic Estimates Methodology: Sector Definitions, Department for Digital, Culture, Media and Sport, https://www.gov.uk/government/publications/dcms-sectors-economic-estimates-methodology.

Drucker, P. (1988, January–February). The coming of the new organization. *Harvard Business Review*, pp. 45–53.

Edmonson, A. (2018). *The fearless organization: Creating psychological safety in the workplace.* John Wiley.

Edmondson, A. C. & Verdin, P. J. (2018). The strategic imperative of psychological safety and organizational error management. In: Hagen, J. (eds) *How could this happen?*. Palgrave Macmillan.

Etzkowitz, H., & Zhou, C. (2018). *The triple helix: University-industry-government innovation and entrepreneurship* (2nd ed.). Routledge.

Financial Times. (2015). Deutsche bank to create innovation hubs to boost technology. https://www.ft.com/content/402ced62-09d0-11e5-a6a8-00144feabdc0#axzz3dyhLXrnl

Flew, T. (2012). *The creative industries: Culture and policy.* SAGE.

Florida, R. (2002). *The rise of the creative class and how it's transforming work, leisure, community and everyday life,* Basic Books.

Fox, A. (1966). *Research papers 3: Industrial sociology and industrial relations.* Her Majesty's Stationery Office.

Gittell, J. H., Seidner, R., & Wimbush, J. (2010). A relational model of how high-performance work systems work. *Organization Science, 21*(2), 490–506. https://doi.org/10.1287/orsc.1090. 0446

Godart, F. C., Shiplov, A. V., & Claes, K. (2014). Making the most of the revolving door: The impact of outward personnel mobility networks on organizational creativity. *Organization Science, 25*(2), 377–400.

Granovetter, M. S. (1973). The strength of weak ties. *The American Journal of Sociology* 78 (6), 1360–1380

Grugulis, I., & Stoyanova, D. (2011). The missing middle: Communities of practice in a freelance labour market. *Work, Employment and Society, 25*(2), 342–351.

Guardian. (2015, 2 June) Dundee: from black sheep of Scottish cities to 'living cultural experiment'. https://www.theguardian.com/cities/2015/jun/22/dundee-scotland -design-v-and-a-culture-regeneration-minecraft-grand-theft-auto

Haas, M., & Mortensen, M. (2016). *The secrets of great teamwork. Harvard Business Review*

Hatch, M. J. (2018). *Organization theory: Modern, Symbolic, and postmodern perspectives* (4th ed.). Oxford University Press.

Hesmondhalgh, D. (2019). *The cultural industries* (4th ed.). SAGE.

Hesmondhalgh, D., & Baker, S. (2010). *Creative labour: Media work in three cultural industries.* Routledge.

Hughes, D. J., Lee, A., Wei Tian, A., Newman, A., & Legood, A. (2018). Leadership, creativity, and innovation: A critical review and practical recommendations. *The Leadership Quarterly, 29*(5), 549–569.

Kanter, R. M. (1983). *The change masters.* Touchstone.

Kanter, R. M. (2009, November 9). Find the 15-minute competitive advantage. *Harvard Business Review* . https://hbr.org/2009/11/find-the-15minute-competitive/

Kanter, R. M. (2013, January). Nine rules for stifling innovation. *Harvard Business Review.* https://hbr.org/2013/01/nine-rules-for-stifling-innova.html

Katzenbach J. R., & Smith, D. K. (1993). *The wisdom of teams: Creating the high performance organization.* Harvard Business School Press.

Kirton, M. (1984). Adaptors and innovators: Why new initiatives get blocked. *Long Range Planning, 17*(2), 137–143.

Kirton, M. (1976). Adaptors and innovators: A description and measure. *Journal of Applied Psychology, 61*(5), 622–629.

Koriat, A. (2015). When two heads are better than one and when they can be worse. The amplification hypothesis. *Journal of Experimental Psychology, 144*(5), 934–950

Ku, G., Wang, C. S., & Galinsky, A. D. (2015). The promise and perversity of perspective-taking in organizations. *Research in Organizational Behaviour, 35,* 79–102.

Mayle, D. (2006). *Managing innovation and change* (3rd ed.). Sage.

McCalman, J., Paton, R., & Siebert, S. (2015). *Change management: A guide to effective implementation* (4th ed.). Sage.

MacKay, R. B., & Chia, R. (2013). Choice, chance, and unintended consequences in strategic change: A process of understanding of the rise and fall of Northco Automotive. *Academy of Management Journal, 56*(1), 208–230.

Martin, G. & Arshed, N. (2020). How and when HR actions, behaviours, and capabilities can transform start-ups into scale-ups? *Academy of Management Proceedings.*

Martin, G., Siebert, S., & Robson, I. (2018). Conformist innovation: And institutional logics perspective on how HR executives construct business school reputations. *International Journal of Human Resource Management, 29*(13), 2027–2053.

Mortensen, M., & Hass, M. R. (2018). Perspective—rethinking teams: From bounded membership to dynamic participation. *Organization Science, 29*(2), 341–355.

OECD. (2005). Organization for economic cooperation and development *oslo manual: Guidelines for collecting and interpreting innovation data* (3rd ed.). http://www.oecd

.org/sti/inno/oslomanualguidelinesforcollectingandinterpretinginnovationdata3 rdedition.htm .

Perry-Smith, J., & Mannucci, P. V. (2015). Social networks, creativity, and entrepreneurship. In C. E. Shelley, M. A. Hitt, & J. Zhou (Eds.), *The Oxford handbook of creativity, innovation, and entrepreneurship* (pp. 205–234). Oxford University Press.

Peters, T. (1989), *Thriving on chaos*. Pan.

Rajkumar, K., Saint-Jaques, G., Bojinov, J., Brynjolfsson, E., & Aral, S (2022). A causal test of the strength of weak ties. *Science, 377*(6612), 1304–1310.

Senior, B. (1997). Team roles and team performance: Is there really a link? *Journal of Occupational and Organizational Psychology, 70,* 241–258.

Senior, B., Swailes, S., & Carnall, C. (2020). *Organisational change* (6th ed.). Financial Times Pearson.

Siebert, S., Martin, G., & Simpson, G. (2020). Rhetorical strategies of legitimation in the professional field of banking. *Journal of Professions and Organization, 7*(2), 134–155.

Smith, D. (2015). *Exploring innovation* (3rd ed.). McGraw Hill.

Straub, V.J. Tsvetkova, M., & Yasseri, T. (2023). The cost of coordination can exceed the benefit of collaboration in performing complex tasks. *Collective Intelligence, 2*(2). https://doi.org/10.1177/26339137231156912

Thornton, P. H., Ocasio, W., & Lounsbury, M. (2012). *The institutional logics perspective: A new approach to culture, structure and process.* Oxford University Press.

Tidd, J., & Bessant, J. (2020). *Managing innovation: Integrating technological, market and organizational change* (7th ed.). Wiley.

Torr, G. (2008). *Managing creative people: Lessons in leadership for the ideas economy.* Wiley.

Townley, B., & Beech, N. (2010). *Managing creativity? Exploring the paradox.* Cambridge University Press.

van Dierendonck, D., & Groen, R. (2011). Belbin revisited: A multitrait–multimethod investigation of a team role instrument. *European Journal of Work and Organizational Psychology, 20*(3), 345–366.

Van Hoye, G., van Hooft, E. A. J. & Lievens, F. (2010). Networking as a job search behaviour: a social networkperspective. *Journal of Occupational and Organizational Psychology, 82,* 661–682.

Von Wittich, D., & Antonakis, J. (2011). The KAI cognitive style inventory: Was it personality all along? *Personality and Individual Differences, 50*(70), 1044–1049.

Wilson, F. (2014). *Organizational behaviour and work; A critical introduction* (4th ed.). Oxford University Press.

Zhou, L., & Rouse, E. D. (2021). *Handbook of research on creativity and innovation.* Edward Elgar.

CHAPTER 10

Managing organizational change and culture

LEARNING OBJECTIVES

By the end of this chapter, you should be able to:

- Understand the issues facing managers in attempting wholesale organizational change.
- Apply different change models to the process of managing organizational change.
- Understand different perspectives on organizational culture change and the problems involved in changing organizational cultures.
- Apply culture change frameworks to organizational culture change problems.
- Propose workable principles of organizational change and the evaluation of change initiatives.

INTRODUCTION

I began this book by examining the nature of management and managers and their roles in a changing world. Following this, we looked at the key contexts of change in contemporary business. In the model of management in Chapter 2, I identified three levels at which managers operate: the individual level, the team level, and the organizational level. I also examined the issues of managing at these different levels in some detail. It remains to examine the change process itself because it is often in this implementation phase that many good ideas fail or remain only good ideas. So, what can managers do to ensure that the changes they introduce, whether they are changes in strategies, systems, products, or processes, become effectively embedded in their organizations?

To begin a discussion on this question, let's look at a case research project that I researched some years ago. This case is as relevant today as it was all those years ago because it shows the impact of some of the contexts discussed in the book – technology, corporate reputation, internationalisation, and knowledge management. It also highlights

DOI: 10.4324/9781003469711-10

some of the problems of managing individual–organizational linkages. I was able to research the case in depth over a long period of time and know the outcomes of the change initiatives. My findings may help you understand how the processes and outcomes of change initiatives are embedded in context and specific time frames. This message will be an important one in this chapter because, as I have already argued, there is no one best practice or way of managing large-scale change; the best we can point to is a series of 'promising practices' that must be related to the context, time, and space when they are applied. We shall look at this idea in more depth at the end of the chapter. After reading the case, I would like you to work through the change frameworks discussed in the two subsequent sections. These frameworks will provide a set of practical tools with which to understand this and other major change problems you may meet in your working lives.

CASE 10.1 AT&T AND NCR: A CLASSIC CASE OF ATTEMPTING TO DEVELOP A GLOBAL BRAND THROUGH CULTURE CHANGE

The history and context of the change programme

The following case is a classic and somewhat typical example of culture change attempted by the headquarters of a US-based multinational enterprise (MNE), which we researched in the early 2000s. We can learn a lot about studying such a case because the outcome is well-known. For those of you who are interested in finding out what happened to the company later, you might want to refer to the company's website.

The case study plant began life as a subsidiary of NCR, a mid-western-based US multinational enterprise (MNE) that underwent significantly changed fortunes during the period 1945–1979. During this period, when the UK plant was used largely as a second-source manufacturing facility to US plants, employment rose dramatically to 6300 employees in 1970 but fell to 820 people in 1980 following a decline in traditional markets. At that time, there were strong rumours the plant was scheduled for closure.

However, by the time of the launch of the cultural change programme in the mid-1990s, the fortunes of the Scottish subsidiary had turned around dramatically, associated with what came to be known locally as the 'Fortress Dundee' policy, in which local management sought and fought for 'independence through local success.' By 1985, it had acquired a significant design and development facility and had become NCR's headquarters for the newly created Self-Service and Financial Systems Division, which designed and developed automatic teller machines (ATMs) for the banking industry. In short, it had turned the tables on its US sister plants and had become something of a star in the US parent company's portfolio of assets. The Scottish subsidiary consistently outperformed sister NCR plants in the USA and Canada as measured by the rate of return on assets, which grew from 54 per cent in 1984 to a yearly average of over 100 per cent from 1987 to 1992. In 2004, it was still the world's leading designer and producer of ATMs, employing some 1700 assembly workers, managers, and design and development engineers (including the largest private sector development community in Scotland), and won the 'Best Factory in Britain' award on two occasions.

This brief history of the changing fortunes of the Scottish subsidiary shows how it became increasingly independent of NCR corporate headquarters for resources. Furthermore, there was a history of opposition or reluctant compliance by the Scottish subsidiary to previous headquarters' initiatives on HRM practices. Much of this reluctance stemmed from headquarters' unsympathetic attitudes towards trade unions, which frequently posed problems for the local management of the highly unionised Scottish plant. This uneasy relationship between corporate and local subsidiary management played itself out in various ways over time. There was local subsidiary criticism and reluctance to adopt certain heavily American HRM practices (e.g., the content and terminology of employee attitude questionnaires), and there was corporate-level coolness towards certain home-grown initiatives in the Scottish subsidiary intended to forge a closer working relationship with its union representatives.

AT&T'S TAKEOVER AND ITS CULTURE CHANGE PROGRAMME

Events in the marketplace in the early 1990s had a major impact on the Dundee company's fortunes. AT&T acquired the NCR Corporation in 1991 following a hostile takeover bid. Initially, the headquarters management of AT&T followed a strategy of controlling only the financial direction of NCR and not its product-market strategy, allowing the Scottish plant to function as a semi-independent unit, largely because its product range fell outside top management's main interests. However, after an agreed period of two years of little or no strategic intervention, AT&T's corporate management team sought to engineer a radical change throughout the corporation using a global branding strategy in which the name of NCR would be exorcised from its history and replaced by AT&T – Global Information Solutions (AT&T (GIS)). This radical change was also viewed to be necessary by headquarters because of the large financial losses incurred by virtually every business unit in NCR that is, apart from the Scottish subsidiary, its only *profitable* arm.

AT&T's president brought in Jerre Stead, a new US-based president for AT&T (GIS), largely because of his high-profile track record in turning around an ailing electrical contracting company and another AT&T unit. Strongly influenced by an American academic guru, the new president sought to re-engineer AT&T (GIS) through a major attempt at 'rebranding', an organizational identity/culture change programme. This rebranding process was marked by: (1) letting go of many of the NCR management team in the USA; (2) developing a more strategic and 'hands-on' approach to strategy and tactics, rather than the purely financial control focus of the previous NCR management team in Dayton; and (3) introducing a cultural change programme that placed employees and customers at the heart of the new corporation's policies. The programme involved two central elements. The first was christened the 'Common Bond': this included a best practice, ethical mission statement, a new values framework, and a set of working principles designed to 'empower employees and customers.' The ethical and empowering features of this programme are worth emphasising at this stage because it has been argued that the 'mutuality model' of HRM (based on treating people with respect) was more likely to lead employees to view the effort positively and accept company actions that might have negative consequences for a minority of employees. Second, the programme involved a further flattening of organizational structures and an attempt to empower the local managers and workforce by, among other techniques, relabelling managers and supervisors as 'coaches' and workers as 'associates'. The list below provides further details of the cultural change programme.

KEY ELEMENTS OF THE CULTURAL CHANGE PROGRAMME

'Opportunities, vision, and values'

1. 'Common Bond' values:
   - respect for individuals;
   - dedication to helping customers;
   - highest standards of integrity;
   - innovation; and
   - teamwork.

2. Accompanying education/communication sessions:
   - opportunity and change: create an awareness of the forces of change and how each associate, by understanding the dynamics of change, could take advantage of the opportunities that arose; and
   - vision and direction forum: to ensure that all associates would understand, through interactive discussions, the major issues affecting the company.

3. Supporting actions:
   - further attempts to flatten the organizational hierarchy;
   - coach and associate labels assigned;
   - casual dress policy introduced;
   - introduction of diversity and harassment policies;
   - employee feedback sessions implemented based on repeated surveys;
   - establishment of a 24 hours a day hotline to the US president and Common Bond champion; and
   - introduction of a new company magazine.

It is important to emphasise five key characteristics of the rebranding and culture change programme:

1. The programme was very much a personalised one that was driven by the new US president of AT&T (GIS), Jerre Stead – and the external US academic consultant who worked closely with him. Although a small number of UK managers were incorporated into the design of the programme, none were from the Scottish subsidiary.

2. The programme was viewed by local management in the Scottish subsidiary as a US-originated and orientated programme. This was because: (a) it was driven

by the two US nationals from headquarters; (b) the language and content of the programme were very US-centric in nature; and (c) its track record of success was based on two US organizations formerly managed by the new appointee.

3. This sense of US parentage was markedly enhanced by an absence of prior consultation and discussion with local management in the Scottish subsidiary, apart from some HRM staff. Quite simply, the views of the prominent and well-respected local CEO, Jim Adamson, and many of his staff had not been sought on the appropriateness of the change initiative in the Scottish context.

4. The president and lead consultant had set themselves very ambitious deadlines for launching the change programme. The stipulated timetable was couched in months rather than years.

5. The president of AT&T (GIS), Jerre Stead, who championed the cultural change programme, remained with the organization for only 18 months. Following his departure, his successor failed to continue to endorse the programme.

Question

1. How do you think the Scottish management team and the workforce would have reacted to the programme?

MODELS OF ORGANIZATIONAL CHANGE

To help you understand the problems raised by this attempt at a wholesale, organization-wide rebranding and identity reconstruction, and to predict the response of employees, you will need a more in-depth understanding of the organizational and cultural change processes. There are several such models and texts on the topic to help you do so (e.g., Burke, 2024; Burnes, 2017; Senior et al., 2020). In these next two sections, I have brought together two generic models used to analyse and guide the process of strategic change in complex organizations, followed by one that deals specifically with culture change. The first generic one, the *intervention strategy model*, has undergone several revisions in a standard text on change. The second one, the strategic change process model, was developed by myself and a colleague, originally based on research into several multinational enterprises but has been updated to reflect some of my recent research into the healthcare sector and scaleup organizations.

The intervention strategy model

The intervention strategy model (ISM), developed by McCalman et al. (2015), is based on the idea of an open systems approach, which we met earlier in this course when discussing technology and people management. An open systems approach views organizations as a series of interlinked and interdependent elements and components of systems and subsystems. However, in defining a system, we should understand the motives and values of those providing the definition and their purposes in providing it because what might be defined as a system in one case may be little more than a component of a much wider system. McCalman et al. (2015) use an example of the motor vehicle, which is made up of a series of elements, such as a gearshift to facilitate driver/ gearbox interaction; components, such as a fuel pump, the job of which is to provide petrol to the combustion chamber; subsystems, such as the gearbox, which is there to engage and influence the driving force of the vehicle; or the engine, which is designed to provide the driving force. Then there is the driver, who manages and controls the technical system. Note that, from the perspective of a car designer, the vehicle itself can be viewed as the complete system to transport people and their luggage/goods. However, from the perspective of transport engineers, the car is only a small part of a wider transport system, comprising roads, rail, waterways, air routes, and so on. From the perspective of the car designer, this wider transport system is its external environment. Note also that this kind of system is a sociotechnical system, comprising a technological subsystem and a human subsystem, the two having to be designed to operate in balance. The same type of analysis can be applied in the healthcare sector. Large hospitals in the acute sector, which are often the focus of much of the attention by the press and public, are increasingly being treated by governments for resource allocation purposes as only one component of a much larger and more complex health and social care system that needs to move away from being an 'ill-health' system. There is a greater focus on health prevention and dealing with public health issues, which often have their roots in economic and health inequalities. This change in focus has important implications for professional autonomy, power, and prestige in areas such as medicine (Martin et al., 2021).

Open systems have certain key properties that it is important to understand in an organizational context. The first of these is *system autonomy*, which refers to the process of mapping out the boundaries of the system and its environment (see the comments on 'problem definition' later in this section). As suggested in the previous paragraph, these boundaries depend on the purposes of the exercise and the person or persons conducting it. The main point when mapping out organizational systems is to ensure that all nonessential relationships are excluded, and all essential ones are included. As McCalman et al. (2015) point out, a *change environment* must include all systems and subsystems directly and indirectly affected. Our healthcare illustration is a good example of such systems thinking, with public health and the care system becoming more important in public policy discussions.

The second key property is *system behaviour*, which refers to three factors:

- The physical processes of the system itself (e.g., how patients are moved through the healthcare system from the 'front door' to the 'back door'– patient flows).
- The communication processes used to handle and transfer information within and between systems (the healthcare system bureaucracy, command centres, bed planning, in-and-out-patient services, workforce planning, HRM, etc.).
- The monitoring processes that maintain the system's stability (e.g., clinical targets, patient safety, workforce targets, risk, and audit reporting systems).

Or, to take an example from a motor vehicle manufacturing plant, we can identify: (a) the physical processes, for example, the speed and nature of a moving assembly line; (b) the communications systems, which plan and provide the assembly-line manufacturing system with the correct materials and amount of labour; and (c) the monitoring systems of production control and quality control, which ensure that what is being produced is on time, at the right cost, and of the right quality.

By examining these linkages, we can determine the extent to which the systems are interdependent and likely to behave in relation to one another. A systems analysis of any change programme should begin with a detailed understanding of these linkages and the change environment or context in which they operate. So, for example, one of the most serious problems facing the healthcare system in the UK is 'bed-blocking' because patients who are otherwise capable of being discharged from hospitals are unable to be released because of a lack of capacity in the social care system to treat them at home with appropriate care packages. This problem at the 'back end' of the chain has major implications at the front end of the chain in creating problems in emergency medicine and a lack of ward space to support in-patient services such as orthopaedic surgery and hospital-based mental health provision.

Thus, a systems approach such as the ISM has the potential to address such problems by providing a set of basic investigative techniques built around the notion of open systems and their key properties. It is linked to three stages of system intervention:

Stage 1: Problem definition
1. Clarifying the objectives of the change.
2. Capturing data and performance indicators.
3. Diagnosing system properties.

Stage 2: The evaluation and design phase
4. Analysing the system.
5. Determining options or solutions.
6. Evaluating options or solutions.

Stage 3: The implementation phase
7. Implementing the chosen option or solution.
8. Appraisal and monitoring.

Problem definition

In stage 1, the objectives of the change and the general problem environment must be made clear. This is followed by a thorough analysis and evaluation of the system and its environment. Thus, for example, it has become common to refer to an entrepreneurial ecosystem, which refers to the actors and factors that coordinate to create entrepreneurial activity and innovation in a regional system. One major problem sometimes encountered at this stage concerns our ability to map out the environment in relation to the organizational systems (Hatch, 2018). Many senior organizational analysts, managers, and entrepreneurs, when asked to discuss their environment, tend to place themselves at the centre of their world and construct (or literally enact) a picture of their environment or ecosystem as revolving around them or radiating from their system. For example, if we asked you to draw a picture of your organization and its environment, it is likely that you would construct something like Figure 10.1. However, the danger of thinking in this way is that the system and its managers become self-referential and egocentric: all analysis and action is made and taken in relation to the organizational system or entrepreneurial firm itself, without stepping outside of the 'centre circle'. To return to our healthcare example, many specialist doctors in the acute sector of healthcare are likely to interpret ecosystem problems as a lack of resources in the acute hospital sector (Martin, Staines et al., 2023), general practitioners (family doctors), community health, and social workers may see it from the perspective of a lack of resources in primary care and the social care sector; whereas public health specialists may see it as a health prevention and education problem, best addressed before people have to use the health and social care system.

So, unless your organization or system is literally in the centre of the circle, say the dominant market player or the headquarters of a highly centralised company, perhaps a more accurate construction of the environment for most organizations would be to place themselves more towards the periphery, while major new competitors, suppliers, customers, service users, or even overseas subsidiaries are at the centre, and the organization and/or its senior managers are at the periphery (see Figure 10.2).

Perhaps the main player in the industry, B, might be a close competitor, while C might be the head office or a key subsidiary division.

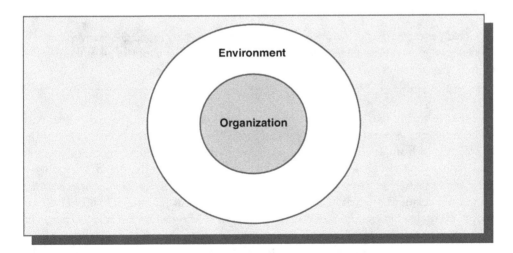

FIGURE 10.1 The egocentric perspective on organizational–environmental relations

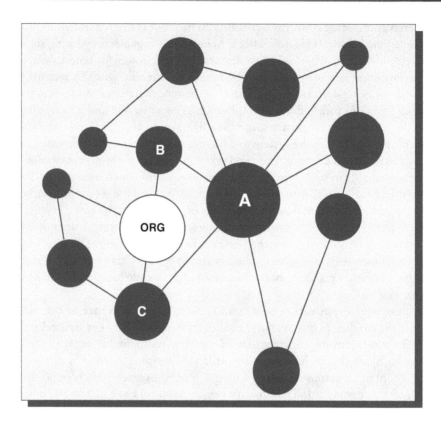

FIGURE 10.2 A more realistic perspective on organizational–environmental relations (*Source*: adapted from Hatch, 2018)

Exercise 10.1

Could Jerre Stead and his advisers have interpreted the organization–environment relationship in a different way that might have helped them avoid some of the problems they encountered? If so, what might this interpretation look like?

Perspective taking has become an important capability among managers to deal with their biases and egocentricity (Ku et al., 2015). This refers to the process of 'imagining the world from another's vantage point or imagining oneself in another's shoes to understand their visual viewpoint, thoughts, motivations, intentions, and/or emotions'. Perspective taking has many claimed benefits such as improved leadership, interpersonal and group relations, cooperative negotiations, and ethical judgements and behaviour. However, it also has potential perverse effects, such as reducing fairness in treatment because of an increased likelihood of giving preferential treatment to people whose shoes you have stepped into, or who you positively stereotype. Awareness of such cognitive biases is critical to effective perspective taking.

The evaluation and design phase

During the evaluation and design phase, organizational change specialists should use the data they collect to analyse the problems in context and arrive at a set of possible solutions. These solutions should then be evaluated. One of the most useful techniques for undertaking evaluation is scenario writing or planning (Ramirez & Wilkinson, 2016). Although forecasting the future has a notoriously poor reputation, organizational change specialists can and need to ask sensible questions about their possible future(s) so that they can anticipate problems and produce possible solutions. Creating strategic scenarios or scenario planning has become an accepted method of engaging with the future by asking such questions and using a more discursive approach than traditional forecasting techniques. Scenario planning has been used effectively in diverse situations, such as Shell Oil's attempt to deal with oil price rises during the 1990s, to stimulate debate on the future of South Africa, and, more recently, to identify potential 'white spaces' between the old and new economies and old and new industries. For example, we were involved in a large-scale, 'what-if' scenario planning exercise for the nascent Scottish online learning industry that helped local companies and education institutions develop more adaptive and relevant strategies for innovating in education and training, many years before COVID-19 forced these organizations to move online (Bell et al., 2004).

Most of the expertise in this field lies not so much in the academic domain as in the large consulting companies. Thus, it is worth quoting Global Business Network (GBN) at length on strategic scenarios because they are acknowledged to be one of the leading consultancy organizations in this field. This consulting company grew out of the well-known Royal Dutch/Shell scenario planning group, whose work in the 1990s promoted the use of this approach.

> Scenarios are tools for ordering one's perceptions about alternative future environments in which today's decisions might be played out. In practice, scenarios resemble a set of stories, written or spoken, built around carefully constructed plots. Stories are an old way of organizing knowledge; when used as strategic tools, they confront denial by encouraging, in fact requiring, the willing suspension of disbelief. Stories can express multiple perspectives on complex events; scenarios give meaning to these events.

Scenarios are powerful planning tools precisely because the future is unpredictable. Unlike traditional forecasting or market research, scenarios present alternative images instead of extrapolating current trends from the present. Scenarios also embrace qualitative perspectives and the potential for sharp discontinuities that econometric models exclude. Consequently, creating scenarios requires decision-makers to question their broadest assumptions about the way the world works so they can foresee decisions that might be missed or denied.

Within an organization, scenarios provide a common vocabulary and an effective basis for communicating complex – sometimes paradoxical – conditions and options. Good scenarios are plausible and surprising, they have the power to break old stereotypes, and their creators assume ownership and put them to work. Using scenarios is rehearsing the future. By recognizing the warning signs and the drama that is unfolding, one can avoid surprises, adapt, and act effectively. Decisions which have been pre-tested against a range of what fate may offer are more likely to stand the test of time, produce robust and resilient strategies, and create distinct competitive advantage. Ultimately, the result of scenario planning is not a more accurate picture of tomorrow but better thinking and an ongoing strategic conversation about the future.

(http://www.gbn.org/AboutScenariosDisplayServlet.srv)

Exercise 10.2

1 The so-called 'law of the instrument' (Kaplan, 1964) states that if you 'give a small boy a hammer and he will find that everyting he encounters needs pounding', or 'every problem becomes a nail.' Does this comment apply to Jerre Stead and his advisers?

2 Apart from the change strategy they chose, what alternative scenarios could Stead and his team have envisaged at the time of the design of the programme?

The implementation phase

Assuming you have followed the advice provided in the two previous phases and you have arrived at a sensible change strategy, there is still no guarantee of success. In fact, many writers in the field of strategy suggest that it is during this third implementation phase that most trouble occurs and where most change programmes fail (Burke, 2024; Burnes, 2017; Senior et al., 2020). Getting the balance right between *thinking* and *doing* (or strategy and action) is a very difficult problem, often with too much emphasis given to the former and not enough to the latter.

Let's go back to the idea of organizations enacting their environments through their sensemaking and behaviour. Enactment refers to how organizations make decisions about what features of their world to focus on, how they collectively define these features, and how they account for and shape these features. For example, we might ask: What aspects of the external change environment did Jerre Stead and his advisers choose to focus on? Could they have made sense of their environment or ecosystem in a different way, perhaps using scenario planning techniques or perspective taking discussed above, which would have allowed them to construct alternative scenarios that reflected local norms? By way of illustration, had they been less US- and head office-centric, could they have created a more accurate picture of the organization and its problems, one that would have allowed them to see the potential for the problems they would create in Scotland, their key subsidiary location? The central point of this message is that managers are active agents, not merely passive recipients or 'puppets' of abstract and external market or institutional forces. Good managers understand how to enact their environment through more intuitive and creative interpretations, re-definitions, and actions (Weick, 2001).

To this end, Weick argued managers are often better advised to 'act their way into thinking' by taking smaller, incremental steps to learn from them, rather than by 'thinking their way into acting' through top-down, transformational planning strategies such as those depicted in the AT&T case. The dangers of a top-down, planning-then-action approach are threefold. First, by making big changes, there is little chance for learning to occur because you don't really know which of the many system components of the change had the most effect. Second, big change involves big commitments and locking oneself into a course of action from which there is no retreat. Third, by constructing a plan that is complex, managers can fall into the trap of 'paralysis by analysis'. Many organizations that spend most of their time analysing and planning often end up like 'rabbits caught in the lights of a car', taking no action at all, either because they don't leave enough time or because they can't decide what to do. In this scenario, planning and strategy-making become the 'endgame', not the means to achieve success.

Think about this example, which is a story borrowed by Karl Weick to illustrate this point and a further, important one. A group of Italian soldiers are out on a winter exercise in the Alps and get lost. They are on the verge of dying in extreme weather conditions when one of them finds a map that points to a direction to go in. They end up safe, but when they get back to base, they find that the map is of the Dolomites, a completely different mountain range, and not the Alps. The moral of this tale is twofold. First, a map is a representation of the territory, not the territory itself. So, it is extremely important to understand that planning is no substitute for doing, and no representation can capture the nuances of life on the ground. Second, one can argue that the real function of the map is to get you going, or 'acting your way into thinking': more like 'fire, ready, aim' as Tom Peters, the management guru put it some years ago. Perhaps too much of a belief in the strategic planning model of management – and all students and managers should take note – is a dangerous thing because you can confuse simple theories (or maps), such as the ubiquitous two-by-two models found in strategy, with reality itself (the territory). Or even worse, as some generals in battle have found out from spectacular and costly failures, their abstract plans may even become objectified as the concrete (real) territory, sometimes labelled the 'fallacy of misplaced concreteness' (Whitehead, 1929) – in which they fight out their battles from headquarters without ever setting foot on the ground. This 'arm's length, officer class' managerialism is one of the dangers associated with having business analysts/planners remote from the day-to-day operations of a business.

The strategic change process model

The second model is one based on our earlier research into the problems of change and change agents at different levels in a range of multinational organizations (Martin & Beaumont, 2001; Martin et al., 2003). Since then, we have developed it further (Martin et al., 2018; Martin et al., 2021) to include more recent research into institutional logics and institutional entrepreneurship (Thornton et al., 2012). The model (see Figure 10.3) complements the ISM framework by explaining the implementation stage in more detail. It focuses on the complex set of events, activities, linguistic practices, emotions, and reactions that help explain:

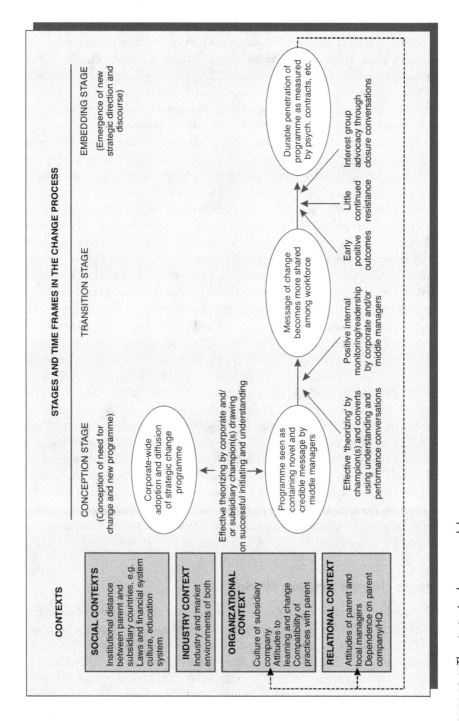

FIGURE 10.3 The strategic change model

(*Source*: based on Martin & Beaumont, 2001, Martin et al., 2018)

- What would be needed for successful change to occur in organizations.
- Why many top-down change initiatives are rarely successful in embedding change in organizations.

Much of the value of this model lies in seeing strategy as sensemaking – a convincing narrative or story that managers and employees co-construct and use to give a sense of mission and purpose to themselves and key stakeholders (Martin & Arshed, 2023). The notion of discourse and change conversations plays a major part in this model.

Box 10.1 Definition: the view of strategy as narrative

Rather than seeing strategy as a set of plans with an objective reality, strategy is sometimes better conceived as stories that managers construct to guide and provide a sense of purpose to key stakeholders, including employees, customers, service users, suppliers, investors, and so on. In effect, they are sensegiving stories (Martin et al., 2023). The most effective strategic stories or strategic discourses are *novel*, *credible*, and *compelling* for others to follow. By discourse, we mean a set of communicative or sensegiving practices that are closely linked to the purposes and interests of powerful groups such as senior managers. Discursive practices in management include strategic conversations that managers use to promote change. Four types of strategic conversation have been identified that effective managers use to promote their change initiatives, all of which involve sensegiving, sensemaking, and, sometimes, sensebreaking:

- *Initiating conversations* are used to get the change process underway, which include assertions, directives, promises, and so on that engage employees and outline what is needed for the organization to succeed in the future. Sometimes these can involve sensebreaking to establish a 'burning platform' for change, i.e., if we don't change, the consequences are going to be dire.
- *Understanding conversations* are used to test the reality of the change propositions and to generate involvement. These conversations focus on claims, evidence, and theories of cause and effect (if we do this, we shall achieve this) to help employees and others understand what managers feel is needed and what will result for the organization and for them. Often, such conversations are aimed at legitimising organizational identities, 'who we are', 'who we want to be', and 'who we definitely do not want to be' (Martin et al., 2018, 2021).
- *Performance conversations* are used to generate action. They focus on conversations, promises, and directives that are intended to produce results (Ford & Ford, 1995). One often used tactic in new ventures is the David versus Goliath rhetoric, used to convince employees that although their company might be small and a new player but that, with real effort, they can knock over the established giants of the industry (Martin et al., 2023).
- *Closure conversations* are assertions and declarations used to signify the successful (or unsuccessful) completion and 'celebration' of the change process. Such conversations must be supported by evidence to give employees hope of achieving a successful future.

Although the model was originally developed to explain the process of strategic change in multinational organizations, such as the one in our AT&T and NCR case study, it can easily be adapted to analyse all forms of complex organization involving centre-subsidiary relations such as those discussed in Chapter 4. To incorporate the problems of managing across international boundaries, we have included the societal context. This refers to the differences in institutional logics (Thornton et al., 2012) between a parent company's home country and those of the countries of subsidiary units, such as the Scottish plant in our case study. Often, national cultures differ according to the logics that dominate decision-making. These include the market, corporate, religious, state, professional, and family logics. Thus, for example, the four regions that make up the National Health Service in the UK differ according to the extent to which market logics shape sector policies and practices. In Scotland, which has devolved powers for health, market logics play less of a role than in the English NHS, whereas the state in the form of the Scottish Government plays a more directive role in managing strategy and operations in the health service in Scotland (Martin et al., 2021).

The key features and stages of the model are as follows:

1. *Receptive contexts for change.* These contexts or situational logics are especially important for successful strategic change to become embedded in complex organizations (Chia & Holt, 2023). In addition to the societal context I have just described, we can identify four others, the industry or sector context, the organizational context, and the relational context. The nature of the industry or sector in a particular locality or country and its environment is important in explaining change, as we saw in Chapter 4 in the case of Innovative Petroleum Engineering, with the different market circumstances between the US parent and the European subsidiary. The organizational context must also be considered. In a multinational environment, this refers to the differences in organizational cultural values, attitudes to issues such as learning, and compatibility of practices between the parent and subsidiaries. These intra-organizational differences are potentially relevant in explaining the success or failure of corporate-wide initiatives such as the branding of firms (Martin et al., 2021). Finally, the attitudes of local managers, including their sense of 'place' as an influence on their identity (Martin, Schreven et al., 2023), and their relative power in relation to the parent company or head office will shape the reception of change programmes, again, as we also saw in the case of Innovative in Chapter 4.

   It is also important to note that the process aspects of the model (the various stages, patterns of events, and language practices) are embedded in these changing contexts over time. This is particularly true of major culture and HR changes, such as the study we undertook in the UK North Sea oil industry (discussed in Chapter 3), in which legislative change in the UK during 1999 left the subsidiaries of multinational drilling companies operating in the UK open to claims for union recognition for the first time since the 1970s (Martin et al., 2003). Despite strong initial resistance from the US headquarters of several of the firms in the industry, a successful and arguably more sophisticated and stable form of employee relations has evolved, based on union recognition and collective bargaining. In that study, we argued that the positive early engagement and experience with the union created the receptive context for further changes towards union recognition and dissipating the anti-union stance and policies of these US-based headquarters of the drilling companies. Without this positive atmosphere created by the unions, further progress would have been impossible.

2. *The conception stage.* This is the stage during which new strategies and new strategic discourses or stories are developed. Note that the process model allows for two-way development of strategic changes in which the ideas are just as likely to come from middle managers, HR specialists, and internal/external change consultants. High-level corporate support, adoption, and sponsorship of the change discourse and programmes are a necessary, but not sufficient, condition for further progress towards successful change.

3. *The transition stage.* For the key messages of change to progress to the transition stage, credible and novel culture changes and HRM strategies (occurring in, and through, effective communications) must be read positively by all levels of management, including main board, subsidiary, and middle-level operational managers. In a study we conducted on ABB, it was evident that the managers in certain subsidiaries of one of the company's major divisions became highly skilled at denying the need for change, using many examples of why such changes in culture were unnecessary and difficult to implement in their specific circumstances (Martin, Beaumont et al., 1998). Chris Argyris (1993) has labelled this process of using skilled communication to deny problems *skilled incompetence.* This is one of the principal reasons for organizational resistance to change, because managers, often for the first time in years, are asked to question the very assumptions on which they have traditionally operated. One of the main reasons for the failure of many programmes of change is that employees are subject to a constant stream of unfinished managerial fads and fashions being forced upon them. Thus, employees become adept at ignoring these programmes of change, most of which have little impact and regularly fail to become embedded in the organization. However, these incomplete programmes, based on fads and fashions in management, result in increased levels of cynicism towards future change initiatives (Pate et al., 2000).

4. *The embedding stage.* For the message of change to continue to progress towards the embedding stage, where a new strategic discourse of change has taken root, the communication of early positive outcomes, supported by evidence of its benefits, is necessary to overcome continued resistance or, often more likely, the kind of benign neglect by employees that often accompanies change programmes. The notion of 'early wins' is one of the most important and enduring in the change literature; it suggests that small-scale experiments and initiatives rather than wholesale, top-down programmes are the best way forward. One of the few near certainties in business is that 'big change invokes big opposition', so it is often necessary to identify the groups that you 'trial out'. We also refer to measures of the extent to which the messages of change are embedded in an organization. Excellent examples of such measures are the state of psychological contracts and the extent of commitment, identification, and psychological ownership of the changes (see Chapters 3 and 6).

5. *The feedback stage.* This stage is critical for continuous change in the organization, during which the outcomes of strategic innovations are fed back into the organizational contexts – particularly new employee attitudes and behaviours, the capacity of employees to unlearn, change, and innovate, and positive attitudes towards the ways in which changes were implemented. This positive feedback loop is likely to set the tone for the reception of future change initiatives. In a study we conducted of a Scottish-based textile company (Martin, Staines et al., 1998), we noted how previously negative experiences with change programmes had led employees to develop strong feelings of cynicism towards senior managers and their efforts to introduce continuous changes in work practices. Such cynicism made future change initiatives almost impossible to implement. This negative spiral of cynicism and resistance to further change has been evident in much of our research into doctors in the NHS (Martin et al., 2021, Martin, Schreven et al., 2023).

The strategic change process model and eight guidelines for evaluating and managing strategic change in organizations

Drawing on my research with various colleagues over several decades, I have developed eight guidelines that might help managers evaluate and manage successful strategic change. These correspond to the four stages discussed above.

The conception stage

1. Without a convincing story and narrative for change, sometimes known as a strategic narrative (Nonaka & Yamaguchi, 2022), which is effectively conceived and put into practice by corporate or mid-level management champions, corporate-wide adoption and the diffusion of major change initiatives are unlikely to progress beyond the conception stage. A novel, credible and compelling story needs to be told and 'fleshed out'. However, it is not always the senior managers that need to do the fleshing out. Much of the advice in this area suggests that broad guidelines, missions, and values are set out but there must be something left for middle managers and employees to contribute to, especially at the level of operational detail. In other words, mission statements may need to be intentionally *equivocal* to allow for employee and middle manager involvement in setting direction.

2. The strategic narrative, the story of the change, and the accompanying narrative of how the story is told should draw on the conversations in Box 10.1, including:
   • Realistic *initiating conversations* set out the reasons for the change.
   • *Understanding conversations*, including those that are directed at enhancing the credibility and novelty of the assertions, the declarations and promises made at the early stages, and the rationale, legitimacy, and evidence used to support these assertions.
   • The *likely actions and benefits* that will result from the proposed changes, especially those that address the 'what's in it for me' question.

3. The messages of change, as set out by leaders, must be interpreted and enacted positively by lower-level managers as containing a credible, compelling, and novel message

to secure their acceptance of the change programme. Active listening, perspective taking, genuine dialogue, and seeking feedback at an early stage of any proposed changes should be sought by senior managers.

The transition stage

4. In the absence of a credible, compelling, and novel message, other corporate and middle managers not yet involved in the change process are unlikely to have the incentive to read the story in a positive light. Instead, they are likely to look for reasons for the changes to be discontinued, resisted, or ignored. Often, middle managers and employees in subsidiaries or on the periphery of organizations become highly skilled in denying the need for change, such as the veracity of company benchmarks, comparisons, or best practices drawn from other companies against which their performance is measured. This is what we mean by skilled incompetence.

5. For the new language of change and its manifestations to become more widely shared by employees at all levels in the organization, the champions of change, aided by their middle management converts, must continue to draw on new understanding conversations and promises or directives that will engage or compel most employees to accept strategic change. Many failed change programmes are aimed at securing the cooperation of a select group of managers or key workers in the organization, a strategy that only serves to reduce its impact in the future.

6. For change to progress towards the embedding stage there needs to be evidence and publicity of early victories for managers, and evidence and publicity of positive outcomes for most employees. The hope of a positive future beyond employees' current circumstances, knowing how to get there, and working in a 'hopeful organization culture' is key to embedding change (Sawyer & Clair, 2022).

7. The champions or leaders of change must continue to embed change in the organization by drawing on *closure conversations* intended to signify the success of these intermediate positive outcomes. US texts and consultants tend to talk about celebrating success and frequently have institutionalised events to demonstrate success, for example, through passing-out or awards ceremonies or 'employee of the month' schemes. However, such events may need to be inclusive of most employees to avoid becoming interpreted as exclusive. They also need to be read as authentic by those whose trust is being sought.

The embedding stage and the emergence of a new discourse

8. The extent to which strategic change is embedded in the organization can be measured by the degree of *penetration* and *durability* of changes in the outcomes of employee psychological contracts, including the effects on employee attitudes, commitment, and satisfaction, and their levels of identification with the organization's goals. This work lies at the heart of the new language of employer branding and corporate reputation management we met earlier, which seeks to align external image with internal employee identity.

Exercise 10.3

Using the ideas from the strategic change process model, particularly the guidelines for evaluating and managing strategic change in organizations, how would you analyse the problems in the AT&T case?

CHANGING ORGANIZATIONAL CULTURES

You should have sensed by now that much of organizational change and people management is concerned, one way or another, with the subject of culture. We have met the notion of culture in previous chapters in the international context, the corporate context, and managing organizations. Although we have preferred to use more precise terms, particularly organizational identity and organizational identification and engagement in our examination of individual–organizational linkages, organizational culture and culture change are topics that have remained 'centre stage' in business and management studies (Collins, 2021; Hatch et al., 2015; Hatch 2018; Sawyer & Clair, 2022). Indeed, according to some authors, creating and sustaining strong organizational cultures has been seen as the single most important factor in designing and managing successful organizations. Although this faith in culture as the key to unlocking organizational success may have been a little optimistic (some might say, misplaced), the interest in culture as an important 'tool in the management box' shows no real signs of diminishing. So, in this section of the chapter, we want to examine the notion of organizational culture to assess its theoretical and practical value to managers. Can we theorise sensibly about an organization's culture, how it forms, and what impact it has on organizational and individual behaviour? And can we manage an organization's culture to bring about desired strategic change?

Organizational culture: Different meanings and key questions

There has been a massive growth in the literature on organizational culture since the 1970s (Nanayakkara & Wilkinson, 2021). Some of the most prominent contributions include Van Mannen and Barley (1984), Schein (1985), Barley (1983), Hatch (1993, 2018), Cameron and Quinn (2011), Pettigrew (2012), Johnson et al. (2012), Hatch et al. (2015), Alvesson and Sveningsson (2016), and Collins (2021). Before we discuss some of the ways in which researchers theorise culture, let's look at what culture means and how it can be observed, sensed, or measured. If you wish to change something, you need to be able to access it. In other words, you must define it and understand what you are trying to change. Organizational culture has caused some controversy among academics and consultants because it can be defined and understood in quite different ways, and is often confused with the notion of organizational identity (Ravasi, 2016). Joanna Martin (2002) made one of the most significant analyses when proposing four different interpretations, all of which have distinctive, practical implications for the effective management of organizational change. These are even more relevant today because the first of these has come to dominate the management consulting industry, 'airport' business books, and much of so-called 'best practice' management:

- The unitary view and monocultures.
- The anthropological view and subcultures.
- The conflict view and 'brandwashing'.
- The fragmented view and paradoxes.

The unitary view and strong monocultures

The unitary view rests on the assumption that organizations, under normal circumstances, are best characterised by common interests and consensus between different stakeholders. For example, unitary cultures assume that employees and managers are broadly in agreement over the aims of the organization and the rights of managers to be able to set the strategic direction and the work of employees, often without interference from bodies such as trade unions or professional associations. When conflict does arise in such organizations, it is attributed to poor leadership or HRM implementation, or disruptive or misguided employees who don't fully understand the nature of the business. From this perspective, an organization is assumed to have a single, overarching culture that can be measured (through surveys) and managed in the same way as you would measure and control employee performance or other key variables. This view is of organizations *having* cultures that can be engineered in much the same way that you can change structures to achieve desired aims (Collins, 2021). In other words, it is based on a machine metaphor of organizations. For example, in our discussion on corporate reputation, we used the term 'organizational personality' to describe something that an organization possesses, just as people possess individual personalities. And, as we discussed in Chapter 5 on the international context, culture as a variable is seen as a set of shared meanings, embracing both the formal and informal aspects of organizations. The key point is that culture, once understood, is treated as a highly manageable feature of organizations. Much of our recent research into the NHS shows that managers hold these assumptions, even though the legitimacy of trade unions and professions is formally acknowledged (Martin et al., 2021). This unitary, engineering perspective of culture appears to be one held by Jerre Stead, the CEO of AT&T (GIS) in the introductory case study.

Such unitary assumptions and analysis can sometimes be a good reflection of organizations in certain contexts and time frames, but in others, they are sometimes misplaced and result in failed attempts to bring about change (Collins, 2021). Ask yourself the questions in the AT&T case: (1) How realistic were the assumptions made by Stead regarding the potential to create a unified culture in the company? (2) Were leadership and communications all that was necessary to overcome barriers to change? Perhaps he could have taken a different view, distinguishing between:

- the *corporate culture*, which is essentially what managers want the organization to be, which is similar to the concept of corporate identity in Chapter 6 and more amenable to control; and
- the *organizational culture and its subcultures*, which are often less amenable to control by managers for a variety of reasons.

The anthropological view

The anthropological view is a quite different perspective from the unitary view. It is much less concerned with managerial control than with understanding organizations. Culture, rather than being treated as something an organization possesses, is seen as the very *essence* of the organization. In other words, culture is something an organization *is* rather than *has*. This view of organizational culture has some fundamental implications, the most important of which is that an organizational culture cannot be 'owned' and managed in the strict sense of these terms by one group or set of interests. Organizational cultures develop and evolve through the collective sensemaking, enactment, and future hopes of *all* employees, not only managers. Even this notion of a monoculture can be questioned because we often find organizations are better characterised as loose groupings of subcultures, although perhaps overlaid with a managerial or corporate culture. This is arguably a better description of the NHS in the UK, which is made of multiple, sometimes competing, interests, professions, and occupations, for example, the different professions within medicine, nursing and allied health professions, estates and maintenance workers, domestic and catering staff, porters, non-clinical managers, and administrators. Overlaid on these professional and occupational identities is a sense of 'place identity' (Ashworth et al., 2023). Places, such as working in a large teaching hospital, out in the community, in remote units in rural areas, or working at home, have a major effect on our well-being, sense of belonging, and sense of who we are (Martin, Schreven et al., 2023). Thus, it is argued, managers have no greater access to the culture of organizations than other employees, and although they can shape culture over time through setting vision, strategic directions, and modelling desired values, they cannot manage or control cultures in the sense of bringing about radical transformation, especially in a short time frame and unreceptive contexts for change, which includes unreceptive places. Perhaps these were points of which Jerre Stead should have been more aware.

Moreover, it is difficult for people who are part of the culture, including managers, who create and recreate culture every day through their enactment of reality, to step outside themselves to change that culture. This is sometimes known as the problem of 'embedded agency'. One of the most important features of culture is that often we cannot see it, especially if we are steeped in an organization's history and way of thinking. In this situation, we require outsiders (researchers or consultants) to 'help us see ourselves as others see us' through perspective taking, which is one way of understanding organizations (Ku et al., 2015).

The conflict view

A third view, widely held among critical organizational theorists, many union officials, and workers, sees culture management as a form of organizational domination and social engineering, in which managers attempt to manipulate organizations for their own aims through sophisticated HRM, especially the selection, induction, engagement, and development process (Boxall & Purcell, 2022). This approach questions the ethics of culture change programmes and rebranding exercises, seeing them as little more than exercises in brainwashing or 'brandwashing'. Naomi Klein's (2001) book *No Logo* and Joel Balkin's (2020) book *The New Corporation*, are good examples of this conflict view on large corporations, arguing that their attempts to brandwash people into accepting the views of business are detrimental to their long-term interests and the interests of society. The case study on AT&T raises some of the issues connected with ethics and the domination perspective, which we shall examine in the review questions at the end of this section. This conflict view is held by the labour process school, which we discussed in the last chapter on technology, and provides one of the intellectual justifications for global opposition groups such as international trade unions. It is also a view that is held by a significant number of medical professionals, many of whom see their work as becoming deprofessionalised (Martin et al., 2021). Consequently, they have become disillusioned with the ways in which the NHS is managed to the point they are seeking early withdrawal from work and going on strike, sometimes for the first time in their careers (Martin, Staines et al., 2023).

The fragmented view

A final view is associated with the postmodernist school of thinking (Hatch, 2018). While the ideas of postmodernism are complex and are not aimed at helping managers, one of its key contributions to management thinking is to question the notion of a single and permanent 'reality' of organizations. Instead, organizations are better depicted as sites of multiple and often conflicting 'realities' that cannot be captured by an overarching narrative such as a corporate or organizational culture. For example, Joanna Martin's (2002) account of culture highlights the fragmentary, contradictory, and paradoxical aspects of organizational culture, especially the gaps that exist between official managerial rhetoric and the behaviour of the same managers who devised the rhetoric. Thus, we often find organizations espousing an official discourse of 'resourceful humans' as 'our most important asset', while treating them as 'human resources' to be cut and controlled like other non-human resources (Martin et al., 2021). We can also observe people at all levels in an organization making apparently contradictory comments and taking contradictory actions. One famous example of this paradox was a 1960s study of workers at a car plant in the south-east of England who were asked to state their degree of agreement with the statement: 'A firm is like a football team with workers and managers on the same side and kicking into the same goal for most of the time.' Seventy-five per cent of the workers agreed with the statement. But three months later they were seen to be marching through the factory, singing the well-known communist anthem, 'The Red Flag', and threatening to hang the industrial relations manager (Goldthorpe et al., 1968). Which just goes to show how time-bound the so-called rhetoric-reality gap can be, although postmodernists would sometimes argue there is no reality other than that created by powerful rhetorics.

Therefore, we must ask ourselves: do employees hold a coherent worldview of their organizations as a unified culture? Obviously, as managers we need to look for generalisations about organizational life, otherwise we couldn't manage effectively. However, this should not blind us to the potential for multiple interpretations of realities and differences of interests and values among groups in organizations, which are sometimes quite fundamental. To return to a point made in earlier chapters, 'what we see depends on where we stand', or perhaps how we talk.

The fragmented view sees organizational cultures as consistent and inconsistent, contradictory, and confused, all at the same time. Academics who adhere to this perspective argue that there is no such thing as strong and endurable corporate or subgroup cultures, and that culture is better described as a jungle, in a permanent state of flux and transformation. Understanding this view of organizations prevents us from placing too much faith in culture management techniques and programmes of culture change since organizations are always in a state of becoming (something else). Often, you are better placed to try to change behaviours through structural change rather than win 'hearts and minds'.

Thus, the answers to the questions posed at the beginning of this section about organizational cultures depend on your definition and perspective of culture. Mintzberg et al. (1998) have synthesised several of these views by linking organizational culture to the strategy-making, organizational design, and change processes in organizations. They argued that strategy can often be seen as a perspective, as an emergent and unintentional process rather than as a rational and intentionally planned one (Chia & Holt, 2023).

1. Strategy formation, organizational design, and leadership form a cultural *process of social interaction*, based on beliefs and shared understandings of members – in other words, culture is co-constructed between leaders and followers (Howieson et al., 2023).

2. Individuals acquire these beliefs through professional or occupation acculturation or socialisation, which is largely tacit and non-verbal (medicine, HR, accounting, etc.), but this sometimes involves a degree of indoctrination through training and induction programmes.

3. Thus, the members of an organization can only partly describe the beliefs that underpin their culture – they cannot describe what they cannot see. Strong cultures, if they exist, can create 'psychic prisons' that blind us to alternative perspectives or at least create a form of myopia.

4. As a result, strategy takes the form of a *perspective* or a worldview, rooted in collective intentions and reflected in patterns of activity embedded in resources or capabilities.

5. Cultures do not normally encourage change; they are largely forces for stability. However, they sometimes allow for shifts in position, which is largely the case in professionally dominated bureaucracies such as academia, healthcare, the law, and banking (Martin, Staines et al., 2023).

They further argue that the linkages between culture and strategic and organizational change are as follows:

• Culture influences decision-making style by influencing the style of analysis and what gets analysed, because we all have different *perceptual filters*, mindsets, or identities and forms of sensemaking.
• Culture can act as a restraint on strategic change because of shared commitments to consistent action and deep-seated beliefs and tacit assumptions, which is often the case in professional bureaucracies and traditional organizations

- Paradoxically, culture can promote change by emphasising innovation, education, and flexibility, which are key characteristics of successful scale-up organizations (Martin et al., 2023).
- So, culturally dominant values can be a key *source of competitive advantage and organizational effectiveness*.
- However, cultures can clash and be the *source of failure* in alliances, mergers, professional bureaucracies, supply chain relationships, and so on, and an explanation of 'why smart managers often do dumb things'.

Exercise 10.4

Of the four perspectives outlined in the previous section, which one helps you best understand the AT&T case? Explain your reasoning.

ALTERNATIVE WAYS OF THEORISING CULTURE

While Joanna Martin's (2002) framework provides key insights into organizational culture, Giorgi et al. (2015) identified alternative ways of seeing culture, some of which add to Martin's insights. In their five-fold framework of how organizational culture can be conceptualised, they pointed to culture as values, culture as stories, culture as frames, culture as toolkits, and finally, culture as categories.

1. Culture as values – is 'what we prefer, hold dear, or desire' (Giorgi et al., 2015, p. 4). Values are the drivers of social structure and action and they are perpetuated through socialisation, leadership, and rituals. Examples of culture as values can be found in banks in the US and in the UK before the Global Financial Crisis of 2007/2008, where some practices normally frowned upon were seen as legitimate and widely used by bankers (Siebert et al., 2020).

2. Culture as stories – like the strategic narrative view, culture consists of stories that convey ideas and meanings (Nonaka & Yamaguchi, 2022). They are 'narratives with causally linked sequences of events that have a beginning, a middle and an end' (Giorgi, et al. 2015: 9). One good example is the study by Linde (2001) of an insurance company in which values are conveyed through repeated stories of its history, and the life and character of its charismatic founder and leader. The story of the company's commercial and ethical success is about development from selling solely car insurance to offering a full service while following the idea that farmers of good moral character should be charged lower rates for car insurance because they run lower risks than drivers in the city.

3. Culture as frames – this perspective builds on the social constructionist perspective (Berger & Luckmann, 1967) and, like Martin's anthropological view, proposes that we cannot objectively assess reality because of our attention or sensemaking is delimited by 'filters' or 'brackets'. Giorgi et al. (2015) argue that frames can be formed within an institutional field where multiple actors negotiate the norms within broader ideological

traditions. This is very much a way of conceptualising culture in the health service, which is the product of such negotiations over many years between the clinical professions, managers, and governments. Few challenge the ideology of a national health service but how it can be best delivered has been the subject of constant definition and redefinition over time.

4. Culture as toolkits – these are 'grab bags' of stories, frames, categories, rituals, and practices that actors draw on to make meaning or to act. The metaphor of the toolkit shifts the emphasis away from values towards 'bits and pieces of culture that can be differently assembled' (Giorgi et al., 2015: 13). Goffee and Jones' (1998) and Cameron and Quinn's (2011) frameworks are good examples of a culture management toolkit. Such toolkits tend to fit with a unitary perspective and, thus, are useful and limited by the context and timeframe in which they take place and the reality of the assumptions on which they are based.

5. Culture as categories – these are 'social constructions or classifications that define and structure the conceptual distinctions between objects, people, and practices. This involves delineating both sameness and distinctiveness with other categories, such as a hierarchical, market, clan or adhocratic cultures' (Cameron & Quinn, 2011) well-known competing values framework. Organizational actors engage in sensemaking and sensegiving as mechanisms for category construction. For example, the famous study by Rao et al. (2005) analyses the erosion of categorical boundaries in opposing category pairs: traditional cuisine and nouvelle cuisine. Elite French chefs, as high-status actors, blended elements from these two rival cuisines, creating new styles of dishes positively evaluated by the critics. By doing that, the chefs redrew the boundaries of culinary categories. Another good example is the notion of hybrid workers, who are able to combine different institutional logics to lead in professions such as medicine, law, and academia.

Arguably, there is some overlap in these categories, and some studies span their boundaries, however, the above classification of the ways in which culture is theorised suggests that the study of culture is a very rich field, in which researchers draw on a wide range of disciplines – psychology, sociology, and anthropology.

EXAMPLES OF A CULTURAL TOOLKIT APPROACH

It is worth looking at a few examples of cultural toolkits. The first, the culture matrix, provides a useful two-by-two map of cultural types that often resonate with the experience of managers and employees. The second, the cultural web, brings values, stories, and frames into the analysis of organizations, again in a way that managers and employees find useful.

The culture matrix

Although a little dated, one of the best researched and most useful of these culture management toolkit approaches is the typology originally developed by Rob Goffee and

Gareth Jones (2003), who wrote about the *character of the corporation* and the *double S* model (see Figure 10.4). Drawing on a wide range of previous research into leadership and organizational behaviour, they identified two dimensions along which organizations can be plotted. These dimensions may be familiar to you from any previous studies in organizational behaviour you have undertaken.

1. *Sociability* refers to the degree of 'friendliness' among members of a community. Sociability comes from mutual esteem and concern for one's colleagues and is reflected in the quality of interpersonal relations among them. High levels of sociability are found in organizations where people take an interest in the well-being and work of colleagues. Low levels of sociability are found in organizations where the focus is purely on the task or work to be done regardless of the well-being of colleagues.

2. *Solidarity* refers to relationships based on mutual interest and thinking alike, regardless of the degree of sociability in the organization. High levels of solidarity are found in organizations in which people are bound together by a focus on achieving common goals such as found in healthcare, voluntary organizations, and armies, regardless of whether employees like or get on with each other. Low levels of solidarity are found in organizations in which employees pursue their own interests first and foremost, such as pay and career progression. The banking sector has often been criticised for people pursuing self-interest and ethical blindness (Siebert et al., 2020).

One of the novel features of this framework is that Goffee and Jones suggested that these two dimensions have their negative as well as their positive sides. So, for example, high levels of sociability, as we have illustrated, can have a 'negative backside' in situations

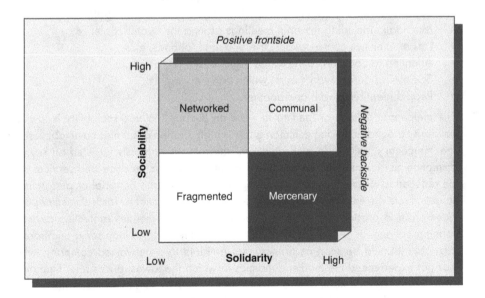

FIGURE 10.4 The culture matrix
(*Source*: based on Goffee & Jones, 2003)

where people cover up for each other to hide poor performance. Similarly, low levels of solidarity can have their positive 'frontside', in so far as pursuing one's self-interest can be the best way to benefit an organization and society, as the famous economist, Adam Smith, pointed out centuries ago. To an extent, paying people based on their individual performance is built on this feature of organizational life and the nature of motivation in certain occupations such as sales and financial services.

Combining these two dimensions, they identify and describe four cultural types, each with a positive frontside and a negative backside. Although none of these cultural types, in and of themselves, are bad, all of them can be damaging if not managed properly.

1. The *networked culture* or *'between friends'*. An organization high on sociability but low on solidarity is referred to as a networked culture. Especially as organizations grow, smaller but more tightly knit sub-organizational entities with a high level of sociability may develop, sometimes at the expense of solidarity. For knowledge-intensive companies with long development cycles and a strong need for knowledge sharing, a networked culture can be a major asset. The same holds true for many companies in marketplaces in which relationships with customers and service are more important than offering them the lowest prices. A typical characteristic of networked companies is great pride in their products and services. Sometimes, however, the focus on the well-being of the organization and its employees has a negative side to it, such as carrying poor performers and 'face-saving' behaviour. Networked cultures have the following characteristics:
    *   Open physical spaces, including social areas.
    *   Decorations, such as photos and other group symbols.
    *   Separated marked spaces to show territory (especially in negative forms).
    *   Much talk, including informal meetings around the 'water cooler'.
    *   Lots of intensive conversations, use of e-mail, phones, etc.
    *   Attention to communicating in the 'right' way.
    *   Socialising during work hours, which can be long.
    *   People identifying with one another.

2. The *mercenary culture*, or *'getting to work on Sunday'*. Where sociability is low, but solidarity around achieving common goals is high, Goffee and Jones have labelled this the 'mercenary' culture. In such situations, the focus is ruthlessly targeted on key performance metrics and the 'bottom line'. The organization's products and services may be reduced to simple means for realising the organization's financial or performance targets. From the employees' perspective, achieving personal rewards sometimes overrides pride in products or services. There are no family-like ties protecting poor-performing colleagues. Although this culture in its extreme form may seem unattractive, arguably it could be seen as a necessary antidote to a networked company, which has not experienced the market dynamics in which the lowest prices rule. Employees of well-run mercenary companies know their competitors, are eager to beat them, and are energised by the mission statement of their company. Arguably, many successful financial services companies run on this basis, as we argued in our study of RBS some years ago (Martin & Gollan, 2012) and the banking sector more generally (Siebert et

al., 2020). It is also sometimes argued that UK universities have been turned into mercenary cultures through the introduction of national performance targets on research performance and student satisfaction. Mercenary cultures tend to have the following characteristics:

- Functional office spaces, which provide basic accommodation and little more than that.
- Displays of awards and recognitions for achievement.
- Communications and talk short and to the point.
- Meetings frequently confrontational.
- Long and unsocial hours when needed, which is often.
- People identify with competing and winning.

3. The *fragmented culture*, or *'all together alone'*. In situations where both sociability and solidarity are low, we find fragmented cultures. Typical examples are research organizations such as some university departments and consulting firms, especially law, accounting, and consulting engineering firms. We might also find some examples in departments of larger companies that employ highly paid specialists, such as investment analysts or economists in the financial services industry. In these cultures, the individuals often see themselves as more important than the groups they are part of and the company for which they work and have an outward orientation to their professional standing and professional careers. Fragmented cultures are characterised by:

- Private offices, or people who work mainly from home.
- Little talk or communications (with little opportunity for casual a chat either).
- Communication and talk focused on specific topics and kept brief.
- Most communication directed to people outside the organization.
- People identify with individualism and value their autonomy.

4. The *communal culture*, or *'we are family'*. Goffee and Jones label the culture in the top right-hand quadrant as 'communal'. A typical example of a company high on solidarity as well as sociability is a business start-up. The founders are often very focused on their mission and employees are hand-picked for the organization to fit the culture, so creating a family-like atmosphere. Such an organizational culture can be extremely powerful, as we found in the case of an organization we researched over several years (Martin et al., 2023). However, it can also have a dark side if the organization becomes self-sufficient and too demanding of its members, like some religious sects. Being high on both solidarity and sociability has an inherent tension built into it, and as communal organizations grow, they are likely to drop on one, or perhaps even both, dimensions. Communal cultures are characterised by:

- Open-plan spaces to facilitate the family atmosphere.
- Highly visible corporate symbols and logos.
- Focus on face-to-face communications.
- Moral persuasion, rather than direction, which often leads to guilt or shame being a motivating force.
- People living to work and working to live, with work–life balance seen as irrelevant.
- High levels of identification with organizational mission and values.

Features of the different cultural types

We have already mentioned that none of these cultures is inherently good or bad. They can all have their functional and dysfunctional sides. A further key finding of Goffee and Jones's work is that organizations may have a dominant culture, but most exhibit several subcultures at the same time. For example, many universities, especially in the USA and UK, that have a strong element of performance measurement, are characterised by a dominant fragmented culture. Nevertheless, some departments in these universities may reflect a communal culture, a networked culture, or even, in the case of some business schools, a mercenary culture, which mirrors the culture of their key clients.

Their research also pointed to the potential for a form of 'life cycle' that resembles an S-shaped transition through the four cultures. For example, a company may be formed as entrepreneurial and prospecting (communal). As it gains success and grows, it may become too 'fat' and too comfortable (networked). This may lead to a lowering of performance, necessitating a turn-around to get the company back in shape (mercenary). However, in the process of changing the culture from high–low to low–high on sociability and solidarity, respectively, the management loses out on both counts and the organization ends up fragmented, with all employees working as if they were independent contractors. This life cycle is not necessarily typical, but it illustrates some of the negative sides of the different cultures and the challenges in managing them. Indeed, this is one of the key strengths of the Goffee and Jones model in assessing how best to deal with organizational change. It is also useful to understand what needs to be compensated for, as each of the cultures has its drawbacks. Furthermore, if a culture is not sustainable, for example, in a growing communal company or in a networked company that is haemorrhaging cash, it can be helpful to know some of the pitfalls to avoid.

The cultural web

The cultural web has its origins in Gerry Johnson's (1992) paper, with the basic premises remaining much the same over the years it has been in popular use. It is probably the best framework that brings together most of the different perspectives on culture we have discussed so far, and is based on three key ideas:

- Organizational culture comprises the taken-for-granted, and often deeply embedded, assumptions and behaviours used and displayed by organizational members to make sense of their context.
- The core assumptions, histories, behaviours, structures, values, symbols, and organizational identity reinforce each other to become what we know as organizational culture.
- Attempts to change or manage organizational culture will be greatly enabled by raising these assumptions, etc., to the surface by using the cultural web as a mapping technique.

Figure 10.5 maps out the components of the cultural web, to which I have added the notion of values that is implicit in Johnson's framework but is worth making explicit. The *cultural paradigm* refers to the basic assumptions that are sometimes widely held and taken for granted in an organization. For example, in healthcare, it is widely held that people are drawn to the sector because they value 'called' work with a moral and social purpose and that one of the key aims of a healthcare organization should be to enable staff to live out their calling. Our research shows that many doctors fail to experience their calling because of their interpretation of resource constraints and poor leadership, which leads them to exit from the system prematurely (Martin, Schreven et al., 2023). *Power,* power hierarchies, and structures are widely discussed concepts in organization studies. One of the most insightful ways of theorising formal and informal power is Steven Lukes' (2021) revised 'three faces of power.' The first face refers to the power to make decisions, which is revealed by who wins out when there are conflicts of interest. Usually, this is associated with formal power, hierarchies, and ruling elites. The second face refers to the ability to manipulate the agenda of decision-making so that some decisions are given high or low priority or are not even discussed (for example, decisions 'behind closed doors' or made in the 'corridors of power'. The third face is ideological power, which refers to the ability of elites to control what people think and/or value. This is manipulative power, which

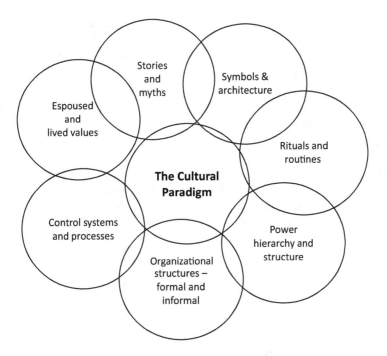

FIGURE 10.5 The amended cultural web
(adapted from G. Johnson et al., 2012, Pearson Publishing)

is sometimes associated with cultural control and brandwashing to determine what is desirable or undesirable behaviour, or even prevent others from realising where their interests might lie.

Organizational structures were the subject of Chapter 4 and not only refer to the formal roles and reporting relationships in an organization but also the informal structures and relationships as identified by organizational theorists many decades ago, with one of the best known being Gouldner (1958). *Control systems* are the formal and informal ways of ensuring staff behave, meet targets, and orient their actions. Key control systems are accounting controls, such as budgeting, and reward systems, particularly those that attempt to relate pay to desirable outcomes. These control systems are specifically designed to shape culture but can sometimes result in dysfunctional behaviour, as we saw during the Global Financial Crisis (Siebert et al., 2020).

Rituals and routines provide one of the most cited perspectives on culture as the 'way we do things around here'. Rituals and routines consist of taken-for-granted customs and practices or habitual behaviours that have become embedded over time. So, for example, the 'Great British Tea Break' and strict demarcation between trades over 'who does what' and who could use certain tools became such a feature of organizational life in many UK companies that they had to be bought out through productivity bargaining and high pay awards to make inroads into British productivity problems during the 1960s. So great were the routines practised by British workers in some industries that the estimate of hours worked during a normal working day was less than a quarter of paid-for time. Organizational rituals are special events or activities that signal or reinforce what is important in an organization. Often, these take place during induction events, training programmes, or how people are selected and appraised. So, for example, organizations in the public sector typically use panel interviews comprising several interviewers in part to signify the importance they attach to fairness and equality. This is despite evidence that suggests such panel interviews are relatively poor in predicting subsequent job performance.

Stories and myths, as we have discussed, are the main means by which organizational members intersubjectively convey and embed the past in the present through their collective sensemaking and sensegiving (Collins, 2021). Such stories are often of heroes and villains, failures, and successes, and what is acceptable, expected, and unacceptable. Psychological contract expectations, which we examined in Chapter 3, are often formed through such stories, while we often rapidly get to know through stories what not to do or say.

Symbols and architecture are objects, acts, events, ways of communicating, or even people that give meaning beyond their material or official purposes. The most obvious physical features are the ways in which offices or workplaces are laid out (Hatch, 2018). The use of space and place to create meaning and to shape how people relate to work are highly influential ways of influencing their experience of meaningful work (Martin, Staines et al., 2023). Similarly, the ways in which senior leaders communicate with staff, either remotely or through direct action, sends a powerful message about the importance of 'resourceful humans' rather than human resources to the organization.

I have added the notion of espoused and lived *values* to this framework to make explicit the importance of formal and informally communicated morals, ethics, and principles, and the theories underlying them, in shaping the assumptions, norms of behaviour, and actions in an organization. Values frameworks are increasingly used in organizations, often in conjunction with codes of ethics, to establish standards of corporate governance, risk, and fairness (see Chapter 11) in sending signals about the kind of reputation the organization seeks to convey with external and internal stakeholders (see Chapter 6), and in shaping accountability and trust relations (see Chapter 11). Notable developments in business education are the various codes of ethics being introduced. These include the Academy of Management Code of Ethics and the Principles for Responsible Management Education (PRME). It remains to be seen how such codes will influence managers and business practice in the coming years, but the signs are positive given the interest of many students in courses in business ethics and the development of ethics committees in business. We also have to understand the distinction between formal espoused values, such as those in vision and values frameworks, and the 'lived values', which refer to how people in the organization experience values being enacted – sometimes referred to as the 'rhetoric-reality gap'.

LESSONS FOR SUCCESSFUL ORGANIZATIONAL CHANGE

I have reviewed some of the key ideas on organizational change and culture change. I hope by now that you are aware of the difficulties involved but have a better understanding of how to go about implementing change in organizations, and how not to do it! As we have discussed, some writers and managers believe that organizations and their cultures can be socially engineered using a set of tools and techniques drawn from organizational development research; indeed, they place great faith in their ability to bring about major changes in performance from such programmes of change. Others, however, are more sceptical and believe that cultures cannot be managed in the sense that they can be controlled through managerial actions alone (Alvesson & Sveningsson, 2016; Collins, 2021). Nor can they be easily changed from the outside, especially by using consultants who can rarely hope to gain the in-depth understanding necessary to help shape cultural change.

My position on this issue is somewhere between the two: that organizational cultures can be shaped by managers and consultants, but usually only with a sensitive and in-depth 'insider' understanding of the issues involved, with the commitment of most employees to change, and through a sustained and sensitive effort by managers and change agents, often over many years to become deeply embedded.

Factors facilitating change

Following years of research (and practice) into this field of study, I have distilled a list of hopefully useful ideas (but not principles) about organizational culture change., which also draw on work from the work of writers/researchers whose ideas seem to make the most sense to me. These are set out in Table 10.1.

TABLE 10.1 Factors facilitating successful organizational change

1. Know where you are starting from. Usually, a receptive context for change together with the managerial ability to create a positive climate for culture change is necessary. One useful maxim that seems to apply is that 'often big change produces big opposition' in threatening the social identities of key players and their investment in the status quo.

2. Establish a sense of urgency by creating the necessary levels of tension (or mechanisms of discomfort) in the organization for change, and by assembling and facilitating a powerful group of people who act as champions to lead the change.

3. Create a vision (though it may, and perhaps should, be imprecise) and values framework which should help direct the culture change effort.

4. Use all possible means to communicate the vision and values deep into the organization (see the use of discourse and strategy as convincing stories) and ensure that managers 'walk the talk' to demonstrate the importance of the new culture and the kinds of behaviour associated with it.

5. Empower others to act by removing structural blockages to the new culture (e.g., organizational and architectural) and encourage innovation and group learning activities.

6. Encourage and use 'deviants' and 'heretics' to critically evaluate existing practices by 'speaking up to power', challenging groupthink, and bringing in fresh ideas.

7. Plan for and create short-term wins to encourage long-term persistence with the change initiatives.

8. Reinforce changes in culture or even emphasise changes in structure over culture using the reward systems to reflect the kinds of behaviour that are appropriate.

9. Be aware of the ethical issues, personal choices, and questions that most people have to face when being asked to commit themselves to culture change. These include: what can people reasonably be expected to do in the name of the organization; what kind of vision and values are people likely to buy into (how do they define the key stakeholders); how closely should the organization touch on peoples' private lives; and what values do they place on different kinds of justice?

10. Finally, be patient and persistent, as major changes in culture and structure may take many years to bring about.

Sources: Pettigrew, 1990; Schoenberger, 1997; Goffee & Jones, 2006; Hatch, 2018, Kotter & Schlesinger, 2008; McCalman et al., 2015; Martin & Siebert, 2016; Alvesson & Sveningsson, 2016.

Evaluating culture change

One final point I have skirted over, but which is crucial to organizational change, is the question: How do you know when the hoped-for changes and/or new culture have taken root in an organization?

We have dealt with this briefly in our strategic change model, but how do you know when organizational change has become embedded in the organization? A summary of existing research has identified five criteria for evaluating change. They are also useful in showing just how difficult and long term a task changing a company's culture might be. Thus, for any change programme to be successful, it must be able to:

- Express a core idea that engages people's feelings by creating a credible, novel, and compelling message.
- Create a universal set of shared values that employees at all levels can buy into.
- Penetrate deep into the organization, beyond the corporate culture to connect the top, middle, and bottom layers of management and employees.
- Adjust to changing contexts and circumstances over time by being sufficiently flexible to cope with unforeseen challenges and opportunities.
- Endure the test of time and the almost natural tendency of managers to introduce further changes.

CASE 10.2 LIVING WITH A PURIST

The Kirk Russell Studio was a highly successful private architectural and interior design practice based in continental Europe, owned by its American founder, Kirk Russell. Its company logo, which dominated all company collateral, is 'Obsession with world-class design is our credo.'

The company was started in 2007 by Russell, who stated that he wasn't interested in beginning a run-of-the-mill architectural practice, tendering for basic contracts. Instead, he sought to develop a 'School of Excellence' for innovative young architects and interior designers, where they could hone and practise their talents on high-profile design work. He made the comment that he wasn't interested in offering these people jobs, but 'a unique experience' that they would always carry with them. And because Russell had a good reputation in the industry in Europe, his purist claims were taken seriously in most quarters.

Russell's approach to potential staff members was a little unorthodox. Instead of offering high salaries and bonuses, he stressed the difficulties of working in a 'School of Excellence.' 'You won't make as much money as you could do elsewhere, and you won't get a high-class office overlooking the Lido,' he used to state in his opening interviews with recruits, 'but you will get the most satisfying and high-profile experience around. However, the quid pro quo is that I demand a purist obsession with design quality and I know, because you are good, that you will produce it.'

Using this approach to talent management, Russell was able to put together a first-class team of architects, designers, and technicians in a short space of time. This image of the School of Excellence was one he also used as a sales pitch to potential clients. 'If you want architects who are merely cost engineers, go elsewhere; if you want the best quality and buildings that will be monuments to their owners, you have come to the best practice in the country.'

The company carved itself out a highly profitable and high-profile niche in the European market and had won several major contracts in Italy, Spain, and the UK. The staff became captivated by Russell's vision of the School of Excellence as time passed, many of them working very long hours way beyond contract. Most of them knew they weren't making the kind of money they might make in London, New York, or other big-city practices, but valued the intangible rewards more. They were working on some of the most high-profile projects in Italy and Spain, which provided them with the kinds of satisfaction and career development that couldn't be gained elsewhere – at least, that was what they told colleagues in other practices when they were out socialising with them or met them on the conference circuit. Some of their colleagues resented having their work degraded during these conversations and did not take kindly to their work and careers being called into question; the implication was always that they were 'in it for the money and not the higher-order values of architectural work'. There was also the issue of taste and judging quality. 'Who says your work is so great? Is designing a school that must meet cost and quality standards not just as valuable as designing a high-profile office or government building?' became a common question and source of increasing friction between members of the 'Russell School' and outsiders during heated arguments in bars.

By the mid-2010s, the Russell School of Excellence, as it was now known informally, had become one of the most respected practices in Europe, and was often invited to submit projects in design competitions for major building projects throughout the continent. Employees became even more committed to the cause, with almost no one leaving and many more joining as the practice expanded. From the perspective of those working in the practice, leisure time and work time became indistinguishable, and they boasted about the family-type culture. Russell himself led by example and was seen as an inspirational leader, with frequent motivational talks around the theme of 'no compromise with quality' and 'designing buildings of great architectural significance.' He was also a man who 'walked the talk', always in the practice, reviewing the work of others, and coaching the newer and often the even more experienced members of the teams. Long hours for everyone were the natural consequence, with excellence and the search for more high-profile projects the bywords.

In 2015, a defining moment occurred, however, when one of the senior and most respected architects was forced to make a choice between family and career. He decided to leave, not feeling able to give the commitment necessary to the company, and his departure was handled smoothly, with a party thrown in. However, in trying to replace this key member of staff, real difficulties were encountered. Russell had decided that every staff member should have a say in who was to be recruited into the 'family,' rationalising his decision on the basis of team-fit and the fact that staff would spend more time with the company's family than with their natural ones. Naturally, staff were enthusiastic that they were involved, and that the new person should embrace the School's mission. However, all interviewees fell short in one way or another. One could not commit the time, another wasn't seen as a team player, and yet another was rejected because she didn't have the right 'attitude.' After several months, the key position remained unfilled.

During this time, Russell had to concentrate on running the business side of the School and began to neglect his coaching and development functions. Everyone saw this happening but thought it was only temporary until the new person was recruited. However, Russell himself began wondering in his private moments if they would ever be able to recapture the spirit of the School of Excellence, especially as the practice was doing well financially, with healthy profits and new projects coming in.

In 2016, another key member left the practice to set up on his own. On returning a few months later, he found Russell on the drawing board filling in for him. While staff still talked about the concern for obsessive quality and felt that it was only a short time before the Academy got back on track, the visitor detected a degree of doubt about the statements made. Employees seemed much less confident than before but weren't going to make it obvious to someone who was now an outsider.

The vacancy for the senior position was never re-advertised. In 2018, while most of the original staff were still with the organization and it was still turning in respectable profits, it wasn't appearing in the trade press quite so much, nor securing such high-profile projects.

Source: this material is based on two real-life cases, including 'Perfection or bust' by Gareth Morgan (1989).

Questions

1. How would you describe the culture of the Kirk Russell Studio?
2. What pieces of advice could be given to Russell to help make his company more effective?

COMPETING PERSPECTIVES ON ORGANIZATIONAL CHANGE

Organizational change is a contested terrain. In their book on managing change, McCalman et al. (2015) emphasise the point that there are multiple ways in which managers can approach change, and managers often face what can be referred to as 'competing narratives'. Rather than ignoring these competing narratives, managers should recognise and see them as a legitimate source of alternative views. One source of difference in the way individuals perceive change is related to their position in the organization. Managers may see change differently from the way their employees do. Also, a top-down change initiated by managers may not be seen in a positive light by the employees, while bottom-up change might unsettle managers who may fear losing control by giving too much power to their employees (Dawson & Buchanan, 2012).

Bearing in mind the preceding 'health warnings', and the concerns expressed about the concept of unitary cultures, managers need to have a set of sophisticated techniques to identify and manage their organizational cultures. For example, in the AT&T case, Jerre Stead and his colleagues might have benefited from constructing alternative scenarios of what the organization might have looked like. More importantly, they would clearly have benefited from an understanding of the nature of the different subcultures in the various subsidiaries of AT&T (GIS).

One way in which these competing perspectives on change might be conceptualised is the notion of pluralism introduced in the 1970s by industrial sociologist Alan Fox (Siebert et al., 2016). In his writing, Fox (1966) and Fox and Flanders (1969) argued that a pluralist frame of reference was a more realistic analysis of industrial relations, and a more relevant model of industrial organization, which was made up of divergent interests and sectional groups. The pluralist view of organizations perceives a multitude of related but separate interests and objectives as the norm. Recognition of divergent interests held by managers and employees also involves an acceptance that there was only a limited degree of common purpose. Understanding the spirit of pluralism with its emphasis on conflicting interests is crucial to managing change. In any change initiative, there are winners and losers, and managing change often involves managing competing interests.

Some studies of change conducted through the lens of institutional theory capture the conflicting interests of organizational stakeholders. These conflicting interests are often closely linked to the differences in power that organizational actors have. Maguire et al. (2004) noted that dominant actors in an organization may have the power to pursue change, but they often do not have the motivation to change the organization for the simple reason that they benefit from the existing institutional arrangements. On the other hand, peripheral actors may have the incentive to promote change, but they may lack the power to change institutions. One way out of implementing change is allowing individuals to break with existing rules and practices associated with the dominant practice and create alternative rules and practices (Battilana, 2006). This process is referred to as institutional entrepreneurship (Maguire et al., 2004; Martin et al., 2018). But it is worth remembering, above all, that organizational change is a political process. Consequently, good advice to take is to develop political skills and build your internal and external networks. However, remember the lessons of the too-much-of-a-good-thing-effect: one of which should read that political managers create political organizations; so, as with most things in life, balance and restraint are probably the best way forward.

LEARNING SUMMARY

In this chapter, I examined the process of changing organizations in light of the different contexts of change. I addressed the key questions of what makes for successful change in an organization and the practical steps that managers can take. The following points should be noted:

- The ISM model is a series of interlinked and interdependent elements of systems and subsystems which depend on the perspective of the developer. The model asks: What are you doing? How could you do it better? How do you effectively implement changes?
- Evaluation and design involve analysing the system, devising and evaluating viable solutions, and scenario planning.
- The implementation phase requires a balance between thinking and doing. Change agents must provide a convincing narrative for change through discourse and language – the *why* factor. Good narratives must be novel, credible, and compelling.
- Organizational culture is one of the defining factors in understanding change. Strategy can be seen as a perspective, requiring social interaction.
- Organizational culture can be analysed according to the extent to which it exhibits sociability and solidarity. Too much or too little of either can be a problem and can mean a shift to the other extreme.
- Cultures can be shaped, not controlled, by managers, but they need an in-depth understanding of the organization's specific needs and context. Toolkits such as the culture web provide a useful way of gaining such an understanding.

REFERENCES

Alvesson, M., & Sveningsson, S. (2016). *Changing organizational culture: Culture change in work* (2nd ed.). Routledge.

Argyris, C. (1993). *Knowledge for action.* Jossey-Bass.

Ashworth, B. E., Caza, B. B., & Meister, A. (2023). My place: How workers become identified with their workplaces and why it matters. *Academy of Management Review.* Retrieved December 13, 2023. https://doi.org/10.5465/amr.2020.0442

Balkin, J. (2020). *The new corporation: How 'good' corporations are bad for democracy.* Vintage Books.

Barley, S. R. (1983). Semiotics and the study of occupational and organizational cultures. *Administrative Science Quarterly*, 28(3), 393–413.

Bate, P. (1996). Towards a strategic framework for changing corporate culture. *Journal of Strategic Change, 5*, 27–42.

Battilana, J. A (2006). Agency and Institutions: The enabling role of individual's social position. *Organization, 13*(5), 653–676.

Bell, M., Martin, G., & Clarke, T. (2004). Engaging in the future of e-Learning: A scenarios-based approach. *Education and Training, 46*(6/7), 296–307.

Berger, P. L. and Luckmann, T. (1967). *The social construction of reality: A treatise in the sociology of knowledge.* New York: Anchor Books.

Boxall, P., & Purcell, J. (2022). *Strategy and human resource management* (5th ed.). Bloomsbury.

Burke, W. W. (2024). *Organization change: Theory and practice* (6th ed.). Sage.

Burnes, B. (2017). *Managing change* (7th ed.). Pearson Publishing.

Cameron, K. S., & Quinn, R. E. (2011). *Diagnosing and changing organizational culture: Based on the competing values framework* (3rd ed.). San Francisco: Jossey-Bass.

Chia, R., & Holt, R. (2023). Strategy, intentionality, and success: four logics for explaining strategic action. *Organization Theory, 4*(3). https://doi.org/10.1177/26317877231186436

Collins, D. (2021). *Rethinking organizational culture: Redeeming culture through stories.* Routledge.

Dawson, P., & Buchanan, D. A. (2012). The way it really happened: Competing narratives in the political process of technological change. In S. Clegg & M. Haugaard (Eds.), *Power and organizations* (pp. 845–864). SAGE.

The Economist. (2005, August 27). Going global: Workers of the world attempt to unite against Wal-Mart, p. 55.

Ford, J. D., & Ford, L. W. (1995). The role of conversations in producing intentional organizational change. *Academy of Management Review, 20,* 541–570.

Fox, A. (1966). *Research papers 3: Industrial sociology and industrial relations.* Her Majesty's Stationery Office.

Fox, A., & Flanders, A. (1969). The reform of collective bargaining: From Donovan to Durkheim. *British Journal of Industrial Relations, 7*(2), 151–180.

Giorgi, S. Lockwood, C., & Glynn, M.A. (2015). The many faces of culture: Making sense of 30 years of research on culture in organization studies. *The Academy of Management Annals, 9*(1), 1–54. doi:10.1080/19416520.2015.1007645

Goffee, R. and Jones, G. (1998). *The character of the corporation.* New York: Harper Business.

Goffee, R., & Jones, G. (2003). *The character of the corporation* (2nd ed.). HarperBusiness.

Goldthorpe, J., Lockwood, D., Bechhofer, F., & Platt, J. (1968). *The affluent worker: Industrial attitudes and behaviour.* Cambridge University Press.

Goffee, R., & Jones G. (2006). *Why should anyone be led by you?* Harvard Business School Publishing.

Goss, T., Pascale, R. T., & Athos, A. (1993, November/December). The reinvention roller coaster: risking the present for a powerful future. *Harvard Business Review, 71*(6), 97–107.

Gouldner, A. W. (1958). Cosmopolitans and locals: Toward an analysis of latent social roles. Part 2. *Administrative Science Quarterly, 2,* 444–480.

Graham, G. (1999). *The internet: A philosophical inquiry.* Routledge.

Gu, G., Wang, C. S., & Galinsky, A. D. (2015). The promise and perversity if perspective-taking in organizations. *Research in Organizational Behavior, 35,* 79–102

Hatch, M. J. (1993). The dynamics of organizational culture. *Academy of Management Review, 18*(4), 657–693

Hatch, M. J. (2018). *Organizational theory: Modern, symbolic and postmodern perspectives* (4th ed.). Oxford University Press.

Hatch, M.J., & Schultz, M. (2008). *Taking brand initiative: How corporations can align strategy, culture and identity through corporate branding.* Wiley/Jossey-Bass.

Hatch, M. J., Schultz, M., & Skov, A. M (2015). Organizational identity and culture in the context of managed change: Transformation in the carlsberg group, 2009–2013. *Academy of Management Discoveries, 1*(1), 58–90

Howieson, W. B., Martin, G., & Bushfield, S. (2023). Medical leadership identity co-construction: claimed but not granted. *European Management Journal*. https://doi.org/10.1016/j.emj.2023.04.012

Johnson, G. N. (1992). Managing strategic change – strategy, culture, and action. *Long Range Planning, 25*, 8–36.

Johnson, G., Whittington, R. & Scholes, K. (2012). *Fundamentals of strategy*. Financial Times/Prentice Hall.

Kanter, R. M. (2013, January). Nine rules for stifling innovation. *Harvard Business Review*. https://hbr.org/2013/01/nine-rules-for-stifling-innova.html

Kaplan, A. (1964). *The conduct of inquiry: Methology for behavioral science*. San Francisco: Chandler.

Klein, N. (2001). *No logo*. Flamingo.

Kotter, J. P. (1995, March/April). Leading change: Why transformation efforts fail. *Harvard Business Review*.

Kotter, J. P., & Schlesinger, L. A. (2008, July–August). Choosing strategies for change. *Harvard Business Review*.

Kotter, J. P., & Heskett, J. (1992). *Corporate culture and performance*. Free Press.

Ku, G., Wang, C. S., & Galinsky, A. D. (2015). The promise and perversity of perspective-taking in organizations. *Research in Organizational Behavior, 35*, 79–102.

Linde, C. (2001). Narrative and social tacit knowledge. *Journal of Knowledge Management, 5*(2), 160–170.

Lukes, S. (2021). *Power: A radical view* (3rd ed.). Bloomsbury.

McCalman, J., Paton, R. A., & Siebert, S. (2015). *Change management: A guide to effective implementation* (4th ed.). Sage.

Maguire, S., C. Hardy, & Lawrence, T. B. (2004). Institutional entrepreneurship in emerging fields: HIV/AIDS treatment advocacy in Canada. *Academy of Management Journal, 47*(5), 657–679.

Martin, G., Beaumont, P. B., & Staines, H. J. (1998). Managing organizational culture. In C. Mabey, T. Clark, & D. Skinner (Eds.), *Experiencing human resource management*. Sage.

Martin, G., Staines, H., & Pate, J. (1998). The new psychological contract: Exploring the relationship between job security and career development. *Human Resource Management Journal, 6*(3), 20–40.

Martin, G., & Beaumont, P. B. (2001). Transforming multinational enterprises: Towards a process model of strategic HRM change in MNEs. *International Journal of Human Resource Management, 10*(6), 34–55.

Martin, G., Beaumont, P. B., & Pate, J. (2003). A process model of strategic change and some case study evidence. In W. Cooke (Ed.), *Multinational companies and transnational workplace issues* (pp. 101–122). Quorum Press.

Martin, G., & Gollan, P. J. (2012). Corporate governance and strategic human resources management (SHRM). in the UK financial services sector: the case of the Royal Bank of Scotland. *International Journal of Human Resource Management, 23*(16), 3295–3314.

Martin G., Siebert S., & Robson I. (2018). Conformist innovation: An institutional logics perspective on how HR executives construct business school reputations.

International Journal of Human Resource Management, 29(13), 2027–2053. doi: 10.1080/09585192.2016.1239118

Martin, G. Bushfield, S., Siebert, S., & Howieson, W. B. (2021). Changing logics in healthcare and their effects on the identity motives and identity work of doctors. *Organization Studies, 42*(9) 1477-1499

Martin, G., Staines, H. J., & Bushfield, S. (2023). *Senior hospital doctors' intentions to retire in NHS Scotland, University of Dundee.* https://discovery.dundee.ac.uk/en/publications/senior-hospital-doctors-intentions-to-retire-in-nhs-scotlanmarti

Martin, G., Schreven, S., Arshed, N., & Martin, A. (2023, July 6–8) *How healthcare staff make sense of their orientations to work(place). – past, present, and future.* Paper presented to the EGOS annual colloquium, University of Cagliari, Italy.

Martin, J. (2002). *Organizational culture: Mapping the terrain (Foundations for Organizational Science series).* Sage.

Mintzberg, H., Ahlstrand, B., & Lampel, J. (1998). *Strategic Safari: A guided tour through the wilds of strategic management.* Free Press.

Morgan, G. (1989). *Creative organizational theory.* Sage.

Nanayakkara, K., & Wilkinson, S. (2021). Organisational culture theories: dimensions of organisational culture and office layouts. In R Appel-Meulenbroek & V. Daniska (Eds.), *A handbook of theories on designing alignment between people and the office environment.* Routledge.

Nonaka, I., & Yamaguchi, I. (2022). Narrative strategy. In I. Nonaka & I. Yamaguchi (Eds.), *Management by eidetic intuition* (pp. 173–189). Palgrave MacMillan.

Pate, J. M., Martin, G., & Staines, H. (2000). Mapping the relationship between psychological contracts and organizational change: A process model and some case study evidence. *Journal of Strategic Change, 9,* 481–493.

Paton, R., MacCalman, J., & Siebert, S. (2015). *Managing change: A guide to effective implementation* (3rd ed.) Sage.

Pettigrew, A. M. (1990). Is corporate culture manageable? In D. C. Wilson & R. H. Rosenfeld (Eds.), *Managing organizations: Text, readings and cases.* McGraw-Hill.

Pettigrew, A. M. (2012). Context and action in the transformation of the firm: A reprise. *Journal of Management Studies, 49*(7), 1304–1328.

Ramirez, R., & Wilkinson, A. (2016). *Strategic reframing: The Oxford scenario planning approach.* Oxford University Press.

Rao, H., Monin, P., & Durand, R. (2005). Border crossing: Bricolage and the Erosion of categorical boundaries in French gastronomy. *American Sociological Review, 70,* 968–991.

Ravasi, D. (2016) Organizational identity, culture, and image. In M. Schultz., B.E. Ashforth & D. Ravasi (Eds.) The Oxford handbook of organizational identity, 65-78, Oxford: Oxford UNiversity Press.

Sawyer, K. B., & Clair, J. A. (2022). Hope cultures in organizations: Tackling the grand challenge of commercial sex exploitation. *Administrative Science Quarterly, 67*(2), 289–338

Schein, E. H. (1985). *Organizational culture and leadership.* Jossey-Bass.

Schoenberger, E. (1997). *The cultural crises of the firm.* Oxford University Press.

Thornton, P. H., Ocasio, W. & Lounsbury, M. (2012). *The institutional logics perspective: A new approach to culture, structure and process*. Oxford: Oxford University Press.

Van Maanen, J., & Barley, S. R. (1984). Occupational communities: Culture and control in organizations. In B. M. Staw & L. L. Cummings (Eds.), *Research in organizational behavior* (Vol. 6, pp. 287–365). JAI Press.

Senior, B., Swailes, S., & Carnall, C. (2020). *Organizational change* (6th ed.). Pearson Education

Siebert, S., Martin, G., & Bozic, B. (2016). Research into employee trust: Epistemological foundations and paradigmatic boundaries. *Human Resource Management Journal*, 26(3), 269–284.

Siebert, S., Martin, G., & Simpson, G. (2020). Rhetorical strategies in the professional field of banking, *Journal of Professions and Organizations*, 7(2), 134–155.

Weick, K. E. (2001). *Making sense of the organization*. Blackwell.

Whitehead, A. N. (1929). *Process and reality*. Harper.

CHAPTER 11

Corporate governance, corporate (social) responsibility, and corporate sustainability

LEARNING OBJECTIVES

By the end of this chapter, you should be able to:

- Define what is meant by good corporate governance.
- Describe and critically evaluate the main theories of corporate governance.
- Critically assess the application of corporate governance theories to cases of poor governance.
- Define what is meant by corporate social responsibility.
- Critically evaluate the business case for corporate social responsibility.
- Critically evaluate measures of the outcomes of corporate social responsibility.
- Apply a model of inputs, mediators, moderators and outcomes of corporate social responsibility to cases and practical decisions facing managers.
- Critically evaluate how the notion of corporate sustainability is changing the corporate social responsibility agenda and our lives.

INTRODUCTION

In this final chapter, we examine three, increasingly prominent, corporate-level concerns, which have a major impact on how people are managed in organizations. These are the related fields of corporate governance (Clarke, 2022), corporate social responsibility (CSR) (Aguinas & Glavas, 2019), or corporate responsibility as it is increasingly coming to be known (Ghobadian et al., 2015), and corporate sustainability (Clarke, 2022; Rasche et al., 2023; George et al., 2022). Let's begin with a short case study from Japan to illustrate the kinds of problems that these bodies of literature attempt

DOI: 10.4324/9781003469711-11

to address. Following reflection on the case, I will present some of the key arguments in these rapidly expanding bodies of literature, including some research of our own on corporate governance models and governance problems.

Box 11.1 Toshiba's fall from grace in 2015

Toshiba is one of Japan's best-known companies, producing consumer electronics on an international scale. As a *Financial Times* article stated in July 2015, it has been a model of corporate governance in Japan and its corporate leaders have frequently been hailed as exemplary in their approach to running a successful multinational company with a strong sense of purpose and corporate culture. Following government reforms to corporate governance legislation in 2001, Japanese firms were required to appoint at least three external directors, which was at odds with conventional practice in Japan. Toshiba embraced the concept wholeheartedly, and in 2013 was ranked very highly among Japanese companies for its corporate governance approach and compliance practices with respect to financial reporting.

However, external auditors uncovered a corporate-wide attempt to inflate profits in July 2015, which caused severe reputational damage to the firm and led directly to the resignation of its CEO and other board members. The report produced by its external auditors showed that the board and internal auditing committee were aware of irregularities in accounting practices since 2008 but took no action because of the overarching requirements set out by its senior leaders to pursue profits and meet earnings targets. This requirement for profits became exceptionally strong following events in 2011/2012 when many Japanese companies were recovering from the tsunami disaster, the Fukushima nuclear accident, and a strong Japanese yen. As the auditors' report noted, the pressure to improve profit margins and generate new sources of business to make the company less reliant on chip-making led to pressure on managers to inflate profit figures.

The report also found that underpinning this drive for profitability in Toshiba was a corporate culture reminiscent of many large Japanese corporations that privileged hierarchy and obedience to senior leaders, with a concomitant failure on the part of divisional-level managers to speak up to power and challenge decisions. Senior leaders in the company 'challenged' managers to continuously improve profit performance and to be intolerant of failure, sometimes threatening them that their divisions would be closed if they failed to achieve targets. This led managers to misreport figures and engage in other forms of deceit to make them look good rather than question the wisdom and authority of the board.

One further factor not noted by the auditors, but which appeared to influence corporate governance and the culture of Toshiba was the failure of previous leaders to give up their positions and hold on company culture on retirement, which led to factional rivalries and unhealthy competition among divisions and managers. The influence of previous generations of leaders on corporate culture and governance in Japanese corporations is especially strong where the corporation is dominated by family shareholdings. One consequence of this traditional hegemony is that women held only 3 per cent of seats on company boards in large Japanese firms in 2015, despite the Japanese government setting out guidelines for 30 per cent of board positions to be held by females to increase diversity and improve innovation.

CORPORATE GOVERNANCE

The Toshiba case deals directly with the problems of internal and external governance (Aguilera et al., 2015). Internal governance raises questions concerned with how boards of directors are constituted and act, who owns/should own the corporation, and how we ensure that managers act in the interests of owners. External governance focuses on how these internal questions are shaped by (a) the legal system, (b) the market for corporate control (i.e., the existence of an active takeover market if a firm is underperforming), (c) the role and power assigned to external auditors, (d) stakeholder activists (celebrity shareholders, socially aware investors, etc.), (e) rating organizations and business/financial analysts, and (f) the business press. Both internal and external governance mechanisms work to create good corporate governance, which Aguilera et al. (p. 485) defined in terms of four principles:

1. 'Good governance should protect the rights of stakeholders and provide the means to enforce those rights by monitoring executives and holding them accountable.'
2. 'Good governance is supposed to help mediate between the different interests and demands of various stakeholders.'
3. 'Good governance provides transparent information disclosure.'
4. 'Good governance involves the provision of strategic and ethical guidance for the firm.'

Question on the Toshiba case

1. To what extent does the Toshiba case violate any or all of the four principles?

Various theories help explain effective corporate governance. However, since corporate governance is a socially constructed concept, what is meant by effective is in the eye of the beholder. So, depending on one's theoretical stance, what is meant by good governance principles may vary. To help us understand some of these debates we need to examine these theories.

The first point to note is that the issue of corporate governance has a long history, first coming to prominence with advances in industrial capitalism during the early part of the twentieth century with the rise of the joint stock company, large-scale enterprises, and the separation of ownership by shareholders from control by professional managers

(Clarke, 2022). The classic works on these developments pointed to a managerial 'revolution' and the beginnings of an early stakeholder theory of the firm, in which managers held effective control over the different interests represented within it (Berle & Means, 1932/1967). Managers were thought to act in such a way as to 'hold the ring' between the competing claims of shareholders, customers, employees, government, and the public in a pluralist theory of industrial government.

Since then, there have been several interesting developments, all of which have tried to answer the question: what is the best means of controlling the supposed controllers (i.e., managers) to protect shareholders and other stakeholders? Four such theories stand out (Clarke, 2022; Mallin, 2017; Martin et al., 2016):

- Agency theory and shareholder value;
- Stakeholder theory;
- Stewardship theory; and
- Enlightened shareholder value.

Agency theory was the response of neo-classical economists to the agency question in positing a contractual view of the firm. They argued there was a legal and metaphorical contract between owners (the financiers of the business and thus the principals) and managers (their agents). Managers raised funds from financiers to operate the business; financiers, in turn, needed managers to generate returns on their investments. In essence, the contract that ensued specified what managers would do with the funds and what the division of returns would be between the principals and agents. The main problem resided in the unforeseeable future contingencies, leaving open the question of residual control rights – the rights to make decisions not foreseen by the contract. However, managers retained substantial control over these residual rights and could exercise great discretion over how to allocate funds. So, agency theory concerned itself with the central problem of how to constrain managers from misallocating funds and acting in their own interests rather than those of the principals.

For neo-classical economists, it is shareholders whose interests should dominate the corporate agenda and for whom the corporation should be run; it is they that bear the residual risk whereas managers effectively get paid whether the firm makes a profit or loss and are simply a charge on the business in the same way as other preferred creditors. Investors, however, only get paid if the firm makes a profit and do not get paid if the firm makes a loss. Consequently, investors have the greatest inherent interest in ensuring that the firm makes the greatest amount of profit and are the party in whose interests the firm should be run. According to agency theorists, maximising shareholder value leads to superior, overall economic performance for the firm and for the economy at large as short-run interests in securing adequate earnings and long-run interests in increasing the capital value of the firm converge (Lan & Heracleous, 2010; Roberts, 2004).

Agency theory assumes efficient markets, including markets for corporate control, managerial labour, and corporate information. Efficiency results from many buyers and sellers, all of whom have perfect information on which to base their interactions. To the extent that efficient markets in these areas exist, managers will bear the costs of any misconduct and, therefore, are much more likely to exercise self-control in awarding themselves excessive pay increases and in conducting business affairs. In essence, a firm is depicted as a market made up of many contractors – owners and managers – negotiating and re-negotiating their interests. In case the assumptions underlying perfect markets are absent for a short while, checks and balances must be built into the system, including an effectively structured board of directors, compensation for managers tied to shareholder interests, and a fully functioning external market for corporate control to discipline managers and incumbent boards. This situation could occur when, for example, there is a temporary shortage of managerial talent or when there is a potential for serious market failure under monopoly conditions.

Newer versions of agency theory complicate the argument by positing a permanent hierarchy of managerial control within organizations, rather than the market metaphor (Aguilera et al., 2015). According to these new institutional economists, firms arise because of the nature of market imperfections and the need to keep down transaction costs among contractors. Nevertheless, attention remains focused on the relationships between shareholders and managers, but this time shareholders are deemed to be facing a diffuse but significant risk of self-interested opportunism by managers because the assets of the firm are too numerous and too ill-defined to fully describe in contractual agreements (Lan & Heracleous, 2010).

Whether in its neo-classical or institutional variants, however, agency theory relies on a mixture of converging economic incentives – pay tied to shareholder value – and power-sharing through bargaining and coalition-building to bring about cooperative behaviour between the two principal parties in governance – shareholders and managers. No other parties are really considered as having long-term and significant interests in the firm. Good examples of firms run according to these principles are firms bought over by new financial intermediaries, such as hedge funds, private equity, or sovereign wealth funds, which are often claimed to be interested only in short-term returns (Appelbaum et al., 2014). However, as both Appelbaum et al. and other researchers in this tradition (e.g., Bacon et al., 2013) argue, there are different types of private equity buyouts and not all such acquisitions are focused on the short term. Instead, both sets of authors conclude that some private equity-backed buyouts do look to the long term and growth, and in doing so, can enhance employees' interests and improve human resource management.

Stakeholder theory adopts a different line of argument. For the proponents of this view, firms are not bundles of assets that belong to shareholders, nor can they be in a modern world when the key assets are largely intangible and under the control of employees. Instead, governance structures and the work of senior managers are aimed at maximising the total wealth of the organization for the benefit of those *inside* it who contribute firm-specific assets, i.e., their knowledge and skills, as well as those outside it (Edward Freeman, Wainwright, Dmytriyev et al., 2023).

This theory fits in well with the assumptions of the corporate reputation approach we examined, which recognises the importance of constituencies including customers, suppliers, employees, business partners, government, the press, investors, and, increasingly, society at large. Stakeholder theory is closer to the models of governance found in continental Europe and in some countries in the Asia-Pacific region than the Anglo-Saxon external focus on the shareholder value model assumed by agency theory (Malin,

2017). See the example of Volkswagen, a multinational German vehicle manufacturer in Box 11.2.

Box 11.2 Stakeholder theory in operation at Volkswagen

Volkswagen, the German automobile manufacturer, is part-owned by the Government of Lower Saxony, which retains 20 per cent of voting rights and gives it the right to veto major decisions and prevent takeovers. In line with many large German companies, it also has a Supervisory Board, which is responsible for:

> monitoring the Management and approving important corporate decisions. Moreover, it appoints the Members of the Board of Management. The Supervisory Board of Volkswagen AG comprises 20 members and conforms to the German Co-determination Act. Half of the overall 20 members of the Supervisory Board are shareholder representatives. In accordance with Article 11(1) of the Articles of Association, the State of Lower Saxony is entitled to appoint two of these share-holder representatives for as long as it directly or indirectly holds at least 15% of the Company's ordinary shares. The remaining shareholder representatives on the Supervisory Board are elected by the Annual General Meeting. The other half of the Supervisory Board consists of employee representatives elected by the employ-ees in accordance with the German Co-determination Act. A total of seven of these employee representatives are Company employees elected by the workforce; the other three employee representatives are representatives of the trade unions elected by the workforce.

Question

1. To what extent does this model of governance ensure that the Government of Lower Saxony and employees' interests are considered?

Stewardship theory is a more recent perspective on governance, which seeks to explain how governance works in practice and how it should work in the future. As we have seen, agency theory proposes a self-interested model of management and in-built conflict with shareholders. Stewardship theory argues that such conflict of interests should not exist because good managers, who have the skill and will, are naturally inclined to act in the interests of shareholders because their interests, and those of other stakeholders in the firm, are broadly similar and contingent on the long-term wealth creation of the organi-zation. Essentially, this is a unitary ('we are all in it together with the same aims') and benign view of organizations, which also posits a strong degree of managerial choice based on their motivations to act as stewards on behalf of everyone in the business and its long-term survival. Although it recognises that there are situations when managers may not always exercise good or well-meaning judgements, stewardship theories are not hung up on the downside risk of managerial misbehaviour that dominates agency theory. Instead, stewardship theorists, such as Colin Mayer (2014) and John Kay (2015), focus on the importance of building trust relationships and social networks to coordinate actors in and across organizations. Building trust between these principal actors, they argue, is characteristic of institutional and funding arrangements more likely to be found in Europe and Asia, for example, networks of banks, privately owned and family-owned firms, and the new forms of organizations we have discussed in the previous chapters.

Is there a possibility of **convergence**? The success of the USA and its new economy during the 1990s, coupled with problems in Asia and continental Europe during the same period, provided a great fillip for outsider, Anglo-Saxon market-based shareholder value models of governance, and the assumptions underpinning them. In countries such as Germany, Sweden, and France, there were enthusiastic calls by certain sections of the business and financial community and supporting political parties to embrace shareholder value principles and rid themselves of stakeholder constraints. However, the problems of companies such as Enron and others in the early 2000s resulted in a re-think of models of governance among American and British companies, which led to the passing of US legislation, including Sarbanes–Oxley in 2002 and attempts by the OECD to set world standards on corporate disclosure and governance. The fallout from the Global Financial Crisis in 2007/2008 and the passing of the Dodd–Frank Wall Street Reform and Consumer Protection Act in 2010 only served to accentuate and accelerate this search for new models of governance, which has led to an enlightened shareholder value model.

Enlightened shareholder value has been proposed by those financial economists and lawyers who remain wedded to the core principles and benefits of agency theory. They seek to balance the interests of investors with those of other stakeholders to ensure that the long-term interests of shareholders are achieved. Such an Anglo-Saxon model is in line with global trends in the internationalisation of finance, equity markets, and various financial instruments, which is forcing organizations from all parts of the world that wish to borrow to conform to certain governance conditions, for example, the OECD's principles of Organization and Governance. This convergence, inevitably, is on the Anglo-Saxon model, though critics argue there are limits to such convergence.

However, as Clarke (2022) and others point out, the sharpest skirmish has been over the idea of shareholder value in any form following the scandals of Enron and the other examples of corporate malfeasance associated with the Global Financial Crisis (Clarke, 2017; Martin & Gollan, 2012; Martin et al., 2016). Nevertheless, there are many Americans and British lawyers, financiers, and businesspeople who stick to the dictums proposed by the neo-classical economist Milton Friedman (1970) 'that the social responsibility of business is to increase profits,' so serving the interests of us all in the long run (Mayer, 2014).

Enron and more recent cases such as RBS in the UK (see Chapter 3) and Toshiba in this chapter have caused economists and moralists to argue that even an enlightened shareholder value model is inappropriate in a modern world, especially given the power and influence of large tech companies (Davis, 2022; Stout, 2013). Critics believe the ability of directors to monitor executive behaviour and the temptations of making enormous gains by cashing in the huge stock options that form the basis of many executive pay packets have created an unworkable system (Bebchuk & Fried, 2010). Enron was the classic example of how self-interested and financially motivated senior leaders could not only poorly serve shareholders, but also customers and employees in bringing companies down. Agency theory has been proven right by Enron in that such managers were all-powerful in governance and shareholders needed protection through governance mechanisms and the introduction of legislation such as Sarbanes–Oxley. However, according to critics, one of agency theory's most sacrosanct principles of tying pay to shareholder value was its undoing. Perhaps as important, the pursuit of shareholder value has disconnected corporations from their moral purposes, according to stakeholder theorists, which is to serve the wider interests represented within firms and changing values in society. Trustee theorists, such as Mayer (2014), also argue that the job of governance is to 'sustain the corporation's assets,' not merely its financial assets. He has proposed the 'trust firm' as a solution that aligns the need for corporations to be efficient with the need for corporations to uphold the values of sustainability.

> The trust firm defines the period and the scope of the corporation's credible commitment. It delineates for how long and over what activities the corporation can credibly commit and the boundaries beyond which it cannot do so. It does this through committing its controlling shareholders to retain their share ownership for pre-determined periods of time and by conferring powers on a board of trustees to prevent the corporation from abusing parties who would otherwise be exposed to its activities.
>
> *(Mayer, 2014, pp. 15–16.).*

It is in the above sense that the calls for a new, more socially responsible, and sustainable theory of governance have been framed, which leads us to a more in-depth discussion of corporate (social) responsibility (CSR) (Clarke, 2017).

CORPORATE SOCIAL RESPONSIBILITY

CSR, or CR as it is increasingly known, has been touched on in most chapters in this book since it is one of the most rapid growth areas of interest for modern businesses and is the basis on which a corporate identity can be built. But what exactly do we mean by CSR, why should it be of interest, especially given the dominance of the shareholder value model of governance among so many companies throughout the world, and how effective is it in changing the nature of business? To answer these questions, we will outline the case for CSR/CR and then examine some of the criticisms of this contested concept from the right, the left, and from within.

The case for CSR. The case that is usually made for CSR is a business case for pursuing socially and environmentally friendly policies, which is rooted in a stakeholder theory of governance and Rawlsian theory of social justice (Latapi Agudelo et al., 2019). Rawlsian ethics are associated with a 'theory of good', which focuses on defining the characteristics of a just society. Imagine a society in which there were no laws, social conventions, or political states. Then ask yourself the question: what principles might reasonable people agree on to guarantee order while placing few constraints on individual freedoms? When applied to organizations, a theory of good states that these principles and the outcomes that result from these principles must be distributed with full consultation so that no organizational stakeholders are losers while others are clear winners. Responsible leaders should place organizational survival and the long-term interests of their stakeholders over any single interest (Mayer, 2014).

Drawing on these ideas, CSR advocates contend there is a fundamental tension between the pursuit of private profit and public good, usually because a pursuit of profit at the expense of society is unsustainable in the long run. The basic argument underlying the business case for CSR is two-fold. First, profit is not pursued by companies for the public good but for private gain, which has little or nothing to do with the public good. If the pursuit of profit is to advance social welfare, it cannot be left to the hidden hand of the market and powerful business leaders, a form of very rough justice. Instead, it often requires active regulation from outside bodies, such as the Financial Conduct Authority in the UK and the 'FED' (Federal Reserve System or central bank) in the USA. Second, in the pursuit of private gain, companies are driven by their internal business logic of maximising revenues and minimising costs to place enormous burdens on society and the environment. Economists call this process one of placing *externalities* on society, defined as companies taking action that affects others' welfare without having the incentive to recognise this impact in their decision-making, nor fully accounting for it in their evaluation of the costs and benefits of decisions. The consequences are that externalities lead to inefficiencies for society if businesses do not pay their fair share of costs (Roberts, 2004). This is the case often levelled against people flying more than they need to because of low-cost airline availability or buying cars with petrol and diesel engines because of their contributions to global warming. Thus, for many governments, NGOs (non-government organizations), and critics of the Anglo-Saxon shareholder value model, the unchecked pursuit of profit yields little or nothing for many ordinary citizens but costs them plenty. Unless it is restrained either by CSR or by government regulation, private enterprise is bound to make losers of everyone apart from private businesses and their owners (Stout, 2012; Davis, 2022).

The business case for CSR. Given the problems that big business has experienced in reputational terms over the last decade or more, especially since the Global Financial Crisis, CSR has itself become big business (Latapi Agudelo et al., 2019). Many governments, business organizations, and professional bodies now promulgate the CSR agenda. Prominent among them was the British government in 2015. The UK government saw CSR as good for society and good for business. They argued that a better understanding of the potential benefits of CSR for the competitiveness of individual companies and national economies would encourage the spread of CSR practice. The Department for Business Innovation and Skills therefore supported work exploring the 'business case' for CSR in a range of publications. Interestingly, since they published their strategy in 2015, there have been no further significant publications on this issue by the UK government at the time of writing. At this point, you may wish to reflect on why.

There are several international networks promoting CSR, including the World Business Council for Sustainable Development. Its membership is made up of 180 multinational enterprises including the European-based Shell, BP, Nokia, Michelin, SKF, Novartis, ABB, Volkswagen, and Daimler-Chrysler, and major US-based Dow

Chemicals, Ford, General Motors, Procter & Gamble, Time Warner, GE, and HP. The Council invites 'companies committed to sustainable development and to promoting the role of Eco-Efficiency, Innovation and Corporate Social Responsibility.' One of the Council's publications acknowledges the legal requirement to promote 'acceptable returns for its shareholders and investors' but argues that 'business and business leaders have … made significant contributions to the societies of which they form part' and that responsible leadership is necessary for business and societal progress.

The Chartered Institute of Personnel and Development in the UK has also been vigorous in pursuing the CSR agenda and in promoting the need for HR specialists to champion CSR. Their position is informed by a stakeholder view of ethics in business, in which employees are one of the principal stakeholders, and a view that employees' beliefs and actions are also the main vehicle for putting CR into action. They see CR as continuing to move up the business and HR agenda, which can become an important instrument of change. To do so, they argued, HR specialists need to broaden their own understanding and skills and take an active role in what they regard as a new form of strategic management.

Box 11.3 A case illustration of corporate social responsibility: Fujitsu (UK)

Fujitsu won an award from the UK Business in the Community organization for being the most 'Responsible Business of the Year' in 2015. The company's entry proclaimed it was 'committed to integrating responsible business issues into core strategy and day to day operations. It is passionate about responding to the unprecedented social and business risks caused by resource scarcity, population growth, an aging society and mass urbanisation by pioneering ICT solutions to create a fairer society.'

The company has led the industry in making data centres, which consume up to 2 per cent of electricity globally, and 27 per cent of Fujitsu's energy, more sustainable. Fujitsu's UK data centres use 100 per cent renewable energy, and the company operates the first European data centre to be certified as Operational Sustainability Gold. It has also worked with suppliers to reduce CO_2 emissions in its supply chain, achieving a 32 per cent decrease.

Fujitsu has commissioned its own 'Collaboration Nation' research on working with SMEs and responded to it by changing its approach, resulting in 23 per cent more contracts being awarded to SMEs year on year.

The company collaborates to innovate and strategically help others. Projects include developing a supercomputing infrastructure which makes high-performance computing capabilities available to SMEs, Kiduku, a research project pioneering sensor technology to help the elderly live well for longer in their own homes, and BITC Connect, which captures the impacts of BITC's Business Connector programme.

Fujitsu is also working to redress the gender imbalance in its sector. Despite males making up over 80 per cent of undergraduates in engineering, technology, and computer science, Fujitsu's graduate female intake has averaged 40 per cent since 2010. Senior leaders across Fujitsu are engaged with and advocate its responsible business agenda, including Duncan Tait, Head of EMEIA, who is a member of BITC's board. The company produces an independently verified annual report against GRI standards including detailed data on non-financial capital, and an independently assured CSR report containing material issues, objectives, targets, and policies.

Measuring CSR. Inevitably, when making a business case for any investment, this turns on the issue of measurement – how do we know there is a payoff for stakeholders? Numbers are language that business leaders understand and need to use to convince the financial community that pursuing goals other than shareholder value is likely to pay off for all in the long run. Managers also need measurement for performance management reasons and to keep them focused. As a result, many of the companies mentioned in this section have adopted the 'triple bottom line' (3BL) as a performance measure. The idea was first proposed by John Elkington (1997), when he described a framework for measuring and reporting corporate performance against economic, social, and environmental parameters. However, he also made a more far-reaching claim:

> At its broadest, the term is used to capture the whole set of values, issues, and processes that companies must address to minimize any harm resulting from their activities and to create economic, social, and environmental value. This involves being clear about the company's purpose and taking into consideration the needs of all the company's stakeholders.

In effect, 3BL has been proposed as a planning and reporting mechanism, and a decision-making framework used to achieve sustainable development. It has been adopted by organizations as diverse as local government in Australia, major corporations such as Monsanto, the BBC, and British Petroleum, and a range of small firms (see, for example, the cases available online at the Business and Sustainable Development Global Website). The financial community is also paying attention to the Dow Jones Sustainability Index, launched in 1999, which tracks the economic, environmental, and social performance of more than 300 global companies, such as Siemens, Citigroup, and Volkswagen, in numerous countries and industries. Not surprisingly, consultants have been at the forefront of CSR. For example, PWC has argued that firms 'need to be a part of a global conversation and movement towards creating responsible business practices that change the world' by measuring how firms build responsible business, improve diversity and inclusion, create community engagement, and develop environmental stewardship.

Criticisms from the right. We have already discussed the shareholder value credo of many businesses – 'the business of business is business' – which was given moral support by neo-classical economists such as Friedman (1970). Currently, there is a battle being waged by economists, corporate lawyers, and business ethics writers who argue there are two reasons for sticking with the shareholder value/agency theory model. The first is the agency theory position that managers of public companies are not owners but are employed by the firms' owners to maximise the long-term value of the owners' assets, within a framework of law that sets out rights and wrongs and the responsibilities and accountabilities of managers and corporate leaders. Some business ethics advocates believe that putting those assets to any other use, such as CSR, is effectively robbing the owners of their just (and ethical) rewards (Sternberg, 2000, 2004, 2012). The ethical decision for a manager who believes that the business s/he is working for is causing harm to society at large is either not to work for that business in the first place or to leave it. Elaine Sternberg, a UK academic and former corporate executive, believes in two principles of business ethics that underlie a shareholder value model. These are *ordinary decency* and *distributive justice*, without which the conduct of business would not be possible. These principles are based on a theory of rights. Paramount among these rights are those of property owners, which must be respected. These, however, do not extend to 'lying, cheating, stealing, killing, coercion, physical violence and most forms of illegality.' Instead, managers should pursue 'honesty and fairness,' reflecting the demands of 'ordinary decency.' Her second component of business ethics, distributive justice, refers to the alignment of organizational rewards and managers' contributions towards achieving shareholder value. Two canons of modern-day HR – performance-linked pay and merit-based promotion – are manifestations of distributive justice within the company. So, for Sternberg and others, promoting people based on anything other than merit or rewarding a manager for anything other than pursuing shareholder value is bad for business and bad ethics. Her arguments were summed up in her 2012 paper, which concluded that organizational mission statements containing a conventional business ethics discourse on corporate responsibility were confused and dangerous. This was because CSR threatened the very basis of business, which was based on private property and individual liberty. Sternberg believes that organizations need to maximise long-term owner value while respecting distributive justice and ordinary decency.

Criticisms from the left. As is often the case in social debate, the right and left of the political spectrum often agree on the analysis but come to entirely different conclusions on the prescriptions. Such is the case with CSR. The left criticism, which has been acknowledged by some business leaders as a legitimate one, was forcibly put by Joel Bakan (2004, 2011, 2020), a North American law professor, who has written several powerful books about the impact of modern corporations on society. His latest one was entitled the 'New Corporation' (Bakan, 2020).

From his examination of legal documents, Bakan (2004) argued that corporations are bound by mandate to pursue relentlessly and without exception self-interested shareholder value, regardless of the harmful consequences it might cause to others. This is an extreme version of agency theory, which few corporate leaders would openly subscribe to. Nevertheless, he claimed, they had very little choice because of the legal, political, and economic logics and structures of capitalist societies. His view was that such mandated corporations have come to dominate our lives in the developed and developing world, determining our lifestyles, culture, employment, and economic and political choices. Moreover, they were having an enormous negative effect on the lives of children, the subject of a later book in 2011, by targeting the growing 'kid market,' creating child health problems and commoditising learning. Aside from the iconography and ideology of modern business, which is all around us, corporations go further in dictating the decisions of national governments and controlling societal decisions that were once part of the public domain and subject to genuine political decisions by ordinary people.

So, according to Bakan, it is corporations that govern society, not governments. Yet, he argued, every thesis brings about its own antithesis: it was the very power of modern, global corporations that left them open to reputational risk in the form of public mistrust, fear, and demands for social and environmental accountability from society. The response has been an acknowledgement by corporate leaders to understand and address the costs of poor reputations and work hard to regain and maintain the trust of 'stakeholders', including an increasingly vociferous investor community and financial press. The vehicle for this identity and image change had been CSR, which is nothing but a means of persuading a sceptical public of the virtues of capitalism. His latest book (Bakan, 2020) continued in much the same vein, claiming that the 'new dawn of corporate American capitalism', which top CEOs claimed would serve the interests not only of shareholders but also of workers, communities, and the environment, was a sham. He pointed out that wages in America have largely stagnated since 2000, poverty and inequality increased markedly, while good jobs and workers' security decreased. In health terms, mortality rates increased from 2014, due to 'deaths of despair' from alcohol, drugs, and suicides. He also argued racism, xenophobia, and toxic masculinity increased, contributing to the rise of demagogues around the world – most notably Donald Trump. With respect to the environment, Bakan also highlighted that the climate crises, much of it caused by American corporations, had reached a point of no return and that, despite their proclamations, American CEOs had done little or nothing about it.

Like many critics from the left (e.g., Stout, 2012; Davis, 2022), Bakan's view of CSR is that it is a largely fraudulent concept because corporations, in the final analysis, cannot do anything other than engage in the 'pathological pursuit of profit and power,' his 2004 book's subtitle. His answer to what can be done largely resides in political change to a 'new and deeper kind of democracy' based on community building and mutual aid. Democratic political movements are his hope for dealing with the climate crisis rather than relying on the motivations of firms to act.

So, what evidence do we have on the motives of firms to engage in CSR? To answer this question, we might want to reflect on some research conducted into CSR in the pharmaceutical industry by Hayley Droppert and Sara Bennet (2015).

Box 11.4 Corporate social responsibility in global health

These authors undertook an exploratory study into the six highest-earning pharmaceutical companies, using publically available data and interviews with key representatives (Droppert & Bennett, 2015). They found that the meaning, motivation, and approach to CSR differed in each of the firms. Four out of the six had clearly defined CSR, with only two setting out clear criteria for what they meant by CSR and three having specific policies. Three had a CSR department but all had a CSR committee or steering group. The most common CSR activities were differential pricing for resource-poor countries, donations of drugs to poor countries, developing mobile or m-health (e.g., by providing text message reminders on when to take drugs), improving product distribution activities in developing countries, and targeting research and development to diseases that disproportionately affected developing countries.

The motivations for undertaking CSR were also varied. However, five of the six reported entering new markets as a key motivation, with four anticipating long-term financial gain. Reputational benefits also figured strongly, particularly in influencing the perception of the firm by consumers and improving employee recruitment and engagement. Finally, all six stressed philanthropic and health benefits, especially improving population health and increasing patient access to necessary medications/health services.

One of their conclusions was that 'pharmaceuticals companies struggle with how other actors perceive and define CSR and that CSR is not even understood in the same way across the pharmaceuticals industry.' However, they did conclude that CSR was playing an increasingly major role in the industry and that it offered real opportunities for developing countries to take advantage of this trend.

Source: based on Droppert & Bennett, 2015.

Questions

1. To what extent does this study confirm the 'view from the left', and does it matter anyway, especially if it is doing good in developing countries?
2. Do the problems of definition cause problems for measuring the impact of CSR?

Criticisms from within. Even some of those advocates of CSR remain unconvinced of the arguments and evidence used to support it. First, the business case for CSR has often rested on the assumption that 'doing good leads to doing well' and that creating product or service differentiation through CSR is a way of satisfying the firm's needs for superior profits and serving societal goals. Aguinas and Glavas (2012), in one of the most cited academic review articles on the topic, concluded that there was wide variation in results supporting this claim. For example, they cited a meta-analysis conducted by Peloza (2009), who found that only 59 per cent of the 128 studies reviewed showed a positive relationship between CSR and financial performance, with 27 per cent showing a mixed/neutral response, and 14 per cent a negative outcome, while a large study of 599 companies in 28 countries by Surroca et al. (2010) found no direct relationship between CSR and financial performance. Thus, according to Aguinas and Glavas, although firms undertook CSR to benefit materially, there was only a small positive financial gain at best. Nevertheless, they concluded that several non-financial outcomes resulted from CSR, including 'better management practices, product quality, operational efficiencies, attractiveness to investors, and enhanced demographic diversity (e.g., women and ethnic minorities)' (p. 943). This finding was followed up in later research by the same authors. who claimed that one of the key benefits of CSR lay in it being an 'ideal conduit to make sense of and find meaningfulness through work' (Aguinas & Glavas, 2019). They explained through a sensemaking lens how employees can experience work more positively, which results in their organizations and stakeholders benefitting. Their reasoning was largely based on the needs of some employees to find a moral and social purpose in their work (a called orientation to work). However, they also pointed to the needs or orientations to work of some employees to enact environmental and ecological values, which they believe are a growing feature of newer generations of employees, especially those brought up in families and national cultures where social responsibility is a prominent value.

Daniel Diermeier (2007, 2011, 2019), a long-time CSR supporter from the University of Chicago, has provided an alternative argument on why firms engage in such behaviour. His view is that long-run cost reduction is the best justification for CSR because it is concerned with managing the downside of reputation risk rather than the upside of differentiation. Note the similarity between this argument and Bakan's view, but for very different reasons.

Like Aguinas and Glavas (2019), Diermeier makes a values case for CSR, claiming that values matter and that the values of the newer generations in advanced industrial societies are more inclined to be post-materialist, with a concern for the environment, tolerance, and social issues that are different from the materialist values of earlier generations that were influenced by hardship. Moreover, he argued that these values would remain relatively permanent throughout the lifetime of this new generation, precisely because their formative years were shaped by times of plenty rather than hardship. The consequences, according to Diermeier, were that the shift to CSR is real and permanent. As a result, companies would be increasingly pressured into responding to these value changes, especially when competing in the global market for talent. In other words, there was a 'market for virtue' and virtue signalling. However, this market only operated under certain conditions.

First, CSR issues are likely to vary in the same way that cultural values vary; some emerging economies not only cannot afford CSR but do not value it so highly because the values of their nationals have been formed under conditions of relative hardship, exacerbated by the growing gaps between rich and poor and by the impact of modern communications in highlighting that gap to the poor.

Second, the consequences of these value changes for competitive positioning were that businesses must be able to adapt their strategies to different segments of product markets (and employment markets), as we have consistently argued throughout this book. As Diermeier argued, for a product differentiation strategy to work by creating and capturing value from customers for socially responsible brands (e.g., Lego, Ben & Jerry's, Starbucks, or Patagonia), three factors must be present:

- Customers must be willing to pay more for socially responsible goods and services to cover the fixed and variable costs of providing them, implying that customers must be willing to pay sufficiently high marginal prices and the market segment must be large enough to cover the fixed costs.
- Socially responsible brands must be difficult to imitate to allow for both socially responsible and non-socially responsible brands to coexist.
- The claims for social responsibility must be credible and customers must be able to verify these claims in some way.

Thus, in sufficiently large markets, it was possible for firms to earn superior profits from socially responsible brands by charging a premium price for them if these three conditions hold. And there are examples of markets in which socially responsible brands do earn superior profits by charging more for their goods and services, such as the food market in which organic and 'fair play' producers have carved out a niche.

However, the case for CSR does not really rest on this 'doing business by doing good' argument, but on lowering long-run costs and reducing reputational risk. According to Diermeier, these were the main arguments for CSR: it does not rest on offering higher consumption value to willing consumers, which is difficult for them to verify anyway, but in delivering goods and services at lower costs to the environment, which is simply a principle of good management and is independent of offering higher value. To support his point, he used the example of the contrast between BP and Shell in the 1990s, when BP attempted to market 'cleaner fuel.' Clearly, there was only a small segment willing to pay higher prices for a commodity product such as petrol for their cars, but, he claimed, BP's strategy was not driven by a need to differentiate themselves in small segment markets; it was driven by its reputation for CSR and in protecting it. Shell, on the other hand, had several problems with its reputation, resulting from its confrontation with Greenpeace, its proposed disposal of rigs in deep water, and its operations in Nigeria where human rights were an issue. As a result, Shell had to invest heavily in CSR to lower its costs arising from reputational risk in the long run and has had to work very hard to catch up with BP in particular markets. However, this would only be worthwhile if the expected savings from avoiding reputational damage were greater than the costs of complying with CSR practices. So, in essence, these are cost-driven strategies, arising from the nature of the markets they operate in, not from price differentiation.

This argument can also be extended to the market for talent. While there may be niche markets for talented people who are attracted by working for companies that offer socially responsible goods and services, more people are likely to be attracted to and remain with organizations with a history of avoiding damage to their reputations, since the individual reputations of talented individuals are likely to suffer from association with firms that have not invested in avoiding reputational damage. This reasoning aligns with Aguinas and Glavas's (2019) sensemaking thesis. Few employees with a strong sense of a called orientation to work are likely to remain with employers whose reputation has been damaged by acting irresponsibly.

Criticisms of measurement. While the idea of a triple bottom line has appeal to several firms and government departments that have used it in their public relations, including BT, AT&T, Shell, Dow Chemicals, the UK government, and state governments in Australia, critics point out some fundamental problems with it, even as a metaphor. These are based on the contention that what is sound about 3BL isn't novel and what is novel isn't measurable (Norman & MacDonald, 2004; MacDonald & Norman, 2007), or in creating compliance (Sridhar & Jones, 2012). The claims of its proponents, in line with stakeholder theories of governance, are that firms should assess their overall long-term contribution to society as well as to shareholders, that the social and environmental impact of firms can be measured in much the same way as the financial impact, and that these individual measures can be aggregated to provide something akin to a societal profit or loss. While those adhering to the strict shareholder value version of corporate governance, such as Elaine Sternberg, may take issue with the first of these claims, in no way could they be regarded as novel, according to Norman and MacDonald, since they have been at the heart of the CSR agenda since the 1980s. The more important criticism, however, lies in the measurement aspects of 3BL.

To date, there are no known, universally accepted standards for measuring an aggregated bottom line, and given different versions of ethics in business, it is probably not theoretically possible. The social and ethical accounting, auditing, and reporting movement (Gray & Laughlin, 2012) has influenced several standard-setting bodies including the Global Reporting Initiative, SA 8000 Workplace/employee relations, AccountAbility 1000 Stakeholders, and ISO 9000 Organization and Governance standards, but would not claim to have provided an aggregate measure of 3BL. Their job has been to identify performance indicators of the social and ethical behaviour of companies and to find ways of auditing it. However, this is some way short of providing valid and reliable aggregate measures of CSR, which was and is the novel claim of 3BL. Indeed, to be plausible, the concept needs to remain vague, qualitative, and generalised; the closer one gets to specifying a measure of 3BL, the less plausible it becomes. Part of the reasoning for this is the 'apples and oranges' argument; there is simply no universal, common currency for equating financial performance with all aspects of social and environmental impact, or even one unit of social good with another, for example, donating money to charity for food aid or donating money to education. So, is this situation simply a case of what is measurable isn't always meaningful, and what is meaningful isn't always measurable? Another part of the reasoning is a more fundamental one and relates to our debate over different versions of governance and their moral stance. CSR and stakeholder theory, according to Norman and MacDonald, are largely premised on a theory of good: how does a business add value to the world? However, this is sometimes at odds with a theory of rights, which underpins the case for shareholder value. This concerns itself, as we noted, with whether individual rights are respected and societal obligations exercised in relation to these individuals. Thus, fulfilling obligations to shareholders may not always have a net positive impact on society but it does respect their rights and discharge society's obligations to them. From a rights perspective, it is not possible to say that maximising three lines of promises to shareholders, employees, and the public at large, as required by 3BL, is better than fulfilling one obligation to shareholders.

PREDICTING THE OUTCOMES OF CSR

So, while there are major issues surrounding the value and measurement of CSR as a way of doing business, is there a way to predict outcomes so that managers have a better understanding of what they are likely to gain, what is necessary in terms of inputs, and what factors may shape this relationship between CSR inputs and outputs? One answer to this question is to return to the work of Aguinas and Glavas (2012, 2019), who provided a model of CSR predictors and outcomes for researchers. We believe that an adapted form of this model can be useful for managers in showing how complex the process is, especially in showing the factors that might 'moderate' and 'mediate' the relationship between inputs and outputs. By moderate, we mean the variables that are likely to affect the strength and direction of the relationship between inputs and outputs, for example, gender differences, nationalities of employees, and levels of salary. By mediate, we mean a variable that explains the relationship between inputs and outputs, for example, perceptions of staff of leadership and values of employees.

The Aguinas and Glavas model also makes an important distinction between the levels of analysis (similar to our change framework in Chapter 10) between the institutional, organizational, and individual levels. So, for example, institutional predictors of CSR outcomes might be the nature of regulation in a society concerning corporate governance – does legislation recognise stakeholders other than investors? Organizational predictors could refer to a corporation's motives for engaging in CSR as illustrated by the case of the pharmaceuticals industry in Box 11.3. Individual predictors might refer to the values of key players in the organization, such as the CEO or Chair.

Figure 11.1 is our adaptation of their model, which shows some of the key relationships and variables that managers might need to consider when introducing any CSR system and what kinds of outcomes they may need to measure to evaluate its success and their motivations for engaging in these kinds of activities.

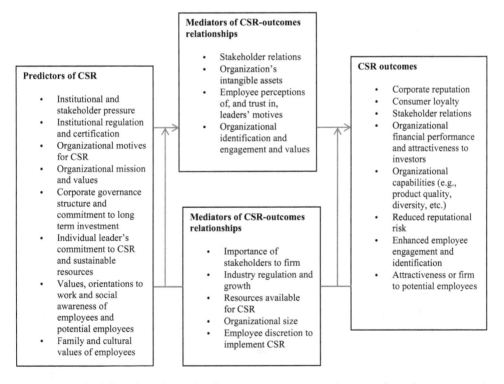

FIGURE 11.1 Modelling the relationship between CSR inputs and outputs (based on Aguinas & Glavas, 2012, p. 952; Aguinas & Glavas, 2019)

Corporate sustainability

Much of what we have looked at so far in relation to social responsibility has been driven by a phenomenon known as the 'Great Acceleration', which refers to how 'humanity has accelerated its population growth, energy use, and the release of greenhouse gases, along with a variety of other environmentally and socio-economically significant trends' since 1950 (Shoshitaishvilli, 2021, p. 1). These trends have driven recent interest in corporate sustainability (Clarke, 2017, 2022; Crane et al., 2019; Howard-Grenville & Lahneman, 2021; Rasche et al., 2023). While environmentalists are concerned with detriment to the environment, the social and economic aspects of the impact of organizations in all sectors on communities and their activities must also be considered (Howard-Grenville & Gapp, 2022; Rasche et al., 2023). This justification is why sustainability has been defined as part of a strategy of social development that meets the needs of the present without compromising the ability of future generations to meet their needs (Crane et al., 2019). Thus, in most communities, there are 'anchor institutions', organizations in the private, public, and third sectors that are central to the local communities and, thus, should have a particular commitment to the sustainability agenda. These anchor institutions include universities, healthcare organizations, and regional governments, as well as large corporates, whose power must be used responsibly (Davis, 2022). Increasingly, these entities are adopting the United Nations 17 Sustainable Development Goals (SDGs) we outlined in Chapter 1.

These goals are specified in more detail in Table 11.1.

It must be acknowledged that these goals are not without their critiques. Criticisms of the merits of economic growth, which is key to the attainment of the SDGs, are often voiced (Hickel, 2020). Researchers have also pointed to the measurability and monitoring of these rather general goals and the potential for conflict between them, for example, between economic growth and environmental and climate goals.

Question: Where do you stand on the potential conflict between economic growth and environmental goals?

To return to the people and organizational theme of this book, our contribution to this debate was to bring together corporate governance and people management to advocate a corporate sustainability approach to governance (Martin et al., 2016). This approach resonates with several of the United Nations SDGs and the Principles for Responsible Management Education (PRME) mission and six principles in arguing that organizations seeking sustainability should consider adopting ten people management practices:

1. A focus on creating a high-trust dynamic among all levels/types of employment and employees.
2. Sustainability, ethics, and diversity as key principles in the management of their own corporate legitimacy.
3. Training for high skill levels, including environmental, ethical, and diversity issues.
4. A focus on sustainable job employment practices.
5. Investment in social capital and networks as a source of innovation, while recognising the need for talented individuals.
6. Providing for genuine employee voice and employee involvement in a corporate sustainability agenda by engaging them in future sensemaking.

TABLE 11.1 The UN Sustainable Development Goals	
Goal	**Aim**
1. No Poverty	End poverty in all its forms everywhere
2. Zero Hunger	End hunger, achieve food security and improved nutrition and promote sustainable agriculture
3. Good Health and Well-Being	Ensure healthy lives and promote well-being for all at all ages
4. Quality Education	Ensure inclusive and equitable quality education and promote lifelong learning opportunities for all
5. Gender Equality	Achieve gender equality and empower all women and girls
6. Clean Water and Sanitation	Ensure availability and sustainable management of water and sanitation for all
7. Affordable and clean energy	Ensure access to affordable, reliable, sustainable, and modern energy for all
8. Decent Work and Economic Growth	Promote sustained, inclusive and sustainable economic growth, full and productive employment and decent work for alldecent work for all
9. Industry, Innovation, and Infrastructure	Build resilient infrastructure, promote inclusive and sustainable industrialization and foster innovation
10. Reduced Inequalities	Reduced inequality within and among countries
11. Sustainable cities and communities	Make cities and human settlements inclusive, safe, resilient, and sustainable
12. Responsible Consumption and Production	Ensuring sustainable consumption and production patterns
13. Climate Action	Take urgent action to combat climate change and its impact
14. Life Below Water	Conserve and sustainably use the oceans, seas and marine resources for sustainable development
15. Life on Land	Protect, restore and promote sustainable use of terrestrial ecosystems, sustainably manage forests, combat desertification, and halt and reverse land degradation and halt biodiversity loss

7. Employee ownership linked to a long-term commitment to organizational value creation as one possible model.
8. Employer brands and branding focused on sustainability, ethics, equality, diversity, and inclusion.
9. Preventing the negative impact of employee actions on the environment, ethics, equality, diversity, and inclusion, and supporting the implementation of environment-friendly systems.
10. Performance management, appraisal, career progression, and rewards linked to sustainability, ethics, and diversity.

I conclude with the hope that by the time I come to write the fourth edition of this book, at least some of these ethical practices will have become embedded in the anchor institutions and large corporations that dominate our economies. Moreover, I also hope that the UN SDGs and PRME will have served their purposes in challenging managers and students to 'think sustainable'. However, we must acknowledge that expert analysis of corporate sustainability as it currently stands, suggests all is not likely to go well in the future if current shareholder value models of governance and the growth paradigm of neo-liberal economics continue to dominate our thinking (Rasche et al., 2023). Moreover, as Howard-Grenville and Lahneman (2021) have argued, our current models of organizational adaptation to the environment, which have changed little since the 1970s and 1980s, will also need to reflect the planetary shifts and the move away from hierarchical organizations to 'panarchical systems,' which are organized in nested hierarchies across space and time. Such a view, which derives from the ecology literature, asks us to think about ecological systems rather than individual organizations as the unit of analysis and how ecosystem 'actors and factors' are connected and often depend on each other for their mutual survival. So, the future is really in the hands of you as readers of books such as this to engage in the kind of reflexivity outlined in Chapter 1 and take appropriate actions to ensure sustainability becomes a key element in the discourse and practice of organizations.

LEARNING SUMMARY

The key learning points from this chapter are:

- Corporate governance is recognised to be one of the most important influences on how firms are organized and managed, especially following corporate governance scandals in the early part of the previous decade and the events surrounding the Global Financial Crisis.
- Different models of corporate governance have been devised to deal with the problem of providing fair rewards to investors and other key stakeholders. Agency theory and shareholder value are the dominant theories underlying corporate governance practice in Anglo-Saxon economies, but these have been criticised for

their lack of fairness and short-term time horizon. Stakeholder theory, stewardship theory, and enlightened shareholder value have been implemented to deal with the problems of shareholder value thinking, but all models create problems in balancing out the competing claims on firms to create wealth, protect wealth, and distribute wealth on a sustainable basis.

- Corporate social responsibility (or corporate responsibility) has arisen as a means of dealing with problems of good governance, especially in addressing the needs and demands of key stakeholders who are not investors in firms.
- The argument for private sector organizations to engage in socially responsible behaviour is usually made by managers through reference to a 'business case' and future financial outcomes. However, the evidence on the links between CSR and financial outcomes is not strong, and other outcomes need to be taken into account to justify CSR initiatives.
- Being socially responsible depends on where you stand. Proponents of the business case for CSR, critics of CSR from the left and right, and advocates of CSR who believe in firms doing well by doing good all see things differently and use different measures of CSR effectiveness.
- Our model of the inputs, mediators, moderators, and outcomes of CSR shows how complex the process of implementing successful initiatives is likely to be. Managers need to consider a complex range of factors at the institutional, organizational, and individual levels of analysis if they want to create sustainable organizations.

REFERENCES

Abito, J.M., Besanko, D., & Diermeier, D. (2019). *Corporate social responsibility, reputation and private politics: the strategic interaction between activists and firms.* Oxford University Press.

Aguilera, R. V., Desender, K., Bednar, M. K., & Lee, J. H. (2015). Connecting the dots: bringing external corporate governance into the corporate governance puzzle. *The Academy of Management Annals, 9*(1), 483–573.

Aguinis, H., & Glavas, A. (2012). What we know and don't know about corporate social responsibility: A review and research agenda. *Journal of Management, 38*, 932–968.

Aguinas, H., & Glavas, A, (2019). On corporate social responsibility, sensemaking, and the search for meaningfulness through work. *Journal of Management, 45*(3), 1057–1086.

Appelbaum, E., Batt, R., & Lee, J. E. (2014). Financial intermediaries in the United States: Development and impact on firms and employment relations. In H. Gospel, A. Pendleton, & S. Vitols (Eds.), *Financialization, new investment funds, and labour: An international comparison.* Oxford University Press.

Bacon, N., Wright, M., & Ball, R. (2013). Private equity, HRM and employment. *Academy of Management Perspectives, 27*(1), 7–21.

Bakan, J. (2004). *The corporation: The pathological pursuit of power.* Free Press.

Bakan, J. (2011). *Childhood under siege: How big business targets your children*. Simon & Schuster.

Bakan, J. (2020). *The new corporation: How "good" corporations are bad for democracy*. Allen Lane.

Bebchuk, L. A., & Fried, J. M. (2010). Paying for long-term performance. *University of Pennsylvania Law Review, 158*, 1915–1959.

Berle, A. A., & Means, G. C. (1967). *The modern corporation and private property* (2nd ed.). Harcourt Brace

Clarke, T. (Ed.). (2017). *International corporate governance: A comparative approach* (2nd ed.). Routledge.

Clarke, T. (2022). *Comparative corporate governance: A research overview*. Routledge.

Crane, A., Matten, D., Glozer, S., & Spence, L.J. (2019). *Business ethics: Managing corporate citizenship and sustainability in the age of globalization* (5th ed.). Oxford University Press.

Davis, G. F. (2009). The rise and fall of finance and the end of the society of organizations. *Academy of Management Perspectives, 29*(3), 27–44.

Davis, G. F. (2022). *Taming corporate power in the 21st century*. Cambridge University Press.

Diermeier, D. (2007). Introduction: From corporate social responsibility to values-based management. In A. Dayal-Gulati & M. Finn (Eds.), *Global corporate citizenship* (pp. 1–23). North Western University Press.

Diermeier, D. (2011). *Reputation rules: Strategies for building your company's most valuable asset*. McGraw-Hill.

Droppert, H., & Bennett, S. (2015). Corporate social responsibility in global health: An exploratory study of multinational pharmaceutical firms, *Globalization and Health*. Retrieved July 23, 2015, from http://www.globalizationandhealth.com/content/11/1/15

Edward Freeman, R. Wainwright, L., Dmytriyev, S., & Strand, R. G. (2023). Stakeholder approaches to corporate sustainability. In A. Rasche, M. Morsing, J. Moon, & A. Kourula (Eds.), *Corporate sustainability: Managing responsible business in a globalised world* (2nd ed., pp. 75–95). Cambridge University Press.

Elkington, J. (1997). *Cannibals with forks: The triple bottom line of 21st century business*. Capstone.

Friedman, M . (1970, September 13). The social responsibility of business is to increase its profits. *New York Times Magazine*.

George, G., Haas, M.R., Joshi, H., McGahan, A.M. & Tracey, P. (Eds.) (2022). *Handbook of business sustainability: the organization, implementation and practice of sustainable growth*, Edward Elgar.

Ghobadian, A., Money, K. & Hillenbrand, C. (2015) Corporate responsibility research: past-present-future. *Group and Organization Management, 40*(3), 271–294.

Gray, R., & Laughlin, R. (2012). It was 20 years ago today: Sgt pepper, accounting, auditing and & accountability journal, green accounting and the blue meanies. *Accounting, Auditing and & Accountability Journal, 25*(2), 228–225.

Hickel, J. (2020). *Less is more: How degrowth will save the world*. Penguin Publishing.

Howard-Grenville, J., & Lahneman, B. (2021). Bringing the biophysical to the fore: re-envisioning organizational adaptation in the era of planetary shifts. *Strategic Organization, 19*(3), 478–493.

Howard-Grenville, J., & Gapp, T. (2022). Organizational culture for sustainability. In G. George, M. R., Haas, H. Joshi, A. M. McGahan, & P. Tracey (Eds.), *Handbook on the business of sustainability: The organization, implementation, and practice of sustainable growth* (pp. 138–151). Edward Elgar.

Kay, J. (2015). *Other people's money: Masters of the universe or servants of the people.* Perseus Academic.

Latapi Agudelo, M. A., Jóhannsdóttir, L., & Davídsdóttir, B. (2019). A literature review of the history and evolution of corporate social responsibility. *International Journal of Corporate Social Responsibility, 4*(1). https://doi.org/10.1186/s40991-018-0039-y

Lan, L. L., & Heracleous, L. (2010). Rethinking agency theory: The view from law. *Academy of Management Review, 35*, 294–314

MacDonald, C., & Norman, W. (2007). Rescuing the baby from the triple bottom line bathwater: A reply to Pava. *Business Ethics Quarterly, 17*(1), 111–114.

Malin, C. A. (2017). *Corporate goverance* (sixth edition). Oxford: Oxford University Press.

Martin, G., & Gollan, P. J. (2012). Corporate governance and strategic human resources management in the UK financial services sector: The case of the RBS. *International Journal of Human Resource Management, 23*(16), 3295–3314.

Martin, G., Farndale, E., Paauwe, J., & Stiles, P. G. (2016). Corporate governance and strategic human resource management: Four archetypes and proposals for a new approach to corporate sustainability. *European Management Journal, 34*(1), 22–35.

Mayer, C. (2014). *Firm commitment: Why the corporation is failing.* Oxford University Press.

Norman, W., & MacDonald, C. (2004). Getting to the bottom of the 'triple bottom line'. *Business Ethics Quarterly, 14*(2), 243–262.

Peloza, N. (2009). The challenge of measuring financial impacts from investments in corporate social performance. *Journal of Management, 35*, 1518–1541.

Rasche, A., Morsing, M., Moon, J., & Kourula, A. (Eds.). 2023. *Corporate sustainability: Managing responsible business in a globalised world* (2nd ed.). Cambridge University Press.

Roberts, J. (2004). *The modern firm: Organizational design for performance and growth.* Oxford: Oxford University Press.

Shoshitaishvili, B. (2021). From Anthropocene to noosphere: The great acceleration. *Earth's Future, 9*, 1–9. https://doi.org/10.1029/2020EF001917

Sridhar, K., & Jones, G. (2012). The three fundamental criticisms of the triple bottom lone approach: An empirical study to link sustainability reports in companies based on the Asia-Pacific region and TBL shortcomings. *Asian Journal of Business Ethics, 2*(1), 91–111.

Sternberg, E. (2000). *Just business: Business ethics in action.* Oxford University Press.

Sternberg, E. (2004). *Corporate governance: Accountability in the marketplace.* Institute of Economic Affairs.

Sternberg, E. (2012). How serious is CSR? A Critical Perspective. In C. Crouch & C. Maclean (Eds.), *The responsible corporation in the global economy* (pp. 29–54). Oxford University Press .

Stout, L. A. (2012). *The shareholder value myth: How putting shareholders first harms investors, corporations and the public.* Berrett-Koehler.

Stout, L. A. (2013). The Shareholder Value Myth European Financial Review, April-May 2013.

Surroca, J., Tribo, J. A., & Waddock, S. (2010). Corporate responsibility and financial performance: the role of intangible resources. *Strategic Management Journal, 31,* 463–490.

Index